Real World Issues, Real World Companies

To emphasize its business orientation, *Fundamental Accounting Principles* incorporates a variety of actual companies into its examples, applied principles, discussions, and end-of-chapter material. The financial statements of several companies are also included for analysis. This real world aspect demonstrates the relevance of the text's accounting material to decision-making in today's business world. These real world companies serve as a reminder that the matter under study is truly relevant to your future.

3M	Exxon	PepsiCo, Inc.
Accessory	Federal Express Corporation	Pier 1
Albertson, Inc.	Federated Department Stores	Pitney-Bowes Corp.
Alcoa	Footlocker	Proctor & Gamble
America West Airlines	Ford Motor Company	Quaker Oats Company
American Express	The GAP	Reader's Digest
American Greetings Corp.	General Electric	Reebok
Apple Computer, Inc.	General Motors	Rubbermaid Incorp.
AT&T	Globe Metallurgical, Inc.	Safeway Inc.
Avis	Greyhound	Sara Lee Corp.
Ben & Jerry's	H&R Block	Score Board, Inc.
Binny & Smith Inc.	Harley-Davidson, Inc.	Sears
Blockbuster Video	Hewlett-Packard Co.	Seven Up
Boeing	Honda	Sony
Boise Cascade	IBM	Southern Company
Chiquita Brands Int'l.	International Dairy Queen	Sprint Corp.
Chrysler Corporation	J.C. Penney Co., Inc.	Texaco
CIT Group/Commercial Services	L.A. Gear, Inc.	Texas Instruments
The Clorox Company	La-Z-Boy	Toyota
Coca-Cola	Marriott	Tyco
Colgate-Palmolive Co.	Mattel, Inc.	U S WEST
Compaq Corp	Maybelline, Inc.	W. T. Grant
Corning, Inc.	Merrill Lynch	Wal-Mart
Deere & Company	Microsoft Corp.	Walt Disney Co.
Dell Computer Corporation	Motorola, Inc.	Wendy's
Delta	New York Times	Whirlpool
Digital Equipment	Nike, Inc.	Wm. Wrigley Jr. Co.
Dr. Pepper	Nissan	Woolco
Duracell International, Inc.	Olympic Stain	Woolworth
E. I. duPont de Nemours	Pennzoil	Xerox Corporation

VOLUME II   CHAPTERS 13–25

F.A.S.T. EDITION
FULLY ANNOTATED SUPPORT FOR TEACHING

FUNDAMENTAL

ACCOUNTING PRINCIPLES

FOURTEENTH EDITION

VOLUME II   CHAPTERS 13–25

F.A.S.T. EDITION
FULLY ANNOTATED SUPPORT FOR TEACHING

FUNDAMENTAL

ACCOUNTING PRINCIPLES

FOURTEENTH EDITION

KERMIT D. LARSON
University of Texas–Austin

Contributing Author
BARBARA CHIAPPETTA
Nassau Community College

IRWIN

Chicago • Bogotá • Boston • Buenos Aires • Caracas
London • Madrid • Mexico City • Sydney • Toronto

*D*edicated to
Nancy, Julie, Tim, Cindy, Albrecht, and Megan

Cover image: Stuart Simons

© Richard D. Irwin, a Times Mirror Higher Education Group, Inc. company, 1955, 1959, 1963, 1966, 1969, 1972, 1975, 1978, 1981, 1984, 1987, 1990, 1993, and 1996

Irwin Book Team

Executive editor:	Jeff Shelstad
Developmental editors:	Margaret Haywood, Jackie Scruggs, Stephen Isaacs
Marketing manager:	Cindy L. Ledwith
Production supervisor:	Bob Lange
Assistant manager, desktop services:	Jon Christopher
Assistant manager, graphics	Charlene R. Breeden
Photo researcher:	Keri Kunst
Project editor:	Denise Santor-Mitzit
Designer:	Heidi J. Baughman
Graphics supervisor:	Heather D. Burbridge
Compositor:	York Graphic Services, Inc.
Typeface:	10/12 Times Roman
Printer:	Von Hoffmann Press, Inc.

Times Mirror
Higher Education Group

Library of Congress Cataloging-in-Publication Data

Larson, Kermit D.
    Fundamental accounting principles/Kermit D. Larson,
    with contributions by Barbara Chiappetta.—14th ed.
       p.   cm.
    Includes index.
    ISBN 0-256-19645-1 0-256-17842-9 (F.A.S.T. edition)
    1. Accounting. I. II. Chiappetta, Barbara.
  III. Title.
  HF5635.P975 1996
  657—dc20   95–20806

Printed in the United States of America
1 2 3 4 5 6 7 8 9 0 VH 2 1 0 9 8 7 6 5

About the Author

Kermit D. Larson is the Arthur Andersen & Co. Alumni Professor of Accounting Emeritus at The University of Texas at Austin. He served as chairman of the U.T. Department of Accounting and was Visiting Associate Professor at Tulane University. His scholarly articles have been published in a variety of journals, including *The Accounting Review, Journal of Accountancy,* and *Abacus.* He is the author of several books, including *Financial Accounting* and *Fundamentals of Financial and Managerial Accounting,* both published by Richard D. Irwin, Inc.

Professor Larson is a member of The American Accounting Association, the Texas Society of CPAs, and the American Institute of CPAs. His activities with the AAA have involved serving as Vice President, as Southwest Regional Vice President, and as chairperson of several committees, including the Committee on Concepts and Standards. He was a member of the committee that planned the first AAA Doctoral Consortium and served as its Director.

Professor Larson currently is President of the Richard D. Irwin Foundation. His other activities have included serving on the Accounting Accreditation Committee and on the Accounting Standards Committee of the AACSB. He was a member of the Constitutional Drafting Committee of the Federation of Schools of Accountancy and a member of the Commission on Professional Accounting Education. He has been an expert witness on cases involving mergers, antitrust litigation, consolidation criteria, franchise taxes, and expropriation of assets by foreign governments. Professor Larson served on the Board of Directors and Executive Committee of Tekcon, Inc., and on the National Accountants Advisory Board of Safe-Guard Business Systems. In his leisure time, he enjoys skiing and is an avid sailor and golfer.

About the Contributing Author

Barbara Chiappetta received her BBA in Accounting and MS in Education from Hofstra University and is a tenured full professor at Nassau Community College. For the past 14 years she has been an active Executive Board member of the Teachers of Accounting at Two-Year Colleges (TACTYC), serving ten years as Vice President and currently as the President since the fall of 1993. As an active member of the American Accounting Association, she has served as a Northeast Regional Representative of the Two-Year Section, is currently a member of the Northeast Region Steering Committee, and continues to chair (for the third year) the Curriculum Revision Committee for the Two-Year Section. Chiappetta co-chaired the Curriculum Revision Project at Nassau Community College. She received the Dean of Instruction's Faculty Distinguished Achievement Award in the spring of 1995.

Ms. Chiappetta has two sons, Michael and David, and both will be celebrating graduations in 1996. Michael, a Colgate University graduate, will receive his law degree from USC, and David will graduate from Syracuse University. Her husband, Robert, is an entrepreneur in the leisure sport industry. Barbara enjoys downhill skiing; she is also an avid tennis player and plays on a USTA team. Barbara also enjoys the challenge of duplicate and tournament bridge.

Contents in Brief

Preface

The 14th edition has changed *Fundamental Accounting Principles* in many important ways. Extensive input obtained through surveys, focus groups, reviewers, and personal correspondence has driven the revision plan. Instructors confirm several trends that are affecting the world of accounting. The trends most prevalent in accounting education today include the demand for change, the visual orientation of students, the need for flexibility and innovation in the classroom, new pedagogy, and the impact of technology. The many changes that have been integrated throughout this revision are in response to these trends.

To emphasize the business orientation of this edition, the text incorporates a variety of features that expose students to real-world situations and show the relevance of the material to real decisions. These features include the following:

EXTENSIVE INTEGRATION OF COMPANY EXAMPLES

- Several actual company references in each chapter describe how the companies have applied the concepts being discussed. Typically, each reference is accompanied by a photo that draws attention to the nature of the business or the specific company.

If **TYCO Toys, Inc.'s** management made the preceding comparison, the resulting figures might motivate them to investigate how this compares to last year and how they could improve this ratio. Continuation of a financially sound business requires continuous monitoring of the liquidity of the firm's assets.

- End-of-chapter questions relate to the financial statements of Apple Computer, Inc.; Ben & Jerry's Homemade, Inc.; and Federal Express Corporation. These statements are provided in appendixes to the book. Apple Computer, Inc., serves as the basis for a Financial Statement Analysis Case in most chapters. Other chapters draw on the Apple Computer annual report for a managerial decision case or managerial analysis problem.

- An actual company scenario at the beginning of each chapter implicitly or explicitly raises questions related to the material covered in the chapter. Later in the chapter, one or more references show how the ideas being explained at that point apply to the company described in the chapter opening. Even before students read a chapter, they realize from the opening scenarios that what they will be learning is useful in solving real problems.

- The financial statements of Microsoft Corporation are used throughout Chapter 17 as a basis for discussing financial statement analysis. In this way, we emphasize the relevance of the discussion to actual decision situations.
- This edition continues the practice of having several chapters incorporate boxed quotations and biographical sketches of persons in business, accounting, and public service. In addition to providing role models for students, these individuals explain how the information in the chapter is relevant to their decision-making situations. This feature is called "As a Matter of Opinion."

As a Matter of Opinion

Diana Scott is a graduate of Wittenberg University. She worked for Price Waterhouse in its national office in New York before joining the FASB staff as a project manager in 1985. After leaving that position in 1991, she joined the management consulting firm of Towers Perrin in Chicago, where she is an accounting and financial consultant in the Technical Services Group.

Over the past several years, accountants have begun to pay much more attention to the potential future payments that businesses may be obligated to make as a result of current op-

made. The standard requires them to provide information about their obligations and to recognize the expenses for probable future payments.

Are there other obligations that we presently ignore but someday may have to recognize as liabilities? I would not be surprised. One that comes to mind is potential claims from injuries to product users. Some juries have given large awards many years after a product was sold. Another possible liability is the cost of cleaning up toxic wastes discarded before anyone was aware of the danger.

Diana J. Scott, CPA

Instructors and reviewers have uniformly called for a new commitment to show students the relevance of accounting information and to teach them how to use the information. The Accounting Education Change Commission also has emphasized the importance of this approach. In response, this revision places much greater emphasis on the use of accounting information by managers, business owners, lenders, and other interested parties.

This shift in focus has been accomplished while maintaining the appropriate goal of showing students how the information is developed. Too often, the importance of this understanding to managers and other nonaccountant decision makers has been overlooked or dismissed. By gaining an introductory understanding of the processes by which accounting information and reports are generated, future decision makers learn the limits of accounting information. They learn to avoid overstating or misinterpreting the information. Thus, they are less apt to confuse such things as book values and market values, accumulated depreciation and spendable funds, or product costs and variable costs.

In every chapter, students learn and practice how to use accounting information in evaluating companies and making decisions. For example, "Using the Information" sections in the financial accounting chapters gradually expand students' understanding of financial ratios and other forms of analysis. Some of the Using the Information topics are:

Debt ratio—Chapter 2

Business segment information—Chapter 6

Return on total assets—Chapter 11

Price-earnings ratio—Chapter 14

Cash flow analyses—Chapter 16

INCREASED FOCUS ON USING ACCOUNTING INFORMATION

After studying this and the previous chapters, you have learned about all of the important classes of assets that businesses own. Recall from Chapter 10 that in evaluating the efficiency of a company in using its assets, a ratio that is often calculated and reviewed is total asset turnover. Another ratio that provides information about a company's efficiency in using its assets is **return on total assets.** You can calculate the return on total assets with this formula:

$$\text{Return on total assets} = \frac{\text{Net income}}{\text{Average total assets}}$$

For example, **Reebok International,** a worldwide distributor of sports and fitness products, earned a net income of $222.4 million during 1993. At the beginning of 1993, Reebok had total assets of $1,345.3 million, and at the end of the year total assets were $1,391.7 million. If the average total assets owned during the year is approximated by averaging the beginning and ending asset balances, Reebok's return on total assets for 1993 was:

USING THE INFORMATION— RETURN ON TOTAL ASSETS

LO 5

Explain the use of return on total assets in evaluating a company's efficiency in using its assets.

In Chapter 17, we review and discuss the relationships between all of the ratios using the annual report from Microsoft Corporation as a basis for discussion. We also discuss vertical and horizontal analyses and the use of other financial disclosures. The cost and managerial chapters continue this increased emphasis on using accounting information in decision making.

CHANGES TO PROMOTE STUDENT MOTIVATION AND STUDY TIME EFFECTIVENESS

Several changes in this edition are intended to motivate students and help them study more effectively.

A Shorter, Less Imposing Book

Perhaps the most obvious improvement in the new edition is that it is a more stream-lined book. This was accomplished by new restrictions on topical coverage, a renewed emphasis on concise writing, a new design, and the publication of the alternate problems in a separate booklet available at no extra charge. We believe *Fundamental Accounting Principles* is a text students will look forward to reading and be happy to carry—to class and to study groups.

Integrated Progress Checks with Answers

Progress Check
(Answers to Progress Checks are provided at the end of the chapter.)

2–1   Which of the following are examples of accounting source documents? *(a)* Journals and ledgers; *(b)* Income statements and balance sheets; *(c)* External transactions and internal transactions; *(d)* Bank statements and sales tickets; *(e)* All of the above.

2–2   What kinds of economic events affect a company's accounting equation?

2–3   Why are business papers called source documents?

A new feature in this edition is a series of Progress Checks integrated in each chapter. These review questions generally follow the discussion related to a learning objective. Occasionally, Progress Checks are presented more frequently. The goal is to have students stop momentarily and reflect on whether they should spend more time studying a given section of the text before moving on. Answers to the Progress Check questions are provided at the end of each chapter.

Pervasive Demonstration of Real-World Relevance

Motivation is typically stimulated by a reminder that the matter under study is truly relevant to life. *Fundamental Accounting Principles* brings these reminders in a variety of ways. For example, marginal notes in several chapters describe how an accounting principle being explained at that point is applied by a widely recognized company. The integration of the opening chapter scenarios with later portions of the chapters serves a similar purpose, as does the extensive use of actual company examples.

PRINCIPLE APPLICATION
Matching Principle, p. 108
In 1993, J.C. Penney Company had retail sales of $18,983 million. In addition to bad debt expenses, the credit costs the company matched with these revenues included operating expenses and third-party credit costs of $260 million.

In the last two entries, notice that the credit card expense was not recorded until cash was received from the credit card company. This practice is merely a matter of convenience. By following this procedure, the business avoids having to calculate and record the credit card expense each time sales are recorded. Instead, the expense related to many sales can be calculated once and recorded when cash is received. However, the *matching principle* requires reporting credit card expense in the same period as the sale. Therefore, if the sale and the cash receipt occur in different periods, you must accrue and report the credit card expense in the period of the sale by using an adjusting entry at the end of the year. For example, this year-end adjustment accrues $24 of credit card expense on a $600 receivable that the Credit Card Company has not yet paid.

Concept Testers

To encourage additional study of important glossary terms, selected chapters conclude the assignment material with a *concept tester* in the form of a short crossword puzzle. These puzzles are supported by the Working Papers.

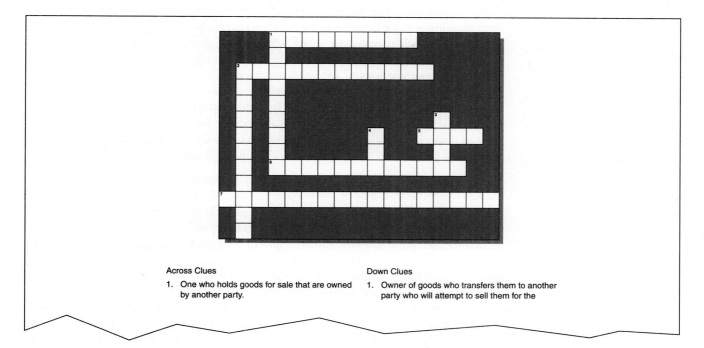

Across Clues

1. One who holds goods for sale that are owned by another party.

Down Clues

1. Owner of goods who transfers them to another party who will attempt to sell them for the

---

Some instructors have described today's students as the MTV generation. Increased exposure to television, computer screens, and movies has honed a visual orientation that influences how students learn most effectively. This edition has been designed with this visual orientation in mind. The design is intended to capture and hold the students' attention.

VISUAL ORIENTATION

Use of Color

Conscious, deliberate thought and effort have gone into the use of color to add more interest and appeal to the book. More importantly, color is used as a code to aid in learning. Blue indicates financial statements and reports that provide accounting information to be used in decision making. The primary documents that accountants generate for themselves as they develop informative statements and reports are green. Finally, documents that serve as sources of the data that go into accounting reports are yellow.

Other Visual Tools

Several other elements will also capture the students' interest via visual concepts. Crossword puzzles at the end of several chapters serve as an excellent method to reinforce verbal learning with a visual tool. Photographs of events and companies help show students how accounting fits into the real world. Supplementary videos make it possible for students to study accounting using television. PowerPoint software programs combine words and illustrations on one computer screen that students will enjoy being exposed to in a classroom environment.

FLEXIBILITY FOR INNOVATION

A common topic of discussion among introductory accounting instructors is the conflict between the extensive nature of traditional topical content and the need for new emphases on using accounting information in decision making, developing critical thinking, enhancing communication skills, and working in groups. Instructors clearly need more flexibility to innovate and develop an appropriate integration of these goals.

A dominant theme of the extensive input we received from instructors was that authors should facilitate these goals by taking a more proactive role in limiting the depth and range of topical coverage in the introductory accounting course. The clear imperative is that the text should reverse the trend toward being a complete resource for all possible combinations of topical development.

As a result, in close contact with reviewers and other instructors, we have taken numerous steps to avoid technical matters better left to intermediate level courses. In addition, we have deleted topics that have become less relevant in the changing climate of business practices. Instead, this edition focuses on the relevant topics that students need to know to be effective users of financial information.

Expanded Prologue

An important change in this direction was to prepare an expanded Prologue that now describes the accounting function in the context of other organizational functions such as finance, human resources, research and development, production, marketing, and executive management. The Prologue also explains the work accountants do, accounting certifications, the fields in which accountants work, and the pervasive importance of ethics in accounting. This accomplishes two basic improvements: First, as a separate learning unit, the Prologue emphasizes the overall importance of these topics to an understanding of the role accounting plays in providing information to a variety of decision makers. Instructors who want to give more attention to these topics, as suggested by the AECC, will find the Prologue especially appealing.

Financial Statement Orientation of Chapter 1

Second, as a result of the Prologue revision, Chapter 1 is now a much shorter and more manageable learning unit with a clear focus on financial statements. This includes the information contained in the statements, the basic concepts that guide the development and use of accounting information, and the relationship of the statements to the transactions and events in the life of a business.

Deletions in Chapters 4 and 5

Reviewers and adopters have overwhelmingly encouraged limiting the early examples in the book to proprietorships. As a result, the discussion of corporations has been deleted from Chapter 4 and from the illustrations in Chapter 5. Corporations are considered in the early chapters only as necessary to support student interaction with the financial statements at the back of the book and to recognize the existence of alternative forms of business organization.

Work sheets now are presented as an *optional* step in the accounting cycle. However, we also describe several reasons why an understanding of work sheets is useful. In addition, a more concise discussion of the adjusting entry method of accounting for inventories has eliminated the need for a separate appendix at the end of Chapter 5.

Discounting Notes Receivable

The revision of Chapter 8 recognizes the fact that an increasing number of companies routinely convert their receivables into cash without waiting to receive customer payments. In dealing with this modern business practice, the discussion of discounting notes receivable has been replaced with a more general examination of the various ways receivables may be converted into cash.

Topics Related to Inventories

Because perpetual inventory records are rarely maintained on a LIFO basis, LIFO has been deleted from the discussion of perpetual inventories in Chapter 9. Also, the discussion of lower of cost or market has been simplified to avoid the details of considering ceiling and floor limits on market value. Finally, the treatment of markups and markdowns has been eliminated from the discussion of the retail inventory method. Reviewers agree that all of these topics are better left to intermediate level courses.

Topics Related to Property, Plant, and Equipment

Sum-of-the-years' digits has been deleted from the discussion of accelerated depreciation, as has the apportioning of accelerated depreciation between accounting periods. To help students appreciate the differences between financial accounting and tax accounting, we continue to discuss MACRS. However, the discussion has been condensed to exclude the calculations that underlie MACRS tax rate tables. We also eliminated the discussions of plant asset subsidiary records and tax rules that govern plant asset exchanges.

Consolidated Financial Statements

Adopters indicate that the consolidated statements chapter in prior editions was the one they most frequently omitted. Nevertheless, long-term investments are an important financial consideration in evaluating many companies. The answer was to eliminate the consolidated statements chapter and to develop a more balanced set of asset chapters. As a result, Chapter 11 completes the asset coverage by discussing natural resources, intangible assets, and long-term investments. The long-term investments portion naturally concludes with a discussion of investments in international operations.

Leases and Deferred Income Tax Liabilities

In Chapter 12, the discussion of leases has been significantly shortened. Students learn the differences between capital and operating leases without having to journalize the entries related to capital leases. Also, the appendix on deferred income taxes has been deleted as a technical issue better left to intermediate level courses. The appendix on payroll records has been moved to the back of the book.

Streamlined Coverage of Partnerships

Reviewers and focus group participants suggested that we compress the coverage of partnerships. In response, we have streamlined the discussion and combined it with the introductory discussion of corporations in Chapter 13. This eliminated the separate chapter on partnerships.

Deletion of Cash Flows Appendix and Direct Method Worksheet

In explaining cash flows from operating activities in Chapter 16, we first explain the direct method, which is most relevant to managerial evaluations and predictions. However, the direct method work sheet has been deleted. We then explain the indirect method as the dominant method used in financial reporting. This approach eliminates the need for a separate appendix dealing with the indirect method.

Segmental Reporting

The illustration and discussion of segmental reporting has been eliminated from Chapter 17. However, a short section at the close of Chapter 6 recognizes that operating in several business segments complicates the design of the accounting system. Then, the use of business segment information by decision makers is briefly discussed.

Integrated Coverage of Mark-to-Market Accounting (*SFAS 115*)

The issuance of *SFAS 115* represents an accounting milestone in its break from the traditional cost and lower-of-cost-or-market bases of reporting. As a result, we incorporate this new development in several sections of the book. These include short-term investments in Chapter 8, long-term investments in Chapter 11, and alternative valuation methods in Appendix D.

Expanded Coverage of Activity-Based Costing

The practice of managerial accounting in United States industry continues to undergo a wide range of significant changes. Among these, the increasing implementation of activity-based costing systems is particularly noticeable. Accordingly, the introductory coverage of activity-based costing in Chapter 21 has been expanded in this new edition.

Emphasis on New Teaching Methods

The instructor's Fully Annotated Support for Teaching (F.A.S.T.) Edition of the text contains suggested ways of using selected problem assignments as the basis for group projects. Each chapter includes at least one group project suggestion. The group projects help students learn the skill of working effectively in teams and also encourage more active student participation in the classroom.

In addition to the hardcover version of the text, the first 12 chapters and the last 13 chapters are available in separate softcover versions that include Working Papers. A variety of special packaging and/or custom publishing options also is available depending on the unique needs of each school. Consult your Irwin representative for details.

A new supplement, *Student Learning Tools* (with an accompanying instructor's manual), is designed to facilitate both the development of interpersonal skills and a conceptual approach with a user emphasis. The introduction is aimed at motivating the student to participate by developing an understanding of the need for and the value of active learning. Tips for writing and recommended research/writing projects are also included.

END-OF-CHAPTER MATERIAL

The 14th edition includes several improvements in the end-of-chapter material. Many of these improvements have been added in response to calls for change from the AECC.

Enhanced Emphasis on Critical Thinking, Analysis, and Communication Skills

The assignment material in the book has been completely revised. Many assignments have been reoriented to increase the emphasis on critical thinking and communication skills. For example, the requirements for selected problems in each chapter now include a *Preparation Component* and a separate *Analysis Component.*

The Analysis Component generally requires students to think about the financial statement consequences of alternative situations. Students learn to consider the consequences of alternatives and the resulting effects on their interpretation of the results. This complements the more usual preparation component of end-of-chapter assignments.

Analysis component:

2. In comparing the results of the three alternatives, how would they change if MDI had been experiencing declining prices in the acquisition of additional inventory?

3. What specific advantages and disadvantages are offered by using LIFO and by using FIFO assuming the cost trends given at the beginning of this problem?

In addition, a new category of assignments is described as Critical Thinking: Essays, Problems, and Cases. Typical assignments in this category are:

Analytical Essays—Students evaluate a situation such as alternative facts related to another problem assignment and express their findings in writing.

Business Communication Cases—Students prepare a variety of correspondence items such as letters to customers, memoranda of record, or internal letters of explanation.

Financial Reporting Problems—Students examine the factual situation of a company and determine the financial statement consequences of alternative procedures.

Managerial Analysis Problems—Students analyze accounting information from the perspective of nonaccountant managers.

Financial Statement Analysis Cases—Students extract and interpret information from the financial information contained in Apple Computer Inc.'s annual report.

Management Decision Cases—Students assume the role of nonaccountant managers and use accounting information to reach various business decisions.

Ethical Issues Essays—Students are asked to consider the ethical implications of the "As A Matter of Ethics" cases presented in the chapters and express their personal conclusions regarding the appropriate actions that should be taken.

CRITICAL THINKING: ESSAYS, PROBLEMS, AND CASES

On March 26, Summerfield Office Supply received Miles Brokaw's check number 629, dated March 24, in the amount of $1,420. The check was to pay for merchandise Brokaw had purchased on February 25. The merchandise was shipped from Summerfield's office at 1715 Westgate Boulevard, Austin, Texas, 78704 to Brokaw's home at 823 Congress, Austin, Texas, 78701. On March 27, Summerfield's cashier deposited the check in the company's bank account. The bank returned the check to Summerfield with the March 31 bank statement. Also included was a debit memorandum indicating that Brokaw's check was returned for nonsufficient funds and the bank was charging Summerfield a $25 NSF processing fee. Immediately after reconciling

Business Communications Case

(LO 5)

Also, a number of the exercises and problems require students to think analytically by working "backward" from outputs to inputs or by analyzing the consequences of errors or omissions.

Instructors indicate an increasing reliance on shorter problem material for use as in-class illustrations and as homework assignments. Undoubtedly, the prospect of solving problems in a short time and the rapid feedback of having done so successfully are motivating factors that lead students to extend their study efforts. Accordingly, this edition contains a new category of very short exercises that are identified as Quick Study. At least one quick study is provided for each learning objective.

QUICK STUDY (Five-Minute Exercises)

QS 10–1
(LO 1)

Explain the difference between *(a)* plant assets and long-term investments; *(b)* plant assets and inventory; and *(c)* plant assets and current assets.

QS 10–2
(LO 1)

Mattituck Lanes installed automatic score-keeping equipment. The electrical work required to prepare for the installation was $12,000. The invoice price of the equipment was $120,000. Additional costs were $2,000 for delivery and $8,400, sales tax. During the installation, a component of the equipment was damaged because it was carelessly left on a lane and hit by the automatic lane cleaning machine during a daily maintenance run. The cost of repairing the component was $1,500. What is the cost of the automatic scorekeeping equipment?

THE IMPACT OF TECHNOLOGY

An increasing number of schools are moving toward multimedia education and a more interactive learning environment. Inevitably, this is a gradual process that requires a great deal of evaluation and reassessment along the way. Initial attempts to incorporate new technologies nearly always require modification and readjustment before the most effective applications are discovered. In light of these facts, the goal of our author-publisher team has been, and continues to be, to facilitate and encourage but not dictate the nature of the changes implemented by our adopters.

Given this objective, we have attempted to lead with technological innovations during the last two editions of *Fundamental Accounting Principles.* In 1990, for example, we began to offer the Telecourse option, teaming with Kirkwood Community College in Cedar Rapids, Iowa, to promote distance learning and interactive, telecommunicating options. In 1993, we offered the first CD-ROM version of an accounting principles package. This included the full text and all supporting supplemental material.

Further innovation is scheduled for this new edition. New *multimedia practice sets* will give the students a portable, exciting learning environment. Our new PowerPoint *Ready Slides, Ready Shows,* and *Ready Notes* give the instructor and student increased flexibility for classroom instruction and student retention. We also offer *computerized practice sets* covering a variety of companies and situations. Our *GLAS* and *SPATS* software provide unusually flexible general ledger and spreadsheet applications in both a DOS and Windows format.

Acknowledgments

We are grateful for the encouragement, suggestions, reviews, and counsel provided by students, colleagues, and instructors from across the nation. A tremendous amount of useful information was gained from the participants in the nationwide *Fundamental Accounting Principles* focus groups organized by the publisher. They include:

Ron Beckman
Sam Houston State University

Frank Beil
Lincoln University

Clifford Bellers
Washtenaw Community College

Kathy Bent
Cape Cod Community College

Lucille Berry
Webster University

Rick Bowden
Oakland Community College,
Auburn Hills

Sheila Bradford
Tulsa Junior College, Metro

Stewart Brown
Bristol Community College

Carol Buchl
Northern Michigan University

Robert Carpenter
Eastfield College

Janet Cassagio
Nassau Community College

Bruce Cassel
Dutchess Community College

Barbara Chiappetta
Nassau Community College

Sue Cook
Tulsa Junior College, S.E.

Jim Cosby
John Tyler Community College

Doris deLespinasse
Adrian College

Pam Dinville
Bellevue College

Irene Douma
Montclair State College

Bill Engel
Longview Community College

Mike Foland
Belleville Community College

Linda Frye
NW Missouri State University

Kathy Gardner
Johnson & Wales University

Mike Garms
Henry Ford Community College

John Godfrey
Springfield Technical Community
College

Glenn Goodale
Castleton State College

Robert Gronstal
Metro Community College

Margie Hamilton
Lewis and Clark Community
College

Robert Hardin
Henry Ford Community College

Linda Herrington
Community College of Alleghany
County

Bob Hildenbrand
Albuquerque TVI, Main

Bob Holman
Longview Community College,
Blue Springs Campus

Patty Holmes
Des Moines Area Community
College

Zach Holmes
Oakland Community College

Susan Honig
Herbert Lehman College

Gloria Jackson
San Antonio College

Doug Johnson
Southeast Community College

George Katz
San Antonio College

Randy Kidd
Penn Valley Community College

Tom Knoll
DeVry Institute of Technology

Frank Korman
Mountain View College

Robert Landry
Massasoit Community College

Cathy Larson
Middlesex Community College

Douglas Larson
Salem State College

Paul Lospennato
Northshore Community College

Nancy Lynch
West Virginia University

Andrea Murowski
Brookdale Community College

Paul Nieman
Sanford Brown College

Vincent Osaghae
Chicago State University

Reed Peoples
Austin Community College,
Rio Grande

Pat Prugh
East Central College

Allan Rabinowitz
Pace University, NYC

Michael Raff
Prince Georges Community College

Alan Rainford
Greenfield Community College

George Ritchey
Harrisburg Community College

Nancy Ruhe
West Virginia University

Helena Ruhl
Three Rivers Community College

Marilyn Scheiner
Montgomery College, Rockville

James Skidmore
Grand Rapids Community College

Dan Small
J. Sargeant Reynolds Community
College

Charles Spector
SUNY, Oswego

Linda Spotts-Michael
Maple Woods Community College

Mary Ston
Oakland Community College

Kathy Tam
Tulsa Junior College, N.E.

Leslie Thysell
John Tyler Community College

John Vaccaro
Bunker Hill Community College

Cynthia Vest
Tarrant County Junior College

Joe Webster
TVI-Montoya

Kathleen Wessman
Montgomery College, Rockville

Jeff Wright
Johnson County Community
College

Marilyn Young
Tulsa Junior College, S.E.

Those who reviewed various portions of the manuscript or participated in our in-depth survey were especially helpful. They include:

John Aheto
Pace University

Rodger Brannan
University of Minnesota, Duluth

Harvey J. Cooke
Penn Valley Community College

S.T. Desai
Cedar Valley College

Kayla Fessler
Oklahoma City Community College

George Gardner
Bemidji St. College

Bonnie Givens
Avila College

Frank Korman
Mountain View College

Linda Lessing
SUNY College of Technology, Farmingdale

Noel McKeon
Florida Community College, Jacksonville

Linda Spotts-Michael
Maple Woods Community College

Dick Schneider
Winona State

Sara Sadon
Evergreen College

Mary Ston
Oakland Community College

Al Taccone
Dean Junior College

Dick Wasson
Southwestern College, Chula Vista

Jane Wiese
Valencia Community College

I particularly want to thank Barbara Chiappetta of Nassau Community College for her participation in *Fundamental Accounting Principles*. Thanks also to Debra Smith of the University of Puget Sound and to Barbara Schnathorst for their important contributions. I am especially indebted to Paul Miller of the University of Colorado, Colorado Springs, whose previous work and continued counsel have helped shape this and future editions. Finally, I will always be grateful for Betsey Jones and Sue Ann Meyer, whose talents and dedication were essential to this project.

SUPPLEMENTS THAT SUPPORT THE TEXT

Fundamental Accounting Principles is supported by a full range of supplements. They include:

FAST HINT
Alternative Example:
If the fair values of these investments on December 31 was $70,000, what entry would be made?
Answer:
Unrealized Holding
  Gain (Loss)   3,000
    Long-Term Invest.,
     Fair Value
     Adjustments   3,000

	Book Value	Fair (Market) Value
Candice Corp. bonds payable	$30,000	$29,050
Intex Corp. common stock, 500 shares	43,000	45,500
Total	$73,000	$74,550

- *Fully Annotated Support for Teaching Edition.* Marginal annotations labeled Fast Hints have been expanded. We continue to include Important Points to Remember, Critical Thought Questions, and Alternative Examples. New to this edition are Additional Insights, Class Discussion Issues, Relevant Exercises, Group Projects, and Relevant Quick Studies.

- *Solutions Manuals.* The solutions manuals contain completely revised solutions for all assignment material. The solutions manuals are available in a new electronic format in both Lotus and Excel.

- *Working Papers.* These volumes include papers for the Exercises, the Problems or Alternate Problems, the Comprehensive Problems, the Serial Problem, and the Concept Testers.

- *Study Guides.* For each chapter and appendix, these guides review the learning objectives and the summaries, outline the topical coverage, and provide a variety of practice problems with solutions.

- *Student Learning Tools.* Written by Barbara Chiappetta, this supplement contains material for students' use in an active learning environment. The materials coordinate with the active learning applications or lessons described in the accompanying instructor's manual. For instructors who additionally address preparation/procedural issues, accounting forms (journal paper, 2 and 3 column paper, and T accounts) are provided for reproduction. Working papers for selected problems from *Fundamental Accounting Principles* are also provided.

- *Instructor's Manual for Student Learning Tools.* This manual illustrates how to use a traditional text and meet the objectives set forth by the Accounting Education Change Commission. The approach employs a concept and user focus. Specific applications using active learning techniques, coordinated with *Student Learning Tools,* are provided. The manual was designed to provide instructors with the materials necessary to create an active learning environment to facilitate the development of interpersonal skills. Active learning strategies and structures, group formation, and assessment techniques are discussed. Visuals coordinated with the applications are available in the form of PowerPoint displays or acetate teaching transparencies.

- *Alternate Problems.* A booklet containing alternate problems is available. Updated yearly, this booklet is free of charge for adopters.

- *Practice Sets.* These give the student practice with the procedures presented in the text. There are several practice sets accompanying this book:

  Fast Mart, Inc. Provides a narrative of transactions and features a retail corporation.

  Cog Hill Camping Equipment Company. A practice set involving a sole proprietorship that includes business papers for a retailing company.

  Republic Lighting Company. A narrative of transactions for a sole proprietorship; it illustrates special journals and includes a work sheet for a retailing company.

  Republic Lighting Company: Extended Version. This is similar to Republic Lighting Company above, but covering two accounting periods.

  KJC Manufacturers, Inc. A narrative of transactions featuring a manufacturing company.

  Freewheel Corporation. A narrative of transactions for a corporate practice set with special journals.

- *Computerized Practice Sets.* From Leland Mansuetti and Keith Weidkamp, both of Sierra College, these computerized practice sets are available in DOS and Windows versions; they offer an alternative to manual sets.

  Granite Bay Jet Ski, Level One. This package simulates a single proprietorship involved in the sales, service, and storage of Kawasaki Jet Ski personal watercraft and other watercraft equipment. It is intended for use after coverage of the accounting cycle and accounting for cash.

  Granite Bay Jet Ski, Level Two. This adds a corporate level to the business presented in Level One. It is intended for use after coverage of depreciation of plant and equipment, current and long-term liabilities, and corporations.

  Thunder Mountain Snowmobile. Comparable to Granite Bay Jet Ski, Level One; the two sets may be alternated to provide variety each semester.

Gold Run Snowmobile, Inc. Comparable to Granite Bay Jet Ski, Level Two; the two sets may be alternated to provide variety each semester.

Wild Goose Marina, Inc. This offers a complete corporate simulation using a business that generates revenue through new and used houseboat sales, accessory sales, service sales, and moorage fees. It is intended for use after coverage of stocks, bonds, and cash flows.

Ramblewood Manufacturing, Inc. This package introduces students to job order cost accounting with a company that specializes in customized fencing. This full corporation simulation is intended for use after coverage of job order cost accounting.

- *Multimedia Practice Sets.* These incorporate sound and video into our best-selling Mansuetti and Weidkamp sets. These new alternatives could provide a more dynamic learning environment for your students.

- *Real World Accounting Series.* These practice sets from Timothy Louwers and William Pasewark offer students hands-on experience in analyzing and understanding corporate annual reports. They show the big picture at the end of the accounting process, emphasizing interpretation and analysis rather than preparation of financial statements.

  Athletronics, Inc. This practice set emphasizes the effect of generally accepted accounting principles on decisions based on accounting data. The student is required to perform financial analysis on the data contained in the manual.

  Shoe Business, Inc. This humorous yet realistic practice set focuses on the frequent overemphasis of bottom-line net income by investors. The student is led through extensive analysis of footnote disclosures, financial ratios, and bankruptcy prediction models.

  Understanding Corporate Annual Reports. This practice set contains instructions for obtaining an annual report from a publicly traded corporation.

- *Testbank.* The testbank contains a wide variety of test questions, including true-false, multiple-choice, quantitative, matching, and essay questions of varying levels of difficulty.

- *Computest.* A computerized version of the manual testbank for more efficient use is available in Macintosh, Windows, or DOS versions. The extensive features of this test generator program include random question selection based on the user's specification of learning objectives, type of question, and level of difficulty.

- *Teletest.* By calling a toll free number, users can specify the content of exams and have laser printed copies of the exams mailed to them.

- *Achievement Tests.* These are available in quantity to adopters. A solutions guide is included with each packet.

- *GLAS (General Ledger Applications Software).* This revised package contains most of the features of commercial accounting software, yet is easily used by students with little or no computer background. A large number of problem assignments are preloaded on the package, and it can be used to solve any problem that calls for journal entries. Both DOS and Windows versions are available.

- *SPATS (Spreadsheet Applications Template Software).* This includes Lotus 1–2–3 (or the equivalent) templates for selected problems and exercises from the text. The templates gradually become more complex, requiring students to build a variety of formulas. What-if questions are added to show the power of spreadsheets and a simple tutorial is included. Instructors may request a free master template for students to use or copy, or students can buy shrinkwrapped versions for a nominal fee. Both DOS and Windows versions are available.

- *Tutorial Software.* Multiple-choice, true-false, journal entry review, and glossary review questions are randomly accessed by students. Explanations of right and wrong answers are provided and scores are tallied. Instructors may request a free master template for students to use or copy, or students can buy shrinkwrapped versions for a nominal fee. Both DOS and Windows versions are available.

- *Solutions Transparencies.* These transparencies are set in large, boldface type to maximize their effectiveness in large classrooms.

- *Ready Shows, Ready Slides, Ready Notes.* These teaching enhancement packages were prepared by Jon A. Booker, Charles W. Caldwell, Susan C. Galbreath, and Richard S. Rand, all of Tennessee Technological University.

  Ready Shows. This is a package of multimedia lecture enhancement aids that uses PowerPoint software to illustrate chapter concepts.

  Ready Slides. These selected four-color teaching transparencies are printed from the PowerPoint Ready Shows.

  Ready Notes. This booklet of Ready Show screen printouts enables students to take notes during Ready Show or Ready Slide presentations.

- *Lecture Enhancement Video Series.* These short, action-oriented videos provide the impetus for lively classroom discussion. The *Financial Accounting Video Library* includes videos with the Financial Accounting Standards Board, Ben & Jerry's, and a video with Art Wyatt discussing the impact of the International Accounting Standards Committee. The *Managerial Accounting Video Library* includes videos featuring George Bush at the Baldrige Award ceremony, on-site footage from manufacturers such as Ford, and service corporations such as First National Bank of Chicago.

- *Lecture Review Videos.* This completely updated video series, produced in conjunction with Kirkwood Community College, provides a complete review by topic for those students who may miss a class or struggle with a topic. Sixty-five tapes, each one approximately 15 minutes in length, provide a complete review of *Fundamental Accounting Principles,* 14th edition.

Kermit D. Larson

Contents

Appendixes

To the Student

Fundamental Accounting Principles is designed to get you actively involved in the learning process so you will learn quickly and more thoroughly. The more time you spend expressing what you are learning, the more effectively you will learn. In accounting, you do this primarily by answering questions and solving problems. But this is not the only way to learn. You also can express your ideas by using the book's wide margins for taking notes, summarizing a phrase, or writing down a question that remains unanswered in your mind. Ideas that pop into your head can lead to fruitful exploration. These notes will assist in your later review of the material, and the simple process of writing them will help you learn.

To guide your study, *learning objectives* are listed near the beginning of each chapter. Read these objectives to form some expectations about what you will learn from studying the chapter. Think of them as your goals while you study. Each learning objective is repeated in the margin at the point the chapter begins to provide material related to that objective. You will find each objective repeated at the end of each chapter in the summary. The exercises and problem assignments following each chapter also are coded to these objectives.

As you progress in your study of each chapter, you will periodically encounter Progress Check questions relating to the material you have just studied. Answer the questions and compare your answers with the correct answers at the end of each chapter. If you are not able to answer the questions correctly, review the preceding section of the chapter before going on.

Several features of the text emphasize the real-world usefulness of the material in the book. For example, the *opening paragraphs* of each chapter raise questions about a real business. As you progress through the chapter, keep a sharp eye out for points in the discussion that apply to the scenario in the opening paragraphs. Also be aware of *photographs* in the text that locate instances where the material under discussion is applied to a real company. You also will find brief inserts entitled "As a Matter of Opinion" in which business and community leaders tell how they use accounting in making decisions.

The use of color in the book has been carefully planned to facilitate your learning. For example, the **financial statements** and **reports** that accounting provides as information to be used in decision making are blue. The **primary documents that accountants generate for their own use** as they develop informative

statements and reports are green. **Documents that serve as sources of the data** that go into an accounting system are yellow.

As you read the text, you will learn many important new terms. These **key terms** are printed in **black boldface** the first time they appear, and they are listed again in a *glossary* after each chapter. In addition, you can find these key terms in the index at the end of the book. As a reinforcement to learning, but also as a light break from regular study, several chapters close with a *crossword puzzle* that involves some of the glossary terms.

Computer technology is changing the way businesses operate and will continue to be a driving force in the 21st century. To reflect this change and to give you practice with software, some of the assignments in the book are preloaded on a general ledger software package called *GLAS*. The following logo identifies these assignments:

In addition, some of the problem assignments are preloaded on a set of computer spreadsheet templates called *SPATS*. These assignments are identified with the following logo:

Ask your instructor or check your school's bookstore for information about other supplemental items that are available to assist your study. The *tutorial software* contains multiple-choice, true-false, journal entry review, and glossary review questions to help you prepare for exams. The *study guide* reviews learning objectives and provides practice problems for each chapter. *Working papers* provide familiarity with the actual framework used in creating accounting information.

Accounting can be an informative, relevant, and engaging field of inquiry. *Fundamental Accounting Principles* offers many tools to lead you into an understanding of the importance of accounting. Read, discuss, and enjoy! What you learn in this course will be useful in your personal and professional affairs for the rest of your life.

Corporations and Partnerships

*B*ecause his father worked for Mobil Corporation for 30 years until retirement, Barry Foster has been interested in the company since childhood. He has always been impressed by the fact that Mobil has paid dividends every year since 1902. It has operations in more than 100 countries involving oil and gas, petrochemicals, plastics, mining, and land development. In 1993, these operations generated total revenues in excess of $63 billion.

Late in 1994, Foster began to examine the company's dividend record more closely. In doing so, he noted that during the 10-year period from 1983 to 1993, dividends to common stock increased from $2.00 per share to $3.25 per share. Dividends in 1994 were running at a rate that would accumulate to $3.40 per share. In attempting to evaluate the company, Foster also gathered information about several other companies. However, he was unsure about how to compare them.

Company	Common Dividend per Share		November 1994 Stock Price
	1994*	1993	
Mobil Corporation	$3.40	$3.25	$82¼
Minnesota Mining & Manufacturing Co.	1.76	1.66	53¼
Texaco Inc.	3.20	3.20	60⅞
AT&T Corp.	1.32	1.32	54
GAP, Inc.	0.48	0.38	37⅞
Microsoft Corp.	0	0	64½

*Estimated 1994 amounts.

LEARNING OBJECTIVES

After studying Chapter 13, you should be able to:

1. **Explain the unique characteristics of the corporate form of business.**
2. **Record the issuance of par value stock and no-par stock with or without a stated value, and explain the concept of minimum legal capital.**
3. **Record transactions that involve dividends and stock subscriptions and explain the effects of stock subscriptions on the balance sheet.**
4. **State the differences between common and preferred stock, and allocate dividends between the common and preferred stock of a corporation.**
5. **Describe convertible preferred stock and explain the meaning of the par value, call price, market value, and book value of corporate stock.**
6. **Explain the concepts of mutual agency and unlimited liability for a partnership, record the investments and withdrawals of partners, and allocate the net incomes or losses of a partnership among the partners.**
7. **Calculate dividend yield and describe its meaning.**
8. **Define or explain the words and phrases listed in the chapter glossary.**

Of the three common types of business organizations (proprietorships, partnerships, and corporations), corporations are fewest in number. However, they transact more business than the other two combined. Large businesses like Mobil Corporation are almost all corporations. In the United States, the dollar sales volume of corporations is approximately nine times the combined sales of unincorporated businesses. Thus, from an overall economic point of view, corporations are clearly the most important form of business organization. As you study this chapter, you will learn how corporations are organized and operated, and about some of the procedures used to account for corporations. You will also learn about partnerships.

CORPORATIONS

CHARACTERISTICS OF CORPORATIONS

LO 1

Explain the unique characteristics of the corporate form of business.

Corporations have become the dominant type of business because of the advantages created by their unique characteristics. We describe these characteristics in the following sections.

Corporations Are Separate Legal Entities

A corporation is a separate legal entity. As a separate entity, a corporation conducts its affairs with the same rights, duties, and responsibilities as a person. However, because it is not a real person, a corporation can act only through its agents, who are its officers and managers.

Stockholders Are Not Liable for the Corporation's Debts

Because a corporation is a separate legal entity, it is responsible for its own acts and its own debts. Its shareholders are not liable for either. From the viewpoint of an investor, this lack of stockholders' liability is, perhaps, the most important advantage of the corporate form of business.

FAST HINT

Important Point to Remember:
The business entity principle introduced in Chapter 1 requires a business to be accounted for separately from its owners.

Ownership Rights of Corporations Are Easily Transferred

The ownership of a corporation is represented by shares of stock that, in general, are easily bought or sold. Also, the transfer of shares from one stockholder to another usually has no effect on the corporation or its operations.[1] Many companies have thousands or even millions of their shares bought and sold every day through major stock exchanges located throughout the world. For example, *The Wall Street Journal* reported that on  November 15, 1994, 5,552,600 shares of **American Express Company** stock were traded on the New York Stock Exchange.

Corporations Have Continuity of Life

A corporation's life may continue indefinitely because it is not tied to the physical lives of its owners. In some cases, a corporation's life may be initially limited by the laws of the state of its incorporation. However, the corporation's charter can be renewed and its life extended when the stated time expires. Thus, a corporation may have a perpetual life as long as it continues to be successful.

Stockholders Are Not Agents of the Corporation

As we previously stated, a corporation acts through its agents, who are the officers or managers of the corporation. Stockholders who are not officers or managers of the corporation do not have the power to bind the corporation to contracts. Instead, stockholders participate in the affairs of the corporation only by voting in the stockholders' meetings.

Ease of Capital Accumulation

Buying stock in a corporation often is more attractive to investors than investing in other forms of business. Stock investments are attractive because: (1) stockholders are not liable for the corporation's actions and debts, (2) stock usually can be transferred easily, (3) the life of the corporation is not limited, and (4) stockholders are not agents of the corporation. These advantages make it possible for some corporations to accumulate large amounts of capital from the combined investments of many stockholders. In a sense, a corporation's capacity for raising capital is limited only by its ability to convince investors that it can use their funds profitably.

Governmental Regulation of Corporations

Corporations are created by fulfilling the requirements of a state's incorporation laws. These laws subject a corporation to state regulation and control. Single proprietorships and partnerships may escape some of these regulations. In addition, they may avoid having to file some governmental reports required of corporations.

Taxation of Corporations

Corporations are subject to the same property and payroll taxes as single proprietorships and partnerships. In addition, corporations are subject to taxes that are not levied

---

[1] However, a transfer of ownership can create significant effects if it brings about a change in who controls the company's activities.

on either of the other two. The most burdensome of these are federal and state income taxes that together may take 40% or more of a corporation's pretax income. However, the tax burden does not end there. The income of a corporation is taxed twice, first as income of the corporation and again as personal income to the stockholders when cash is distributed to them as dividends. This differs from single proprietorships and partnerships, which are not subject to income taxes as business units. Their income is taxed only as the personal income of their owners.[2]

The tax situation of a corporation is generally viewed as a disadvantage. However, in some cases, it can work to the advantage of stockholders because corporation and individual tax rates are progressive. That is, higher levels of income are taxed at higher rates and lower levels of income are taxed at lower rates. Therefore, taxes may be saved or at least delayed if a large amount of income is divided among two or more tax-paying entities. Thus, an individual who has a large personal income and pays taxes at a high rate may benefit if some of the income is earned by a corporation that person owns, as long as the corporation avoids paying dividends. By not paying dividends, the corporation's income is taxed only once at the lower corporate rate, at least temporarily until dividends are paid.

FAST HINT
Important Point to Remember:
The double-taxation effect is not as severe as it might appear when we consider that the owner/manager of a corporation can legitimately collect a reasonable salary that is taxed only once.

FAST HINT
Relevant Quick Study:
To apply these concepts, work QS 13–1.

ORGANIZING A CORPORATION

A corporation is created by securing a charter from a state government. The requirements that must be met to be chartered vary among the states. Usually, a charter application must be signed by three or more subscribers to the prospective corporation's stock (such persons are called the *incorporators* or *promoters*). Then, the application must be filed with the appropriate state official. When it is properly completed and all fees are paid, the charter is issued and the corporation is formed. The subscribers then purchase the corporation's stock, meet as stockholders, and elect a board of directors. The directors are responsible for guiding the company's business affairs.

ORGANIZATION COSTS

The costs of organizing a corporation, such as legal fees, promoters' fees, and amounts paid to secure a charter, are called **organization costs.** On the corporation's books, these costs are debited to an asset account called Organization Costs. In a sense, this intangible asset benefits the corporation throughout its life. Thus, you could argue that the cost should be amortized over the life of the corporation, which may be unlimited. However, generally accepted accounting principles require any intangible asset to be amortized over a period that is no longer than 40 years.[3]

Income tax rules permit a corporation to write off organization costs as a tax deduction over a minimum of five years. Thus, to make record-keeping simple, many corporations use a five-year amortization period for financial statement purposes. Although the five-year period is arbitrary, it is widely used in practice. Because organization costs usually are not material in amount, the *materiality principle* also supports the arbitrarily short amortization period.

MANAGEMENT OF A CORPORATION

Although the organizational structures of all corporations are not always the same, the ultimate control of a corporation rests with its stockholders. However, this control is exercised only indirectly through the election of the board of directors. Indi-

---

[2]Some corporations that have a limited number of shareholders can elect to be treated like a partnership for tax purposes. These companies are called *Sub-Chapter S Corporations.*

[3]FASB, *Accounting Standards—Current Text* (Norwalk, CT, 1994), sec. I60.110. First published in *APB Opinion No. 17,* par. 29.

vidual stockholders' rights to participate in management begin and end with a vote in the stockholders' meetings, where each of them has one vote for each share of stock owned.

Normally, a corporation holds a stockholders' meeting once each year to elect directors and transact other business as required by the corporation's bylaws. A group of stockholders that owns or controls the votes of 50% plus one share of a corporation's stock can easily elect the board and thereby control the corporation. However, in many companies, very few stockholders attend the annual meeting or even care about getting involved in the voting process. As a result, a much smaller percentage may be able to dominate the election of board members.

Stockholders who do not attend stockholders' meetings must be given an opportunity to delegate their voting rights to an agent. A stockholder does this by signing a document called a **proxy** that gives a designated agent the right to vote the stock. Prior to a stockholders' meeting, a corporation's board of directors typically mails to each stockholder an announcement of the meeting and a proxy that names the existing board chairperson as the voting agent of the stockholder. The announcement asks the stockholder to sign and return the proxy.

A corporation's board of directors is responsible for and has final authority for managing the corporation's activities. However, it can act only as a collective body. An individual director has no power to transact corporate business. Although the board has final authority, it usually limits its actions to establishing broad policy. Day-to-day direction of corporate business is delegated to executive officers appointed by the board.

Traditionally, the chief executive officer (CEO) of the corporation is the president. Under the president, several vice presidents may be assigned specific areas of management responsibility, such as finance, production, and marketing. In addition, the corporation secretary keeps the minutes of the meetings of the stockholders and directors and ensures that all legal responsibilities are fulfilled. In a small corporation, the secretary is also responsible for keeping a record of the stockholders and the changing amounts of their stock interest.

Many corporations have a different structure in which the chairperson of the board of directors is also the chief executive officer. With this arrangement, the president is usually designated the chief operating officer (COO), and the rest of the structure is essentially the same.

STOCK CERTIFICATES AND THE TRANSFER OF STOCK

When investors buy a corporation's stock, they may receive a stock certificate as proof that they purchased the shares.[4] In many corporations, only one certificate is issued for each block of stock purchased. This certificate may be for any number of shares. Other corporations may use preprinted certificates, each of which represents 100 shares, plus blank certificates that may be made out for any number of shares.

When selling shares of a corporation, a stockholder completes and signs a transfer endorsement on the back of the certificate and sends it to the corporation's secretary or the transfer agent. The secretary or agent cancels and files the old certificate, and issues a new certificate to the new stockholder. If the old certificate represents more shares than were sold, the corporation issues two new certificates. One certificate goes to the new stockholder for the sold shares and the other to the original stockholder for the remaining unsold shares.

---

[4] The issuance of certificates is less common than it used to be. Instead, many stockholders maintain accounts with the corporation or their stockbrokers and never receive certificates.

Registrar and Transfer Agent

If a corporation's stock is traded on a major stock exchange, the corporation must have a *registrar* and a *transfer agent.* The registrar keeps the stockholder records and prepares official lists of stockholders for stockholders' meetings and for dividend payments. Registrars and transfer agents usually are large banks or trust companies that have the computer facilities and staff to carry out this kind of work.

When a corporation has a transfer agent and a stockholder wants to transfer ownership of some shares to another party, the owner completes the transfer endorsement on the back of the stock certificate and sends the certificate to the transfer agent, usually with the assistance of a stockbroker. The transfer agent cancels the old certificate and issues one or more new certificates and sends them to the registrar. The registrar enters the transfer in the stockholder records and sends the new certificate or certificates to the proper owners.

Progress Check

(Answers to Progress Checks are provided at the end of the chapter.)

13-1   Which of the following is not a characteristic of the corporate form of business?
(a) Ease of capital accumulation;   (b) Stockholders are liable for corporate debts;
(c) Ownership rights are easily transferred.

13-2   Why is the income of a corporation said to be taxed twice?

13-3   What is a proxy?

AUTHORIZATION AND ISSUANCE OF STOCK

LO 2

Record the issuance of par value stock and no-par stock with or without a stated value, and explain the concept of minimum legal capital.

When a corporation is organized, its charter authorizes it to issue a specified number of shares of stock. If all of the authorized shares have the same rights and characteristics, the stock is called **common stock.** However, a corporation may be authorized to issue more than one class of stock, including different classes of common stock and preferred stock. (We discuss preferred stock later in this chapter.) For example, **American Greetings Corporation** has two types of common stock outstanding. Class A stock has one vote per share and Class B stock has ten votes per share.

Because a corporation cannot issue more than the number of shares authorized in its charter, its founders usually obtain authorization to issue more shares than they plan to sell when the company is first organized. By doing so, the corporation avoids having to get the state's approval to sell more shares when additional capital is needed to finance an expansion of the business. A corporation's balance sheet must disclose the numbers of shares authorized and issued. These facts are reported in the stockholders' equity section of the statement. For example, **Federal Express Corporation's** balance sheet in Appendix G shows this information:

	1993	1992
Common stock, $.10 par value; 100,000,000 shares authorized, 54,743,000 and 54,100,000 shares issued	$5,474,300	$5,410,000

Sale of Stock for Cash

When stock is sold for cash and immediately issued, an entry like the following is made to record the sale and issuance:

June	5	Cash	300,000.00	
		Common Stock, $10 Par Value		300,000.00
		Sold at par and issued 30,000 shares of $10 par value common stock.		

Exchanging Stock for Noncash Assets

A corporation may accept assets other than cash in exchange for its stock. In the process, the corporation also may assume some liabilities, such as a mortgage on some of the property. These transactions are recorded with an entry like this:

June	10	Machinery	10,000.00	
		Buildings	65,000.00	
		Land	15,000.00	
		Long-Term Notes Payable		50,000.00
		Common Stock, $10 Par Value		40,000.00
		Exchanged 4,000 shares of $10 par value common stock for machinery, buildings, and land.		

This entry records the acquired assets and the new liability at their fair market values as of the date of the transaction. It also records the difference between the combined fair values of the assets and the liability as an increase in stockholders' equity. If reliable fair values for the assets and liabilities cannot be determined, the fair market value of the stock may be used to estimate their values.

A corporation also may give shares of its stock to its promoters in exchange for their services in organizing the company. In this case, the corporation receives the intangible asset of being organized in exchange for its stock. The company's bookkeeper records this transaction as follows:

June	5	Organization Costs	5,000.00	
		Common Stock, $10 Par Value		5,000.00
		Gave the promoters 500 shares of $10 par value common stock in exchange for their services in organizing the corporation.		

Many stocks have a **par value,** which is an arbitrary value assigned to the stock when it is authorized. A corporation may choose to issue stock with a par value of any amount. For example, **Sara Lee Corporation's** common stock has a par value of $1.33⅓. Widely used par values are $100, $25, $10, $5, $1, and $0.01. When a corporation issues par value stock, the par value is printed on each certificate and used in accounting for the stock.

PAR VALUE AND MINIMUM LEGAL CAPITAL

In many states, the par value of a corporation's stock also establishes the **minimum legal capital** for the corporation. Laws that establish minimum legal capital normally require stockholders to invest assets equal in value to at least that amount.

Otherwise, the stockholders are liable to the corporation's creditors for the deficiency. Usually, the minimum legal capital is defined as the par value of the issued stock. In other words, persons who buy stock from a corporation must give the corporation assets equal in value to at least the par value of the stock or be subject to making up the difference later. For example, if a corporation issues 1,000 shares of $100 par value stock, the minimum legal capital of the corporation is $100,000. Minimum legal capital requirements also make it illegal to pay any dividends if they will reduce the stockholders' equity below the minimum amount.

The requirements for minimum legal capital are intended to protect the creditors of a corporation. Because a corporation's creditors cannot demand payment from the personal assets of the stockholders, the assets of the corporation are all that is available to satisfy the creditors' claims. To protect a corporation's creditors under these conditions, the minimum legal capital requirement limits a corporation's ability to distribute its assets to its stockholders. The idea is that assets equal to the amount of minimum legal capital cannot be paid to the stockholders unless all creditor claims are paid first.

Because par value determines the amount of minimum legal capital in many states, it is traditionally used in accounting for the part of stockholders' equity derived from the issuance of stock. However, par value does not establish a stock's market value or the price at which a corporation must issue the stock. If purchasers are willing to pay more, a corporation may sell and issue its stock at a price above par.

STOCK PREMIUMS AND DISCOUNTS

Premiums on Stock

When a corporation sells its stock at a price above the par value, the stock is said to be issued at a premium. For example, if a corporation sells and issues its $10 par value common stock at $12 per share, the stock is sold at a $2 per share premium. A **premium on stock** is an amount in excess of par paid by the purchasers of newly issued stock. It is not a revenue and does not appear on the income statement. Rather, a premium is reported on the balance sheet as part of the stockholders' investment.

In accounting for stock sold at a price greater than its par value, the premium is recorded separately from the par value and is called *contributed capital in excess of par value.* For example, assume that a corporation sells and issues 10,000 shares of its $10 par value common stock for cash at $12 per share. The sale is recorded as follows:

Dec.	1	Cash	120,000.00	
		Common Stock, $10 Par Value		100,000.00
		Contributed Capital in Excess of Par Value, Common		
		Stock		20,000.00
		Sold and issued 10,000 shares of $10 par value common		
		stock at $12 per share.		

When a balance sheet is prepared, any contributed capital in excess of par value is added to the par value of the stock in the equity section, as shown in the following example:

Stockholders' Equity

Common stock, $10 par value, 25,000 shares authorized, 20,000 shares issued and outstanding	$200,000
Contributed capital in excess of par value, common stock ..	30,000
Total contributed capital	$230,000
Retained earnings	82,400
Total stockholders' equity	$312,400

Discounts on Stock

If stock is issued at a price below par value, the difference between par and the issue price is called a **discount on stock.** Most states prohibit the issuance of stock at a discount because the stockholders would be investing less than minimum legal capital. In states that allow stock to be issued at a discount, its purchasers usually become contingently liable to the corporation's creditors for the amount of the discount. Therefore, stock is seldom issued at a discount. However, if stock is issued at less than par, the discount is not an expense and does not appear on the income statement. Rather, the amount of the discount is debited to a discount account that is contra to the common stock account. The balance of the discount account is subtracted from the par value of the stock on the balance sheet.

NO-PAR STOCK

At one time, all stocks were required to have a par value. Today, nearly all states permit the issuance of stocks that do not have a par value. The primary advantage of **no-par stock** is that it may be issued at any price without having a discount liability attached. Also, printing a par value of, say, $100 on a stock certificate may cause an inexperienced person to think that the share must be worth $100. Therefore, eliminating par value may encourage a closer analysis of the factors that give a stock value. These factors include such things as expected future earnings and dividends, and prospects for the economy as a whole.

In some states, the entire proceeds from the sale of no-par stock becomes minimum legal capital. In this case, the entire proceeds are credited to a no-par stock account. For example, if a corporation issues 1,000 shares of no-par stock at $42 per share, the transaction is recorded like this:

Oct.	20	Cash	42,000.00	
		Common Stock, No-Par		42,000.00
		Sold and issued 1,000 shares of no-par common stock at $42 per share.		

In other states, the board of directors of a corporation places a **stated value** on its no-par stock. The stated value becomes the minimum legal capital and is credited to the no-par stock account. If the stock is issued at an amount in excess of stated value, the excess is credited to Contributed Capital in Excess of Stated Value, No-Par Common Stock. For example, suppose that a corporation issues 1,000 shares of no-par common stock with a stated value of $25 per share for cash of $42 per share. The transaction is recorded as follows:

Oct.	20	Cash	42,000.00	
		Common Stock, No-Par		25,000.00
		Contributed Capital in Excess of		
		Stated Value, No-Par Common Stock		17,000.00
		Sold 1,000 shares of no-par stock having a $25 per share stated value at $42 per share.		

FAST HINT
Relevant Exercise:
To apply these concepts, work Exercise 13–1 or 13–2.

Progress Check

13-4 **A company issued 7,000 shares of its $10 par value common stock in exchange for equipment valued at $105,000. The entry to record the transaction would include a credit to:**
   a. **Contributed Capital in Excess of Par Value, Common Stock for $35,000;**
   b. **Retained Earnings for $35,000;**
   c. **Common Stock, $10 Par Value for $105,000.**

13–5   What is a stock premium?

13–6   Who is intended to be protected by minimum legal capital?

SALE OF STOCK THROUGH SUBSCRIPTIONS

LO 3

Record transactions that involve stock subscriptions and explain the effects of stock subscriptions on the balance sheet.

FAST HINT

Important Point to Remember:
The par value of shares subscribed is recorded in the Common Stock Subscribed account. When the stock is paid for and issued, the Common Stock Subscribed account balance is transferred to the Common Stock account.

FAST HINT

Important Point to Remember:
The Contributed Capital in Excess of Par Value account is credited when the subscription is initially taken. This account is not affected later when the shares are actually issued.

Usually, stock is sold for cash and immediately issued. However, corporations sometimes sell stock through **stock subscriptions.** For example, when a new corporation is formed, the organizers may realize that the new business has limited immediate needs for cash but will need additional capital in the future. To get the corporation started on a sound footing, the organizers may sell the stock to investors who agree to contribute some cash now and to make additional contributions in the future. When stock is sold through subscriptions, the investor agrees to buy a certain number of the shares at a specified price. The agreement also states when payments are to be made.

To illustrate the sale of stock through subscriptions, assume that Northgate Corporation accepted subscriptions on May 6 to 5,000 shares of its $10 par value common stock at $12 per share. The subscription contracts called for a 10% down payment with the balance to be paid in two equal installments due after three and six months. Northgate records the subscriptions with the following entry:

May	6	Subscriptions Receivable, Common Stock	60,000.00	
		Common Stock Subscribed		50,000.00
		Contributed Capital in Excess of Par Value, Common Stock		10,000.00
		Accepted subscriptions to 5,000 shares of $10 par value common stock at $12 per share.		

At the time that subscriptions are accepted, the firm debits the Subscriptions Receivable account for the sum of the stock's par value and premium. This is the total amount the subscribers agreed to pay. Notice that the *Common Stock Subscribed* account (an equity) is credited for par value and that the premium is credited to Contributed Capital in Excess of Par Value, Common Stock.

The receivables are converted into cash when the subscribers pay for their stock. And, when all the payments are received, the subscribed stock is issued. Northgate records the receipt of the down payment and the two installment payments with these entries:

May	6	Cash	6,000.00	
		Subscriptions Receivable, Common Stock		6,000.00
		Collected 10% down payments on the common stock subscriptions.		
Aug.	6	Cash	27,000.00	
		Subscriptions Receivable, Common Stock		27,000.00
		Collected the first installment payments on the common stock subscriptions.		
Nov.	6	Cash	27,000.00	
		Subscriptions Receivable, Common Stock		27,000.00
		Collected the second installment payments on the common stock subscriptions.		

In this case, the down payments accompanied the subscriptions. Therefore, the accountant could have combined the May 6 entries to record the subscriptions and the down payments as follows:

May	6	Cash	6,000.00	
		Subscriptions Receivable, Common Stock	54,000.00	
		Common Stock Subscribed		50,000.00
		Contributed Capital in Excess of Par		
		Value, Common Stock		10,000.00
		Accepted subscriptions to 5,000 shares of $10 par value common stock at $12 per share and received down payments of 10% of the subscription price.		

When stock is sold through subscriptions, the stock usually is not issued until the subscriptions are paid in full. Also, if dividends are declared before subscribed stock has been issued, the dividends go only to the holders of outstanding shares, not to the subscribers. However, as soon as the subscriptions are paid, the stock is issued. The entry to record the issuance of the Northgate common stock is as follows:

Nov.	6	Common Stock Subscribed	50,000.00	
		Common Stock, $10 Par Value		50,000.00
		Issued 5,000 shares of common stock sold through subscriptions.		

FAST HINT
Relevant Exercise:
To apply these concepts, work Exercise 13–4.

Subscriptions are usually collected in full, but not always. Sometimes, a subscriber fails to pay the agreed amount. When this default happens, the subscription contract is canceled. If the subscriber has made a partial payment on the contract, the amount may be refunded. Or, the company may issue a smaller amount of stock with a fair value equal to the partial payment. Or, the state law may allow the subscriber's partial payment to be kept by the corporation to compensate it for any damages.

Subscriptions Receivable and Subscribed Stock on the Balance Sheet

If the collection of stock subscriptions is questionable, they should be subtracted from contributed capital on the balance sheet. Otherwise, if the corporation is confident of collection, they may be reported on the balance sheet as current or long-term assets, depending on when collection is expected. If a corporation prepares a balance sheet after accepting subscriptions to its stock but before the stock is issued, both the issued stock and the subscribed stock should be reported on the balance sheet as follows:

FAST HINT
Critical Thought Question:
Are shares of common stock subscribed included in the number of total authorized shares? Total issued shares?

Common stock, $10 par value, 25,000 shares authorized, 20,000 shares issued and outstanding	$200,000	
Common stock subscribed, 5,000 shares	50,000	
Total common stock issued and subscribed . .	$250,000	
Contributed capital in excess of par value, common stock		40,000
Total contributed capital		$290,000

Many corporations pay cash dividends to their stockholders in regular amounts at regular dates. These cash flows provide a return to the investors and usually affect the stock's market value. Three dates are involved in the process of declaring dividends.

The day the directors vote to pay a dividend is called the **date of declaration.** Stockholders receive a dividend only if the directors formally vote to declare one. By

CORPORATE DIVIDENDS

declaring a dividend, the directors create a legal liability of the corporation to its stockholders.

In its declaration, the directors specify a future date on which the persons listed in the corporation's records are identified as those who will receive the dividend. In most cases, this **date of record** follows the date of declaration by at least two weeks. Persons who buy stock in time to be recorded as stockholders on the date of record will receive the dividend.

The declaration by the board of directors also specifies a **date of payment,** which follows the date of record by enough time to allow the corporation to prepare checks payable to the stockholders. If a balance sheet is prepared between the date of declaration and the date of payment, the liability for the dividend is reported as a current liability.

Accounting for Dividends

Because the act of declaring a dividend creates a liability for the corporation, the accountant needs to record the new obligation. This entry would be recorded if the directors of a company with 5,000 outstanding shares declare a $1 per share dividend on January 9, payable on February 1:

Jan.	9	Cash Dividends Declared	5,000.00	
		Common Dividend Payable		5,000.00
		Declared a $1 per share cash dividend on the common stock.		

Cash Dividends Declared is a temporary account that accumulates information about the total dividends declared during the reporting period. It serves the same purpose as the Withdrawals account for a proprietorship. Note that it is not an expense account. The credited account describes the corporation's liability to its stockholders.

No entry is needed at the date of record. And on the payment date, the following entry records the settlement of the liability and the reduction of the cash balance:

Feb.	1	Common Dividend Payable	5,000.00	
		Cash		5,000.00
		Paid the $1 per share cash dividend to the common stockholders.		

At the end of the annual reporting period, the balance of the Cash Dividends Declared account is closed to Retained Earnings. For example, if the company declared four quarterly dividends of $5,000, the account has a $20,000 balance at the end of the year, and the accountant makes this closing entry:

Dec.	31	Retained Earnings	20,000.00	
		Cash Dividends Declared		20,000.00
		To close the Cash Dividends Declared account.		

If one of the declared dividends remains unpaid on December 31, this closing entry is still recorded because the act of declaration reduces retained earnings. The liability account continues to have a balance until the dividends are paid, and its amount is presented on the December 31 balance sheet.

Deficits and Dividends

A corporation with a debit balance of retained earnings is said to have a **deficit**. A deficit arises when a company incurs cumulative losses and pays dividends greater than the cumulative profits earned in other years. A deficit is deducted on a corporation's balance sheet, as in this example:

FAST HINT
Relevant Quick Study:
To apply these concepts, work QS 13–5.

Stockholders' Equity

Common stock, $10 par value, 5,000 shares authorized and outstanding	$50,000
Deduct retained earnings deficit	(6,000)
Total stockholders' equity	$44,000

In most states, a corporation with a deficit is not allowed to pay a cash dividend to its stockholders. This legal restriction is designed to protect the creditors of the corporation by preventing the distribution of assets to stockholders at a time when the company is in financial difficulty.

Progress Check

13–7 Siskel Co. accepted subscriptions for 9,000 shares of $10 par value common stock at $48 per share. A 10% down payment was made on the date of the contract, the balance to be paid in full in six months. The entries to record receipt of the final balance and the issuance of the stock would include a credit to: *(a)* Subscriptions Receivable, Common Stock for $432,000; *(b)* Common Stock Subscribed for $432,000; *(c)* Common Stock, $10 Par Value for $90,000.

13–8 How is the Common Stock Subscribed account classified on the balance sheet?

13–9 In accounting for cash dividends that have been declared but not paid, the Cash Dividends Declared account is: *(a)* Reported on the balance sheet as a liability; *(b)* Closed to Income Summary; *(c)* Closed to Retained Earnings.

13–10 What three dates are normally involved in the declaration and payment of a cash dividend?

When investors buy a corporation's common stock, they acquire all the *specific* rights granted by the corporation's charter to its common stockholders. They also acquire the *general* rights granted stockholders by the laws of the state in which the company is incorporated. State laws vary, but common stockholders usually have the following general rights:

1. The right to vote at stockholders' meetings.
2. The right to sell or otherwise dispose of their stock.
3. The right of first opportunity to purchase any additional shares of common stock issued by the corporation. This right is called the common stockholders' **preemptive right**. It gives stockholders the opportunity to protect their proportionate interest in the corporation. For example, a stockholder who owns 25% of a corporation's common stock has the first opportunity to buy 25% of any new common stock issued. This arrangement enables the stockholder to maintain a 25% interest.

RIGHTS OF COMMON STOCKHOLDERS

LO 4

State the differences between common and preferred stock, and allocate dividends between the common and preferred stock of a corporation.

FAST HINT
Critical Thought Question:
If a corporation bought back its
own shares on the open market,
would the corporation then have
the right to vote and the right to
receive dividends?

4.   The right to share equally with other common stockholders in any dividends, with the result that each common share receives the same amount.
5.   The right to share equally in any assets that remain after creditors are paid when the corporation is liquidated, with the result that each common share receives the same amount.

In addition, stockholders have the right to receive timely reports that describe the corporation's financial position and the results of its activities.

PREFERRED STOCK

As mentioned earlier in this chapter, a corporation may be authorized to issue more than one kind or class of stock. If two classes of common stock are issued, the primary difference between them often is only a matter of voting rights. However, some companies issue two classes of stock with one class being a **preferred stock** and the other class being a common stock.

Preferred stock often has a par value, but like common stock, may be sold at a price that differs from par. Separate contributed capital accounts are used to record the issuance of preferred stock. For example, if 50 shares of preferred stock with a $100 par value are issued for $6,000 cash, the entry is:

June	1	Cash	6,000.00	
		Preferred Stock		5,000.00
		Contributed Capital in Excess of Par		
		Value, Preferred Stock		1,000.00
		Issued preferred stock for cash.		

The term *preferred* is used because the preferred shares have a higher priority (or senior status) relative to common shares in one or more ways. These typically include a preference for receiving dividends and a preference in the distribution of assets if the corporation is liquidated.

In addition to the preferences it receives, preferred stock carries all the rights of common stock, unless they are nullified in the corporation's charter. For example, most preferred stock does not have the right to vote.

Preferred Dividends

A preference for dividends gives preferred stockholders the right to receive their dividends before the common stockholders receive a dividend. In other words, a dividend cannot be paid to common stockholders unless preferred stockholders also receive one. The amount of dividends that the preferred stockholders must receive is usually expressed as a dollar amount per share or as a percentage applied to the par value. For example, the December 31, 1993, balance sheet of **Pitney Bowes, Inc.**, showed that the company had 4%, $50 par value, preferred stock outstanding. These shares required the company to pay quarterly dividends of $0.50 per share (an annual rate of $2 or 4% of par) before the common shareholders could receive a dividend.

A preference for dividends does not, however, grant an absolute right to dividends. If the board of directors does not declare a dividend, neither the preferred nor the common stockholders receive one.

Cumulative and Noncumulative Preferred Stock

Most preferred stock is **cumulative** but some is **noncumulative**. For noncumulative, the right to receive dividends is forfeited in any year that the dividends are not declared. When preferred stock is cumulative and the board of directors fails to declare a dividend to the preferred stockholders, the unpaid dividend is called a **dividend in arrears.** The accumulation of dividends in arrears on cumulative preferred stock does not guarantee that they will be paid. However, the cumulative preferred stockholders must be paid both the current dividend and all dividends in arrears before any dividend can be paid to the common stockholders.

To show the difference between cumulative and noncumulative preferred stock, assume that a corporation's outstanding stock includes 1,000 shares of $100 par, 9% preferred stock and 4,000 shares of $50 par, common stock. During 19X1, the first year of the corporation's operations, the board of directors declared cash dividends of $5,000. During 19X2, it declared $42,000. The allocations of the total dividends are as follows:

	Preferred	Common
Assuming noncumulative preferred:		
19X1	$ 5,000	$ 0
19X2:		
First: current preferred dividend	$ 9,000	
Remainder to common		$33,000
Assuming cumulative preferred:		
19X1	$ 5,000	$ 0
19X2:		
First: dividends in arrears	$ 4,000	
Next: current preferred dividend	9,000	
Remainder to common		$29,000
Totals	$13,000	$29,000

Notice that the allocation of the 19X2 dividends depends on whether the preferred stock is noncumulative or cumulative. With noncumulative preferred stock, the preferred stockholders never receive the $4,000 that was skipped in 19X1. However, when the preferred stock is cumulative, the $4,000 in arrears is paid in 19X2 before the common stockholders receive a dividend.

Disclosure of Dividends in Arrears in the Financial Statements

Dividends are not like interest expense, which is incurred as time passes and therefore must be accrued. A liability for a dividend does not come into existence until the dividend is declared by the board of directors. Thus, if a preferred dividend date passes and the corporation's board fails to declare the dividend on its cumulative preferred stock, the dividend in arrears is not a liability. However, when preparing the financial statements, the *full-disclosure principle* requires the corporation to report the amount of preferred dividends in arrears as of the balance sheet date. Normally, this information is given in a footnote.

Participating Preferred Stock—A Defense Against Hostile Takeovers

The dividends on most preferred stocks are limited to a maximum amount each year. The maximum is defined as a stated percentage of the stock's par value or as a specific dollar amount per share. Once the preferred stockholders receive this amount, the common stockholders receive any and all additional dividends. Preferred stocks that have this limitation are called *nonparticipating*. However, the owners of **participating preferred stock** have the right to share with the common stockholders in any additional dividends paid in excess of the stated percentage dividend on the preferred.

Although many corporations are authorized to issue participating preferred stock, the shares are rarely issued. That is, companies obtain authorization to issue the shares even though management does not expect to ever sell them. They do this to defend against a *takeover* of the corporation by an unfriendly investor (or a group of investors) who would buy enough voting common stock to gain control over operations. Using terminology from spy novels, the financial world refers to this kind of a plan as a *poison pill* that the company will swallow if it is threatened with capture by an enemy.

A typical poison pill works as follows: The common stockholders on a given date are granted the right to purchase a large amount of participating preferred stock at a very low price. This right cannot be transferred. Thus, if the stock is sold, the buyer does not gain the right. In addition, this right cannot be exercised unless the directors identify a buyer of a large block of common shares as an unfriendly buyer.

If an unfriendly investor were identified and the preferred stock were issued, future dividends would be divided between the preferred shares and the common shares. This would transfer some of the value of the common shares to the preferred shares. As a result, the stock owned by the unfriendly buyer would lose much of its value and be worth much less than the buyer's cost. The ultimate effect is to eliminate the potential benefit of attempting a hostile takeover.

WHY PREFERRED STOCK IS ISSUED

A corporation might issue nonparticipating preferred stock for several reasons. One reason is to raise capital without sacrificing control of the corporation. For example, suppose that the organizers of a business have $100,000 cash to invest but wish to organize a corporation that needs $200,000 of capital to get off to a good start. If they sold $200,000 of common stock, they would have only 50% control and would have to negotiate extensively with the other stockholders in making policy. However, if they issue $100,000 of common stock to themselves and can sell outsiders $100,000 of 8%, cumulative preferred stock that has no voting rights, they can retain control of the corporation.

A second reason for issuing preferred stock is to boost the return earned by the common stockholders. Using the previous example to illustrate, suppose that the corporation's organizers expect the new company to earn an annual after-tax income of $24,000. If they sell and issue $200,000 of common stock, this income produces a 12% return on the $200,000 of common stockholders' equity. However, if they issue $100,000 of 8% preferred stock to the outsiders and $100,000 of common stock to themselves, their own return increases to 16% per year, as shown here:

FAST HINT
Relevant Exercise:
To apply these concepts, work
Exercise 13–7.

Net after-tax income	$24,000
Less preferred dividends at 8%	(8,000)
Balance to common stockholders (equal to 16% on their $100,000 investment)	$16,000

In this case, the common stockholders earn 16% because the assets contributed by the preferred stockholders are invested to earn $12,000 while the preferred dividend payments amount to only $8,000.

The use of preferred stock to increase the return to common stockholders is an example of **financial leverage.** Whenever the dividend rate on preferred stock is less than the rate that the corporation earns on its assets, the effect of issuing preferred stock is to increase (or *lever*) the rate earned by common stockholders. Financial leverage also occurs when debt is issued and paid an interest rate less than the rate earned from using the assets the creditors loaned to the corporation.

There are other reasons for issuing preferred stock. For example, a corporation's preferred stock may appeal to some investors who believe that its common stock is too risky or that the dividend rate on the common stock will be too low. Also, if a corporation's management wants to issue common stock but believes the current market price for the common stock is too low, the corporation may issue preferred stock that is convertible into common stock. If and when the price of the common stock increases, the preferred stockholders can convert their shares into common shares.

FAST HINT
Important Point to Remember:
Financial leverage is a primary reason for borrowing funds when the borrowing company can earn a rate of return on the borrowed funds in excess of the interest rate.

Progress Check

13-11 **In what ways may preferred stock have a priority status to common stock?**

13-12 **Increasing the return to common stockholders by including preferred stock in the capital structure is an example of: (a) Financial leverage; (b) Cumulative earnings; (c) Dividends in arrears.**

13-13 **MBI Corp. has 9,000 shares of $50 par value, 10% cumulative and nonparticipating preferred stock and 27,000 shares of $10 par value common stock issued and outstanding. No dividends have been declared for the past two years, but during the current year, MBI declares a $288,000 dividend. The amount to be paid to common shareholders is: (a) $243,000; (b) $153,000; (c) $135,000.**

As we just mentioned, an issue of preferred stock can be made more attractive to some investors by giving them the right to exchange the preferred shares for a fixed number of common shares. **Convertible preferred stock** offers investors a higher potential return than does nonconvertible preferred stock. If the company prospers and its common stock increases in value, the convertible preferred stockholders can share in the prosperity by converting their preferred stock into the more valuable common stock. Conversion is at the option of the investors and therefore does not occur unless it is to their advantage. (The investors can enjoy the results of the increased value of the common stock without converting the preferred stock because the preferred stock's market value reflects the change in the common stock's value.)

In addition to a par value, stocks may have a *call price,* a *market value,* and a *book value.*

Call Price of Callable Preferred Stock

Some issues of preferred stock are callable. This means that the issuing corporation has the right to retire the **callable preferred stock** by paying a specified amount to the preferred stockholders. The amount that must be paid to call and retire a preferred share is its **call price** or *redemption value.* This amount is set at the time the stock is issued. Normally, the call price includes the par value of the stock plus a premium that provides the stockholders with some additional return on their investment. When the issuing corporation calls and retires a preferred stock, it must pay not only the call price but also any dividends in arrears.

CONVERTIBLE PREFERRED STOCK

LO 5

Explain convertible preferred stock and describe the meaning of the par value, call price, market value, and book value of corporate stock.

STOCK VALUES

FAST HINT
Relevant Exercise:
To apply these concepts, work Exercise 13–8.

Illustration 13-1
Stockholders' Equity with
Preferred and Common
Stock

Stockholders' Equity		
Preferred stock, $100 par value, 7% cumulative, 2,000 shares authorized, 1,000 shares issued and outstanding	$100,000	
Contributed capital in excess of par value, preferred stock	5,000	
Total capital contributed by preferred stockholders		$105,000
Common stock, $25 par value, 12,000 shares authorized, 10,000 shares issued and outstanding	$250,000	
Contributed capital in excess of par value, common stock	10,000	
Total capital contributed by common stockholders		260,000
Total contributed capital		$365,000
Retained earnings		82,000
Total stockholders' equity		$447,000

FAST HINT

Critical Thought Question:
Who generally has the right or option to exchange convertible preferred stock for common stock? Who has the right or option to retire callable preferred stock?

Market Value

The market value of a share of stock is the price at which it can be bought or sold. Market values are influenced by a wide variety of factors including expected future earnings, dividends, and events in the economy at large. Market values of frequently traded stocks are reported daily in newspapers such as *The Wall Street Journal*. The market values of stocks that are not actively traded can be more difficult to determine. Analysts use a variety of techniques to estimate the value of such stocks, and most of these techniques use accounting information as an important input to the valuation process.

Book Value

FAST HINT

Important Point to Remember:
Analysts may take book value per share into consideration in estimating the market value of a share, but book value normally does not approximate a share's liquidation value or market value.

The **book value of a share of stock** equals the share's portion of the stockholders' equity as it is recorded in the company's accounts. If a corporation has only common stock, the book value per share equals the total stockholders' equity divided by the number of outstanding shares. For example, if a company has 10,000 outstanding shares and total stockholders' equity of $285,000, the stock's book value is $28.50 per share ($285,000/10,000 shares).

Computing the book value of stock is more complex when both common and preferred shares are outstanding. To calculate the book values of each class of stock, you begin by allocating the total stockholders' equity between the two classes. The preferred stockholders' portion equals the preferred stock's call price (or par value if the preferred is not callable) plus any cumulative dividends in arrears. Then allocate the remaining stockholders' equity to the common shares. To determine the book value per share of preferred, divide the portion of stockholders' equity assigned to preferred by the number of preferred shares outstanding. Similarly, the book value per share of common is the stockholders' equity assigned to common divided by the number of outstanding common shares. For example, assume a corporation has the stockholders' equity as shown in Illustration 13–1.

If the preferred stock is callable at $108 per share and two years of cumulative preferred dividends are in arrears, the book values of the corporation's shares are calculated as follows:

Total stockholders' equity		$ 447,000
Less equity applicable to preferred shares:		
Call price (1,000 × $108)	$108,000	
Cumulative dividends in arrears ($100,000 × 7% × 2) . . .	14,000	(122,000)
Equity applicable to common shares		$ 325,000
Book value of preferred shares ($122,000/1,000)		$ 122.00
Book value of common shares ($325,000/10,000)		$ 32.50

FAST HINT
Alternative Example:
If the preferred shares had no
call price, would the book value
of the preferred (and common)
be higher or lower?
Answer: Because the par value
is less than the call price, the
book value of the preferred
shares would be lower while
book value of the common
shares would be higher.

In their annual reports to shareholders, corporations sometimes report the increase in the book value of the corporation's shares that has occurred during a year. Also, book value may have significance in contracts. For example, a stockholder may enter into a contract to sell shares at their book value at some future date. However, remember that book value normally does not approximate market value. For example, the book value per share of Anheuser-Busch Companies, Inc.'s common stock on December 31, 1993, was $15.94; this is significantly lower than its $49.125 market value on the same date.

Similarly, book value should not be confused with the liquidation value of a stock. If a corporation is liquidated, its assets probably will sell at prices that are quite different from the amounts at which they are carried on the books.

FAST HINT
Relevant Quick Study:
To apply these concepts, work
QS 13–6.

Progress Check

13–14   Potter Co.'s outstanding stock includes 1,000 shares of $90 par value cumulative preferred stock and 12,000 shares of $20 par value common stock. The call price of the preferred stock is $90 and dividends of $18,000 are in arrears. Total stockholders' equity is $630,000. What is the book value per share of the common shares?

13–15   The price at which a share of stock can be bought or sold is the: *(a)* Call price;   *(b)* Redemption value;   *(c)* Market value.

PARTNERSHIPS

A **partnership** can be defined as *an unincorporated association of two or more persons to carry on a business for profit as co-owners.* Many businesses, such as small retail and service businesses, are organized as partnerships. Also, many professional practitioners—including physicians, lawyers, and certified public accountants—have traditionally organized their practices as partnerships.

LO 6

Explain the concepts of mutual agency and unlimited liability for a partnership, record investments and withdrawals of partners, and allocate the net incomes or losses of a partnership among the partners.

A partnership is a voluntary association between the partners. All that is required to form a partnership is that two or more legally competent people (that is, people who are of age and of sound mental capacity) must agree to be partners. Their agreement becomes a **partnership contract.** Although it should be in writing, the contract is binding even if it is only expressed orally.[5]

The life of a partnership is always limited. Death, bankruptcy, or anything that takes away the ability of one of the partners to enter into or fulfill a contract

CHARACTERISTICS OF PARTNERSHIPS

---

[5] In some cases, courts have ruled that partnerships have been created by the actions of the partners, even when there was no expressed agreement to form a partnership.

FAST HINT
Important Point to Remember:
A person cannot be forced into
being a partner with another
person. For example, when a
new partner is to be admitted,
all parties involved must agree
to the admission. In large partnerships, this right may be
waived by the partners.

automatically ends a partnership. In addition, a partnership may be terminated at will
by any one of the partners. Before agreeing to join a partnership, you should understand clearly two important characteristics of a partnership: mutual agency and unlimited liability.

Mutual Agency

Generally, the relationship between the partners in a partnership involves **mutual
agency.** Under normal circumstances, every partner is a fully authorized agent of the
partnership. As its agent, a partner can commit or bind the partnership to any contract that is within the apparent scope of the partnership's business. For example, a
partner in a merchandising business can sign contracts that bind the partnership to
buy merchandise, lease a store building, borrow money, or hire employees. These activities are all within the scope of the business of a merchandising firm. On the other
hand, a partner in a law firm, acting alone, cannot bind his or her partners to a contract to buy merchandise for resale or rent a retail store building. These actions are
not within the normal scope of a law firm's business.

Partners may agree to limit the power of any one or more of the partners to nego-
tiate certain contracts for the partnership. Such an agreement is binding on the partners and on outsiders who know that it exists. However, it is not binding on outsiders
who do not know that it exists. Outsiders who are not aware of the agreement have
the right to assume that each partner has normal agency powers for the partnership.

Because mutual agency exposes all partners to the risk of unwise actions by any
one partner, people should carefully evaluate potential partners before agreeing to join
a partnership. The importance of this advice is underscored by the fact that most partnerships are also characterized by unlimited liability.

Unlimited Liability of Partners

FAST HINT
Relevant Exercise:
To apply these concepts, work
Exercise 13–9.

When a partnership cannot pay its debts, the creditors normally can satisfy their claims
from the *personal* assets of the partners. Also, if some partners do not have enough
assets to meet their share of the partnership's debts, the creditors can turn to the assets of the remaining partners who are able to pay. Because partners may be called
on to pay all the debts of the partnership, each partner is said to have **unlimited liability** for the partnership's debts. Mutual agency and unlimited liability are the main
reasons why most partnerships have only a few members.

Limited Partnerships and Limited Liability Partnerships

Partnerships in which all of the partners have unlimited liability are called **general
partnerships.** Sometimes, however, individuals who want to invest in a partnership
are not willing to accept the risk of unlimited liability. Their needs may be met by
using a **limited partnership.** A limited partnership has two classes of partners, general and limited. At least one partner has to be a **general partner** who must assume
unlimited liability for the debts of the partnership. The remaining **limited partners**
have no personal liability beyond the amounts that they invest in the business. Usually, a limited partnership is managed by the general partner or partners. The limited
partners have no active role except for major decisions specified in the partnership
agreement.

A similar form of partnership that an increasing number of states are allowing pro-
fessionals such as lawyers to use is the **limited liability partnership.** This type of
partnership is designed to protect innocent partners from malpractice or negligence
claims that result from the acts of another partner. When a partner provides service

that results in a malpractice claim, that partner has personal liability for the claim. The remaining partners who were not responsible for the actions that resulted in the claim are not personally liable for the claim. However, all partners have personal liability for other partnership debts.

Accounting for a partnership does not differ from accounting for a proprietorship except for transactions that directly affect the partners' equity. Because ownership rights in a partnership are divided among the partners, partnership accounting:

- Uses a capital account for each partner.
- Uses a withdrawals account for each partner.
- Allocates net incomes or losses to the partners according to the provisions of the partnership agreement.

When partners invest in a partnership, their capital accounts are credited for the invested amounts. Partners' withdrawals of assets are debited to their withdrawals accounts. In closing the accounts at the end of the year, the partners' capital accounts are credited or debited for their shares of the net income or loss. Finally, the withdrawals account of each partner is closed to that partner's capital account. These closing procedures are like those used for a single proprietorship. The only difference is that separate capital and withdrawals accounts are maintained for each partner.

Because they are its owners, partners are not employees of the partnership. If partners devote their time and services to the affairs of their partnership, they are understood to do so for profit, not for salary. Therefore, when the partners calculate the net income of a partnership, salaries to the partners are not deducted as expenses on the income statement. However, when the net income or loss of the partnership is allocated among the partners, the partners may agree to base part of the allocation on salary allowances that reflect the relative values of service provided by the partners.

Partners are also understood to have invested in a partnership for profit, not for interest. Nevertheless, partners may agree that the division of partnership earnings should include a return based on their invested capital. For example, if one partner contributes five times as much capital as another, it is only fair that this fact be considered when earnings are allocated among the partners. Thus, a partnership agreement may provide for interest allowances based on the partners' capital balances. Like salary allowances, interest allowances are not expenses to be reported on the income statement.

FAST HINT
Important Point to Remember: Entries for the declaration and payment of a cash dividend in a corporation have the same effect as the entry to record a withdrawal in a partnership. In both cases, owner's equity and cash are reduced as cash is paid to owners.

In the absence of a contrary agreement, the law states that the income or loss of a partnership should be shared equally by the partners. However, partners may agree to any method of sharing. If they agree on how they will share income but say nothing about losses, then losses are shared in the same way as income.

Several methods of sharing partnership earnings can be used. Three frequently used methods divide earnings: (1) on a stated fractional basis, (2) in the ratio of capital investments, or (3) using salary and interest allowances and any remainder in a fixed ratio.

Earnings Allocated on a Stated Fractional Basis

An easy way to divide partnership earnings is to give each partner a fraction of the total. All that is necessary is for the partners to agree on the fractional share that each will receive. For example, assume that the partnership agreement of B. A. Jones and

Illustration 13-2
Sharing Income When
Income Exceeds Salary and
Interest Allowances

	Share to Stanley	Share to Breck	Income to be Allocated
Total net income			$70,000
Allocated as salary allowances:			
Stanley	$36,000		
Breck		$24,000	
Total allocated as salary allowances			60,000
Balance of income after salary allowances			$10,000
Allocated as interest:			
Stanley (10% on $30,000)	3,000		
Breck (10% on $10,000)		1,000	
Total allocated as interest			4,000
Balance of income after salary and			
interest allowances			$ 6,000
Balance allocated equally:			
Stanley	3,000		
Breck		3,000	
Total allocated equally			6,000
Balance of income			$ 0
Shares of the partners	$42,000	$28,000	
Percentages of total net income	60%	40%	

S. A. Meyers states that Jones will receive two-thirds and Meyers will receive one-third of the partnership earnings. If the partnership's net income is $30,000, the earnings are allocated to the partners and the Income Summary account is closed with the following entry:

Dec.	31	Income Summary	30,000.00	
		B. A. Jones, Capital		20,000.00
		S. A. Meyers, Capital		10,000.00
		To close the Income Summary account and allocate the earnings.		

When earnings are shared on a fractional basis, the fractions may reflect the relative capital investments of the partners. For example, suppose that B. Donner and H. Flack formed a partnership and agreed to share earnings in the ratio of their investments. Because Donner invested $50,000 and Flack invested $30,000, Donner will receive five-eighths of the earnings ($50,000/$80,000) while Flack will receive three-eighths of the earnings ($30,000/$80,000).

Salaries and Interest as Aids in Sharing

As we have mentioned, the service contributions and capital contributions of the partners often are not equal. If the service contributions are not equal, salary allowances can compensate for the differences. Or, when capital contributions are not equal, interest allowances can compensate for the unequal investments. When both investment and service contributions are unequal, the allocation of net incomes and losses may include both interest and salary allowances.

For example, in Kathy Stanley and David Breck's new partnership, Stanley is to provide services that they agree are worth an annual salary of $36,000. Breck is less

	Share to Stanley	Share to Breck	Income to be Allocated
Total net income			$ 50,000
Allocated as salary allowances:			
Stanley	$36,000		
Breck		$24,000	
Total allocated as salary allowances			60,000
Balance of income after salary allowances			$ (10,000)
Allocated as interest:			
Stanley (10% on $30,000)	3,000		
Breck (10% on $10,000)		1,000	
Total allocated as interest			4,000
Balance of income after salary and			
interest allowances			$ (14,000)
Balance allocated equally:			
Stanley	(7,000)		
Breck		(7,000)	
Total allocated equally			(14,000)
Balance of income			$ 0
Shares of the partners	$32,000	$18,000	
Percentages of total net income	64%	36%	

Illustration 13-3
Sharing Income When
Interest and Salary
Allowances Exceed Income

experienced in the business, so his service contribution is worth only $24,000. Also, Stanley will invest $30,000 in the business and Breck will invest $10,000. To compensate Stanley and Breck fairly in light of the differences in their service and capital contributions, they agree to share incomes or losses as follows:

1. Annual salary allowances of $36,000 to Stanley and $24,000 to Breck.
2. Interest allowances equal to 10% of each partner's beginning-of-year capital balance.
3. The remaining balance of income or loss is to be shared equally.

Note that the provisions for salaries and interest in this partnership agreement are called *allowances*. These allowances are not reported on the income statement as salaries and interest expense. They are only a means of splitting up the net income or net loss of the partnership.

FAST HINT
Relevant Exercise:
To apply these concepts, work
Exercise 13–14.

Under the Stanley and Breck partnership agreement, a first year's net income of $70,000 is shared as shown in Illustration 13–2. Notice that Stanley gets $42,000, or 60% of the income, while Breck gets $28,000, or 40%.

In Illustration 13–2, notice that the $70,000 net income exceeds the salary and interest allowances of the partners. However, the method of sharing agreed to by Stanley and Breck must be followed even if the net income is smaller than the salary and interest allowances. For example, if the first year's net income was $50,000, it would be allocated to the partners as shown in Illustration 13–3. Notice that this circumstance provides Stanley with 64% of the total income, while Breck gets only 36%.

A net loss would be shared by Stanley and Breck in the same manner as the $50,000 net income. The only difference is that the income-and-loss-sharing procedure would begin with a negative amount of income because of the net loss. After the salary and interest allowances, the remaining balance to be allocated equally would then be a larger negative amount.

Progress Check

13–16   A partnership is automatically terminated in the event: *(a)* The partnership agreement is not in writing; *(b)* A partner dies; *(c)* A partner exercises mutual agency.

13–17   Mixon and Reed form a partnership by contributing $70,000 and $35,000 respectively. They agree to an interest allowance equal to 10% of each partner's capital balance at the beginning of the year with the remaining income to be shared equally. Allocate the first-year net income of $40,000 to the partners.

13–18   What does the term *unlimited liability* mean when it is applied to a partnership?

USING THE INFORMATION— DIVIDEND YIELD

LO 7

Calculate dividend yield and describe its meaning.

Investors buy shares of a company's stock in anticipation of receiving a return from cash dividends and from increases in the stock's value. Stocks that pay large dividends on a regular basis are sometimes called *income stocks.* They are attractive to investors who want dependable cash flows from their investments. In contrast, other stocks pay few or no dividends, but are still attractive to investors because they expect the market value of the stocks to increase rapidly. The stocks of companies that do not distribute cash but use it to finance rapid expansion are often called *growth stocks.*

One way to evaluate whether a company stock should be viewed as an income stock or growth stock is to examine the **dividend yield.** The following formula shows that this ratio is a rate of return based on the annual cash dividends and the stock's market value:

$$\text{Dividend yield} = \frac{\text{Annual cash dividends per share}}{\text{Market value per share}}$$

Dividend yield may be calculated on a historical basis using the prior year's actual dividends or on an expected basis. For example, recall from the first page of this chapter the discussion of Mobil Corporation and the dividend and stock price information for several companies. The dividend yields for those companies were as follows:

FAST HINT
Relevant Quick Study:
To apply these concepts, work QS 13–8.

Company	Common Dividend per share		November 1994 Stock Price	Dividend Yield	
	1994*	1993		1994*	1993
Mobil Corporation	$3.40	$3.25	$82¼	4.1%	4.0%
Minnesota Mining & Mfg. Co.	1.76	1.66	53¼	3.3	3.1
Texaco Inc.	3.20	3.20	60⅞	5.3	5.3
AT&T Corp.	1.32	1.32	54	2.4	2.4
GAP, Inc.	0.48	0.38	37⅞	1.3	1.0
Microsoft Corp.	0	0	64½	—	—

*Estimated 1994 amounts.

An investor can compare these dividend yields to evaluate the relative importance of dividends to the prices of the stocks. Current dividends obviously have no impact on Microsoft Corp.'s stock price and very little impact on the GAP, Inc.'s stock price. The values of these two stocks must stem from expected increases in their stock prices (and the eventual dividends that may be paid.)

On the other hand, Mobil Corporation and Texaco Inc. pay substantial dividends of 4.0 to 5.3%. These are less than one would expect from investments in corporate debt securities, but still high enough to conclude that dividends are a very important factor in establishing their stock prices.

Although income stocks tend to have relatively stable market values, their values can vary substantially in anticipation of changes in the company's ability to pay future dividends or changes in rates of returns on other available investments. Thus, investors should examine much more information in addition to the dividend yield before deciding to buy, sell, or keep a stock.

Progress Check

13-19   Which of the following produces an expected dividend yield of 10% for common stock?

a. Dividends of $100,000 are expected to be paid next year and expected net income is $1,000,000.

b. Dividends of $50,000 were paid during the prior year and net income was $500,000.

c. Dividends of $2 per share are expected to be paid next year and the current market value of the stock is $20 per share.

SUMMARY OF THE CHAPTER IN TERMS OF LEARNING OBJECTIVES

LO 1. Explain the unique characteristics of the corporate form of business. Corporations are separate legal entities. As such, their stockholders are not liable for the corporate debts. Stocks issued by corporations are easily transferred between stockholders, and the life of corporations does not end with the incapacity or death of a stockholder. A corporation acts through its agents, who are its officers and managers, not its stockholders. Corporations tend to be closely regulated by government and are subject to income taxes.

LO 2. Record the issuance of par value stock and no-par stock with or without a stated value, and explain the concept of minimum legal capital. When stock is issued, the par or stated value is credited to the stock account and any excess is credited to a separate contributed capital account. If the stock has no par or stated value, the entire proceeds are credited to the stock account. Stockholders must contribute assets equal to the minimum legal capital of a corporation or be potentially liable for the deficiency. And, as long as any liabilities remain unpaid, the minimum legal capital cannot be paid to stockholders.

LO 3. Record transactions that involve dividends and stock subscriptions and explain the effects of stock subscriptions on the balance sheet. If a corporation sells stock through subscriptions, the unpaid portion is recorded as a receivable, and the subscribers' equity is recorded in contributed capital accounts. The balance of the Common Stock Subscribed account is transferred to the Common Stock account when the shares are issued, which normally occurs after all payments are received. Three dates are involved when cash dividends are distributed to stockholders. The board of directors binds the company to pay the dividend on the date of declaration. The recipients of the dividend are identified on the date of record. The cash is paid to the stockholders on the date of payment.

LO 4. State the differences between common and preferred stock, and allocate dividends between the common and preferred stock of a corporation. Preferred stock has a priority (or senior status) relative to common stock in one or more ways. Usually, common stockholders cannot be paid dividends unless a specified amount of dividends also is paid to preferred shareholders. Preferred stock also may have a priority status if the corporation is liquidated. The dividend preference for most preferred stocks is cumulative. Many companies are authorized to issue participating preferred stocks as a poison pill against hostile takeovers.

LO 5. Describe convertible preferred stock and explain the meaning of the par value, call price, market value, and book value of corporate stock. Convertible preferred stock can be exchanged by its holders for common stock. If preferred stock is callable, the amount that must be paid to retire the stock is its call price plus any dividends in arrears. Market value is the price that a stock commands when it is bought or sold. The book value of preferred stock is any dividends in arrears plus its par value or, if it is callable, its call price. The remaining stockholders' equity is divided by the number of outstanding common shares to determine the book value per share of the common stock.

LO 6. Explain the concepts of mutual agency and unlimited liability for a partnership, record the investments and withdrawals of partners, and allocate the net incomes or losses of a partnership among the partners. Mutual agency means that every partner can bind a partnership to contracts that are within the normal scope of the business. In a general partnership, each partner has unlimited liability for the debts of the partnership. A partnership agreement should specify the method for allocating the partnership's net income or loss among the partners. This allocation may be done on a fractional basis, or it may use salary and interest allowances to compensate partners for differences in their service and capital contributions.

LO 7. Calculate dividend yield and describe its meaning. The dividend yield is the ratio between a stock's annual dividends per share and its market value per share. It describes the rate of return provided to the stockholders from the company's dividends. The yield can be compared with the rates of return offered by other kinds of investments to determine whether the stock should be viewed as an income or growth stock.

DEMONSTRATION PROBLEM

Barton Corporation was created on January 1, 19X1. The following transactions relating to stockholders' equity occurred during the first two years of the company's operations. Prepare the journal entries to record these transactions. Also prepare the balance sheet presentation of the organization costs, liabilities, and stockholders' equity as of December 31, 19X1, and December 31, 19X2. Include appropriate footnotes.

19X1

Jan. 1   Authorized the issuance of 2 million shares of $5 par value common stock and 100,000 shares of $100 par value preferred stock. The preferred stock pays a 10% annual dividend and is cumulative.

1   Issued 200,000 shares of common stock for cash at $12 per share.

1   Issued 100,000 shares of common stock in exchange for a building valued at $820,000 and merchandise inventory valued at $380,000.

1   Accepted subscriptions for 150,000 shares of common stock at $12 per share. The subscribers made no down payments, and the full purchase price was due on April 1, 19X1.

1   Paid a cash reimbursement to the company's founders for $100,000 of organization costs; these costs are to be amortized over 10 years.

1   Issued 12,000 shares of preferred stock for cash at $110 per share.

Apr. 1   Collected the full subscription price for the January 1 common stock and issued the stock.

Dec. 31   The Income Summary account for 19X1 had a $125,000 credit balance before being closed to Retained Earnings; no dividends were declared on either the common or preferred stocks.

19X2

June 4   Issued 100,000 shares of common stock for cash at $15 per share.

Dec. 10   Declared dividends payable on January 10, 19X3, as follows:

To preferred stockholders for 19X1	$120,000
To preferred stockholders for 19X2	120,000
To common stockholders for 19X2	300,000

31   The Income Summary account for 19X2 had a $1 million credit balance before being closed to Retained Earnings.

Record journal entries for the events in 19X1 and 19X2.

Close the accounts related to retained earnings at the end of each year.

Determine the balances for the 19X1 and 19X2 balance sheets, including the following amounts to use in the balance sheet and the accompanying note:

a. The number of shares issued.

b. The amount of dividends in arrears.

c. The unamortized balance of organization costs.

Prepare the specified portions of the 19X1 and 19X2 balance sheets.

Planning the Solution

Solution to Demonstration Problem

19X1				
Jan.	1	Cash	2,400,000.00	
		Common Stock		1,000,000.00
		Contributed Capital in Excess of Par Value, Common Stock		1,400,000.00
		Issued 200,000 shares of common stock.		
	1	Building	820,000.00	
		Merchandise Inventory	380,000.00	
		Common Stock		500,000.00
		Contributed Capital in Excess of Par Value, Common Stock		700,000.00
		Issued 100,000 shares of common stock.		
Jan.	1	Subscriptions Receivable	1,800,000.00	
		Common Stock Subscribed		750,000.00
		Contributed Capital in Excess of Par Value, Common Stock		1,050,000.00
		Accepted subscriptions for 150,000 shares of common stock.		
	1	Organization Costs	100,000.00	
		Cash		100,000.00
		Reimbursed the founders for organization costs.		
	1	Cash	1,320,000.00	
		Preferred Stock		1,200,000.00
		Contributed Capital in Excess of Par Value, Preferred Stock		120,000.00
		Issued 12,000 shares of preferred stock.		
Apr.	1	Cash	1,800,000.00	
		Subscriptions Receivable		1,800,000.00
		Collected balance due on subscribed common stock.		
	1	Common Stock Subscribed	750,000.00	
		Common Stock		750,000.00
		Issued 150,000 shares of subscribed common stock.		
Dec.	31	Income Summary	125,000.00	
		Retained Earnings		125,000.00
		To close the Income Summary account and update Retained Earnings.		

19X2				
June	4	Cash	1,500,000.00	
		Common Stock		500,000.00
		Contributed Capital in Excess of		
		Par Value, Common Stock		1,000,000.00
		Issued 100,000 shares of common stock.		
Dec.	10	Cash Dividends Declared	540,000.00	
		Common Dividend Payable		300,000.00
		Preferred Dividend Payable		240,000.00
		Declared current dividends and dividends in		
		arrears to common and preferred stockholders,		
		payable on January 10, 19X3.		
	31	Income Summary	1,000,000.00	
		Retained Earnings		1,000,000.00
		To close the Income Summary account and		
		update Retained Earnings.		
	31	Retained Earnings	540,000.00	
		Cash Dividends Declared		540,000.00
		To close the Cash Dividends Declared		
		account.		

Balance sheet presentations:

	As of December 31,	
	19X1	**19X2**
Assets		
Organization costs	$ 90,000	$ 80,000
Liabilities		
Common dividend payable		$ 300,000
Preferred dividend payable		240,000
Total liabilities		$ 540,000
Stockholders' Equity		
Contributed capital:		
Preferred stock, $100 par value,		
10% cumulative dividends, 100,000		
shares authorized, 12,000 shares issued		
and outstanding	$1,200,000	$1,200,000
Contributed capital in excess of		
par value, preferred stock	120,000	120,000
Total capital contributed by		
preferred stockholders	$1,320,000	$1,320,000
Common stock, $5 par value, 2,000,000		
shares authorized, 450,000 shares		
issued and outstanding in 19X1, and		
550,000 shares in 19X2	$2,250,000	$2,750,000
Contributed capital in excess of par value,		
common stock	3,150,000	4,150,000
Total capital contributed by		
common stockholders	$5,400,000	$6,900,000
Total contributed capital	$6,720,000	$8,220,000
Retained Earnings (see Note 1)	125,000	585,000
Total stockholders' equity	$6,845,000	$8,805,000

Note 1: As of December 31, 19X1, there were $120,000 of dividends in arrears on the
preferred stock.

GLOSSARY

Book value of a share of stock one share's portion of the stockholders' equity recorded in the accounts. p. 500

Callable preferred stock preferred stock that the issuing corporation, at its option, may retire by paying a specified amount (the call price) to the preferred stockholders plus any dividends in arrears. p. 499

Call price of preferred stock the amount that must be paid to call and retire a preferred share. p. 499

Common stock stock of a corporation that has only one class of stock, or if there is more than one class, the class that has no preferences over the corporation's other classes of stock. p. 488

Convertible preferred stock a preferred stock that can be exchanged for shares of the issuing corporation's common stock at the option of the preferred stockholder. p. 499

Cumulative preferred stock preferred stock on which undeclared dividends accumulate until they are paid; common stockholders cannot receive a dividend until all cumulative dividends have been paid. p. 497

Date of declaration the date on which a corporation's board of directors votes to pay a dividend; the dividend becomes a liability on this date. p. 493

Date of payment the date on which a corporation actually disburses a cash dividend directly to the stockholders. p. 494

Date of record the date on which the corporation's records are examined to identify the stockholders who will receive a dividend. p. 494

Deficit a debit balance in the Retained Earnings account; this situation arises when a company's cumulative losses and dividends are greater than the cumulative profits earned in other years. p. 495

Discount on stock the difference between the par value of stock and its issue price when it is issued at a price below par value. p. 491

Dividend in arrears an unpaid dividend on cumulative preferred stock; it must be paid before any regular dividends on the preferred stock and before any dividends on the common stock. p. 497

Dividend yield a company's annual cash dividends per share divided by the market value per share. p. 506

Financial leverage the achievement of an increased return on common stock by paying dividends on preferred stock or interest at a rate that is less than the rate of return earned with the assets invested in the corporation by the preferred stockholders or creditors. p. 499

General partner a partner who assumes unlimited liability for the debts of the partnership; the general partner in a limited partnership is usually responsible for its management. p. 502

General partnership a partnership in which all partners have unlimited liability for partnership debts. p. 502

Limited liability partnership a partnership in which each partner is not personally liable for malpractice claims unless the partner was responsible for providing the service that resulted in the claim. p. 502

Limited partners partners who have no personal liability for debts of the partnership beyond the amounts they have invested in the partnership. p. 502

Limited partnership a partnership that has two classes of partners, limited partners and one or more general partners. p. 502

Minimum legal capital an amount of assets defined by state law that stockholders must invest and leave invested in a corporation; this provision is intended to protect the creditors of the corporation. p. 489

Mutual agency the legal relationship among the partners whereby each partner is an agent of the partnership and is able to bind the partnership to contracts within the apparent scope of the partnership's business. p. 502

Noncumulative preferred stock a preferred stock on which the right to receive dividends is forfeited for any year that the dividends are not declared. p. 497

No-par stock a class of stock that does not have a par value; no-par stock can be issued at any price without creating a discount liability. p. 491

Organization costs the costs of bringing a corporation into existence, including legal fees, promoters' fees, and amounts paid to the state to secure the charter. p. 486

Par value an arbitrary value assigned to a share of stock when the stock is authorized. p. 489

Participating preferred stock preferred stock that gives its owners the right to share in dividends in excess of the stated percentage or amount. p. 498

Partnership an unincorporated association of two or more persons to carry on a business for profit as co-owners. p. 501

Partnership contract the agreement between partners that sets forth the terms under which the affairs of the partnership will be conducted. p. 501

Preemptive right the right of common stockholders to protect their proportionate interest in a corporation by having the first opportunity to buy additional shares of common stock issued by the corporation. p. 495

Preferred stock stock that gives its owners a priority status over common stockholders in one or more ways, such as the payment of dividends or the distribution of assets upon liquidation. p. 496

Premium on stock the difference between the par value of stock and its issue price when it is issued at a price above par value. p. 490

Proxy a legal document that gives an agent of a stockholder the power to exercise the voting rights of that stockholder's shares. p. 487

Stated value of no-par stock an arbitrary amount assigned to no-par stock by the corporation's board of directors; this amount is credited to the no-par stock account when the stock is issued. p. 491

Stock subscription a contractual commitment by an investor to purchase unissued shares of stock and become a stockholder. p. 492

Unlimited liability of partners the legal relationship among general partners that makes each of them responsible for paying all the debts of the partnership if the other partners are unable to pay their shares. p. 502

QUESTIONS

1. Who is responsible for directing the affairs of a corporation?
2. What are organization costs? List several examples of these costs.
3. How are organization costs classified on the balance sheet?
4. What are the duties and responsibilities of a corporation's registrar and transfer agent?
5. List the general rights of common stockholders.
6. What is the preemptive right of common stockholders?
7. What is the main advantage of no-par stock?
8. What is the difference between the par value and the call price of a share of stock?
9. Why would an investor find convertible preferred stock attractive?
10. Kurt and Ellen are partners in operating a store. Without consulting Kurt, Ellen contracts to purchase merchandise for the store. Kurt contends that he did not authorize the order and refuses to take delivery. Is the partnership obligated to pay? Why or why not?

11. Would your answer to Question 10 differ if Kurt and Ellen were partners in a public accounting firm?
12. Examine the balance sheet for Ben & Jerry's Homemade, Inc., in Appendix G at the end of the book and determine the classes of stock that the company has issued.

    BEN&JERRY'S
    VERMONT'S FINEST • ICE CREAM & FROZEN YOGURT.

13. Examine the statement of changes in stockholders' equity (called the *consolidated statement of changes in common stockholders' investment*) for Federal Express Corporation in Appendix G at the end of the book and determine how many shares of common stock the company issued during the year ended May 31, 1993. Examine the company's balance sheet and determine the par value per share.

QUICK STUDY (Five-Minute Exercises)

**QS 13–1
(LO 1)**

Of the following statements, which are true for the corporate form of business?

a. Capital often is more easily accumulated than with other forms of organization.

b. It has a limited life.

c. Owners have unlimited liability for corporate debts.

d. Distributed income is taxed twice in normal circumstances.

e. It is a separate legal entity.

f. Ownership rights cannot be easily transferred.

g. Owners are not agents of the corporation.

**QS 13–2
(LO 2)**

On June 1, YMI Corporation issued 25,000 shares of $5 par value common stock for $168,000 cash. Present the entry to record this transaction.

**QS 13–3
(LO 3)**

On August 15, Retro Company accepted subscriptions to 12,000 shares of $1 par value common stock at $10 per share. A 20% down payment was made on this date with the remainder to be paid in six months. Prepare an entry to record this transaction.

Nosar Company's stockholders' equity includes 50,000 shares of $5 par value, 8%, cumulative, nonparticipating preferred stock and 200,000 shares of $1 par value common stock. Nosar did not declare any dividends during the prior year and now declares and pays a $72,000 cash dividend. Determine the amount distributed to each class of stockholders.

**QS 13–4
(LO 4)**

Prepare journal entries to record the following transactions for Gruene Corporation:

**QS 13–5
(LO 4)**

June 15 Declared a $24,000 cash dividend payable to common stockholders.

July 31 Paid the dividend declared on June 15.

Dec. 31 Closed the Cash Dividends Declared account.

The stockholders' equity section of Roscoe Company's balance sheet follows:

**QS 13–6
(LO 5)**

Stockholders' Equity

Preferred stock, 5% cumulative, $10 par value, 20,000 shares authorized, issued and outstanding	$ 200,000
Common stock, $5 par value, 200,000 shares authorized, 150,000 shares issued and outstanding	750,000
Retained earnings	890,000
Total stockholders' equity	$1,840,000

The call price of the preferred stock is $45 and one year's dividends are in arrears. Determine the book value per share of the common stock.

Fred Earnest and Jackie Magness are partners in a business they started two years ago. The partnership agreement states that Earnest should receive a salary allowance of $15,000 and that Magness should receive $20,000. Any remaining income or loss is to be shared equally. Determine each partner's share of the current year's net income of $52,000.

**QS 13–7
(LO 6)**

SOS Company expects to pay out a $4.50 per share cash dividend next year on its common stock. The current market price per share is $52.20. Calculate the expected dividend yield on the SOS stock.

**QS 13–8
(LO 7)**

EXERCISES

Present the general journal entries that an accountant would prepare to record the following issuances of stock in three different situations:

**Exercise 13–1
Recording stock issuances
(LO 2)**

a. Two thousand shares of $10 par value common stock are issued for $35,000 cash.

b. One thousand shares of no-par common stock are issued to the corporation's promoters in exchange for their efforts in creating it. Their efforts are estimated to be worth $15,000, and the stock has no stated value.

c. One thousand shares of no-par common stock are issued to the corporation's promoters in exchange for their efforts in creating it. Their efforts are estimated to be worth $15,000, and the stock has a $1 per share stated value.

Printers, Inc., issued 4,000 shares of its common stock for $96,000 cash on March 16. Present the journal entries that the company's accountant would use to record this event under each of the following situations:

**Exercise 13–2
Accounting for par and
no-par stock issuances
(LO 2)**

a. The stock has no par or stated value.

b. The stock has a stated value of $8 per share.

c. The stock has a $20 par value.

Exercise 13–3
Interpreting journal entries for stock issuances and subscriptions
(LO 2, 3)

Each of these entries was recently recorded by a different corporation. Provide an explanation for the event or transaction described by each entry.

a.	Cash	40,000.00	
	Common Stock, No-Par		40,000.00
b.	Merchandise Inventory	45,000.00	
	Machinery	65,000.00	
	Notes Payable		72,000.00
	Common Stock, $25 Par Value		20,000.00
	Contributed Capital in Excess of		
	Par Value, Common Stock		18,000.00
c.	Organization Costs	45,000.00	
	Common Stock, No-Par		33,000.00
	Contributed Capital in Excess of		
	Stated Value, No-Par Common Stock		12,000.00
d.	Cash	25,000.00	
	Subscriptions Receivable, Common Stock	75,000.00	
	Common Stock Subscribed		60,000.00
	Contributed Capital in Excess of		
	Par Value, Common Stock		40,000.00

Exercise 13–4
Stock subscriptions
(LO 3)

On February 15, Quality Care Corp. accepted subscriptions at $19 per share for 8,000 shares of its $10 par value common stock. The subscriptions called for 40% of the subscription price to be paid as a down payment with the balance due on April 15. Show the journal entries that the company's accountant would make to record these three events:

a.   Accepting the subscriptions and the down payments.

b.   Receiving the balance of the subscriptions on the due date.

c.   Issuing the stock on the same date.

Exercise 13–5
Dividends on common and noncumulative preferred stock
(LO 4)

The outstanding stock of D. B. Copper Corp. includes 20,000 shares of noncumulative preferred stock with a $10 par value and a 7.5% dividend rate, as well as 50,000 shares of common stock with a $1 par value. During its first four years of operation, the corporation declared and paid the following total amounts of dividends:

19X1	$ 5,000
19X2	12,000
19X3	50,000
19X4	98,000

Determine the amount of dividends paid in each year to each class of stockholders. Also determine the total dividends paid to each class in the four years combined.

Exercise 13–6
Dividends on common and cumulative preferred stock
(LO 4)

Use the data in Exercise 13–5 to determine the amount of dividends paid in each year to each class of stockholders, assuming that the preferred stock is cumulative. Also determine the total dividends paid to each class in the four years combined.

Exercise 13–7
Using preferred stock to create leverage
(LO 4)

An individual entrepreneur is planning to start a new business and needs $625,000 of start-up capital. This person has $500,000 in personal assets that can be invested and thus needs to raise another $125,000 in cash. The founder will buy 10,000 shares of common stock for $500,000 and has two alternative plans for raising the additional cash. One plan is to sell 2,500 shares of common stock to one or more other investors for $125,000 cash. The second is to sell 1,250 shares of cumulative preferred stock to one or more investors for $125,000 cash (this stock has a $100 par value, an annual 8% dividend rate, and would be issued at par).

1. If the business is expected to earn $90,000 of after-tax net income in the first year, what rate of return on beginning equity will the founder earn under each alternative? Which of the two plans will provide the higher return to the founder?

2. If the business is expected to earn $21,000 of after-tax net income in the first year, what rate of return on beginning equity will the founder earn under each alternative? Which of the two plans will provide the higher return to the founder?

Match each of the numbered descriptions with the characteristic of preferred stock that it best describes. Indicate your answer by writing the letter for the correct characteristic in the blank space next to each description.

Exercise 13–8
Identifying characteristics of preferred stock
(LO 5)

A. Callable
B. Convertible
C. Cumulative

D. Noncumulative
E. Nonparticipating
F. Participating

__1. The holders of the stock can exchange it for shares of common stock.

__2. The issuing corporation can retire the stock by paying a prearranged price.

__3. The holders of the stock are entitled to receive dividends in excess of the stated rate under some conditions.

__4. The holders of the stock are not entitled to receive dividends in excess of the stated rate.

__5. The holders of the stock lose any dividends that are not declared.

__6. The holders of the stock are entitled to receive current and all past dividends before common stockholders receive any dividends.

On the following list of eight general characteristics of business organizations, write a brief description of how each characteristic applies to corporations and partnerships.

Exercise 13–9
Characteristics of corporations and partnerships
(LO 1, 6)

		Corporations	Partnerships
1.	Life		
2.	Owners' liability		
3.	Legal status		
4.	Tax status of income		
5.	Owners' authority		
6.	Ease of formation		
7.	Transferability of ownership		
8.	Ability to raise large amounts of capital		

Andy Anderson and Bobbie Buelow created a new business on April 11 when they each invested $60,000 cash in the company. On December 15, they decided that they would each receive $15,000 of the company's cash as a distribution. The checks were prepared and given to Anderson and Buelow on December 20. On December 31, the company's accountant determined that the company's net income was $44,000.

Exercise 13–10
Comparative entries for partnership and corporation
(LO 1, 6)

1. Assume that this company is a partnership and present the journal entries that the accountant would make to record these events: *(a)* investments by the owners, *(b)* the

cash distribution to the owners, and *(c)* the closing of the Income Summary and the owners' withdrawals accounts.

2. Assume that this company is a corporation and present the journal entries that the accountant would make to record these events: *(a)* investments by the owners, *(b)* the cash distribution to the owners, and *(c)* the closing of the Income Summary and dividends accounts. When the company was created, each owner acquired 2,000 shares of $25 par value common stock.

Exercise 13–11
Book value per share of stock
(LO 5)

The balance sheet for High Beams, Inc., includes the following information:

Stockholders' Equity

Preferred stock, 6% cumulative, $50 par value, $60 call price, 5,000 shares issued and outstanding	$ 250,000
Common stock, $20 par value, 40,000 shares issued and outstanding	800,000
Retained earnings	535,000
Total stockholders' equity	$1,585,000

Determine the book value per share of the preferred and common stock under these two situations:

a. No preferred dividends are in arrears.

b. Three years of preferred dividends are in arrears.

Exercise 13–12
Income allocation for a partnership
(LO 6)

Sells and Haskins began a partnership by investing $120,000 and $80,000, respectively. During its first year, the partnership earned $40,000. Show how the partnership's income would be allocated to the partners under each of the following situations:

a. The partners did not establish a method of sharing income.

b. The partners agreed to share incomes and losses in proportion to their initial investments.

c. The partners agreed to share incomes and losses with an $18,000 per year salary allowance to Sells, a $10,000 per year salary allowance to Haskins, 8% interest on their initial investments, and the balance equally.

Exercise 13–13
Calculating dividend yield
(LO 7)

Calculate the dividend yield for each of these situations:

		Annual Dividend per Share	Stock's Market Price per Share
a.	. . . . . .	$6.00	$ 64.00
b.	. . . . . .	3.00	30.50
c.	. . . . . .	5.50	65.00
d.	. . . . . .	0.60	43.00
e.	. . . . . .	1.00	25.00
f.	. . . . . .	7.50	108.00

PROBLEMS

Problem 13–1
Stock subscriptions
(LO 2, 3, 4)

On March 1, Mercer Corporation received authorization to issue up to 20,000 shares of $10 par value preferred stock that pays a 9% cumulative dividend. The company also is authorized to issue up to 100,000 shares of common stock that has no par value; however, the board of directors established a $2 stated value for this stock. The company then completed these transactions over the next three months:

Mar. 6   Accepted subscriptions to 15,000 shares of common stock at $5 per share. The subscribers each made down payments of 30% of the subscription price. The balance is due on May 6.

 20   Issued 1,000 shares of common stock to the corporation's promoters for their services in organizing the corporation. The board valued the services at $5,000.

 30   Accepted subscriptions to 4,000 shares of preferred stock at $12 per share. The subscribers each made down payments of 40% of the subscription price. The balance is due on May 30.

May 6   Collected the balance due on the March 6 common stock subscriptions and issued the shares.

 12   Accepted subscriptions to 2,500 shares of preferred stock at $14 per share. The subscribers each made down payments of 40% of the subscription price. The balance is due on July 12.

 30   Collected the balance due on the March 30 preferred stock subscriptions and issued the shares.

At the end of May, the balance of retained earnings is $16,000.

Required

Use the information about the transactions to prepare the stockholders' equity section of the company's balance sheet as of May 31. (Note: You will find it useful to prepare journal entries for the transactions to help you process the data.)

CHECK FIGURE:
Total equity, $179,000

Alabama Energy, Inc., was chartered at the beginning of the year and engaged in a number of transactions. The following journal entries affected its stockholders' equity during its first year of operations:

Problem 13–2
Stockholders' equity transactions
(LO 2, 3, 5, 7)

a.	Cash	300,000.00	
	Common Stock, $25 Par Value		250,000.00
	Contributed Capital in Excess of		
	Par Value, Common Stock		50,000.00
b.	Organization Costs	150,000.00	
	Common Stock, $25 Par Value		125,000.00
	Contributed Capital in Excess of		
	Par Value, Common Stock		25,000.00
c.	Cash	43,000.00	
	Accounts Receivable	15,000.00	
	Office Equipment	21,500.00	
	Building	60,000.00	
	Accounts Payable		22,000.00
	Notes Payable		37,500.00
	Common Stock, $25 Par Value		50,000.00
	Contributed Capital in Excess of		
	Par Value, Common Stock		30,000.00
d.	Cash	120,000.00	
	Common Stock, $25 Par Value		75,000.00
	Contributed Capital in Excess of		
	Par Value, Common Stock		45,000.00
e.	Cash Dividends Declared	15,000.00	
	Common Dividend Payable		15,000.00
f.	Common Dividend Payable	15,000.00	
	Cash		15,000.00

g.	Income Summary	60,000.00	
	Retained Earnings		60,000.00
h.	Retained Earnings	15,000.00	
	Cash Dividends Declared		15,000.00

Required

1. Provide explanations for the journal entries.
2. Prepare answers for the following questions:
    a. What is the net income for the year?
    b. How many shares of common stock are outstanding?
    c. What is the minimum legal capital?
    d. What is the total contributed capital?
    e. What is the total retained earnings?
    f. What is the total stockholders' equity?
    g. What is the book value per share of the common stock at the end of the year?
    h. The dividend yield on this stock is 2%. Expected dividends for the upcoming year are $1 per share. What is the stock's current market value?
    i. The market interest rate on bonds ranges from 8 to 10%. Does the value of this company's stock appear to be based on income or growth?

CHECK FIGURE:
Total equity, $695,000

Problem 13–3
Allocating dividends between preferred and common stock
(LO 4)

Moving Along, Inc., has 5,000 outstanding shares of $100 par value, 5% preferred stock and 40,000 shares of $1 par value common stock. During the last seven-year period, the company paid out the following total amounts in dividends to its preferred and common stockholders:

19X1	$ 5,000
19X2	11,000
19X3	22,500
19X4	65,000
19X5	18,000
19X6	35,000
19X7	45,000

CHECK FIGURE:
Requirement *b:* total to common, $26,500

No dividends were in arrears for years prior to 19X1.

Required

1. Determine the amounts of dividends paid to the two classes of stock in each year and for all seven years combined under these two assumptions:
    a. The preferred stock is noncumulative.
    b. The preferred stock is cumulative.
2. Comment on the difference between the answers in requirement 1.

Problem 13–4
Calculating book values
(LO 5)

Duplex Communications, Inc.'s common stock is currently selling on a stock exchange today at $85 per share, and a recent balance sheet shows the following information:

Stockholders' Equity

Preferred stock, 5%, $? par value, 1,000 shares authorized, issued and outstanding	$ 50,000
Common stock, $? par value, 4,000 shares authorized, issued, and outstanding	80,000
Retained earnings	150,000
Total stockholders' equity	$280,000

Required

Preparation component:

1. What is the market value of the corporation's common stock?
2. What are the par values of the preferred stock and the common stock?
3. If no dividends are in arrears, what are the book values of the preferred stock and the common stock?
4. If two years' preferred dividends are in arrears, what are the book values of the preferred stock and the common stock?

CHECK FIGURE:
Requirement 4: book value of common, $56.25

5. If two years' preferred dividends are in arrears and the preferred stock is callable at $55 per share, what are the book values of the preferred stock and the common stock?

Analysis component:

6. What are some factors that may contribute to the difference between the book value of common stock and its market value?

Tinker, Evers, and Chance created a partnership and invested $42,000, $83,000, and $75,000, respectively, at the beginning of the year. During its first year, the partnership achieved a net income of $78,000. Tinker, Evers, and Chance each withdrew $15,000 cash from the partnership on December 31.

Problem 13–5
Allocating partnership income
(LO 6)

Required

Preparation component:

1. Prepare schedules that show how the partners would allocate the partnership's net income among themselves under each of the following agreements:

    a. The partners divide the income equally.

    b. The partners share the income in proportion to their initial investments.

    c. The partners agreed to provide annual salary allowances of $30,000 to Tinker, $13,000 to Evers, and $13,000 to Chance and 8% interest allowances on the partners' initial investments. Any remaining income (or deficit) is to be shared equally.

CHECK FIGURE:
Agreement c: income to Evers, $21,640

2. Prepare a schedule that shows the equity balances of each of the three partners as of the end of the year under agreement *c*.

Analysis component:

3. For each of the partnership agreements in requirement 1, describe a probable situation which would result in the partners agreeing that the agreement was a fair allocation of future earnings.

CRITICAL THINKING: ESSAYS, PROBLEMS, AND CASES

Jan Carston and Carey Glenwood want to create a new software development business. Each of them can contribute fairly large amounts of capital. However, they know that the business will need additional equity capital from other investors after its first year. With respect to their individual activities, they are both planning to devote full-time effort to getting the first products out the door within the year. They plan to hire three employees initially and expect to distribute a substantial amount of cash every year for their personal expenses Carston has proposed organizing the business as a general partnership, but Glenwood thinks that a corporation offers more advantages. They have asked you to prepare a brief analysis that supports choosing the corporate form. What main points would you include in your analysis?

Analytical Essay
(LO 1, 6)

Financial Reporting Problem

(LO 2, 6)

For a number of years, Berry Benson and Connie Karle have operated a retailing company called We've Got It. They organized the company as a partnership and have shared income and losses in a 2:3 ratio. (Benson gets 40% while Karle gets 60%.) Because the business is growing beyond their ability to keep up with it, they have agreed to accept a third person, Mickey Rogers, into the business. Part of the new arrangement involves creating a new corporation, called We've Got It, Inc. The corporate charter authorizes 50,000 shares of $10 par value common stock. The deal requires three steps. First, the partners must settle up the old business by revaluing the assets to their fair market values and dividing the previously unrecognized gains and losses. Second, the partnership must transfer its assets and liabilities to the corporation, which will issue shares to the partners in exchange for their equity in the partnership. The shares will be considered to be worth $10 each when the exchange is made. Third, Rogers will pay $10 cash for all authorized shares not issued to the former partners. You have been engaged to help the three phases of the deal go smoothly.

The following spreadsheet has been developed to help you accomplish the first phase of modifying the partnership's accounts to reflect the fair market values for the assets and to modify the partners' equity balances:

WE'VE GOT IT
Account Modification Spreadsheet
July 31

Accounts	Unmodified Trial Balance	Modifications (a)	(b)	(c)	(d)	(e)	Modified Trial Balance
Debits:							
Cash	21,000						
Accounts receivable	31,000						
Merchandise inventory	150,000	(25,000)					
Store equipment	128,000						
Buildings	280,000						
Land	87,000						
Total	697,000						____
							====
Credits:							
Allowance for doubtful accounts	(3,000)						
Accum. depreciation, equip.	(48,000)						
Accum. depreciation, bldgs.	(82,000)						
Accounts Payable	(32,000)						
Notes payable	(172,000)						
Benson, capital	(160,000)	10,000					
Karle, capital	(200,000)	15,000					
Total	(697,000)						____
							====

Numbers in parentheses are credits.

The partners have agreed that the following modifications need to be included in the first phase (they will divide any gains and losses from the changes in recorded value according to their regular income and loss ratio):

a. The merchandise inventory is to be written down to its fair value of $125,000.

b. An account receivable from a customer for $1,000 is known to be uncollectible and will be written off against the allowance for doubtful accounts.

c. After writing off that account, the allowance for doubtful accounts will be adjusted to 5% of the gross accounts receivable.

d. The net recorded value of the store equipment will be decreased to $65,000 by increasing the balance of the accumulated depreciation account.

e. The gross recorded value of the building is to be increased to its replacement cost of $360,000. At the same time, the balance of the accumulated depreciation account is to be adjusted to equal 25% of the replacement cost to represent the fact the building's fair market value is 75% of its replacement cost.

Your first task is to complete the spreadsheet by entering the effects of each of the five modifications as debits and credits to the affected accounts. The first items have been entered in the spreadsheet as an example. You should provide supporting calculations as needed. Second, determine how many shares each partner is entitled to receive in exchange for the partner's equity. Third, determine how many shares Rogers will purchase for cash. Fourth, present the journal entries that the corporation will use to record the issuance of the shares to all three stockholders. Finally, present a balance sheet for the corporation immediately after the transactions are completed (the notes payable are due within 90 days).

Financial Statement Analysis Cases

FSAC 13-1
(LO 4)

Having received a large lump sum of severance pay, Lou Franklin is thinking about investing the money in one of two securities, either Endor Corporation common stock or the preferred stock issued by Kenobe Company. The companies manufacture similar products and compete in the same market, and both have been operating about the same length of time—four years for Endor and three years for Kenobe. The two companies also have similar amounts of stockholders' equity, as shown here:

Endor Corporation

Common stock, $1 par value, 800,000 shares authorized, 500,000 shares issued and outstanding . .	$ 500,000
Retained earnings	820,000
Total stockholders' equity	$1,320,000

Kenobe Company

Preferred stock, $50 par value, 6% cumulative, 6,000 shares authorized, issued, and outstanding . . .	$ 300,000*
Common stock, $20 par value, 50,000 shares authorized, issued, and outstanding	1,000,000
Retained earnings	60,000
Total stockholders' equity	$1,360,000

*The current and two prior years' dividends are in arrears on the preferred stock.

Endor did not pay a dividend on its common stock during its first year's operations; however, it has paid a cash dividend of $0.09 per share in each of the past three years. The stock is currently selling for $3.00 per share. In contrast, the preferred stock of Kenobe Company is selling for $45 per share. Franklin has expressed a leaning for the preferred stock as an investment because it appears to be a bargain at $5 below par value and $14 below book value. Besides, Franklin has told you, "The dividends are guaranteed because it is a preferred stock." Franklin also believes that the common stock of Endor is overpriced at 14% above book value and 200% above par value, while it is paying only a $0.09 per share dividend. In conclusion, your friend asks how anyone could prefer a common stock yielding only 3% to a preferred stock that is supposed to pay 6%.

1. Is the preferred stock of Kenobe Company actually selling at $14 below its book value, and is the common stock of Endor Corporation actually selling at 14% above book value and 200% above par?

2. Analyze the stockholders' equity sections and express your opinion of the two stocks as investments by describing some of the factors Franklin should consider in choosing between them.

FSAC 13-2
(L.O. 3, 4, 5, 7)

Use the information provided in the financial statements of Apple Computer, Inc., and the footnotes in Appendix F to answer the following questions:

1. Does it appear that Apple has been authorized to issue any preferred stock? If so, has any been issued as of September 24, 1993?

2. How many shares of common stock have been authorized? How many have been issued as of September 24, 1993?

3. What is the par value of the common stock? What is its book value at September 24, 1993?

4. Are any shares of common stock subscribed? Are there any shares that cannot be issued to the public because they have been promised to others?

5. What was the highest market value of the stock during 1993? What was the lowest?

6. Did Apple declare any dividends on its capital stock during 1993? If so, how large were the dividends (in total, and per share)? If the price of the stock was $48 per share at the end of fiscal year 1993, and dividends were expected to continue at the same rate, what was the dividend yield of the stock? Does it appear that Apple is a growth or income stock?

ANSWERS TO PROGRESS CHECKS

13–1   *b*

13–2   A corporation must pay taxes on its income and its stockholders must pay personal income taxes on dividends received from the corporation.

13–3   A proxy is a legal document used to transfer a stockholder's right to vote to another person.

13–4   *a*

13–5   A stock premium is an amount in excess of par paid by purchasers of newly issued stock.

13–6   Creditors of the corporation are intended to be protected by minimum legal capital.

13–7   *c*

13–8   Common Stock Subscribed is classfied as contributed capital in the stockholders' equity section of the balance sheet.

13–9   *c*

13–10 The three dates are the date of declaration, the date of record, and the date of payment.

13–11 Typically, preferred stock has a preference in receiving dividends and in the distribution of assets in the case of a company's liquidation.

13–12 *a*   Total dividend $288,000
13–13 *b*   To preferred shareholders 135,000*
                    Remainder to common shareholders $153,000

                    *9,000 × $50 × .10 × 3 = $135,000

13–14 Total stockholders' equity $630,000
       Less equity applicable to preferred shares:
         Call price (1,000 × $90) $90,000
         Dividends in arrears 18,000   108,000
       Equity applicable to common shares $522,000

       Book value of common shares ($522,000/12,000) .... $ 43.50

13–15 *c*
13–16 *b*

13–17

	Mixon	Reed	Income to be Allocated
Total net income			$40,000
Allocated as interest	$ 7,000	$ 3,500	10,500
Remaining balance			$29,500
Balance allocated equally	14,750	14,750	29,500
Remaining balance			$ –0–
Shares of partners	$21,750	$18,250	

13–18 Unlimited liability means that the creditors of a partnership have the right to require each partner to be personally responsible for all partnership debts.

13–19 *c*

CHAPTER 14

Additional Corporate Transactions; Reporting Income and Retained Earnings; Earnings per Share

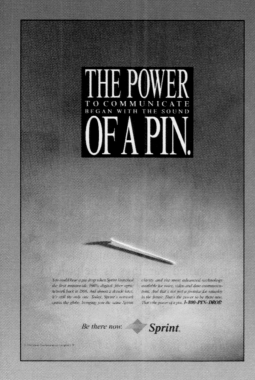

*S*print Corporation is a diversified telecommunications company that provides global voice, data, and video conferencing services and related products. The company's 1993 annual report stated that net operating revenues had tripled since 1984, increasing from $3.7 to $11.4 billion. During the three-year period from 1991 to 1993, income from continuing operations increased from $472.7 to $480.6 million. Nevertheless, during the same three years, the earnings applicable to common stock declined from $516.1 to $52.1 million.

Considering the sharp differences in these trends, a common stockholder might wonder how to assess the company's future prospects. How might Sprint describe the results in its financial statements? What additional information would you expect to find in the income statement beyond the items in the following table?

Sprint Corporation
(In millions)

	1993	1992	1991
Net operating revenues	$11,367.8	$10,420.3	$9,933.3
Income from continuing operations	480.6	496.1	472.7
Net income	54.9	502.8	520.2
Preferred stock dividends	(2.8)	(3.5)	(4.1)
Earnings applicable to common stock	52.1	499.3	516.1

LEARNING OBJECTIVES

After studying Chapter 14 you should be able to:

1. **Describe stock dividends and stock splits and explain their effects on a corporation's assets and stockholders' equity.**

2. **Record purchases and sales of treasury stock and retirements of stock and describe their effects on stockholders' equity. Also, describe restrictions and appropriations of retained earnings and explain how they are described in financial reports.**

3. **Explain how to report the income effects of discontinued segments, extraordinary items, changes in accounting principles and estimates, and prior period adjustments.**

4. **Calculate earnings per share for companies with simple capital structures and explain the difference between primary and fully diluted earnings per share.**

5. **Calculate the price-earnings ratio and describe its meaning.**

6. **Define or explain the words and phrases listed in the chapter glossary.**

Corporations often enter into special financing transactions that involve changes in stockholders' equity. The first section of this chapter explains several of these transactions, including stock dividends, stock splits, and transactions involving the company's own stock. The second section of the chapter expands your understanding of financial statements by explaining how information about income and retained earnings is classified and reported. The third section explains how corporations report earnings per share. Understanding these topics will help you interpret and use financial statements. In fact, the discussion in this chapter helps clarify some of the reporting issues implied by the previous discussion of Sprint Corporation.

CORPORATE DIVIDENDS AND OTHER STOCK TRANSACTIONS

In Chapter 1, we briefly described a corporation's retained earnings as the stockholders' equity that is created by the company's profitable activities. It is equal to the total cumulative amount of the reported net income less any net losses and dividends declared since the company started operating. In effect, retained earnings are the stockholders' residual interest in the corporation that was not created by their investments. Information about retained earnings is helpful to investors and other users of financial statements for predicting future cash flows for dividends and other events.

RETAINED EARNINGS AND DIVIDENDS

LO 1

Describe stock dividends and stock splits and explain their effects on a corporation's assets and stockholders' equity.

FAST HINT
Critical Thought Question:
How does a cash dividend affect working capital and stockholders' equity?

Most state laws allow a corporation to pay cash dividends if retained earnings exist. However, in addition to retained earnings, a corporation must have enough cash to pay the dividend. And, even if there is sufficient cash and retained earnings, the directors may decide against declaring a dividend because the cash is needed in the business. Although cash may be paid out in dividends, companies also keep some cash in reserve to meet emergencies, to take advantage of unexpected opportunities, or to avoid having to borrow for future expansion.

Chapter 13 described how cash dividends are recorded in the accounts. The declaration of a dividend reduces the retained earnings and creates a current liability to the stockholders. On the date of record, the recipients of the dividend are identified, but no entry is recorded in the accounts. On the date of payment, cash is sent to the qualifying stockholders and the liability is removed from the books.

Generally, the Dividends Declared account is closed to the Retained Earnings account. However, in limited circumstances, some state laws allow cash dividends to be paid as a return of capital contributed by the stockholders. If so, the Dividends Declared account is closed with a debit entry to one of the contributed capital accounts instead of Retained Earnings. Because these dividends return part of the original investment to the stockholders, they are often called **liquidating dividends.** They usually occur when the company is completing a major downsizing, perhaps in preparation for a merger or even dissolution. In most cases, the equity that originated from the par or stated value of the outstanding stock cannot be used as a basis for liquidating dividends until all creditors have been paid. This situation normally occurs only when the corporation is actually going out of business.

FAST HINT
Important Point to Remember: Although it often is said that a dividend is a distribution of retained earnings, retained earnings are not assets and actually cannot be distributed. It is more precise to describe a dividend as a distribution of assets that satisfies stockholders' equity claims.

Sometimes, a corporation's directors may declare a **stock dividend.** This means the company distributes additional shares of its own stock to its stockholders without receiving any payment in return. Stock dividends and cash dividends are very different. A cash dividend reduces the corporation's assets and stockholders' equity, and a stock dividend does neither. A stock dividend simply transfers some equity from retained earnings into contributed capital.

STOCK DIVIDENDS

Why Stock Dividends Are Distributed

If stock dividends do not affect assets or total stockholders' equity, why are they declared and distributed? Directors can use stock dividends to keep the market value of the stock affordable. For example, if a profitable corporation grows but does not pay cash dividends, the price of its common stock increases in anticipation of continued growth and future dividends. Eventually, the price of a share may become so high that it discourages some investors from buying the stock. Thus, the corporation may declare stock dividends to increase the number of outstanding shares and thereby keep the per share price of its stock low enough to be attractive to smaller investors.

Another reason for declaring a stock dividend is to provide tangible evidence of management's confidence that the company is doing well. The stock dividend may substitute for a cash dividend, thereby saving cash that can be used to expand the business.

The Effect of Stock Dividends on Stockholders' Equity Accounts

Although a stock dividend does not affect the corporation's assets or total stockholders' equity, it does affect the components of stockholders' equity. This effect is recorded by transferring part of the retained earnings to the contributed capital accounts. Because this treatment increases the company's contributed capital, it is often described as *capitalizing* retained earnings.

If a corporation declares a **small stock dividend,** accounting principles require it to capitalize retained earnings equal to the market value of the shares to be distributed. This practice is based on the concept that a small stock dividend is likely to be perceived as similar to a cash dividend because it has a small impact on the price of the stock. A dividend is considered small if it is less than or equal to 25% of the previously outstanding shares.

A **large stock dividend,** one that distributes more than 25% of the outstanding shares before the dividend, is likely to have a noticeable effect on the stock's market price per share. It is not likely to be perceived as a substitute for a cash dividend. Therefore, a large stock dividend is recorded by capitalizing an amount of retained earnings only to the minimum required by the state law governing the corporation. In most cases, the law requires capitalizing retained earnings equal to the par or stated value of the shares.

For example, assume that Northwest Corporation's stockholders' equity consists of the following amounts just before the declaration of a stock dividend:

NORTHWEST CORPORATION
Stockholders' Equity
December 31, 19X1

Common stock, $10 par value, 15,000 shares authorized, 10,000 shares issued and outstanding	$100,000
Contributed capital in excess of par value, common stock . .	8,000
Total contributed capital	$108,000
Retained earnings	35,000
Total stockholders' equity	$143,000

Recording a Small Stock Dividend

To illustrate how a small stock dividend is recorded, let's assume that the directors of Northwest Corporation declare a 10% stock dividend on December 31. The 1,000 dividend shares (10% of the 10,000 outstanding shares) are to be distributed on January 20 to the January 15 stockholders of record.

If the market value of Northwest Corporation's stock on December 31 is $15 per share, the dividend declaration is recorded with this entry:

Dec.	31	Stock Dividends Declared	15,000.00	
		Common Stock Dividend Distributable		10,000.00
		Contributed Capital in Excess of Par Value, Common Stock		5,000.00
		To record the declaration of a 1,000-share common stock dividend.		

FAST HINT
Critical Thought Question:
Could Northwest have declared this stock dividend if the retained earnings had been less than $15,000? Explain.

FAST HINT
Important Point to Remember:
The credit to Contributed Capital in Excess of Par Value is recorded when the stock dividend is declared in anticipation of issuing the stock. This account is not affected later when stock is distributed.

The debit is recorded in the temporary account called Stock Dividends Declared. This account serves the same purpose as the Cash Dividends Declared account described in the preceding chapter. A complete chart of accounts includes separate accounts for cash and stock dividends because the financial statements must report stock and cash dividends as separate events. If stock dividends are not frequently declared, a company can get by without a separate account for Stock Dividends Declared. Instead, it can record the debit directly to Retained Earnings. This approach is acceptable as long as the information is reported correctly in the financial statements.

In the previous entry, the first credit puts the par value of the dividend shares in a contributed capital account called Common Stock Dividend Distributable. This account balance exists only until the shares are actually issued. The second credit records the premium on the dividend shares at this time, even though the shares have not yet been issued. This account is the same one that is used for all other issuances at an amount more than par value.

Illustration 14–1
The Effect of Northwest
Corporation's 10% Stock
Dividend

Before the 10% stock dividend
Stockholders' equity:

Common stock (10,000 shares)	$100,000
Contributed capital in excess of par value, common stock . .	8,000
Retained earnings	35,000
Total stockholders' equity	$143,000

Book value per share = $143,000/10,000 shares = $14.30
Book value of Johnson's 200 shares = $14.30 × 200 = $2,860

After the 10% stock dividend
Stockholders' equity:

Common stock (11,000 shares)	$110,000
Contributed capital in excess of par value, common stock . .	13,000
Retained earnings	20,000
Total stockholders' equity	$143,000

Book value per share = $143,000/11,000 shares = $13.00
Book value of Johnson's 220 shares = $13 × 220 = $2,860

As part of the year-end closing process, the accountant for the Northwest Corporation closes the Stock Dividends Declared account to Retained Earnings with this entry:

FAST HINT
Relevant Quick Study:
To apply these concepts, work QS 14–1.

Dec.	31	Retained Earnings	15,000.00	
		Stock Dividends Declared		15,000.00
		To close the Stock Dividends Declared account.		

On January 20, the company distributes the new shares to the stockholders and records the event with this entry:

Jan.	20	Common Stock Dividend Distributable	10,000.00	
		Common Stock		10,000.00
		To record the distribution of a 1,000-share common		
		stock dividend.		

The combined effect of these three entries is the transfer (or capitalization) of $15,000 of retained earnings to contributed capital. The amount of capitalized retained earnings equals the market value of the 1,000 issued shares ($15 × 1,000 shares).

This example demonstrates that a stock dividend has no effect on the corporation's assets or total stockholders' equity. Nor does the dividend affect the percentage of the company owned by individual stockholders. For example, assume that Pat Johnson owned 200 shares of Northwest Corporation's stock prior to the 10% stock dividend. When the corporation sent each stockholder one new share for each 10 shares held, Johnson received 20 new shares (10% × 200 shares).

Looking at Illustration 14–1, you can see what the 10% stock dividend does to Northwest Corporation's total contributed capital and retained earnings. Note that nothing happens to the total book value of Johnson's shares. Before the stock dividend, Johnson owned 2% of the corporation's stock, which is 200 of the 10,000 outstanding shares. The book value of this holding was $2,860 (2% × $143,000, or 200

FAST HINT
Critical Thought Question:
How does a small stock dividend affect working capital?

× $14.30 per share). After the dividend, Johnson holds 220 shares, but the holding still equals 2% of the 11,000 shares now outstanding. The book value is still $2,860 (2% × $143,000, or 220 × $13.00 per share). In other words, the only change in Johnson's 2% investment is that now it is represented by 220 shares instead of 200 shares. Also, the only effect on the stockholders' equity is a transfer of $15,000 from retained earnings to contributed capital. There is no change in the corporation's total assets, in its total equity, or in the percentage of equity owned by Johnson. Of course, Johnson's main concern is whether the 220 shares are now worth more than the 200 shares used to be.

Stock Dividends on the Balance Sheet

Because a stock dividend does not reduce the corporation's assets, it is never a liability on a balance sheet prepared between the declaration and distribution dates. Instead, the amount of any declared but undistributed stock dividend appears on the balance sheet as a component of the contributed capital in the stockholders' equity section. For example, the stockholders' equity of Northwest Corporation looks like this just after the 10% stock dividend is declared on December 31:

NORTHWEST CORPORATION
Stockholders' Equity
December 31, 19X1

Common stock, $10 par value, 15,000 shares authorized, 10,000 shares issued and outstanding	$100,000
Common stock dividend distributable, 1,000 shares	10,000
Total common stock issued and to be issued	$110,000
Contributed capital in excess of par value, common stock . .	13,000
Total contributed capital	$123,000
Retained earnings	20,000
Total stockholders' equity	$143,000

This updated section of the balance sheet is changed in three ways. First, the amount of equity attributed to the common stock increased from $100,000 to $110,000 because 1,000 additional shares are ready to be issued. Second, the contributed capital in excess of par increased by $5,000, which equals the excess of the $15 per share market value over the $10 per share par value for the 1,000 shares. Finally, the balance of retained earnings decreased by $15,000 from the predividend amount of $35,000 to $20,000.

Recording a Large Stock Dividend

When a stock dividend exceeds 25% of the outstanding shares, the corporation capitalizes retained earnings equal to the minimum amount required by the law. Usually, that is the par or stated value of the newly issued shares. For example, suppose Northwest Corporation's board declared a 30% stock dividend on December 31 instead of 10%. Because the dividend is greater than the arbitrary limit of 25%, it is considered to be large. As a result, only the par value of the new 3,000 shares is capitalized. Thus, the company would record the declaration with this entry:

FAST HINT
Critical Thought Question:
What are the similarities between the Common Stock Dividend Distributable and the Common Stock Subscribed accounts?

Dec.	31	Stock Dividends Declared	30,000.00	
		Common Stock Dividend Distributable		30,000.00
		To record the declaration of a 3,000-share stock dividend at par value.		

This entry causes the company's retained earnings to be decreased by the $30,000 par value of the dividend shares. It also causes the company's contributed capital to increase by the same amount.

STOCK SPLITS

Recall that one goal for stock dividends is to reduce the stock's market price. Stock dividends divide the company into a larger number of smaller pieces. The total value of the company is unchanged, but the price of each new share is smaller. The same result can be accomplished through a **stock split.** When a stock split occurs, the corporation calls in its outstanding shares and issues two or more new shares in exchange for each of the old ones.[1]

Suppose that a company has 100,000 outstanding shares of $20 par value common stock that have a current market value of $88 per share. The market value can be cut in half by a two-for-one split. The split replaces the 100,000 $20 par value shares with 200,000 $10 par value shares that have a market value in the neighborhood of $44 per share.

Splits can be accomplished at any ratio, including two-for-one, three-for-one, or even higher. In fact, it is possible for the ratio to be less than one to one, causing stockholders to end up with fewer shares. These **reverse stock splits** are intended to increase the stock's market price per share.

A stock split does not affect the total stockholders' equity reported on the balance sheet. It also does not affect a stockholder's percentage interest in the corporation. The contributed capital and retained earnings accounts are unchanged by a split, and no journal entry is made. The only effect on the accounts is a change in the account title used for the common stock. The earlier example described a two-for-one split for a $20 par value stock. After the split, the account name would be changed to Common Stock, $10 Par Value. Although nothing else changes in the accounts, the disclosures about the stock on the balance sheet are changed to reflect the additional outstanding shares and the revised par value per share.

Many companies accomplish the effect of a stock split by declaring large stock dividends. This practice avoids a great deal of the administrative cost that would be incurred by splitting the stock. **Harley-Davidson, Inc.,** accomplished the effect of a 2-for-1 stock split in 1992 by distributing one new share for each old share.

FAST HINT
Relevant Exercise:
To apply these concepts, work Exercise 14–2.

Progress Check
(Answers to Progress Checks are provided at the end of the chapter.)

14–1 Which of the following statements is correct?

a. A large stock dividend is recorded by capitalizing retained earnings equal to the market value of the distributable shares.

b. Stock dividends and stock splits have the same effect on the total assets and retained earnings of the issuing corporation.

c. A stock dividend does not transfer corporate assets to the stockholders but does require that retained earnings be capitalized.

14–2 What distinguishes a large stock dividend from a small stock dividend?

14–3 When accounting for a small stock dividend, what amount of retained earnings should be capitalized?

---

[1]To reduce the administrative cost, most splits are accomplished by simply issuing new certificates to the stockholders for the additional shares they are entitled to receive. The stockholders do not have to turn in the old certificates.

TREASURY STOCK

LO 2

Record purchases and sales of treasury stock and retirements of stock and describe their effects on stockholders' equity. Also, describe restrictions and appropriations of retained earnings and explain how they are described in financial reports.

For a variety of reasons, corporations often acquire shares of their own stock. They may use the shares to acquire control of other corporations. Sometimes, they repurchase shares to avoid a hostile takeover by an investor seeking control of the company. Many buy shares and reissue them to employees as compensation. For example, **Hewlett-Packard Company** reports that it has a stock repurchase program to meet future employee stock plan requirements. In 1993, the company purchased 4,345,000 shares under this program.

Less frequently, a corporation may buy a large number of shares to maintain a suitable market for the stock. This practice was widespread in 1987 after many stocks lost a great deal of market value very quickly. By buying the shares, corporations helped their stockholders get a better price and brought more stability to the market.

Regardless of the reason for their acquisition, a corporation's reacquired shares are called **treasury stock.** In many respects, treasury stock is similar to unissued stock. Neither unissued nor treasury stock is an asset of the corporation. Neither receive cash or stock dividends, and no one can exercise the vote attached to the shares. However, treasury stock does have one potentially significant difference from unissued stock. Specifically, if treasury stock was originally issued at its par value or higher, the company can resell the stock at less than par without having the buyers incur a discount liability.

In addition, treasury stock purchases require management to exercise ethical sensitivity. Corporate funds are being paid to specific stockholders instead of all stockholders. As a result, managers must be careful to be sure that the purchase is in the best interest of all the stockholders. These concerns cause most companies to be very open with their stockholders about their treasury stock and other activities related to stock. Read As a Matter of Ethics and consider whether Falcon Corporation's management is showing proper consideration for its stockholders.

PURCHASING TREASURY STOCK

The act of purchasing treasury stock reduces the corporation's assets and stockholders' equity by equal amounts.[2] This effect is illustrated by the two balance sheets of the Curry Corporation in Illustrations 14–2 and 14–3. The first balance sheet shows the account balances on April 30, 19X1, before a treasury stock purchase. The sec-

---

[2]This text discusses the *cost method* of accounting for treasury stock; it is the most widely used. The *par value* method is discussed in more advanced accounting courses.

Illustration 14-2
Curry Corporation's Balance
Sheet Prior to the Purchase
of Treasury Stock

CURRY CORPORATION
Balance Sheet
April 30, 19X1

Assets		Stockholders' Equity		
Cash	$ 30,000	Contributed capital:		
Other assets	95,000	Common stock, $10 par value, authorized and issued		
		10,000 shares	$100,000	
		Retained earnings	25,000	
Total assets	$125,000	Total stockholders' equity	$125,000	

Illustration 14-3
Curry Corporation's Balance
Sheet Immediately after
Purchasing Treasury Stock

CURRY CORPORATION
Balance Sheet
April 30, 19X1

Assets		Stockholders' Equity	
Cash	$ 18,500	Contributed capital:	
Other assets	95,000	Common stock, $10 par value, authorized and issued 10,000 shares, of which 1,000 are in the treasury	$100,000
		Retained earnings, of which $11,500 is restricted by the purchase of treasury stock	25,000
		Total	$125,000
		Less cost of treasury stock	(11,500)
Total assets	$113,500	Total stockholders' equity	$113,500

ond balance sheet shows the account balances after the company purchased 1,000 of its own shares for $11,500 cash.

This entry records the purchase of the 1,000 shares:

May	1	Treasury Stock, Common	11,500.00	
		Cash		11,500.00
		Purchased 1,000 shares of treasury stock at $11.50 per share.		

The entry reduces the stockholders' equity by debiting the Treasury Stock account, which is *contra* to equity. To see the effects of the transaction, look at the balance sheet in Illustration 14–3.

Notice that the purchase reduces the company's cash, total assets, and total equity by $11,500. The equity reduction is reflected on the balance sheet by deducting the cost of the treasury stock in the equity section. The purchase does not reduce the balance of either the Common Stock account or the Retained Earnings account. However, two disclosures in this section describe the effects of the transaction. First, the statement tells the reader that 1,000 of the issued shares are in the treasury of the corporation. Thus, only 9,000 shares are outstanding. Second, the purchase has placed a restriction on the company's retained earnings. This restriction is described in the next section.

FAST HINT
Important Point to Remember:
Even though the Treasury Stock account is debited when the stock is purchased, it is not an asset account. This contra account is not simply subtracted from Retained Earnings. Instead, it is subtracted from the combined balances of all the equity accounts.

FAST HINT
Alternative Example:
As an alternative to the facts reflected in Illustration 14–3, what amounts would be reported for common stock and total stockholders' equity if the company had purchased 1,000 shares of treasury stock at $9 per share ($1 less than par value)? *Answer:* The common stock balance would be unchanged at $100,000 but the total stockholders' equity would be $116,000.

FAST HINT
Relevant Exercise:
To apply these concepts, work Exercise 14–3.

Restricting Retained Earnings by the Purchase of Treasury Stock

Cash dividends and purchases of treasury stock have a similar effect on a corporation's assets and stockholders' equity. That is, they both transfer corporate cash to stockholders and reduce assets and equity. Therefore, most states restrict the amount of cash dividends and treasury stock purchases to the amount of retained earnings.

Unlike a cash dividend, a treasury stock purchase does not directly reduce the balance of the Retained Earnings account. However, the corporation should disclose any statutory restrictions on retained earnings. Thus, the balance sheet in Illustration 14–3 identifies the amount of the **restricted retained earnings** created by the treasury stock purchase. In many cases, the restriction is described in a footnote to the financial statements. In addition to this restriction, other limits on dividends may be established by statute and by contract.

Appropriated Retained Earnings

In contrast to statutory or contractual retained earnings restrictions, a corporation's directors may voluntarily limit dividends because of a special need for cash, such as to purchase new facilities. When the directors do this, management usually explains in a letter attached to the financial statements why dividends have not been declared. However, they may notify the stockholders and other financial statement users of this change in policy by setting up an amount of **appropriated retained earnings.** These appropriations are strictly voluntary and nonbinding. They serve only to notify the statement readers of the directors' decision to not pay out cash.

REISSUING TREASURY STOCK

Treasury stock may be reissued by selling it at cost, above cost, or below cost. If it is reissued by being sold at its cost, the entry is the opposite of the entry that was made to record the purchase.

If treasury stock is sold for more than cost, the amount received in excess of cost is credited to a special account called Contributed Capital, Treasury Stock Transactions. For example, if Curry Corporation receives $12 cash per share for 500 treasury shares originally purchased at $11.50 per share, the accountant records the transaction with the following entry:

June	3	Cash	6,000.00	
		Treasury Stock, Common		5,750.00
		Contributed Capital, Treasury Stock Transactions		250.00
		Received $12 per share for 500 treasury shares that cost $11.50 per share.		

Notice that the company does not report a gain from this transaction.

When treasury stock is sold at less than its cost, the entry to record the sale depends on whether there is a credit balance in the Contributed Capital, Treasury Stock Transactions account. If there is no balance, the excess of cost over the sales price is debited to Retained Earnings. However, if the contributed capital account has a credit balance, the excess of the cost over the sales price is debited for an amount up to the balance in that account. When the credit balance in the contributed capital account is eliminated, any remaining difference between the cost and the selling price is debited to Retained Earnings.

For example, if Curry Corporation sells its remaining 500 shares of treasury stock at $10 per share, the company's equity is reduced by $750 (500 shares ×$1.50 per share excess of cost over selling price). The reissuance is recorded with this entry:

July	10	Cash	5,000.00	
		Contributed Capital, Treasury Stock Transactions	250.00	
		Retained Earnings	500.00	
		Treasury Stock, Common		5,750.00
		Received $10 per share for 500 treasury shares that cost $11.50 per share.		

This entry eliminates the $250 credit balance in the contributed capital account created on June 3 and then reduces the Retained Earnings balance by the remaining $500 of the excess of the cost over the selling price. Thus, the purchase and reissuance of the treasury shares caused the Curry Corporation to incur a $500 decrease in retained earnings and total stockholders' equity. Notice that the company does not report a loss from this transaction.

FAST HINT
Relevant Quick Study:
To apply these concepts, work QS 14–2.

RETIRING STOCK

Instead of acquiring treasury stock with the intent of reissuing it in the future, a corporation may simply purchase its own stock and retire it. It cancels the shares, which become the same as unissued stock. For example, the **Wm. Wrigley Jr. Company** reported in the notes to its 1993 financial statements that "on August 19, 1992, the Board of Directors adopted a resolution retiring the entire balance of shares of Common Stock held in the corporate treasury at that time and all subsequent acquisitions to the extent not required for issuance [under the company's management Incentive Plan.]" Like purchases of treasury stock, purchases and retirements of stock are permissible under state laws only if they do not jeopardize the best interests of creditors and other stockholders.

When stock is purchased for retirement, the accountant must remove all the contributed capital amounts related to the retired shares. If the purchase price for the shares exceeds the net amount removed from contributed capital, the excess is debited to Retained Earnings. On the other hand, if the purchase price is less than the net amount removed from contributed capital, the difference is credited to a special contributed capital account.

For example, assume that the Carolina Corporation originally issued its $10 par value common stock at $12 per share. As a result, the $2 per share premium was credited to the Contributed Capital in Excess of Par Value, Common Stock account. When the corporation purchased and retired 1,000 shares of this stock at $12 per share on April 12, it recorded the effects of this event with this entry:

Apr.	12	Common Stock	10,000.00	
		Contributed Capital in Excess of Par Value, Common Stock	2,000.00	
		Cash		12,000.00
		Purchased and retired 1,000 shares of common stock at $12 per share.		

This entry restores the accounts to the balances that they would have had if the stock had never been issued.

On the other hand, if the corporation paid only $11 per share instead of $12, the retirement causes equity to increase by $1 per share, the difference between cost and the original issuance price. This increase in equity is recorded as follows:

Apr.	12	Common Stock	10,000.00	
		Contributed Capital in Excess of Par Value, Common Stock	2,000.00	
		Cash		11,000.00
		Contributed Capital from the Retirement of		
		Common Stock		1,000.00
		Purchased and retired 1,000 shares of common stock at		
		$11 per share.		

FAST HINT
Critical Thought Question:
Can you suggest a reason why the increase in total equity from retiring stock is not credited to a gain account and reported on the income statement?

Even though this transaction increased equity, the amount is not a gain. The concept underlying this treatment is that transactions in a corporation's own stock cannot affect income or increase retained earnings.

The same idea governs the accounting for a retirement accomplished with a purchase price that is greater than the stock's original issuance price. For example, suppose that the Carolina Corporation retired 1,000 shares of its stock at $15 per share, which is $3 per share greater than the $12 original issue price. This entry would be used to account for the event:

Apr.	12	Common Stock	10,000.00	
		Contributed Capital in Excess of Par Value, Common Stock	2,000.00	
		Retained Earnings	3,000.00	
		Cash		15,000.00
		Purchased and retired 1,000 shares of common stock at		
		$15 per share.		

FAST HINT
Alternative Example:
How would this entry to record the retirement at $15 per share be different if the company had a $1,000 credit balance in the account called Contributed Capital from the Retirement of Common Stock?
Answer: The entry also would include a $1,000 debit to Contributed Capital from the Retirement of Common Stock to bring that account balance to zero and a $2,000 debit to Retained Earnings.

FAST HINT
Relevant Exercise:
To apply these concepts, work Exercise 14–5.

Even though this transaction decreased equity, the $3 per share is not a loss. In this case, the $3,000 is debited to Retained Earnings. If there had been a credit balance in a contributed capital account related to retirements, it would have been debited up to the amount of its balance.

All three retirement examples reduced the company's assets and equity by the amount paid for the stock. However, no income effects are recognized. The only effects on equity are recorded in the contributed capital and retained earnings accounts.

Progress Check

14-4   A corporation's purchase of treasury stock: *(a)* Has no effect on total assets; *(b)* Reduces total assets and total stockholders' equity by equal amounts; *(c)* Is recorded with a debit to Retained Earnings.

14-5   Southern Co. purchased shares of Northern Corp. Should these shares be classified as treasury stock by either company?

14-6   How does treasury stock affect the number of authorized, issued, and outstanding shares of stock?

14-7   When a corporation purchases treasury stock: *(a)* Retained earnings is restricted by the amount paid for the stock; *(b)* It is recorded with a credit to Appropriated Retained Earnings; *(c)* It is always retired.

REPORTING INCOME AND RETAINED EARNINGS INFORMATION

When a company's only revenue and expense transactions are created by routine, continuing operations, a single-step income statement is adequate for describing the results of its activities. This format shows the revenues followed by a list of operating expenses and the net income. In today's complex business world, however, activities often include many income-related events that are not part of a company's continuing and otherwise normal activities.

The accountant's goal is to provide useful information in a format that helps the statement users understand the past-period events and predict future-period results. To see how this goal is accomplished, look at the income statement in Illustration 14–4. Notice that the income statement is separated into five different sections.

LO 3

Explain how to report the income effects of discontinued segments, extraordinary items, changes in accounting principles and estimates, and prior period adjustments.

CONTINUING OPERATIONS

Section 1 of the income statement shows the revenues, expenses, and income generated by the company's continuing operations. This portion looks like the single-step income statement that we first discussed in Chapter 5. Income statement users rely on the information in this section to develop predictions of what will happen in the future. As such, this section usually contains the most important information in the income statement. Previous chapters have explained the nature of the items and measures included in income from continuing operations.

FAST HINT
Relevant Exercise:
To apply these concepts, work Exercise 14–6 or 14–7.

DISCONTINUED SEGMENTS

Most large companies have several different lines of business and deal with different groups of customers. For example, **International Business Machines** not only produces and sells computer hardware and software but also delivers system design and repair services. Information about these **segments of the business** is of particular interest to users of the company's financial statements. According to GAAP, a segment is a component of a company's operations that serves a  particular line of business or class of customers. A segment has assets, activities, and financial results of operations that can be distinguished from other parts of the business. Large companies with operations in different segments are required to provide supplemental footnote information about each of their major segments.

Reporting Income Statement Information about Discontinued Segments

When a company incurs a gain or loss from selling or closing down a segment, the gain or loss must be reported in a separate section of the income statement.[3] Section 2 of the income statement in Illustration 14–4 includes this information. Note that the income from operating the discontinued segment prior to its disposal also is reported in section 2. When the income statement presents the results of several years side by side, it is necessary to go back and restate the prior years' results to separate out the revenues and expenses of the discontinued segment.

Separate information about a discontinued segment can be useful on its own. However, the primary purpose of reporting the gains or losses from discontinued operations separately is to more clearly present the results of continuing operations. The effect is to provide useful information for predicting the income that will be earned by the segments that continue to operate in the future.

---

[3]FASB, *Accounting Standards—Current Text* (Norwalk, CT, 1994), sec. I13.105. Originally published as *APB Opinion No. 30,* par. 8.

Illustration 14-4 Income Statement for a Corporation

CONNELLY CORPORATION
Income Statement
For Year Ended December 31, 19X4

1	Net sales		$8,440,000
	Gain on sale of equipment		38,000
	Total		$8,478,000
	Expenses:		
	Cost of goods sold	$5,950,000	
	Depreciation expense	35,000	
	Other selling, general, and administrative expenses	515,000	
	Interest expense	20,000	
	Income taxes expense	595,500	
	Total expenses		(7,115,500)
	Unusual loss on relocating a plant		(45,000)
	Infreqent gain on sale of surplus land		72,000
	Income from continuing operations		$1,389,500
	Discontinued segment:		
2	Income from operating Division A (net of $180,000 income taxes)	$ 420,000	
	Loss on disposal of Division A (net of $66,000 tax benefit)	(154,000)	266,000
	Income before extraordinary items and cumulative effect of a change in accounting principle		$1,655,500
	Extraordinary items:		
3	Gain on sale of unused land condemned by the state for a highway interchange (net of $61,200 income taxes)	$ 142,800	
	Loss from earthquake damage (net of $270,000 income tax benefit)	(630,000)	(487,200)
	Cumulative effect of a change in accounting principle:		
4	Effect on prior years' income (through December 31, 19X3) of changing to a different depreciation method (net of $24,000 income taxes)		56,000
	Net income		$1,224,300
	Earnings per common share (200,000 outstanding shares):		
5	Income from continuing operations		$ 6.95
	Discontinued operations		1.33
	Income before extraordinary items and cumulative effect of a change in accounting principle		$ 8.28
	Extraordinary items		(2.44)
	Cumulative effect of a change in accounting principle		0.28
	Net income		$ 6.12

Distinguishing the Results of Operating a Discontinued Segment from the Gain or Loss on Disposal

Section 2 of Illustration 14–4 reports both the income from operating the discontinued Division A during the year and the loss that occurred from disposing of the division's assets. The income tax effects of operating and disposing of the segment are also disclosed in section 2. As a result, the tax effects related to the discontinued segment are separated from the presentation of continuing operations in section 1. If the tax effects of the discontinued segment were not separated from the continuing operations, the result would not be as useful.

This discussion presents only a highly summarized description of the requirements for reporting the results of discontinued segments. The details are covered in more advanced accounting courses.

EXTRAORDINARY ITEMS

Section 3 of the income statement in Illustration 14–4 reports **extraordinary gains and losses** that occurred during the year. Extraordinary gains and losses are both unusual and infrequent. An **unusual gain or loss** is abnormal or otherwise unrelated to the ordinary activities and environment of the business. An **infrequent gain or loss** is not expected to occur again in the company's operating environment.[4] Reporting extraordinary items in a separate category makes it easier for users to predict what will happen in the future, apart from these extraordinary events.

In light of these definitions of *unusual* and *infrequent,* very few items qualify as extraordinary gains or losses by meeting both criteria. For example, none of the following events are considered extraordinary:

1. Write-downs or write-offs of assets, unless the change in value is caused by a major unusual and infrequent calamity, a condemning or expropriating of property by a domestic or foreign government, or a prohibition against using the assets under a newly enacted law.

2. Gains or losses from exchanging foreign currencies or translating account balances expressed in one currency into another currency.

3. Gains and losses from disposing of a business segment.

4. Effects of a labor action, including one against the company, its competitors, or its major suppliers.

5. Adjustment of accruals on long-term contracts.[5]

Gains or losses that are neither unusual nor infrequent are reported as part of the results of continuing operations. Gains or losses that are either unusual or infrequent but not both are not extraordinary. These items are listed on the income statement in the continuing operations section below the regular revenues, expenses, gains, and losses. For example, **Duracell International Inc.'s** 1993 income statement reported a $65 million charge for restructuring. The charge related to organizational integration and streamlining, including the closure of a Brazilian manufacturing facility and upgrading global manufacturing capabilities.

Section 1 of Illustration 14–4 includes a "Gain on sale of equipment" that is neither unusual nor infrequent with the revenues. However, an unusual loss and an infrequent gain are reported at the end of the section. The proper classification of these items is not always clear without carefully examining the circumstances.

In addition, GAAP require a few items to be reported as extraordinary gains or losses, even if they do not otherwise meet the normal criteria. For example, *FASB Statement No. 4* requires a gain or loss from retiring debt to be reported as extraordinary. Thus, in 1992, **Maybelline, Inc.** reported an extraordinary loss of $13,568,000 from the retirement of debt.

---

[4]Ibid., sec. I17.107. Originally published as *APB Opinion No. 30*, par. 20.

[5]Ibid., sec. I17.110. Originally published as *APB Opinion No. 30*, par. 23.

Illustration 14–5   Calculating the Cumulative Effect of a Change in Accounting Principle

Year	Double-Declining-Depreciation Amount	Straight-Line Depreciation Amount	Pre-Tax Difference	Tax Rate	After-Tax Cumulative Effect
Prior to change:					
19X1	$ 80,000	$ 35,000	$45,000		
19X2	60,000	35,000	25,000		
19X3	45,000	35,000	10,000		
Subtotal	$185,000	$105,000	$80,000	30%	$56,000†
Year of change:					
19X4	$ 33,750	35,000*			
Years after change:					
19X5		35,000			
19X6		35,000			
19X7		35,000			
19X8		35,000			
Total		$210,000			

*Reported on the 19X4 income statement as depreciation expense.
†Reported on the 19X4 income statement as the cumulative adjustment for differences in the three years prior to the change in 19X4, net of $24,000 additional taxes to be paid (30% × $80,000).

CHANGES IN ACCOUNTING PRINCIPLES

In general, the *consistency principle* requires a company to continue applying a specific accounting method or principle once it is chosen. (In this context, the term *accounting principles* describes accounting methods, such as FIFO and straight-line depreciation.) However, a company may change from one acceptable accounting principle to another as long as it justifies the change as an improvement in the information provided in its financial statements. In addition, companies often change accounting principles when they adopt new standards issued by the FASB.

When a company changes accounting principles, it usually affects the amount of reported income in more than one way. For example, let's consider Connelly Corporation's income statement in Illustration 14–4. The company purchased its only depreciable asset early in 19X1 for $320,000. The asset has a $40,000 salvage value and has been depreciated with the double-declining balance method for three of the eight years in its predicted useful life. (This company is subject to a 30% income tax rate.) During 19X4, the company decided that its income statement would be more useful if the annual depreciation were calculated with the straight-line method instead of double-declining balance.

In Illustration 14–5, we compare the results of applying the two depreciation methods to the first three years in the asset's service life and show how the company would determine what to report on its 19X4 income statement. The table shows that the accelerated method caused $185,000 of depreciation to be allocated to 19X1 through 19X3. If the straight-line method had been used from the beginning, only $105,000 of depreciation would have been allocated to those years. To give the accounts the balances that they would have had under the straight-line method, the company needs to decrease accumulated depreciation for this asset by the $80,000 gross difference. Offsetting this debit is a credit of $24,000 (30% × $80,000) to a deferred income tax liability for additional taxes to be paid in the future. The remaining $56,000 is the resulting credit to equity created by this change. Because the change increases equity, the company adds it to the income for the year in which the change is made effective.

Reporting Requirements for Changes in Accounting Principles

The income statement in Illustration 14–4 on page 538 shows the acceptable method of reporting the effects of a change in accounting principles by the Connelly Corporation. Section 1 of the income statement includes $35,000 of depreciation expense for the current year. This amount is shown in the straight-line method column for 19X4 in Illustration 14–5. Thus, the income for the year of the change is based on the new accounting principle. The annual depreciation of $35,000 also will be used in 19X5 through 19X8. In Illustration 14–5, we calculate the $56,000 catch-up adjustment reported in section 4 of the income statement in Illustration 14–4. This item is the cumulative effect of the change in accounting principle.

In many cases, the cumulative effect may be millions or even billions of dollars. Many large companies reported cumulative effects when they changed their accounting for employees' benefits other than pensions and income taxes. These changes were made because the FASB implemented *Statement No. 106*. For example, **Deere & Company** reported a $1,095 million reduction in net income when it first applied *Statement No. 106* in 1993.

In addition to the information in the financial statements, two points about the change should be explained: First, a footnote should describe the change and why it is an improvement over the old principle. Second, the footnote should describe what 19X4's income would have been under the old method if the change had not occurred. For this example, the footnote would reveal that leaving the method unchanged would have caused the depreciation for 19X4 to be $33,750 under double-declining instead of $35,000 under straight-line. This footnoted amount appears in Illustration 14–5 as the declining balance depreciation for 19X4.

Section 5 of Illustration 14–4 provides detailed information about earnings per share results for the year. This information is included on the face of the income statement in accordance with GAAP. This section is more complete than the minimum reporting requirements to show the possible categories companies can and often do report. A later section of the chapter explains the basic procedures to compute earnings per share.

Companies do not report the effect of a **prior period adjustment** on their current income statements. Instead, prior period adjustments appear in the statement of retained earnings (or the statement of changes in stockholders' equity), net of any income tax effects. Prior period adjustments modify the beginning balance of retained earnings for events occurring prior to the earliest year described in the financial statements. Under GAAP, prior period adjustments only record the effects of correcting material errors in earlier years. These errors include arithmetic mistakes, using unacceptable accounting principles, or failing to consider relevant facts.[6] An error would occur if an accountant mistakenly omits depreciation, applies an unacceptable depreciation method, or overlooks important facts in predicting an asset's useful life. For example, assume that the accountant for the Connelly Corporation failed to detect an error

FAST HINT
Relevant Exercise:
To apply these concepts, work Exercise 14–8.

EARNINGS PER SHARE SECTION OF THE INCOME STATEMENT

PRIOR PERIOD ADJUSTMENTS FOR CORRECTING MATERIAL ERRORS

---

[6]Ibid, sec. A35.104. Originally published as *APB Opinion No. 20*, par. 13.

in a 19X2 journal entry for the purchase of land incorrectly debited to an expense account. This statement of retained earnings includes a prior period adjustment to correct this error discovered in 19X4:

CONNELLY CORPORATION
Statement of Retained Earnings
For Year Ended December 31, 19X4

Retained earnings, December 31, 19X3, as previously stated . .	$4,745,000
Prior period adjustment:	
Cost of land incorrectly charged to expense	
(net of $63,000 income taxes)	147,000
Retained earnings, December 31, 19X3, as adjusted	$4,892,000
Plus net income	1,162,500
Less cash dividends declared	(240,000)
Retained earnings, December 31, 19X4	$5,814,500

CHANGES IN ACCOUNTING ESTIMATES

Many of the items disclosed in financial statements are based on estimates and predictions. Future events are certain to reveal that some of these estimates and predictions were inaccurate, even though they were based on the best data available at the time. Because these inaccuracies are not the result of mistakes, they are not considered to be accounting errors. Thus, any corrections of these estimates are not reported as prior period adjustments. Instead, they are **changes in accounting estimates.** For example, depreciation is based on predicted useful lives and salvage values. As new information becomes available, it may be used to change the predictions and modify the amounts reported as depreciation expense. Unlike changes in accounting principles, changes in accounting estimates are not accounted for with cumulative catch-up adjustments. Instead, the revised estimates are applied in determining revenues and expenses for the current and future periods. In Chapter 10, we explained one common change in an accounting estimate when we discussed revising depreciation rates.

STATEMENT OF CHANGES IN STOCKHOLDERS' EQUITY

Most corporations actually do not present a separate statement of retained earnings. Instead, they provide a **statement of changes in stockholders' equity** that lists the beginning and ending balances of each equity account and describes all the changes that occurred during the year. For example, **Albertson's Inc.,** which operates a large chain of retail food-drug stores, presents this information in a format that provides a column for each component of equity, and uses the rows to describe the events of the year. (See Illustration 14–6.) Notice that the company acquired treasury stock in fiscal year 1994 and then either sold or retired all the shares. The statement also indicates a stock split, but the credit to the Common Stock account reveals it was actually a 100% stock dividend. (For reasons not explained in the report, the dividend was recorded with a partial transfer of contributed capital in excess of par to the common stock account.)

Progress Check

14–8   **Which of the following is an extraordinary item?** *(a)* **A settlement paid to a customer injured while using the company's product;** *(b)* **A loss from damages to a plant caused by a meteorite;** *(c)* **A loss from selling old equipment.**

Illustration 14-6

	Common Stock $1.00 Par Value	Capital in Excess of Par	Retained Earnings	Treasury Stock	Total
ALBERTSON'S INC. Consolidated Stockholders' Equity (In thousands, except per share data)					
Balance at January 30, 1992	$132,131	$ 718	$1,066,603		$1,199,452
Exercise of stock options	199	4,191			4,390
Cash dividends, $0.32 per share . .			(84,631)		(84,631)
Net earnings			269,217		269,217
Balance at January 28, 1993	132,330	4,909	1,251,189		1,388,428
Exercise of stock options	245	4,238			4,483
Purchase treasury shares				$(517,526)	(517,526)
Issue treasury shares		19,615		244,912	264,527
Retire treasury shares	(5,788)	(25,010)	(241,816)	272,614	
Two-for-one stock split	126,620	(1,635)	(124,985)		
Other			953		953
Cash dividends, $0.36 per share . .			(91,167)		(91,167)
Net earnings			339,681		339,681
Balance at February 3, 1994	$253,407	$ 2,117	$1,133,855		$1,389,379

Courtesy of Albertson's Inc.

14-9 Identify the four possible major sections of the income statement that might appear below income from continuing operations.

14-10 A company that used FIFO for the past 15 years has decided to switch to LIFO. The effect of this event on past years' net income should be: *(a)* Reported as a prior period adjustment to retained earnings; *(b)* Ignored as it is a change in an accounting estimate; *(c)* Reported on the current year's income statement.

EARNINGS PER SHARE

Among the most widely quoted items of accounting information is **earnings per share.** This number represents the amount of income earned by each share of a corporation's common stock. For example, this excerpt from *The Wall Street Journal* reported the earnings per share **J. C. Penney Co.** achieved and expected to achieve:

LO 4

Calculate earnings per share for companies with simple capital structures and explain the difference between primary and fully diluted earnings per share.

> J. C. Penney Co. expects to post another record year for earnings and revenue, William R. Howell, chairman and chief executive, said at the company's annual meeting. Mr. Howell said he is comfortable with analysts' estimates of earnings between $4.15 and $4.22 a share for the fiscal year ending Jan. 29, 1995, a gain of 10% to 12% from fiscal 1994 earnings of $944 million, or $3.77 a share.[7]

---

[7]"J. C. Penney Expects to have Record Year for Sales and Profit," *The Wall Street Journal,* May 23, 1994, p. C16.

As this excerpt suggests, investors and their advisers use earnings per share to evaluate a corporation's past performance, project its future performance, and compare its prospects with other investment opportunities.

Because of the importance and widespread use of earnings per share numbers, accountants have developed detailed guidelines for calculating it. One important factor that shapes the presentation of earnings per share is the company's capital structure, which can be either simple or complex.

COMPANIES WITH SIMPLE CAPITAL STRUCTURES

Earnings per share calculations can be simple or complicated, depending on a company's situation. The calculations are not difficult for a company with a **simple capital structure** because it has only common stock and perhaps nonconvertible preferred stock outstanding. That is, a simple capital structure cannot include any options or rights to purchase common stock or any convertible preferred stock or bonds.

Calculating Earnings per Share When the Number of Common Shares Does Not Change

The earnings per share calculation is simple if: (1) a company has only common stock and nonconvertible preferred stock outstanding, and (2) the number of outstanding common shares does not change during the period. In this situation, the calculation involves determining the amount of the net income that is available to the common stockholders and dividing it by the number of common shares. The amount of income available to the common stockholders is the year's net income less any dividends declared or accumulated on the preferred stock. (If the preferred stock is cumulative, the current year's dividend must be subtracted even if it was not declared.) The following formula applies:

$$\text{Earnings per share} = \frac{\text{Net income} - \text{Preferred dividends}}{\text{Outstanding common shares}}$$

For example, assume that Blackwell Company earned $40,000 net income in 19X1 and declared dividends of $7,500 on its noncumulative preferred stock. The company had 5,000 common shares outstanding throughout the entire year. Thus:

$$\text{Earnings per share} = \frac{\$40,000 - \$7,500}{5,000 \text{ shares}} = \$6.50$$

The calculation is more complex if the number of outstanding shares changes during the year. The number of shares outstanding may change for a variety of reasons such as sales of additional shares, purchases of treasury stock, and stock dividends or splits.

Finding the Denominator When a Company Sells or Purchases Common Shares

If a company sells additional shares or purchases treasury shares during the year, the denominator of the formula is the weighted-average number of outstanding shares. The idea behind this change is to produce an average amount of earnings accruing to the average number of shares outstanding during the year the income was earned.

For example, suppose that Blackwell Company earned $40,000 in 19X2 and declared preferred dividends of $7,500. As a result, the earnings available to the common stock is again $32,500. Also assume that Blackwell sold 4,000 additional common shares on July 1, 19X2, and purchased 3,000 treasury shares on November 1, 19X2. As a result, 5,000 shares were outstanding for six months, 9,000 shares were outstanding for four months, and 6,000 shares were outstanding for two months. We calculate the weighted-average number of shares outstanding as follows:

Time Period	Outstanding Shares	Fraction of Year	Weighted Average
January–June	5,000	6/12	2,500
July–October	9,000	4/12	3,000
November–December	6,000	2/12	1,000
Weighted-average outstanding shares ..			6,500

Using the weighted-average number of common shares outstanding for Blackwell, the earnings per share calculation is:

$$\text{Earnings per share} = \frac{\$40,000 - \$7,500}{6,500 \text{ shares}} = \$5.00$$

Blackwell reports this number at the bottom of its 19X2 income statement.

Adjusting the Denominator for Stock Splits and Stock Dividends

The number of outstanding shares also can be affected by a stock split or stock dividend during the year. These events do not bring in any additional assets; thus, they do not affect the company's ability to produce earnings for the common stockholders. In effect, the earnings for the year are simply spread out over a larger number of shares. As a result, in calculating the weighted-average number of shares outstanding, stock splits and stock dividends are not treated like stock sales and purchases.

When a stock split or stock dividend occurs, the number of shares that were outstanding earlier in the year are retroactively restated to reflect the effects of the stock split or dividend as if it occurred at the beginning of the year. For example, reconsider the Blackwell Company example and assume that the stock transactions in 19X2 included a two-for-one stock split on December 1. This split caused the percentage ownership of each share to be cut in half while doubling the number of outstanding shares. The situation is described by this table:

Time Period	Original Shares	Effect of Split	Post-Split Shares
January–June	5,000	2	10,000
July–October	9,000	2	18,000
November	6,000	2	12,000

Then, the numbers in the third column can be inserted into the weighted-average calculation for the new shares:

Time Period	Post-Split Shares	Fraction of Year	Weighted Average
January–June	10,000	6/12	5,000
July–October	18,000	4/12	6,000
November–December	12,000	2/12	2,000
Weighted-average outstanding shares			13,000

The Blackwell Company's earnings per share for 19X2 under this set of assumptions are:

$$\text{Earnings per share} = \frac{\$40,000 - \$7,500}{13,000 \text{ shares}} = \$2.50$$

The same sort of modification is used when stock dividends occur. For example, if the two-for-one stock split had been a 10% stock dividend, the numbers of old outstanding shares would have been multiplied by 1.1 instead of two.

Companies with **complex capital structures** have outstanding options or rights to purchase common stock and/or securities such as bonds or preferred stock that are convertible into common stock. Earnings per share calculations for companies with complex capital structures are more complicated. Often, such companies must present two types of earnings per share calculations. One is called **primary earnings per share,** and the other is called **fully diluted earnings per share.**

Suppose that a corporation has convertible preferred stock outstanding throughout the current year. However, consider what the effects would have been if the preferred shares had been converted at the beginning of the year. The result of this assumed conversion would have been to increase the number of common shares outstanding and to reduce preferred dividends. The net result may have been to reduce earnings per share, or to increase earnings per share. When the assumed conversion of a security reduces earnings per share, the security is said to be **dilutive;** those that increase earnings per share are **antidilutive.**

Primary Earnings per Share

Based on detailed rules, convertible securities are evaluated at the time they are issued.[8] If eventual conversion appears highly probable, the convertible security is called a **common stock equivalent.** Primary earnings per share is calculated as if dilutive common stock equivalents had already been converted at the beginning of the period.

Fully Diluted Earnings per Share

Common stock equivalents have terms that make their eventual conversion very probable. Other convertible securities are less apt to be converted. Nevertheless, if we assume those securities were converted at the beginning of the period, the effect may be to reduce earnings per share; in other words, the assumed conversion may have a dilutive effect. Fully diluted earnings per share is calculated as if all dilutive securities had already been converted.

Because information about earnings per share is important, corporations must report it on the face of their income statements. Furthermore, they usually report the amount of earnings per share for net income and each of the four subcategories of income (continuing operations, discontinued segments, extraordinary items, and the effect of accounting principle changes). Illustration 14–4 on page 538 shows Connelly Corporation's earnings per share in section 5.

Even though GAAP is flexible in where some earnings per share information should be reported, many companies present all the details in one place for the convenience of the financial statement users. Illustration 14–7 provides real earnings per share presentations by **Sprint Corporation** and the **Colgate-Palmolive Company.**

FAST HINT
Relevant Exercise:
To apply these concepts, work Exercise 14–10 or 14–11.

COMPANIES WITH COMPLEX CAPITAL STRUCTURES

FAST HINT
Additional Insight:
In 1994, the FASB created a project that could reduce the complexity of primary earnings per share by omitting common stock equivalents from the denominator. The goal is to simplify the calculations and bring the United States in line with practices used in virtually all other countries.

FAST HINT
Important Point to Remember:
The calculation for primary earnings per share includes the assumed conversion of all dilutive common stock equivalents. The calculations for fully diluted earnings per share includes the assumed conversion of all other dilutive securities as well. It is not necessary to report fully diluted earnings per share if they equal 97% or more of primary earnings.

PRESENTING EARNINGS PER SHARE ON THE INCOME STATEMENT

Illustration 14–7 Reporting Earnings per Share on the Income Statement

SPRINT CORPORATION:
Showing multiple components:

	1993	1992	1991
Earnings per common share			
Continuing operations	$1.39	$1.46	$1.41
Discontinued operations	(0.04)		0.15
Extraordinary item	(0.08)	(0.05)	(0.01)
Cumulative effect of changes in accounting principles	(1.12)	0.07	
Total	$0.15	$1.48	$1.55

COLGATE-PALMOLIVE COMPANY
Showing primary and fully diluted results:

	1993	1992	1991
Earnings per common share, primary			
Income before changes in accounting	$ 3.38	$2.92	$0.77
Cumulative effect on prior years of accounting changes	(2.30)		
Net income	$ 1.08	$2.92	$0.77
Earnings per common share, fully diluted			
Income before changes in accounting	$ 3.15	$2.74	$0.75
Cumulative effect on prior years of accounting changes	(2.10)		
Net income	$ 1.05	$2.74	$0.75

Courtesy of Sprint Corporation and Colgate-Palmolive Company.

Sprint shows the per-share effects of the various components of its income for three fiscal years. Colgate-Palmolive shows the primary and fully diluted results for the same three years.

Progress Check

14–11 **During 19X1, FDI Co. had net income of $250,000 and paid preferred dividends of $70,000. On January 1, the company had 25,000 outstanding common shares and purchased 5,000 treasury shares on July 1. Earnings per share for 19X1 is: (a) $8.00; (b) $9.00; (c) $10.00.**

14–12 **How are stock splits and stock dividends treated in calculating the weighted-average number of outstanding common shares?**

14–13 **What two sets of earnings per share results are reported for a company with a complex capital structure?**

You learned in Chapter 13 that a stock's market value is largely affected by the stream of future dividends expected to be paid out to stockholders. Market value is also affected by expected future changes in value. By comparing the company's earnings per share and its market price per share, investors and other decision makers can obtain information about the stock market's apparent expectations for growth in future earnings, dividends, and market values.

Although it would be possible to make this comparison as a rate of return by dividing the earnings per share by the market price per share, the ratio has traditionally been turned upside-down and calculated as the **price-earnings ratio.** Thus, this ratio is found by dividing the stock's market price by the earnings per share, as shown in this formula:

$$\text{Price-earnings ratio} = \frac{\textbf{Market value per share}}{\textbf{Earnings per share}}$$

USING THE INFORMATION— THE PRICE-EARNINGS RATIO

LO 5
Calculate the price-earnings ratio and describe its meaning.

FAST HINT
Additional Insight:
Average PE ratios for traded U.S. stocks have increased over the last two or three decades. Although some market analysts have interpreted this trend to be a signal that the stock market is overpriced, the higher ratios may actually reflect that most changes in GAAP over this period have reduced reported earnings by increasing the recognized amounts for many different expenses.

FAST HINT
Relevant Quick Study:
To apply these concepts, work QS 14–5.

FAST HINT
Relevant Exercise:
To apply these concepts, work Exercise 14–14.

The ratio may be calculated using the earnings per share reported in the past period. However, analysts often calculate the ratio based on the expected earnings per share for the next period. Suppose, for example, that the stock's current market price is $100 per share and that its next year's earnings are expected to be $8 per share. Its price-earnings ratio (often abbreviated as the PE ratio) is found as $100/$8, which is 12.5.

As a general rule, stocks with higher PE ratios (generally greater than 12 to 15) are considered more likely to be overpriced while stocks with lower PE ratios (generally less than 5 to 8) are considered more likely to be underpriced. Thus, some investors prefer to sell or avoid buying stocks with high PE ratios while they prefer to buy or hold stocks that have low PE ratios. Investment decisions are not quite that simple, however, because a stock with a high PE ratio may prove to be a good investment if its earnings increase rapidly. On the other hand, a stock with a low PE ratio may prove to be a low performer. Although the price-earnings ratio is clearly important for investment decisions, it is only one piece of information that investors should consider.

Progress Check

14-14   Calculate the price-earnings ratio for a company with earnings per share of $4.25 and stock with a market value of $34.00.

14-15   Two companies in the same industry face similar levels of risk, have nearly the same level of earnings, and are expected to continue their historical record of paying $1.50 annual dividends per share. Yet, one of the companies has a PE ratio of 6 while the other has a PE ratio of 10. Which company does the market apparently expect to have a higher future growth rate in earnings?

SUMMARY OF CHAPTER IN TERMS OF LEARNING OBJECTIVES

LO 1. Describe stock dividends and stock splits and explain their effects on a corporation's assets and stockholders' equity. In contrast to cash dividends, stock dividends do not transfer corporate assets to stockholders. Stock dividends and stock splits do not affect assets, total stockholders' equity, or the equity attributed to each stockholder. Small stock dividends (≤25%) are recorded by capitalizing retained earnings equal to the market value of the distributed shares. Large stock dividends (>25%) are recorded by capitalizing retained earnings equal to the par or stated value of the issued shares. Stock splits are not recorded through journal entries but should lead to changing the account title for the common stock if it includes the par or stated value.

LO 2. Record purchases and sales of treasury stock and retirements of stock and describe their effects on stockholders' equity. Also, describe restrictions and appropriations of retained earnings and explain how they are described in financial reports. When outstanding treasury shares are repurchased by the corporation that issued them, the cost of the shares is debited to Treasury Stock. Its balance is subtracted from total stockholders' equity in the balance sheet. When treasury stock is later reissued, the amount of any proceeds in excess of cost is credited to Contributed Capital, Treasury Stock Transactions. If the proceeds are less than cost, the difference is debited to Contributed Capital, Treasury Stock Transactions to the extent a credit balance exists in that account. Any remaining amount is debited to Retained Earnings.

Most states limit dividends and treasury stock purchases to the amount of retained earnings. Companies also enter into contracts that may limit the amount of dividends, even though the companies have both the cash and the retained earnings to pay them.

Corporations may voluntarily appropriate retained earnings to inform stockholders why dividends are not larger. Often, however, this information is expressed in a letter to the stockholders.

LO 3. Explain how to report the income effects of discontinued segments, extraordinary items, changes in accounting principles and estimates, and prior period adjustments. If a company has decided to discontinue a segment, the income effects of operating and disposing of the segment are separately reported on the income statement below income from continuing operations. Extraordinary gains or losses also are separated from continuing operations and reported lower in the income statement. A similar treatment is required for the cumulative effects of changes in accounting principles. Prior period adjustments for error corrections are not reported on the income statement, but appear on the retained earnings statement or the statement of changes in stockholders' equity. Changes in accounting estimates arise when new information shows the old estimates to be inaccurate. If an accounting estimate is changed, the firm uses the new estimate to calculate income in the current and future periods.

LO 4. Calculate earnings per share for companies with simple capital structures and explain the difference between primary and fully diluted earnings per share. The outstanding securities of companies with simple capital structures do not include any securities that are convertible into common stock. These companies calculate earnings per share by dividing net income (less any preferred dividends) by the weighted-average number of outstanding common shares. Companies with complex capital structures have issued securities that are convertible into common stock. These companies often have to report both primary earnings per share and fully diluted earnings per share.

LO 5. Calculate the price-earnings ratio and describe its meaning. The price-earnings ratio of a common stock is closely watched by investors and other decision makers. The ratio is calculated by dividing the current market value per share by earnings per share. A high ratio may suggest that a stock is overvalued while a low ratio may suggest that a stock is undervalued. However, selecting stocks to buy or sell requires a great deal more information.

DEMONSTRATION PROBLEM

The Precision Company began 19X1 with the following balances in its stockholders' equity accounts:

Common stock, $10 par, 500,000 shares authorized, 200,000 shares issued and outstanding	$2,000,000
Contributed capital in excess of par	1,000,000
Retained earnings	5,000,000
Total	$8,000,000

All of the outstanding stock was issued for $15 when the company was created.

Part 1

Prepare journal entries to account for the following transactions during 19X1:

Mar. 31 Declared a 20% stock dividend. The market value of the stock was $18 per share.

Apr. 15 Distributed the stock dividend declared on March 31.

June 30 Purchased 30,000 shares of treasury stock at $20 per share.

Aug. 31 Sold 20,000 treasury shares at $26 per share.

Nov. 30 Purchased and retired 50,000 shares at $24 per share.

Part 2

Use the following information to prepare an income statement for 19X1, including earnings per share results for each category of income.

Cumulative effect of a change in depreciation method (net of tax benefit)	$ (136,500)
Expenses related to continuing operations	(2,072,500)
Extraordinary gain on debt retirement (net of tax)	182,000
Gain on disposal of discontinued segment's assets (net of tax). .	29,000
Gain on sale of stock investment.	400,000
Loss from operating discontinued segment (net of tax benefit). .	(120,000)
Income taxes on income from continuing operations.	(225,000)
Prior period adjustment for error (net of tax benefit).	(75,000)
Sales.	4,140,000
Infrequent loss.	(650,000)

Planning the Solution

* Decide whether the stock dividend is a small or large dividend. Then, analyze each event to determine the accounts affected and the appropriate amounts to be recorded.
* Based on the shares of outstanding stock at the beginning of the year and the transactions during the year, calculate the weighted-average number of outstanding shares for the year.
* Assign each of the listed items to an appropriate income statement category.
* Prepare an income statement similar to Illustration 14–4, including appropriate earnings per share results.

Solution to Demonstration Problem

Part 1

Mar.	31	Stock Dividends Declared	720,000.00	
		Common Stock Dividend Distributable		400,000.00
		Contributed Capital in Excess of Par		
		Value, Common Stock		320,000.00
		Declared a small stock dividend of 20% or 40,000 shares; market value is $18 per share.		
Apr.	15	Common Stock Dividend Distributable	400,000.00	
		Common Stock		400,000.00
		Distributed 40,000 shares of common stock.		
June	30	Treasury Stock, Common	600,000.00	
		Cash		600,000.00
		Purchased 30,000 shares of common stock at $20 per share.		
Aug.	31	Cash	520,000.00	
		Treasury Stock, Common		400,000.00
		Contributed Capital, Treasury Stock Transactions . .		120,000.00
		Sold 20,000 shares of treasury stock at $26 per share.		

Nov.	30	Common Stock	500,000.00		
		Contributed Capital in Excess of Par Value,			
		Common Stock	250,000.00		
		Retained Earnings	450,000.00		
		Cash		1,200,000.00	
		Purchased and retired 50,000 shares at $24 per share.			

Part 2

Calculating the weighted average of outstanding shares:

Time Period	Original Shares	Effect of Dividend	Post-Dividend Shares
January–April 15	200,000	1.2	240,000

Time Period	Post-Dividend Shares	Fraction of Year	Weighted Average
January–June	240,000	6/12	120,000
July–August	210,000	2/12	35,000
September–November	230,000	3/12	57,500
December	180,000	1/12	15,000
Weighted-average outstanding shares			227,500

PRECISION COMPANY
Income Statement
For Year Ended December 31, 19X1

Sales		$4,140,000
Expenses		(2,072,500)
Income taxes		(225,000)
Gain on sale of stock investment		400,000
Infrequent loss		(650,000)
Income from continuing operations		$1,592,500
Discontinued operations:		
Loss from operating discontinued segment (net of tax benefit)	$(120,000)	
Gain on disposal of discontinued segment's assets (net of tax)	29,000	
Loss from discontinued division		(91,000)
Income before extraordinary items and cumulative effect of a change in accounting principle		$1,501,500
Extraordinary items:		
Extraordinary gain on debt retirement (net of tax)		182,000
Cumulative effect of a change in accounting principle:		
Cumulative effect of a change in depreciation method (net of tax benefit)		(136,500)
Net income		$1,547,000

Earnings per share (227,500 average shares outstanding):	
Income from continuing operations	$ 7.00
Loss from discontinued segment	(0.40)
Income before extraordinary gain and cumulative effect of change in accounting principle	$ 6.60
Extraordinary gain	0.80
Cumulative effect of change in accounting principle	(0.60)
Net income	$ 6.80

GLOSSARY

Antidilutive securities securities the assumed conversion or exercise of which has the effect of decreasing earnings per share. p. 546

Appropriated retained earnings retained earnings that are voluntarily restricted as a way of informing stockholders that dividends will not be paid. p. 534

Changes in accounting estimates modifications to previous estimates or predictions about future events and outcomes, such as salvage values and the useful lives of operating assets. p. 542

Common stock equivalent a convertible or exercisable security the eventual conversion of which is highly probable. p. 546

Complex capital structure a capital structure that includes outstanding rights or options to purchase common stock or securities that are convertible into common stock. p. 546

Dilutive securities securities the assumed conversion or exercise of which has the effect of decreasing earnings per share. p. 546

Earnings per share the amount of income earned by each share of a company's common stock. p. 543

Extraordinary gain or loss a gain or loss that is reported separate from continuing operations because it is both unusual and infrequent. p. 539

Fully diluted earnings per share earnings per share calculated as if all dilutive securities had already been converted. p. 546

Infrequent gain or loss a gain or loss that is not expected to occur again, given the operating environment of the business. p. 539

Large stock dividend a stock dividend that is more than 25% of the corporation's previously outstanding shares. p. 528

Liquidating dividends distributions of corporate assets as a dividend that returns part of the original investment to the stockholders; these distributions are charged to contributed capital accounts. p. 527

Price-earnings ratio the ratio between a company's current market value and its earnings per share; used to gain understanding of the market's expectations for the stock. p. 547

Primary earnings per share earnings per share calculated as if dilutive common stock equivalents had already been converted or exercised. p. 546

Prior period adjustment a correction of an error in a previous year that is reported in the statement of retained earnings. p. 541

Restricted retained earnings retained earnings that are not available for dividends because of legal or contractual limitations. p. 534

Reverse stock split an act by a corporation to call in its stock and replace each share with less than one new share. p. 531

Segment of a business a component of a company's operations that serves a particular line of business or class of customers and that has assets, activities, and financial results of operations that can be distinguished from other parts of the business. p. 537

Simple capital structure a capital structure that consists of no more than common stock and nonconvertible preferred stock; it cannot include any options or rights to purchase common stock or any convertible preferred stocks or bonds. p. 544

Small stock dividend a stock dividend that is 25% or less of the corporation's previously outstanding shares. p. 527

Statement of changes in stockholders' equity a financial statement that lists the beginning and ending balances of each equity account and describes all the changes that occurred during the year. p. 542

Stock dividend a corporation's distribution of its own stock to its stockholders without receiving any payment in return. p. 527

Stock split an act by a corporation to call in its stock and replace each share with more than one new share. p. 531

Treasury stock stock that was reacquired and is still held by the issuing corporation. p. 532

Unusual gain or loss a gain or loss that is abnormal or otherwise unrelated to the ordinary activities and environment of the business. p. 539

QUESTIONS

1. Why is the term *liquidating dividend* used to describe cash dividends that are debited against contributed capital accounts?

2. What effects does declaring a stock dividend have on the corporation's assets, liabilities, and total stockholders' equity? What effects does the distribution of the stock have?

3. What is the difference between a stock dividend and a stock split?

4. Courts have determined that a stock dividend is not taxable income to stockholders. What concept justifies this decision?

5. How does the purchase of treasury stock affect the purchaser's assets and total stockholders' equity?

6. Why do state laws place limits on purchases of treasury stock?

7. Where on the income statement would a company report an abnormal gain that is not expected to occur more often than once every two years?

8. After taking five years' straight-line depreciation expense for an asset that was expected to have an eight-year useful life, a company decided that the asset would last another six years. Is this decision a change in accounting principle? How would the financial statements describe this change?

9. How are earnings per share results calculated for a corporation with a simple capital structure?

10. Refer to the statement of changes in common stockholders' investment for Federal Express Corporation in Appendix G at the end of the book. Can you determine the purpose for the company's annual purchases of treasury stock?

11. Refer to the balance sheet for Ben & Jerry's Homemade, Inc., in Appendix G at the end of the book. How many treasury shares of Class A and Class B stock did the company have at the end of its 1992 fiscal year?

QUICK STUDY (Five-Minute Exercises)

The stockholders' equity section of Baylor Co.'s balance sheet as of June 1 follows:

QS 14–1
(LO 1)

Common stock, $5 par value, 250,000 shares authorized, 100,000 shares issued and outstanding.	$ 500,000
Contributed capital in excess of par value, common stock	235,000
Total contributed capital	$ 735,000
Retained earnings.	422,000
Total stockholders' equity	$1,157,000

On June 1, Baylor declares and distributes a 10% stock dividend. The market value of the stock on this date is $25. Prepare the stockholders' equity section for Baylor immediately following the stock dividend.

On September 2, Garrett Corp. purchased 2,000 shares of its own stock for $18,000. On December 5, Garrett reissued 500 shares of the treasury stock for $4,725. Prepare the December 5 journal entry Garrett should make to record the sale of the treasury stock.

QS 14–2
(LO 2)

Answer the questions about each of the following items related to a company's activities for the year:

QS 14–3
(LO 3)

a. After using an expected useful life of seven years and no salvage value to depreciate its office equipment over the preceding three years, the company decided early this year that the equipment will last only two more years. How should the effects of this decision be reported in the current financial statements?

b. In reviewing the notes payable files, it was discovered that last year the company reported the entire amount of a payment on an installment note payable as interest expense. The mistake had a material effect on the amount of income in the prior year. How should the correction be reported in the current year financial statements?

On January 1, Star Company had 50,000 shares of common stock issued and outstanding. On April 1, it purchased 4,000 treasury shares and on June 5, declared a 20% stock dividend. Calculate Star's weighted-average outstanding shares for the year.

QS 14–4
(LO 4)

Calculate a company's price-earnings ratio if its common stock has a market value of $63 per share and if its earnings per share is $7.20.

QS 14–5
(LO 5)

EXERCISES

Exercise 14–1
Stock dividends and per share values
(LO 1)

The stockholders' equity of Porter Construction, Inc., on March 8 consisted of the following:

Common stock, $25 par value, 100,000 shares
   authorized, 40,000 shares issued and outstanding $1,000,000
Contributed capital in excess of par value, common stock 350,000
Total contributed capital $1,350,000
Retained earnings..................................... 450,000
Total stockholders' equity $1,800,000

On March 8, the stock's market value was $40. On that date, the directors declared a 20% stock dividend distributable on March 31 to the March 20 stockholders of record. The stock's market value was $38 on April 10.

Required

1. Prepare entries to record the dividend declaration and distribution.

2. One stockholder owned 500 shares on March 8. Calculate the per share and total book values of the investor's shares immediately before and after the dividend on March 8.

3. Calculate the market values of the investor's shares as of March 8 and April 10.

Exercise 14–2
Stock dividends and splits
(LO 1)

On March 31, 19X1, Pacific Management Corporation's common stock was selling for $62 per share and the following information appeared in the stockholders' equity section of its balance sheet as of that date:

Common stock, $20 par value, 60,000 shares
   authorized, 25,000 shares issued and outstanding .... $ 500,000
Contributed capital in excess of par value, common stock 200,000
Total contributed capital .... $ 700,000
Retained earnings..................................... 660,000
Total stockholders' equity $1,360,000

Required

1. Assume that the company declares and immediately distributes a 100% stock dividend. The event is recorded by capitalizing the required minimum amount of retained earnings. Answer these questions about the stockholders' equity as it exists after issuing the new shares:

   a. What is the retained earnings balance?

   b. What is the total amount of stockholders' equity?

   c. How many shares are outstanding?

2. Assume that the company implements a two-for-one stock split instead of the stock dividend. Answer these questions about the stockholders' equity as it exists after issuing the new shares:

   a. What is the retained earnings balance?

   b. What is the total amount of stockholders' equity?

   c. How many shares are outstanding?

3. Briefly explain the difference, if any, that an investor would experience if new shares are distributed under a large dividend or a stock split.

Exercise 14–3
Reporting a treasury stock purchase
(LO 2)

On August 15, the stockholders' equity section of the balance sheet for Indelible, Inc., included this information:

Stockholders' Equity

Contributed capital:
　　Common stock, $10 par value, 12,000 shares authorized,
　　　　issued, and outstanding. . . . .　$120,000
　　Contributed capital in excess of par value, common stock . . . .　　36,000
　　Total contributed capital. . . . .　$156,000
　　Retained earnings . . . .　144,000
　　Total stockholders' equity . . . .　$300,000

On the next day, the corporation purchased 1,500 shares of treasury stock at $30 per share. Present the stockholders' equity section as it would appear immediately after the purchase.

Use the information in Exercise 14–3 to develop the accountant's journal entries to record these events for Indelible, Inc.:

1.　The purchase of the treasury shares on August 16.

2.　The sale of 400 treasury shares on September 1 for cash at $36 per share.

3.　The sale of all the remaining treasury shares on September 29 for cash at $25 per share.

Exercise 14–4
Journal entries for treasury stock transactions
(LO 2)

This information appeared in the stockholders' equity section of Winter Sports, Inc.'s balance sheet as of December 31, 19X1:

Common stock, $5 par value, 40,000 shares
　　authorized, 15,000 shares issued and outstanding . . . .　$ 75,000
Contributed capital in excess of par value, common stock. . .　165,000
Total contributed capital. . . . .　$240,000
Retained earnings . . . .　190,000
Total stockholders' equity . . . .　$430,000

Exercise 14–5
Journal entries for stock retirements
(LO 2)

On January 1, 19X2, the company purchased and retired 800 shares of common stock.

1.　Determine the average amount of contributed capital per share of outstanding stock.

2.　Prepare the journal entries to record the retirement under the following separate situations:

　　a.　The stock was purchased for $13 per share.

　　b.　The stock was purchased for $16 per share.

　　c.　The stock was purchased for $30 per share.

During 19X1, Simon's Club, Inc., sold its assets in a chain of wholesale outlets. This sale took the company out of the wholesaling business completely. The company still operates its retail outlets. Following is a lettered list of sections of an income statement:

Exercise 14–6
Income statement categories
(LO 3)

A.　Income from continuing operations

B.　Income from operating a discontinued segment

C.　Gain or loss from disposing of a discontinued segment

D.　Extraordinary gain or loss

E.　Cumulative effect of a change in accounting principle

Indicate where each of the nine income-related items for the company would appear on the 19X1 income statement by writing the letter of the appropriate section in the blank beside each item.

		Debit	Credit
_____ 1.	Depreciation expense	$175,000	
_____ 2.	Gain on sale of segment (net of tax)		$ 450,000
_____ 3.	Loss from operating segment (net of tax)	370,000	
_____ 4.	Salaries expense	360,000	
_____ 5.	Sales		1,800,000
_____ 6.	Gain on state's condemnation of company property (net of tax)		220,000
_____ 7.	Cost of goods sold	920,000	
_____ 8.	Effect of change from declining-balance to straight-line depreciation (net of tax)		90,000
_____ 9.	Income taxes expense	138,000	

Exercise 14–7
Income statement
presentation
(LO 3)

Use the data for the company described in Exercise 14–6 to present the income statement for 19X1.

Exercise 14–8
Accounting for a change in
accounting principle
(LO 3)

The Long Company put an asset in service on January 1, 19X1. Its cost was $900,000, its predicted service life was six years, and its expected salvage value was $90,000. The company decided to use double-declining-balance depreciation and recorded these amounts of depreciation expense in the first two years of the asset's life:

19X1 .... $300,000
19X2 200,000

The scheduled depreciation expense for 19X3 was $133,000. After consulting with the company's auditors, management decided to change to straight-line depreciation in 19X3, without changing either the predicted service life or salvage value. Under this system, the annual depreciation expense for all years in the asset's life would be $135,000. The company faces a 35% income tax rate.

1. Prepare a table like Illustration 14–5 that deals with this situation.

2. How much depreciation expense will be reported on the company's income statement for this asset in 19X3 and in each of the remaining years of the asset's life?

3. What amount will be reported on the company's 19X3 income statement as the after-tax cumulative effect of the change?

Exercise 14–9
Weighted-average
outstanding shares and
earnings per share
(LO 4)

A company reported $450,000 of net income for 19X1. It also declared $65,000 of dividends on preferred stock for the same year. At the beginning of 19X1, the company had 90,000 outstanding shares of common stock. These two events changed the number of outstanding shares during the year:

Apr. 30 Sold 60,000 common shares for cash.

Oct. 31 Purchased 36,000 shares of common stock for the treasury.

a. What is the amount of net income available to the common stockholders?
b. What is the weighted-average number of shares of common stock for the year?
c. What is the earnings per share for the year?

Exercise 14–10
Weighted-average shares
outstanding and earnings
per share
(LO 4)

A company reported $240,000 of net income for 19X1. It also declared $32,500 of dividends on preferred stock for the same year. At the beginning of 19X1, the company had 25,000 outstanding shares of common stock. These three events changed the number of outstanding shares during the year:

June 1 Sold 15,000 common shares for cash.

Aug. 31 Purchased 6,500 shares of common stock for the treasury.

Oct. 1 Completed a three-for-one stock split.

a.   What is the amount of net income available to the common stockholders?

b.   What is the weighted-average number of shares of common stock for the year?

c.   What is the earnings per share for the year?

Use the following information to calculate the price-earnings ratio for each case:

	Earnings per Share	Market Value per Share
a.	$ 4.50	$ 43.00
b.	18.00	120.00
c.	3.25	45.00
d.	0.75	18.00
e.	5.00	83.00

Exercise 14–11
Computing the price-earnings ratio
(LO 5)

Match each of the numbered definitions with the term it best defines. Indicate your answer by writing the letter for the correct term in the blank space next to each description.

Exercise 14–12
Identifying corporate capital structure terms
(LO 6)

A.   Common stock equivalent

B.   Extraordinary gain or loss

C.   Large stock dividend

D.   Reverse stock split

E.   Small stock dividend

F.   Stock split

G.   Treasury stock

___ 1.   Gain or loss that is reported separate from continuing operations because it is both unusual and infrequent.

___ 2.   Stock that was reacquired and is still held by the issuing corporation.

___ 3.   Stock dividend that is more than 25% of the corporation's previously outstanding shares.

___ 4.   Action by a corporation to call in its stock and replace it with less than one new share.

___ 5.   Convertible or exercisable security that is reasonably expected to be converted or exercised.

___ 6.   Action by a corporation to call in its stock and replace it with more than one new share.

___ 7.   Stock dividend that is 25% or less of the corporation's previously outstanding shares.

PROBLEMS

The balance sheet for Elizabeth Manufacturing, Inc., reported the following components of stockholders' equity on December 31, 19X1:

Problem 14–1
Treasury stock transactions and stock dividends
(LO 1, 2)

Common stock, $10 par value, 100,000 shares authorized,
    40,000 shares issued and outstanding. $400,000
Contributed capital in excess of par value, common stock   60,000
Retained earnings   270,000
Total stockholders' equity $730,000

The company completed these transactions during 19X2:

Jan.   6   Purchased 4,000 shares of treasury stock at $20.00 cash per share.

Mar. 10   The directors declared a $1.50 per share cash dividend payable on April 10 to the April 2 stockholders of record.

Apr. 10   Paid the dividend declared on March 10.

Aug.   1   Sold 1,500 of the treasury shares at $24.00 per share.

Sept. 6   Sold 2,500 of the treasury shares at $17.00 per share.

Dec. 10   The directors declared a $1.60 per share cash dividend payable on January 10, 19X3, to the December 15 stockholders of record. They also declared a 20% stock dividend distributable on January 10, 19X3, to the December 15 stockholders of record. The market value of the stock was $25.00 per share.

        31   Closed the $388,000 credit balance in the Income Summary account to Retained Earnings.

        31   Closed the Cash Dividends Declared and Stock Dividends Declared accounts.

Required

CHECK FIGURE:
Retained earnings,
Dec. 31, 19X2,
$338,500

1. Prepare general journal entries to record the transactions and closings for 19X2.
2. Prepare a statement of retained earnings for 19X2.
3. Prepare the stockholders' equity section of the company's balance sheet as of December 31, 19X2.

Problem 14–2
Describing equity changes
with journal entries and
account balances
(LO 1)

At September 30, the end of the third quarter for Astronomical Adventures, Inc., these balances existed in its stockholders' equity accounts:

Common stock, $12 par value	$360,000
Contributed capital in excess of par value	90,000
Retained earnings	320,000

Over the next three months, the following journal entries were recorded in the company's equity accounts:

Oct.	5	Cash Dividends Declared	60,000.00	
		Common Dividend Payable		60,000.00
	20	Common Dividend Payable	60,000.00	
		Cash		60,000.00
	31	Stock Dividends Declared	75,000.00	
		Common Stock Dividend Distributable		36,000.00
		Contributed Capital in Excess of Par Value, Common Stock		39,000.00
Nov.	15	Common Stock Dividend Distributable	36,000.00	
		Common Stock, $12 Par Value		36,000.00
Dec.	1	Memo—change the title of the common stock account to reflect the new par value of $4 per share.		
	31	Income Summary	210,000.00	
		Retained Earnings		210,000.00
	31	Retained Earnings	135,000.00	
		Cash Dividends Declared		60,000.00
		Stock Dividends Declared		75,000.00

Required

CHECK FIGURE:
Total equity, Dec. 31,
$920,000

1. Provide explanations for each of the journal entries.
2. Complete the following table showing the balances of the company's equity accounts (including the dividends declared accounts) at each of the indicated dates:

Date	Oct. 5	Oct. 20	Oct. 31	Nov. 15	Dec. 1	Dec. 31
Common stock	$	$	$	$	$	$
Stock dividend distributable						
Contributed capital in excess of par						
Retained earnings						
Less:						
Cash dividends declared ..						
Stock dividends declared ..						
Combined balances of equity accounts	$	$	$	$	$	$

The equity sections from the 19X1 and 19X2 balance sheets of New Haven Corporation appeared as follows:

Problem 14–3
Changes in retained earnings
(LO 1, 2)

Stockholders' Equity
(As of December 31, 19X1)

Common stock, $4 par value, 100,000 shares authorized, 40,000 shares issued and outstanding	$160,000
Contributed capital in excess of par value, common stock ..	120,000
Total contributed capital	$280,000
Retained earnings	320,000
Total stockholders' equity	$600,000

Stockholders' Equity
(As of December 31, 19X2)

Common stock, $4 par value, 100,000 shares authorized, 47,400 shares issued, 3,000 in the treasury	$189,600
Contributed capital in excess of par value, common stock ..	179,200
Total contributed capital	$368,800
Retained earnings ($30,000 restricted)	400,000
Total	$768,800
Less cost of treasury stock	(30,000)
Total stockholders' equity	$738,800

The following events occurred during 19X2:

Jan. 10 A $0.50 per share cash dividend was declared, and the date of record was five days later.

Mar. 17 The treasury stock was purchased.

Apr. 10 A $0.50 per share cash dividend was declared, and the date of record was five days later.

July 10 A $0.50 per share cash dividend was declared, and the date of record was five days later.

Aug. 15 A 20% stock dividend was declared when the market value was $12.00 per share.

Sept. 8 The dividend shares were issued.

Oct. 10 A $0.50 per share cash dividend was declared, and the date of record was five days later.

Required

1. How many shares were outstanding on each of the cash dividend dates?
2. How large were each of the four cash dividends?
3. How large was the capitalization of retained earnings for the stock dividend?
4. What was the price per share paid for the treasury stock?
5. How much income did the company achieve during 19X2?

CHECK FIGURE:
Net income, $248,000

Problem 14–4
Presenting items in an
income statement
(LO 3)

The following table shows the balances from various accounts in the adjusted trial balance for McHenry Corp. as of December 31, 19X1:

		Debit	Credit
a.	Interest earned		$ 8,000
b.	Depreciation expense, equipment	$ 24,000	
c.	Loss on sale of office equipment	16,500	
d.	Accounts payable		28,000
e.	Other operating expenses	65,000	
f.	Accumulated depreciation, equipment		49,000
g.	Gain from settling a lawsuit		28,000
h.	Cumulative effect of change in accounting principle (pre-tax)	42,000	
i.	Accumulated depreciation, buildings		109,000
j.	Loss from operating a discontinued segment (pre-tax)	13,000	
k.	Gain on early settlement of debt (pre-tax)		19,000
l.	Sales		647,000
m.	Depreciation expense, buildings	36,000	
n.	Correction of overstatement of prior year's sales (pre-tax)	10,000	
o.	Gain on sale of discontinued segment's assets (pre-tax)		22,000
p.	Loss from settling a lawsuit	16,000	
q.	Income taxes expense	?	
r.	Cost of goods sold	325,000	

Required

Answer each of these questions by providing detailed schedules:

1. Assuming that the company's income tax rate is 30%, what are the tax effects and after-tax measures of the items labeled as pre-tax?
2. What is the amount of the company's income from continuing operations before income taxes? What is the amount of the company's income taxes expense? What is the amount of the company's income from continuing operations?
3. What is the amount of after-tax income associated with the discontinued segment?
4. What is the amount of income before extraordinary items and the cumulative effect of the change in principle?
5. What is the amount of net income for the year?

CHECK FIGURE:
Net income, $130,550

Problem 14–5
Changes in accounting
principles
(LO 3)

On January 1, 19X1, Fields, Inc., purchased some equipment. Its cost was $400,000 and it was expected to have a salvage value of $20,000 at the end of its five-year useful life. Depreciation was allocated to 19X1, 19X2, and 19X3 with the declining-balance method at twice the straight-line rate. Early in 19X4, the company concluded that changing to the straight-line method would produce more useful financial statements because it would be consistent with the practices of other firms in the industry.

Required

Preparation component:

1. Do generally accepted accounting principles allow Fields, Inc., to change depreciation methods in 19X4?
2. Prepare a schedule that shows the amount of depreciation expense allocated to 19X1 through 19X3 under the declining-balance method.
3. Prepare a schedule that shows the amount of depreciation expense that would have been allocated to 19X1 through 19X3 under the straight-line method.
4. Combine the information from your answers to Requirements 2 and 3 in a table like Illustration 14–5 that computes the before- and after-tax cumulative effects of the change.

CHECK FIGURE:
After-tax cumulative effect, $59,920

The company's income tax rate is 30%. (For simplicity, round your answers to the nearest dollar.)

5. How should the cumulative effect be reported by the company? Does the cumulative effect increase or decrease net income?

6. How much depreciation expense will be reported on the income statement for 19X4?

Analysis component

7. Assume that in error, Fields, Inc., treats the change in depreciation methods as a change in an accounting estimate. Using your answers from requirements 2, 3, and 4, describe the effect this error would have on the 19X4 financial statements.

The income statements for Safeco, Inc., presented the following information when they were first published in 19X2, 19X3, and 19X4:

Problem 14–6
Earnings per share
calculations and presentation
(LO 4)

	19X2	19X3	19X4
Sales	$740,000	$850,000	$825,000
Expenses	465,000	520,000	491,000
Income from continuing operations	$275,000	$330,000	$334,000
Loss on discontinued segment	(105,000)		
Income before extraordinary items	$170,000	$330,000	$334,000
Extraordinary gain (loss)		66,000	(140,000)
Net income	$170,000	$396,000	$194,000

The company also experienced some changes in the number of outstanding shares through the following events:

Outstanding shares on December 31, 19X1	10,000
19X2:	
Treasury stock purchase on April 1	− 1,000
Issuance of new shares on June 30	+ 3,000
10% stock dividend on October 1	+ 1,200
Outstanding shares on December 31, 19X2	13,200
19X3:	
Issuance of new shares on July 1	+ 4,000
Treasury stock purchase on November 1	− 1,200
Outstanding shares on December 31, 19X3	16,000
19X4:	
Issuance of new shares on August 1	+ 5,000
Treasury stock purchase on September 1	− 1,000
Three-for-one split on October 1	+ 40,000
Outstanding shares on December 31, 19X4	60,000

Required

Preparation component:

1. Calculate the weighted average of the outstanding common shares as of the end of 19X2.

2. Calculate the 19X2 earnings per share amounts to report on the 19X2 income statement for income from continuing operations, loss on discontinued segment, and net income.

3. Calculate the weighted average of the outstanding common shares as of the end of 19X3.

4. Calculate the 19X3 earnings per share amounts to report on the 19X3 income statement for income from continuing operations, the extraordinary gain, and net income.

5. Calculate the weighted average of the outstanding common shares as of the end of 19X4.

CHECK FIGURE:
19X4 earnings per share
for net income, $3.64

6. Calculate the 19X4 earnings per share amounts to report on the 19X4 income statement for income from continuing operations, the extraordinary gain, and net income.

Analysis component:

7. Write a brief explanation of how you would use the earnings per share statistics from requirement 6 to estimate earnings per share for 19X5.

CRITICAL THINKING: ESSAYS, PROBLEMS, AND CASES

Analytical Essays

AE 14-1
(LO 1)

As of December 31, the balance sheet for Helmer Corporation provided this information about the stockholders' equity:

Common stock, $10 par value, 50,000 shares authorized, 30,000 shares issued and outstanding . .	$300,000
Contributed capital in excess of par value, common stock	150,000
Retained earnings	500,000
Total stockholders' equity	$950,000

The company's board of directors wants to decrease the market value of the company's outstanding stock from its current level of $50 per share by increasing the number of outstanding shares from 30,000 to 60,000. They are considering a choice between a two-for-one stock split and a 100% stock dividend.

Required

Write a short essay describing the difference between the two alternatives in terms of:

1. Their effects on the stock.
2. How they would be recorded in the accounts.
3. Their effects on the balance sheet.

AE 14-2
(LO 4)

The bookkeeper for Catamaran Corporation, who has almost finished preparing the 19X1 financial statements, has come to you for some advice. This draft of the balance sheet accurately describes the company's stockholders' equity situation:

Preferred stock, $80 par value, 5%, cumulative, 10,000 shares authorized, 6,000 shares issued and outstanding . .	$480,000
Common stock, $1 par value, 50,000 shares authorized, 36,000 shares issued and outstanding	36,000
Contributed capital in excess of par value, common stock	260,000
Retained earnings	125,000
Total stockholders' equity	$901,000

The net income for 19X1 has been correctly measured as $250,000, and the accounts show that no cash dividends were declared on the preferred or common stock. In fact, the only stock transaction that occurred during the year was the sale of 3,000 shares of common stock on May 1, 19X1. The bookkeeper has tentatively calculated earnings per share as follows:

$$\frac{\text{Net income}}{\text{Outstanding common plus preferred as of Dec. 31}} = \frac{\$250,000}{36,000 + 6,000} = \$5.95$$

Required

1. Describe any errors that you find in the calculation of earnings per share and specify the corrections that should be made.

2. Explain how the calculation would be different if the preferred stock is not cumulative and if the additional common shares had been issued through a stock dividend instead of a sale.

Financial Reporting Problems

On January 1, 19X1, QualTech, Inc., had the following balances in its stockholders' equity accounts:

FRP 14-1 (LO 1, 2)

Common stock	$ 750,000
Contributed capital in excess of par value, common stock ..	150,000
Retained earnings	650,000
Total	$1,550,000

The company was authorized to issue 100,000 shares, but had issued only 25,000 shares as of January 1, 19X1. The par value per share was $30. The common stock had the following book values as of December 31:

19X1	....	$70.00
19X2	....	30.00
19X3	....	36.00

At the end of each year, the company paid the following dividends per share:

19X1	....	$3.50
19X2	....	1.00
19X3	....	2.00

On March 1, 19X1, the company declared a 20% stock dividend. The market value of the shares was $40 per share. On August 10, 19X2, the stockholders approved a three-for-one split by increasing the number of authorized shares and reducing the par value per share. On April 5, 19X3, the company purchased 10,000 shares of treasury stock at the price of $50 per share.

Required

Use the preceding facts to find the following information (present your work in appropriate schedules):

1. Determine the par value per share of common stock as of the end of 19X1, 19X2, and 19X3.

2. Determine the number of authorized, issued, and outstanding shares as of the end of 19X1, 19X2, and 19X3.

3. Determine the total par value of the issued shares as of the end of 19X1, 19X2, and 19X3.

4. Determine the balance of contributed capital in excess of par as of the end of 19X1, 19X2, and 19X3.

5. Use the book value per share to determine the total stockholders' equity at the end of 19X1, 19X2, and 19X3.

6. Determine the total amount of retained earnings as of the end of 19X1, 19X2, and 19X3.

7. Use the answer to requirement 6 and information about the dividends to determine the amount of net income reported in 19X1, 19X2, and 19X3.

Finally, use the information to complete this table:

	1/1/X1	12/31/X1	12/31/X2	12/31/X3
Common stock:				
Par value per share	____	____	____	____
Authorized shares	____	____	____	____
Issued shares	____	____	____	____
Treasury shares	____	____	____	____
Outstanding shares	____	____	____	____
Account balances:				
Common stock	____	____	____	____
Contributed capital in		)		
excess of par	____	____	____	____
Retained earnings	____	____	____	____
Total	____	____	____	____
Less treasury stock	____	____	____	____
Total stockholders' equity	____	____	____	____

FRP 14-2

(LO 3)

Over the last three years, Commonwealth Enterprises, Inc., has experienced the following income results (all numbers are rounded to the nearest thousand dollars):

	19X1	19X2	19X3
Revenues	$11,000	$11,900	$14,600
Expenses	(7,000)	(7,900)	(7,700)
Gains	3,200	2,400	0
Losses	(1,200)	(1,900)	(3,900)
Net income	$ 6,000	$ 4,500	$ 3,000

Part 1

Use the information to develop a general prediction of the company's net income for 19X4.

Part 2

A closer analysis of the information shows that the company discontinued a segment of its operations in 19X3. The company's accountant has determined that the discontinued segment produced the following amounts of income:

	19X1	19X2	19X3
Revenues	$7,000	$2,600	$1,600
Expenses	(5,000)	(5,000)	(4,000)
Gains		400	
Losses	(1,200)	(1,500)	(900)
Loss on disposal of segment assets			(1,200)

Use the information to calculate the company's income without the discontinued segment and then develop a general prediction of the company's net income for 19X4.

Part 3

A more in-depth analysis of the company's activity reveals that the company experienced these extraordinary items during the three years when it retired some of its debts before their scheduled maturity dates:

	19X1	19X2	19X3
Extraordinary gain	$2,200	$2,000	
Extraordinary loss			$(1,700)

Use the information to calculate the company's income from continuing operations and to develop a general prediction of the company's net income for 19X4.

The financial statements and footnotes from Apple's 1993 annual report are presented in Appendix F at the end of the book. Use that information to answer the following questions:

1. Does Apple have a simple or complex capital structure?

2. What was Apple's earnings per share in fiscal year 1993? How does this figure compare with the results for 1992?

3. What was the dollar amount of cash dividends declared during 1993?

4. What was the dollar amount of cash dividends paid during 1993? How does this number compare with the dividends declared?

5. What is the par value of the common stock?

6. How many shares of common stock were outstanding at the end of the 1993 fiscal year?

7. Does Apple own shares of treasury stock?

8. Did Apple have any extraordinary gains or losses during 1993?

9. Did Apple have any gains or losses on the disposal of a business segment during 1993?

Financial Statement Analysis Case
(LO 1, 2, 3, 4)

Review the As a Matter of Ethics case on page 532 and discuss the ethical implications of the directors' tentative decision to avoid announcing Falcon Corporation's new government contract. What actions would you take if you were the financial vice president?

Ethical Issues Essay

FAST HINT
Group Project:
Create a role-playing situation in which different members of the class act out the individuals described in the ethics case; watch for some interesting interactions.

CONCEPT TESTER

(LO 6)

Test your understanding of the concepts introduced in this chapter by completing the following crossword puzzle:

Across Clues

2. Three words; the calling in of stock to replace each share with less than one new share.
5. Three words; a distribution of shares to stockholders without receiving anything in return.
7. Three words; stock that was reacquired and is still held by the issuing corporation.
8. Three words; a gain that is both infrequent and unusual.

Down Clues

1. Three words; replacing each share of a corporation's stock with more than one new share.
3. Three words; the amounmt of income earned by each share of a corporation's stock.
6. Two words; a gain that is not expected to occur again, given the environment of the business.

ANSWERS TO PROGRESS CHECKS

14–1 *c*

14–2 A small stock dividend is 25% or less of the previous oustanding shares. A large stock dividend is greater than 25%.

14–3 Retained earnings equal to the market value of the distributable shares should be capitalized.

14–4 *b*

14–5 No. The shares are an investment for Southern Co. and issued outstanding shares for Northern Corp.

14–6 Treasury stock does not affect the number of both authorized and issued shares. It reduces the amount of outstanding shares.

14–7 *a*

14–8 *b*

14–9 The four major sections are discontinued segments, extraordinary items, cumulative effects of changes in accounting principles, and earnings per share.

14–10 *c*

14–11 *a* Weighted-average shares: $(25,000 \times 6/12) + (20,000 \times 6/12) = 22,500$

Earnings per share: $(\$250,000 - \$70,000)/22,500 = \$8.00$

14–12 The number of shares previously outstanding are retroactively restated to reflect the stock split or stock dividend as if it occurred at the beginning of the year.

14–13 The two sets are primary earnings per share and fully diluted earnings per share.

14–14 $\$34.00/\$4.25 = \$8.00$

14–15 The company with the highest PE ratio.

Installment Notes Payable and Bonds

L. A. Gear Inc. designs, develops, and markets a broad range of athletic and lifestyle footwear for adults and children. Its innovative products include lighted shoes sold under the names of *L. A. LIGHTS*™ and *Light Gear*™. The company's 1993 annual report disclosed the sale of approximately 4.5 million pairs of children's lighted shoes during 1993. Based on industry estimates for 1993, the company had the fourth largest share of the United States market for branded athletic footwear.

Nevertheless, during the three-year period of 1991 through 1993, L. A. Gear experienced substantial net losses that resulted from reduced sales. Fiscal year net losses decreased from $66,200,000 in 1991 to $32,513,000 in 1993. To counter this trend, the company initiated a long-term restructuring plan late in 1991. That effort, which continued throughout the 1993 year, included a program of international expansion. Primarily to finance that effort, the company issued $50 million of bonds payable during December of 1992. These bonds were described on the company's November 30, 1993, balance sheet as 7¾% convertible subordinated debentures due 2002.

L. A. Gear Inc. (In thousands)	1993	1992	1991
Net sales	$398,358	$430,194	$619,175
Net income (loss)	(32,513)	(71,901)	(66,200)
Total assets	254,613	250,144	327,751
Convertible subordinated debentures	50,000	—	—
Shareholders' equity	46,797	87,451	131,715

LEARNING
OBJECTIVES

After studying Chapter 15, you should be able to:

1. **Calculate the payments on an installment note payable and describe their effects on the financial statements.**

2. **Describe the various characteristics of different types of bonds and prepare entries to record bond issuances and retirements.**

3. **Estimate the price of bonds issued at a discount and describe their effects on the issuer's financial statements.**

4. **Estimate the price of bonds issued at a premium and describe their effects on the issuer's financial statements.**

5. **Calculate and describe how to use the ratio of pledged assets to secured liabilities.**

6. **Define or explain the words and phrases listed in the chapter glossary.**

In Chapter 12, you learned that some notes payable require a single payment on the date the note matures. In those cases, the single payment includes the borrowed amount plus interest. You also learned about other notes requiring a series of payments that include interest plus a part of the principal. We begin this chapter with a more complete discussion of these installment notes. Then, we turn to bonds, which are securities issued by corporations and government bodies. The discussion explains the nature of bonds such as the convertible subordinated debentures issued by **L. A. Gear, Inc.**

INSTALLMENT
NOTES PAYABLE

LO 1

Calculate the payments on an installment note payable and describe their effects on the financial statements.

When an **installment note** is used to borrow money, the borrower records the note with an entry similar to the one used for a single-payment note. That is, the increase in cash is recorded with a debit and the increase in the liability is recorded with a credit to Notes Payable. For example, suppose that a company borrows $60,000 by signing an 8% installment note that requires six annual payments. The borrower records the note as follows:

19X1				
Dec.	31	Cash	60,000.00	
		Notes Payable		60,000.00
		Borrowed $60,000 by signing an 8% installment note.		

Installment notes payable like this one require the borrower to pay back the debt with a series of periodic payments. Usually, each payment includes all interest expense that has accrued up to the date of the payment plus some portion of the original amount borrowed (the *principal*). Installment notes generally specify one of two alternative payment patterns. Some notes require payments that include interest and equal amounts of principal while other notes simply call for equal payments.

Installment Notes with Payments of Accrued Interest and Equal Amounts of Principal

Installment note agreements requiring payments of accrued interest plus equal amounts of principal create cash flows that decrease in size over the life of the note. This pattern occurs because each payment reduces the liability's principal balance, with the result that the following period's interest expense is reduced. The next payment is smaller because the amount of interest is reduced. For example, suppose the $60,000,

Illustration 15–1 Installment Note with Payments of Accrued Interest and Equal Amounts of Principal

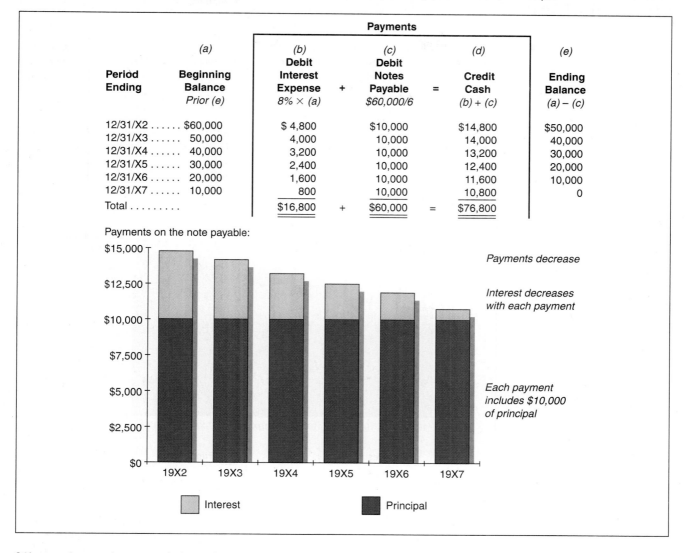

	(a)	(b)		(c)		(d)	(e)
		Payments					
Period Ending	**Beginning Balance** Prior (e)	**Debit Interest Expense** 8% × (a)	+	**Debit Notes Payable** $60,000/6	=	**Credit Cash** (b) + (c)	**Ending Balance** (a) − (c)
12/31/X2	$60,000	$ 4,800		$10,000		$14,800	$50,000
12/31/X3	50,000	4,000		10,000		14,000	40,000
12/31/X4	40,000	3,200		10,000		13,200	30,000
12/31/X5	30,000	2,400		10,000		12,400	20,000
12/31/X6	20,000	1,600		10,000		11,600	10,000
12/31/X7	10,000	800		10,000		10,800	0
Total		$16,800	+	$60,000	=	$76,800	

Payments on the note payable:

Payments decrease

Interest decreases with each payment

Each payment includes $10,000 of principal

☐ Interest   ■ Principal

8% note that we just recorded requires the borrower to make six payments at the end of each year equal to the accrued interest plus $10,000 of principal.

We describe the payments, interest, and changes in the balance of this note in Illustration 15–1. Column *a* of the illustration contains the beginning balance of the note. Columns *b*, *c*, and *d* describe each cash payment and how it is divided between interest and principal. Column *b* calculates the interest expense that accrues during each year at 8% of the beginning balance. Column *c* shows the portion of the payment applied to principal. It shows that each payment reduces the liability with a $10,000 debit to the Notes Payable account. Column *d* calculates each annual payment, which consists of the interest in column b plus $10,000. (Notice that the credit to the Cash account equals the sum of the debits to the expense and the liability account.) Finally, column *e* shows the ending balance of the liability, which equals the beginning balance in column *a* minus the principal portion of the payment in column *c*. Over the life of the note, the table shows that the total interest expense is $16,800 and the total reduction in principal is $60,000. Thus, the total cash payments are $76,800.

The graph in the lower section of Illustration 15–1 shows these three points: (1) the total payment gets smaller as the loan balance is reduced, (2) the amount of interest included in each payment gets steadily smaller, and (3) the amount of principal in each payment remains constant at $10,000.

FAST HINT
Relevant Exercise:
To apply these concepts, work Exercise 15–1.

Illustration 15–2
Installment Note with Equal
Payments

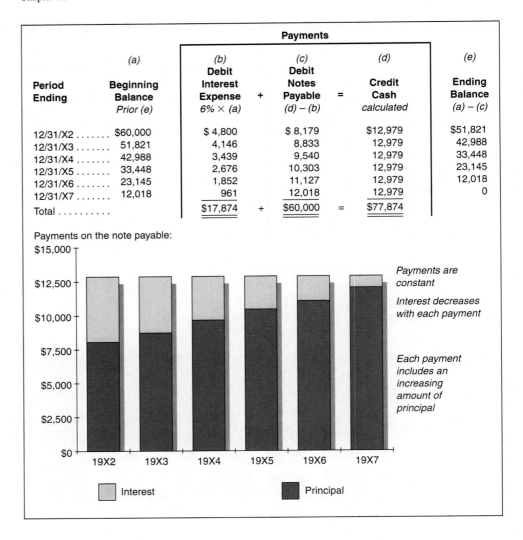

Period Ending	(a) Beginning Balance *Prior (e)*	Payments			(e) Ending Balance *(a) − (c)*
		(b) Debit Interest Expense *6% × (a)* +	(c) Debit Notes Payable *(d) − (b)* =	(d) Credit Cash *calculated*	
12/31/X2	$60,000	$ 4,800	$ 8,179	$12,979	$51,821
12/31/X3	51,821	4,146	8,833	12,979	42,988
12/31/X4	42,988	3,439	9,540	12,979	33,448
12/31/X5	33,448	2,676	10,303	12,979	23,145
12/31/X6	23,145	1,852	11,127	12,979	12,018
12/31/X7	12,018	961	12,018	12,979	0
Total		$17,874 +	$60,000 =	$77,874	

Payments on the note payable:

Payments are constant

Interest decreases with each payment

Each payment includes an increasing amount of principal

The borrower records the effects of the first two payments with these entries:

19X2 Dec.	31	Interest Expense	4,800.00	
		Notes Payable	10,000.00	
		Cash		14,800.00
		To record first installment payment.		

19X3 Dec.	31	Interest Expense	4,000.00	
		Notes Payable	10,000.00	
		Cash		14,000.00
		To record second installment payment.		

After all six payments are recorded, the balance of the Notes Payable account for the note is eliminated.

Installment Notes with Equal Payments

In contrast to the previous pattern, many installment notes require the borrower to make a series of equal payments. These payments consist of changing amounts of interest and principal. To demonstrate this type of note, assume that a $60,000 note requires the borrower to make a series of six equal payments of $12,979 at the end of each year. Illustration 15–2 shows the effects of making the payments on this note. (The payments are $12,979 because $60,000 is the present value of an annuity of six annual payments of $12,979, discounted at 8%. We show you how to make this calculation later in this section.)

Allocating Each Payment between Interest and Principal. Each payment of $12,979 includes both interest and principal. Look at Illustration 15–2 to see how an accountant allocates the total amount of each payment between interest and principal.

The table is essentially the same as the table in Illustration 15–1. Again, column *a* shows the liability's beginning balance for each year. Column *b* presents the interest that accrues each year at 8% of the beginning balance. Column *c* calculates the change in the principal of the liability caused by each payment. The debit to the liability account in this column is the difference between the total payment in column *d* and the interest expense in column *b*. Finally, column *e* presents the ending balance after each payment is made.

Even though all six payments are equal, the amount of interest decreases each year because the balance of the liability gets smaller. Then, because the amount of interest gets smaller, the amount of the payment applied to the principal gets larger. This effect is presented graphically in Illustration 15–2. Because the tables in Illustrations 15–1 and 15–2 show how the principal balance is reduced (or amortized) by the periodic payments, they are often referred to as *installment note amortization schedules*.[1]

The bookkeeper records the effects of the first two payments with these journal entries:

19X2 Dec.	31	Interest Expense	4,800.00	
		Notes Payable	8,179.00	
		Cash		12,979.00
		To record first installment payment.		

19X3 Dec.	31	Interest Expense	4,146.00	
		Notes Payable	8,833.00	
		Cash		12,979.00
		To record second installment payment.		

The amounts in these entries come from the table in Illustration 15–2. The borrower would record similar entries for each of the remaining payments. Over the six years, the Notes Payable account balance will be eliminated.

FAST HINT
Critical Thought Question:
Have you ever signed an installment note? What was the reason? Did the payments include an equal amount of principal, or were they all the same size? (Most consumer notes require a series of equal payments.)

FAST HINT
Critical Thought Question:
How would the payment schedule in Illustration 15–2 be changed if the payments were to be made semiannually or quarterly?

FAST HINT
Important Point to Remember:
The Truth-in-Lending Act requires lenders to provide consumers with information about the true cost of their loans. The information describes up-front finance charges and the annual interest percentage rate. The idea behind the law is to help consumers compare the costs of alternative sources of credit.

---

[1]Many business calculators are programmed to make these amortization calculations for annuities.

To be sure that you understand the differences between the two payment patterns, compare the numbers and graphs in Illustrations 15–1 and 15–2. Notice that the series of equal payments leads to a greater amount of interest expense over the life of the note. This result occurs because the first three payments in Illustration 15–2 are smaller and thus do not reduce the principal as quickly as the first three payments in Illustration 15–1.

Calculating the Equal Periodic Payments on an Installment Note. In the previous example, we simply gave you the size of the equal annual payments on the installment note. Now, we show you how to calculate the size of the payment.

When a note requires a series of equal payments, you can calculate the size of each payment with a present value table for an annuity such as Table 15–2 on page 594.[2] To make the calculation with the table, start with this equation:

$$\textbf{Payment} \times \textbf{Annuity table value} = \textbf{Present value of the annuity}$$

Then, modify the equation to get this version:

$$\textbf{Payment} = \frac{\textbf{Present value of the annuity}}{\textbf{Annuity table value}}$$

Because the balance of an installment note equals the present value of the series of payments, the equation can again be modified to become this formula:

$$\textbf{Payment} = \frac{\textbf{Note balance}}{\textbf{Annuity table value}}$$

For this example, the initial note balance is $60,000. The annuity table value in the formula is based on the note's interest rate and the number of payments. The interest rate is 8% and there are six payments. Therefore, enter Table 15–2 on the sixth row and go across to the 8% column, where you will find the value of 4.6229. These numbers now can be substituted into the formula to find the payment:

$$\textbf{Payment} = \frac{\$60,000}{4.6229} = \$12,979$$

This formula can be used for all installment notes that require equal periodic payments.[3]

FAST HINT

Alternative Example:
Suppose that the $60,000 installment loan has an 8% interest rate with eight equal annual payments. How large should each payment be?
Answer: Use Table 15–2 to find the solution: $60,000/5.7466 = $10,441

FAST HINT

Relevant Exercise:
To apply these concepts, work Exercise 15–3.

FAST HINT

Class Discussion:
Ask a student who has a business calculator to demonstrate how to determine the size of a payment for an installment note with equal payments.

Progress Check
(Answers to Progress Checks are provided at the end of the chapter.)

15–1　Which of the following is true for an installment note that requires a series of equal payments?
    a. The payments consist of an increasing amount of interest and a decreasing amount of principal.
    b. The payments consist of changing amounts of principal, but the interest portion of the payment remains constant.
    c. The payments consist of a decreasing amount of interest and an increasing amount of principal.

15–2　How is the interest portion of an installment note payment calculated?

15–3　When a borrower records an interest payment on an installment note, how are the balance sheet and income statement affected?

---

[2]Appendix E provides present value tables that include additional interest rates and additional periods (or payments). You should use them to solve the exercises and problems at the end of the chapter.

[3]Business calculators can also be used to find the size of the payments.

Illustration 15–3
Financing with Bonds or Stock

	Plan A Don't Expand	Plan B Increase Equity	Plan C Issue Bonds
Income before interest ..	$ 100,000	$ 225,000	$ 225,000
Interest			(50,000)
Net income	$ 100,000	$ 225,000	$ 175,000
Equity	$1,000,000	$1,500,000	$1,000,000
Return on equity	10.0%	15.0%	17.5%

BORROWING BY ISSUING BONDS

LO 2

Describe the various characteristics of different types of bonds and prepare entries to record bond issuances and retirements.

Business corporations often borrow money by issuing **bonds.**[4] Bonds involve written promises to pay interest at a stated annual rate and to make a final payment of an amount identified on the bonds as the **par value of the bonds.** Most bonds require the borrower to pay the interest semiannually. The par value of the bonds (also known as the *face amount*) is paid at a specified future date called the *maturity date of the bonds*. The amount of interest that must be paid each year is determined by multiplying the par value of the bonds by the stated rate of interest established when the bonds were issued.

Differences between Notes Payable and Bonds

When a business borrows money by signing a note payable, the money is generally obtained from a single lender, such as a bank. In contrast, a group of bonds (often called a *bond issue*) typically consists of a large number of bonds, usually in denominations of $1,000, that are sold to many different lenders. After bonds are originally issued, they often are bought and sold by these investors. Thus, any particular bond may actually be owned by a number of people before it matures.

FAST HINT
Alternative Example:
Suppose that the earnings under Plan A would be $150,000 instead of $100,000. How large would the return on equity be under each plan?
Answer:
Plan A = 15%   ($150/$1,000)
Plan B = 18.3%   ($275/$1,500)
Plan C = 22.5%   ($225/$1,000)

Differences between Stocks and Bonds

Stocks and bonds are different types of securities. A share of stock represents an ownership right in the corporation. For example, a person who owns 1,000 of a corporation's 10,000 outstanding shares controls one-tenth of the total stockholders' equity. On the other hand, if a person owns a $1,000, 11%, 20-year bond, the bondholder has a receivable from the issuer. The bond owner has the right to receive 11% interest ($110) each year that the bond is outstanding and $1,000 when the bond matures 20 years after its issue date. The issuing company is obligated to make these payments and thus has a liability to the bondholder.

ADVANTAGES OF ISSUING BONDS

Companies that issue bonds are usually trying to increase their rate of return on equity. For example, assume a company that has $1 million of equity is considering spending $500,000 to expand its capacity. Management predicts that the $500,000 will allow the company to earn an additional $125,000 of income before paying any interest. The managers are considering three possible plans. Under Plan A, the expansion will not occur. Under Plan B, the expansion will occur, and the needed funds will be obtained from the owners. Under Plan C, the company will sell $500,000 of bonds that pay 10% annual interest ($50,000). Illustration 15–3 shows how the plans would affect the company's net income, equity, and return on equity.

---

[4]Bonds are also issued by nonprofit corporations, as well as the federal government and other governmental units, such as cities, states, and school districts. Although the examples in this chapter deal with business situations, all issuers use the same practices to account for their bonds.

FAST HINT
Important Point to Remember:
Using debt to increase the return to common stockholders is the primary method of generating financial leverage for a company. Leverage also can be achieved with preferred stock.

CHARACTERISTICS OF BONDS

FAST HINT
Critical Thought Question:
What is the likely effect of a sinking fund requirement on the risk and market interest rate for the bonds?

Analysis of the alternatives in the illustration shows that the owners will enjoy a greater rate of return and be better off if the expansion is made and if the funds are obtained by issuing the bonds. Even though the projected total income under Plan C would be smaller than Plan B's income, the rate of return on the equity would be larger because there would be less equity. This result occurs whenever the expected rate of return from the new assets is greater than the rate of interest on the bonds. In addition, issuing bonds allows the current owner or owners of a business to remain in control of the company.

Over the years, financial experts have created many different kinds of bonds with various characteristics. We describe some of the more common features of bonds in the following paragraphs.

Serial Bonds

Some companies issue several groups of bonds that mature at different dates. As a result, the bonds are repaid gradually over a number of years. Because these bonds mature in series, they are called **serial bonds.** For example, $1 million of serial bonds might mature at the rate of $100,000 each year from 6 to 15 years after the bonds were issued. There would be 10 groups (or series) of bonds of $100,000 each. One series would mature after six years, another after seven years, and another each successive year until the final series is repaid.

Sinking Fund Bonds

As an alternative to serial bonds, **sinking fund bonds** all mature on the same date. To reduce some of the risk for owners, these bonds require the issuer to create a *sinking fund,* which is a separate pool of assets used only to retire the bonds at maturity. In effect, the issuer must start to set aside the cash to pay off the bonds long before they mature.

Convertible Bonds

Some companies issue **convertible bonds** that can be exchanged by the bondholders for a fixed number of shares of the issuing company's common stock. These bonds offer issuers the advantage that they might be settled without paying back the cash initially borrowed. Convertible bonds also offer the bondholders the potential to participate in future increases in the market value of the stock. However, if the stock does not appreciate, the bondholders continue to receive periodic interest and will receive the par value when the bond matures. In most cases, the bondholders can decide whether and when to convert the bonds to stock. However, the issuer can force conversion by exercising an option to buy the bonds back at a price less than the market value of the stock.

Registered Bonds and Bearer Bonds

A company that issues **registered bonds** keeps a record of the names and addresses of the bonds' owners. Then, over the life of the bonds, the company makes interest payments by sending checks to these registered owners. When one investor sells a bond to another investor, the issuer must be notified of the change. Registered bonds offer the issuer the practical advantage of not having to actually issue bond certificates to the investors. This arrangement also protects investors against loss or theft of the bonds.

Unregistered bonds are called **bearer bonds,** because they are payable to whoever holds them (the *bearer*). Since there may be no record of sales or exchanges, the holder of a bearer bond is presumed to be its rightful owner. As a result, lost or stolen bonds are difficult to replace.

Many bearer bonds are also **coupon bonds.** This term reflects the fact that interest coupons are attached to each bond. Each coupon matures on a specific interest payment date. The owner detaches each coupon when it matures and presents it to a bank or broker for collection. At maturity, the owner follows the same process and presents the bond certificates to a bank or broker. Because there is no readily available record of who actually receives the interest, the income tax law discourages companies from issuing new coupon bonds.

FAST HINT
Important Point to Remember:
Congress discourages the issuance of new coupon bonds by not allowing the issuers to deduct the interest as an expense in computing their taxable income. This apparent inequity is justified as a means of preventing the abuse by some taxpayers who would own the coupon bonds but not report the income on their tax returns.

Secured Bonds and Debentures

When bonds are secured, specific assets of the issuing company are pledged (or *mortgaged*) as collateral. This arrangement gives the bondholders additional protection against default by the issuer. If the issuing company fails to pay the interest or maturity value, the secured bondholders can demand that the collateral be sold and the proceeds used to repay the debt.

In contrast to secured bonds, unsecured bonds are potentially more risky because they are supported by only the issuer's general credit standing. Unsecured bonds are also called **debentures.** Because of the greater risk of default, a company generally must be financially strong to successfully issue debentures at a favorable rate of interest.

FAST HINT
Relevant Quick Study:
To apply these concepts, work QS 15–2.

Sometimes, companies issue debentures that rank below certain other unsecured liabilities of the company. Debentures such as this are called subordinated debentures. Recall from the discussion at the beginning of the chapter that **L. A. Gear Inc.** issued *subordinated debentures.* In a liquidation, the subordinated debentures would not be repaid until the claims of the more senior, unsecured liabilities were first satisfied.

Bond Market Values

Bonds are securities and can be easily traded between investors. Because they are bought and sold in the market, they have a market value. As a matter of convenience, bond market values are expressed as a percentage of their face value. For example, a company's bonds might be trading at $103\frac{1}{2}$, which means that they can be bought or sold for 103.5% of their par value. If other bonds are trading at 95, they can be bought or sold at 95% of their par value.

When a company issues bonds, it normally sells them to an investment firm called an *underwriter.* In turn, the underwriter resells the bonds to the public. In some situations, the issuer may sell the bonds directly to investors as the cash is needed.

THE PROCESS OF ISSUING BONDS

The legal document that identifies the rights and obligations of the bondholders and the issuer is called the **bond indenture.** In effect, the bond indenture is the legal contract between the issuer and the bondholders. Although the practice is less common today, each bondholder may receive an actual bond certificate as evidence of the company's debt. However, most companies reduce their costs by not issuing certificates to registered bondholders.

If the underwriter sells the bonds to a large number of investors, the bondholders' interests are represented and protected by a *trustee.* The trustee monitors the issuer's actions to ensure that it complies with the obligations in the bond indenture. Most trustees are large banks or trust companies.

Accounting for the Issuance of Bonds

Before bonds are issued, the terms of the indenture are drawn up and accepted by the trustee. If the bonds are to be offered to the general public by the underwriter, they must be registered with the Securities and Exchange Commission (SEC), which means that the issuer must provide extensive financial information in special reports.

For example, suppose that the Barnes Company receives authorization from the SEC to issue $800,000 of 9%, 20-year bonds dated January 1, 1995, that are due on December 31, 2014. They will pay interest semiannually on each June 30 and December 31. After the bond indenture is accepted by the trustee on behalf of the bondholders, all or a portion of the bonds may be sold to the underwriter. If all the bonds are sold at their par value, Barnes Company makes this entry to record the sale:

1995				
Jan.	1	Cash	800,000.00	
		Bonds Payable		800,000.00
		Sold bonds at par.		

This entry reflects the fact that the company's cash and long-term liabilities are increased.

Six months later, the first semiannual interest payment is made, and Barnes records the payment with this entry:

FAST HINT
Relevant Exercise:
To apply these concepts, work
Exercise 15–5.

1995				
June	30	Interest Expense	36,000.00	
		Cash		36,000.00
		Paid semiannual interest on bonds.		
		(9% × $800,000 × 1/2).		

When the bonds mature 20 years later, Barnes Company will record its payment of the maturity value with the following entry:

2014				
Dec.	31	Bonds Payable	800,000.00	
		Cash		800,000.00
		Paid bonds at maturity.		

SELLING BONDS BETWEEN INTEREST DATES

Like the previous example, many bonds are sold on their original issue date. However, circumstances may cause a company to actually sell some of the bonds later. If so, it is likely that the selling date will fall between interest payment dates. When this happens, the purchasers normally pay the issuer the purchase price plus any interest accrued since the issue date or the preceding interest payment date. This accrued interest is then refunded to the purchasers on the next interest date. For example, assume that the Fields Company sold $100,000 of its 9% bonds at par on March 1, 19X1, which was two months after the original issue date. The interest on the bonds is payable semiannually on each June 30 and December 31. Because two months have passed, the issuer collects two months' interest from the buyer at the time of the sale. This amount is $1,500 ($100,000 × 9% × 2/12). This situation is represented by the following diagram:

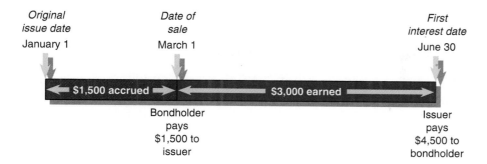

The issuer's entry to record the sale is:

Mar.	1	Cash	101,500.00	
		Interest Payable		1,500.00
		Bonds Payable		100,000.00
		Sold $100,000 of bonds with two months' accrued interest.		

Note that the liabilities for the interest and the bonds are recorded in separate accounts.

When the June 30 semiannual interest date arrives, the issuer pays a full six months' interest of $4,500 ($100,000 × 9% × 1/2) to the bondholder. This payment includes the four months' interest of $3,000 earned by the bondholder from March 1 to June 30 plus the refund of the two months' accrued interest collected by the issuer when the bonds were sold. The issuer's entry to record this first payment is:

June	30	Interest Payable	1,500.00	
		Interest Expense	3,000.00	
		Cash		4,500.00
		Paid semiannual interest on the bonds.		

The practice of collecting and then refunding the accrued interest with the next interest payment may seem like a roundabout way to do business. However, it greatly simplifies the bond issuer's administrative efforts. To understand this point, suppose that a company sells bonds on 15 or 20 different dates between the original issue date and the first interest payment date. If the issuer did not collect the accrued interest from the buyers, it would have to pay different amounts of cash to each of them in accordance with how much time had passed since they purchased their bonds. To make the correct payments, the issuer would have to keep detailed records of the purchasers and the dates on which they bought their bonds. Issuers avoid this extra record-keeping by having each buyer pay in the accrued interest at the time of purchase. Then, the company pays a full six months' interest to all purchasers, regardless of when they bought the bonds.

The interest rate to be paid by the issuer of bonds is specified in the indenture and on the bond certificates. Because it is stated in the indenture, this rate is called the **contract rate** of the bonds. (This rate is also known as the *coupon rate*, the *stated rate*, or the *nominal rate*.) The amount of interest to be paid each year is determined by multiplying the par value of the bonds by the contract rate. The contract rate is

FAST HINT
Alternative Example:
How much interest would be collected from the buyer of $50,000 of these bonds at par on June 1, 19X1?
Answer: $1,875 ($50,000 × 9% × 5/12)

FAST HINT
Relevant Exercise:
To apply these concepts, work Exercise 15–6.

BOND INTEREST RATES

usually stated on an annual basis, even if the interest is to be paid semiannually. For example, suppose that a company issues a $1,000, 8% bond that pays interest semiannually. As a result, the annual interest of $80 (8% × $1,000) will be paid in two semiannual payments of $40 each.

Although the contract rate sets the amount of interest that the issuer pays in *cash,* the contract rate is not necessarily the rate of interest *expense* actually incurred by the issuer. In fact, the interest expense depends on the market value of the issuer's bonds, which depends on the purchasers' opinions about the risk of lending to the issuer. This perceived risk (as well as the supply of and demand for bonds) is reflected in the **market rate** for bond interest. The market rate is the consensus rate that borrowers are willing to pay and that lenders are willing to earn at the level of risk inherent in the bonds. This rate changes often (even daily) in response to changes in the supply of and demand for bonds. The market rate tends to go up when the demand for bonds decreases or the supply increases. The rate tends to go down when the supply of bonds decreases or the demand increases.

Because many factors affect the bond market, various companies face different interest rates for their bonds. The market rate for a specific set of bonds depends on the level of risk investors assign to them. As the level of risk increases, the rate increases. Market rates also are affected by the length of the bonds' life. Long-term bonds generally have higher rates because they are more risky.

Many bond issuers offer a contract rate of interest equal to the rate they expect the market to demand as of the bonds' issuance date. If the contract and market rates are equal, the bonds sell at their par value. However, if the contract and market rates are not equal, the bonds are not sold at their par value. Instead, they are sold at a *premium* above their par value or at a *discount* below their par value. Observe the relationship between the interest rates and the issue price of the bonds' values in this table:

When the contract rate is		The bond sells
Above the market rate	⇒	At a premium
At the market rate	⇒	At par value
Below the market rate	⇒	At a discount

FAST HINT

Important Point to Remember:
In the 1980s, a large number of business acquisitions were financed by issuing junk bonds that promised to pay high rates of interest but offered little security. Although some companies used them wisely to make acquisitions, many investors suffered huge losses when the acquired companies could not generate adequate cash flows to pay the interest.

FAST HINT

Critical Thought Question:
Assuming that a bond is initially issued at a discount, what circumstances might lead an investor to purchase it later at a premium?

Over the last two decades, some companies have issued *zero-coupon bonds* that do not provide any periodic interest payments. Because this contract rate of 0% is always below the market rate, these bonds are always issued at prices less than their face values.

Progress Check

15-4   Unsecured bonds that are backed only by the issuer's general credit standing are called: (a) Serial bonds; (b) Debentures; (c) Registered bonds; (d) Convertible bonds; (e) Bearer bonds.

15-5   How do you calculate the amount of interest a bond issuer will pay each year?

15-6   On May 1, a company sold $500,000 of 9% bonds that pay semiannual interest on each January 1 and July 1. The bonds were sold at par value plus accrued interest since January 1. The bond issuer's entry to record the first semiannual interest payment on July 1 should include: (a) A debit to Interest Payable for $15,000; (b) A debit to Interest Expense for $22,500; (c) A credit to Interest Payable for $7,500.

15-7   When the contract rate is above the market rate, do the bonds sell at a premium or a discount? Do the purchasers pay more or less than the par value of the bonds?

As we described in the previous section, a **discount on bonds payable** arises when a company issues bonds with a contract rate less than the market rate. The expected issue price of the bonds can be found by calculating the *present value* of the expected cash flows, discounted at the market rate of interest.

To illustrate, assume that a company offers to issue bonds with a $100,000 par value, an 8% annual contract rate, and a five-year life. Also assume that the market rate of interest for this company's bonds is 10%.[5] In exchange for the purchase price received from the buyers, these bonds obligate the issuer to pay out two different future cash flows:

1. $100,000 at the end of the bonds' five-year life.
2. $4,000 (4% × $100,000) at the end of each six-month interest period throughout the five-year life of the bonds.

To estimate the bonds' issue price, use the market rate of interest to calculate the present value of the future cash flows. Using an annuity table of present values, you must work with *semiannual* compounding periods. Thus, the annual market rate of 10% is changed to the semiannual rate of 5%. Likewise, the five-year life of the bonds is changed to 10 semiannual periods.

The actual calculation requires two steps: First, you find the present value of the $100,000 maturity payment. Second, find the present value of the annuity of 10 payments of $4,000 each.

The present values can be found by using Table 15–1 (on page 594) for the single maturity payment and Table 15–2 for the annuity. To complete the first step, enter Table 15–1 on row 10 and go across to the 5% column. The table value is 0.6139. Second, enter Table 15–2 on row 10 and go across to the 5% column, where the table value is 7.7217. This schedule shows the results when you multiply the cash flow amounts by the table values and add them together:

Cash Flow	Table	Table Value	Amount	Present Value
Par value	15–1	0.6139	$100,000	$61,390
Interest (annuity) ..	15–2	7.7217	4,000	30,887
Total				$92,277

Table 15–1 (on page 594)

If 5% is the appropriate semiannual interest rate for the bonds in the current market, the maximum price that informed buyers would offer for the bonds is $92,277. This amount is also the minimum price that the issuer would accept.

If the issuer accepts $92,277 cash for its bonds on the original issue date of December 31, 19X1, it records the event with this entry:

19X1					
Dec.	31	Cash	92,277.00	
		Discount on Bonds Payable	7,723.00	
		Bonds Payable		100,000.00
		Sold bonds at a discount on the original issue date.		

BONDS SOLD AT A DISCOUNT

LO 3

Estimate the price of bonds issued at a discount and describe their effects on the issuer's financial statements.

FAST HINT
Class discussion:
Ask a student who has a business calculator to demonstrate how it can be used to determine the present value of the cash flows from a bond.

---

[5] The spread between the contract rate and the market rate of interest on a new bond issue is seldom more than a fraction of a percent. However, we use a difference of 2% here to emphasize the effects.

This entry causes the bonds to appear in the long-term liability section of the issuer's balance sheet as follows:

Long-term liabilities:		
Bonds payable, 8%, due December 31, 19X6 ..	$100,000	
Less discount	7,723	$92,277

FAST HINT
Relevant Exercise:
To apply these concepts, work Exercise 15–7.

This presentation shows that the discount is deducted from the par value of the bonds to produce the **carrying amount** of the bonds payable. As we saw in the last chapter for notes payable, the carrying amount is the net amount at which the bonds are reflected on the balance sheet.

Allocating Interest and Amortizing the Discount

In the previous example, the issuer received $92,277 for its bonds and will pay the bondholders $100,000 after five years have passed. Because the $7,723 discount is eventually paid to the bondholders at maturity, it is part of the cost of using the $92,277 for five years. This table shows that the total interest cost of $47,723 is the difference between the amount repaid and the amount borrowed:

Amount repaid:	
Ten payments of $4,000	$ 40,000
Maturity amount	100,000
Total repaid	$140,000
Less amount borrowed	(92,277)
Total interest expense	$ 47,723

The total expense also equals the sum of the 10 cash payments and the discount:

Ten payments of $4,000	$40,000
Plus discount	7,723
Total interest expense	$47,723

In describing these bonds and the interest expense, the issuer's accountant must accomplish two things: First, the total interest expense of $47,723 must be allocated among the 10 six-month periods in the bonds' life. Second, the carrying value of the bonds must be updated for each balance sheet. Two alternative methods accomplish these objectives. They are the straight-line and the interest methods of allocating interest. Because the process involves reducing the original discount on the bonds over the life of the bonds, it is also called *amortizing the bond discount.*

Straight-Line Method. The **straight-line method** of allocating the interest is the simpler of the two methods. This method allocates an equal portion of the total interest expense to each of the six-month interest periods.

In applying the straight-line method to the present example, the accountant divides the five years' total expense of $47,723 by 10 (the number of semiannual periods in the bonds' life). The result is $4,772 per period.[6] The same number can be found by

---

[6] For simplicity, all calculations have been rounded to the nearest whole dollar. Use the same practice when solving the exercises and problems at the end of the chapter.

dividing the $7,723 original discount by 10. That result is $772, which is the amount of discount to be amortized in each interest period. When the $772 of amortized discount is added to the $4,000 cash payment, the total interest expense for each six-month period is $4,772.

When the semiannual cash payment is made, the issuer uses the following entry to record the interest expense and update the balance of the bond liability:

19X2					
June	30	Interest Expense	4,772.00		
		Discount on Bonds payable		772.00	
		Cash			4,000.00
		To record six months' interest and discount amortization			

Note that the $772 credit to the Discount on Bonds Payable account actually *increases* the bonds' carrying value. The increase comes about by *decreasing* the balance of the contra account that is subtracted from the Bonds Payable account.

As an example of this, **Chiquita Brands International's** 1993 Annual Report disclosed debentures with a par value of $110,820,000 and a contract rate of $10\frac{1}{2}\%$. A footnote explained that the bonds had an "imputed interest rate of 12.1%" and "unamortized discount of $10,391,000 and $10,887,000" at the end of 1993 and 1992, respectively. The carrying value was $100,429,000 and $99,933,000 at the end of 1993 and 1992, respectively. Thus, the unamortized discount decreased by $496,000 and the carrying value of the bonds increased by exactly the same amount.

Illustration 15–4 presents a table similar to the amortization tables that you have studied for notes payable. It shows how the interest expense is allocated among the 10 six-month periods in the bonds' life. It also shows how amortizing the bond discount causes the balance of the net liability to increase until it reaches $100,000 at the end of the bonds' life. Notice the following points as you analyze Illustration 15–4:

1. The $92,277 beginning balance in column *a* equals the cash received from selling the bonds. It also equals the $100,000 face amount of the bonds less the initial $7,723 discount from selling the bonds for less than par.

2. The semiannual interest expense of $4,772 in column *b* for each row equals the amount obtained by dividing the total expense of $47,723 by 10.

3. The credit to the Discount on Bonds Payable account in column *c* equals one-tenth of the total discount of $7,723.

4. The $4,000 interest payment in column *d* is the result of multiplying the $100,000 par value of the bonds by the 4% semiannual contract rate of interest.

5. The ending balance in column *e* equals the beginning balance in column *a* plus the $772 discount amortization in column *c*. This ending balance then becomes the beginning balance on the next row in the table.

6. The balance in column *e* continues to grow each period by the $772 of discount amortization until it finally equals the par value of the bonds when they mature.

The three payment columns show that the company incurs a $4,772 interest expense

Illustration 15–4　Allocating Interest Expense and Amortizing the Bond Discount with the Straight-Line Method

	(a)	Payments (b) Debit Interest Expense	(c) Credit Discount on Bonds	(d) Credit Cash	(e)
Period Ending	Beginning Balance		=	+	Ending Balance
	Prior (e)	$47,723/10	$7,723/10	4% × $100,000	(a) + (c)
6/30/X2	$92,277	$ 4,772	$ 772	$ 4,000	$ 93,049
12/31/X2	93,049	4,772	772	4,000	93,821
6/30/X3	93,821	4,772	772	4,000	94,593
12/31/X3	94,593	4,772	772	4,000	95,365
6/30/X4	95,365	4,772	772	4,000	96,137
12/31/X4	96,137	4,772	772	4,000	96,909
6/30/X5	96,909	4,772	772	4,000	97,681
12/31/X5	97,681	4,772	772	4,000	98,453
6/30/X6	98,453	4,772	772	4,000	99,225
12/31/X6	99,225	4,775 *	775	4,000	100,000
Total		$47,723 =	$7,723 +	$40,000	

*Adjusted for rounding.

FAST HINT
Relevant Exercise:
To apply these concepts, work Exercise 15–8.

FAST HINT
Important Point to Remember:
The straight-line method was widely used before the development of inexpensive computers increased the calculating power available to companies and accountants. With this technology at hand, the simplicity of straight-line is no longer considered to be an effective reduction of effort.

each period, but pays only $4,000. The $772 unpaid portion of the expense is appropriately added to the balance of the liability. It is added to the liability by being taken from the contra account balance. This table shows you how the balance of the discount is partially amortized every six months until it is eliminated:

Period Ending	Beginning Discount Balance	Amount Amortized	Ending Discount Balance
6/30/X2	$7,723	$ (772)	$6,951
12/31/X2	6,951	(772)	6,179
6/30/X3	6,179	(772)	5,407
12/31/X3	5,407	(772)	4,635
6/30/X4	4,635	(772)	3,863
12/31/X4	3,863	(772)	3,091
6/30/X5	3,091	(772)	2,319
12/31/X5	2,319	(772)	1,547
6/30/X6	1,547	(772)	775
12/31/X6	775	(775)	0
Total		$(7,723)	

Interest Method. Straight-line allocations of interest used to be widely applied in practice. However, generally accepted accounting principles now allow the straight-line method to be used only if the results do not differ materially from those obtained by using the **interest method** to allocate the interest over the life of the bonds.[7]

The interest method is exactly the same process for allocating interest that you first learned in Chapter 12 for notes payable. Interest expense for a period is found by multiplying the balance of the liability at the beginning of that period by the original market interest rate.

---

[7] FASB, Accounting Standards—Current Text (Norwalk, CT, 1994), sec. I69.108. First published in *APB Opinion No. 21,* par. 15.

Illustration 15–5 Allocating Interest Expense and Amortizing the Bond Discount with the Interest Method

Period Ending	(a) Beginning Balance	(b) Debit Interest Expense	=	(c) Credit Discount on Bonds	+	(d) Credit Cash	(e) Ending Balance
	Prior (e)	5% × (a)		(b) − (d)		4% × $100,000	(a) + (c)
6/30/X2	$92,277	$ 4,614		$ 614		$ 4,000	$ 92,891
12/31/X2	92,891	4,645		645		4,000	93,536
6/30/X3	93,536	4,677		677		4,000	94,213
12/31/X3	94,213	4,711		711		4,000	94,924
6/30/X4	94,924	4,746		746		4,000	95,670
12/31/X4	95,670	4,784		784		4,000	96,454
6/30/X5	96,454	4,823		823		4,000	97,277
12/31/X5	97,277	4,864		864		4,000	98,141
6/30/X6	98,141	4,907		907		4,000	99,048
12/31/X6	99,048	4,952		952		4,000	100,000
Total		$47,723	=	$7,723	+	$40,000	

In Illustration 15–5, we present an amortization table for our example. The key difference between Illustrations 15–4 and 15–5 lies in the calculation of the interest expense in column *b*. Instead of assigning an equal amount of interest to each interest period, the interest method assigns an increasing amount of interest over the bonds' life because the balance of the liability increases over the five years. The interest expense in column *b* equals the original 5% market interest rate times the balance of the liability at the beginning of each period. Notice that both methods allocate the same $47,723 of total expense among the five years, but with different patterns.

The amount of discount amortized in any period is the difference between the interest expense in column *b* and the cash payment in column *d*. In effect, the accrued but unpaid portion of the interest expense in column *c* is added to the net liability in column *a* to get the ending balance in column *e*.

In the following table, you can see how the balance of the discount is amortized by the interest method until it reaches zero:

FAST HINT
Class discussion:
Ask a student familiar with a spreadsheet computer program to describe to the class how the amortization in Illustration 15–5 could be produced.

Period Ending	Beginning Discount Balance	Amount Amortized	Ending Discount Balance
6/30/X2	$7,723	$ (614)	$7,109
12/31/X2	7,109	(645)	6,464
6/30/X3	6,464	(677)	5,787
12/31/X3	5,787	(711)	5,076
6/30/X4	5,076	(746)	4,330
12/31/X4	4,330	(784)	3,546
6/30/X5	3,546	(823)	2,723
12/31/X5	2,723	(864)	1,859
6/30/X6	1,859	(907)	952
12/31/X6	952	(952)	0
Total		$(7,723)	

Except for the differences in the amounts, journal entries that record the expense and update the liability balance are the same under the interest method and the straight-line method. For example, the entry to record the interest payment at the end of the first interest period is:

19X2				
June	30	Interest Expense	4,614.00	
		Discount on Bonds Payable		614.00
		Cash		4,000.00
		To record six months' interest and discount amortization.		

FAST HINT
Relevant Exercise:
To apply these concepts, work Exercise 15–9.

The accountant uses the numbers in Illustration 15-5 to make similar entries throughout the five-year life of the bonds.

Comparing the Straight-Line and Interest Methods. With this background in place, we can now look more closely at the differences between the straight-line and interest methods of allocating interest among the periods in the bonds' life. In Illustration 15–6, the two graphs illustrate the differences for bonds issued at a discount.

The horizontal line in the first graph in Illustration 15–6 represents the amounts of interest expense reported each period under straight-line. The upward sloping line represents the increasing amounts of interest reported under the interest method. The amounts increase because the constant 5% rate is applied to the growing balance of the liability.

The horizontal line in the second graph represents the constant rate of 5% that the interest method uses to determine the interest expense for every six-month period. The downward sloping line represents the changing interest rates produced by the straight-line method when the bond is issued at a discount. The interest rates decrease each period because the amount of interest expense remains constant while the balance of the liability increases.

The interest method is preferred over the straight-line method because it provides a more reasonable description of the growth of the liability and the amount of interest expense incurred each period. As we mentioned, the straight-line method can be used only if the results do not differ materially from those obtained by using the interest method.

Progress Check

A company recently issued a group of five-year, 6% bonds with a $100,000 par value. The interest is to be paid semiannually, and the market interest rate was 8% on the issue date. Use this information to answer the following questions:

15–8   What is the bonds' selling price? *(a)* $100,000; *(b)* $92,393; *(c)* $91,893; *(d)* $100,321; *(e)* $92,016.

15–9   What is the journal entry to record the sale?

15–10   What is the amount of interest expense recorded at the time of the first semiannual cash payment *(a)* using the straight-line method of allocating interest and *(b)* using the interest method of allocating interest?

BONDS SOLD AT A PREMIUM

LO 4

Estimate the price of bonds issued at a premium and describe their effects on the issuer's financial statements.

When bonds carry a contract interest rate that is greater than the market rate, the bonds sell at a price greater than the par value and the difference between the par and market values is called the **premium.** In effect, buyers bid up the price of the bonds until it reaches the level that creates the current market rate of interest. As we explained for the discount situation, this premium market price can be estimated by finding the present value of the expected cash flows from the bonds at the market interest rate.

Illustration 15-6 Comparing the Straight-Line and Interest Methods of Allocating Interest on a Bond Sold at a Discount

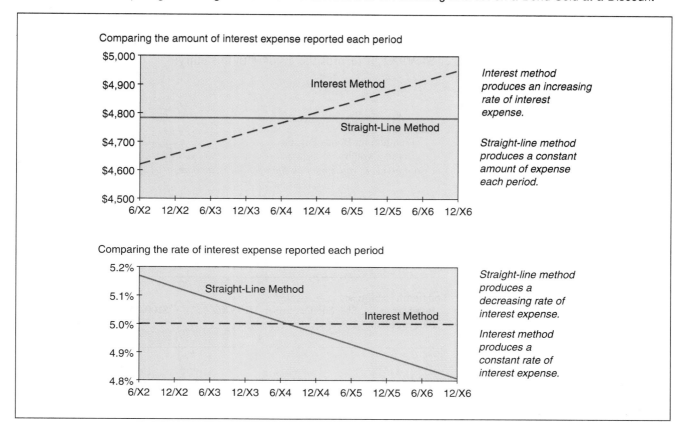

For example, assume that a company decides to issue bonds with a $100,000 par value, a 12% annual contract rate, and a five-year life. On the issue date, the market interest rate for the bonds is only 10%. Thus, potential buyers of these bonds bid up their market price until the effective rate equals the market rate. To estimate this price, we use the 5% semiannual market rate to find the present value of the expected cash flows. The cash flows consist of:

1. $100,000 at the end of the bonds' five-year life.
2. $6,000 (6% × $100,000) at the end of each six-month interest period throughout the five-year life of the bonds.

The present values can be found by using Table 15–1 (page 594) for the single maturity payment and Table 15–2 for the annuity. To complete the first step, enter Table 15–1 on row 10 and go across to the 5% column. The table value is 0.6139. Second, enter Table 15–2 on row 10 and go across to the 5% column, where the table value is 7.7217. Finally, use these table values to reduce the future cash flows to their present value. This schedule shows the results when you multiply the cash flow amounts by the table values and add them together:

Cash Flow	Table	Table Value	Amount	Present Value
Par value	15–1	0.6139	$100,000	$ 61,390
Interest (annuity)	15–2	7.7217	6,000	46,330
Total				$107,720

If 5% is the appropriate semiannual interest rate for the bonds in the current market, the maximum price that informed buyers would offer for the bonds is $107,720. This amount is also the minimum price that the issuer would accept.

If the issuer does accept $107,720 cash for its bonds on the original issue date of December 31, 19X1, it records the event with this entry:

19X1					
Dec.	31	Cash	107,720.00	
		Premium on Bonds Payable		7,720.00
		Bonds Payable		100,000.00
		Sold bonds at a premium on the original issue date.		

This entry causes the bonds to appear in the long-term liability section of the issuer's balance sheet as follows:

Long-term liabilities:		
Bonds payable, 8%, due December 31, 19X6	$100,000	
Plus premium	7,720	$107,720

FAST HINT
Relevant Exercise:
To apply these concepts, work Exercise 15–10.

This presentation shows that the premium is added to the par value of the bonds to produce their carrying amount.

Allocating Interest Expense and Amortizing the Premium

Over the life of these premium bonds, the issuer pays back $160,000, which consists of the 10 periodic interest payments of $6,000 plus the $100,000 par value. Because it borrowed $107,720, the total interest expense will be $52,280. This table shows the calculation:

Amount repaid:	
Ten payments of $6,000	$ 60,000
Maturity amount	100,000
Total repaid	$160,000
Less amount borrowed	(107,720)
Total interest expense	$ 52,280

The following calculation confirms that the total expense also equals the difference between the 10 cash payments and the premium:

Ten payments of $6,000	$ 60,000
Less premium	(7,720)
Total interest expense	$ 52,280

Illustration 15-7   Allocating Interest Expense and Amortizing the Bond Premium with the Interest Method

	(a)	(b) Debit Interest Expense	+	(c) Debit Premium on Bonds	=	(d) Credit Cash	(e) Ending Balance
Period Ending	Beginning Balance						
	Prior (e)	5% × (a)		(d) − (b)		6% × $100,000	(a) − (c)
6/30/X2	$107,720	$ 5,386		$ 614		$ 6,000	$107,106
12/31/X2	107,106	5,355		645		6,000	106,461
6/30/X3	106,461	5,323		677		6,000	105,784
12/31/X3	105,784	5,289		711		6,000	105,073
6/30/X4	105,073	5,254		746		6,000	104,327
12/31/X4	104,327	5,216		784		6,000	103,543
6/30/X5	103,543	5,177		823		6,000	102,720
12/31/X5	102,720	5,136		864		6,000	101,856
6/30/X6	101,856	5,093		907		6,000	100,949
12/31/X6	100,949	5,051*		949		6,000	100,000
Total		$52,280	+	$7,720	=	$60,000	

*Adjusted for rounding.

The premium is subtracted because it will not be paid to the bondholders when the bonds mature.

This total interest expense can be allocated over the 10 semiannual periods with either the straight-line or the interest method. Because the interest method is preferred, it is the only one illustrated for these bonds. Illustration 15–7 shows an amortization schedule for the bonds using this method.

Again, column *a* of the illustration shows the beginning balance, and column *b* shows the amount of expense at 5% of the beginning balance. But, the amount of cash paid out in column *d* is larger than the expense because the payment is based on the higher 6% contract rate. As a result, the excess payment over the expense reduces the principal. These amounts are shown in column *c*. Finally, column *e* shows the new ending balance after the amortized premium in column *c* is deducted from the beginning balance in column *a*.

The following table shows how the premium is reduced by the amortization process over the life of the bonds:

FAST HINT
Alternative Example:
If the issuer were to use straight-line allocation for this bond issued at a premium, how much interest expense would be allocated to each six-month period? How much would the premium be amortized each six-month period?
Answer:
Semiannual interest = $52,280/10 = $5,228
Semiannual amortization = $7,720/10 = $772

Period Ending	Beginning Premium Balance	Amount Amortized	Ending Premium Balance
6/30/X2	$7,720	$ (614)	$7,106
12/31/X2	7,106	(645)	6,461
6/30/X3	6,461	(677)	5,784
12/31/X3	5,784	(711)	5,073
6/30/X4	5,073	(746)	4,327
12/31/X4	4,327	(784)	3,543
6/30/X5	3,543	(823)	2,720
12/31/X5	2,720	(864)	1,856
6/30/X6	1,856	(907)	949
12/31/X6	949	(949)	0
Total		$(7,720)	

The effect of premium amortization on interest expense and on the liability can be seen in this journal entry on June 30, 19X2, when the issuer makes the first semiannual interest payment:

19X2				
June	30	Interest Expense	5,386.00	
		Premium on Bonds Payable	614.00	
		Cash		6,000.00
		To record six months' interest and premium amortization.		

FAST HINT
Relevant Exercise:
To apply these concepts, work Exercise 15-11.

ACCOUNTING FOR ACCRUED INTEREST EXPENSE

Similar entries are recorded at each payment date until the bonds mature at the end of 19X6. However, the interest method causes the company to report decreasing amounts of interest expense and increasing amounts of premium amortization.

If a bond's interest period does not coincide with the issuing company's accounting period, an adjusting entry is necessary to recognize the interest expense that has accrued since the most recent interest payment. For example, assume that the bonds described in Illustration 15–7 were issued on September 1, 19X1, instead of December 31, 19X1. As a result, four months' interest (and premium amortization) accrue before the end of the 19X1 calendar year. Because the reporting period ends on that date, an adjusting entry is needed to capture this information about the bonds.

Interest for the four months ended December 31, 19X1, equals $3,591, which is 4/6 of the first six months' interest of $5,386. The premium amortization is $409, which is 4/6 of the first six months' amortization of $614. The sum of the interest expense and the amortization is $4,000 ($3,591 + $409), which also equals 4/6 of the $6,000 cash payment that is due on March 1, 19X2. The accountant records these effects with this adjusting entry:

19X1				
Dec.	31	Interest Expense	3,591.00	
		Premium on Bonds Payable	409.00	
		Interest Payable		4,000.00
		To record four months' accrued interest and premium amortization.		

Similar entries are made on each December 31 throughout the five-year life of the bonds.

When the $6,000 cash payment occurs on the next interest date, the journal entry recognizes the interest expense and amortization for January and February of 19X2 and eliminates the interest payable liability created by the adjusting entry. For this example, the accountant makes the following entry to record the payment on March 1, 19X2:

19X2				
Mar.	1	Interest Payable	4,000.00	
		Interest Expense ($5,386 × 2/6)	1,795.00	
		Premium on Bonds Payable ($614 × 2/6)	205.00	
		Cash		6,000.00
		To record two months' interest and amortization and eliminate the accrued interest liability.		

The interest payments made each September are recorded normally because the entire six-month interest period is included within a single fiscal year.

Progress Check

On December 31, 19X1, Cello Corporation issued 16%, 10-year bonds with a par value of $100,000. Interest is paid on June 30 and December 31. The bonds were sold to yield a 14% annual market rate of interest. Use this information to solve the following:

15-11   What is the selling price of the bonds?

15-12   Using the interest method of allocating interest expense, Cello would record the second interest payment (on December 31, 19X2) with a debit to Premium on Bonds Payable in the amount of: *(a)* $7,470;   *(b)* $7,741;   *(c)* $259;   *(d)* $530;   *(e)* $277.

15-13   How would the bonds appear in the long-term liability section of Cello's balance sheet as of December 31, 19X2?

For various reasons, companies may want to retire some or all of their bonds prior to maturity. For example, if market interest rates decline significantly, a company may wish to replace old high-interest debt obligations with new lower-interest debt. Many companies reserve the right to retire bonds early by issuing **callable bonds.** This means the bond indenture gives the issuing company an option to *call* the bonds before they mature by paying the par value plus a *call premium* to the bondholders. When interest rates were high in the 1980s, **AT&T Corporation** and many other companies issued callable bonds. When market rates dropped dramatically in the early 1990s, many of these bonds were called and retired.

RETIRING BONDS PAYABLE

LO 2

Describe the various characteristics of different types of bonds and prepare entries to record bond issuances and retirements.

Even if a specific bond issue is not callable, the issuer may be able to retire its bonds by repurchasing them on the open market at the current market price. Whether bonds are called or repurchased, the issuer is unlikely to pay a price that equals the bonds' carrying value. In a repurchase, this is because a bond's market value changes as the market interest rate changes.

If there is a difference between the bonds' carrying value and the amount paid in a bond retirement transaction, the issuer must record a gain or loss equal to the difference.[8] For example, in **Mattel Inc.'s** 1993 Annual Report, a footnote to the financial statements explained that in July 1991, the company "redeemed its 14³/₄% debentures with a remaining principal amount of $99.1 million at 105.9% of par. The write-off of unamortized discount associated with the debt together with the early redemption premium resulted in an extraordinary charge of $4.5 million, net of an income tax benefit of $2.6 million."

As another example, assume that a company issued callable bonds with a par value of $100,000. The call option required the issuer to pay a call premium of $3,000 to the bondholders in addition to the par value. Also

---

[8]Any material gain or loss from retiring bonds or other debt must be reported on the debtor's income statement as an extraordinary gain or loss. FASB, *Accounting Standards—Current Text* (Norwalk, CT, 1994), sec. D14.104. First published in FASB, *Statement of Financial Accounting Standards No. 4,* par. 8.

assume that immediately after a June 30 interest payment, the bonds had a carrying value of $104,500. Then, on July 1, the issuer called all of the bonds and paid $103,000 to the bondholders. The issuer must recognize a $1,500 gain as a result of the difference between the bonds' carrying value of $104,500 and the retirement price of $103,000. This entry records the bond retirement:

July	1	Bonds Payable	100,000.00	
		Premium on Bonds Payable	4,500.00	
		Gain on Retirement of Bonds		1,500.00
		Cash		103,000.00
		To record the retirement of bonds.		

Although a company generally must call all of its bonds when it exercises a call option, it may retire as many or as few bonds as it desires through open market transactions. If it retires less than the entire set of bonds, it recognizes a gain or loss for the difference between the carrying value of those bonds and the amount paid to acquire them.

Earlier in this chapter, we said that some bonds are secured by collateral agreements, while others, called *debentures,* are not secured. These risk-reducing arrangements also are widely used for notes payable, including car and home loans. Unsecured bonds and notes are more risky because the issuer's obligation to pay interest and principal has the same priority as all other unsecured liabilities in the event of bankruptcy. If the company's financial troubles leave it unable to pay its debts in full, the unsecured creditors (including the holders of debentures) lose a proportion or all of their balances.

Thus, a company's ability to borrow money with or without collateral agreements depends on its credit rating. In many cases, debt financing is simply unavailable if the borrower cannot provide security to the creditors with a collateral agreement. Even if unsecured loans are available, the creditors are likely to charge a higher rate of interest to compensate for the additional risk. To borrow the funds at a more economical rate, many notes payable and bonds are secured by collateral agreements called *mortgages.*

A **mortgage** is a legal agreement that helps protect a lender if a borrower fails to make the required payments on a note payable or on bonds payable. A mortgage gives the lender the right to be paid out of the cash proceeds from the sale of the borrower's specific assets identified in the mortgage.

A separate legal document, called the *mortgage contract,* describes the terms of a mortgage. The mortgage contract is given to the lender who accepts a note payable or to the trustee for the bondholders. Mortgage contracts usually require a borrower to pay all property taxes on the mortgaged assets, to maintain them properly, and to carry adequate insurance against fire and other types of losses. These requirements are designed to keep the property from losing value and thus avoid diminishing the lender's security. Importantly, mortgage contracts grant the lender the right to *foreclose* on the property if the borrower fails to pay in accordance with the terms of the debt agreement. If a foreclosure occurs, a court either orders the property to be sold or simply grants legal title of the mortgaged property to the lender. If the property is sold, the proceeds are first applied to court costs and then to the claims of the mortgage holder. If there are any additional proceeds, the borrower is entitled to receive them. However, this cash is subject to any claims from the company's unsecured creditors.

FAST HINT
Important Point to Remember:
It is also possible to achieve essentially the same result as retiring bonds by placing assets in an irrevocable trust that pays the interest and maturity value of the bonds. The rules applying to these "in-substance defeasances" are described in *FASB Statement No. 76.*

FAST HINT
Relevant Exercise:
To apply these concepts, work Exercise 15–12.

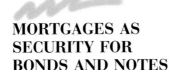

MORTGAGES AS SECURITY FOR BONDS AND NOTES

FAST HINT
Critical Thought Question:
Even though a mortgage is provided to protect the lender, are there circumstances in which the lender would hesitate to foreclose on the property?

Given the relevance of information about a company's security agreements with its lenders, the footnotes to the financial statements may describe the amounts of assets pledged as security against liabilities. The next section describes a ratio that can be used to assess a borrower's situation with respect to its security agreements.

Progress Check

15-14 Six years ago, a company issued $500,000 of 6%, 8-year bonds at a price of 95. The current carrying value is $493,750. The company retired 50% of the bonds by buying them on the open market at a price of 102½. What is the amount of gain or loss on retirement of the bonds?

15-15 A mortgage is:
   a. A promissory note that requires the borrower to make a series of payments consisting of interest and principal.
   b. A legal agreement that protects a lender by giving the lender the right to be paid out of the cash proceeds from the sale of specific assets owned by the borrower.
   c. A company's long-term liability that requires periodic payments of interest and a final payment of its par value when it matures.

As you have learned in this chapter, creditors can reduce their risk with agreements that can force borrowers to sell specific assets to settle overdue debts. Investors who consider buying a company's secured debt obligations need to determine whether the pledged assets of the debtor provide adequate security. One method of evaluating this is to calculate the ratio of **pledged assets to secured liabilities.** This is calculated by dividing the book value of the company's assets pledged as collateral by the book value of the liabilities secured by these collateral agreements:

$$\text{Pledged assets to secured liabilities} = \frac{\textbf{Book value of pledged assets}}{\textbf{Book value of secured liabilities}}$$

For example, suppose that a company has assets with a book value of $2,300,000 that are pledged to secure liabilities with a balance of $1,000,000. The ratio is $2,300,000/$1,000,000 = 2.3 to 1. Although there are no hard and fast guidelines for interpreting the values of this ratio, 2.3 to 1 may be sufficiently high to provide the existing secured creditors with some comfort that the debts are safely covered by the assets.

The pledging of assets for the benefit of secured creditors also affects unsecured creditors. As an increasing portion of the assets are pledged, the unsecured creditors are less likely to receive a full repayment. In evaluating their position, unsecured creditors may gain some information from the ratio of pledged assets to secured creditors. For two reasons, an unusually large ratio may suggest that the unsecured creditors are at risk. First, secured creditors may have demanded an unusually large ratio because the value of the assets in liquidation is low. Second, the secured creditors may perceive that the ability of the company to meet its obligations from operating cash flows is weak.

In using this ratio, a creditor must be aware that the reported book value of the company's assets is unlikely to reflect their fair value. Thus, creditors would have better information if they could determine the assets' current market value and then use it in the ratio instead of book value. Major creditors may be able to get this information directly by asking the borrower to provide recent appraisals or other evidence of the assets' fair value. Other creditors may not have this option. In addition, using the ratio requires knowledge about the amounts of secured liabilities and pledged assets. This information may or may not be clearly identified in the financial statements.

USING THE INFORMATION — PLEDGED ASSETS TO SECURED LIABILITIES

LO 5

Calculate and describe how to use the ratio of pledged assets to secured liabilities.

FAST HINT
Relevant Quick Study:
To apply these concepts, work QS 15–5.

FAST HINT
Critical Thought Question:
Suppose that a company's ratio of pledged assets to secured liabilities declined from 2.0 to 1.5. Should the company's unsecured creditors be concerned? Explain.

Progress Check

15-16   At the end of 19X3, A to Z Company has $350,000 of unsecured liabilities and $575,000 of secured liabilities. The book value of pledged assets is $1,265,000. Calculate the ratio of pledged assets to secured liabilities.

15-17   Would the secured creditors or the unsecured creditors be more concerned if A to Z's ratio of pledged assets to secured liabilities was 1.7 to 1 the previous year?

PRESENT VALUE TABLES

Table 15-1
Present Value of $1

| | Rate | | | | | | | |
Periods	3%	4%	5%	6%	7%	8%	10%	12%
1	0.9709	0.9615	0.9524	0.9434	0.9346	0.9259	0.9091	0.8929
2	0.9426	0.9246	0.9070	0.8900	0.8734	0.8573	0.8264	0.7972
3	0.9151	0.8890	0.8638	0.8396	0.8163	0.7938	0.7513	0.7118
4	0.8885	0.8548	0.8227	0.7921	0.7629	0.7350	0.6830	0.6355
5	0.8626	0.8219	0.7835	0.7473	0.7130	0.6806	0.6209	0.5674
6	0.8375	0.7903	0.7462	0.7050	0.6663	0.6302	0.5645	0.5066
7	0.8131	0.7599	0.7107	0.6651	0.6227	0.5835	0.5132	0.4523
8	0.7894	0.7307	0.6768	0.6274	0.5820	0.5403	0.4665	0.4039
9	0.7664	0.7026	0.6446	0.5919	0.5439	0.5002	0.4241	0.3606
10	0.7441	0.6756	0.6139	0.5584	0.5083	0.4632	0.3855	0.3220
20	0.5537	0.4564	0.3769	0.3118	0.2584	0.2145	0.1486	0.1037
30	0.4120	0.3083	0.2314	0.1741	0.1314	0.0994	0.0573	0.0334

Table 15-2   Present Value of an Annuity of $1

| | Rate | | | | | | | |
Payments	3%	4%	5%	6%	7%	8%	10%	12%
1	0.9709	0.9615	0.9524	0.9434	0.9346	0.9259	0.9091	0.8929
2	1.9135	1.8861	1.8594	1.8334	1.8080	1.7833	1.7355	1.6901
3	2.8286	2.7751	2.7232	2.6730	2.6243	2.5771	2.4869	2.4018
4	3.7171	3.6299	3.5460	3.4651	3.3872	3.3121	3.1699	3.0373
5	4.5797	4.4518	4.3295	4.2124	4.1002	3.9927	3.7908	3.6048
6	5.4172	5.2421	5.0757	4.9173	4.7665	4.6229	4.3553	4.1114
7	6.2303	6.0021	5.7864	5.5824	5.3893	5.2064	4.8684	4.5638
8	7.0197	6.7327	6.4632	6.2098	5.9713	5.7466	5.3349	4.9676
9	7.7861	7.4353	7.1078	6.8017	6.5152	6.2469	5.7590	5.3282
10	8.5302	8.1109	7.7217	7.3601	7.0236	6.7101	6.1446	5.6502
20	14.8775	13.5903	12.4622	11.4699	10.5940	9.8181	8.5136	7.4694
30	19.6004	17.2920	15.3725	13.7648	12.4090	11.2578	9.4269	8.0552

SUMMARY OF THE CHAPTER IN TERMS OF LEARNING OBJECTIVES

LO 1. Calculate the payments on an installment note payable and describe their effects on the financial statements. Typical installment notes require one of two alternative payment patterns: *(a)* payments that include interest plus equal amounts of principal or *(b)* equal payments. In either case, interest is allocated to each period in a note's life by multiplying the carrying value by the original interest rate. If a note is repaid with equal payments, the payment's size is found by dividing the borrowed amount by the annuity table value for the interest rate and the number of payments.

LO 2. Describe the various characteristics of different types of bonds and prepare entries to record bond issuances and retirements. Bonds usually are issued to many investors. Serial bonds mature at different points in time. Companies that issue sinking fund bonds must accumulate a fund of assets to use to pay out the par value of the bonds at the maturity date. Convertible bonds can be exchanged by the bondholders for shares of the issuing company's stock. When bonds are registered, each bondholder's name and address is recorded by the issuing company. In contrast, bearer bonds are payable to whoever holds the bonds.

Some bonds are secured by mortgages on the issuer's assets while other bonds, called debentures, are unsecured. When bonds are sold between interest dates, the accrued interest is collected from the purchasers, who are then refunded that amount on the next interest payment date. Bonds can be retired early by the issuer by exercising a call option or by purchases on the open market. The issuer must recognize a gain or loss for the difference between the amount paid out and the bonds' carrying value.

LO 3. Estimate the price of bonds issued at a discount and describe their effects on the issuer's financial statements. The cash paid to bondholders on semiannual interest payment dates is calculated as one-half of the result of multiplying the par value of the bonds by their contract interest rate. The market value of a bond can be estimated by using the market interest rate to find the present values of the interest payments and the par value. Bonds are issued at a discount when the contract rate is less than the market rate. Then, the issuer records the issuance with a credit to the Bonds Payable account for the par value and a debit to Discount on Bonds Payable. The amount of interest assigned to each interest period can be allocated with the straight-line method if the result is not materially different from the results of applying the interest method. The interest method assigns interest to a period by multiplying the beginning carrying value by the original market interest rate.

LO 4. Estimate the price of bonds issued at a premium and describe their effects on the issuer's financial statements. Bonds are issued at a premium when the contract rate is higher than the market interest rate. The issuer records the premium in a supplemental account. The balance of this account is reduced over the life of the bonds through the interest allocation process.

LO 5. Calculate and describe how to use the ratio of pledged assets to secured liabilities. Secured and unsecured creditors are both concerned about the relationship between the amounts of assets owned by the debtor and the amounts of secured liabilities. The secured creditors are safer when the ratio of pledged assets to secured liabilities is larger, while the risks of unsecured creditors may be increased in this circumstance.

DEMONSTRATION PROBLEM

The Staley Tile Company patented and successfully test-marketed a new product. However, to expand its ability to produce and market the product, the company needed to raise $800,000 of additional financing. On January 1, 19X1, the company borrowed the money under these arrangements:

a. Staley signed a $400,000, 10% installment note that will be repaid with five equal annual installments. The payments will be made on December 31 of 19X1 through 19X5.

b. Staley issued five-year bonds with a par value of $400,000. The bonds have a 12% annual contract rate and pay interest on June 30 and December 31. The annual market interest rate for the bonds was 10% on January 1, 19X1.

Required

1. For the installment note, (a) calculate the size of each payment, (b) prepare an amortization table, and (c) present the entry for the first payment.

2. For the bonds, *(a)* estimate the issue price of the bonds; *(b)* present the January 1, 19X1, entry to record issuing the bonds; *(c)* prepare an amortization table using the interest method; *(d)* present the June 30, 19X1, entry to record the first payment of interest; and *(e)* present an entry to record retiring the bonds at the call price of $416,000 on January 1, 19X3.

Planning the Solution

*   For the installment note, divide the borrowed amount by the annuity table factor (from Table 15–2 on page 594) for 10% and five payments. Prepare a table similar to Illustration 15–2 and use the numbers in the first line for the entry.
*   For the bonds, estimate the issue price by using the market rate to find the present values of the bonds' cash flows. Then, use this result to record issuing the bonds. Next, develop an amortization table like Illustration 15–7, and use it to get the numbers that you need for the journal entry. Finally, use the table to find the carrying value as of the date of the retirement of the bonds that you need for the journal entry.

Solution to Demonstration Problem

Part 1:

Payment = Note balance/Table value = $400,000/3.7908 = $105,519

Table value is for 5 payments and an interest rate of 10%.

Table:

		Payments			
	(a)	*(b)*	*(c)*	*(d)*	*(e)*
Period Ending	**Beginning Balance**	**Debit Interest Expense** +	**Debit Notes Payable** =	**Credit Cash**	**Ending Balance**
19X1	$400,000	$ 40,000	$ 65,519	$105,519	$334,481
19X2	334,481	33,448	72,071	105,519	262,410
19X3	262,410	26,241	79,278	105,519	183,132
19X4	183,132	18,313	87,206	105,519	95,926
19X5	95,926	9,593	95,926	105,519	0
Total		$127,595	$400,000	$527,595	

Journal entry:

19X1					
Dec.	31	Interest Expense	40,000.00	
		Notes Payable	65,519.00	
		Cash		105,519.00
		To record first installment payment.		

Part 2:

Estimated issue price of the bonds:

Cash Flow	Table	**Table Value**	Amount	**Present Value**
Par value	15–1	0.6139	$400,000	$245,560
Interest (annuity)	15–2	7.7217	24,000	185,321
Total				$430,881

Table value is for 10 payments and an interest rate of 5%.

Journal entry:

19X1					
Jan.	1	Cash	430,881.00		
		Premium on Bonds Payable		30,881.00	
		Bonds Payable		400,000.00	
		Sold bonds at a premium.			

Table:

		Payments			
	(a)	*(b)*	*(c)*	*(d)*	*(e)*
Period Ending	**Beginning Balance**	**Debit Interest Expense** +	**Debit Premium on Bonds** =	**Credit Cash**	**Ending Balance**
	Prior (e)	*5% × (a)*	*(d) – (b)*	*6% × $400,000*	*(a) – (c)*
6/30/X1	$430,881	$ 21,544	$ 2,456	$ 24,000	$428,425
12/31/X1	428,425	21,421	2,579	24,000	425,846
6/30/X2	425,846	21,292	2,708	24,000	423,138
12/31/X2	423,138	21,157	2,843	24,000	420,295
6/30/X3	420,295	21,015	2,985	24,000	417,310
12/31/X3	417,310	20,866	3,134	24,000	414,176
6/30/X4	414,176	20,709	3,291	24,000	410,885
12/31/X4	410,885	20,544	3,456	24,000	407,429
6/30/X5	407,429	20,371	3,629	24,000	403,800
12/31/X5	403,800	20,200*	3,800	24,000	400,000
Total		$209,119	$30,881	$240,000	

*Adjusted for rounding.

Journal entries:

19X1					
June	30	Interest Expense	21,544.00		
		Premium on Bonds Payable	2,456.00		
		Cash		24,000.00	
		Paid semiannual interest on the bonds.			
19X3					
Jan.	1	Bonds Payable	400,000.00		
		Premium on Bonds Payable	20,295.00		
		Cash		416,000.00	
		Gain on Retirement of Bonds		4,295.00	
		To record the retirement of bonds (carrying value			
		determined as of December 31, 19X2).			

GLOSSARY

Bearer bonds   bonds that are made payable to whoever holds them (called the bearer); these bonds are not registered. p. 576

Bond   a company's long-term liability that requires periodic payments of interest and final payment of its par value when it matures; usually issued in denominations of $1,000. p. 575

Bond indenture   the contract between the bond issuer and the bondholders; it identifies the rights and obligations of the parties. p. 577

Callable bonds   bonds that give the issuer an option of retiring them before they mature. p. 591

Carrying amount the net amount at which bonds are reflected on the balance sheet; equals the par value of the bonds less any unamortized discount or plus any unamortized premium. p. 582

Contract rate the interest rate specified in the bond indenture; it is multiplied by the par value of the bonds to determine the amount of interest to be paid each year. p. 579

Convertible bonds bonds that can be exchanged by the bondholders for a fixed number of shares of the issuing company's common stock. p. 576

Coupon bonds bonds that have interest coupons attached to their certificates; the bondholders detach the coupons when they mature and present them to a bank for collection. p. 577

Debentures unsecured bonds that are supported by only the general credit standing of the issuer. p. 577

Discount on bonds payable the difference between the par value of a bond and its lower issue price or paying amount; arises when the contract rate is lower than the market rate. p. 581

Installment notes promissory notes that require the borrower to make a series of payments consisting of interest and principal. p. 570

Interest method (interest allocation) a method that allocates interest expense to a reporting period by multiplying the beginning paying value by the original market interest rate. p. 584

Market rate the consensus interest rate that borrowers are willing to pay and that lenders are willing to earn at the level of risk inherent in the bonds. p. 580

Mortgage a legal agreement that protects a lender by giving the lender the right to be paid out of the cash proceeds from the sale of the borrower's specific assets identified in the mortgage. p. 592

Par value of a bond the amount that the bond issuer agrees to pay at maturity and the amount on which interest payments are based; also called the *face amount*. p. 575

Pledged assets to secured liabilities the ratio of the book value of a company's pledged assets to the book value of its secured liabilities. p. 593

Premium on bonds payable the difference between the par value of a bond and its higher issue price or paying amount; arises when the contract rate is higher than the market rate. p. 586

Registered bonds bonds owned by investors whose names and addresses are recorded by the issuing company; the interest payments are made with checks to the bondholders. p. 576

Serial bonds bonds that mature at different dates with the result that the entire debt is repaid gradually over a number of years. p. 576

Sinking fund bonds bonds that require the issuing company to make deposits to a separate pool of assets; the bondholders are repaid at maturity from the assets in this pool. p. 576

Straight-line method (interest allocation) a method that allocates an equal amount of interest to each accounting period in the life of bonds. p. 582

QUESTIONS

1. Describe two alternative payment patterns for installment notes.
2. What is the difference between notes payable and bonds payable?
3. What is the primary difference between a share of stock and a bond?
4. What is the main advantage of issuing bonds instead of obtaining funds from the company's owners?
5. What is a bond indenture? What provisions are usually included in an indenture?
6. What are the duties of a trustee for bondholders?
7. Why does a company that issues bonds between interest dates collect accrued interest from the bonds' purchasers?
8. What are the *contract* and *market interest rates* for bonds?
9. What factors affect the market interest rates for bonds?

10. If you know the par value of bonds, the contract rate and the market interest rate, how can you estimate the market value of the bonds?
11. Does the straight-line or interest method produce an allocation of interest that creates a constant rate of interest over a bond's life? Explain your answer.
12. What is the cash price of a $2,000 bond that is sold at 98$1/4$? What is the cash price of a $6,000 bond that is sold at 101$1/2$?
13. Explain why unsecured creditors should be alarmed when the pledged assets to secured liabilities ratio for a borrower has grown substantially.
14. Refer to the financial statements for Ben & Jerry's Homemade, Inc., presented in Appendix G. Is there any indication in the balance sheet that the company has issued bonds?

QUICK STUDY (Five-Minute Exercises)

QS 15–1
(LO 1)

The owner of Ripley's Restaurant borrowed $80,000 from a bank and signed an installment note that calls for eight annual payments of equal size, with the first payment due one year after the note was signed. Use Table 15–2 on page 594 to calculate the size of the annual payment for each of the following annual interest rates: *a.* 5%, *b.* 7%, *c.* 10%.

Match the following terms and phrases by entering the letter of the phrase that best describes each term in the blank next to the term.

QS 15–2
(LO 2)

_____ serial bonds	_____ bearer bonds
_____ sinking fund bonds	_____ secured bonds
_____ convertible bonds	_____ debentures
_____ registered bonds	_____ bond indenture

a. Issuer records the bondholders' names and addresses.

b. Unsecured; backed only by the issuer's general credit standing.

c. Varying maturity dates.

d. Identifies the rights and responsibilities of the issuer and bondholders.

e. Can be exchanged for shares of the issuer's common stock.

f. Unregistered; interest is paid to whoever possesses them.

g. Issuer maintains a separate pool of assets from which bondholders are paid at maturity.

h. Specific assets of the issuer are mortgaged as collateral.

The Carraway Co. issued 10%, 10-year bonds with a par value of $200,000. On the issue date, the annual market rate of interest for the bonds was 12%, and they sold for $177,059. The straight-line method is used to allocate the interest.

QS 15–3
(LO 3)

a. What is the total amount of interest expense that will be recognized over the life of the bonds?

b. What is the amount of interest expense recorded on the first interest payment date?

The Downhome Co. issued 12%, 10-year bonds with a par value of $60,000 and semiannual interest payments. On the issue date, the annual market rate of interest for the bonds was 10%, and they were sold for $67,478. The interest method is used to allocate the interest.

QS 15–4
(LO 4)

a. What is the total amount of interest expense that will be recognized over the life of the bonds?

b. What is the amount of interest expense recorded on the first interest payment date?

Use the following information to compute the ratio of pledged assets to secured liabilities for both companies:

QS 15–5
(LO 5)

	Red Co.	Blue Co.
Pledged assets	$155,000	$ 87,000
Total assets	180,000	300,000
Secured liabilities	90,000	66,000
Unsecured liabilities	140,000	160,000

EXERCISES

When solving the following exercises, round all dollar amounts to the nearest whole dollar. Also assume that none of the companies use reversing entries.

On December 31, 19X1, Akron Co. borrowed $16,000 by signing a four-year, 5% installment note. The note requires annual payments of accrued interest and equal amounts of principal on December 31 of each year from 19X2 through 19X5.

Exercise 15–1
Installment note with payments of accrued interest and equal amounts of principal
(LO 1)

a. How much principal will be included in each of the four payments?

b. Prepare an amortization table for this installment note like the one presented in Illustration 15–1 on page 571.

Use the data in Exercise 15–1 to prepare journal entries that Akron Co. would make to record the loan on December 31, 19X1, and the four payments starting on December 31, 19X2, through the final payment on December 31, 19X5.

Exercise 15–2
Entries for payments of accrued interest and equal amounts of principal
(LO 1)

Exercise 15–3
Installment note with equal payments
(LO 1)

On December 31, 19X1, Gates Co. borrowed $10,000 by signing a four-year, 5% installment note. The note requires four equal payments of accrued interest and principal on December 31 of each year from 19X2 through 19X5.

a.   Calculate the size of each of the four equal payments.

b.   Prepare an amortization table for this installment note like the one presented in Illustration 15–2 on page 572.

Exercise 15–4
Journal entries for a note with equal payments
(LO 1)

Use the data in Exercise 15–3 to prepare journal entries that Gates Co. would make to record the loan on December 31, 19X1, and the four payments starting on December 31, 19X2, through the final payment on December 31, 19X5.

Exercise 15–5
Journal entries for bond issuance and interest payments
(LO 2)

On January 1, 19X1, the Tennyson Co. issued $300,000 of 20-year bonds that pay 8% interest semiannually on June 30 and December 31. The bonds were sold to investors at their par value.

a.   How much interest will the issuer pay to the holders of these bonds every six months?

b.   Show the journal entries that the issuer would make to record (1) the issuance of the bonds on January 1, 19X1, (2) the first interest payment on June 30, 19X1, and (3) the second interest payment on December 31, 19X1.

Exercise 15–6
Journal entries for bond issuance with accrued interest
(LO 2)

On March 1, 19X1, the Tennyson Co. issued $300,000 of 20-year bonds dated January 1, 19X1. The bonds pay 8% interest semiannually on June 30 and December 31. The bonds were sold to investors at their par value plus the two months' interest that had accrued since the original issue date.

a.   How much accrued interest was paid to the issuer by the purchasers of these bonds on March 1, 19X1?

b.   Show the journal entries that the issuer would make to record (1) the issuance of the bonds on March 1, 19X1; (2) the first interest payment on June 30, 19X1; and (3) the second interest payment on December 31, 19X1.

Exercise 15–7
Calculating the present value of a bond and recording the issuance
(LO 3)

The Sesame Co. issued bonds with a par value of $150,000 on their initial issue date. The bonds mature in 15 years and pay 8% annual interest in two semiannual payments. On the issue date, the annual market rate of interest for the bonds turned out to be 10%.

a.   What is the size of the semiannual interest payment for these bonds?

b.   How many semiannual interest payments will be made on these bonds over their life?

c.   Use the information about the interest rates to decide whether the bonds were issued at par, a discount, or a premium.

d.   Estimate the market value of the bonds as of the date they were issued.

e.   Present the journal entry that would be made to record the bonds' issuance.

Exercise 15–8
Straight-line allocation of interest for bonds sold at a discount
(LO 3)

The Columbia Company issued bonds with a par value of $50,000 on January 1, 19X2. The annual contract rate on the bonds is 8%, and the interest is paid semiannually. The bonds mature after three years. The annual market interest rate at the date of issuance was 12%, and the bonds were sold for $45,085.

a.   What is the amount of the original discount on these bonds?

b.   How much total interest expense will be recognized over the life of these bonds?

c.   Present an amortization table like Illustration 15–4 on page 584 for these bonds; use the straight-line method of allocating the interest and amortizing the discount.

Exercise 15–9
Interest method allocation of interest for bonds sold at a discount
(LO 3)

The Cheyenne Company issued bonds with a par value of $30,000 on January 1, 19X2. The annual contract rate on the bonds is 8%, and the interest is paid semiannually. The bonds mature after three years. The annual market interest rate at the date of issuance was 10%, and the bonds were sold for $28,477.

a. What is the amount of the original discount on these bonds?

b. How much total interest expense will be recognized over the life of these bonds?

c. Present an amortization table like Illustration 15–5 on page 585 for these bonds; use the interest method of allocating the interest and amortizing the discount.

The Allan Co. issued bonds with a par value of $25,000 on their initial issue date. The bonds mature in 15 years and pay 8% annual interest in two semiannual payments. On the issue date, the annual market rate of interest for the bonds turned out to be 6%.

Exercise 15–10
Calculating the present value of a bond and recording the issuance
(LO 3)

a. What is the size of the semiannual interest payment for these bonds?

b. How many semiannual interest payments will be made on these bonds over their life?

c. Use the information about the interest rates to decide whether the bonds were issued at par, a discount, or a premium.

d. Estimate the market value of the bonds as of the date they were issued.

e. Present the journal entry that would be made to record the bonds' issuance.

The Cypress Company issued bonds with a par value of $40,000 on January 1, 19X2. The annual contract rate on the bonds was 12%, and the interest is paid semiannually. The bonds mature after three years. The annual market interest rate at the date of issuance was 10%, and the bonds were sold for $42,030.

Exercise 15–11
Interest method allocation of interest for bonds sold at a premium
(LO 3)

a. What is the amount of the original premium on these bonds?

b. How much total interest expense will be recognized over the life of these bonds?

c. Present an amortization table like Illustration 15–7 on page 589 for these bonds; use the interest method of allocating the interest and amortizing the premium.

On January 1, 19X1, the Amsterdam Co. issued $700,000 of its 10%, 15-year bonds at a price of 95$1/2$. Three years later, on January 1, 19X4, the company retired 30% of these bonds by buying them on the open market at 105$3/4$. All interest had been properly accounted for and paid through December 31, 19X3, the day before the purchase. The company used the straight-line method to allocate the interest and amortize the original discount.

Exercise 15–12
Retiring bonds payable
(LO 2)

a. How much money did the company receive when it first issued the entire group of bonds?

b. How large was the original discount on the entire group of bonds?

c. How much amortization did the company record on the entire group of bonds between January 1, 19X1, and December 31, 19X3?

d. What was the carrying value of the entire group of bonds as of the close of business on December 31, 19X3? What was the carrying value of the retired bonds on this date?

e. How much money did the company pay on January 1, 19X4, to purchase the bonds that it retired?

f. What is the amount of the gain or loss from retiring the bonds?

g. Provide the general journal entry that the company would make to record the retirement of the bonds.

The Schaffner Co. issued bonds with a par value of $100,000 and a five-year life on May 1, 19X1. The contract interest rate is 7%. The bonds pay interest on October 31 and April 30. They were issued at a price of $95,948.

Exercise 15–13
Straight-line amortization table and accrued interest
(LO 3, 4, 5)

a. Prepare an amortization table for these bonds that covers their entire life. Use the straight-line method of allocating interest.

b. Show the journal entries that the issuer would make to record the first two interest payments and to accrue interest as of December 31, 19X1.

PROBLEMS

When solving the following problems, round all dollar amounts to the nearest whole dollar. Also assume that none of the companies use reversing entries.

Problem 15–1
Installment notes
(LO 1)

On November 30, 19X1, the Stanley Company borrowed $50,000 from a bank by signing a four-year installment note bearing interest at 12%. The terms of the note require equal payments each year on November 30.

Required

1. Calculate the size of each installment payment. (Use Table 15–2 on page 594.)
2. Complete an installment note amortization schedule for this note similar to Illustration 15–2 on page 594.
3. Present the journal entries that the borrower would make to record accrued interest as of December 31, 19X1 (the end of the annual reporting period) and the first payment on the note.
4. Now assume that the note does not require equal payments but does require four payments that include accrued interest and an equal amount of principal in each payment. Complete an installment note amortization schedule for this note similar to Illustration 15–1 on page 591. Present the journal entries that the borrower would make to record accrued interest as of December 31, 19X1 (the end of the annual reporting period) and the first payment on the note.

CHECK FIGURE:
Requirement 2: Interest for period ending 11/30/X4, $3,339

Problem 15–2
Calculating bond prices and recording issuances with journal entries
(LO 2, 3, 4)

Helmer Co. issued a group of bonds on January 1, 19X1, that pay interest semiannually on June 30 and December 31. The par value of the bonds is $40,000, the annual contract rate is 8%, and the bonds mature in 10 years.

Required

For each of these three situations, *(a)* determine the issue price of the bonds and *(b)* show the journal entry that would record the issuance.

CHECK FIGURE:
Requirement 1: Premium, $5,952

1. The market interest rate at the date of issuance was 6%.
2. The market interest rate at the date of issuance was 8%.
3. The market interest rate at the date of issuance was 10%.

Problem 15–3
Straight-line method of allocating interest and amortizing a bond discount
(LO 3)

Abbot Company issued $125,000 of bonds that pay 6% annual interest with two semiannual payments. The date of issuance was January 1, 19X1, and the interest is paid on June 30 and December 31. The bonds mature after 10 years and were issued at the price of $108,014.

Required

1. Prepare a general journal entry to record the issuance of the bonds.
2. Determine the total interest expense that will be recognized over the life of these bonds.
3. Prepare the first four lines of an amortization table like Illustration 15–4 based on the straight-line method of allocating the interest.
4. Prepare the first four lines of a separate table that shows the beginning balance of the discount, the amount of straight-line amortization of the discount, and the ending balance.
5. Present the journal entries that the bond issuer would make to record the first two interest payments.

CHECK FIGURE:
Total interest expense, $91,986

Problem 15–4
Interest method of allocating bond interest and amortizing a discount
(LO 2, 3)

The Martin Company issued $50,000 of bonds that pay 4% annual interest with two semiannual payments. The date of issuance was January 1, 19X1, and the interest is paid on June 30 and December 31. The bonds mature after three years and were issued at the price of $47,292. The market interest rate was 6%.

Required

Preparation component:

1. Prepare a general journal entry to record the issuance of the bonds.
2. Determine the total interest expense that will be recognized over the life of these bonds.
3. Prepare the first four lines of an amortization table like Illustration 15–5 based on the interest method.
4. Prepare the first four lines of a separate table that shows the beginning balance of the discount, the amount of interest method amortization of the discount, and the ending balance.
5. Present the journal entries that the bond issuer would make to record the first two interest payments.

Analysis component:

6. Instead of the facts described in the problem, assume that the market interest rate on January 1, 19X1, was 3% instead of 6%. Without presenting any specific numbers, describe how this change would affect the amounts presented on the company's financial statements.

CHECK FIGURE:
Total interest expense, $8,708

The Jones Company issued $100,000 of bonds that pay 9% annual interest with two semiannual payments. The date of issuance was January 1, 19X1, and the interest is paid on June 30 and December 31. The bonds mature after three years and were issued at the price of $102,619. The market interest rate was 8%.

Problem 15–5
Interest method of amortizing bond premium and retiring bonds
(LO 2, 4)

Required

1. Prepare a general journal entry to record the issuance of the bonds.
2. Determine the total interest expense that will be recognized over the life of these bonds.
3. Prepare the first four lines of an amortization table like Illustration 15–7 based on the interest method.
4. Prepare the first four lines of a separate table that shows the beginning balance of the premium, the amount of interest method amortization of the premium, and the ending balance.
5. Present the journal entries that the bond issuer would make to record the first two interest payments.
6. Present the journal entry that would be made to record the retirement of these bonds on December 31, 19X2, at the price of 98.

CHECK FIGURE:
Requirement 3: Interest for period ending 6/30/X2, $4,073

The Briggs Company issued bonds with a par value of $80,000 and a five-year life on January 1, 19X1. The bonds pay interest on June 30 and December 31. The contract interest rate is 8.5%. The bonds were issued at a price of $81,625. The market interest rate was 8% on the original issue date.

Problem 15–6
Bond premium amortization and finding the present value of remaining cash flows
(LO 3, 4)

Required

1. Prepare an amortization table for these bonds that covers their entire life. Use the interest method.
2. Show the journal entries that the issuer would make to record the first two interest payments.
3. Use the original market interest rate to calculate the present value of the remaining cash flows for these bonds as of December 31, 19X3. Compare your answer with the amount shown on the amortization table as the balance for that date, and explain your findings.

CHECK FIGURE:
Balance as of 6/30/X3, $80,894

On January 1, 19X2, Alpha Company issued $45,000 of 10%, five-year bonds secured by a mortgage that specifies assets totaling $75,000 as collateral. On the same date, Beta Company isssued 10%, five-year bonds with a par value of $20,000. Beta is securing its bonds with a

Problem 15–7
Computing and analyzing ratio of pledged assets to secured liabilities
(LO 5)

mortgage that includes $50,000 of pledged assets. Following is December 31, 19X1, balance sheet information for both companies:

	Alpha Co.	Beta Co.
Total assets	$300,000*	$150,000†
Liabilities:		
Secured	$ 70,000	$ 25,000
Unsecured	50,000	55,000
Owners' equity	180,000	70,000
Total liabilities and owners' equity	$300,000	$150,000
Footnote	*33% pledged	†42% pledged

Required

Preparation component:

CHECK FIGURE:
Alpha: 1.5 to 1; Beta: 2.5 to 1

1. Calculate the ratio of pledged assets to secured liabilities for each company after January 1, 19X2.

Analysis component:

2. Which company's bonds appear to offer the best security? What other information might be helpful in evaluating the risk of the bonds?

CRITICAL THINKING: ESSAYS, PROBLEMS, AND CASES

When solving the following, round all dollar amounts to the nearest whole dollar.

Analytical Essay

(LO 5)

An unsecured major creditor of the Hawkins Company has been monitoring the company's financing activities. Two years before, the ratio of its pledged assets to secured liabilities had been 1.4. One year ago, the ratio had climbed to 2.0, and the most recent financial report shows that the ratio value is now 3.1. Briefly describe what this trend may indicate about the company's activities, specifically from the point of view of this creditor.

Management Decision Case

(LO 2, 3, 4)

Star Manufacturing Company is planning major additions to its operating capacity and needs approximately $400,000 to finance the expansion. The company has been considering three alternative proposals for issuing bonds that pay annual interest over the eight years in their lives. The alternatives are:

    Plan A: Issue $400,000 of 8% bonds.
    Plan B: Issue $450,000 of 6% bonds.
    Plan C: Issue $360,000 of 10% bonds.

The market rate of interest for all of these bonds is expected to be 8%.

Required

1. For each plan, calculate:
    a. The expected cash proceeds from issuing the bonds.
    b. The expected annual cash outflow for interest.
    c. The expected interest expense for the first year. (Use the interest method to amortize bond premium or discount.)
    d. The amount that must be paid at maturity.

2. Which plans have the smallest and largest cash demands on the company prior to the final payment at maturity? Which plans require the smallest and largest payment at maturity?

The Angela Company issued $500,000 of zero-coupon bonds on January 1, 19X1. These bonds are scheduled to mature seven years later on December 31, 19X7. Under the terms of the bond agreement, the company will pay out $500,000 to the bondholders on the maturity date without making any periodic interest payments. The market rate of interest for these bonds was 10% when they were issued.

Financial Reporting Problem

(LO 3)

Required

1. Estimate the amount of cash that Angela received when it issued these bonds (assume annual compounding).

2. Present the journal entry that Angela's accountant would use to record the issuance of these bonds.

3. Calculate the total amount of interest expense that will be incurred over the life of the bonds.

4. Prepare an amortization table that shows the amount of interest expense that will be allocated to each year in the bonds' life with the interest method.

5. Present the journal entry that Angela's accountant would use to record the interest expense from these bonds for the year ended December 31, 19X1.

Use the financial statements and the footnotes in Appendix F to answer these questions about Apple Computer, Inc.

Financial Statement Analysis Case

(LO 1)

a. Has Apple issued any bonds or long-term notes payable?

b. What is the carrying value of Apple's short-term notes payable at the end of the 1993 fiscal year?

c. Are the notes payable secured or unsecured?

d. What was the average life of the notes?

e. What was the average interest rate on the notes outstanding at the end of the 1993 fiscal year?

ANSWERS TO PROGRESS CHECKS

15–1 c

15–2 The interest portion of an installment payment equals the beginning balance for the period multiplied by the original interest rate.

15–3 On the balance sheet, the balances of the liability and cash are decreased. On the income statement, interest expense is increased.

15–4 b

15–5 Multiply the par value of the bonds by the contract rate of interest.

15–6 a

15–7 The bonds sell at a premium, and the purchasers pay more than the par value of the bonds.

15–8 c. (Present values of $100,000 and a semiannual annuity of $3,000, both at 4% for 10 semiannual periods.)

15–9
Cash	91,893.00	
Discount on Bonds Payable	8,107.00	
Bonds Payable		100,000.00

15–10 a. $3,811 (Total interest equal to $38,107, or 10 payments of $3,000 plus the $8,107 discount, divided by 10 periods.)
b. $3,676 (Beginning balance of $91,893 times 4% market interest rate.)

15–11 $110,592 (Present value of $100,000 plus the semiannual annuity of $8,000, both at 7% for 20 semiannual periods.)

15–12   *e.* (On 6/30/X2: $110,592 $\times$ 7% = $7,741 interest expense;
         $8,000 $-$ $7,741 = $259 premium amortization; $110,592 $-$ $259 = $110,333
         ending balance. On 12/31/X2: $110,333 $\times$ 7% = $7,723 interest expense;
         $8,000 $-$ $7,723 = $277 premium amortization.)

15–13   Bonds payable, 16%, due December 31,
         19X0 . . . . $100,000
         Plus premium 10,056* $110,056

         *Beginning premium balance of $10,592 less $259 and $277 amortized on 6/30/X2
          and 12/31/X2.

15–14 . $9,375 loss (Difference between repurchase price of $256,250 [50% of ($500,000 $\times$
         102.5%)] and carrying value of $246,875 [50% of $493,750].)

15–15   *b*

15–16   2.2 to 1 ($1,265,000/$575,000)

15–17   Unsecured creditors. They may be less likely to receive full repayment if the portion
         of assets pledged increases.

Reporting and Using Cash Flows in Decision Making

*F*inancial news reports indicate that Hollywood studios and other corporations in the entertainment industries are battling to take over television studios. In 1994, *The Wall Street Journal* described a widespread rumor that The Walt Disney Company considered bidding to acquire NBC. Supposedly, the initial offer being considered was $5 billion. Why might Disney have been interested? Cash flow! The networks' libraries of TV episodes are considered to be major prizes in winning acquisitions. Episodes of "Home Improvement," a successful sitcom owned by Disney, are selling for $3.4 million an episode, and Paramount Pictures' production of "Seinfeld" is expected to sell for $2 to $3 million per episode! (*The Wall Street Journal*, Sept. 9, 1994, p. R4)

As the following excerpt from Disney's 1993 annual report shows, the company's cash position had declined substantially since 1991. Continued drains on cash were expected as a result of ongoing renovations and expansion of theme parks and stores, plans to build cruise ships, new parks, and the demands of EuroDisney. Under these circumstances, management must pay particular attention to cash inflows and outflows.

THE WALT DISNEY COMPANY—CONSOLIDATED STATEMENT OF CASH FLOW
(In millions)

Year ended September 30	1993	1992	1991
Increase (Decrease) in Cash and Cash Equivalents	$(401.8)	$(121.3)	$ 66.3
Cash and Cash Equivalents, Beginning of Year	764.8	886.1	819.8
Cash and Cash Equivalents, End of Year	$363.0	$764.8	$886.1

LEARNING OBJECTIVES

After studying Chapter 16, you should be able to:

1. **Explain why cash flow information is important to decision making and describe the information in a statement of cash flows and the methods used to disclose noncash investing and financing activities.**

2. **Calculate cash inflows and outflows by inspecting the noncash account balances and prepare a statement of cash flows using the direct method.**

3. **Calculate the net cash provided or used by operating activities according to the indirect method and prepare the statement of cash flows.**

4. **Prepare a working paper for a statement of cash flows so that the net cash flow from operating activities is calculated by the indirect method.**

5. **Define or explain the words or phrases listed in the chapter glossary.**

Up to this point in your study of accounting, profitability may have seemed to be the sole focus of business managers. Profits certainly are important to business success. However, a business cannot achieve or maintain profitability without carefully managing its cash. Cash is the lifeblood of a business enterprise. In a sense, cash is the fuel that keeps a business moving forward.

Managers and external parties such as investors and creditors pay close attention to a company's cash position and the events and transactions causing that position to change. Information about these events and transactions is reported in a financial statement called the **statement of cash flows.** By studying this chapter, you will learn how to prepare and interpret a statement of cash flows. You will also begin to appreciate the importance of cash flow information as the basis for projecting future cash flows and making a variety of decisions.

WHY CASH FLOW INFORMATION IS IMPORTANT

LO 1

Explain why cash flow information is important to decision making and describe the information in a statement of cash flows and the methods used to disclose noncash investing and financing activities.

FAST HINT
Important Point to Remember:
Under the accrual basis of accounting, revenues are recognized when earned, not when received, and expenses are recorded when incurred, not when paid. Thus an accrual basis income statement provides little information regarding the company's cash flows or its ability to meet current obligations. *SFAS 95* requires companies to report a statement of cash flows.

Information about cash flows can influence decision makers in many ways. For example, if a company's regular operations bring in more cash than they use, investors will value the company higher than if property and equipment must be sold to finance operations. Information about cash flows can help creditors decide whether a company will have enough cash to pay its existing debts as they mature. And, investors, creditors, managers, and other users of financial statements use cash flow information to evaluate a company's ability to meet unexpected obligations. Cash flow in-

formation is used by decision makers outside as well as inside the firm to evaluate a company's ability to take advantage of new business opportunities that may arise. Managers within a company use cash flow information to plan day-to-day operating activities and make long-term investment decisions.

An example of how careful analysis and management of cash flows can lead to improved financial stability is **R. H. Macy & Company's** dramatic turnaround. The company obtained temporary protection from the bankruptcy court in January 1992 and desperately needed to improve its cash flows. Management did so by engaging in aggressive cost-cutting measures. As a result of this effort, Macy's cash inflow rose to $210 million in its fiscal year ended July 1993 from a negative cash flow of $38.9 million in fiscal 1992. This improvement allowed Macy's to avoid bankruptcy and probably influenced its combination with Federated Department Stores.

The story of **W. T. Grant Co.** is a classic example of why cash flow information should be considered in predicting a firm's future stability and performance. From

1970 to 1973, Grant was reporting net income of more than $40 million per year. At the same time, it was experiencing an alarming decrease in cash provided by operations. Net cash *outflow* exceeded $90 million by 1973.[1] In spite of its earnings performance, Grant went bankrupt within a few years.

The **W. T. Grant** investors who relied solely on earnings per share figures in the early 1970s were unpleasantly surprised. In more recent years, investors generally have learned to evaluate cash flows as well as income statement and balance sheet information as they make their investment decisions.[2]

The importance of cash flow information to decision makers has directly influenced the thinking of accounting authorities. For example, the FASB's objectives of financial reporting clearly reflect the importance of cash flow information. The FASB stated that financial statements should include information about:

- How a business obtains and spends cash.
- Its borrowing and repayment activities.
- The sale and repurchase of its ownership securities.
- Dividend payments and other distributions to its owners.
- Other factors affecting a company's liquidity or solvency.[3]

To accomplish these objectives, a financial statement is needed to summarize, classify, and report the periodic cash inflows and outflows of a business. This information is provided in a statement of cash flows.

In November 1987, the FASB issued *Statement of Financial Accounting Standards No. 95,* "Statement of Cash Flows." This standard requires businesses to include a statement of cash flows in all financial reports that contain both a balance sheet and an income statement. The purpose of this statement is to present information about a company's cash receipts and disbursements during the reporting period.

Illustration 16–1 is a diagram of the information reported in a statement of cash flows. The illustration shows three categories of cash flows: cash flows from operating activities, cash flows from investing activities, and cash flows from financing activities. Both inflows and outflows are included within each category. Because all cash inflows and outflows are reported, the statement reconciles the beginning-of-period and end-of-period balances of cash plus cash equivalents.

Direct Method of Presenting Cash Flows from Operating Activities

When preparing a statement of cash flows, you can calculate the net cash provided (or used) by operating activities two different ways. One is the **direct method of calculating net cash provided (or used) by operating activities.** The other is the indirect method. When using the direct method, you separately list each major class of operating cash receipts (for example, cash received from customers) and each major

FAST HINT
Additional Insight:
Cash flow problems contributed to the farm crisis in the 1980s. When market prices fell, many farmers were forced to liquidate assets to meet payments on outstanding debt. As a result, the market values of farmland and operating assets spiraled downward.

STATEMENT OF CASH FLOWS

FAST HINT
Relevant Quick Study:
To apply these concepts, work QS 16–1.

---

[1]James Largay and Clyde Stickney, "Cash Flow, Ratio Analysis and the W. T. Grant Company Bankruptcy," *Financial Analysts Journal,* July–August 1980, pp. 51–56.

[2]Marc J. Epstein and Moses L. Pava, "How Useful Is the Statement of Cash Flows," *Management Accounting,* July 1992.

[3]FASB, *Statement of Financial Accounting Concepts No. 1,* "Objectives of Financial Reporting by Business Enterprises" (Norwalk, CT, 1978), par. 49.

class of cash payments (such as payments for merchandise). Then, you subtract the payments from the receipts to determine the net cash provided (or used) by operating activities.

Indirect Method of Presenting Cash Flows from Operating Activities

The **indirect method of calculating net cash provided (or used) by operating activities** is not as informative as the direct method. The indirect method is not as informative because it does not disclose the individual categories of cash inflows and outflows from operating activities. Instead, the indirect method discloses only the net cash provided (or used) by operating activities.

When using the indirect method, list net income first. Next, adjust it for items that are necessary to reconcile net income to the net cash provided (or used) by operating activities. For example, in the calculation of net income, we subtract depreciation expense. However, depreciation expense does not involve a current cash payment. Therefore, add depreciation expense back to net income in the process of reconciling net income to the net cash provided (or used) by operating activities.

The direct method is most informative and is the method that the FASB recommends. However, most companies use the indirect method in spite of the FASB's recommendation. By learning the direct method first, you will find the indirect method easier to understand. Also, managers use the direct method to predict future cash requirements and cash availability. Thus, we explain the direct method next.

FAST HINT
Additional Insight:
To gain an overview of the difference between the direct method and indirect method statements, ask students to examine and note the differences between Illustration 16–2 and Illustration 16–10.

The Format of the Statement of Cash Flows (Direct Method)

Illustration 16–2 shows the statement of cash flows for Grover Company. Notice that the major classes of cash inflows and cash outflows are listed separately in the operating activities section of the statement. This is the format of the direct method. The operating cash outflows are subtracted from the operating cash inflows to determine the net cash provided (or used) by operating activities.

Also observe in Illustration 16–2 the other two categories of cash flows reported on the statement of cash flows. In both categories—investing activities and financing activities—we subtract the cash outflows from the cash inflows to determine the net cash provided (or used).

Illustration 16-1 Categories of Information in the Statement of Cash Flows

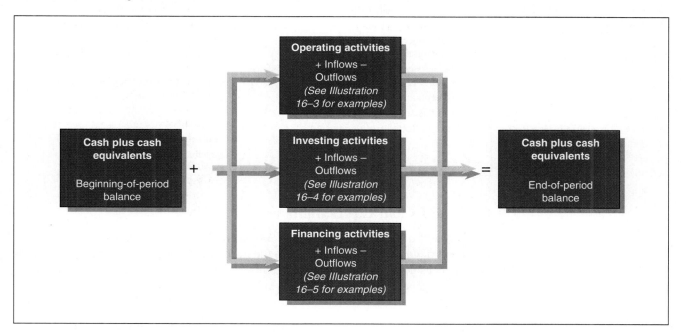

Illustration 16-2
Statement of Cash Flows
(Direct Method)

GROVER COMPANY
Statement of Cash Flows
For Year Ended December 31, 19X2

Cash flows from operating activities:		
Cash received from customers	$570,000	
Cash paid for merchandise	(319,000)	
Cash paid for wages and other operating expenses ..	(218,000)	
Cash paid for interest	(8,000)	
Cash paid for taxes	(5,000)	
Net cash provided by operating activities		$20,000
Cash flows from investing activities:		
Cash received from sale of plant assets	$12,000	
Cash paid for purchase of plant assets	(10,000)	
Net cash provided by investing activities		2,000
Cash flows from financing activities:		
Cash received from issuing stock	$15,000	
Cash paid to retire bonds	(18,000)	
Cash paid for dividends	(14,000)	
Net cash used in financing activities		(17,000)
Net increase in cash		$ 5,000
Cash balance at beginning of 19X2		12,000
Cash balance at end of 19X2		$17,000

Compare the statement in Illustration 16–2 with the chart in Illustration 16–1. Notice that the beginning and ending balances are called *cash plus cash equivalents* in Illustration 16–1. However, in Illustration 16–2, the beginning and ending balances refer only to *cash*. The balances in Illustration 16–2 are called *cash* because Grover Company does not own any cash equivalents.

Illustration 16–3
Cash Flows from Operating
Activities

FAST HINT
Important Point to Remember:
Students may incorrectly classify *cash dividends* and *interest received* as investment inflows and *interest paid* as financing outflows. However, the FASB decided these cash flows should be reported as operating activities.

Cash Inflows	**Cash Outflows**
Cash sales to customers.	Payments to employees for salaries and wages.
Cash collections from credit customers.	Payments to suppliers of goods and services.
Receipts of cash dividends from stock investments in other entities.	Payments to government agencies for taxes, fines, and penalties.
Receipts of interest payments.	Interest payments, net of amounts capitalized.
Refunds from suppliers.	Cash refunds to customers.
Cash collected from a lawsuit.	Contributions to charities.

Cash and Cash Equivalents

In *Statement of Financial Accounting Standards No. 95,* the FASB concluded that a statement of cash flows should explain the difference between the beginning and ending balances of cash and cash equivalents. Prior to this new standard, cash equivalents were generally understood to be short-term, temporary investments of cash. As you learned in Chapter 7, however, a cash equivalent must satisfy these two criteria:

1. The investment must be readily convertible to a known amount of cash.
2. The investment must be sufficiently close to its maturity date so that its market value is relatively insensitive to interest rate changes.

In general, only investments purchased within three months of their maturity dates satisfy these criteria.[4]

The idea of classifying short-term, highly liquid investments as cash equivalents is based on the assumption that companies make these investments to earn a return on idle cash balances. Sometimes, however, items that meet the criteria of cash equivalents are not held as temporary investments of idle cash balances. For example, an investment company that specializes in the purchase and sale of securities may buy cash equivalents as part of its investing strategy. Companies that have such investments are allowed to exclude them from the cash equivalents category. However, the companies must develop a clear policy for determining which items to include and which to exclude. These policies must be disclosed in the footnotes to the financial statements and must be followed consistently from period to period.

CLASSIFYING CASH TRANSACTIONS

On a statement of cash flows, cash and cash equivalents are treated as a single item. In other words, the statement reports the changes in cash plus cash equivalents. Therefore, cash payments to purchase cash equivalents and cash receipts from selling cash equivalents do not appear on the statement. All other cash receipts and payments are classified and reported on the statement as operating, investing, or financing activities. Within each category, individual cash receipts and payments are summarized in a manner that clearly describes the general nature of the company's cash transactions. Then, the summarized cash receipts and payments within each category are netted against each other. A category provides a net cash inflow if the receipts in the category exceed the payments. And, if the payments in a category exceed the receipts, the category is a net cash outflow during the period.

---

[4]FASB, *Accounting Standards—Current Text* (Stamford, CT, 1994), sec. C25.106. First published in *Statement of Financial Accounting Standards No. 95,* par. 8.

Cash Inflows	Cash Outflows
Proceeds from selling productive assets (for example, land, buildings, equipment, natural resources, and intangible assets).	Payments to purchase property, plant, and equipment or other productive assets (excluding merchandise inventory).
Proceeds from selling investments in the equity securities of other companies.	Payments to acquire equity securities of other companies.
Proceeds from selling investments in the debt securities of other entities, except cash equivalents.	Payments to acquire debt securities of other entities, except cash equivalents.
Proceeds from collecting the principal amount of loans.	Payments in the form of loans made to other parties.
Proceeds from the sale (discounting) of loans made by the enterprise.	

Operating Activities

Look at the cash flows classified as **operating activities** in Illustration 16–2. Notice that operating activities generally include transactions that relate to the calculation of net income. However, some income statement items are not related to operating activities. We discuss these items later.

As disclosed in a statement of cash flows, operating activities involve the production or purchase of merchandise and the sale of goods and services to customers. Operating activities also include expenditures that relate to administering the business. In fact, cash flows from operating activities include all cash flows from transactions that are not defined as investing or financing activities. Illustration 16–3 shows typical cash inflows and outflows from operating activities.

Investing Activities

Transactions that involve making and collecting loans or that involve purchasing and selling plant assets, other productive assets, or investments (other than cash equivalents) are called **investing activities.** Usually, investing activities involve the purchase or sale of assets classified on the balance sheet as plant and equipment, intangible assets, or long-term investments. However, the purchase and sale of short-term investments other than cash equivalents are also investing activities. Illustration 16–4 shows examples of cash flows from investing activities.

The fourth type of receipt listed in Illustration 16–4 involves proceeds from collecting the principal amount of loans. Regarding this item, carefully examine any cash receipts that relate to notes receivable. If the notes resulted from sales to customers, classify the cash receipts as operating activities. Use this classification even if the notes are long-term notes. But, if a company loans money to other parties, classify the cash receipts from collecting the principal of the loans as inflows from investing activities. Nevertheless, the FASB concluded that collections of interest are not investing activities. Instead, they are reported as operating activities.

Financing Activities

The **financing activities** of a business include transactions with its owners and transactions with creditors to borrow money or to repay the principal amounts of loans. Financing activities include borrowing and repaying both short-term loans and long-term debt. However, cash payments to settle credit purchases of merchandise, whether

FAST HINT
Critical Thought Question:
Refer to Illustration 16–3. What might be the reason for classifying the cash collected from a lawsuit as a cash inflow from operating activities?

FAST HINT
Critical Thought Question:
Why is cash flow information more useful to investors, creditors, and managers when it is organized in the three categories?

FAST HINT
Relevant Quick Study:
To apply these concepts, work QS 16–2.

FAST HINT
Critical Thought Question:
Interest payments on a loan are classified as cash outflows from operating activities, but payments of loan principal are cash outflows from financing activities. What might be the reason for this distinction?

Illustration 16–5
Cash Flows from Financing
Activities

Cash Inflows	**Cash Outflows**
Proceeds from issuing equity securities (e.g., common and preferred stock).	Payments of dividends and other distributions to owners.
Proceeds from issuing bonds and notes payable.	Payments to purchase treasury stock.
Proceeds from other short- or long-term borrowing transactions.	Repayments of cash loans.
	Payments of the principal amounts involved in long-term credit arrangements.

Illustration 16–6
Decco Company—Footnote
Describing Noncash
Investing and Financing
Activities

The company issued 1,000 shares of common stock for the purchase of land and buildings with fair values of $5,000 and $15,000, respectively.

The company entered into a capital lease obligation of $12,000 for new computer equipment.

The company exchanged old machinery with a fair value of $7,000 and a book value of $8,000 for new machinery valued at $12,000. The balance of $5,000 was paid in cash.

NONCASH INVESTING AND FINANCING ACTIVITIES

FAST HINT
Critical Thought Question:
Does an increase of $100,000 in plant assets, disclosed on comparative balance sheets, tell us that the firm purchased plant assets that cost $100,000? Can we tell from the balance sheet if plant assets were acquired using cash?

FAST HINT
Relevant Exercise and Quick Study:
To apply these concepts, work Exercise 16–2 and QS 16–3.

on account or by note, are operating activities. Payments of interest expense are also operating activities. Illustration 16–5 shows examples of cash flows from financing activities.

Some important investing and financing activities do not involve cash receipts or payments during the current period. For example, a company might purchase land and buildings and finance 100% of the purchase by giving a long-term note payable. Although this transaction clearly involves both investing and financing activities, we do not report it in the current period's statement of cash flows because it does not involve a cash inflow or outflow.

Other investing and financing activities may involve some cash receipt or payment as well as giving or receiving other types of consideration. For example, suppose that you purchase machinery for $12,000 by paying cash of $5,000 and trading in old machinery that has a market value of $7,000. In this case, the statement of cash flows reports only the $5,000 cash outflow for the purchase of machinery. As a result, this $12,000 investing transaction is only partially described in the statement of cash flows.

The noncash portions of investing and financing activities should *not* be reported in the statement of cash flows. However, they are important events that should be disclosed. To accomplish this disclosure, a company may describe its noncash investing and financing activities in a footnote or a separate schedule. Illustration 16–6 shows an example of how a company might disclose its noncash investing and financing activities.

In Illustration 16–6, notice that the last item describes an exchange of machinery including both the cash and noncash aspects of this transaction. The $5,000 cash payment is reported in Decco Company's statement of cash flows as an investing activity. Nevertheless, the description of noncash investing and financing activities includes both the cash and noncash aspects of the transaction.

Examples of transactions that must be disclosed as noncash investing and financing activities include the following:

- The retirement of debt securities by issuing equity securities.
- The conversion of preferred stock to common stock.

- The leasing of assets in a transaction that qualifies as a capital lease.
- The purchase of long-term assets by issuing a note payable to the seller.
- The exchange of a noncash asset for other noncash assets.
- The purchase of noncash assets by issuing equity or debt securities.

FAST HINT
Additional Insight:
A transfer from retained earnings to common stock, including any credit to additional paid-in capital in a stock dividend transaction, is not considered a noncash financing activity because the company receives no consideration for the shares it issues.

Progress Check
(Answers to Progress Checks are provided at the end of the chapter.)

16–1 **Does a statement of cash flows disclose payments of cash to purchase cash equivalents? Does it disclose receipts of cash from the liquidation of cash equivalents?**

16–2 **What are the categories of cash flows reported separately on the statement of cash flows?**

16–3 **Concerning the direct and indirect methods of presenting cash flows from operating activities, which is most informative? Which is used most often in practice?**

16–4 **Identify the category for each of the following cash flow activities:** *(a)* **purchase of equipment for cash;** *(b)* **payment of wages;** *(c)* **sale of common stock;** *(d)* **receipt of cash dividends on stock investment;** *(e)* **collection from customers;** *(f)* **issuance of bonds for cash.**

The information you need to prepare a statement of cash flows comes from a variety of sources. These include comparative balance sheets at the beginning and the end of the accounting period, an income statement for the period, and a careful analysis of each noncash balance sheet account in the general ledger. However, because cash inflows and cash outflows are to be reported, you might wonder why we do not focus our attention on the Cash account. For the moment, we should at least consider this approach.

PREPARING A STATEMENT OF CASH FLOWS

LO 2
Calculate cash inflows and outflows by inspecting the noncash account balances and prepare a statement of cash flows using the direct method.

Analyzing the Cash Account

All of a company's cash receipts and cash payments are recorded in the Cash account in the General Ledger. Therefore, the Cash account would seem to be the logical place to look for information about cash flows from operating, investing, and financing activities. To demonstrate, review this summarized Cash account of Grover Company:

Summarized Cash Account

Balance, 12/31/X1	12,000		
Receipts from customers	570,000	Payments for merchandise	319,000
Proceeds from sale of plant		Payments for wages and other	
assets	12,000	operating expenses	218,000
Proceeds from stock issuance	15,000	Interest payments	8,000
		Tax payments	5,000
		Payments for purchase of	
		plant assets	10,000
		Payments to retire bonds	18,000
		Dividend payments	14,000
Balance, 12/31/X2	17,000		

In this account, the individual cash transactions are already summarized in terms of major types of receipts and payments. For example, the account has only one debit entry for the total receipts from all customers. All that remains is to determine whether each type of cash inflow or outflow is an operating, investing, or financing activity and then place it in its proper category on the statement of cash flows. The completed statement of cash flows appears in Illustration 16–2 on page 611.

Illustration 16-7   Why an Analysis of the Noncash Accounts Explains the Change in Cash

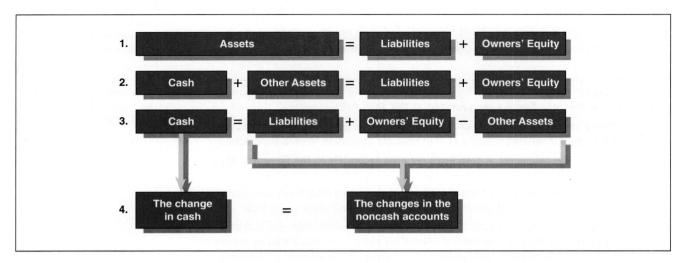

While an analysis of the Cash account may appear to be an easy way to prepare a statement of cash flows, it has two serious drawbacks. First, most companies have so many individual cash receipts and disbursements that it is not practical to review them all. Imagine what a problem this analysis would present for IBM, General Motors, Kodak, or Exxon, or even for a relatively small business. Second, the Cash account usually does not contain a description of each cash transaction. Therefore, even though the Cash account shows the amount of each debit and credit, you generally cannot determine the type of transaction by looking at the Cash account. Thus, the Cash account does not readily provide the information you need to prepare a statement of cash flows. To obtain the necessary information, you must analyze the changes in the noncash accounts.

Analyzing Noncash Accounts to Determine Cash Flows

When a company records cash inflows and outflows with debits and credits to the Cash account, it also records credits and debits in other accounts. Some of these accounts are balance sheet accounts. Others are revenue and expense accounts that are closed to Retained Earnings, a balance sheet account. As a result, all cash transactions eventually affect noncash balance sheet accounts. Therefore, we can determine the nature of the cash inflows and outflows by examining the changes in the noncash balance sheet accounts. Illustration 16–7 shows this important relationship between the Cash account and the noncash balance sheet accounts.

In Illustration 16–7, notice that the balance sheet equation labeled (1) is expanded in (2) so that cash is separated from the other assets. Then, the equation is rearranged in (3) so that cash is set equal to the sum of the liability and equity accounts less the noncash asset accounts. The illustration then points out in (4) that changes in one side of the equation (cash) must be equal to the changes in the other side (noncash accounts). Part (4) shows that you can fully explain the changes in cash by analyzing the changes in liabilities, owners' equity, and noncash assets.

This overall process has another advantage. The examination of each noncash account also identifies any noncash investing and financing activities that occurred during the period. As you learned earlier, these noncash items must be disclosed, but not on the statement of cash flows.

Illustration 16–8   Analysis of the Noncash Accounts Explains the Change in Cash

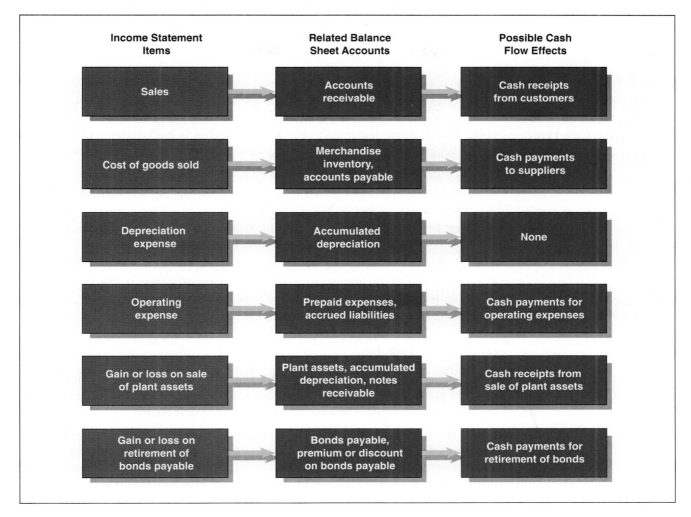

When beginning to analyze the changes in the noncash balance sheet accounts, recall that Retained Earnings is affected by revenues, expenses, and dividend declarations. Therefore, look at the income statement accounts to help explain the change in Retained Earnings. In fact, the income statement accounts provide important information that relates to the changes in several balance sheet accounts.

Illustration 16–8 summarizes some of these relationships between income statement accounts, balance sheet accounts, and possible cash flows. For example, to determine the cash receipts from customers during a period, adjust the amount of sales revenue for the increase or decrease in Accounts Receivable.[5] If the Accounts Receivable balance did not change, the cash collected from customers is equal to sales revenue. On the other hand, if the Accounts Receivable balance decreased, cash collections must have been equal to sales revenue *plus* the reduction in Accounts Receivable. And, if the Accounts Receivable balance increased, the cash collected from customers must have been equal to Sales *less* the increase in Accounts Receivable.

---

[5]This introductory explanation assumes that there is no bad debts expense. However, if bad debts occur and are written off directly to Accounts Receivable, the change in the Accounts Receivable balance will be due in part to the write-off. The remaining change results from credit sales and from cash receipts. This chapter does not discuss the allowance method of accounting for bad debts since it would make the analysis unnecessarily complex at this time.

By analyzing all noncash balance sheet accounts and related income statement accounts in this fashion, you can obtain the necessary information for a statement of cash flows. Next, we illustrate this process by examining the noncash accounts of Grover Company.

Grover Company's December 31, 19X1, and 19X2 balance sheets and its 19X2 income statement are presented in Illustration 16–9. Our objective is to prepare a statement of cash flows that explains the $5,000 increase in cash, based on these financial statements and this additional information about the 19X2 transactions:

a. All accounts payable balances resulted from merchandise purchases.

b. Plant assets that cost $70,000 were purchased by paying $10,000 cash and issuing $60,000 of bonds payable to the seller.

c. Plant assets with an original cost of $30,000 and accumulated depreciation of $12,000 were sold for $12,000 cash. The result was a $6,000 loss.

d. The proceeds from issuing 3,000 shares of common stock were $15,000.

e. The $16,000 gain on the retirement of bonds resulted from paying $18,000 to retire bonds that had a book value of $34,000.

f. Cash dividends of $14,000 were declared and paid.

FAST HINT
Important Point to Remember:
Refer students to Illustration 16–9 and identify Grover's $5,000 change in cash. Point out that this is what we want to explain. In preparing a statement of cash flows, the $5,000 serves as a check figure.

Operating Activities

We begin the analysis by calculating the cash flows from operating activities. In general, this process involves adjusting the income statement items that relate to operating activities for changes in their related balance sheet accounts.

Cash Received from Customers The calculation of cash receipts from customers begins with sales revenue. If all sales are for cash, the amount of cash received from customers is equal to sales. However, when sales are on account, you must adjust the amount of sales revenue for the change in Accounts Receivable.

In Illustration 16–9, look at the Accounts Receivable balances on December 31, 19X1, and 19X2. The beginning balance was $40,000, and the ending balance was $60,000. The income statement shows that sales revenue was $590,000. With this information, you can reconstruct the Accounts Receivable account and determine the amount of cash received from customers, as follows:

Accounts Receivable

Balance, 12/31/X1	40,000		
Sales, 19X2	590,000	Collections =	570,000
Balance, 12/31/X	260,000		

FAST HINT
Alternative Example:
If the ending balance of accounts receivable had been only $20,000, what amount would be reported as cash received from customers?
Answer: $610,000

This account shows that the balance of Accounts Receivable increased from $40,000 to $60,000. It also shows that cash receipts from customers are $570,000, which is equal to sales of $590,000 plus the $40,000 beginning balance less the $60,000 ending balance. This calculation can be restated in more general terms like this:

Cash received from customers = Sales − Increase in accounts receivable

And, if the balance of Accounts Receivable decreases, the calculation is:

Cash received from customers = Sales + Decrease in accounts receivable

FAST HINT
Relevant Exercise and
Quick Study:
To apply these concepts, work Exercise 16–3 and QS 16–4.

Now turn back to Illustration 16–2 on page 611. Note that the $570,000 of cash Grover Company received from customers appears on the statement of cash flows as a cash inflow from operating activities.

Illustration 16-9
Financial Statements

GROVER COMPANY
Balance Sheet
December 31, 19X2 and 19X1

		19X2		19X1
Assets				
Current assets:				
Cash		$ 17,000		$ 12,000
Accounts receivable		60,000		40,000
Merchandise inventory		84,000		70,000
Prepaid expenses		6,000		4,000
Total current assets		$167,000		$126,000
Long-term assets:				
Plant assets	$250,000		$210,000	
Less accumulated depreciation	60,000	190,000	48,000	162,000
Total assets		$357,000		$288,000
Liabilities				
Current liabilities:				
Accounts payable		$ 35,000		$ 40,000
Interest payable		3,000		4,000
Income taxes payable		22,000		12,000
Total current liabilities		$ 60,000		$ 56,000
Long-term liabilities:				
Bonds payable		90,000		64,000
Total liabilities		$150,000		$120,000
Stockholders' Equity				
Contributed capital:				
Common stock, $5 par value	$ 95,000		$ 80,000	
Retained earnings	112,000		88,000	
Total stockholders' equity		207,000		168,000
Total liabilities and				
stockholders' equity		$357,000		$288,000

GROVER COMPANY
Income Statement
For Year Ended December 31, 19X2

Sales		$590,000
Cost of goods sold	$300,000	
Wages and other operating expenses ..	216,000	
Interest expense	7,000	
Income taxes expense	15,000	
Depreciation expense	24,000	(562,000)
Loss on sale of plant assets		(6,000)
Gain on retirement of debt		16,000
Net income		$ 38,000

Cash Payments for Merchandise. The calculation of cash payments for merchandise begins with cost of goods sold and merchandise inventory. For a moment, suppose that all merchandise purchases are for cash and that the ending balance of Merchandise Inventory is unchanged from the beginning balance. In this case, the total cash paid for merchandise equals the cost of goods sold. However, this case is not typical. Usually, you expect some change in a company's Merchandise Inventory balance during a period. Also, purchases of merchandise usually are made on account, causing some change in the Accounts Payable balance.

FAST HINT
Critical Thought Question:
Does an increase in accounts payable generally represent an inflow or an outflow of cash? Explain.

When the balances of Merchandise Inventory and Accounts Payable change, you must adjust cost of goods sold for the changes in these accounts to determine the cash payments for merchandise. This adjustment has two steps. First, combine the change in the balance of Merchandise Inventory with cost of goods sold to determine the cost of purchases during the period.[6] Second, combine the change in the balance of Accounts Payable with the cost of purchases to determine the total cash payments to suppliers of merchandise.

Consider again the Grover Company example. Begin by combining the reported amount of cost of goods sold ($300,000) with the Merchandise Inventory beginning balance ($70,000) and with the ending balance ($84,000) to determine the amount that was purchased during the period. To accomplish this, reconstruct the Merchandise Inventory account as follows:

Merchandise Inventory

Balance, 12/31/X1	70,000		
Purchases =	**314,000**	Cost of goods sold	300,000
Balance, 12/31/X2	84,000		

This account shows that we add the $14,000 increase in merchandise inventory to cost of goods sold of $300,000 to get purchases of $314,000.

To determine the cash paid for merchandise, you adjust purchases for the change in accounts payable. This can be done by reconstructing the Accounts Payable account as follows:

Accounts Payable

		Balance, 12/31/X1	40,000
Payments =	**319,000**	Purchases	314,000
		Balance, 12/31/X2	35,000

In this account, purchases of $314,000 plus a beginning balance of $40,000 less the ending balance of $35,000 equals cash payments of $319,000. In other words, purchases of $314,000 plus the $5,000 decrease in accounts payable equals cash payments of $319,000.

FAST HINT
Alternative Example:
If the ending balances of inventory and accounts payable had been $60,000 and $50,000 respectively, what amount of cash would have been paid for merchandise during the year?
Answer: $280,000

To summarize the adjustments to cost of goods sold that are necessary to calculate cash payments for merchandise:

$$\text{Purchases} = \text{Cost of goods sold} \begin{bmatrix} + \text{ Increase in merchandise inventory} \\ or \\ - \text{ Decrease in merchandise inventory} \end{bmatrix}$$

And,

$$\text{Cash payments for merchandise} = \text{Purchases} \begin{bmatrix} + \text{ Decrease in accounts payable} \\ or \\ - \text{ Increase in accounts payable} \end{bmatrix}$$

Now, look at Illustration 16–2 on page 611. Notice that Grover Company's payments of $319,000 for merchandise are reported on the statement of cash flows as a cash outflow for operating activities.

Cash Payments for Wages and Other Operating Expenses. Grover Company's income statement shows wages and other operating expenses of $216,000 (see Illustration 16–9 on page 619). To determine the amount of cash paid during the period for wages and other operating expenses, we need to combine this amount with the changes in any related balance sheet accounts. In Grover Company's beginning and ending balance sheets in Illustration 16–9, you must look for prepaid expenses and any accrued liabilities that relate to wages and other operating expenses. In this example, the balance sheets show that Grover Company has prepaid expenses but does

---

[6]The amount of purchases is also in the Purchases account in the General Ledger.

not have any accrued liabilities. Thus, the adjustment to the expense item is limited to the change in prepaid expenses. The amount of the adjustment can be determined by assuming that all cash payments of wages and other operating expenses were originally debited to Prepaid Expenses. With this assumption, we can reconstruct the Prepaid Expenses account as follows:

Prepaid Expenses				
Balance, 12/31/X1	4,000			
Payments =	218,000	Wages and other operating expenses	216,000	
Balance, 12/31/X2	6,000			

FAST HINT
Important Point to Remember:
An increase in prepaid expenses indicates that the cash purchase of additional prepaid expenses exceeded the amount that expired and was charged against income during the year. Adjusting entries for prepaid expenses were presented in Chapter 3.

This account shows that prepaid expenses increased by $2,000 during the period. Therefore, the cash payments for wages and other operating expenses were $2,000 greater than the reported expense. Thus, the amount paid for wages and other operating expenses is $216,000 plus $2,000, or $218,000.

In reconstructing the Prepaid Expenses account, we assumed that all cash payments for wages and operating expenses were debited to Prepaid Expenses. However, this assumption does not have to be true for the analysis to work. If cash payments were debited directly to the expense account, the total amount of cash payments would be the same. In other words, the cash paid for operating expenses still equals the $216,000 expense plus the $2,000 increase in prepaid expenses.

On the other hand, if Grover Company's balance sheets had shown accrued liabilities, we would have to adjust the expense for the change in those accrued liabilities. In general terms, the calculation is as follows:

FAST HINT
Relevant Exercises and Quick Study:
To apply these concepts, work Exercises 16–3 and 16–4 and QS 16–6.

$$
\begin{array}{l}
\text{Cash paid for} \\
\text{wages and other} \\
\text{operating} \\
\text{expenses}
\end{array}
=
\begin{array}{l}
\text{Wages and} \\
\text{other} \\
\text{operating} \\
\text{expenses}
\end{array}
\left[
\begin{array}{c}
\textbf{+ Increase in prepaid} \\
\textbf{expenses} \\
\textit{or} \\
\textbf{− Decrease in prepaid} \\
\textbf{expenses}
\end{array}
\right]
\left[
\begin{array}{c}
\textbf{+ Decrease in accrued} \\
\textbf{liabilities} \\
\textit{or} \\
\textbf{− Increase in accrued} \\
\textbf{liabilities}
\end{array}
\right]
$$

Payments for Interest and Taxes. Grover Company's remaining operating cash flows involve cash payments for interest and for taxes. The analysis of these items is similar because both require adjustments for changes in related liability accounts. Grover Company's income statement shows interest expense of $7,000 and income taxes expense of $15,000. To calculate the related cash payments, adjust interest expense for the change in interest payable and adjust income taxes expense for the change in income taxes payable. These calculations are accomplished by reconstructing the liability accounts as follows:

FAST HINT
Relevant Exercise:
To apply these concepts, work Exercise 16–4.

Interest Payable					Income Taxes Payable		
		Balance, 12/31/X1	4,000			Balance, 12/31/X1	12,000
Interest paid =	8,000	Interest expense	7,000	Income taxes paid =	5,000	Income taxes expense	15,000
		Balance, 12/31/X2	3,000			Balance, 12/31/X2	22,000

These reconstructed accounts show that interest payments were $8,000 and income tax payments were $5,000. The general form of each calculation is:

FAST HINT
Alternative Example:
What journal entries would have been made to record the change in the balance of interest payable?
Answer:
Interest Expense   7,000
    Interest Payable   7,000
Interest Payable   8,000
    Cash   8,000

$$
\textbf{Cash payment} = \textbf{Expense}
\left[
\begin{array}{c}
\textbf{+ Decrease in related payable} \\
\textit{or} \\
\textbf{− Increase in related payable}
\end{array}
\right]
$$

Both of these cash payments appear as operating items on Grover Company's statement of cash flows in Illustration 16–2 on page 611.

Investing Activities

Investing activities usually involve transactions that affect long-term assets. Recall from the information provided about Grover Company's transactions that the company purchased and also sold plant assets. Both of these transactions are investing activities.

Purchase of Plant Assets. Grover Company purchased plant assets that cost $70,000 by issuing $60,000 of bonds payable to the seller and paying the $10,000 balance in cash. The $10,000 payment is reported as a cash outflow on the statement of cash flows (see Illustration 16–2). Also, because $60,000 of the purchase was financed by issuing bonds payable, this transaction involves noncash investing and financing activities. It might be described in a footnote as follows:

Noncash investing and financing activities:	
Purchased plant assets	$70,000
Issued bonds payable to finance purchase . .	60,000
Balance paid in cash	$10,000

FAST HINT
Alternative Example:
Assume a plant asset with a $40,000 cost and $37,000 accumulated depreciation was sold at a $1,000 loss. What is the cash flow? Assume that same asset was sold at a gain of $3,000. What is the cash flow?
Answers: + $2,000; + $6,000

Sale of Plant Assets. Grover Company sold plant assets that cost $30,000 when they had accumulated depreciation of $12,000. The result of the sale was a loss of $6,000 and a cash receipt of $12,000. This cash receipt is reported in the statement of cash flows as a cash inflow from investing activities (see Illustration 16–2).

Recall from Grover Company's income statement that depreciation expense was $24,000. Depreciation does not use or provide cash. Note, however, the effects of depreciation expense, the plant asset purchase, and the plant asset sale on the Plant Assets and Accumulated Depreciation accounts. These accounts are reconstructed as follows:

Plant Assets					Accumulated Depreciation, Plant Assets		
Balance, 12/31/X1	210,000					Balance, 12/31/X1	48,000
Purchase	70,000	Sale	30,000	Sale	12,000	Depreciation expense	24,000
Balance, 12/31/X2	250,000					Balance, 12/31/X2	60,000

FAST HINT
Relevant Exercise and Quick Study:
To apply these concepts, work Exercise 16–5 and QS 16–7.

The beginning and ending balances of these accounts were taken from Grover Company's balance sheets (Illustration 16–9). Reconstructing the accounts shows that the beginning and ending balances of both accounts are completely reconciled by the purchase, the sale, and the depreciation expense. Therefore, we did not omit any of the investing activities that relate to plant assets.

FAST HINT
Critical Thought Question:
Would it be possible for a real estate investment to generate a net loss yet create a positive cash flow? Explain.

Financing Activities

Financing activities usually relate to a company's long-term debt and stockholders' equity accounts. In the information about Grover Company, four transactions involved financing activities. We already discussed one of these, the $60,000 issuance of bonds payable to purchase plant assets, as a noncash investing and financing activity. The remaining three transactions were the retirement of bonds, the issuance of common stock, and the payment of cash dividends.

Payment to Retire Bonds Payable. Grover Company's December 31, 19X1, balance sheet showed total bonds payable of $64,000. Included within this beginning balance for 19X2 were bonds with a carrying value of $34,000 that were retired for an $18,000 cash payment during the year. The income statement reports the $16,000 difference as a gain. The statement of cash flows shows the $18,000 payment as a cash outflow for financing activities (see Illustration 16–2 on page 611).

Notice that the beginning and ending balances of Bonds Payable are reconciled by the $60,000 issuance of new bonds and the retirement of $34,000 of old bonds. The following reconstructed Bonds Payable account shows the results of these activities:

		Bonds Payable	
		Balance, 12/31/X1	64,000
Retired bonds	34,000	Issued bonds	60,000
		Balance, 12/31/X2	90,000

Receipt from Common Stock Issuance.

During 19X2, Grover Company issued 3,000 shares of common stock at par for $5 per share. This $15,000 cash receipt is reported on the statement of cash flows as a financing activity. Look at the December 31, 19X1, and 19X2 balance sheets in Illustration 16–9. Notice that the Common Stock account balance increased from $80,000 at the end of 19X1 to $95,000 at the end of 19X2. Thus, the $15,000 stock issue explains the change in the Common Stock account.

Payment of Cash Dividends.

According to the facts provided about Grover Company's transactions, it paid cash dividends of $14,000 during 19X2. This payment is reported as a cash outflow for financing activities. Also, note that the effects of this $14,000 payment and the reported net income of $38,000 fully reconcile the beginning and ending balances of Retained Earnings. This is shown in the reconstructed Retained Earnings account that follows:

		Retained Earnings	
		Balance, 12/31/X1	88,000
Cash dividend	14,000	Net income	38,000
		Balance, 12/31/X2	112,000

We have described all of Grover Company's cash inflows and outflows and one noncash investing and financing transaction. In the process of making these analyses, we reconciled the changes in all of the noncash balance sheet accounts. The change in the Cash account is reconciled by the statement of cash flows, as seen in Illustration 16–2 on page 611.

FAST HINT
Critical Thought Question:
Which of the following events affects cash flow?
a. Declaration of a cash dividend.
b. Payment of a cash dividend.
c. Declaration of a stock dividend.
d. Payment of a stock dividend.
e. A stock split.

FAST HINT
Relevant Quick Study:
To apply these concepts, work QS 16–9.

Progress Check

16–5 Net sales during a period were $590,000, beginning accounts receivable were $120,000, and ending accounts receivable were $90,000. What amount was collected from customers during the period?

16–6 Merchandise Inventory account balance decreased during a period from a beginning balance of $32,000 to an ending balance of $28,000. Cost of goods sold for the period was $168,000. If the Accounts Payable balance increased $2,400 during the period, what was the amount of cash paid for merchandise?

16–7 Hargrave Inc. reports wages and other operating expenses incurred totaled $112,000. At the end of last year prepaid expenses totaled $1,200 and this year the balance was $4,200. The current balance sheet does show wages payable of $5,600 whereas last year's did not show any accrued liabilities. How much was paid for wages and other operating expenses this year?

16–8 Equipment that cost $80,000 and had accumulated depreciation of $30,000 was sold at a loss of $10,000. What was the cash receipt from the sale? In what category of the statement of cash flows should it be reported?

Illustration 16–10
Statement of Cash Flows
(Indirect Method)

GROVER COMPANY
Statement of Cash Flows
For Year Ended December 31, 19X2

Cash flows from operating activities:			
Net income		$ 38,000	
Adjustments to reconcile net income to net			
cash provided by operating activities:			
(1)	Increase in accounts receivable	(20,000)	
	Increase in merchandise inventory . . .	(14,000)	
	Increase in prepaid expenses	(2,000)	
	Decrease in accounts payable	(5,000)	
	Decrease in interest payable	(1,000)	
	Increase in income taxes payable	10,000	
(2)	Depreciation expense	24,000	
(3)	Loss on sale of plant assets	6,000	
	Gain on retirement of bonds	(16,000)	
Net cash provided by operating activities			$ 20,000
Cash flows from investing activities:			
Cash received from sale of plant assets . . .		$ 12,000	
Cash paid for purchase of plant assets		(10,000)	
Net cash provided by investing activities . .			2,000
Cash flows from financing activities:			
Cash received from issuing stock		$ 15,000	
Cash paid to retire bonds		(18,000)	
Cash paid for dividends		(14,000)	
Net cash used in financing activities			(17,000)
Net increase in cash			$ 5,000
Cash balance at beginning of 19X2			12,000
Cash balance at end of 19X2			$ 17,000

RECONCILING NET INCOME TO NET CASH PROVIDED (OR USED) BY OPERATING ACTIVITIES

As you learned earlier, the FASB recommends that the operating activities section of the statement of cash flows be prepared according to the direct method. Under this method, the statement reports each major class of cash inflows and outflows from operating activities. *However, when the direct method is used, the FASB also requires that companies disclose a reconciliation of net income to the net cash provided (or used) by operating activities.* This reconciliation is precisely what is accomplished by the *indirect* method of calculating the net cash provided (or used) by operating activities. We explain the indirect method next.

THE INDIRECT METHOD OF CALCULATING NET CASH PROVIDED (OR USED) BY OPERATING ACTIVITIES

LO 3

Calculate the net cash provided or used by operating activities according to the indirect method and prepare the statement of cash flows.

When using the indirect method, list net income first. Then, adjust net income to reconcile its amount to the net amount of cash provided (or used) by operating activities. To see the results of the indirect method, look at Illustration 16–10. This illustration shows Grover Company's statement of cash flows with the reconciliation of net income to the net cash provided by operating activities.

In Illustration 16–10, notice that the net cash provided by operating activities is $20,000. This is the same amount that was reported on the statement of cash flows (direct method) in Illustration 16–2 on page 611. However, these illustrations show entirely different ways of calculating the $20,000 net cash inflow. Under the direct method in Illustration 16–2, we subtracted major classes of operating cash outflows from major classes of cash inflows. By comparison, we include none of the individual cash inflows or cash outflows under the indirect method used in Illustration 16–10. Instead, we modify net income to exclude those amounts included in the determination of net income but not involved in operating cash inflows or outflows during the period. Net income also is modified to include operating cash inflows and outflows not recorded as revenues and expenses.

Illustration 16–10 shows three types of adjustments to net income. The adjustments grouped under section (1) are for changes in noncash current assets and current liabilities that relate to operating activities. Adjustment (2) is for an income statement item that relates to operating activities but that did not involve a cash inflow or outflow during the period. The adjustments grouped under (3) eliminate gains and losses that resulted from investing and financing activities. These gains and losses do not relate to operating activities.

To help you understand why adjustments for changes in noncash current assets and current liabilities are part of the reconciliation process, we use the transactions of a very simple company as an example. Assume that Simple Company's income statement shows only two items, as follows:

ADJUSTMENTS FOR CHANGES IN CURRENT ASSETS AND CURRENT LIABILITIES

Sales	$20,000
Operating expenses	(12,000)
Net income	$ 8,000

For a moment, assume that all of Simple Company's sales and operating expenses are for cash. The company has no current assets other than cash and has no current liabilities. Given these assumptions, the net cash provided by operating activities during the period is $8,000, which is the cash received from customers less the cash paid for operating expenses.

Adjustments for Changes in Noncash Current Assets

Now assume that Simple Company's sales are on account. Also assume that its Accounts Receivable balance was $2,000 at the beginning of the year and $2,500 at the end of the year. Under these assumptions, cash receipts from customers equal sales of $20,000 minus the $500 increase in Accounts Receivable, or $19,500. Therefore, using the *direct* method, the net cash provided by operating activities is $7,500 ($19,500 − $12,000).

When the *indirect* method is used to calculate the net cash flow, net income of $8,000 is adjusted for the $500 increase in Accounts Receivable to get $7,500 as the net amount of cash provided by operating activities. Both calculations are as follows:

FAST HINT
Critical Thought Question:
Looking at Illustration 16–10 and Illustration 16–2, explain how the two different approaches can result in the same amount of cash flows from operating activities. Which method do you prefer?

Direct Method:	
Receipts from customers ($20,000 − $500)	$19,500
Payments for operating expenses	(12,000)
Cash provided (or used) by operating activities . .	$ 7,500
Indirect Method:	
Net income	$8,000
Less the increase in accounts receivable	(500)
Cash provided (or used) by operating activities . .	$7,500

Notice that the direct method calculation subtracts the increase in Accounts Receivable from Sales, while the indirect method calculation subtracts the increase in Accounts Receivable from net income.

As another example, assume instead that the Accounts Receivable balance decreased from $2,000 to $1,200. Under this assumption, cash receipts from customers equal sales of $20,000 plus the $800 decrease in Accounts Receivable, or $20,800. By the direct method, the net cash provided by operating activities is $8,800 ($20,800 − $12,000). And, when the indirect method is used, the $800 decrease in Accounts Receivable is *added* to the $8,000 net income to get $8,800 net cash provided by operating activities.

When the indirect method is used, adjustments like those for Accounts Receivable are required for all noncash current assets related to operating activities. When a noncash current asset increases, part of the assets derived from operating activities goes into the increase. This leaves a smaller amount as the net cash inflow. Therefore, when you calculate the net cash inflow using the indirect method, subtract the noncash current asset increase from net income. But, when a noncash current asset decreases, additional cash is produced, and you should add this amount to net income. These modifications of income for changes in current assets related to operating activities are as follows:

Net income
Add: Decreases in current assets
Subtract: Increases in current assets
Net cash provided (or used) by operating activities

Adjustments for Changes in Current Liabilities

To illustrate the adjustments for changes in current liabilities, return to the original assumptions about Simple Company. Sales of $20,000 are for cash, and operating expenses are $12,000. However, assume now that Simple Company has Interest Payable as its only current liability. Also assume that the beginning-of-year balance in Interest Payable was $500 and the end-of-year balance was $900. This increase means that the operating expenses of $12,000 were $400 larger than the amount paid in cash during the period. Therefore, the cash payments for operating expenses were only $11,600, or ($12,000 − $400). Under these assumptions, the direct method calculation of net cash provided by operating activities is $8,400, or $20,000 receipts from customers less $11,600 payments for expenses. The indirect method calculation of $8,400 is net income of $8,000 plus the $400 increase in Interest Payable.

Alternatively, if the Interest Payable balance decreased, for example by $300, the cash outflow for operating expenses would have been the $12,000 expense plus the $300 liability decrease, or $12,300. Then, the direct calculation of net cash flow is $20,000 − $12,300 = $7,700. The indirect calculation is $8,000 − $300 = $7,700. In other words, when using the indirect method, subtract a *decrease* in Interest Payable from net income.

Using the indirect method requires adjustments like those for Interest Payable for all current liabilities related to operating activities. When a current liability decreases, part of the cash derived from operating activities pays for the decrease. Therefore, subtract the decrease from net income to determine the remaining net cash inflow. And, when a current liability increases, it finances some operating expenses. In other words, cash was not used to pay for the expense and the liability increase must be *added* to net income when you calculate cash provided by operating activities. These adjustments for changes in current liabilities related to operating activities are:

Net income
Add: Increases in current liabilities
Subtract: Decreases in current liabilities
Net cash provided (or used) by operating activities

One way to remember how to make these modifications to net income is to observe that a *debit* change in a noncash current asset or a current liability is *subtracted* from net income. And, a *credit* change in a noncash current asset or a current liability is *added* to net income.

Adjustments for Operating Items that Do Not Provide or Use Cash

Some operating items that appear on an income statement do not provide or use cash during the current period. One example is depreciation. Other examples are amortization of intangible assets, depletion of natural resources, and bad debts expense.

Record these expenses with debits to expense accounts and credits to noncash accounts. They reduce net income but do not require cash outflows during the period. Therefore, when adjustments to net income are made under the indirect method, add these noncash expenses back to net income.

In addition to noncash expenses such as depreciation, net income may include some revenues that do not provide cash inflows during the current period. An example is equity method earnings from a stock investment in another entity (see Chapter 11). If net income includes revenues that do not provide cash inflows, subtract the revenues from net income in the process of reconciling net income to the net cash provided by operating activities.

The indirect method adjustments for expenses and revenues that do not provide or use cash during the current period are as follows:

> Net income
> Add: Expenses that do not use cash
> Subtract: Revenues that do not provide cash
> Net cash provided (or used) by operating activities

FAST HINT
Critical Thought Question:
Can you think of other examples of operating items that do not provide or use cash?

FAST HINT
Relevant Exercise:
To apply these concepts, work Exercises 16–6 and 16–7.

Adjustments for Nonoperating Items

Some income statement items are not related to the operating activities of the company. These gains and losses result from investing and financing activities. Examples are gains or losses on the sale of plant assets and gains or losses on the retirement of bonds payable.

Remember that the indirect method reconciles net income to the net cash provided (or used) by operating activities. Therefore, net income must be modified to exclude gains and losses created by investing and financing activities. In making the modifications under the indirect method, subtract gains from financing and investing activities from net income and add losses back to net income:

> Net income
> Add: Losses from investing or financing activities
> Subtract: Gains from investing or financing activities
> Net cash provided (or used) by operating activities

FAST HINT
Relevant Exercise:
To apply these concepts, work Exercise 16–8.

Progress Check

16–9   Determine the net cash provided (or used) by operating activities based on the fol-
        lowing data:

Net income	$74,900
Decrease in accounts receivable	4,600
Increase in inventory	11,700
Decrease in accounts payable	1,000
Loss on sale of equipment	3,400
Payment of dividends	21,500

16–10   Why are expenses such as depreciation and amortization of goodwill added to net
        income when cash flow from operating activities is calculated by the indirect
        method?

16–11   A company reports a net income of $15,000 that includes a $3,000 gain on the sale
        of plant assets. Why is this gain subtracted from net income in calculating cash
        flow from operating activities according to the indirect method?

APPLYING THE INDIRECT METHOD TO GROVER COMPANY

LO 4

Prepare a working paper for a statement of cash flows so that the net cash flow from operating activities is calculated by the indirect method.

Determining the net cash flows provided (or used) by operating activities according to the indirect method requires balance sheets at the beginning and end of the period, the current period's income statement, and other information about selected transactions. Illustration 16–9 on page 619 shows the income statement and balance sheet information for Grover Company. Based on this information, Illustration 16–10 presents the indirect method of reconciling net income to net cash provided by operating activities.

Preparing the Indirect Method Working Paper

When a company has a large number of accounts and many operating, investing, and financing transactions, the analysis of noncash accounts can be difficult and confusing. In these situations, a working paper can help organize the information you need to prepare a statement of cash flows. A working paper also makes it easier to check the accuracy of your work.

In addition to Grover Company's comparative balance sheets and income statement presented in Illustration 16–9, the information needed to prepare the working paper follows. The letters identifying each item of information also cross-reference related debits and credits in the working paper.

a. Net income was $38,000.

b. Accounts receivable increased by $20,000.

c. Merchandise inventory increased by $14,000.

d. Prepaid expenses increased by $2,000.

e. Accounts payable decreased by $5,000.

f. Interest payable decreased by $1,000.

g. Income taxes payable increased by $10,000.

h. Depreciation expense was $24,000.

i. Loss on sale of plant assets was $6,000; assets that cost $30,000 with accumulated depreciation of $12,000 were sold for $12,000 cash.

j. Gain on retirement of bonds was $16,000; bonds with a book value of $34,000 were retired with a cash payment of $18,000.

k. Plant assets that cost $70,000 were purchased; the payment consisted of $10,000 cash and issuing $60,000 of bonds payable.

Illustration 16–11

GROVER COMPANY
Working Paper for Statement of Cash Flows (Indirect Method)
For Year Ended December 31, 19X2

	December 31, 19X1	Analysis of Changes Debit	Analysis of Changes Credit	December 31, 19X2
Balance sheet—debits:				
Cash	12,000			17,000
Accounts receivable	40,000	(b) 20,000		60,000
Merchandise inventory	70,000	(c) 14,000		84,000
Prepaid expenses	4,000	(d) 2,000		6,000
Plant assets	210,000	(k1) 70,000	(i) 30,000	250,000
	336,000			417,000
Balance sheet—credits:				
Accumulated depreciation	48,000	(i) 12,000	(h) 24,000	60,000
Accounts payable	40,000	(e) 5,000		35,000
Interest payable	4,000	(f) 1,000		3,000
Income taxes payable	12,000		(g) 10,000	22,000
Bonds payable	64,000	(j) 34,000	(k2) 60,000	90,000
Common stock, $5 par value	80,000		(l) 15,000	95,000
Retained earnings	88,000	(m) 14,000	(a) 38,000	112,000
	336,000			417,000
Statement of cash flows:				
Operating activities:				
Net income		(a) 38,000		
Increase in accounts receivable ...			(b) 20,000	
Increase in merchandise inventory .			(c) 14,000	
Increase in prepaid expenses			(d) 2,000	
Decrease in accounts payable			(e) 5,000	
Decrease in interest payable			(f) 1,000	
Increase in income taxes payable ..		(g) 10,000		
Depreciation expense		(h) 24,000		
Loss on sale of plant assets		(i) 6,000		
Gain on retirement of bonds			(j) 16,000	
Investing activities:				
Receipts from sale of plant assets .		(i) 12,000		
Payment for purchase of plant assets .			(k1) 10,000	
Financing activities:				
Payments to retire bonds			(j) 18,000	
Receipts from issuing stock		(l) 15,000		
Payments of dividends			(m) 14,000	
Noncash investing and financing activities:				
Purchase of plant assets financed by bonds		(k2) 60,000	(k1) 60,000	
		337,000	337,000	

l. Sold 3,000 shares of common stock for $15,000.

m. Paid cash dividends of $14,000.

Illustration 16–11 shows the indirect method working paper for Grover Company. Notice that the beginning and ending balance sheets are recorded on the working paper the same as when using the direct method. Following the balance sheets, we enter information in the Analysis of Changes columns about cash flows from

FAST HINT
Relevant Quick Study:
To apply these concepts, work QS 16–10.

operating, investing, and financing activities and about noncash investing and financing activities. Note that the working paper does not reconstruct the income statement. Instead, net income is entered as the first item used in computing the amount of cash flows from operating activities.

Entering the Analysis of Changes on the Working Paper

After the balance sheets are entered, we recommend using the following sequence of procedures to complete the working paper:

1. Enter net income as an operating cash inflow (a debit) and as a credit to Retained Earnings.

2. In the Statement of Cash Flows section, adjustments to net income are entered as debits if they increase cash inflows and as credits if they decrease cash inflows. Following this rule, adjust net income for the change in each noncash current asset and current liability related to operating activities. For each adjustment to net income, the offsetting debit or credit should reconcile the beginning and ending balances of a current asset or current liability.

3. Enter the adjustments to net income for income statement items, such as depreciation, that did not provide or use cash during the period. For each adjustment, the offsetting debit or credit should help reconcile a noncash balance sheet account.

4. Adjust net income to eliminate any gains or losses from investing and financing activities. Because the cash associated with a gain must be excluded from operating activities, the gain is entered as a credit in the operating activities section. On the other hand, losses are entered with debits. For each of these adjustments, the related debits and/or credits help reconcile balance sheet accounts and also involve entries to show the cash flow from investing or financing activities.

5. After reviewing any unreconciled balance sheet accounts and related information, enter the reconciling entries for all remaining investing and financing activities. These include items such as purchases of plant assets, issuances of long-term debt, sales of capital stock, and dividend payments. Some of these may require entries in the noncash investing and financing activities section of the working paper.

6. Confirm the accuracy of your work by totaling the Analysis of Changes columns and by determining that the change in each balance sheet account has been explained.

For Grover Company, these steps were performed in Illustration 16–11:

Step	Entries
1	*(a)*
2	*(b)* through *(g)*
3	*(h)*
4	*(i)* through *(j)*
5	*(k)* through *(m)*

Because adjustments *i, j,* and *k* are more complex, we show them in the following debit and credit format. This format is similar to the one used for general journal entries, except that the changes in the Cash account are identified as sources or uses of cash.

i.	Loss from Sale of Plant Assets	6,000.00	
	Accumulated Depreciation	12,000.00	
	Receipt from Sale of Plant Assets	12,000.00	
	Plant Assets		30,000.00
	To describe the sale of plant assets.		
j.	Bonds Payable	34,000.00	
	Payments to Retire Bonds		18,000.00
	Gain on Retirement of Bonds		16,000.00
	To describe the retirement of bonds.		
k1.	Plant Assets	70,000.00	
	Payment to Purchase Plant Assets		10,000.00
	Purchase of Plant Assets Financed by Bonds		60,000.00
	To describe the purchase of plant assets, the cash payment, and the use of noncash financing.		
k2.	Purchase of Plant Assets Financed by Bonds	60,000.00	
	Bonds Payable		60,000.00
	To show the issuance of bonds payable to finance the purchase of plant assets.		

Progress Check

16-12   **In preparing a working paper for a statement of cash flows with the cash flows from operating activities reported according to the indirect method, which of the following is true?**

   (a) **A decrease in accounts receivable is analyzed with a debit in the statement of cash flows section and a credit in the balance sheet section.**

   (b) **A cash dividend paid is analyzed with a debit to retained earnings and a credit in the investing activities section.**

   (c) **The analysis of a cash payment to retire bonds payable at a loss would require one debit and two credits.**

   (d) **Depreciation expense would not require analysis on the working paper because there is no cash inflow or outflow.**

Numerous ratios are used to analyze income statement and balance sheet data. By comparison, ratios related to the statement of cash flows are not widely used.[7] Only one ratio of that nature, cash flow per share, has received much attention. Some financial analysts use that ratio, usually calculated as net income adjusted for noncash items such as depreciation and amortization. Currently, however, the FASB does not allow reporting cash flow per share, apparently because it might be misinterpreted as a measure of earnings performance.

Mary Garza (As a Matter of Opinion, page 610) typifies the attitude of most managers when she emphasizes the importance of understanding and predicting cash flows. Many business decisions are based on cash flow evaluations. For example, creditors evaluate a company's ability to generate cash before deciding whether to loan money to the company. Investors often make similar evaluations before they buy a company's stock. In making these evaluations, cash flows from investing and financing activities are considered. However, special attention is given to the company's ability to generate cash flows from its operations. The cash flows statement facilitates this by separating the investing and financing activity cash flows from the operating cash flows.

USING THE INFORMATION— CASH FLOWS

LO 1

Explain why cash flow information is important to decision making and describe the information in a statement of cash flows and the methods used to disclose noncash investing and financing activities.

---

[7]To consider some suggested cash flow ratios, see Don E. Giacomino and David E. Mielke, "Cash Flows: Another Approach to Ratio Analysis," *Journal of Accountancy,* March 1993.

To see the importance of identifying cash flows as operating, investing, and financing activities, consider the following three companies. Assume they operate in the same industry and have been in business for several years.

	First Company	Second Company	Third Company
Cash provided (used) by operating activities	$90,000	$40,000	$(24,000)
Cash provided (used) by investing activities:			
Proceeds from sale of operating assets			26,000
Purchase of operating assets	(48,000)	(25,000)	
Cash provided (used) by financing activities:			
Proceeds from issuance of debt			13,000
Repayment of debt	(27,000)		
Net increase (decrease) in cash	$15,000	$15,000	$ 15,000

Each of the three companies generated a $15,000 net increase in cash. Their means of accomplishing this, however, were very different. First Company's operating activities provided $90,000, which allowed the company to purchase additional operating assets for $48,000 and repay $27,000 of debt. By comparison, Second Company's operating activities provided only $40,000, enabling it to purchase only $25,000 of operating assets. By comparison, Third Company's net cash increase was obtained only by selling operating assets and incurring additional debt; operating activities resulted in a net cash outflow of $24,000.

The implication of this comparison is that First Company is more capable of generating cash to meet its future obligations than is Second Company; and Third Company is least capable. This evaluation is, of course, tentative and may be contradicted by other information.

Managers analyze cash flows in making a variety of short-term decisions. In deciding whether borrowing will be necessary, managers use the procedures you learned in this chapter to predict cash flows for the next period or periods. These short-term planning situations also may lead to decisions about investing idle cash balances. Another example is deciding whether a customer's offer to buy a product at a reduced price should be accepted or rejected.

Long-term decisions involving new investments usually require detailed cash flow predictions. Companies must estimate cash inflows and outflows over the life of the investment, often extending many years into the future. Other decisions that require cash flow information include deciding whether a product should be manufactured by the company or purchased from an outside supplier, and deciding whether a product or a department should be eliminated or retained.

Progress Check

16-13   Refer to the consolidated statements of cash flows for Ben & Jerry's Homemade, Inc., in Appendix G. What type and amount of investing activities took place during the year ended December 26, 1992? What was the largest source of cash to finance these activities?

SUMMARY OF CHAPTER IN TERMS OF LEARNING OBJECTIVES

LO 1. Explain why cash flow information is important to decision making and describe the information in a statement of cash flows and the methods used to disclose noncash investing and financing activities. Many decisions involve evaluating cash flows. Examples are investor and creditor decisions to invest in or loan money to a company. The evaluations include paying attention to the activities that provide or use cash. Managers evaluate cash flows in deciding whether borrowing is necessary, whether cash balances should be invested, and in a variety of other short-term and long-term decisions.

The statement of cash flows reports cash receipts and disbursements as operating, investing, or financing activities. Operating activities include transactions related to producing or purchasing merchandise, selling goods and services to customers, and performing administrative functions. Investing activities include purchases and sales of noncurrent assets and short-term investments that are not cash equivalents. Financing activities include transactions with owners and transactions to borrow or repay the principal amounts of long-term and short-term debt.

For external reporting, a company must supplement its statement of cash flows with a description of its noncash investing and financing activities. Two examples of these activities are the retirement of debt obligations by issuing equity securities and the exchange of a note payable for plant assets.

LO 2. Calculate cash inflows and outflows by inspecting the noncash account balances and prepare a statement of cash flows using the direct method. To identify the cash receipts and cash payments, analyze the changes in the noncash balance sheet accounts created by income statement transactions and other events. For example, the amount of cash collected from customers is calculated by modifying sales revenues for the change in accounts receivable. Also, cash paid for interest is calculated by adjusting interest expense for the change in interest payable.

In using the direct method to report the net cash provided (or used) by operating activities, major classes of operating cash inflows and outflows are separately disclosed. Then, operating cash outflows are subtracted from operating cash inflows to derive the net inflow or outflow from operating activities. This method is encouraged by the FASB but is not required. Company managers generally use the direct method to predict future cash inflows and outflows.

LO 3. Calculate the net cash provided or used by operating activities according to the indirect method and prepare the statement of cash flows. In using the indirect method to calculate the net cash provided (or used) by operating activities, first list the net income and then modify it for these three types of events: *(a)* changes in noncash current assets and current liabilities related to operating activities, *(b)* revenues and expenses that did not provide or use cash, and *(c)* gains and losses from investing and financing activities. If using the direct method, report the reconciliation between net income and net cash provided (or used) by operating activities on a separate schedule.

LO 4. Prepare a working paper for a statement of cash flows so that the net cash flow from operating activities is calculated by the indirect method. To prepare an indirect method working paper, first enter the beginning and ending balances of the balance sheet accounts in columns 1 and 4. Then, establish the three sections of the statement of cash flows. Net income is entered as the first item in the operating activities section. Then, adjust the net income for events *(a)* through *(c)* identified in the preceding paragraph. This process reconciles the changes in the noncash current assets and current liabilities related to operations. Reconcile any remaining balance sheet account changes and report their cash effects in the appropriate sections. Enter noncash investing and financing activities at the bottom of the working paper.

DEMONSTRATION PROBLEM

The following summarized journal entries show the total debits and credits to the Pyramid Corporation's Cash account during 19X2. Use the information to prepare a statement of cash flows for 19X2. The cash provided (or used) by operating activities should be presented according to the direct method. In the statement, identify the entry that records each item of cash flow. Assume that the beginning balance of cash was $133,200.

a.	Cash	1,440,000.00	
	Common Stock, $10 par value		360,000.00
	Contributed Capital in Excess of		
	Par Value, Common Stock		1,080,000.00
	Issued common stock for cash.		
b.	Cash	2,400,000.00	
	Notes Payable		2,400,000.00
	Borrowed cash with a note payable.		
c.	Purchases	480,000.00	
	Cash		480,000.00
	Purchased merchandise for cash.		
d.	Accounts Payable	1,200,000.00	
	Cash		1,200,000.00
	Paid for credit purchases of merchandise.		
e.	Wages Expense	600,000.00	
	Cash		600,000.00
	Paid wages to employees.		
f.	Rent Expense	420,000.00	
	Cash		420,000.00
	Paid rent for buildings.		
g.	Cash	3,000,000.00	
	Sales		3,000,000.00
	Made cash sales to customers.		
h.	Cash	1,800,000.00	
	Accounts Receivable		1,800,000.00
	Collected accounts from credit customers.		
i.	Machinery	2,136,000.00	
	Cash		2,136,000.00
	Purchased machinery for cash.		
j.	Investments	2,160,000.00	
	Cash		2,160,000.00
	Purchased investments for cash.		
k.	Interest Expense	216,000.00	
	Notes Payable	384,000.00	
	Cash		600,000.00
	Paid notes and accrued interest.		
l.	Cash	206,400.00	
	Dividends Earned		206,400.00
	Collected dividends from investments.		
m.	Cash	210,000.00	
	Loss on Sale of Investments	30,000.00	
	Investments		240,000.00
	Sold investments for cash.		
n.	Cash	720,000.00	
	Accumulated Depreciation, Machinery	420,000.00	
	Machinery		960,000.00
	Gain on Sale of Machinery		180,000.00
	Sold machinery for cash.		
o.	Common Dividend Payable	510,000.00	
	Cash		510,000.00
	Paid cash dividends to stockholders.		

p.	Income Taxes Payable	480,000.00		
	Cash		480,000.00	
	Paid income taxes owed for the year.			
q.	Treasury Stock, Common	228,000.00		
	Cash		228,000.00	
	Acquired treasury stock for cash.			

- Prepare a blank statement of cash flows with sections for operating, investing, and financing activities.

- Examine each journal entry to determine whether it describes an operating, investing, or financing activity and whether it describes an inflow or outflow of cash.

- Enter the cash effects of the entry in the appropriate section of the statement, being sure to combine similar events, including *c* and *d,* as well as *g* and *h.* For entry *k,* identify the portions of the cash flow that should be assigned to operating and financing activities.

- Total each section of the statement, determine the total change in cash, and add the beginning balance to get the ending balance.

Planning the Solution

PYRAMID CORPORATION
Statement of Cash Flows
For Year Ended December 31, 19X2

Solution to Demonstration Problem

Cash flows from operating activities:
g,h.	Cash received from customers	$ 4,800,000	
l.	Cash received as dividends	206,400	
c,d.	Cash paid for merchandise	(1,680,000)	
e.	Cash paid for wages	(600,000)	
f.	Cash paid for rent	(420,000)	
k.	Cash paid for interest	(216,000)	
p.	Cash paid for taxes	(480,000)	
	Net cash provided by operating activities ...		$ 1,610,400

Cash flows from investing activities:
i.	Cash paid for purchases of machinery	$(2,136,000)	
j.	Cash paid for purchases of investments	(2,160,000)	
m.	Cash received from sale of investments	210,000	
n.	Cash received from sale of machinery	720,000	
	Net cash used in investing activities		(3,366,000)

Cash flows from financing activities:
a.	Cash received from issuing stock	$ 1,440,000	
b.	Cash received from borrowing	2,400,000	
k.	Cash paid for repayment of note payable ...	(384,000)	
o.	Cash paid for dividends	(510,000)	
q.	Cash paid for purchases of treasury stock ...	(228,000)	
	Net cash provided by financing activities ...		2,718,000

Net increase in cash		$ 962,400
Beginning balance of cash		133,200
Ending balance of cash		$ 1,095,600

GLOSSARY

Direct method of calculating net cash provided (or used) by operating activities a calculation of the net cash provided or used by operating activities that lists the major classes of operating cash receipts, such as receipts from customers, and subtracts the major classes of operating cash disbursements, such as cash paid for merchandise. p. 609

Financing activities transactions with the owners of a business or transactions with its creditors to borrow money or to repay the principal amounts of loans. p. 613

Indirect method of calculating net cash provided (or used) by operating activities a calculation that begins with net income and then adjusts the net income amount by adding and subtracting items that are necessary to reconcile net income to the net cash provided or used by operating activities. p. 610

Investing activities transactions that involve making and collecting loans or that involve purchasing and selling plant assets, other productive assets, or investments other than cash equivalents. p. 613

Operating activities activities that involve the production or purchase of merchandise and the sale of goods and services to customers, including expenditures related to administering the business. p. 613

Statement of cash flows a financial statement that reports the cash inflows and outflows for an accounting period, and that classifies those cash flows as operating activities, investing activities, and financing activities. p. 608

QUESTIONS

1. What are some examples of items reported on a statement of cash flows as investing activities?

2. What are some examples of items reported on a statement of cash flows as financing activities?

3. When a statement of cash flows is prepared by the direct method, what are some examples of items reported as cash flows from operating activities?

4. If a corporation pays cash dividends, where on the corporation's statement of cash flows should the payment be reported?

5. A company purchases land for $100,000, paying $20,000 cash and borrowing the remainder on a long-term note payable. How should this transaction be reported on a statement of cash flows?

6. What is the direct method of reporting cash flows from operating activities?

7. What is the indirect method of reporting cash flows from operating activities?

8. Is depreciation a source of cash?

9. On June 3, a company borrowed $50,000 by giving its bank a 60-day, interest-bearing note. On the statement of cash flows, where should this item be reported?

10. If a company reports a net income for the year, is it possible for the company to show a net cash outflow from operating activities? Explain your answer.

11. Refer to Federal Express Corporation's consolidated statement of cash flows shown in Appendix G.
   (a) Which method was used to calculate net cash provided by operating activities? *(b)* Why was the increase in receivables subtracted rather than added in the calculation of net cash provided by operating activities during the year ended May 31, 1993?

QUICK STUDY (Five-Minute Exercises)

QS 16–1
(LO 1)

Describe the content of a statement of cash flows.

QS 16–2
(LO 1)

Classify the following cash flows as operating, investing, or financing activities:

1. Purchased merchandise for cash.
2. Paid interest on outstanding bonds.
3. Sold delivery equipment at a loss.
4. Paid property taxes on the company offices.
5. Collected proceeds from sale of long-term investments.

6. Issued common stock for cash.

7. Received payments from customers.

8. Paid wages.

9. Paid dividends.

10. Received interest on investment.

List three examples of transactions that are noncash financing and investing transactions.

QS 16–3
(LO 1)

Use the following information in QS 16–4 through QS 16–9.

QS 16–4
(LO 2)

KUNG ATTIRE, INC.
Comparative Balance Sheet

Assets	19X2	19X1
Cash	$ 47,900	$ 12,500
Accounts receivable (net)	21,000	26,000
Inventory	43,400	48,400
Prepaid expenses	3,200	2,600
Furniture	55,000	60,000
Accumulated depreciation, furniture	(9,000)	(5,000)
Total assets	$161,500	$144,500

Liabilities and Stockholders' Equity		
Accounts payable	$ 8,000	$ 11,000
Wages payable	5,000	3,000
Income taxes payable	1,200	1,800
Notes payable (long-term)	15,000	35,000
Common stock, $5 par value	115,000	90,000
Retained earnings	17,300	3,700
Total liabilities and stockholders' equity	$161,500	$144,500

KUNG ATTIRE, INC.
Income Statement
For Year Ended June 30, 19X2

Sales		$234,000
Cost of goods sold		156,000
Gross profit		$ 78,000
Operating expenses:		
Depreciation expense	$19,300	
Other expenses	28,500	
Total operating expenses		47,800
Net income from operations		$ 30,200
Income taxes		12,300
Net income		$ 17,900

How much cash was received from customers during Year 2?

Refer to the facts in QS 16–4. How much cash was paid for merchandise during 19X2?

QS 16–5
(LO 5)

Refer to the facts in QS 16–4. How much cash was paid for operating expenses during 19X2?

QS 16–6
(LO 2)

Refer to the facts in QS 16–4 and assume furniture that cost $27,000 was sold at its book value and all furniture acquisitions were for cash. What was the cash inflow related to the sale of furniture?

QS 16–7
(LO 2)

| QS 16–8 | Refer to the facts in QS 16–4 and assume that all stock was issued for cash. How much cash |
| (LO 2) | was disbursed for dividends? |

| QS 16–9 | Refer to the facts in QS 16–4. Using the indirect method, calculate cash provided or used from |
| (LO 3) | operating activities. |

| QS 16–10 | When a working paper for a statement of cash flows is prepared, all changes in noncash bal- |
| (LO 4) | ance sheet accounts are accounted for on the working paper. Explain why this occurs. |

EXERCISES

Exercise 16–1
Classifying transactions
on statement of cash flows
(direct method)
(LO 1)

The following events occurred during the year. Assuming that the company uses the direct method of reporting cash provided by operating activities, indicate the proper accounting treatment for each event by placing an *x* in the appropriate column.

		Statement of Cash Flows			Footnote Describing Noncash Investing and Financing Activities	Not Reported on Statement or in Footnote
		Operating Activities	Investing Activities	Financing Activities		
a.	Long-term bonds payable were retired by issuing common stock.	___	___	___	___	___
b.	Surplus merchandise inventory was sold for cash.	___	___	___	___	___
c.	Borrowed cash from the bank by signing a nine-month note payable.	___	___	___	___	___
d.	Paid cash to purchase a patent.	___	___	___	___	___
e.	A six-month note receivable was accepted in exchange for a building that had been used in operations.	___	___	___	___	___
f.	Recorded depreciation expense on all plant assets.	___	___	___	___	___
g.	A cash dividend that was declared in a previous period was paid in the current period.	___	___	___	___	___

Exercise 16–2
Organizing the statement of
cash flows and supporting
footnote
(LO 1)

Use the following information about the 19X2 cash flows of Forrest Company to prepare a statement of cash flows under the direct method and a footnote describing noncash investing and financing activities.

Cash and cash equivalents balance, December 31, 19X1 ..	$ 50,000
Cash and cash equivalents balance, December 31, 19X2 ..	140,000
Cash received as interest	5,000
Cash paid for salaries	145,000
Bonds payable retired by issuing common stock (there was no gain or loss on the retirement)	375,000
Cash paid to retire long-term notes payable	250,000
Cash received from sale of equipment	122,500
Cash borrowed on six-month note payable	50,000
Land purchased and financed by long-term note payable ..	212,500
Cash paid for store equipment	47,500
Cash dividends paid	30,000
Cash paid for other expenses	80,000
Cash received from customers	970,000
Cash paid for merchandise	505,000

In each of the following cases, use the information provided about the 19X1 operations of Benzar Company to calculate the indicated cash flow:

Exercise 16–3
Calculating cash flows
(LO 2)

Case A: Calculate cash received from customers:
Sales revenue $255,000
Accounts receivable, January 1 12,600
Accounts receivable, December 31 17,400

Case B: Calculate cash paid for insurance:
Insurance expense .... $ 34,200
Prepaid insurance, January 1 5,700
Prepaid insurance, December 31 8,550

Case C: Calculate cash paid for salaries:
Salaries expense $102,000
Salaries payable, January 1 6,300
Salaries payable, December 31 7,500

In each of the following cases, use the information provided about the 19X1 operations of CNA Company to calculate the indicated cash flow:

Exercise 16–4
Calculating cash flows
(LO 2)

Case A: Calculate cash paid for rent:
Rent expense .... $ 20,400
Rent payable, January 1 4,400
Rent payable, December 31 3,600

Case B: Calculate cash received from interest:
Interest revenue .... $ 68,000
Interest receivable, January 1 6,000
Interest receivable, December 31 7,200

Case C: Calculate cash paid for merchandise:
Cost of goods sold $352,000
Merchandise inventory, January 1 106,400
Accounts payable, January 1 45,200
Merchandise inventory, December 31 87,600
Accounts payable, December 31 56,000

Use the following income statement and information about changes in noncash current assets and current liabilities to present the cash flows from operating activities using the direct method:

Exercise 16–5
Cash flows from operating
activities (direct method)
(LO 2)

ALAMO DATA COMPANY
Income Statement
For Year Ended December 31, 19X1

Sales		$606,000
Cost of goods sold		297,000
Gross profit from sales		$309,000
Operating expenses:		
Salaries expense	$82,845	
Depreciation expense	14,400	
Rent expense	16,200	
Amortization expense, patents	1,800	
Utilities expense	6,375	121,620
Total		$187,380
Gain on sale of equipment		2,400
Net income		$189,780

Changes in current asset and current liability accounts during the year, all of which related to operating activities, were as follows:

Accounts receivable	$13,500 increase
Merchandise inventory	9,000 increase
Accounts payable	4,500 decrease
Salaries payable	1,500 decrease

Exercise 16–6
Cash flows from operating
activities (indirect method)
(LO 3)

Refer to the information about Alamo Data Company presented in Exercise 16–5. Use the indirect method and calculate the cash provided (or used) by operating activities.

Exercise 16–7
Cash flows from operating
activities (indirect method)
(LO 3)

Trador Company's 19X1 income statement showed the following: net income, $728,000; depreciation expense, $90,000; amortization expense, $16,400; and gain on sale of plant assets, $14,000. An examination of the company's current assets and current liabilities showed that the following changes occurred because of operating activities: accounts receivable decreased $36,200; merchandise inventory decreased $104,000; prepaid expenses increased $7,400; accounts payable decreased $18,400; other payables increased $2,800. Use the indirect method to calculate the cash flow from operating activities.

Exercise 16–8
Classifying transactions on
statement of cash flows (indirect
method)
(LO 3)

The following events occurred during the year. Assuming that the company uses the indirect method of reporting cash provided by operating activities, indicate the proper accounting treatment for each event listed below by placing an *x* in the appropriate column.

	Statement of Cash Flows			Footnote Describing Noncash Investing and Financing Activities	Not Reported on Statement or in Footnote
	Operating Activities	**Investing Activities**	**Financing Activities**		
a. Land for a new plant was purchased by issuing common stock.	_____	_____	_____	_____	_____
b. Recorded depreciation expense.	_____	_____	_____	_____	_____
c. Income taxes payable increased by 15% from prior year.	_____	_____	_____	_____	_____
d. Declared and paid a cash dividend.	_____	_____	_____	_____	_____
e. Paid cash to purchase merchandise inventory.	_____	_____	_____	_____	_____
f. Sold plant equipment at a loss.	_____	_____	_____	_____	_____
g. Accounts receivable decreased during the year.	_____	_____	_____	_____	_____

PROBLEMS

Problem 16–1
Statement of cash flows
(direct method)
(LO 1, 2)

Helix Corporation's 19X2 and 19X1 balance sheets carried the following items:

	December 31	
Debits	**19X2**	**19X1**
Cash	$116,000	$ 78,000
Accounts receivable	62,000	54,000
Merchandise inventory	406,000	356,000
Equipment	222,000	198,000
Totals	$806,000	$686,000

Credits		
Accumulated depreciation, equipment	$104,000	$ 68,000
Accounts payable	46,000	64,000
Income taxes payable	18,000	16,000
Common stock, $2 par value	388,000	372,000
Contributed capital in excess of par value, common stock	132,000	108,000
Retained earnings	118,000	58,000
Totals	$806,000	$686,000

An examination of the company's activities during 19X2, including the income statement, shows the following:

a. Sales (all on credit) $1,328,000
b. Credits to Accounts Receivable during the
    period were receipts from customers.
c. Cost of goods sold $796,000
d. Purchases of merchandise were on credit.
e. Debits to Accounts Payable during the period
    resulted from payments for merchandise.
f. Depreciation expense   36,000
g. Other operating expenses (paid with cash)   334,000
h. Income taxes expense   28,000   1,194,000
i. The only decreases in Income Taxes Payable
    were payments of taxes.
j. Net income .... $ 134,000
k. Equipment was purchased for $24,000 cash.
l. Eight thousand shares of stock were issued for cash at $5 per share.
m. The company declared and paid $74,000 of cash dividends during the year.

Required

Prepare a statement of cash flows that reports the cash inflows and outflows from operating activities according to the direct method. Show your supporting calculations.

Refer to Helix Corporation's balance sheets presented in Problem 16–1. The additional information about the company's activities during 19X2 is restated as follows:

a. Net income was $134,000.

b. Accounts receivable increased.

c. Merchandise inventory increased.

d. Accounts payable decreased.

e. Income taxes payable increased.

f. Depreciation expense was $36,000.

g. Equipment was purchased for $24,000 cash.

h. Eight thousand shares of stock were issued for cash at $5 per share.

i. The company declared and paid $74,000 of cash dividends during the year.

Required

Prepare a statement of cash flows that reports the cash inflows and outflows from operating activities according to the indirect method.

Refer to the facts about Helix Corporation presented in Problem 16–1 and Problem 16–2. Prepare a statement of cash flows working paper that follows the indirect method of calculating cash flows from operating activities. Identify the debits and credits in the Analysis of Changes columns with letters that correspond to the list in Problem 16–2.

Purcell Company's 19X2 and 19X1 balance sheets included the following items:

	December 31	
Debits	**19X2**	**19X1**
Cash	$ 107,750	$153,250
Accounts receivable	130,000	99,250
Merchandise inventory	547,500	505,000
Prepaid expenses	10,750	12,500
Equipment	319,000	220,000
Totals	$1,115,000	$990,000

FAST HINT
Group Project:
After assigning Problems 16–1 and 16–2, ask students in small groups to compare their solutions and resolve any discrepancies. Then, ask the groups to be prepared in 10 minutes to defend or refute this statement: "The direct method of reporting cash flows from operations is a more informative basis for predicting cash flows." They should use data from Problems 16–1 and 16-2 to illustrate and substantiate positions taken.

CHECK FIGURE:
Net cash provided by operating activities, $96,000

Problem 16–2
Statement of cash flows (indirect method)
(LO 3)

CHECK FIGURE:
Net cash provided by operating activities, $96,000

Problem 16–3
Cash flows working paper (indirect method)
(LO 4)

CHECK FIGURE:
Analysis of Changes column totals, $386,000

Problem 16–4
Statement of cash flows (direct method)
(LO 1, 2)

| Credits | December 31 | |
	19X2	19X1
Accumulated depreciation, equipment ..	$ 69,250	$ 88,000
Accounts payable	176,250	233,250
Short-term notes payable	20,000	12,500
Long-term notes payable	187,500	107,500
Common stock, $5 par value	337,500	312,500
Contributed capital in excess of		
par value, common stock	65,000	
Retained earnings	259,500	236,250
Totals	$1,115,000	$990,000

Additional information about the 19X2 activities of the company is as follows:

a. Sales revenue, all on credit $992,500
b. Credits to Accounts Receivable during the period
    were receipts from customers.
c. Cost of goods sold $500,000
d. All merchandise purchases were on credit.
e. Debits to Accounts Payable during the period
    resulted from payments to creditors.
f. Depreciation expense   37,500
g. Other expenses   273,000
h. The other expenses were paid in advance and were
    initially debited to Prepaid Expenses.
i. Income taxes expense (paid with cash)   24,250
j. Loss on sale of equipment   10,250   845,000
    The equipment cost $93,750, was depreciated by
    $56,250, and was sold for $27,250.
k. Net income $147,500

l. Equipment that cost $192,750 was purchased by paying cash of
    $50,000 and by signing a long-term note payable for the balance.
m. Borrowed $7,500 by signing a short-term note payable.
n. Paid $62,750 to reduce a long-term note payable.
o. Issued 5,000 shares of common stock for cash at $18 per share.
p. Declared and paid cash dividends of $124,250.

Required

Preparation component:

1. Prepare a statement of cash flows that reports the cash inflows and outflows from oper-
    ating activities according to the direct method. Show your supporting calculations. Also
    prepare a footnote describing noncash investing and financing activities.

CHECK FIGURE:
Net cash provided by operating
activities, $66,750

Analysis component:

2. Analyze and discuss the information contained in your answer to requirement 1, giving
    special attention to the wisdom of the dividend payment.

Problem 16–5
Statement of cash flows
(indirect method)
(LO 3)

Refer to Purcell Company's balance sheets presented in Problem 16–4. The additional information about the company's activities during 19X2 is restated as follows:

a. Net income was $147,500.
b. Accounts receivable increased.
c. Merchandise inventory increased.
d. Prepaid expenses decreased.
e. Accounts payable decreased.
f. Depreciation expense was $37,500.
g. Equipment that cost $93,750 with accumulated depreciation of $56,250 was sold for
    $27,250 cash, which caused a loss of $10,250.

h. Equipment that cost $192,750 was purchased by paying cash of $50,000 and (*i*) by signing a long-term note payable for the balance.

j. Borrowed $7,500 by signing a short-term note payable.

k. Paid $62,750 to reduce a long-term note payable.

l. Issued 5,000 shares of common stock for cash at $18 per share.

m. Declared and paid cash dividends of $124,250.

Required

Prepare a statement of cash flows that reports the cash inflows and outflows from operating activities according to the indirect method.

Refer to the facts about Purcell Company presented in Problem 16–4 and Problem 16–5. Prepare a statement of cash flows working paper that follows the indirect method of calculating cash flows from operating activities. Identify the debits and credits in the Analysis of Changes columns with letters that correspond to the list for the company presented in Problem 16–5.

CHECK FIGURE:
Net cash provided by operating activities, $66,750

Problem 16–6
Cash flows working paper (indirect method)
(LO 4)

CHECK FIGURE:
Analysis of Changes column totals, $1,030,750

CRITICAL THINKING: ESSAYS, PROBLEMS, AND CASES

Analytical Essays

Write a brief essay explaining why, in preparing a statement of cash flows according to the direct method, it is generally better to determine the changes in cash by analyzing the changes in the noncash accounts rather than by examining the Cash account directly. You should include in your essay an explanation of why the changes in cash for the period equal the changes in the noncash balance sheet accounts.

AE 16–1
(LO 2)

The following items might be found on a working paper for a statement of cash flows. Write a brief essay describing where each item appears on a working paper for a statement of cash flows according to the indirect method. Also describe the nature of any debits and/or credits that should be entered in the Analysis of Changes columns next to each item, and any balancing entries.

AE 16–2
(LO 4)

a. Accounts receivable.

b. Depreciation expense.

c. Payment for purchase of plant assets.

Financial Reporting Problem

(LO 4)

Griffin Company's 19X2 statement of cash flows appeared as follows:

Cash flows from operating activities:
Cash received from customers	$903,600	
Cash paid for merchandise	(473,550)	
Cash paid for other operating expenses	(244,500)	
Cash paid for income taxes	(26,100)	
Net cash provided by operating activities		$159,450
Cash flows from investing activities:		
Cash received from sale of office equipment ..	$ 13,950	
Cash paid for store equipment	(21,000)	
Net cash used in investing activities		(7,050)
Cash flows from financing activities:		
Cash paid to retire bonds payable	$(76,650)	
Cash paid for dividends	(37,500)	
Net cash used in financing activities		(114,150)
Net increase in cash		$ 38,250
Cash balance at beginning of year		47,850
Cash balance at end of year		$ 86,100

Griffin's beginning and ending balance sheets were as follows:

	December 31	
Debits	**19X2**	**19X1**
Cash	$ 86,100	$ 47,850
Accounts receivable	68,250	79,650
Merchandise inventory	312,000	292,950
Prepaid expenses	7,200	3,300
Equipment	271,650	293,400
Totals	$745,200	$717,150
Credits		
Accumulated depreciation, equipment ..	$123,900	$ 95,100
Accounts payable	57,600	67,500
Income taxes payable	10,200	8,850
Dividends payable	–0–	9,000
Bonds payable	–0–	75,000
Common stock, $10 par value	337,500	337,500
Retained earnings	216,000	124,200
Totals	$745,200	$717,150

An examination of the company's statements and accounts showed:

a. All sales were made on credit.

b. All merchandise purchases were on credit.

c. Accounts Payable balances resulted from merchandise purchases.

d. Prepaid expenses relate to other operating expenses.

e. Equipment that cost $42,750 with accumulated depreciation of $22,200 was sold for cash.

f. Equipment was purchased for cash.

g. The change in the balance of Accumulated Depreciation resulted from depreciation expense and from the sale of equipment.

h. The change in the balance of Retained Earnings resulted from dividend declarations and net income.

Required

Present Griffin's income statement for 19X2. Show your supporting calculations.

Look in Appendix F at the end of the book to find Apple Computer, Inc.'s statement of cash flows. Based on your examination of that statement, answer the following questions:

1. Was Apple's statement of cash flows prepared according to the direct method or the indirect method?

2. During each of the fiscal years 1993, 1992, and 1991, was the cash provided by operating activities more or less than the cash paid for dividends?

3. What was the major reason for the difference between net income and cash flow from operating activities?

4. Describe the major cash inflows and outflows during 1993.

5. Describe the major differences in Apple's 1993 cash flows compared to its 1992 cash flows.

Financial Statement Analysis Case

(LO 1)

ANSWERS TO PROGRESS CHECKS

16–1 No. The statement of cash flows reports changes in the sum of cash plus cash equivalents. It does not report transfers between cash and cash equivalents.

16–2 The three categories of cash inflows and outflows are operating activities, investing activities, and financing activities.

16–3 The direct method is most informative. The indirect method is used most often.

16–4   *a.* Investing
     b. Operating
     c. Financing
     d. Operating
     e. Operating
     f. Financing

16–5 $590,000 + ($120,000 − $90,000) = $620,000

16–6 $168,000 − ($32,000 − $28,000) − $2,400 = $161,600

16–7 $112,000 + ($4,200 − $1,200) − $5,600 = $109,400

16–8 $80,000 − $30,000 − $10,000 = $40,000
The $40,000 cash receipt should be reported as an investment activity.

16–9 $74,900 + $4,600 − $11,700 − $1,000 + $3,400 = $70,200

16–10 In the calculation of net income, expenses such as depreciation and amortization are subtracted because these expenses do not require current cash outflows. Therefore, adding these expenses back to net income eliminates noncash items from the net income number, converting it to a cash basis.

16–11 In the process of reconciling net income to net cash provided (or used) by operating activities, a gain on the sale of plant assets is subtracted from net income because a sale of plant assets is not an operating activity; it is an investing activity.

16–12 *a*

16–13 Investing activities during the year ended December 26, 1992, used net cash of $36,378,580. Cash outflows that contributed to this included additions to property, plant, and equipment for $10,447,007; increase in investments amounting to $25,200,000; and changes in other assets amounting to $836,657. An investing activity that produced a cash inflow was the sale of property, plant, and equipment for $105,084. The largest source of cash to finance these activities was $33,661,528 obtained through the issuance of common stock.

Analyzing Financial Statements

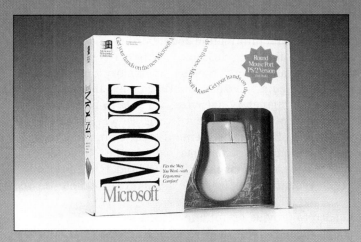

A group of high-tech wizards have a vision and a desire to create a computer software corporation. In their enthusiasm, they have told a few potential investors that their proposed company was likely to be so successful it would rival the current giants in the industry. Microsoft Corporation was named as an example of what the new venture was likely to become. The investors were quite familiar with the history of Microsoft and suggested that the wizards might be wise to be a little more moderate in their expectations. When the wizards disagreed, the investors pointed out that Microsoft was formed in 1975 and by 1993 had revenues of $3.75 billion. They added that it operated in 41 countries and had revenues outside the United States of more than $2 billion.

In concluding the conversation, the investors gave the wizards a copy of Microsoft's 1993 annual report and suggested that they study it carefully to see if it really represented a goal they could achieve.

MICROSOFT CORPORATION
Growth percentages increase

	Year Ended June 30				
	1993	1992	1991	1990	1989
Net revenues	36%	50%	56%	47%	36%
Net income	35	53	66	63	38
Earnings per share	31	47	58	55	37
Book value per share	43	56	44	57	47

LEARNING OBJECTIVES

After studying Chapter 17, you should be able to:

1. **Explain the relationship between financial reporting and general purpose financial statements.**

2. **Describe, prepare, and interpret comparative financial statements and common-size comparative statements.**

3. **Calculate and explain the interpretation of the ratios, turnovers, and rates of return used to evaluate (a) short-term liquidity, (b) long-term risk and capital structure, and (c) operating efficiency and profitability.**

4. **State the limitations associated with using financial statement ratios and the sources from which standards for comparison may be obtained.**

5. **Define or explain the words and phrases listed in the chapter glossary.**

Chapter 17 demonstrates how to use the information in financial statements to evaluate the activities and financial status of a business. By explaining how you can relate the numbers in financial statements to each other, this chapter expands your ability to interpret the ratios we described in previous chapters.

FINANCIAL REPORTING

LO 1

Explain the relationship between financial reporting and general purpose financial statements.

FAST HINT
Important Point to Remember:
Financial statement analysis is frequently a topic on the CPA, CMA, and CIA exams.

FAST HINT
Important Point to Remember:
Decision makers rely on financial statement analysis to help them gain a better understanding of the financial position and profitability of a business. Auditors use financial statement analysis to assess the reasonableness of amounts presented in the statements.

FAST HINT
Relevant Quick Study:
To apply these concepts, work QS 17–1.

Many people receive and analyze financial information about business firms. These people include managers, employees, directors, customers, suppliers, current and potential owners, current and potential lenders, brokers, regulatory authorities, lawyers, economists, labor unions, financial advisors, and financial analysts. Some of these, such as managers and some regulatory agencies, are able to gain access to specialized financial reports that meet their specific interests. However, the others must rely on the **general purpose financial statements** that companies publish periodically. General purpose financial statements include the (1) income statement, (2) balance sheet, (3) statement of changes in stockholders' equity (or statement of retained earnings), (4) statement of cash flows, and (5) footnotes related to the statements.

Financial reporting is intended to provide useful information to investors, creditors, and others for making investment, credit, and similar decisions. The information should help the users assess the amounts, timing, and uncertainty of prospective cash inflows and outflows.

Financial reporting includes communicating through a variety of means in addition to the financial statements. Some examples are reports filed with the Securities and Exchange Commission, news releases, and management letters or analyses included in annual reports. For an example, in Appendix F look at the section of **Apple Computer, Inc.'s** annual report called Management Discussion and Analysis of Financial Condition and Results of Operations.

Progress Check
(Answers to Progress Checks are provided at the end of the chapter.)

17-1   Who are the intended users of general purpose financial statements?

17-2   What statements are usually included in the general purpose financial statements published by corporations?

In analyzing financial information, individual items usually are not very revealing. However, important relationships exist between items and groups of items. As a result, financial statement analysis involves identifying and describing relationships between items and groups of items and changes in those items.

You can see changes in financial statement items more clearly when amounts for two or more successive accounting periods are placed side by side in columns on a single statement. Statements prepared in this manner are called **comparative statements.** Each financial statement can be presented in this comparative format.

In its simplest form, a comparative balance sheet consists of the amounts from two or more successive balance sheet dates arranged side by side. However, the usefulness of the statement can be improved by also showing each item's dollar amount of change and percentage change. When this is done, large dollar or percentage changes are more readily apparent. Illustration 17–1 shows this type of comparative balance sheet for Microsoft Corporation.

A comparative income statement is prepared in the same way. Amounts for two or more successive periods are placed side by side, with dollar and percentage changes in additional columns. Look at Illustration 17–2 to see **Microsoft Corporation's** comparative income statement.

Calculating Percentage Increases and Decreases

To calculate the percentage increases and decreases on comparative statements, divide the dollar increase or decrease of an item by the amount shown for the item in the base year. If no amount is shown in the base year, or if the base year amount is negative (such as a net loss), a percentage increase or decrease cannot be calculated.

In this text, percentages and ratios typically are rounded to one or two decimal places. However, there is no uniform practice on this matter. In general, percentages should be carried out far enough to be meaningful. They should not be carried out so far that the important relationships become lost in the length of the numbers.

Analyzing and Interpreting Comparative Statements

In analyzing comparative data, study any items that show significant dollar or percentage changes. Then, try to identify the reasons for each change and, if possible, determine whether they are favorable or unfavorable. For example, in Illustration 17–1, the first item, "Cash and short-term investments," shows a $945 million increase (70.3%). To a large extent, this may be explained by the increase in two other items: the $429 million increase in "Common stock and paid-in capital" and the $620 million increase in "Retained earnings."

Note that **Microsoft Corporation's** liabilities increased by $116 million. In light of this, the $945 million increase in "Cash and short-term investments" might appear to be an excessive investment in highly liquid assets that usually earn a low return. However, the company's very strong and liquid financial position indicates an outstanding ability to respond to new opportunities such as the acquisition of other companies.

Now look at the comparative income statement for

Illustration 17-1

	MICROSOFT CORPORATION Comparative Balance Sheet June 30, 1993, and June 30, 1992 (in millions)			
	June 30		Amount of Increase or (Decrease) during 1993	Percentage Increase or (Decrease) during 1993
	1993	1992		
Assets				
Current assets:				
Cash and short-term investments	$2,290	$1,345	$ 945	70.3
Accounts receivable, net of				
allowances of $76 and $57	338	270	68	25.2
Inventories	127	86	41	47.7
Other	95	69	26	37.7
Total current assets	$2,850	$1,770	$1,080	61.0
Property, plant, and equipment—net	867	767	100	13.0
Other assets	88	103	(15)	(14.6)
Total assets	$3,805	$2,640	$1,165	44.1
Liabilities and Stockholders' Equity				
Current liabilities:				
Accounts payable	$ 239	$ 196	$ 43	21.9
Accrued compensation	86	62	24	38.7
Income taxes payable	127	73	54	74.0
Other	111	116	(5)	(4.3)
Total current liabilities	$ 563	$ 447	$ 116	26.0
Commitments and contingencies	—	—		
Stockholders' equity:				
Common stock and paid-in capital—				
shares authorized 500; issued and				
outstanding 282 and 272	$1,086	$ 657	$ 429	65.3
Retained earnings	2,156	1,536	620	40.4
Total stockholders' equity	$3,242	$2,193	$1,049	47.8
Total liabilities and stockholders' equity . .	$3,805	$2,640	$1,165	44.1

FAST HINT

Alternative Example:

If cash and short-term investments had been used during 1993 to buy an additional $500 million of property, plant, and equipment, what would have been the percentage increase in cash and short-term investments? *Answer:* ($2,290 – $500)/$1,345 = 33.1%

Microsoft in Illustration 17–2. Microsoft's rapid growth is reflected by its 36% increase in net revenues. In fact, we should point out that the growth in 1993 continued a very strong trend established in prior years. (Later, we present data showing that net revenues in 1993 were 467% of net revenues in 1989.) Perhaps the most fundamental reason for this is the company's commitment to research and development. Note that research and development expenses were $470 million in 1993, up $118 million from 1992.

All of the income statement items (except "Other") reflect the company's rapid growth. The increases ranged from 30.7 to 46.4%. Especially note the large $351 million or 41.1% increase in "Sales and marketing." This suggests the company's leadership and strong response to competition in the software industry. Although the dollar increase in "Interest income—net" was only $26 million, this amounted to a 46.4% increase. This is consistent with the large increase in Cash and short-term investments reported on the balance sheet.

Illustration 17-2

MICROSOFT CORPORATION
Comparative Income Statement
For Years Ended June 30, 1993, and 1992
(in millions)

	Years Ended June 30		Amount of Increase or (Decrease) during 1993	Percentage Increase or (Decrease) during 1993
	1993	**1992**		
Net revenues	$3,753	$2,759	$994	36.0
Cost of revenues	633	467	166	35.6
Gross profit	$3,120	$2,292	$828	36.1
Operating expenses:				
Research and development	$ 470	$ 352	$118	33.5
Sales and marketing	1,205	854	351	41.1
General and administrative	119	90	29	32.2
Total operating expenses	$1,794	$1,296	$498	38.4
Operating income	$1,326	$ 996	$330	33.1
Interest income—net	82	56	26	46.4
Other*	(7)	(11)	(4)	(36.4)
Income before income taxes	$1,401	$1,041	$360	34.6
Provision for income taxes	448	333	115	34.5
Net income	$ 953	$ 708	$245	34.6
Earnings per share	$ 3.15	$ 2.41	$0.74	30.7
Weighted-average shares outstanding	303	294		

*On this line, the (7) and (11) are shown in parentheses because they represent expenses that are subtracted in the calculation of income. The (4) is in parentheses because the Other item decreased from 11 to 7. In the third column, the expense decrease (4) must be added to the $330 and $26 increases in operating income and interest income to reconcile the $360 increase in Income before income taxes.

Trend Percentages

Trend percentages (also known as *index numbers*) can be used to describe changes that have occurred from one period to the next. They are also used to compare data that cover a number of years. To calculate trend percentages:

1. Select a base year and assign each item on the base year statement a weight of 100%.
2. Express each item from the statements for the other years as a percentage of its base year amount. To determine these percentages, divide the amounts in the nonbase years by the amount of the item in the base year.

For example, consider the following data for Microsoft Corporation:

	1993	1992	1991	1990	1989
Net revenues	$3,753	$2,759	$1,843	$1,183	$804
Cost of revenues	633	467	362	253	204
Gross profit	$3,120	$2,292	$1,481	$ 930	$600

Using 1989 as the base year, we calculate the trend percentages for each year by dividing the dollar amounts in each year by the 1989 dollar amounts. When the percentages are calculated, the trends for these items appear as follows:

FAST HINT
Important Point to Remember:
An alternative method for calculating percentage increases or decreases is to divide the current year's total by last year's amount and subtract 1.0. For example, net revenues in Illustration 17–2 increased by 36.0% ($3,753/$2,759) − 1.0 = 36%).

Illustration 17–3 Trend Lines Showing Percentage Changes in Net Revenues, Cost of Revenues, and Gross Profit

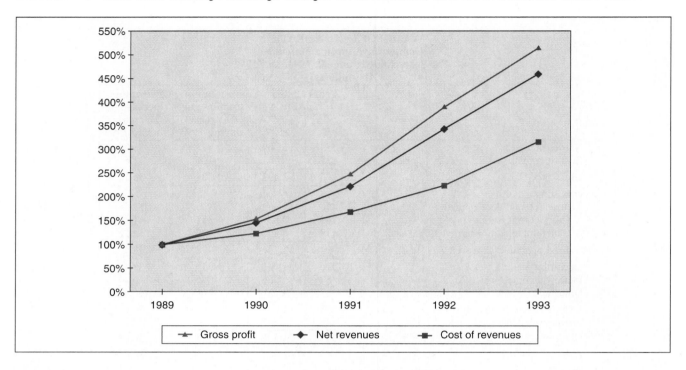

FAST HINT
Relevant Exercise:
To apply these concepts, work
Exercise 17–1.

	1993	1992	1991	1990	1989
Net revenues	466.8%	343.2%	229.2%	147.1%	100%
Cost of revenues	310.3	228.9	177.5	124.0	100
Gross profit	520.0	382.0	246.8	155.0	100

Illustration 17–3 presents the same data in a graph. A graph can help you identify trends and detect changes in their strength or direction. For example, note that the gross profit line and the net revenues line were bending upward from 1989 to 1991 but were essentially straight from 1991 to 1993. In other words, the rates of increase were improving from 1989 to 1991 but were basically unchanged from 1991 to 1993.

A graph also may help you identify and understand the relationships between items. For example, the graph in Illustration 17–3 shows that through 1993, cost of revenues increased at a rate that was somewhat less than the increase in net revenues. Further, the differing trends in these two items had a clear effect on the percentage changes in gross profit. That is, gross profit increased each year at a faster rate than net revenues or cost of revenues.

The analysis of financial statement items also may include the relationships between items on different financial statements. For example, note the following comparison of Microsoft's total assets and net revenues:

	1993	1989	1993 Amount as a Percentage of 1989
Net revenues	$3,753	$804	466.8%
Total assets (fiscal year-end)	3,805	721	527.7

The rate of increase in total assets was even larger than the increase in net revenues. Was this change favorable? We cannot say for sure. It might suggest that the

Illustration 17–4

	June 30		Common-size Percentages	
	1993	**1992**	**1993**	**1992**
MICROSOFT CORPORATION **Common-Size Comparative Balance Sheet** **June 30, 1993, and June 30, 1992** **(in millions)**				
Assets				
Current assets:				
Cash and short-term investments	$2,290	$1,345	60.2	50.9
Accounts receivable, net of				
allowances of $76 and $57	338	270	8.9	10.2
Inventories	127	86	3.3	3.3
Other	95	69	2.5	2.6
Total current assets	$2,850	$1,770	74.9	67.0
Property, plant, and equipment—net	867	767	22.8	29.1
Other assets	88	103	2.3	3.9
Total assets	$3,805	$2,640	100.0	100.0
Liabilities and Stockholders' Equity				
Current liabilities:				
Accounts payable	$ 239	$ 196	6.3	7.4
Accrued compensation	86	62	2.3	2.3
Income taxes payable	127	73	3.3	2.8
Other	111	116	2.9	4.4
Total current liabilities	$ 563	$ 447	14.8	16.9
Commitments and contingencies	—	—		
Stockholders' equity:				
Common stock and paid-in capital—				
shares authorized 500; issued and				
outstanding 282 and 272	$1,086	$ 657	28.5	24.9
Retained earnings	2,156	1,536	56.7	58.2
Total stockholders' equity	$3,242	$2,193	85.2	83.1
Total liabilities and stockholders' equity . .	$3,805	$2,640	100.0	100.0

company is no longer able to use its assets as efficiently as in earlier years. On the other hand, it might mean that the company is poised for even greater growth in future years. Financial statement analysis often leads the analyst to ask questions, without providing one clear answer.

Common-Size Comparative Statements

Although the comparative statements illustrated so far show how each item has changed over time, they do not emphasize the relative importance of each item. Changes in the relative importance of each financial statement item are shown more clearly by **common-size comparative statements.**

In common-size statements, each item is expressed as a percentage of a *base amount.* For a common-size balance sheet, the base amount is usually the amount of total assets. This total is assigned a value of 100%. (Of course, the total amount of liabilities plus owners' equity also equals 100%.) Then, each asset, liability, and owners' equity item is shown as a percentage of total assets (or total liabilities plus owners' equity). If you present a company's successive balance sheets in this way, changes in the mixture of the assets or liabilities and equity are more readily apparent.

FAST HINT
Important Point to Remember:
Common-size statements also can be used to compare two or more companies in the same industry.

Illustration 17-5

	Years Ended June 30		Common-size Percentages	
	1993	**1992**	**1993**	**1992**
Net revenues	$3,753	$2,759	100.0	100.0
Cost of revenues	633	467	16.9	16.9
Gross profit	$3,120	$2,292	83.1	83.1
Operating expenses:				
Research and development	$ 470	$ 352	12.5	12.8
Sales and marketing	1,205	854	32.1	31.0
General and administrative	119	90	3.2	3.3
Total operating expenses	$1,794	$1,296	47.8	47.0*
Operating income	$1,326	$ 996	35.3	36.1
Interest income—net	82	56	2.2	2.0
Other	(7)	(11)	(0.2)	(0.4)
Income before income taxes	$1,401	$1,041	37.3	37.7
Provision for income taxes	448	333	11.9	12.1
Net income	$ 953	$ 708	25.4	25.7*
Earnings per share	$ 3.15	$ 2.41		
Weighted-average shares outstanding	303	294		

MICROSOFT CORPORATION
Common-Size Comparative Income Statement
For Years Ended June 30, 1993, and 1992
(in millions)

*Does not foot due to rounding.

FAST HINT
Relevant Exercise:
To apply these concepts, work
Exercise 17–3.

For example, look at the common-size comparative balance sheet for Microsoft in Illustration 17–4. Note that Cash and short-term investments amounted to 50.9% of total assets at the end of the 1992 fiscal year. By comparison, they were 60.2% of total assets at the end of 1993.

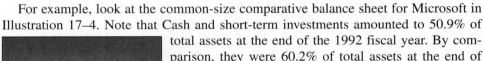

In producing a common-size income statement, the amount of net sales is usually the base amount and is assigned a value of 100%. Then, each statement item appears as a percentage of net sales. If you think of the 100% sales amount as representing one sales dollar, the remaining items show how each sales dollar was distributed among costs, expenses, and profit. For example, the comparative income statement in Illustration 17–5 shows that for each dollar of **Microsoft's** net revenue during 1993, research and development expenses amounted to 12.5 cents. In 1992, research and development consumed 12.8 cents of each sales dollar. Common-size percentages help the analyst see any potentially important changes in a company's expenses. For Microsoft, the relative size of each expense changed very little from 1992 to 1993.

Many corporate annual reports include graphic presentations such as those in Illustration 17–6 from Microsoft's 1993 Annual Report. The pie chart on the left side of the illustration shows the revenues generated by each of the company's product groups. The pie chart on the right shows the revenues by sales channel. In that chart, OEM refers to original equipment manufacturers. In the annual report, the data for these charts did not appear in the financial statements. Instead, they were included as part of the discussion and analysis by management.

Illustration 17-6   Pie-Chart Presentations, Microsoft Corporation

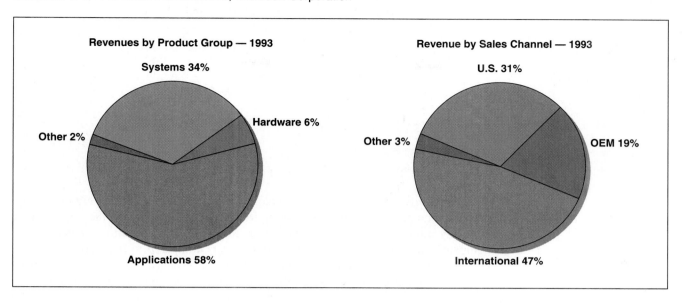

Progress Check

17-3   **On common-size comparative statements, which of the following is true?**   *(a)* **Each item is expressed as a percentage of a base amount;**   *(b)* **Total assets is assigned a value of 100%;**   *(c)* **Amounts from two or more successive periods are placed side by side;**   *(d)* **All of the above are true.**

17-4   **What is the difference between between the percentages shown on a comparative income statement and those shown a common-size comparative income statement?**

17-5   **Trend percentages:**   *(a)* **Are shown on the comparative income statement and balance sheet;**   *(b)* **Are shown on common-size comparative statements;**   *(c)* **Are also known as index numbers.**

The amount of current assets less current liabilities is called the **working capital** or *net working capital* of a business. A business must maintain an adequate amount of working capital to meet current debts, carry sufficient inventories, and take advantage of cash discounts. Indeed, a business that runs out of working capital cannot meet its current obligations or continue operations.

Current Ratio

When evaluating the working capital of a business, you must look beyond the dollar amount of current assets less current liabilities. Also consider the relationship between the amounts of current assets and current liabilities. Recall from Chapter 3 that the *current ratio* describes a company's ability to pay its short-term obligations. The current ratio relates current assets to current liabilities, as follows:

$$\text{Current ratio} = \frac{\text{Current assets}}{\text{Current liabilities}}$$

ANALYSIS OF SHORT-TERM LIQUIDITY

LO 3

Calculate and explain the interpretation of the ratios, turnovers, and rates of return used to evaluate *(a)* short-term liquidity, *(b)* long-term risk and capital structure, and *(c)* operating efficiency and profitability.

For example, using the information in Illustration 17–1, Microsoft's working capital positions and current ratios at the end of its 1993 and 1992 years were:

	June 30, 1993	June 30, 1992
(In millions)		
Current assets	$2,850	$1,770
Current liabilities	563	447
Working capital	$2,287	$1,323
Current ratio:		
$2,850/$563	5.1 to 1	
$1,770/$447		4.0 to 1

A high current ratio generally indicates a strong position because a high ratio suggests the company is capable of meeting its current obligations. On the other hand, a company might have a current ratio that is too high. This condition means that the company has invested too much in current assets compared to its needs. Normally, current assets do not generate very much additional revenue. Therefore, if a company invests too much in current assets, the investment is not being used efficiently.

Years ago, bankers and other creditors often used a current ratio of 2 to 1 as a rule of thumb in evaluating the debt-paying ability of a credit-seeking company. A company with a 2 to 1 current ratio was generally thought to be a good credit risk in the short run. However, most lenders realize that the 2 to 1 rule of thumb is not a good test of debt-paying ability. Whether a company's current ratio is good or bad depends on at least three factors:

1. The nature of the company's business.
2. The composition of its current assets.
3. The turnover rate for some of its current assets.

Whether a company's current ratio is adequate depends on the nature of its business. A service company that has no inventories other than supplies and that grants little or no credit may be able to operate on a current ratio of less than 1 to 1 if its sales generate enough cash to pay its current liabilities on time. On the other hand, a company that sells high-fashion clothing or furniture may occasionally misjudge customer demand. If this happens, the company's inventory may not generate as much cash as expected. A company that faces risks like these may need a current ratio of much more than 2 to 1 to protect its liquidity.

Therefore, when you study the adequacy of working capital, consider the type of business under review. Before you decide that a company's current ratio is too low or too high, compare the company's current ratio with ratios of other successful companies in the same industry. Another important source of insight is to observe how the ratio has changed over time.

Keep in mind that the current ratio can be affected by a company's choice of an inventory flow assumption. For example, a company that uses LIFO tends to report a smaller amount of current assets than if it uses FIFO. Therefore, consider the underlying factors before deciding that a given current ratio is acceptable.

Also consider the composition of a company's current assets when you evaluate its working capital position. Cash and short-term investments are more liquid than accounts and notes receivable. And, short-term receivables normally are more liquid than merchandise inventory. Cash can be used to pay current debts at once. But, accounts receivable and merchandise inventory must be converted into cash before payments can be made. Therefore, an excessive amount of receivables and inventory could weaken the company's ability to pay its current liabilities.

One way to take the composition of current assets into account is to evaluate the acid-test ratio. We discuss this next; then, we examine the turnover rates for receivables and inventories.

Acid-Test Ratio

Recall from Chapter 5 that an easily calculated check on current asset composition is the *acid-test ratio,* also called the *quick ratio.* Quick assets are cash, short-term investments, accounts receivable, and notes receivable. These are the most liquid types of current assets. Calculate the ratio as follows:

$$\text{Acid-test ratio} = \frac{\text{Quick assets}}{\text{Current liabilities}}$$

Using the information in Illustration 17–1, we calculate Microsoft's acid-test ratios as follows:

	June 30, 1993	June 30, 1992
(In millions)		
Cash and short-term investments	$2,290	$1,345
Accounts receivable, net of allowances	338	270
Total quick assets	$2,628	$1,615
Current liabilities	$ 563	$ 447
Acid-test ratio:		
$2,628/$563	4.7 to 1	
$1,615/$447		3.6 to 1

A traditional rule of thumb for an acceptable acid-test ratio is 1 to 1. However, as is true for all financial ratios, you should be skeptical about rules of thumb. The working capital requirements of a company are also affected by how frequently the company converts its current assets into cash. Thus, a careful analysis of a company's short-term liquidity should include additional analyses of its receivables and inventories.

FAST HINT
Relevant Exercise:
To apply these concepts, work Exercise 17–4.

Accounts Receivable Turnover

One way to measure how frequently a company converts its receivables into cash is to calculate the accounts receivable turnover. As you learned in Chapter 8, this is calculated as follows:

$$\text{Accounts receivable turnover} = \frac{\text{Net sales}}{\text{Average accounts receivable}}$$

Although this ratio is widely known as accounts receivable turnover, all short-term receivables from customers normally are included in the denominator. Thus, if a company has short-term notes receivable, those balances should be included with the accounts receivable. In the numerator, the calculation would be more precise if credit sales were used. Usually, however, net sales is used because information about credit sales is not available.

Applying the formula to Microsoft's 1993 fiscal year results, the company's accounts receivable turnover was:

$$\frac{\$3,753}{(\$338 + \$270)/2} = 12.3 \text{ times}$$

FAST HINT
Alternative Example:
Refer to the financial statements for Federal Express in Appendix G. What was the company's accounts receivable turnover for 1993?
Answer:
($922,727 + $899,773)/2
= $911,250
$7,808,043/$911,250 = 8.6 times

If accounts receivable are collected quickly, the accounts receivable turnover is high. In general, this is favorable because it means that the company does not have to commit large amounts of capital to accounts receivable. However, an accounts receivable turnover may be too high. This might occur when credit terms are so restrictive they negatively affect sales volume.

Sometimes, the ending accounts receivable balance can substitute for the average balance in calculating accounts receivable turnover. This is acceptable if the effect is not significant. Also, some analysts prefer using gross accounts receivable before subtracting the allowance for doubtful accounts. However, balance sheets may report only the net amount of accounts receivable.

Days' Sales Uncollected

Accounts receivable turnover is only one way to measure how frequently a company collects its accounts. Another method is to calculate the days' sales uncollected, which we defined in Chapter 7 as:

$$\text{Days' sales uncollected} = \frac{\text{Accounts receivable}}{\text{Net sales}} \times 365$$

Although this formula takes the usual approach of placing accounts receivable in the numerator, short-term notes receivable from customers should be included. To illustrate, we refer to the information about Microsoft in Illustrations 17–1 and 17–2. The days' sales uncollected on June 30, 1993, was:

$$\frac{\$338}{\$3,753} \times 365 = 32.9 \text{ days}$$

Days' sales uncollected has more meaning if you know the credit terms. A rule of thumb is that days' sales uncollected: *(a)* should not exceed one and one-third times the days in the credit period, if discounts are not offered; *(b)* should not exceed one and one-third times the days in its discount period, if discounts are offered.

Turnover of Merchandise Inventory

Working capital requirements are also affected by how long a company holds merchandise inventory before selling it. This effect can be measured by calculating merchandise turnover, which we defined in Chapter 9 as:

$$\text{Merchandise turnover} = \frac{\text{Cost of goods sold}}{\text{Average merchandise inventory}}$$

Using the cost of revenues and inventories information in Illustrations 17–1 and 17–2, we calculate Microsoft's merchandise turnover during 1993 as follows (cost of goods sold is called cost of revenues on Microsoft's income statement):

$$\frac{\$633}{(\$127 + \$86)/2} = 5.9 \text{ times}$$

In this calculation, the average inventory was estimated by averaging the beginning and the ending inventories for 1993. In case the beginning and ending inventories do not represent the amount normally on hand, an average of the quarterly inventories may be used, if that is available.

From a working capital point of view, a company with a high turnover requires a smaller investment in inventory than one that produces the same sales with a low turnover. On the other hand, the merchandise turnover may be too high if a company keeps such a small inventory that sales volume is restricted.

FAST HINT
Important Point to Remember:
The days' sales uncollected ratio reflects the number of days in the average collection period of a business. The average collection period can be estimated by dividing 365 by the accounts receivable turnover ratio. For example, 365 divided by an accounts receivable turnover of 12 would indicate a 30-day average collection period.

FAST HINT
Critical Thought Question:
How would using LIFO affect the calculation of merchandise turnover?

Days' Stock on Hand

Recall from Chapter 9 that days' stock on hand is another means of evaluating the liquidity of a company's inventory. It relates to inventory in a similar fashion as day's sales uncollected relates to receivables. The calculation is:

$$\text{Days' stock on hand} = \frac{\text{Ending inventory}}{\text{Cost of goods sold}} \times 365$$

Applying the formula to Microsoft's 1993 information, we calculate days' stock on hand as:

$$\frac{\$127}{\$633} \times 365 = 73.2 \text{ days}$$

Assuming the particular products in inventory are those customers demand, the formula estimates that the inventory will be converted into receivables (or cash) in 73.2 days. If all of Microsoft's sales were credit sales, the conversion of inventory to receivables in 73.2 days plus the conversion of receivables to cash in 32.9 days would suggest that the inventory would be converted into cash in about 106 days (73.2 + 32.9 = 106.1).

FAST HINT
Relevant Exercise:
To apply these concepts, work Exercise 17–5.

Progress Check

17-6   The following is taken from the 12/31/X2 balance sheet of Paff Company: cash, $820,000; accounts receivable, $240,000; inventories, $470,000; plant and equipment, $910,000; accounts payable, $350,000; and income taxes payable, $180,000. Calculate the *(a)* current ratio and *(b)* acid-test ratio.

17-7   On 12/31/X1, Paff Company (see 17-6) had accounts receivable of $290,000 and inventories of $530,000. Also, during 19X2, net sales amounted to $2,500,000 and cost of goods sold was $750,000. Calculate the *(a)* accounts receivable turnover, *(b)* days' sales uncollected, *(c)* merchandise turnover, and *(d)* days' stock on hand.

An analysis of working capital evaluates the short-term liquidity of the company. However, analysts are also interested in a company's ability to meet its obligations and provide security to its creditors over the long run. Indicators of this ability include *debt* and *equity* ratios, the relationship between *pledged assets* and *secured liabilities,* and the company's capacity to earn *sufficient income to pay its fixed interest charges.*

Debt and Equity Ratios

Financial analysts are always interested in the portion of a company's assets contributed by its owners and the portion contributed by creditors. This relationship is described by the debt ratio you learned about in Chapter 2. Recall that the debt ratio expresses total liabilities as a percentage of total assets. The **equity ratio** provides complementary information by expressing total stockholders' equity as a percentage of total assets.

We calculate the debt and equity ratios of Microsoft Corporation as follows:

	1993	1992
a. Total liabilities (all short-term)	$ 563	$ 447
b. Total stockholders' equity	3,242	2,193
c. Total liabilities and stockholders' equity	$3,805	$2,640
Percentages provided by creditors: (a/c)	14.8%	16.9%
Percentages provided by stockholders: (b/c)	85.2%	83.1%

ANALYSIS OF LONG-TERM RISK AND CAPITAL STRUCTURE

LO 3

Calculate and explain the interpretation of the ratios, turnovers, and rates of return used to evaluate *(a)* short-term liquidity, *(b)* long-term risk and capital structure, and *(c)* operating efficiency and profitability.

FAST HINT
Additional Insight:
Bank examiners from the FDIC and other regulatory agencies use debt and equity ratios to monitor compliance with regulatory capital requirements imposed on commercial banks and S&Ls.

Microsoft's financial statements reflect very little debt compared to most companies. It has no long-term liabilities and, at the end of the 1993 year, its current liabilities provide only 14.8% of the total assets. In general, a company is less risky if it has only a small amount of debt in its capital structure. The larger the portion provided by stockholders, the more losses can be absorbed by stockholders before the remaining assets become inadequate to satisfy the claims of creditors.

From the stockholders' point of view, however, including debt in the capital structure of a company may be desirable, so long as the risk is not too great. If a business can earn a return on borrowed capital that is higher than the cost of borrowing, the difference represents increased income to stockholders. Because debt can have the effect of increasing the return to stockholders, the inclusion of debt is sometimes described as financial leverage. Companies are said to be highly leveraged if a large portion of their assets is financed by debt.

Pledged Assets to Secured Liabilities

In Chapter 15, we explained how to use the ratio of pledged assets to secured liabilities to evaluate the risk of nonpayment faced by secured creditors. Recall that the ratio also may provide information of interest to unsecured creditors. The ratio is calculated as follows:

$$\text{Pledged assets to secured liabilities} = \frac{\text{Book value of pledged assets}}{\text{Secured liabilities}}$$

Regardless of how helpful this ratio might be in evaluating the risk faced by creditors, the information needed to calculate the ratio is seldom presented in published financial statements. Thus, it is used primarily by persons who have the ability to obtain the information directly from the company managers.

The usual rule-of-thumb minimum value for this ratio is 2 to 1. However, the ratio needs careful interpretation because it is based on the book value of the pledged assets. As you know, book values are not intended to reflect the amount that would be received for the assets in a liquidation sale. Also, the long-term earning ability of the company with pledged assets may be more important than the value of the pledged assets. Creditors prefer that a debtor be able to pay with cash generated by operating activities rather than with cash obtained by liquidating assets.

Times Fixed Interest Charges Earned

As you learned in Chapter 12, the times fixed interest charges earned ratio is often calculated to describe the security of the return offered to creditors. The amount of income before the deduction of interest charges and income taxes is the amount available to pay the interest charges. Calculate the ratio as follows:

$$\text{Times fixed interest charges earned} = \frac{\text{Income before interest and income taxes}}{\text{Interest expense}}$$

The larger this ratio, the greater the security for the lenders. A rule of thumb for this statistic is that creditors are reasonably safe if the company earns its fixed interest charges two or more times each year. Look in Illustration 17–2 and observe that Microsoft did not report interest expense as a separate item. Apparently interest expense is not material; probably it is offset against interest income which is reported as "Interest income—net." Also recall from Illustration 17–1 that Microsoft did not have any long-term debt. Furthermore, few if any of the company's current liabilities would be likely to generate interest expense. As a result, we are not able to calculate a times fixed interest charges earned ratio for Microsoft. Yet, we should again recognize that there appears to be little risk for Microsoft's creditors.

FAST HINT
Critical Thought Question:
Why are the times fixed interest charges earned ratio and the debt and equity ratios of special interest to commercial bank lending officers?

FAST HINT
Relevant Exercise:
To apply these concepts, work Exercise 17-6.

Financial analysts are especially interested in the ability of a company to use its assets efficiently to produce profits for its owners and thus provide cash flows to them. Several ratios are available to help you evaluate operating efficiency and profitability.

Profit Margin

The operating efficiency of a company can be expressed in two components. The first is the company's *profit margin.* As you learned in Chapter 4, this ratio describes a company's ability to earn a net income from sales. It is measured by expressing net income as a percentage of revenues. For example, we can use the information in Illustration 17–2 to calculate **Microsoft's** 1993 profit margin as follows:

$$\text{Profit margin} = \frac{\text{Net income}}{\text{Revenues}} = \frac{\$953}{\$3,753} = 25.4\%$$

To evaluate the profit margin of a company, consider the nature of the industry in which the company operates. For example, a publishing company might be expected to have a profit margin between 10 and 15%, while a retail supermarket might have a normal profit margin of 1 or 2%.

Total Asset Turnover

The second component of operating efficiency is *total asset turnover,* which describes the ability of the company to use its assets to generate sales. In Chapter 10, you learned to calculate this ratio as follows:

$$\text{Total asset turnover} = \frac{\text{Net sales}}{\text{Average total assets}}$$

In calculating Microsoft's total asset turnover for 1993, we follow the usual practice of averaging the total assets at the beginning and the end of the year. Taking the information from Illustrations 17-1 and 17-2, the calculation is:

$$\frac{\$3,753}{(\$3,805 + \$2,640)/2} = 1.165 \text{ times*}$$

*Carried to three decimal places to avoid later rounding error.

Both profit margin and total asset turnover describe the two basic components of operating efficiency. However, they also evaluate management performance because the management of a company is fundamentally responsible for its operating efficiency.

Return on Total Assets

Because operating efficiency has two basic components (profit margin and total asset turnover), analysts frequently calculate a summary measure of these components. This summary measure is the *return on total assets* that we discussed in Chapter 11. Recall that the calculation is:

$$\text{Return on total assets} = \frac{\text{Net income}}{\text{Average total assets}}$$

Applying this to Microsoft's 1993 year, we calculate return on total assets as:

$$\frac{\$953}{(\$3,805 + \$2,640)/2} = 29.6\%$$

ANALYSIS OF OPERATING EFFICIENCY AND PROFITABILITY

FAST HINT
Critical Thought Question:
Why would earnings per share be the most commonly used measure of profitability?

FAST HINT
Alternative Example:
Refer to the financial statements for Federal Express in Appendix G. What was the company's return on total assets in 1993?
Answer:
($5,793,064 + $5,463,186)/2 = $5,628,125
$53,866/$5,628,125 = 1.0%

Microsoft's 29.6% return on total assets appears very favorable compared to most businesses. However, you should make comparisons with competing companies and alternative investment opportunities before reaching a final conclusion. Also, you should evaluate the trend in the rates of return earned by the company in recent years.

Earlier, we said that the return on total assets summarizes the two components of operating efficiency—profit margin and total asset turnover. The following calculation shows the relationship between these three measures. Notice that both profit margin and total asset turnover contribute to overall operating efficiency, as measured by return on total assets.

FAST HINT
Relevant Exercise:
To apply these concepts, work Exercise 17–7.

Profit margin	$\times$	Total asset turnover	$=$	Return on total assets
$\dfrac{\text{Net income}}{\text{Net sales}}$	$\times$	$\dfrac{\text{Net sales}}{\text{Average total assets}}$	$=$	$\dfrac{\text{Net income}}{\text{Average total assets}}$

For Microsoft Corporation:

25.4%	$\times$	1.165	$=$	29.6%

Return on Common Stockholders' Equity

Perhaps the most important reason for operating a business is to earn a net income for its owners. The *return on common stockholders' equity* measures the success of a business in reaching this goal. In Chapter 1, we simplified this calculation by basing it on the beginning balance of owners' equity. However, many companies have frequent transactions that involve issuing and perhaps repurchasing stock during each year. Thus, you should allow for these events by calculating the return based on the average stockholders' equity, as follows:

$$\text{Return on common stockholders' equity} = \frac{\text{Net income} - \text{Preferred dividends}}{\text{Average common stockholders' equity}}$$

Recall from Illustration 17–1 that Microsoft did not have any preferred stock outstanding. As a result, we determine Microsoft's 1993 return as follows:

$$\frac{\$953}{(\$3,242 + \$2,193)/2} = 35.1\%$$

When preferred stock is outstanding, the denominator in the calculation should be the book value of the common stock. In the numerator, the dividends on cumulative preferred stock must be subtracted whether they were declared or are in arrears. If the preferred is not cumulative, the dividends are subtracted only if declared.

Price Earnings Ratio

Recall from Chapter 14 that the price earnings ratio is calculated as follows:

$$\text{Price earnings ratio} = \frac{\text{Market price per share}}{\text{Earnings per share}}$$

FAST HINT
Important Point to Remember:
The PE ratio can be thought of as an indicator of investors' expected growth and risk for a corporation's stock. A high level of perceived risk suggests a low PE ratio. A high growth rate suggests a high PE ratio.

Sometimes, the predicted earnings per share for the next period is used in the denominator of the calculation. Other times, the reported earnings per share for the most recent period is used. In either case, the ratio is an indicator of the future growth of and risk related to the company's earnings as perceived by investors who establish the market price of the stock.

During the last three months of Microsoft's 1993 year, the market price of its common stock ranged from a low of $65.50 to a high of $98. Using the $3.15 earnings per share that was reported after the year-end, the price earnings ratios for the low and the high were:

$$\text{Low: } \frac{\$65.50}{\$3.15} = 20.8 \qquad \text{High: } \frac{\$98.00}{\$3.15} = 31.1$$

In its 1993 annual report, Microsoft's management reported that it did not expect the 1994 revenue growth rates to be as high as those for 1993. Management also indicated that operating expenses as a percentage of revenues might increase. Nevertheless, the price earnings ratios are much higher than for most companies. No doubt, Microsoft's high ratios reflect the expectation of investors that the company would continue to grow at a much higher rate than most companies.

Dividend Yield

As you learned in Chapter 13, *dividend yield* is a statistic used to compare the dividend-paying performance of different investment alternatives. The formula is:

$$\text{Dividend yield} = \frac{\text{Annual dividends per share}}{\text{Market price per share}}$$

Some companies may not declare dividends because they need the cash in the business. For example, Microsoft's 1993 Annual Report stated that the company had not declared any dividends.

Progress Check

17-8 Which ratio describes the security of the return offered to creditors? *(a)* Debt ratio; *(b)* Equity ratio; *(c)* Times fixed interest charges earned; *(d)* Pledged assets to secured liabilities.

17-9 Which ratio measures the success of a business in earning net income for its owners? *(a)* Profit margin; *(b)* Return on common stockholders' equity; *(c)* Price earnings ratio; *(d)* Dividend yield.

17-10 If BK Company has net sales of $8,500,000, net income of $945,000, and total asset turnover of 1.8 times, what is BK's return on total assets?

To evaluate short-term liquidity, use these ratios:

$$\text{Current ratio} = \frac{\text{Current assets}}{\text{Current liabilities}}$$

$$\text{Acid-test ratio} = \frac{\text{Cash + Short-term investments + Current receivables}}{\text{Current liabilities}}$$

$$\text{Accounts receivable turnover} = \frac{\text{Net sales}}{\text{Average accounts receivable}}$$

$$\text{Days' sales uncollected} = \frac{\text{Accounts receivable}}{\text{Net sales}} \times 365$$

$$\text{Merchandise turnover} = \frac{\text{Cost of goods sold}}{\text{Average merchandise inventory}}$$

$$\text{Days' stock on hand} = \frac{\text{Ending inventory}}{\text{Cost of goods sold}} \times 365$$

To evaluate long-term risk and capital structure, use these ratios:

$$\text{Debt ratio} = \frac{\text{Total liabilities}}{\text{Total assets}}$$

$$\text{Equity ratio} = \frac{\text{Total stockholders' equity}}{\text{Total assets}}$$

FAST HINT
Critical Thought Question:
Why would some investors avoid stocks with high price earnings multiples?

FAST HINT
Relevant Exercise:
To apply these concepts, work Exercise 17–8.

FAST HINT
Additional Insight:
Corporate PE ratios and dividend yields can be found by looking at daily stock market quotations listed in *The Wall Street Journal, Investor's Business Daily*, or the business section of many local newspapers.

REVIEW OF FINANCIAL STATEMENT RATIOS AND STATISTICS FOR ANALYSIS

FAST HINT
Important Point to Remember:
Accounts receivable turnover can also be calculated by dividing 365 by days' sales uncollected.

$$\text{Pledged assets to secured liabilities} = \frac{\text{Book value of pledged assets}}{\text{Secured liabilities}}$$

$$\text{Times fixed interest charges earned} = \frac{\text{Income before interest and taxes}}{\text{Interest expense}}$$

To evaluate operating efficiency and profitability, use these ratios:

$$\text{Profit margin} = \frac{\text{Net income}}{\text{Net sales}}$$

$$\text{Total asset turnover} = \frac{\text{Net sales}}{\text{Average total assets}}$$

$$\text{Return on total assets} = \frac{\text{Net income}}{\text{Average total assets}}$$

$$\text{Return on common stockholders' equity} = \frac{\text{Net income} - \text{Preferred dividends}}{\text{Average common stockholders' equity}}$$

$$\text{Price earnings ratio} = \frac{\text{Market price per common share}}{\text{Earnings per share}}$$

$$\text{Dividend yield} = \frac{\text{Annual dividends per share}}{\text{Market price per share}}$$

STANDARDS OF COMPARISON

LO 4

State the limitations associated with using financial statement ratios and the sources from which standards for comparison may be obtained.

After computing ratios and turnovers in the process of analyzing financial statements, you have to decide whether the calculated amounts suggest good, bad, or merely average performance by the company. To make these judgments, you must have some bases for comparison. The following are possibilities:

1. An experienced analyst may compare the ratios and turnovers of the company under review with *subjective* standards acquired from past experiences.

2. For purposes of comparison, an analyst may calculate the ratios and turnovers of a selected group of competing companies in the same *industry*.

3. *Published* ratios and turnovers (such as those provided by Dun & Bradstreet) may be used for comparison.

4. Some local and national trade associations gather data from their members and publish *standard* or *average* ratios for their trade or industry. When available, these data can give the analyst a useful basis for comparison.

5. *Rule-of-thumb* standards can be used as a basis for comparison.

Of these five standards, the ratios and turnovers of a selected group of competing companies normally are the best bases for comparison. Rule-of-thumb standards should be applied with great care and then only if they seem reasonable in light of past experience and the industry's norms.

FAST HINT
Relevant Quick Study:
To apply these concepts, work QS 17–4.

Progress Check

17-11 Which of the following would not be used as a basis for comparison when analyzing ratios and turnovers?
   a. Companies in different industries.
   b. Subjective standards from past experience.
   c. Rule-of-thumb standards.
   d. Averages within a trade or industry.

17-12 Which of the typical bases of comparison is usually best?

LO 1. Explain the relationship between financial reporting and general purpose financial statements. Financial reporting is intended to provide information that is useful to investors, creditors, and others in making investment, credit, and similar decisions. The information is communicated in a variety of ways, including general purpose financial statements. These statements normally include an income statement, balance sheet, statement of changes in stockholders' equity or statement of retained earnings, statement of cash flows, and the related footnotes.

LO 2. Describe, prepare, and interpret comparative financial statements and common-size comparative statements. Comparative financial statements show amounts for two or more successive periods, sometimes with the changes in the items disclosed in absolute and percentage terms. In common-size statements, each item is expressed as a percentage of a base amount. The base amount for the balance sheet is usually total assets, and the base amount for the income statement is usually net sales.

LO 3. Calculate and explain the interpretation of the ratios, turnovers, and rates of return used to evaluate (*a*) short-term liquidity, (*b*) long-term risk and capital structure, and (*c*) operating efficiency and profitability. To evaluate the short-term liquidity of a company, calculate a current ratio, an acid-test ratio, the accounts receivable turnover, the days' sales uncollected, the merchandise turnover, and the days' stock on hand.

In evaluating the long-term risk and capital structure of a company, calculate debt and equity ratios, pledged assets to secured liabilities, and the number of times fixed interest charges were earned.

In evaluating operating efficiency and profitability, calculate profit margin, total asset turnover, return on total assets, and return on common stockholders' equity. Other statistics used to evaluate the profitability of alternative investments include the price earnings ratio and the dividend yield.

LO 4. State the limitations associated with using financial statement ratios and the sources from which standards for comparison may be obtained. In deciding whether financial statement ratio values are satisfactory, too high, or too low, you must have some bases for comparison. These bases may come from past experience and personal judgment, from ratios of similar companies, or from ratios published by trade associations or other public sources. Traditional rules of thumb should be applied with great care and only if they seem reasonable in light of past experience.

SUMMARY OF THE CHAPTER IN TERMS OF LEARNING OBJECTIVES

DEMONSTRATION PROBLEM

Use the financial statements of Precision Co. to satisfy the following requirements:

1. Prepare a comparative income statement showing the percentage increase or decrease for 19X2 over 19X1.
2. Prepare a common-size comparative balance sheet for 19X2 and 19X1.
3. Compute the following ratios as of December 31, 19X2, or for the year ended December 31, 19X2:

   a. Current ratio.
   b. Acid-test ratio.
   c. Accounts receivable turnover.
   d. Days' sales uncollected.
   e. Merchandise turnover.
   f. Debt ratio

   g. Pledged assets to secured liabilities.
   h. Times fixed interest charges earned.
   i. Profit margin.
   j. Total asset turnover.
   k. Return on total assets.
   l. Return on common stockholders' equity.

PRECISION COMPANY
Comparative Income Statement
For Years Ended December 31, 19X2 and 19X1

	19X2	19X1
Sales	$2,486,000	$2,075,000
Cost of goods sold	1,523,000	1,222,000
Gross profit from sales	$ 963,000	$ 853,000
Operating expenses:		
Advertising expense	$ 145,000	$ 100,000
Sales salaries expense	240,000	280,000
Office salaries expense	165,000	200,000
Insurance expense	100,000	45,000
Supplies expense	26,000	35,000
Depreciation expenses	85,000	75,000
Miscellaneous expense	17,000	15,000
Total operating expenses	$ 778,000	$ 750,000
Operating income	$ 185,000	$ 103,000
Less interest expense	44,000	46,000
Income before taxes	$ 141,000	$ 57,000
Income taxes	47,000	19,000
Net income	$ 94,000	$ 38,000
Earnings per share	$ 0.99	$ 0.40

PRECISION COMPANY
Comparative Balance Sheet
December 31, 19X2, and December 31, 19X1

	19X2	19X1
Assets		
Current assets:		
Cash	$ 79,000	$ 42,000
Short-term investments	65,000	96,000
Accounts receivable (net)	120,000	100,000
Merchandise inventory	250,000	265,000
Total current assets	$ 514,000	$ 503,000
Plant and equipment:		
Store equipment (net)	$ 400,000	$ 350,000
Office equipment (net)	45,000	50,000
Buildings (net)	625,000	675,000
Land	100,000	100,000
Total plant and equipment	$1,170,000	$1,175,000
Total assets	$1,684,000	$1,678,000
Liabilities		
Current liabilities:		
Accounts payable	$ 164,000	$ 190,000
Short-term notes payable	75,000	90,000
Taxes payable	26,000	12,000
Total current liabilities	$ 265,000	$ 292,000
Long-term liabilities:		
Notes payable (secured by mortgage on building and land)	400,000	420,000
Total liabilities	$ 665,000	$ 712,000
Stockholders' Equity		
Contributed capital:		
Common stock, $5 par value	$ 475,000	$ 475,000
Retained earnings	544,000	491,000
Total stockholders' equity	$1,019,000	$ 966,000
Total liabilities and stockholders' equity	$1,684,000	$1,678,000

- Set up a four-column income statement; enter the 19X2 and 19X1 amounts in the first two columns, and then enter the dollar change in the third column and the percentage change from 19X1 in the fourth column.
- Set up a four-column balance sheet; enter the 19X2 and 19X1 amounts in the first two columns, and then compute and enter the amount of each item as a percent of total assets.
- Compute the given ratios using the provided numbers; be sure to use the average of the beginning and ending amounts where appropriate.

Planning the Solution

1.

Solution to Demonstration Problem

PRECISION COMPANY
Comparative Income Statement
For Years Ended December 31, 19X2 and 19X1

	19X2	19X1	Increase (Decrease) in 19X2 Amount	Increase (Decrease) in 19X2 Percentage
Sales	$2,486,000	$2,075,000	$411,000	19.8
Cost of goods sold	1,523,000	1,222,000	301,000	24.6
Gross profit from sales	$ 963,000	$ 853,000	$110,000	12.9
Operating expenses:				
Advertising expense	$ 145,000	$ 100,000	$ 45,000	45.0
Sales salaries expense	240,000	280,000	(40,000)	(14.3)
Office salaries expense ...	165,000	200,000	(35,000)	(17.5)
Insurance expense	100,000	45,000	55,000	122.2
Supplies expense	26,000	35,000	(9,000)	(25.7)
Depreciation expense	85,000	75,000	10,000	13.3
Miscellaneous expenses ...	17,000	15,000	2,000	13.3
Total operating expenses ..	$ 778,000	$ 750,000	$ 28,000	3.7
Operating income	$ 185,000	$ 103,000	$ 82,000	79.6
Less interest expense	44,000	46,000	(2,000)	(4.3)
Income before taxes	$ 141,000	$ 57,000	$ 84,000	147.4
Income taxes	47,000	19,000	28,000	147.4
Net income	$ 94,000	$ 38,000	$ 56,000	147.4
Earnings per share	$ 0.99	$ 0.40	$ 0.59	147.5

2.

PRECISION COMPANY
Common-Size Comparative Balance Sheet
December 31, 19X2, and December 31, 19X1

	December 31 19X2	December 31 19X1	Common-size Percentages 19X2*	Common-size Percentages 19X1*
Assets				
Current assets:				
Cash	$ 79,000	$ 42,000	4.7	2.5
Short-term investments	65,000	96,000	3.9	5.7
Accounts receivable (net)	120,000	100,000	7.1	6.0
Merchandise inventory	250,000	265,000	14.8	15.8
Total current assets	$ 514,000	$ 503,000	30.5	30.0
Plant and equipment:				
Store equipment (net)	$ 400,000	$ 350,000	23.8	20.9
Office equipment (net)	45,000	50,000	2.7	3.0
Buildings (net)	625,000	675,000	37.1	40.2
Land	100,000	100,000	5.9	6.0
Total plant and equipment	$1,170,000	$1,175,000	69.5	70.0
Total assets	$1,684,000	$1,678,000	100.0	100.0

	December 31		Common-size Percentages	
	19X2	**19X1**	**19X2***	**19X1***
Liabilities				
Current liabilities:				
Accounts payable	$ 164,000	$ 190,000	9.7	11.3
Short-term notes payable	75,000	90,000	4.5	5.4
Taxes payable	26,000	12,000	1.5	0.7
Total current liabilities	$ 265,000	$ 292,000	15.7	17.4
Long-term liabilities:				
Notes payable (secured by mortgage on building and land)	400,000	420,000	23.8	25.0
Total liabilities	$ 665,000	$ 712,000	39.4	42.4
Stockholders' Equity				
Contributed capital:				
Common stock, $5 par value	$ 475,000	$ 475,000	28.2	28.3
Retailed earnings	544,000	491,000	32.3	29.3
Total stockholders' equity	$1,019,000	$ 966,000	60.5	57.6
Total liabilities and equity	$1,684,000	$1,678,000	100.0	100.0

*Columns may not foot due to rounding.

3. Ratios for 19X2:

a. Current ratio: $514,000/$265,000 = 1.9 to 1

b. Acid-test ratio: ($79,000 + $65,000 + $120,000)/$265,000 = 1.0 to 1

c. Average receivables: ($120,000 + $100,000)/2 = $110,000
Accounts receivable turnover: $2,486,000/$110,000 = 22.6 times

d. Days' sales uncollected: ($120,000/$2,486,000) × 365 = 17.6 days

e. Average inventory: ($250,000 + $265,000)/2 = $257,500
Merchandise turnover: $1,523,000/$257,500 = 5.9 times

f. Debt ratio: $665,000/$1,684,000 = 39.5%

g. Pledged assets to secured liabilities:
($625,000 + $100,000)/$400,000 = 1.8 to 1

h. Times fixed interest charges earned: $185,000/$44,000 = 4.2 times

i. Profit margin: $94,000/$2,486,000 = 3.8%

j. Average total assets: ($1,684,000 + $1,678,000)/2 = $1,681,000
Total asset turnover: $2,486,000/$1,681,000 = 1.48 times

k. Return on total assets: $94,000/$1,681,000 = 5.6% or 3.8% × 1.48 = 5.6%

l. Average total equity: ($1,019,000 + $966,000)/2 = $992,500
Return on common stockholders' equity: $94,000/$992,500 = 9.5%

GLOSSARY

Common-size comparative statements comparative financial statements in which each amount is expressed as a percentage of a base amount. In the balance sheet, the amount of total assets is usually selected as the base amount and is expressed as 100%. In the income statement, net sales is usually selected as the base amount. p. 653

Comparative statement a financial statement with data for two or more successive accounting periods placed in columns side by side, sometimes with changes shown in dollar amounts and percentages. p. 649

Equity ratio the portion of total assets provided by stockholders' equity, calculated as stockholders' equity divided by total assets. p. 659

Financial reporting the process of providing information that is useful to investors, creditors, and others in making investment, credit, and similar decisions. p. 648

General purpose financial statements statements published periodically for use by a wide variety of interested parties; include the income statement, balance sheet, statement of changes in stockholders' equity (or statement of retained earnings), statement of cash flows, and related footnotes. p. 648

Working capital current assets minus current liabilities. p. 655

QUESTIONS

1. Explain the difference between financial reporting and financial statements.

2. What is the difference between comparative financial statements and common-size comparative statements?

3. Which items are usually assigned a value of 100% on a common-size comparative balance sheet and a common-size comparative income statement?

4. Why is working capital given special attention in the process of analyzing balance sheets?

5. What are three factors that would influence your decision as to whether a company's current ratio is good or bad?

6. Suggest several reasons why a 2 to 1 current ratio may not be adequate for a particular company.

7. What does a relatively high accounts receivable turnover indicate about a company's short-term liquidity?

8. What is the significance of the number of days' sales uncollected?

9. Why does merchandise turnover provide information about a company's short-term liquidity?

10. Why is the capital structure of a company, as measured

by debt and equity ratios, of importance to financial statement analysts?

11. Why must the ratio of pledged assets to secured liabilities be interpreted with caution?

12. Why would a company's return on total assets be different from its return on common stockholders' equity?

13. What ratios would you calculate for the purpose of evaluating management performance?

14. Using the financial statements for Federal Express Corporation in Appendix G, calculate Federal Express's return on total assets for the fiscal year ended May 31, 1993.

15. Refer to the financial statements for Ben & Jerry's Homemade, Inc., in Appendix G. Calculate Ben & Jerry's equity ratio as of December 26, 1992.

QUICK STUDY (Five-Minute Exercises)

Which of the following items are means of accomplishing the objective of financial reporting but are not included within general purpose financial statements? *(a)* Income statements; *(b)* Company news releases; *(c)* Balance sheets; *(d)* Certain reports filed with the Securities and Exchange Commission; *(e)* Statements of cash flows; *(f)* Management discussions and analyses of financial performance.

**QS 17–1
(LO 1)**

Given the following information for Moyers Corporation, determine *(a)* the common-size percentages for gross profit from sales, and *(b)* the trend percentages for net sales, using 19X1 as the base year.

**QS 17–2
(LO 2)**

	19X2	19X1
Net sales	$134,400	$114,800
Cost of goods sold	72,800	60,200

a. Which two terms describe the difference between current assets and current liabilities?

b. Which two short-term liquidity ratios measure how frequently a company collects its accounts?

c. Which two ratios are the basic components in measuring a company's operating efficiency? Which ratio is the summary of these two components?

**QS 17–3
(LO 3)**

What are five possible bases of comparison you can use when analyzing financial statement ratios? Which of these is generally considered to be the most useful? Which one is least likely to provide a good basis for comparison?

**QS 17–4
(LO 4)**

EXERCISES

Exercise 17–1
Calculating trend percentages
(LO 2)

Calculate trend percentages for the following items, using 19X0 as the base year. Then, state whether the situation shown by the trends appears to be favorable or unfavorable.

	19X4	19X3	19X2	19X1	19X0
Sales	$377,600	$362,400	$338,240	$314,080	$302,000
Cost of goods sold	172,720	164,560	155,040	142,800	136,000
Accounts receivable	25,400	24,400	23,200	21,600	20,000

Exercise 17–2
Reporting percentage changes
(LO 2)

Where possible, calculate percentages of increase and decrease for the following:

	19X2	19X1
Short-term investments	$145,200	$110,000
Accounts receivable	28,080	32,000
Notes payable	38,000	–0–

Exercise 17–3
Calculating common-size percentages
(LO 2)

Express the following income statement information in common-size percentages and assess whether the situation is favorable or unfavorable:

CLEARWATER CORPORATION
Comparative Income Statement
For Years Ended December 31, 19X2, and 19X1

	19X2	19X1
Sales	$960,000	$735,000
Cost of goods sold	576,000	382,200
Gross profit from sales	$384,000	$352,800
Operating expenses	216,000	148,470
Net income	$168,000	$204,330

Exercise 17–4
Evaluating short-term liquidity
(LO 3)

TGA Company's December 31 balance sheets included the following data:

	19X3	19X2	19X1
Cash	$ 61,600	$ 71,250	$ 73,600
Accounts receivable, net	177,000	125,000	98,400
Merchandise inventory	223,000	165,000	106,000
Prepaid expenses	19,400	18,750	8,000
Plant assets, net	555,000	510,000	459,000
Total assets	$1,036,000	$890,000	$745,000
Accounts payable	$ 257,800	$150,500	$ 98,500
Long-term notes payable secured by mortgages on plant assets	195,000	205,000	165,000
Common stock, $10 par value	325,000	325,000	325,000
Retained earnings	258,200	209,500	156,500
Total liabilities and stockholders' equity	$1,036,000	$890,000	$745,000

Required

Compare the short-term liquidity positions of the company at the end of 19X3, 19X2, and 19X1 by calculating: (*a*) the current ratio and (*b*) the acid-test ratio. Comment on any changes that occurred.

Refer to the information in Exercise 17–4 about TGA Company. The company's income statements for the years ended December 31, 19X3, and 19X2 included the following data:

	19X3	19X2
Sales	$1,345,000	$1,060,000
Cost of goods sold	$ 820,450	$ 689,000
Other operating expenses	417,100	267,960
Interest expense	22,200	24,600
Income taxes	17,050	15,690
Total costs and expenses	$1,276,800	$ 997,250
Net income	$ 68,200	$ 62,750
Earnings per share	$ 2.10	$ 1.93

Required

For the years ended December 31, 19X3, and 19X2, assume all sales were on credit and calculate the following: (a) days' sales uncollected, (b) accounts receivable turnover, (c) merchandise turnover, and (d) days' stock on hand. Comment on any changes that occurred from 19X2 to 19X3.

Refer to the information in Exercises 17–4 and 17–5 about TGA Company. Compare the long-term risk and capital structure positions of the company at the end of 19X3 and 19X2 by calculating the following ratios: (a) debt and equity ratios, (b) pledged assets to secured liabilities, and (c) times fixed interest charges earned. Comment on any changes that occurred.

Refer to the financial statements of TGA Company presented in Exercises 17–4 and 17–5. Evaluate the operating efficiency and profitability of the company by calculating the following: (a) profit margin, (b) total asset turnover, and (c) return on total assets. Comment on any changes that occurred.

Refer to the financial statements of TGA Company presented in Exercises 17–4 and 17–5. This additional information about the company is known:

Common stock market price, December 31, 19X3	$30.00
Common stock market price, December 31, 19X2	28.00
Annual cash dividends per share in 19X3	.60
Annual cash dividends per share in 19X2	.30

Required

To evaluate the profitability of the company, calculate the following for 19X3 and 19X2: (a) return on common stockholders' equity, (b) price earnings ratio on December 31, and (c) dividend yield.

Common-size and trend percentages for a company's sales, cost of goods sold, and expenses follow:

Exercise 17–9
Determining income effects
from common-size and trend
percentages
(LO 2)

	Common-Size Percentages			**Trend Percentages**		
	19X3	**19X2**	**19X1**	**19X3**	**19X2**	**19X1**
Sales	100.0%	100.0%	100.0%	106.5%	105.3%	100.0%
Cost of goods sold	64.5	63.0	60.2	104.1	102.3	100.0
Expenses	16.4	15.9	16.2	96.0	94.1	100.0

Required

Determine whether the company's net income increased, decreased, or remained unchanged during this three-year period.

PROBLEMS

Problem 17–1
Calculating ratios and percentages
(LO 2, 3)

The condensed statements of Stellar Company follow:

STELLAR COMPANY
Comparative Income Statement
For Years Ended December 31, 19X3, 19X2, and 19X1
($000)

	19X3	19X2	19X1
Sales	$148,000	$136,000	$118,000
Cost of goods sold	89,096	85,000	75,520
Gross profit from sales	$ 58,904	$ 51,000	$ 42,480
Selling expenses	$ 20,898	$ 18,768	$ 15,576
Administrative expenses	13,379	11,968	9,735
Total expenses	$ 34,277	$ 30,736	$ 25,311
Income before taxes	$ 24,627	$ 20,264	$ 17,169
State and federal income taxes	4,588	4,148	3,481
Net income	$ 20,039	$ 16,116	$ 13,688

STELLAR COMPANY
Comparative Balance Sheet
December 31, 19X3, 19X2, and 19X1
($000)

	19X3	19X2	19X1
Assets			
Current assets	$24,240	$18,962	$25,324
Long-term investments	–0–	250	1,860
Plant and equipment	45,000	48,000	28,500
Total assets	$69,240	$67,212	$55,684
Liabilities and Stockholders' Equity			
Current liabilities	$10,100	$ 9,980	$ 9,740
Common stock	36,000	36,000	27,000
Other contributed capital	4,500	4,500	3,000
Retained earnings	18,640	16,732	15,944
Total liabilities and stockholders' equity . .	$69,240	$67,212	$55,684

Required

Preparation component:

1. Calculate each year's current ratio.

CHECK FIGURE:
19X3, total assets, 124.34

2. Express the income statement data in common-size percentages.

3. Express the balance sheet data in trend percentages with 19X1 as the base year.

Analysis component:

4. Comment on any significant relationships revealed by the ratios and percentages.

Problem 17–2
Calculation and analysis of trend percentages
(LO 2)

The condensed comparative statements of Jasper Company follow:

JASPER COMPANY
Comparative Income Statement
For Years Ended December 31, 19X7–19X1
($000)

	19X7	19X6	19X5	19X4	19X3	19X2	19X1
Sales	$797	$698	$635	$582	$543	$505	$420
Cost of goods sold	573	466	401	351	326	305	250
Gross profit from sales	$224	$232	$234	$231	$217	$200	$170
Operating expenses	170	133	122	90	78	77	65
Net income	$ 54	$ 99	$112	$141	$139	$123	$105

JASPER COMPANY
Comparative Balance Sheet
December 31, 19X7–19X1
($000)

	19X7	19X6	19X5	19X4	19X3	19X2	19X1
Assets							
Cash	$ 34	$ 44	$ 46	$ 47	$ 49	$ 48	$ 50
Accounts receivable, net	240	252	228	175	154	146	102
Merchandise inventory	869	632	552	466	418	355	260
Other current assets	23	21	12	22	19	19	10
Long-term investments	0	0	0	68	68	68	68
Plant and equipment, net . . .	1,060	1,057	926	522	539	480	412
Total assets	$2,226	$2,006	$1,764	$1,300	$1,247	$1,116	$902
Liabilities and Equity							
Current liabilities	$ 560	$ 471	$ 309	$ 257	$ 223	$ 211	$136
Long-term liabilities	597	520	506	235	240	260	198
Common stock	500	500	500	420	420	320	320
Other contributed capital . . .	125	125	125	90	90	80	80
Retained earnings	444	390	324	298	274	245	168
Total liabilities and equity . .	$2,226	$2,006	$1,764	$1,300	$1,247	$1,116	$902

Required

Preparation component:

1. Calculate trend percentages for the items of the statements using 19X1 as the base year.

CHECK FIGURE:
19X7 total assets, 246.8

Analysis component:

2. Analyze and comment on the situation shown in the statements.

The 19X2 financial statements of Oltorf Corporation follow:

Problem 17–3
Calculation of financial statement ratios
(LO 3)

OLTORF CORPORATION
Income Statement
For Year Ended December 31, 19X2

Sales		$697,200
Cost of goods sold:		
Merchandise inventory, December 31, 19X1	$ 64,800	
Purchases	455,800	
Goods available for sale	$520,600	
Merchandise inventory, December 31, 19X2	62,300	
Cost of goods sold		458,300
Gross profit from sales		$238,900
Operating expenses		122,700
Operating income		$116,200
Interest expense		7,100
Income before taxes		$109,100
Income taxes		17,800
Net income		$ 91,300

OLTORF CORPORATION
Balance Sheet
December 31, 19X2

Assets		Liabilities and Stockholders' Equity	
Cash	$ 18,000	Accounts payable	$ 32,600
Short-term investments	14,700	Accrued wages payable	4,200
Accounts receivable, net	55,800	Income taxes payable	4,800
Notes receivable (trade)	6,200	Long-term note payable,	
Merchandise inventory	62,300	secured by mortgage on	
Prepaid expenses	2,800	plant assets	125,000
Plant assets, net	306,300	Common stock, $1 par value .	180,000
		Retained earnings	119,500
		Total liabilities and	
Total assets	$466,100	stockholders' equity	$466,100

Assume that all sales were on credit. On the December 31, 19X1, balance sheet, the assets totaled $367,500, common stock was $180,000, and retained earnings were $86,700.

Required

Calculate the following: (*a*) current ratio, (*b*) acid-test ratio, (*c*) days' sales uncollected, (*d*) merchandise turnover, (*e*) days' stock on hand, (*f*) ratio of pledged assets to secured liabilities, (*g*) times fixed interest charges earned, (*h*) profit margin, (*i*) total asset turnover, (*j*) return on total assets, and (*k*) return on common stockholders' equity.

Problem 17–4
Comparative analysis of financial statement ratios
(LO 3)

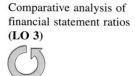

Two companies that compete in the same industry are being evaluated by a bank that can lend money to only one of them. Summary information from the financial statements of the two companies follows:

	Payless Company	Capital Company
Data from the current year-end balance sheets:		
Assets		
Cash	$ 37,400	$ 66,000
Accounts receivable	73,450	112,900
Notes receivable (trade)	16,200	13,100
Merchandise inventory	167,340	263,100
Prepaid expenses	8,000	11,900
Plant and equipment, net	568,900	606,400
Total assets	$ 871,290	$1,073,400
Liabilities and Stockholders' Equity:		
Current liabilities	$ 120,200	$ 184,600
Long-term notes payable	159,800	210,000
Common stock, $5 par value	350,000	410,000
Retained earnings	241,290	268,800
Total liabilities and stockholders' equity ...	$ 871,290	$1,073,400
Data from the current year's income statements:		
Sales	$1,325,000	$1,561,200
Cost of goods sold	970,500	1,065,000
Interest expense	14,400	23,000
Income tax expense	24,840	38,700
Net income	135,540	210,400
Beginning-of-year data:		
Accounts receivable, net	$ 57,800	$ 106,200
Notes receivable	–0–	–0–
Merchandise inventory	109,600	212,400
Total assets	776,400	745,100
Common stock, $5 par value	350,000	410,000
Retained earnings	189,300	181,200

Required

1. Calculate the current ratio, acid-test ratio, accounts (including notes) receivable turnover, merchandise turnover, days' stock on hand, and days' sales uncollected for the two companies. Then, identify the company that you consider to be the better short-term credit risk and explain why.

2. Calculate the profit margin, total asset turnover, return on total assets, and return on common stockholders' equity for the two companies. Assuming that each company paid cash dividends of $2.00 per share and each company's stock can be purchased at $25 per share, calculate their price earnings ratios and dividend yields. Also, identify which company's stock you would recommend as the better investment and explain why.

Metro Corporation began the month of March with $750,000 of current assets, a current ratio of 2.5 to 1, and an acid-test ratio of 1.1 to 1. During the month, it completed the following transactions:

Problem 17–5
Analysis of working capital
(LO 3)

Mar. 4 Bought $85,000 of merchandise on account. (The company uses a perpetual inventory system.)

10 Sold merchandise that cost $68,000 for $113,000.

12 Collected a $29,000 account receivable.

17 Paid a $31,000 account payable.

19 Wrote off a $13,000 bad debt against the Allowance for Doubtful Accounts account.

24 Declared a $1.25 per share cash dividend on the 40,000 shares of outstanding common stock.

28 Paid the dividend declared on March 24.

29 Borrowed $85,000 by giving the bank a 30-day, 10% note.

30 Borrowed $100,000 by signing a long-term secured note.

31 Used the $185,000 proceeds of the notes to buy additional machinery.

Required

Prepare a schedule showing Metro's current ratio, acid-test ratio, and working capital after each of the transactions. Round calculations to two decimal places.

CRITICAL THINKING: ESSAYS, PROBLEMS, AND CASES

Analytical Essays

Kerbey Company and Telcom Company are similar firms that operate within the same industry. The following information is available:

AE 17–1
(LO 3)

FAST HINT
Group Project:
Ask small groups to assume that the two companies have applied for a one-year loan. The task of the group is to itemize any additional information the companies must provide before the group can make a loan decision.

	Kerbey			Telcom		
	19X3	**19X2**	**19X1**	**19X3**	**19X2**	**19X1**
Current ratio	1.8	1.9	2.2	3.3	2.8	2.0
Acid-test ratio	1.1	1.2	1.3	2.9	2.6	1.7
Accounts receivable						
turnover	30.5	25.2	29.2	16.4	15.2	16.0
Merchandise turnover	24.2	21.9	17.1	14.5	13.0	12.6
Working capital	$65,000	$53,000	$47,000	$126,000	$98,000	$73,000

Required

Write a brief essay comparing Kerbey and Telcom based on the preceding information. Your discussion should include their relative ability to meet current obligations and to use current assets efficiently.

**AE 17–2
(LO 3)**

Snowden Company and Comet Company are similar firms that operate within the same industry. Comet began operations in 19X7 and Snowden in 19X1. In 19X9, both companies paid 7% interest to creditors. The following information is available:

	Snowden			Comet		
	19X9	**19X8**	**19X7**	**19X9**	**19X8**	**19X7**
Total asset turnover	3.3	3.0	3.2	1.9	1.7	1.4
Return on total assets . . .	9.2	9.8	9.0	6.1	5.8	5.5
Profit margin	2.6	2.7	2.5	3.0	3.2	3.1
Sales	$800,000	$740,000	$772,000	$400,000	$320,000	$200,000

Required

Write a brief essay comparing Snowden and Comet based on the preceding information. Your discussion should include their relative ability to use assets efficiently to produce profits. Also comment on their relative success in employing financial leverage in 19X9.

Financial Statement Analysis Cases

**FSAC 17–1
(LO 2, 3)**

In your position as controller of Skinner Company, you are responsible for keeping the board of directors informed about the financial activities and status of the company. In preparing for the next board meeting, you have calculated the following ratios, turnovers, and percentages to enable you to answer questions:

	19X6	**19X5**	**19X4**
Sales trend	137.00	125.00	100.00
Selling expenses to net sales	9.8%	13.7%	15.3%
Sales to plant assets	3.5 to 1	3.3 to 1	3.0 to 1
Current ratio	2.6 to 1	2.4 to 1	2.1 to 1
Acid-test ratio	0.8 to 1	1.1 to 1	1.2 to 1
Merchandise turnover	7.5 times	8.7 times	9.9 times
Accounts receivable turnover	6.7 times	7.4 times	8.2 times
Total asset turnover	2.6 times	2.6 times	3.0 times
Return on total assets	8.8%	9.4%	10.1%
Return on stockholders' equity . . .	9.75%	11.50%	12.25%
Profit margin	3.3%	3.5%	3.7%

Required

Using the preceding data, answer each of the following questions and explain your answers:

a. Is it becoming easier for the company to meet its current debts on time and to take advantage of cash discounts?

b. Is the company collecting its accounts receivable more rapidly?

c. Is the company's investment in accounts receivable decreasing?

d. Are dollars invested in inventory increasing?

e. Is the company's investment in plant assets increasing?

f. Is the stockholders' investment becoming more profitable?

g. Is the company using its assets efficiently?

h. Did the dollar amount of selling expenses decrease during the three-year period?

Refer to the 11-year financial history and the consolidated balance sheet contained in the financial statements of Apple Computer, Inc., in Appendix F, to answer the following questions:

FSAC 17–2
(LO 2, 3)

a. Using 1991 as the base year, calculate trend percentages for 1991–1993 for the total net sales, total costs and expenses, operating income, and net income.

b. Calculate common-size percentages for 1993 and 1992 for the following categories of assets: total current assets; net property, plant, and equipment; and other assets.

c. Calculate the high and low price earnings ratio for 1993.

d. Calculate the dividend yield for 1993 using the high stock price for the year.

e. Calculate the debt and equity ratios for 1993.

ANSWERS TO PROGRESS CHECKS

17–1 General purpose financial statements are intended for the large variety of users who are interested in receiving financial information about a business but who do not have the ability to require the company to prepare specialized financial reports designed to meet their specific interests.

17–2 General purpose financial statements include the income statement, balance sheet, statement of changes in stockholders' equity (or statement of retained earnings), and statement of cash flows, plus footnotes related to the statements.

17–3 d

17–4 Percentages on a comparative income statement show the increase or decrease in each item from one period to the next. On a common-size comparative income statement, each item is shown as a percentage of net sales for a specific period.

17–5 c

17–6 (a) ($820,000 + $240,000 + $470,000)/($350,000 + $180,000) = 2.9 to 1

(b) ($820,000 + $240,000)/($350,000 + $180,000) = 2 to 1

17–7 (a) $2,500,000/[($290,000 + $240,000)/2] = 9.43 times

(b) ($240,000/$2,500,000) × 365 = 35 days

(c) $750,000/[($530,000 + $470,000)/2] = 1.5 times

(d) ($470,000/$750,000) × 365 = 228.7 days

17–8 c

17–9 b

17–10 Profit margin × Total asset turnover = Return on total assets ($945,000/$8,500,000) × 1.8 = 20%

17–11 a

17–12 The ratios and turnovers of a selected group of competing companies.

CHAPTER 18

An Introduction to Managerial Accounting and Cost Accounting Concepts

Jane Stone graduated from the University of Washington and spent three years with a Big-Six firm before accepting a position as manager of special projects with Olympic Stain, a former division of the Clorox Company. Her job was to assist managers with financial analysis. During Stone's first week, she met with managers in marketing, sales, purchasing, and manufacturing. Purchasing wanted help in setting criteria for selecting vendors. Manufacturing wanted help deciding between two machine purchases. Marketing needed to understand the financial implications of a new promotion plan before committing to the advertising. The sales manager wanted to redesign the sales compensation plan to focus on key targets in marketing's new promotion plan.

Stone took notes, asked questions, and reviewed the financial statements for the past six months. Nowhere did she see the information she needed. Discouraged, she went to Controller John Dickson with a summary of the requests. Stone concluded, " I thought I knew all about accounting, but the answers aren't in the data we are gathering for our accounting records. Where do I start?"

Dickson said, "Welcome to the world of management accounting. You must recognize that you are looking at new alternatives, so looking at data about the past doesn't help much. It may be a beginning, but in most cases you have to look outside the accounting system for your answers. Decide what you want to know and then come back when you have a list of questions. I will steer you in the right direction. You will learn a lot about operations before your projects are complete."

LEARNING OBJECTIVES

After studying Chapter 18, you should be able to:

1. **Describe five differences between financial and managerial accounting.**
2. **Describe the basic differences between the financial statements of manufacturing companies and merchandising companies.**
3. **Prepare a manufacturing statement and explain its purpose and relationship to the primary financial statements.**
4. **Describe the unique accounts manufacturing companies use in a general accounting system.**
5. **Describe the flow of manufacturing costs in a general accounting system and prepare entries to record them.**
6. **Explain the procedures for periodically assigning costs to the inventories owned by manufacturing companies.**
7. **Define or explain the words and phrases listed in the chapter glossary.**

Managerial and financial accounting both provide information that helps people make decisions. However, this chapter describes five major differences between managerial and financial accounting.

The chapter also compares the accounting and reporting practices used by manufacturing and merchandising companies. Both types of companies earn revenues by selling goods. On one hand, a merchandising company sells goods without changing their condition. On the other hand, a manufacturing company buys raw materials and turns them into finished products that it sells to customers. The differences between merchandising and manufacturing create needs for different kinds of information that in turn lead to different accounting practices.

INTRODUCTION TO MANAGERIAL ACCOUNTING

LO 1

Describe five differences between financial and managerial accounting.

FAST HINT
Important Point to Remember:
Manufacturing costs are important to managers because they affect both the financial position and profitability of a business. Managerial accounting assists the analysis, planning, and control of manufacturing costs.

Most of the discussions in the first 17 chapters of this book focus on financial accounting that provides information primarily to people who are not managers of an organization. As described in the first chapter, *managerial accounting,* or *management accounting,* provides information to the managers of an organization. Thus, both financial and managerial accounting share the common purpose of providing information. Financial and managerial accounting also share the common practice of reporting monetary information. In fact, they even report some of the same information. We have already seen some areas in which the two types of accounting overlap. For example, the financial statements for a company contain information that is useful for both the managers of a company (insiders) and other persons who are interested in the company (outsiders).

This chapter takes a more careful look at managerial accounting information, how accountants gather it, and how managers use it. The main topic of this chapter and Chapters 19 and 20 is accounting for manufacturing activities. We look at the concepts and procedures used to determine the costs of the products that a company manufactures and sells. A firm reports these costs on its balance sheet as inventory and on its income statement as cost of goods sold.

Information about the cost of products is also very important for managers. For example, managers use information about the past cost of producing goods to predict the future cost of producing the same or similar items. Then, they use the predicted cost to set an appropriate selling price. Sometimes, the manufacturer cannot set the price because it is determined in the marketplace. Then, managers may use the predicted cost in deciding whether the product can be produced profitably.

	Financial Accounting	**Managerial Accounting**
1. Users of the information	Investors, creditors, and other users external to the organization	Managers internal to the organization
2. Purpose of the information	Assist external users in making investment, credit, and other financial decisions	Assist managers in planning and controlling the organization's activities
3. Flexibility of practices	Tends to be rigid; controlled by GAAP	Relatively flexible
4. Timeliness and time dimension of the information reported	Available only after the audit is completed; minimal predictions	Available quickly without the need to wait for an audit; many projections and estimates
5. Subject of the information	Primary focus is on whole organization	Includes focus on specific projects and subdivisions of the organization

Illustration 18–1
Differences between Financial and Managerial Accounting

Managers also use information about costs as they control the production process. For example, information about manufacturing costs helps managers identify costs that should be reduced. In later chapters, you will learn more about how managers use cost information in controlling business operations.

Differences between Financial and Managerial Accounting

Despite the overlap of financial and managerial accounting, there are a number of differences between them. The following paragraphs discuss the five major differences summarized in Illustration 18–1.

Users of the Information. Companies accumulate, process, and report financial accounting and managerial accounting for different groups of people. They provide financial accounting information primarily to external users, including investors, creditors, and others. These external users do not have a part in managing the activities of the organization. Companies provide managerial accounting information to internal users, who are responsible for making and implementing decisions about the organization's activities.

Purpose of the Information. Investors, creditors, and other users of financial accounting information must decide whether to invest in or lend to the organization, and on what terms. If they have already invested in the organization or loaned to it, they must decide whether to continue holding the stock or the loan.

Managers must plan the future of the organization to take advantage of opportunities or to overcome obstacles. Managers also try to control present activities to ensure that they are being carried out efficiently. Managerial accounting information helps managers make both planning and control decisions.

Flexibility of Practices. Because external users make comparisons between companies and because external users need to be protected against false or misleading information, financial accounting practices tend to have a rigid structure. Firms usually present financial accounting information in the form of general purpose financial statements. By providing these statements with footnotes, financial accountants try to report the relevant information that most external users need. Thus, an extensive set of rules and guidelines that the business world refers to as generally accepted accounting principles (GAAP) governs financial accounting practices.

FAST HINT
Critical Thought Question:
Would it be desirable to accumulate information for management reports in a database that is separate from financial accounting records? Why or why not?

FAST HINT
Important Point to Remember:
Financial statements are usually issued months after the end of a company's fiscal year. However, GAAP requires the presentation of information about important events that occur during the time the statements are being prepared. These events are called *subsequent events.*

FAST HINT
Important Point to Remember:
Independent auditors do test the integrity of managerial accounting records that provide amounts used in the financial statements.

The internal users of managerial accounting information are not in the same position as the external users. The authoritative standards that make up GAAP do not limit managerial accounting. The managers of a company can decide for themselves what information they want and how they want it reported. Since they have access to all company data, managers require less protection against false or misleading information than external parties. Thus, managerial accounting practices are flexible. This flexibility allows different companies to design individualized managerial accounting systems. Even within a single company, different managers often can design their own systems to meet their special needs. This flexibility also allows managers to modify their systems quickly in response to changes in the environment.

Timeliness and Time Dimension of the Information Reported. Formal financial statements, which primarily report events and transactions that occurred in the past, are not immediately available to outside parties. In most cases, independent certified public accountants must audit the financial statements a company sends to external users. Because audits can take two to three months to complete, annual financial reports to outsiders usually are not available to users until well after the end of the year. Further, to protect external users from excessive optimism, financial reports according to GAAP deal primarily with the results of past activities and conditions that exist in the present. Although some predictions are necessary, such as the service lives and salvage values of plant assets, financial accounting avoids predictions whenever possible.

On the other hand, managerial accounting information can be forwarded to the managers quickly since external auditors do not have to review it and estimates and projections are perfectly acceptable. However, to get the information quickly, managers may have to accept some lack of precision in the reports.

For example, an early internal report to management produced right after the end of the year might indicate that net income for the year was between $4,200,000 and $4,750,000. Later, the audited income statement might show that net income for the year was $4,550,000. Even though the internal report is not precise, the information may be more useful because it is available so much earlier. Also, in contrast to financial accounting, managerial accounting often includes predictions of future conditions and events. For example, an important managerial accounting report is a budget that predicts sales, expenses, and other costs. If managerial accounting reports were restricted to the past and present, managers would not be able to use budgets and would not be able to manage very effectively.

Although accounting reports to managers can be provided without waiting for the completion of an audit, internal auditing has had an increasingly important role to play in private companies since Congress enacted the Foreign Corrupt Practices Act in 1978. The act made corporate management responsible for preventing and detecting fraudulent activities in their corporations. Companies responded by strengthening their internal audit functions. For example, the CEO and chief financial officer of **Chrysler Corporation** reported that "the company maintains a strong internal auditing program that independently assesses the effectiveness of the internal controls and recommends possible improvements." (*1993 Report to Shareholders,* p. 45) The internal auditors evaluate the flow of information inside the company as well as the flow of information to outsiders. These internal audits help to avoid situations such as the one described in As a Matter of Ethics.

As a Matter of Ethics

Three former college classmates got together to have dinner at an expensive restaurant to talk over the past and to share recent news about what they and their companies were doing. The evening was long but entertaining and fruitful with respect to business ideas. When the check arrived, it was grabbed by one of the three. Because he was a self-employed entrepreneur, he said, "Here, let me pay it—I'll deduct it as a business expense on my tax return, and it won't cost me as much." One of the others was the vice president of a medium-size corporation. She snatched the check out of his hand and said, "I'll put this on a company credit card, and it won't

cost us anything at all." The third, who was a factory manager for a company that sold products to the government, smiled and folded his hands. When his silence got the attention of the other two, he said, "Neither of you understands the system yet. I'll put this on my company's credit card and call it overhead on a cost-plus contract* my company has with the government. That way, my company will pay for our dinner *and* make a profit on it."

*Under a cost-plus contract, the seller receives its costs plus a percentage of those costs.

Texas Instruments, Inc., is a leader in the area of corporate ethics. The company has had a written statement of corporate ethics for more than 30 years and

established an Ethics Office almost 10 years ago. TI uses ongoing training and communications programs to help employees understand what type of behavior is expected and what resources are available to assist them make the right decisions. Ethical behavior at TI goes far beyond simple compliance with laws, regulations and policies—it revolves around values and principles.

Subject of the Information. Although a corporation might organize itself into divisions and departments, investors do not buy stock in one division or department of a corporation. Neither do creditors lend money to a single division or department of a company. Instead, they own shares in or make loans to the whole company. Thus, since these external parties want to know about the whole company, the financial accounting information that goes to external users is focused primarily on the organization as a whole. GAAP requires large companies to report separate information on various segments of their operations. However, the purpose of this requirement is to help external users understand more about the whole company.

The focus of managerial accounting is quite different. Only the top-level managers are responsible for managing the entire organization. Most managers of the organization are responsible for much smaller sets of activities. These middle- and lower-level managers need managerial accounting reports that deal with the specific activities, projects, and subdivisions for which they are responsible. For example, division sales managers are directly responsible only for the results achieved in their divisions. While they may want to see the results for all divisions, they may not need a companywide sales report. What division sales managers need to improve their sales personnel's performance is detailed information about the results achieved in their specific divisions. This information would include the level of success achieved by each salesperson in each division.

The following diagrams indicate the difference in organizational detail reported on external reports and internal reports.

FAST HINT
Relevant Quick Study:
To apply these concepts, work
QS 18–1.

Organizational Detail

External reports

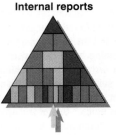

Internal reports

Details reported
on entire firm

Details reported
on each department,
division, or area

A Reminder. Although the preceding paragraphs have emphasized the differences between financial and managerial accounting, you should not conclude that they are completely separate. Much information is useful to both external and internal users. In particular, information about the costs of manufacturing products is useful to both external investors and creditors and internal managers.

Both financial and managerial accounting can affect the way people behave. Remember the story at the beginning of the chapter about Jane Stone's job at **Olympic Stain.** Stone's understanding of accounting was essential to her task of quantifying future costs and revenues associated with each project. But equally important was an understanding that people make the decisions that cause the costs or revenues to happen.

For example, Stone's design of a new sales compensation plan would affect the behavior of the sales force. Stone would also have to estimate the effects of the new promotion plan and the new sales compensation plan on the buying patterns of customers. These estimates would affect the equipment decision for manufacturing and may affect the vendor selection criteria established by purchasing. Thus, Stone had to recognize that all of the projects were related.

So that you can understand more about manufacturing activities, the next section highlights the differences between merchandising firms and manufacturing firms.

Progress Check
(Answers to the Progress Checks are provided at the end of the chapter.)

18–1   Managerial accounting produces information that is:
    a. Designed to meet the needs of a company's internal managers.
    b. Prepared to meet the specific needs of the user.
    c. Often focused heavily on the future.
    d. All of the above.

18–2   What is the difference between the intended users of financial and managerial accounting information?

18–3   Do generally accepted accounting principles control the practice of managerial accounting?

As we mentioned at the beginning of the chapter, the basic difference between merchandising and manufacturing companies is that merchandisers buy goods ready for sale while manufacturers produce goods from raw materials. For example, a shoe store buys and sells shoes without doing anything to physically change them. In contrast, the shoe manufacturer must buy leather, cloth, plastic, rubber, glue, and laces and then use its employees' labor in a factory to convert these raw materials into shoes. These unique operations of a manufacturer require special accounting practices.

In prior chapters, we focused on the financial statements of merchandising and service companies. However, manufacturing is different from selling merchandise and providing services. As a result, the financial statements for manufacturing companies have some unique features.

The Balance Sheet

Manufacturers have several kinds of assets that other companies do not have. In particular, manufacturers usually have three inventories instead of the single inventory that is held by merchandising companies. For example, in Illustration 18–2, notice the three different inventories in the current asset section of the balance sheet for Sample Manufacturing Company.

The first inventory consists of the **raw materials** the company acquires to use in making products. It uses these materials in two ways—directly and indirectly. Most raw materials physically become part of the product and therefore are clearly identified with specific units or batches of product. Raw materials used in this manner are called **direct materials.** Other materials used in support of the production process are not as clearly identified with specific units or batches of product. For example, companies need lubricants for machinery and supplies for cleaning up the factory. These materials are called **indirect materials** because they do not become a part of the product and are not clearly identified with specific units or batches of product. Items used as indirect materials often appear on the balance sheet as factory supplies. In other cases, they are included in raw materials.

Another inventory held by manufacturers is the **goods in process inventory,** also called the *work in process inventory.* It consists of products in the process of being manufactured but not yet complete. The goods in process inventory may or may not be large, depending on the nature of the production process. If the time required to produce a unit of product is very short, the goods in process inventory is likely to be small. But, if weeks or months are needed to produce a unit, the goods in process inventory is larger.

The third inventory owned by a manufacturer is the **finished goods inventory,** consisting of completed products waiting to be sold. This inventory is similar to the merchandise inventory owned by a retailing company because both inventories contain items ready for sale.

Manufacturers also have unique plant assets such as *small tools, factory buildings,* and *factory equipment.* An intangible asset often owned by manufacturers is *patents.* Companies use these assets to manufacture products. The balance sheet in Illustration 18–2 shows that Sample Manufacturing Company owns all of these assets. Some manufacturers invest millions or even billions of dollars in their production facilities and patents. For example, **E. I. duPont de Nemours Company's**

COMPARING MERCHANDISING AND MANUFACTURING ACTIVITIES

FINANCIAL STATEMENTS FOR A MANUFACTURING COMPANY

LO 2
Describe the basic differences between the financial statements of manufacturing companies and merchandising companies.

FAST HINT
Important Point to Remember:
Reducing the size of inventories can save storage costs and free capital for other uses. A just-in-time manufacturing system reduces inventories to the bare minimum. This approach to production management is explained in Chapter 20.

Illustration 18–2

SAMPLE MANUFACTURING COMPANY
Balance Sheet
December 31, 19X2

Assets

Current assets:		
Cash		$ 11,000
Accounts receivable	$32,000	
Allowance for doubtful accounts	(1,850)	30,150
Raw materials inventory		9,000
Goods in process inventory		7,500
Finished goods inventory		10,300
Supplies		350
Prepaid insurance		300
Total current assets		$ 68,600
Plant assets:		
Small tools		$ 1,100
Delivery equipment	$ 9,000	
Accumulated depreciation	(4,000)	5,000
Office equipment	$ 1,700	
Accumulated depreciation	(400)	1,300
Factory machinery	$72,000	
Accumulated depreciation	(6,500)	65,500
Factory building	$90,000	
Accumulated depreciation	(3,300)	86,700
Land		9,500
Total plant assets		$169,100
Intangible assets:		
Patents		$ 11,200
Total assets		$248,900

Liabilities and Stockholders' Equity

Current liabilities:		
Accounts payable	$ 14,000	
Wages payable	540	
Interest payable	2,000	
Income taxes payable	32,600	
Total current liabilities	$ 49,140	
Long-term liabilities:		
Long-term notes payable	50,000	
Total liabilities		$ 99,140
Stockholders' equity:		
Common stock, $5 par value	$100,000	
Retained earnings	49,760	
Total stockholders' equity		149,760
Total liabilities and stockholders' equity		$248,900

1993 balance sheet shows a net investment in property, plant, and equipment of $21.4 billion, most of which involves production facilities.

The Income Statement

One difference between the income statements of manufacturers and merchandisers is the way they describe the elements that make up the cost of goods sold. Observe these cost of goods sold schedules for a merchandiser and a manufacturer:

Merchandising Company		Manufacturing Company	
Cost of goods sold:		Cost of goods sold:	
Beginning *merchandise* inventory	$ 14,200	Beginning *finished goods* inventory	$ 11,200
Cost of goods *purchased*	234,150	Cost of goods *manufactured* (see the	
Goods available for sale	$248,350	manufacturing statement)	170,500
Ending *merchandise* inventory	12,100	Goods available for sale	$181,700
Cost of goods sold	$236,250	Ending *finished goods* inventory	10,300
		Cost of goods sold	$171,400

Notice that the merchandiser uses the term *merchandise* inventory while the manufacturer uses the term *finished goods* inventory. (The manufacturer's inventories of raw materials and goods in process are not included because they are not available for sale.) Next, observe that the manufacturing company shows the cost of goods *manufactured* instead of the cost of goods *purchased*. This difference exists because the manufacturer produces its goods instead of purchasing them ready for sale. The line showing the cost of goods manufactured also includes a reference to the manufacturing statement, which we discuss later in this chapter.

Other than these differences, the cost of goods sold calculations appear the same for both companies. However, we want to emphasize that the numbers used in the calculations represent different activities. The merchandiser's cost of goods purchased is the cost of buying the products to be sold. The manufacturer's cost of goods manufactured includes the sum of the materials, labor, and overhead costs incurred by the manufacturer in producing the products.

In Illustration 18–3, notice that the operating expenses of Sample Manufacturing Company include sales salaries, office salaries, and depreciation of the delivery and office equipment. However, the operating expenses do not include manufacturing costs such as factory workers' wages and depreciation of the production equipment and the factory. These are not reported as operating expenses. Instead, they are included in cost of goods sold. In the next section, we explain how this is accomplished.

You have already learned in prior chapters that some costs are capitalized or debited to asset accounts and other costs are charged to expense as they are incurred. Costs are capitalized if they produce benefits that are expected to have value in the future. Costs are expensed if their benefits appear to expire as the costs are incurred. For manufacturing companies, costs that are capitalized as inventory are called **product costs.** Costs that are charged to expense as they are incurred are called **period costs.**

Illustration 18–4 shows the difference between the product costs and period costs incurred by a manufacturer during 19X2. The period costs flow directly to the 19X2 income statement as expenses because they do not produce assets. In contrast, product costs are initially assigned to inventory accounts.

The final treatment of product costs depends on what happens to the finished goods. That is, the finished goods are either sold in 19X2 or are still on hand at the end of the year. The product costs of the items sold in 19X2 are reported on the 19X2 income statement as the cost of goods sold. The costs of the unsold inventories are carried forward to the balance sheet at the end of 19X2. Then, assuming the goods are sold in 19X3, their cost appears on the income statement for that year.

The difference between period and product costs explains why the income statement of Sample Manufacturing Company does not report expenses in 19X2 for

FAST HINT
Relevant Quick Study:
To apply these concepts, work QS 18–2

FAST HINT
Additional Insight:
Labor and overhead are sometimes called *conversion costs* because they are incurred in the process of converting raw materials to finished goods.

THE DIFFERENCE BETWEEN PERIOD AND PRODUCT COSTS

FAST HINT
Relevant Exercise:
To apply these concepts, work Exercise 18–2.

Illustration 18–3

SAMPLE MANUFACTURING COMPANY
Income Statement
For Year Ended December 31, 19X2

Sales		$310,000
Cost of goods sold:		
Finished goods inventory, December 31, 19X1 ..	$ 11,200	
Cost of goods manufactured (see		
manufacturing statement)	170,500	
Goods available for sale	$181,700	
Finished goods inventory, December 31, 19X2 ..	(10,300)	
Cost of goods sold		171,400
Gross profit		$138,600
Operating expenses:		
Selling expenses:		
Sales salaries expense	$18,000	
Advertising expense	5,500	
Delivery wages expense	12,000	
Shipping supplies expense	250	
Insurance expense, delivery equipment	300	
Depreciation expense, delivery equipment ...	2,100	
Total selling expenses	$38,150	
General and administrative expenses:		
Office salaries expense	$15,700	
Miscellaneous expenses	200	
Bad debts expense	1,550	
Office supplies expense	100	
Depreciation expense, office equipment	200	
Interest expense	4,000	
Total general and administrative expenses	21,750	
Total operating expenses		59,900
Income before income taxes		$ 78,700
Less income taxes expense		(32,600)
Net income		$ 46,100
Net income per common share (20,000 shares) ...		$2.31

factory workers' wages or for depreciation on the factory buildings and equipment. Instead, these costs are combined with the cost of the raw materials to determine the product cost of the finished goods. Some of these manufacturing costs appear on the income statement as cost of goods sold in 19X2, and some of them remain on the balance sheet at the end of 19X2 as the cost of the raw materials, goods in process, and finished goods inventories.

MANUFACTURING ACTIVITIES AND THE MANUFACTURING STATEMENT

The manufacturing activities of a company are described in a special financial report called the **manufacturing statement.** This report is also called the *schedule of manufacturing activities* or the *schedule of cost of goods manufactured.* The amounts and types of costs incurred in the manufacturing process are summarized on this statement. To help you understand the manufacturing statement, however, we examine the manufacturer's activities that relate to inventories.

Manufacturing Activities that Relate to Inventories

Illustration 18–5 represents the flow of a manufacturer's activities that relate to its inventories. Note that the diagram has three sections. The top section represents the flow of raw materials. A company starts an accounting period with a beginning raw

Illustration 18-4   Product and Period Costs in the Financial Statements

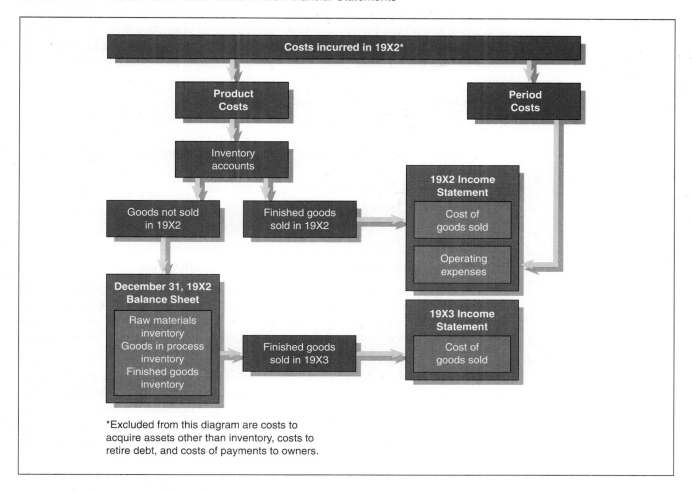

*Excluded from this diagram are costs to acquire assets other than inventory, costs to retire debt, and costs of payments to owners.

materials inventory. During the period, it acquires additional raw materials. When the purchases are added to the beginning inventory, the result is the raw materials available for use in production. Then, either they are used in production or they remain on hand at the end of the period for use in the next period.

The middle section of Illustration 18–5 shows four factors that come together in the production activity of the period. They are direct materials, direct labor, factory overhead, and the beginning goods in process inventory.

Direct Materials.   The first factor used in production is the direct materials that come into the manufacturing process from the raw materials inventory. Recall that direct materials are clearly associated with specific units or batches of production because the materials go into and become part of the finished products.

Direct Labor.   The second factor, shown in the middle section of Illustration 18–5, is **direct labor.** Direct labor is clearly associated with specific units or batches of production because direct labor converts raw materials into finished products.

Factory Overhead.   The third factor applied in production is **factory overhead,** also called *manufacturing overhead* or *factory burden.* Although they are incurred as part of the manufacturing process, factory overhead costs are not clearly associated with specific units of product or batches of production. Factory overhead includes all manufacturing costs other than direct materials and direct labor costs.

FAST HINT
Important Point to Remember:
Direct material and direct labor costs increase in proportion to increases in production volume. Some overhead costs also vary with production, but others remain constant. Variable and fixed costs are described in Chapter 22.

An example of a factory overhead cost is **indirect labor.** This labor is not clearly associated with specific units or batches of product because it is the labor of manufacturing employees who do not work specifically on converting direct materials into finished products. Indirect labor includes such activities as supervising employees, maintaining factory equipment, and cleaning the plant. Other factory overhead costs are:

- Indirect materials: Cleaning supplies and lubricants.
- Indirect labor (including related payroll taxes and fringe benefits): Maintenance and supervision.
- Depreciation and amortization: Factory building, factory equipment, patents, and tools.
- Factory utilities: Electricity, natural gas, and water.
- Insurance on factory buildings and equipment.
- Property taxes on factory buildings and equipment.
- Property taxes on raw materials and work in process inventories.
- Repairs and maintenance on factory buildings and equipment.

Factory overhead excludes selling and administrative expenses because they are not incurred in the process of manufacturing products. Even though these costs are sometimes called *selling and administrative overhead,* they are expensed on the income statement as period costs and are not capitalized as part of the cost of the finished goods.

Goods in Process Inventory. The fourth factor in production is the beginning *goods in process inventory.* In many situations, companies direct their labor, material, and overhead to completing all units of product that were incomplete at the beginning of the period. Then, they start new units. Most of the new units are completed during the period. Those units remaining incomplete at the end of the period are the goods in process inventory.

Once units are completed, they pass out of the goods in process inventory and become part of the finished goods inventory. As shown in the bottom section of Illustration 18–5, these newly completed units are combined with the beginning finished goods inventory to make up the finished goods available for sale during the period. Finished goods either are sold during the period or remain on hand at the end of the period. When they are sold, their cost is reported on the income statement as the cost of goods sold. If they are not sold, their cost appears on the balance sheet as the ending finished goods inventory.

Progress Check

18-4   **What are three inventories unique to manufacturers?**

18-5   **What is the difference between product and period costs?**

18-6   **How is indirect labor treated in accounting for production?**

18-7   **What is the difference between direct and indirect materials?**

The Manufacturing Statement

LO 3

Prepare a manufacturing statement and explain its purpose and relationship to the primary financial statements.

Illustration 18–6 presents the manufacturing statement of Sample Manufacturing Company for 19X2. This statement summarizes the costs of the manufacturing activity that took place during the period.

The top section of the statement calculates the cost of the raw materials used. The calculation starts with the beginning raw materials inventory of $8,000. Then, pur-

Illustration 18-5 Flows of Resources through the Inventories and the Production Process to Customers

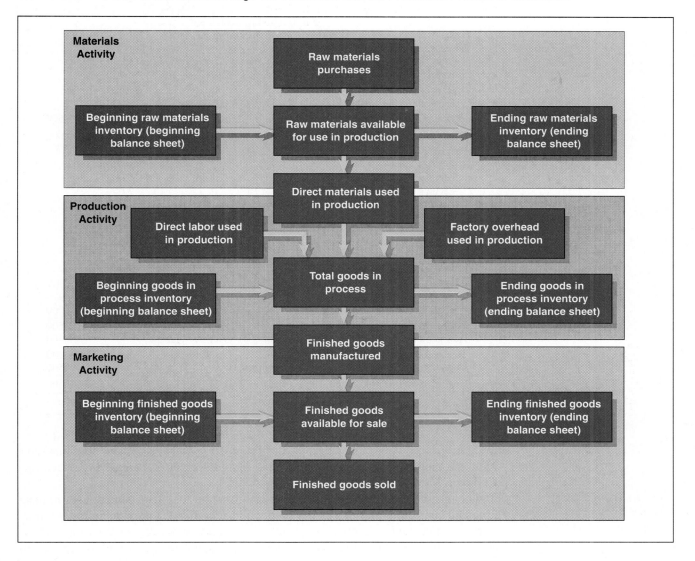

chases of $86,500 are added to get the $94,500 cost of raw materials available for use in 19X2. Based on a physical count, the ending raw materials inventory is estimated to be $9,000. The total cost of raw materials used during the period is calculated as $85,500 ($94,500 − $9,000).

The total direct labor cost of $60,000 includes related payroll taxes and fringe benefits. Note that the statement lists the cost of each factory overhead item and shows the total factory overhead cost for the year was $30,000. Some companies show only the total factory overhead on the manufacturing statement. Then, a separate schedule of overhead items is prepared in support of the manufacturing statement.

In Illustration 18–6, notice that the total manufacturing cost incurred during the year is calculated as $175,500 ($85,500 + $60,000 + $30,000). Then, in the bottom section of the statement, this amount is added to the beginning goods in process inventory of $2,500 to compute the $178,000 total cost of goods that were in process during the year. Because the ending goods in process inventory had an estimated cost of $7,500, the net cost of goods manufactured (or cost of goods completed) during

Illustration 18–6

SAMPLE MANUFACTURING COMPANY
Manufacturing Statement
For Year Ended December 31, 19X2

Direct materials:

Raw materials inventory, December 31, 19X1	$ 8,000	
Raw materials purchases	86,500	
Raw materials available for use	$94,500	
Raw materials inventory, December 31, 19X2	(9,000)	
Direct materials used		$ 85,500
Direct labor		60,000

Factory overhead costs:

Indirect labor	$ 9,000	
Factory supervision	6,000	
Factory utilities	2,600	
Repairs, factory equipment	2,500	
Property taxes, factory building	1,900	
Factory supplies used	600	
Factory insurance expired	1,100	
Small tools written off	200	
Depreciation, factory equipment	3,500	
Depreciation, factory building	1,800	
Amortization, patents	800	
Total factory overhead costs		30,000
Total manufacturing costs		$175,500
Add goods in process inventory, December 31, 19X1		2,500
Total goods in process during the year		$178,000
Deduct goods in process inventory, December 31, 19X2		(7,500)
Cost of goods manufactured		$170,500

---

the year was $170,500. Now turn to Illustration 18–3 on page 688 and find this same item and amount listed in the cost of goods sold section of Sample Manufacturing Company's income statement.

The manufacturing statement contains information that management uses in planning and controlling the company's production activities. To provide timely information, the statement is likely to be produced monthly or weekly or even more often. Although the manufacturing statement may contain information useful to outside parties, it is not a general purpose financial statement. Because GAAP does not require companies to publish the statement, most of them do not.

FAST HINT
Relevant Exercise:
To apply these concepts, work Exercise 18–5.

ACCOUNTING FOR MANUFACTURING ACTIVITIES WITH A GENERAL ACCOUNTING SYSTEM

So far, our focus has been on how the reports generated by the accounting system reflect what happens when production activities take place. We now turn to the accounting procedures used to compile the information presented in the reports. In this chapter, we describe manufacturing accounting systems based on *periodic* inventories. These systems estimate the costs of the raw materials, goods in process, and finished goods inventories based on physical counts of the quantities on hand at the end of each period. This information is then used to compute the amounts consumed, finished, and sold during the period. A manufacturing company that applies these periodic inventory procedures is said to have a **general accounting system.**

Many manufacturing companies use more complex accounting systems based on *perpetual* inventories. These systems are called **cost accounting systems.** By keeping running records of the costs of materials, goods in process, and finished goods inventories, these systems provide more timely information about those inventories and changes in their levels. They also provide timely information about manufacturing costs per unit of product, which managers use in their efforts to control costs.

Chapter 19 describes job order cost accounting systems that provide more detailed information about the costs of unique products manufactured individually or in small batches. Chapter 20 describes process cost accounting systems used to provide information about the costs of products manufactured in large quantities.

Despite their differences, general accounting systems and cost accounting systems have similar features. They both focus on the three elements of manufacturing cost: *direct materials, direct labor,* and *factory overhead.* They also provide information about the three inventories—raw materials, goods in process, and finished goods. However, they do not keep these records in the same way. The next sections describe how general accounting systems work.

FAST HINT
Additional Insight:
Direct material and direct labor are sometimes referred to as prime costs in companies where they are the main focus of management's attention.

Progress Check

18-8 **A manufacturing statement:** *(a)* **Calculates the cost of goods manufactured during the period;** *(b)* **Calculates the cost of goods sold during the period;** *(c)* **Reports operating expenses incurred during the period.**

18-9 **Does GAAP require companies to publish the manufacturing statement?**

18-10 **How are the beginning and ending goods in process inventories reported on the manufacturing statement?**

Accounts Unique to a General Accounting System

Many of the accounts used by manufacturing companies and merchandising companies are the same. Both have accounts for cash, accounts receivable, accounts payable, common stock, retained earnings, sales, and selling and administrative expenses. However, because of the complexity of a manufacturing company's operations, its General Ledger usually contains more accounts than a merchandising company's ledger. The accounts used only by manufacturing companies include Factory Equipment, Accumulated Depreciation on Factory Equipment, Factory Supplies, Factory Supplies Used, Raw Materials Inventory, Raw Materials Purchases, Direct Labor, Factory Overhead, Goods in Process Inventory, Finished Goods Inventory, and Manufacturing Summary. The last seven accounts in this list are explained next.

LO 4

Describe the unique accounts manufacturing companies use in a general accounting system.

Raw Materials Inventory. Under a periodic inventory system, a firm records the cost of the raw materials on hand at the end of the period in the Raw Materials Inventory account. Throughout the following accounting period, this amount remains in the account as its beginning balance. Then, when the period ends, the balance is updated in the closing process.

Companies determine the end-of-period cost of raw materials by counting the materials on hand and assigning costs to them based on historical purchase prices. Management may choose to assign costs to the account based on FIFO, LIFO, weighted average, or specific invoice prices. To avoid unnecessary complexity, we assume a FIFO flow in this discussion.

Raw Materials Purchases. In a general accounting system, the cost of raw materials purchased during a period is debited to the Raw Materials Purchases account. This account is similar to the Purchases account that you have used for merchandise purchases. Raw Materials Purchases is a temporary holding account for costs later allocated between the ending raw materials inventory and the production of the period. The account starts each period with a zero balance. The balance increases as materials purchases are recorded and returns to zero when the account is closed at the end of the period.

Many companies use supplemental and contra accounts to record other events that affect the cost of the purchased materials. For example, the ledger might include accounts for transportation-in, materials purchases returns and allowances, and materials purchases discounts. To simplify the illustrations in this chapter, we do not include these accounts in the examples.

Direct Labor. General accounting systems use a special temporary account to record direct labor costs. The Direct Labor account is similar to the Raw Materials Purchases account because it accumulates direct labor costs until they are allocated to other accounts at the end of the year. The account begins the year with a zero balance, receives debits throughout the year as direct labor costs are incurred, and then is closed at the end of the period. When the Direct Labor account is closed, the accumulated costs are assigned to the fully and partially completed units of product manufactured during the year.

To help managers control direct labor costs, the accounting system may include several accounts for different categories of direct labor costs. Other accounts distinguish base pay from fringe benefits and payroll taxes. However, all these costs end up being assigned to products. To simplify the discussion, the illustrations in the chapter use only one Direct Labor account.

Factory Overhead. Firms use another temporary holding account to record manufacturing overhead costs. The Factory Overhead account is like the Direct Labor account because it starts the year with a zero balance. During the year, it is debited as overhead costs are incurred. Then, when the accumulated costs are allocated to products in the year-end closing process, the account balance is returned to zero.

As with direct labor, a company may use a group of individual overhead accounts to accumulate information about different overhead costs. This information often helps management control specific overhead costs such as indirect labor, indirect materials, and utilities. Although the upcoming example uses only a single overhead account, it shows how multiple overhead accounts could be used.

Goods in Process Inventory. As we described earlier, a manufacturing company often has an inventory of partially completed goods in process. These units have received at least some of their direct materials and probably some direct labor and overhead costs. However, the units remain unfinished. At the end of the period, the estimated cost of the unfinished units is debited to the Goods in Process Inventory account.

Because a general accounting system is based on periodic inventory methods, the balance of this account remains unchanged throughout the following period. In other words, the account is not updated during a period to reflect the completion of units or the introduction of new units into production. Finally, the next year-end closing process updates the account balance to reflect the cost of the ending goods in process inventory.

The costs to be recorded in the Goods in Process Inventory account can seldom be determined with precision under a periodic system. Even though the number of units might be countable, the process of assigning costs to those units is not precise. Imagine, for example, a workshop with 120 partially completed lawn mowers. Some of them are just barely started, others are part way along in production, and still others are nearly complete. Determining the cost of these mowers involves many estimates and compromises. We describe these measurement problems in more detail later in the chapter.

Finished Goods Inventory. Finished goods are completed units ready for sale. Like the other two inventory accounts, the initial balance of the Finished Goods Inventory account equals the cost of the prior year's ending inventory. As additional units are completed and sales occur, the account is not updated. No entries are made to the account until it is updated by the year-end closing process to reflect the estimated cost of the finished goods on hand.

FAST HINT
Important Point to Remember:
A manufacturing company may use numerous subsidiary ledgers to accumulate detailed information concerning production costs and inventories. A subsidiary ledger for accounts receivable was described in Chapter 6.

A physical count of the ending finished goods inventory provides some of the information needed to determine the ending balance in the account. However, with a general accounting system, accountants often encounter measurement difficulties when they assign costs to completed goods. The difficulties arise because the system does not keep precise records of costs incurred in producing each unit. The next two chapters show how perpetual inventory systems provide more precise measures of unit costs. As a result, the valuation of the goods in process and finished goods inventories is more precise.

Manufacturing Summary. A general accounting system also uses the Manufacturing Summary account. This temporary account is similar to the Income Summary account. The Manufacturing Summary account has a zero balance throughout the year until the closing process starts. During closing, all manufacturing costs are transferred to this account. Then, the account balance is returned to zero as this total cost is allocated among the three ending inventory accounts and the cost of goods sold.

FAST HINT
Relevant Exercise:
To apply these concepts, work Exercise 18–8.

Progress Check

18-11   Which of the following statements is true with regard to a general accounting system for a manufacturing company?
   a. Raw materials purchased are debited to Goods in Process Inventory.
   b. The Goods in Process Inventory account is updated in the year-end closing process.
   c. The FIFO cost pricing method must be used.

18-12   What is the difference between a general accounting system for manufacturers and a cost accounting system?

18-13   Name an account that has a function similar to the Manufacturing Summary account.

Now that you have a background for manufacturing and general accounting systems, we can describe the flow of manufacturing costs and the related entries that account for manufacturing activities. The entries are based on the following information about the inventories and events for Sample Manufacturing Company for 19X2:

COST FLOWS AND JOURNAL ENTRIES UNDER A GENERAL ACCOUNTING SYSTEM

LO 5
Describe the flow of manufacturing costs in a general accounting system and prepare entries to record them.

Beginning inventories:	
Raw materials	$ 8,000
Goods in process	2,500
Finished goods	11,200
Production costs for the year:	
Raw materials purchases	$86,500
Direct labor	60,000
Factory overhead	30,000
Ending inventories:	
Raw materials	$ 9,000
Goods in process	7,500
Finished goods	10,300

For now, the costs of the ending inventories are assumed. Later, we describe how you can determine the amounts.

Beginning Balances

In the upper section of Illustration 18–7, the five boxes on the left represent the sources of manufacturing costs. They include the beginning materials inventory, the beginning goods in process inventory, purchases of raw materials, direct labor costs, and factory overhead. In the lower section of the illustration, notice that the Raw Materials Inventory, Goods in Process Inventory, and Finished Goods Inventory accounts have balances at the beginning of the period. The amounts of $8,000, $2,500, and $11,200 are carried forward from the end of 19X1.

Recording the Period's Manufacturing Activities

In the upper section of Illustration 18–7, the arrows labeled 1 represent the manufacturing events of the year. These arrows symbolize purchasing raw materials for $86,500, using direct labor at a cost of $60,000, and incurring $30,000 of factory overhead costs.

In the lower section of Illustration 18–7, notice that Cash, Accounts Payable, and Other Accounts are used with Raw Materials Purchases, Direct Labor, and Factory Overhead to record the production costs for 19X2. The debits and credits connected by the arrows labeled 1 summarize the journal entries to record these 19X2 activities. For example, the arrows pointing to Accounts Payable and Raw Material Purchases summarize all of the credit purchases of raw materials during the period. In general journal form, one of those transactions would be recorded as follows:

FAST HINT

Alternative Example:

What entry would be made to record the purchase of $1,000 of raw materials for cash?

Answer:

Raw Materials
    Purchases   1,000
  Cash   1,000

19X2				
May	15	Raw Materials Purchases	800.00	
		Accounts Payable		800.00
		Purchased raw materials on credit.		

This entry increases the balance of Raw Materials Purchases by the cost of the acquired materials. It also increases the balance of Accounts Payable to reflect the new liability created by the transaction.

As another example, the arrows pointing to Direct Labor and Other Accounts represent all of the 19X2 accruals of direct labor costs. Again in general journal form, one of those transactions (ignoring withholdings) would be recorded as follows:

Aug.	21	Direct Labor	2,550.00	
		Wages Payable		2,550.00
		To accrue direct labor payroll.		

This entry increases the balance of the temporary Direct Labor account and increases Wages Payable (Other Accounts in the illustration) by the amount accrued. To simplify the diagram, Illustration 18–7 uses Other Accounts to represent all accounts other than Cash and Accounts Payable that are credited during the year in recording manufacturing costs.

The arrow pointing to Factory Overhead represents all overhead costs incurred during the year. The illustration uses only one Factory Overhead account instead of the many detailed accounts that a company might use.

Illustration 18-7   The Flow of Manufacturing Costs

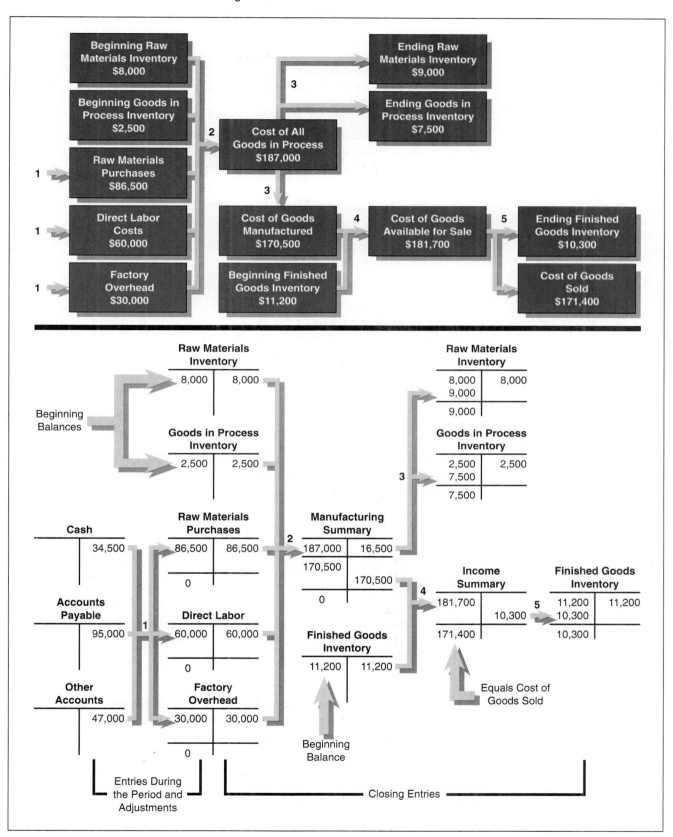

An example of factory overhead would be $1,800 of depreciation on the factory building. The following adjusting entry records this cost:

Dec.	31	Factory Overhead	1,800.00	
		Accumulated Depreciation, Building		1,800.00
		To record depreciation on the factory building.		

At the bottom of Illustration 18–7, notice that the arrows labeled 1 represent all of the entries made during the period plus the adjusting entries. The cost flows labeled 2, 3, 4, and 5 are all recorded with closing entries.

Closing the Temporary Manufacturing Accounts

In the upper section of Illustration 18–7, arrow 2 indicates that the five sources of manufacturing costs generated a total cost of $187,000 to be accounted for during 19X2. We calculate this total as follows:

Beginning inventories:	
Raw materials	$ 8,000
Goods in process	2,500
Production costs for the year:	
Raw materials purchases	86,500
Direct labor	60,000
Factory overhead	30,000
Total costs to be accounted for during 19X2 ..	$187,000

In the lower section of Illustration 18–7, entry 2 transfers the balances of the five accounts into the temporary Manufacturing Summary account at the end of 19X2. In general journal form, this closing entry appears as follows:

19X2				
Dec.	31	Manufacturing Summary	187,000.00	
		Raw Materials Inventory		8,000.00
		Goods in Process Inventory		2,500.00
		Raw Materials Purchases		86,500.00
		Direct Labor		60,000.00
		Factory Overhead		30,000.00
		To close the production accounts to Manufacturing		
		Summary.		

This example uses only one Factory Overhead account. However, recall from the discussion of the Factory Overhead account on page 694 that a company may collect its factory overhead costs in several accounts. When several overhead accounts are used, the previous closing entry includes a credit to each of them. For example, assume that a separate account is used for each of the specific overhead costs listed in the manufacturing statement in Illustration 18–6 on page 692. In that case, the preceding closing entry would be replaced by the following:

19X2				
Dec.	31	Manufacturing Summary	187,000.00	
		Raw Materials Inventory		8,000.00
		Goods in Process Inventory		2,500.00
		Raw Materials Purchases		86,500.00
		Direct Labor		60,000.00
		Indirect Labor		9,000.00
		Factory Supervision		6,000.00
		Factory Utilities		2,600.00
		Repairs, Factory Equipment		2,500.00
		Property Taxes on Factory Building		1,900.00
		Factory Supplies Used		600.00
		Factory Insurance Expired		1,100.00
		Small Tools Written Off		200.00
		Depreciation of Factory Equipment		3,500.00
		Depreciation of Factory Building		1,800.00
		Amortization of Patents		800.00
		To close the production accounts to Manufacturing Summary.		

FAST HINT
Critical Thought Question:
The factory overhead accounts shown in this entry include an account for factory supervision. Under what circumstances might a supervisor's salary be included with direct labor?

Recording the Ending Balances of the Manufacturing Inventory Accounts

In Illustration 18–7, look at the arrows labeled 3. They indicate that $9,000 of the $187,000 total cost for 19X2 is allocated to the ending inventory of raw materials and another $7,500 is allocated to the ending goods in process inventory. The remaining $170,500 is the cost of the units completed during the period.

In the lower section of the illustration, arrow 3 shows the entry to record the cost of the ending raw materials and goods in process inventories. In general journal form, entry 3 is:

19X2				
Dec.	31	Raw Materials Inventory	9,000.00	
		Goods in Process Inventory	7,500.00	
		Manufacturing Summary		16,500.00
		To update the raw materials and goods in process inventories.		

Notice that the $170,500 cost of completed units temporarily remains as the balance of Manufacturing Summary. Look at Illustration 18–6 on page 692 to see this amount on the bottom line of the Manufacturing Statement. You can also see it in the Cost of Goods Sold section of the income statement in Illustration 18–3 on page 688.

Closing the Manufacturing Summary Account and Updating the Finished Goods Inventory Account

The next flow of cost, arrow 4 in Illustration 18–7, recognizes the cost of goods available for sale. In the lower section of the illustration, arrow 4 shows that this involves transferring the Manufacturing Summary balance and the beginning Finished Goods Inventory to Income Summary.

The complete closing entry is not represented in Illustration 18–7 because the focus of the illustration is on the manufacturing costs. The following complete closing entry closes all the 19X2 expense accounts for Sample Manufacturing Company. The balances of the expense accounts are taken from the 19X2 income statement in Illustration 18–3.

19X2				
Dec.	31	Income Summary	274,200.00	
		Manufacturing Summary		**170,500.00**
		Finished Goods Inventory		**11,200.00**
		Sales Salaries Expense		18,000.00
		Advertising Expense		5,500.00
		Delivery Wages Expense		12,000.00
		Shipping Supplies Expense		250.00
		Insurance Expense, Delivery Equipment		300.00
		Depreciation Expense, Delivery Equipment		2,100.00
		Office Salaries Expense		15,700.00
		Miscellaneous Expenses		200.00
		Bad Debts Expense		1,550.00
		Office Supplies Expense		100.00
		Depreciation Expense, Office Equipment		200.00
		Interest Expense		4,000.00
		Income Taxes Expense		32,600.00
		To close the Manufacturing Summary and expense accounts, and to clear the Finished Goods Inventory account.		

In the upper section of the illustration, arrow 5 allocates the cost of goods available for sale between the ending inventory of finished goods and the cost of goods sold. In the lower section of Illustration 18–7, entry 5 completes the process of accounting for Sample Manufacturing Company's manufacturing costs during 19X2. Notice that the entry leaves the $171,400 cost of goods sold remaining in the Income Summary account.

Although Illustration 18–7 does not show the Sales account, the complete closing entry also includes a debit to Sales:

FAST HINT
Critical Thought Question:
A credit balance in the Income Summary account prior to closing indicates that the company has experienced net income for the period. Is it possible for the Manufacturing Summary account to have a credit balance prior to closing? Explain.

19X2				
Dec.	31	Finished Goods Inventory	10,300.00	
		Sales	310,000.00	
		Income Summary		320,300.00
		To close the Sales account and update the Finished Goods Inventory account.		

After this entry is posted, the Income Summary account has a credit balance of $46,100, which equals the net income for 19X2. The following entry closes the Income Summary account and updates the Retained Earnings account:

FAST HINT
Relevant Quick Studies:
To apply these concepts, work QS 18–5 and 18–6.

19X2				
Dec.	31	Income Summary	46,100.00	
		Retained Earnings		46,100.00
		To close Income Summary and update Retained Earnings.		

Observe that the last closing entry is exactly the same whether the company is engaged in merchandising, manufacturing, or providing services.

Illustration 18–8 shows how manufacturing cost information flows from managerial accounting reports to the financial statements. In the illustration, overhead cost information flows from a schedule of overhead costs to the manufacturing statement and on to the income statement. Note that the individual factory overhead costs are listed in a separate schedule. The schedule supports and explains the total factory overhead cost item shown on the manufacturing statement. Recall that some companies include a detailed list of overhead costs on the manufacturing statement and others use a supporting schedule. The manufacturing statement includes the total factory overhead in its calculation of the cost of goods manufactured. Then, the cost of goods manufactured is carried over to the income statement and shown as part of the cost of goods sold calculation.

As we mentioned earlier, the manufacturing statement and the supporting schedule of overhead items are prepared for managers. They are rarely published. Nevertheless, the manufacturing statement explains part of and is consistent with the income statement. As you already know, the financial statements published for outsiders' use always include an income statement. Thus, you can see that even though managerial accounting and financial accounting are designed to serve different users, some managerial reports are closely related to the financial statements.

REPORTING OVERHEAD COSTS TO MANAGERS AND TO EXTERNAL PARTIES

Progress Check

18-14 In preparing closing entries for a manufacturing company that uses a general accounting system, the beginning balance of Finished Goods Inventory is:
a. Debited to Finished Goods Inventory and credited to Income Summary.
b. Debited to Finished Goods Inventory and credited to Manufacturing Summary.
c. Credited to Finished Goods Inventory and debited to Income Summary.

18-15 What accounts are summarized in the Manufacturing Summary account?

18-16 What accounts are summarized in the Income Summary account?

When a company uses a general accounting system, it bases the ending inventories of raw materials, goods in process, and finished goods on physical counts of the units on hand. Assigning cost to the raw materials inventory does not involve a new problem. It is no different than assigning cost to the merchandise inventory of a retailer. The items in both inventories are generally in the same condition as when they were purchased.

However, determining the costs of goods in process and finished goods inventories is more complex. Because these inventories have been partially or wholly converted from raw materials into finished products, firms simply cannot measure the costs of goods in process and finished goods as the amounts paid to suppliers. Instead, the manufacturing cost of these inventories must be estimated.

Estimating Direct Material and Direct Labor Costs in the Ending Inventories

In some manufacturing processes, the direct materials and direct labor costs in the goods in process and finished goods inventories can be determined precisely. More often, however, a production manager who understands the manufacturing process must estimate these costs.

INVENTORY VALUATION PROBLEMS UNDER A GENERAL ACCOUNTING SYSTEM

LO 6

Explain the procedures for periodically assigning costs to the inventories owned by manufacturing companies.

Illustration 18–8   Relationships between Overhead Items, the Manufacturing Statement, and the Income Statement

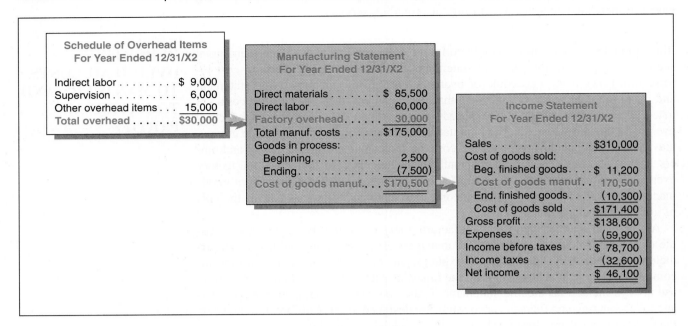

After the manager estimates the quantity of direct materials in each unit, costs are assigned based on a cost flow assumption such as FIFO. Finally, the estimated direct material costs for the units in the inventory are totaled to approximate the direct material cost of the entire inventory. The same process is used to calculate the cost of direct materials in the finished goods inventory.

The procedures for estimating the direct labor cost of goods in process are similar to those used for direct materials. Normally, a production manager estimates the hours of direct labor that have been applied to the units in the inventory. Then, based on the cost per hour of labor, the manager calculates the total direct labor cost of the units. The manager makes similar estimates of the direct labor cost added to the finished goods on hand.

Estimating Factory Overhead Cost in the Ending Inventories

Because factory overhead is not clearly associated with specific units or batches of product, estimating the overhead cost that should be assigned to the ending inventories is a challenging problem. The traditional approach to assigning overhead relates factory overhead to some other factor used throughout most of the manufacturing process.

For example, a company may express total factory overhead cost as a percentage of total machine hours used in production. Then, the firm assigns overhead cost to units of product by multiplying that percentage by the number of machine hours used to produce each unit. Another alternative is to express total factory overhead cost as a percentage of direct labor cost. If this approach is taken, the company assigns overhead cost to units of product by multiplying that percentage by the direct labor cost assigned to each unit.

To see how this procedure is followed, consider the example of Sample Manufacturing Company. The company's total overhead costs for 19X2 were $30,000 and its total direct labor costs were $60,000. Thus, $1 of factory overhead cost was incurred for each $2 of direct labor cost. In other words, overhead costs as a percentage of direct labor cost were:

$$\frac{\text{Factory overhead, \$30,000}}{\text{Direct labor, \$60,000}} = 50\%$$

Next, Sample applies this percentage to management's estimates of direct labor cost per unit to determine the factory overhead cost per unit.

The following table shows the assignments of all three types of cost to the units in the ending inventories:

	Goods in Process			Finished Goods		
	Cost per Unit	Units of Product	Total Cost	Cost per Unit	Units of Product	Total Cost
Direct materials (estimated)	$3.75	1,000	$3,750	$11.00	515	$ 5,665
Direct labor (estimated)	2.50	1,000	2,500	6.00	515	3,090
Factory overhead (50% of direct labor)	1.25	1,000	1,250	3.00	515	1,545
Total cost			$7,500			$10,300

The table shows that management estimated direct materials costs at $3.75 per unit in process and $11 per finished unit. The estimates of direct labor cost were $2.50 per unit in process and $6.00 per finished unit. Then, factory overhead cost was assigned at the rate of 50% of the direct labor cost. Physical counts of the ending inventories showed that there were 1,000 partially finished units in process and 515 units in the finished goods inventory. Finally, each per unit cost was multiplied by the number of units in each inventory to calculate the total cost assigned to the two inventories. Notice that the $7,500 cost of the ending goods in process and the $10,300 cost of the ending finished goods inventory are the amounts used in Illustration 18–8.

Companies commonly relate factory overhead to direct labor when assigning overhead to inventories. However, alternative methods may be used. For example, factory overhead may be related to machine hours used in manufacturing. Thus, if the products are manufactured on a machine, total overhead cost may be divided by total machine hours used to get overhead cost per machine hour. Then, firms can assign overhead to units based on the number of machine hours it takes to produce a unit.

Other factors, such as the quantity of direct materials used in production, may also be used as the basis for assigning overhead to inventories. However, all assignment methods are somewhat arbitrary. They are all based on the assumption that the amount of overhead incurred in producing a unit of product is proportional to the amount of the related factor (such as direct labor) that it takes to produce a unit. Chapter 21 describes a more sophisticated approach to the problem called *activity-based costing*.

FAST HINT
Alternative Example:
Suppose that Sample's total overhead costs were $45,000. What would be the estimated total cost for ending inventories of goods in process and finished goods if overhead costs are assigned in proportion to direct labor cost?
Answer:
Goods in Process = $ 8,125
Finished Goods   = $11,073

FAST HINT
Relevant Exercise:
To apply these concepts, work Exercise 18–12.

Progress Check

18-17 Why are the assignments of direct material and direct labor costs to goods in process and finished goods inventories usually based on estimates by managers familiar with the production process?

18-18 Republic Company used an overhead rate of 60% of direct labor cost to add overhead cost to the cost of the items of its goods in process inventory. Given that the manufacturing statement of the company reported total overhead cost of $156,000, how much direct labor did it report?

LO 1. Describe five differences between financial and managerial accounting. Despite their similarities, financial and managerial accounting differ in many ways. These include who uses the information, what they use the information for, why they need it, and the flexibility of the practices. The information provided by financial and managerial accounting also differs in its timeliness, the periods to which it relates, and its subject matter.

LO 2. Describe the basic differences between the financial statements of manufacturing companies and merchandising companies. The financial statements of manufacturers and merchandisers are different in their descriptions of inventories and cost of goods sold. In the cost of goods sold calculations, manufacturers report the cost of goods manufactured while merchandisers report the cost of purchases. The balance sheets of manufacturers include three inventories (raw materials, goods in process, and finished goods) while merchandisers report only merchandise inventory. Manufacturers also may identify some of their plant assets as factory equipment and buildings.

LO 3. Prepare a manufacturing statement and explain its purpose and relationship to the primary financial statements. The manufacturing statement presents a calculation of the cost of goods manufactured during the period. It begins by showing the period's costs for direct materials, direct labor, and overhead, and then combines these numbers with the beginning and ending inventories of goods in process to calculate the cost of the completed goods.

LO 4. Describe the unique accounts manufacturing companies use in a general accounting system. Unique accounts used by manufacturers with general accounting systems include Raw Materials Inventory, Raw Materials Purchases, Direct Labor, Factory Overhead, Goods in Process Inventory, Finished Goods Inventory, and Manufacturing Summary. Additional accounts may provide more detailed information for management use in planning and controlling operations.

LO 5. Describe the flow of manufacturing costs in a general accounting system and prepare entries to record them. During each period, manufacturers use separate accounts to record their raw materials purchases, direct labor costs, and factory overhead costs. After end-of-period adjustments are recorded in the closing process, all manufacturing costs are transferred to the Manufacturing Summary account. Next, the Manufacturing Summary balance is allocated to cost of goods manufactured (Income Summary) and to the ending inventories of materials and goods in process. At the same time, the beginning finished goods inventory balance is transferred to Income Summary. Another closing entry records the ending finished goods inventory.

LO 6. Explain the procedures for periodically assigning costs to the inventories owned by manufacturing companies. When determining the costs of ending inventories, a manufacturer allocates the raw materials and direct labor costs to goods in process and finished goods based on estimates by production managers. Factory overhead cost is related to another factor used in production, such as direct labor or machine hours. Then, the manufacturer allocates overhead cost to the ending work in process and finished goods inventories based on the estimated quantity of direct labor or machine hours used to produce the units in the inventories.

**DEMONSTRATION
PROBLEM**

The following account balances and other information were taken from the accounting records of Sunny Corporation for the year ended December 31, 19X2. Use the information to prepare a schedule of factory overhead costs, a manufacturing statement (show only the total overhead cost), and an income statement.

Advertising expense	$ 85,000
Amortization of patents	16,000
Bad debts expense	28,000
Depreciation expense, office equipment	37,000
Depreciation of factory building	133,000
Depreciation of factory equipment	78,000
Direct labor	250,000
Factory insurance expired	62,000
Factory supervision	74,000
Factory supplies used	21,000
Factory utilities	115,000
Finished goods inventory, December 31, 19X1	15,000
Finished goods inventory, December 31, 19X2	12,500
Goods in process inventory, December 31, 19X1	8,000
Goods in process inventory, December 31, 19X2	9,000
Income taxes expense	53,400
Indirect labor	26,000
Interest expense	25,000
Miscellaneous expenses	55,000
Property taxes on factory equipment	14,000
Raw materials inventory, December 31, 19X1	60,000
Raw materials inventory, December 31, 19X2	78,000
Raw materials purchases	313,000
Repairs, factory equipment	31,000
Salaries expense	150,000
Sales	1,630,000

Planning the Solution

- Analyze the list of the costs and select those items that are factory overhead.
- Arrange these costs in a schedule of factory overhead costs for 19X2.
- Analyze the items remaining on the list and select the ones related to production activity for the year; the selected items should include the materials and goods in process inventories and direct labor.
- Prepare a manufacturing statement for 19X2 showing the calculation of the cost of materials used in production, the cost of direct labor, and the total factory overhead cost. When presenting the overhead cost on this statement, show only the total overhead cost from the schedule of overhead costs for 19X2. Then, show the costs of the beginning and ending goods in process inventory to determine the total cost of goods manufactured.
- Combine the remaining revenue and expense items from the list into the income statement for 19X2. Combine the cost of goods manufactured from the manufacturing statement with the finished goods inventory amounts to calculate the cost of goods sold for 19X2.

Solution to Demonstration Problem

SUNNY CORPORATION
Schedule of Factory Overhead Costs
For Year Ended December 31, 19X2

Amortization of patents	$ 16,000
Depreciation of factory building	133,000
Depreciation of factory equipment	78,000
Factory insurance expired	62,000
Factory supervision	74,000
Factory supplies used	21,000
Factory utilities	115,000
Indirect labor	26,000
Property taxes on factory equipment	14,000
Repairs, factory equipment	31,000
Total factory overhead	$570,000

SUNNY CORPORATION
Manufacturing Statement
For Year Ended December 31, 19X2

Direct materials:		
Raw materials inventory, December 31, 19X1	$ 60,000	
Raw materials purchases	313,000	
Raw materials available for use	$373,000	
Raw materials inventory, December 31, 19X2	(78,000)	
Direct materials used		$ 295,000
Direct labor		250,000
Factory overhead costs		570,000
Total manufacturing costs		$1,115,000
Goods in process inventory, December 31, 19X1		8,000
Total goods in process		$1,123,000
Goods in process inventory, December 31, 19X2		(9,000)
Cost of goods manufactured		$1,114,000

SUNNY CORPORATION
Income Statement
For Year Ended December 31, 19X2

Sales		$1,630,000
Cost of goods sold:		
Finished goods inventory, December 31, 19X1	$ 15,000	
Cost of goods manufactured	1,114,000	
Goods available for sale	$1,129,000	
Finished goods inventory, December 31, 19X2	(12,500)	
Cost of goods sold		(1,116,500)
Gross profit		$ 513,500
Operating expenses:		
Advertising expense	$ 85,000	
Bad debts expense	28,000	
Depreciation expense, office equipment	37,000	
Interest expense	25,000	
Miscellaneous expenses	55,000	
Salaries expense	150,000	
Total operating expenses		(380,000)
Income before taxes		$ 133,500
Income taxes expense		(53,400)
Net income		$ 80,100

GLOSSARY

Cost accounting system a system of accounting for manufacturing operations that uses perpetual inventory records. p. 692

Direct labor labor with a cost that is clearly associated with specific units or batches of product because the labor is used to convert raw materials into finished products. p. 689

Direct materials raw materials that physically become part of the product and therefore are clearly identified with specific units or batches of product. p. 685

Factory overhead costs that are incurred as part of the manufacturing process but are not clearly associated with specific units of product or batches of production; includes all manufacturing costs other than direct material and direct labor costs. p. 689

Finished goods inventory products that have completed the manufacturing process and are ready to be sold by the manufacturer. p. 685

General accounting system a system of accounting for manufacturing operations that uses periodic inventories. p. 692

Goods in process inventory products that are in the process of being manufactured but not yet complete. p. 685

Indirect labor labor that is not clearly associated with specific units or batches of product because it is the labor of manufacturing employees who do not work specifically on converting direct materials into finished products. p. 690

Indirect materials materials that are used in support of the production process but that do not become a part of the product and are not clearly identified with units or batches of product. p. 685

Manufacturing statement a financial report that summarizes the amounts and types of costs that were incurred in the manufacturing process during the period. p. 688

Period costs costs that are charged to expense because their benefits appear to expire as the costs are incurred. p. 687

Product costs costs that are capitalized as inventory because they produce benefits expected to have value in the future. p. 687

Raw materials materials that are purchased for use in making products; most are used as direct materials but some are used as indirect materials. p. 685

QUESTIONS

1. Why does the structure of financial accounting tend to be rigid while managerial accounting is relatively flexible?

2. Why does managerial accounting tend to include more predictions of the future than financial accounting?

3. In addition to inventories, what other assets may appear on the balance sheet of a manufacturer but not on the balance sheet of a merchandiser?

4. What are the three categories of manufacturing cost?

5. List several examples of factory overhead costs.

6. What is the difference between factory overhead and selling and administrative overhead?

7. Which inventories of a manufacturing company appear on its manufacturing statement? Which appear on the income statement? Which appear on the balance sheet?

8. Identify the seven accounts used in general accounting systems for manufacturers that are not used by merchandising or service companies.

9. If a general accounting system is used, at what point in the accounting cycle are the costs of raw materials purchases, direct labor, and factory overhead allocated to the cost of goods sold and to the ending raw materials, goods in process, and finished goods inventories?

10. Describe the relationships among the income statement, the manufacturing statement, and a detailed schedule of factory overhead costs.

11. A footnote to the Lands' End, Inc., financial statements includes "Inventory, primarily merchandise held for sale." What other types of inventories might the company hold?

12. Notice that the current assets on the balance sheet of Federal Express in Appendix G do not include any inventories. Explain why this situation is not unusual.

QUICK STUDY (Five-Minute Exercises)

State whether each of the following most likely describes financial accounting or managerial accounting:

**QS 18–1
(LO 1)**

a. The practice tends to be flexible.

b. The users are managers of the corporation.

c. The primary focus is on the organization as a whole.

d. The information is available only after the audit is completed.

e. The purpose of the information is to assist external users in making investment, credit, and other financial decisions.

Calculate cost of goods sold using the following information:

**QS 18–2
(LO 2)**

Finished goods inventory, December 31, 19X1 . . .	$321,500
Goods in process inventory, December 31, 19X1 . .	74,550
Goods in process inventory, December 31, 19X2 . .	81,200
Cost of goods manufactured	972,345
Finished goods inventory, December 31, 19X2 . . .	297,200

QS 18–3
(LO 3)

Halton Company's manufacturing statement includes the following information. Determine the cost of goods manufactured.

Direct materials used	$189,760
Direct labor	65,100
Total factory overhead costs	24,720
Goods in process, December 31, 19X1	299,400
Goods in process, December 31, 19X2	234,210

QS 18–4
(LO 4)

Complete the following sentences about accounts unique to a manufacturing company:

a. The temporary account that has a zero balance until the closing process starts and is similar to Income Summary is the _____ _____ account.

b. The temporary accounts in which manufacturing costs are recorded throughout the period are _____, _____, and _____.

QS 18–5
(LO 5)

The Intermat Company manufactures products and accounts for its activities using a general accounting system. The following account balances are taken from the company's ledger at the end of the year before closing:

Raw materials inventory	$ 20,000
Goods in process inventory	16,000
Raw materials purchases	84,000
Direct labor	110,000
Factory overhead	220,000

Physical counts at the end of the year show:

Raw materials inventory	$ 18,000
Goods in process inventory	17,600

Prepare the closing entries that should be made to the Manufacturing Summary account, except for the entry to the Income Summary account.

QS 18–6
(LO 5)

These additional account balances are taken from the ledger of the Intermat Company described in QS 18–5.

Finished goods inventory	$ 30,000
Sales	800,000
Selling expenses	122,000
General and administrative expenses	87,000
Income taxes expense	73,440

A physical count at the end of the year shows:

Finished Goods Inventory	$ 37,000

Prepare the closing entries that should be made to the Income Summary account. Assume that the balance of the Manufacturing Summary account is $414,400 (debit) after the entries in QS 18–5 are posted.

QS 18–7
(LO 6)

Secor Company incurred the following manufacturing costs for the period:

Direct labor	$468,000
Direct materials	354,500
Factory overhead	117,000

Calculate overhead cost as a percentage of (a) direct labor and (b) direct materials.

EXERCISES

Calculate the cost of goods sold for these two companies:

	Landry Retail	Koslow Manufacturing
Beginning inventory:		
Merchandise	$250,000	
Finished goods		$500,000
Purchases	460,000	
Cost of goods manufactured		886,000
Ending inventory:		
Merchandise	150,000	
Finished goods		644,000

Exercise 18–1
Calculating cost of goods sold
(LO 2)

The following costs were incurred by a manufacturing company. Classify each one as either a product or a period cost:

Direct materials used.
Payroll taxes for production supervisor.
Accident insurance on factory workers.
Bad debts expense.
Depreciation of factory building.
Advertising.

State and federal income taxes.
Amortization of patents.
Interest on long-term debt.
Factory utilities.
Small tools used.
Office supplies used.

Exercise 18–2
Classifying product costs and period costs
(LO 2)

The following information was taken from the accounting records of Unos Company and FCI Company.

	Unos Company	FCI Company
Beginning finished goods inventory	$ 15,000	$17,800
Beginning goods in process inventory ...	12,400	22,000
Beginning raw materials inventory	6,400	8,240
Depreciation of factory equipment	24,000	35,000
Direct labor	10,000	14,000
Ending finished goods inventory	12,300	21,800
Ending goods in process inventory	15,400	19,000
Ending raw materials inventory	4,600	3,400
Factory utilities	6,000	4,400
Factory supplies used	3,600	4,800
General and administrative expenses	34,000	50,000
Indirect labor	1,300	1,920
Repairs, factory equipment	3,320	5,100
Raw materials purchases	27,000	32,600
Sales salaries	30,000	28,000

Exercise 18–3
Calculating the cost of goods manufactured and the cost of goods sold
(LO 2, 3)

Calculate the cost of goods manufactured and the cost of goods sold for each company.

For each of the following account balances in a manufacturing company's ledger, indicate by a ✓ in the appropriate column whether it will appear on the balance sheet, the income statement, the manufacturing statement, or a detailed schedule of factory overhead costs. Assume that the income statement shows the calculation of cost of goods sold and the manufacturing statement shows only the total amount of factory overhead.

    Note that an account balance may appear on more than one report. For example, the ending inventory of finished goods appears on both the balance sheet and the income statement.

Exercise 18–4
Identifying components of financial statements
(LO 3)

Account	Balance Sheet	Income Statement	Manufacturing Statement	Overhead Schedule
Accounts receivable				
Bad debts expense				
Beginning finished goods inventory				
Beginning goods in process inventory				
Beginning raw materials inventory				
Cash				
Depreciation of factory building				
Depreciation of factory equipment				
Depreciation expense, office building				
Depreciation expense, office equipment				
Direct labor				
Ending finished goods inventory				
Ending goods in process inventory				
Ending raw materials inventory				
Factory supervision				
Factory supplies used				
Income taxes				
Insurance on factory building				
Insurance expense, office building				
Office supplies used				
Property taxes on factory building and equipment				
Raw materials purchases				
Sales				

Exercise 18–5
Preparing a manufacturing statement
(LO 3)

After Darvo Corporation posted its adjusting entries on December 31, 19X2, the General Ledger included the following account balances. (Some accounts in the General Ledger have not been listed.)

Sales	$712,500
Raw materials inventory, December 31, 19X1	39,000
Goods in process inventory, December 31, 19X1	45,525
Finished goods inventory, December 31, 19X1	57,375
Raw materials purchases	114,825
Direct labor	136,650
Factory supplies used	13,800
Indirect labor	33,600
Repairs, factory equipment	6,000
Rent on factory building	49,500
Selling expenses	86,400
General and administrative expenses	100,950

The ending inventories are:

Raw materials inventory, December 31, 19X2	$ 35,625
Goods in process inventory, December 31, 19X2	31,650
Finished goods inventory, December 31, 19X2	53,475

Given this information, prepare a manufacturing statement for Darvo Corporation. Include the individual overhead account balances.

Exercise 18–6
Preparing a manufacturing company's income statement
(LO 2, 3)

Use the information provided in Exercise 18–5 to prepare an income statement for Darvo Corporation. Assume that the cost of goods manufactured is $371,625.

The following partially completed flowchart is similar to Illustration 18–5 on page 691. Some of the boxes in the flowchart show cost amounts while other boxes contain question marks. Calculate the cost that should appear in each box containing a question mark.

Exercise 18–7
Understanding the manufacturing process
(LO 2)

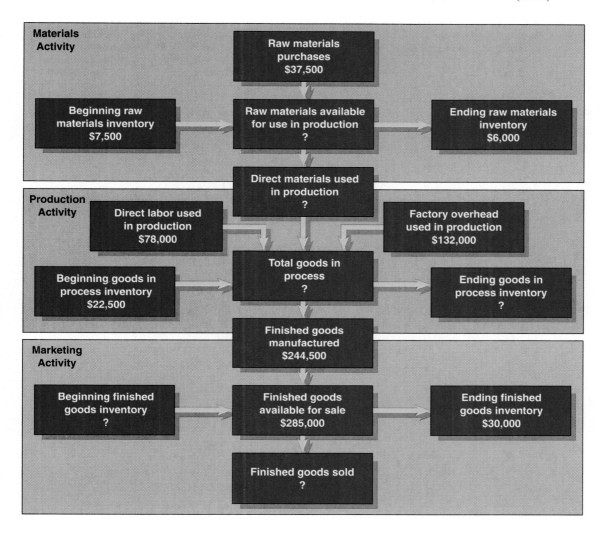

Exercise 18–8
Identifying facts about
manufacturing accounts
(LO 4)

The following chart lists seven accounts in general accounting systems used by manufacturers. Fill in the requested facts for each account. The first row is completed for you.

Account	Balance at Beginning of Year	Entries to Account Prior to Closing	Closing Entries Made to Account	Closed at End of Year?	Financial Statements on Which Balance is Reported
Raw Materials Inventory	Cost of raw materials on hand at end of prior year	None	Credited for beginning balance Debited for ending balance	No	Manufacturing Statement Balance Sheet
Raw Materials Purchases					
Direct Labor					
Factory Overhead					
Goods in Process Inventory					
Finished Goods Inventory					
Manufacturing Summary					

Use the information provided in Exercise 18–5 and prepare closing entries for Darvo Corporation.

Exercise 18–9
Closing entries for a manufacturing company
(LO 5)

The following account balances are taken from the Helix Co.'s accounting records after adjustments as of December 31, 19X2. Also presented are the results of physical counts and valuations of the ending inventories.

Exercise 18–10
Closing entries for a manufacturing company
(LO 5)

Sales	$422,400
Raw materials purchases	67,200
Direct labor	99,120
Factory overhead	81,600
Selling expenses	45,840
General and administrative expenses	41,760
Income taxes expense	47,520
Raw materials inventory	12,480
Goods in process inventory	17,040
Finished goods inventory	10,320
Ending inventories:	
Raw materials	19,440
Goods in process	25,200
Finished goods	15,840

Prepare closing entries for the company.

Cardinal Company uses the proportional relationship between factory overhead and direct labor costs to assign factory overhead to its inventories of goods in process and finished goods. The company incurred the following costs during 19X2:

Exercise 18–11
Overhead rate calculation and analysis
(LO 6)

Direct materials used	$ 637,500
Direct labor	1,440,000
Factory overhead	1,080,000

a. Determine the company's overhead rate.

b. Under the assumption that the company's $57,000 ending goods in process inventory had $18,000 of direct labor costs, determine the inventory's direct material costs.

c. Under the assumption that the company's $337,485 ending finished goods inventory had $195,000 of direct material costs, determine the inventory's direct labor cost and its factory overhead costs.

According to physical counts, Monarch Company's ending goods in process inventory consisted of 4,500 units of partially completed product and its finished goods inventory consisted of 11,700 units of product. The factory manager determined that the goods in process inventory included direct materials cost of $10.50 per unit and direct labor cost of $7.00 per unit. Finished goods were estimated to have $12.80 of direct materials cost per unit and $9.00 of direct labor cost per unit. During the period, the company incurred these costs:

Exercise 18–12
Allocating costs to ending inventories
(LO 6)

Direct materials	$460,000
Direct labor	277,000
Factory overhead	443,200

The company allocates factory overhead to goods in process and finished goods inventories by relating overhead to direct labor cost.

a. Calculate the overhead rate.

b. Calculate the total cost of the two ending inventories.

c. Because this was Monarch's first year, there were no beginning inventories. Calculate the cost of goods sold for the year, and show how much direct material, direct labor, and factory overhead is included in the cost of goods sold.

PROBLEMS

Problem 18–1
Allocating costs to goods in process; preparing the manufacturing statement
(LO 3, 5, 6)

Perdue Company's General Ledger included the following items related to its manufacturing activities for 19X2. The accounts have been adjusted, but have not yet been closed.

Raw materials inventory	$ 84,600
Goods in process inventory	99,360
Raw materials purchases	311,400
Direct labor	450,000
Indirect labor	194,220
Factory utilities	109,440
Repairs, factory equipment	30,060
Rent on factory building	84,600
Property taxes on factory equipment	19,260
Factory insurance expired	16,020
Factory supplies used	34,920
Depreciation of factory equipment	82,800
Amortization of patents	13,680

In addition, the ending inventory of raw materials is known to be $91,080. The ending inventory of goods in process is not known, but it is known that the company makes a single product and 4,500 units of goods were in process on December 31, 19X2. Each unit contained an estimated $18.00 of direct materials and had $7.50 of direct labor cost assigned to it.

Required

Preparation component:

1. Calculate the overhead rate based on the relationship between total factory overhead cost and total direct labor cost. Then, determine the cost of the ending goods in process inventory.

2. Prepare a manufacturing statement for 19X2.

3. Prepare entries to close the manufacturing accounts to Manufacturing Summary and to close the Manufacturing Summary account.

Analysis component:

4. Calculate the overhead rate based on the relationship between total factory overhead and total direct materials used. Then, without providing additional calculations, explain how Perdue's manufacturing statement would be affected if this rate were used instead of one based on direct labor cost.

CHECK FIGURE:
Overhead rate, 130.0%

The following alphabetical list of items was taken from the adjusted trial balance and other records of Greer Company before the year-end closing entries were recorded:

Problem 18–2
Preparing manufacturing and income statements
(LO 2, 3, 4)

Advertising expense	$ 16,200
Depreciation expense, office equipment	6,750
Depreciation expense, selling equipment	8,100
Depreciation of factory equipment	28,350
Direct labor	523,800
Factory supervision	97,200
Factory supplies used	14,850
Factory utilities	27,000
Income taxes expense	109,350
Indirect labor	47,250
Inventories:	
Raw materials, January 1	132,300
Raw materials, December 31	136,350
Goods in process, January 1	10,700
Goods in process, December 31	11,250
Finished goods, January 1	141,750
Finished goods, December 31	113,400
Miscellaneous production costs	6,750
Office salaries expense	56,700
Raw materials purchases	695,250
Rent expense, office space	18,900
Rent expense, selling space	21,600
Rent on factory building	64,800
Repairs, factory equipment	24,300
Sales	2,431,350
Sales discounts	45,900
Sales salaries expense	236,250
Transportation-in on raw materials	20,250

Required

Preparation component:

1. Prepare a manufacturing statement and an income statement for the company. The income statement should present separate categories for *(a)* selling expenses and *(b)* general and administrative expenses.

CHECK FIGURE:
Cost of goods manufactured, $1,545,200

Analysis component:

2. Recall what you learned about merchandise turnover and calculate the turnover rates for Greer's raw materials and finished goods inventories. Then, discuss some possible reasons for the differences between the turnover rates for the two inventories.

Better Products began this year with the following inventories: raw materials, $160,000; goods in process, $240,000; and finished goods, $280,000. The company uses the ratio between its total factory overhead and total direct labor costs to assign overhead cost to its inventories of goods in process and finished goods. At the end of this year, this information was known about the costs of the inventories (one amount is missing):

Problem 18–3
Calculating cost components and preparing the manufacturing statement
(LO 3, 4, 6)

	Raw Materials	Goods in Process	Finished Goods
Direct material	$88,000	$52,000	$ 80,000
Direct labor	–0–	40,000	100,000
Factory overhead	–0–	?	120,000
Totals	$88,000	$?	$300,000

This additional information was available from the company's records:

Total factory overhead costs incurred during the year	$1,440,000
Cost of all goods manufactured during the year	3,600,000

Required

Prepare a manufacturing statement for Better Products for the year. You can develop all the missing data from what you have been given.

Problem 18–4
Adjusting and closing entries, allocating overhead costs
(LO 4, 5, 6)

Following is the unadjusted trial balance of the Titus Company as of December 31, 19X2:

Cash	$ 62,500	
Accounts receivable	250,000	
Raw materials inventory	200,000	
Goods in process inventory	100,000	
Finished goods inventory	225,000	
Factory equipment	500,000	
Accumulated depreciation, factory equipment		$ 112,500
Accounts payable		162,500
Wages payable		
Income taxes payable		
Common stock		397,000
Retained earnings		418,000
Sales		1,562,500
Raw materials purchases	625,000	
Direct labor	232,500	
Indirect labor	87,500	
Factory utilities	67,500	
Repairs, factory equipment	15,000	
Depreciation of factory equipment		
Selling expenses	162,500	
General and administrative expenses	125,000	
Income taxes expense		
Total	$2,652,500	$2,652,500

The following adjusting entries need to be made:

a. Depreciation on the factory equipment for the year is $75,000.

b. Accrued direct labor wages are $17,500.

c. Accrued indirect labor wages are $5,000.

d. Accrued income taxes are estimated to be $80,000.

The raw materials ending inventory was $210,000. These facts were known about the other ending inventories:

	Materials Cost per Unit	Labor Cost per Unit	Units
Goods in process	$25.00	$10.00	2,500
Finished goods	40.00	22.50	6,000

Required

1. Present the prescribed adjusting entries.

2. Determine the total adjusted overhead cost, the total adjusted direct labor cost, and the ratio of overhead cost to direct labor cost.

3. Determine the cost of the ending inventories of goods in process and finished goods.

4. Present the closing entries.

Problem 18–5
Preparing manufacturing schedules and financial statements
(LO 3)

Using the answers to Problem 18–4, prepare the following financial statements for the Titus Company:

1. Schedule of overhead costs for 19X2.

2. Manufacturing statement for 19X2 (show only one line for factory overhead).

3. Income statement for 19X2.

4. Balance sheet for December 31, 19X2.

CRITICAL THINKING: ESSAYS, PROBLEMS, AND CASES

Analytical Essays

Analyze Illustration 18–5 on page 691 and describe how the activities represented by the flow-chart are presented in a company's managerial and financial accounting reports.

AE 18–1
(LO 2, 3, 4)

Several years ago, Thelma Grumbles took over the operation of her family's sailboat manu-facturing company. The company previously manufactured basic sailboats. However, it recently has turned more and more to building custom boats to individual customers' specifications. The seasonal nature of this business means that shop activity is rather slow during October, November, and December when customers are not interested in buying sailboats.

AE 18–2
(LO 6)

Grumbles has tried to increase business during these slow months. However, most prospec-tive customers who come to the business during these months just don't end up buying. When Grumbles quotes a price for a sailboat, most customers during the slow months say that the product is nice but the price is too high, and then leave without placing an order. Grumbles thinks the trouble may lie in using the rule that her father used when he ran the business (be-fore many custom orders were taken). His rule was to "always set the price high enough to make a 10% profit over and above all costs, and be sure that all costs are included."

Grumbles has found that the direct material and direct labor costs are pretty easy to fig-ure but that overhead is another thing. The overhead consists of depreciation of the factory building and machinery, utility costs, property taxes, and so on. In total, these amount to about $15,000 each month, whether she builds any sailboats or not. In applying her father's rule, she finds that she has to charge more for a sailboat built during the slow fourth quarter because the overhead is spread over fewer jobs. She readily admits that this practice seems to drive away business during the months when she could most easily handle extra volume. However, she really finds it hard to break her father's rule because, as she says, "Dad did all right in this business for a long time."

Required

Explain why the old price rule leads to higher bids for sailboats that would be built in De-cember than for those built in May, which is a very busy month. You may want to assume some figures to make your point. Suggest how to solve this pricing problem and still follow the rule.

Managerial Analysis Problem

(LO 4, 6)

Hudson Company has operated for three years. Its business is manufacturing and selling a sin-gle product. Although annual sales increased by 20 and 25% in the last two years, it appears that net income increased by only about 7 and 14%. The company president, Art Bodie, has asked you to analyze the situation and tell him why profits have lagged behind sales. Bodie is primarily a production expert and knows little about accounting. Also, the person who keeps the company's books has a limited understanding of accounting for manufacturing.

The company's condensed income statements for the past three years show:

	19X1	19X2	19X3
Sales	$1,000,000	$1,200,000	$1,500,000
Cost of goods sold:			
Finished goods inventory, beginning	$ –0–	$ 66,000	$ 99,000
Cost of goods manufactured	330,000	437,500	628,000
Goods available for sale	$ 330,000	$ 503,500	$ 727,000
Finished goods inventory, ending	66,000	99,000	145,200
Cost of goods sold	$ 264,000	$ 404,500	$ 581,800
Gross profit from sales	$ 736,000	$ 795,500	$ 918,200
Selling and administrative expenses	160,000	180,000	217,500
Net income	$ 576,000	$ 615,500	$ 700,700

As you have checked into things, you have uncovered the following additional information:

a.   The company sold 5,000 units of its product during the first year it was in business, 6,000 units during the second year, and 7,500 units during the third. All sales were priced at $200 per unit, and no discounts were granted.

b.   The finished goods inventory consisted of 500 units at the end of the first year, 750 at the end of the second, and 1,100 at the end of the third.

c.   The bookkeeper valued the units in each year's ending finished goods inventory at $132 per unit. The amount reported by the bookkeeper on the income statement as the cost of goods manufactured in each year was the sum of the costs for materials, labor, and overhead incurred in each year.

d.   Because the time needed to produce the product is very short, no in-process inventories existed at any of the reporting dates.

Required

Prepare a report for Bodie that shows: (1) the number of units of product manufactured each year, (2) each year's cost to manufacture a unit of product, (3) the cost of each year's ending inventory of finished goods (using FIFO), and (4) each year's selling and administrative expenses per unit of product sold. As part of your report, (5) prepare income statements for all three years showing the net income each year. Finally, (6) provide a possible explanation of why the net income has not kept pace with the rising sales volume.

Financial Statement Analysis Case
(LO 2)

Use the financial statements and related footnotes of the Apple Computer, Inc., annual report shown in Appendix F to complete the following requirements:

a.   What types of inventories does Apple own?

b.   What method does Apple use to value the inventories?

c.   Given the information Apple provides about its inventories, is it certain that Apple is a manufacturing company?

Ethical Issues Case

Examine the ethics case on page 683 and provide answers to these questions, together with explanations for your answers:

1.   Do you think it is ethical for businesspersons to use social occasions to discuss business?

2.   Do you think it is ethical for them to receive tax deductions for the cost of social occasions in which business is discussed?

3.   Do you think it is ethical for a person in business to be reimbursed by an employer for a social occasion in which business is discussed?

4.   Do you think it is ethical that a person's corporate employer is reimbursed and makes a profit for a social occasion in which business is discussed?

CONCEPT TESTER

Test your understanding of the concepts introduced in this chapter by completing the following crossword puzzle:

Across Clues

6. Two words; costs that are capitalized to an inventory account.
7. Two words; labor clearly associated with specific units or batches of production.
8. Two words; materials used in production that are not clearly associated with units of product.
9. Two words; products that have completed the manufacturing process.

Down Clues

1. Two words; labor that is not clearly associated with specific units or batches of product.
2. Two words; materials purchased for use in production, primarily as direct materials.
3. Two words; costs charged to expense because their benefits expire as the costs are incurred.
4. Two words; materials clearly associated with specific units or batches of production.
5. Three words; products that are in the process of being manufactured.

ANSWERS TO PROGRESS CHECKS

18–1 *d*

18–2 Managerial accounting information is intended to be used by company managers and financial accounting information is intended for use primarily by external parties.

18–3 No, managerial accounting practices are not governed by GAAP. However, some of the information produced under GAAP is used in managerial accounting reports.

18–4 The three unique inventories are raw materials, goods in process, and finished goods.

18–5 Product costs are incurred in producing products and are debited to inventory accounts. When the units of product are sold, the costs are included in cost of goods sold on the income statement. Period costs do not appear to produce assets and are expensed as incurred.

18–6 Indirect labor cost is added to the cost of goods manufactured as a part of factory overhead.

18–7 Direct materials are clearly associated with specific units or batches of product. Indirect materials are used in the production process but are included in factory overhead because they cannot be clearly associated with specific units or batches of product.

18–8 *a*

18–9 No.

18–10   The beginning goods in process inventory is added to the total manufacturing costs to yield total goods in process. Then, the ending inventory is subtracted to yield the cost of goods manufactured during the year.

18–11   *b*

18–12   A general accounting system is based on periodic inventory methods while a cost accounting system uses perpetual inventory methods.

18–13   The Manufacturing Summary account is similar to the Income Summary account.

18–14   *c*

18–15   Those accounts that enter into the calculation of cost of goods manufactured are summarized in the Manufacturing Summary account. They include the beginning and ending balances of the Raw Materials Inventory and Goods in Process Inventory accounts, and the preclosing balances of the Raw Materials Purchases, Direct Labor, and Factory Overhead accounts.

18–16   The accounts that enter into the calculation of the year's net income are summarized in the Income Summary account. They include the beginning and ending balances of the Finished Goods Inventory account, the balance of the Manufacturing Summary account, and the balances of all revenue and expense accounts.

18–17   Direct material and direct labor costs of goods in process and finished goods inventories usually must be estimated because the quantities of direct materials and direct labor used on the inventories are not known with certainty.

18–18 $156,000/60\% = \$260,000$

New Production Management Concepts and Job Order Cost Accounting Systems

Binney & Smith Inc. makes Crayola Crayons® and Silly Putty®. Joe Roberts, Binney & Smith's director of customer service, felt dazed after meeting with the vice president of purchasing for a leading mass retailer. The vice president indicated that Binney & Smith's on-time shipping performance of 80% was not acceptable. Neither was its shipping lead time of three weeks between order placement and shipment of the product. The retailer expected an immediate 50% improvement and a plan for continuing improvement ultimately leading to next-day shipment on any order placed.

For Roberts, the most perplexing aspect of the meeting was that Binney & Smith's lead times were normal in its industry. The firm's performance had always been considered acceptable by customers. Binney & Smith had consistently captured a large percentage of the domestic market for drawing tools. Nevertheless, the potential loss of this customer could seriously erode their market share.

Roberts saw this was clearly not an issue of product quality or price. However, it was a challenge to rethink the whole manufacturing process. Back in his office, Roberts reread two articles he received recently from Dan Tretter, the manufacturing operations manager. Both articles, one on the theory of constraints and the other on just-in-time manufacturing, claimed remarkable improvements in manufacturing delivery and lead times. Perhaps meeting the mass retailer's demand would be possible.

LEARNING OBJECTIVES

After studying Chapter 19, you should be able to:

1. **Identify five new production management concepts and explain how they affect the management of manufacturing processes.**

2. **Describe the type of manufacturing operations in which job order cost accounting systems are used.**

3. **Explain how job cost sheets are used in job order cost accounting systems.**

4. **Describe and record the flow of materials, labor, and overhead costs in a job order cost accounting system.**

5. **Explain how the accounts are adjusted for any overapplied or underapplied factory overhead.**

6. **Define or explain the words and phrases listed in the chapter glossary.**

In Chapter 18, you learned some basic concepts about manufacturing and about the general accounting systems that some firms use to account for costs incurred in producing goods. This chapter expands your understanding of manufacturing by looking at five new production management concepts that are changing the way many companies manufacture their products. These concepts are customer orientation, total quality management, just-in-time manufacturing, the theory of constraints, and continuous improvement. Some companies such as Binney & Smith have significantly improved their manufacturing processes by implementing these concepts.

To put these concepts into practice, managers must have more up-to-date and precise information than general accounting systems can provide. General accounting systems are not adequate because they are based on periodic inventory methods. Cost accounting systems based on perpetual inventory methods are much more effective. They constantly track the quantities of materials, goods in process, and finished goods inventories, and thus provide more up-to-date information. In this chapter, we explain one cost accounting system called job order cost accounting. This system is used by companies that manufacture single units or small groups of unique products.

NEW PRODUCTION MANAGEMENT CONCEPTS

LO 1

Identify five new production management concepts and explain how they affect the management of manufacturing processes.

Several factors have encouraged the development of new ideas about how companies should manage their production operations. These factors include increased demands by customers for higher-quality products, for custom-designed products, and for faster delivery. In addition, the movement toward a worldwide economy and increased competition between United States and foreign manufacturers have forced domestic companies to look for new and more effective management processes. During the past decade, for example, Japanese manufacturers such as **Honda Motor Company**, **Nissan Motor Corp.**, and **Toyota Motor Corp.** have increased their collective share of the U.S. auto market by more than 40%.

To encourage an increased emphasis on quality among United States companies, the U.S. Congress established the Malcolm Baldrige National Quality Award in 1987. Entrants must complete a painstaking self-analysis via guidelines furnished by the Baldrige committee and then survive an on-site review of operations.

In 1988, **Globe Metallurgical, Inc.**, distinguished itself as the only small business to have won a Baldrige award. Using computer-controlled systems and statistical process control, Globe set out to monitor and quantify every aspect of its manufacturing process. The resulting system advises workers whether processing targets are being met and identifies production steps most prone to failure. As a result of the new system, worker productivity increased up to 50% in some areas and customer complaints fell 91%.

During the 1970s and 1980s, many companies began to apply several new concepts for managing their manufacturing processes. These new concepts have changed the way they manufacture their products. Many of these changes were not possible earlier because of a lack of computing power. Since that time, dramatic advances in computers have brought about a variety of improvements in manufacturing processes. New kinds of manufacturing equipment, such as computer-controlled robots and machine tools, are now widely used. In addition, the information available to production managers has been greatly expanded. Accounting and other types of information often are available on demand. Coupled with improved communication devices, computers allow companies to transmit data and reports over long distances at low cost, without any delays.

As a result of these forces, new philosophies of management have developed quickly and spread around the world. Among these are five new concepts of how managers should approach their tasks. The following sections of the chapter explain these ideas more completely.

Customer Orientation

The management concept of **customer orientation** means that a company's managers and employees need to be in tune with the wants and needs of customers. This concept extends all the way back into the factory. In effect, customer orientation bends the company's productive ability toward meeting customers' wants and needs. This approach is far different from using advertising and selling efforts to bend customers' wants toward accepting the company's products.

The concept of customer orientation calls for flexible product designs that include options to support individual customer choices. Instead of presenting buyers with products that the seller has already manufactured, the goal is to meet buyers' needs by modifying the products as they are manufactured. The idea is to offer customers more attention and service.

In addition to flexible product designs, the concept of customer orientation calls for flexible production processes that allow a manufacturer to respond quickly to changes in buyers' needs and preferences.

A company that has experienced great success by focusing on its customers is **Xerox Corporation.** The company's Customer Satisfaction Measurement System tracks the behavior and preferences of some 200,000 Xerox equipment owners. The resulting information is used to establish benchmarks for quality improvements.

FAST HINT
Critical Thought Question:
Based on this opening discussion, what role do you believe is appropriate for traditional mass production?

Total Quality Management

A major focus of many companies across the United States and in other countries has been to improve the quality of their products and services. Because of the worldwide attention given to the high quality of several Japanese and German manufacturers and the increased demands of customers for high quality, managers have identified quality as one of the most important keys to success in manufacturing. In an effort to implement this new emphasis on quality, many firms have adopted a concept called **Total Quality Management (TQM).**

Under TQM, all managers and employees strive toward higher standards in their work and in the products and services they offer to customers. (Note that these new concepts of production management apply to the production of both products and services. Customers look for flexibility and quality in services as much as they look for them in products.)

Traditional production processes tend to leave the responsibility for quality in the hands of a somewhat independent group of quality control inspectors. The focus usually is on an inspection of completed products. In contrast, TQM requires a focus on quality throughout the production process. The strategy is to identify defective work when and where it occurs. This constant focus on quality reminds each employee of the need to eliminate defective work at all stages of production activity. The expected results are fewer defects in completed products and potential reductions of costs associated with reworking rejected products.

A company that uses TQM rewards employees who find defects. Without this emphasis, employees are more likely to ignore defects in partially completed units that arrive at their workstations. After all, pointing out problems may require extra effort, paperwork, and hostile reactions from other employees. Thus, an essential ingredient of TQM is changing the attitudes of employees to encourage a new commitment to quality. TQM also encourages employees to try new ways to improve quality. By keeping open minds and rewarding innovation, managers committed to TQM can tap the knowledge and abilities of the people closest to the work.

A company that operates under TQM strongly emphasizes the value of reaching higher quality levels. For example, a TQM company will establish quality standards and measure quality results at each stage of production. Many companies set maximum rejection rates as targets for each workstation. Then, they encourage employees by rewarding those who reach their targets and by displaying actual rejection rates.

Motorola, Inc., began a new emphasis on quality by establishing a training center and spending millions of dollars on worker education. The company uses information from employees along with data gathered through customer surveys, complaint hotlines, and other sources to direct quality improvement and product development. As a result of these efforts, Motorola products have increased their market share domestically and abroad. The company also was recognized for winning the Malcolm Baldrige National Quality Award.

Just-in-Time Manufacturing

Managers recognize that commitments to customers and quality lead to profits only if the company's activities are carried out efficiently. Customer orientation promotes efficiency because fewer unmarketable products are manufactured. Total quality management promotes efficiency because it reduces the cost of reworking or repairing defective products. Another strategy for improving efficiency is to use a **just-in-time (JIT)** manufacturing system.

As a Matter of Fact

In the 1950s, Japanese products were a joke. They lacked quality and many times totally missed the market. But Japanese people spent years learning to understand the United States, and in the 70s the situation changed. The Japanese have applied quality techniques to manufacturing consumer products and the world has benefited.

Following World War II, the United States could make almost any product, and if it was close to usable and affordable, customers would buy it. The United States produced about half of the world's total production, and we consumed an equal amount. We dominated and customers had no choice. Now, we have formidable foreign competition . . . [that] has [an] excellent education, ample capital, and is strongly motivated. There is a beneficial payoff from these advantages in price, performance, and ease of use. If we wish to increase, or even maintain our current living standard, we must be a net contributor in the world market.

American industries need to start employing Total Quality Management, a philosophy that has been credited with the Japanese success. Before embarking on TQM in any organization, there are two basic facts that must be understood.

First, customer focus—satisfying customer needs is the No. 1 reason for the existence of any business. The cars that Chrysler is trying to sell in Japan still have the steering wheel on the left side, [even though the Japanese drive on the left side of the road]. How successful would the Japanese have been in this country if they had insisted on sending us cars with the steering wheel on the right? We must learn to make things the way the customer wants, not the way we dictate.

Second, we must understand that virtually everything we do is a process. A process is defined as having inputs, outputs, and a series of steps between them. It is important to understand that businesses are processes because that allows us to define them, measure them, and make improvements in them.

Let's get on with the task. We need to be totally committed to quality in business, education, and government. We need to be competitive in the world marketplace so that we can contribute to the welfare of others. As author and TQM expert W. Edwards Deming has said, improved quality yields higher productivity through decreased scrap, rework, mistakes, delays, snags, and better use of resources. Higher productivity allows us to capture market share with lower prices and provide more jobs.

Dave Kent, "Bashing Japan Won't Improve Quality in America," *Colorado Springs Gazette-Telegraph*, January 19, 1992, p. G2.

Under a JIT approach, companies acquire or produce inventory only as it is needed. Thus, manufacturing activity is scheduled so that finished products are assembled as they are needed for delivery to customers. Furthermore, firms produce components of the finished product only as needed in the assembly process. In addition, raw materials are obtained from suppliers only when the company is ready to use them. In effect, the company tries to keep no more than bare minimum amounts of finished goods, goods in process, and raw materials inventories.

Installing a JIT system can be a way of implementing the concept of customer orientation. In other words, companies manufacture products in response to predicted or actual customer orders. The orientation of JIT is that products are *pulled* through the manufacturing process by the orders received from customers. This is in contrast to a more traditional approach in which products are *pushed* through production by the insertion of raw materials and the application of labor and overhead. The traditional approach relies on marketing and sales forces to push the finished units on to customers.

In 1991, **Toyota Motor Corp.** announced a striking example of using JIT with a customer orientation. Toyota declared that all automobiles sold in Japan are to be produced only in response to specific orders from individual customers. Under this system, customers place orders through dealers and wait only two weeks to take delivery. The advantages are that customers get exactly what they want after a relatively short wait and that neither the manufacturer nor dealers have to invest in large inventories of automobiles.

FAST HINT
Critical Thought Question:
Identify other industries that might benefit from a just-in-time manufacturing process.

Note that JIT may be applied to raw materials and goods in process as well as to finished products. Consider the following production line for a product that has four components added in sequence as the units move toward completion:

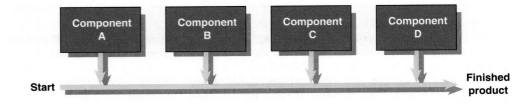

The traditional manufacturer allows inventories of the components to accumulate between the workstations to avoid shutting down the production line because of a shortage of any of the four components. In contrast, the JIT management goal calls for the four components to arrive at the production line *just in time* to be used. When this goal is accomplished, the company has less invested in inventories and uses the money saved to reduce debt or invest in other profitable activities.

A JIT approach can be even more efficient when a product consists of several components manufactured in separate production lines. For example, the components of an air conditioner include a case, a compressor, a fan, a heat exchanger, and a control system. Each component is the output of a separate production line. If the JIT approach can be implemented throughout the entire air conditioner factory, large gains in efficiency are possible.

Not all manufacturing situations allow the use of JIT methods. A JIT company must be able to predict the timing and nature of customer orders. An effective total quality management system must be in place to carefully control the manufacturing processes. Otherwise, unexpected numbers of defective units may cause all production activity to stop. JIT also requires dependable suppliers willing to make frequent shipments of  small quantities. Computers and good communication equipment are essential. For example, some companies use systems that send orders directly from the manufacturer's production line to the supplier's production line. These factors make a JIT manufacturing system more susceptible to disruption than traditional systems. For example, in June 1992, **General Motors Corporation** closed three plants during a three-day rail strike when parts to be delivered by train did not arrive.

Theory of Constraints

The fourth new concept for improving a company's productive operations is called the **theory of constraints (TOC).** Management's basic focus is on looking for the factors that limit or constrain the operations of the business. After the constraints have been identified, management should develop ways of relaxing or overcoming these constraining processes.

From a TOC perspective, the company's overall goal is to minimize the goods in process inventory waiting to be processed while maximizing the throughput. **Throughput** is the added value of finished products processed through the system. The added value per unit is the selling price minus the direct costs of production.

While the theory of constraints can be applied to the operations of the entire company, including production, sales, engineering, distribution, and administration, it has been applied most often in production. The general idea is to synchronize and plan manufacturing operations to minimize the time it takes the company to produce one item or one order. In this way, the company is able to serve customers better with faster deliveries.

TOC maintains that the key to decreasing processing time is to find the **constraint** (bottleneck), the most constraining process or resource, and strategically locate goods in process inventories to maximize its output. Consider the previous example of the production line that combines four components to produce finished goods. If the work-station for adding Component B to the product is the slowest of the four workstations, its output determines the output of the entire line. In this case, the company should provide sufficient inventory in front of Component B workstation and a sufficient inventory storage area behind it to ensure continuous operation. The inventory in front or upstream of the constraint protects the constraint against a shortage of materials to work on. The open space behind or downstream of Component B workstation protects the constraint from being blocked and shut down by problems at later workstations.

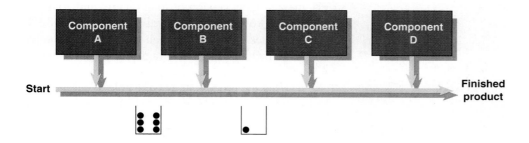

This positioning of inventory enables Component B workstation to continue working even if other stations break down. In contrast, JIT maintains that all problems should be solved so that protective inventory is not required.

Recall the discussion of **Binney & Smith Inc.** at the beginning of the chapter. Binney & Smith used TOC to find and manage the manufacturing bottleneck, rearrange the plant layout, and decide the size of the goods-in-process buffer to be used in the newly created just-in-time inventory system. The results included a decrease in raw materials inventory of 40%, a decrease in goods-in-process inventory of 60%, an on-time shipping performance of 96%, and a reduction in shipping lead time from 12 to 5 days.

Once a constraint is identified and managed as well as possible, management figures out how to relieve it and increase throughput. The solution may be as simple as adding more machinery or extra shifts of workers; or it may require redesigning the production line or the product.

Of course, the company's real problem may be in marketing. The company may be producing the wrong mix of products or may not have identified marketing opportunities.

Applying the theory of constraints is a continuous process. After the first constraint is identified and relieved, you search for the next one. That is, as soon as one problem is cleared up, some other constraint becomes the factor that is limiting throughput. Management attention then focuses on locating and improving the performance of this constraint.

Continuous Improvement

The fifth new production management concept calls for an attitude of **continuous improvement** throughout the entire organization. With this attitude, every manager and employee constantly looks for ways to improve company operations. This includes customer service, product quality, product features, the production process, and employee interactions. An attitude of continuous improvement rejects the possibility that anything is ever good enough. New ideas are constantly being tried and old ideas are constantly being questioned.

The relationship between continuous improvement and the other production management concepts should be clear. With this attitude, the company's employees are committed to meeting customers' needs, to improving quality, and to increasing efficiency. With continuous improvement, there is no place for resistance to change. Instead, managers and employees seek every opportunity for growth and increased profitability. Because of the intense competition in today's world economy, a company is less likely to fall behind if its employees are committed to continuous improvement.

Binney & Smith, Inc. developed and implemented their version of total quality and continuous improvement by integrating both TOC and JIT principles. They called their effort High Velocity Manufacturing. By encouraging their workforce to solve problems and accept responsibility for improving the process, they were able to cut the time it takes to change from running one color of crayon to another color. The change-over time went from two hours to one-half hour. An integral part of their continuous improvement program was shifting responsibility for quality control from an end-of-the-line inspector to the machine operators. As a result, their defect rate decreased from 12% in 1992 to 6% in 1993. The mass retailer continues to be Binney & Smith's customer.

FAST HINT
Critical Thought Question:
Would it be effective to implement all five new production management concepts simultaneously? Explain.

FAST HINT
Relevant Quick Study:
To apply these concepts, work QS 19–1.

PRODUCTION MANAGEMENT AND COST ACCOUNTING

With this background in place, we now begin to examine cost accounting systems that help management gain control over the production process. In Chapter 18, you learned several basic concepts of manufacturing. You saw that companies employ three components of production (materials, labor, and overhead) and move products through three inventories (raw materials, goods in process, and finished goods). Chapter 18 explained how to use a general accounting system to account for manufacturing activity. Although general accounting systems are still used by smaller companies, cost accounting systems generate more timely and more precise information.

Under a general accounting system, managers have to wait for physical counts of the inventories to learn what has happened. Even then, the information may not be very precise because the costs of the goods in process and finished goods inventories are based on subjective estimates.

Under a cost accounting system, production information is available quickly. Because perpetual records are used for the inventories, the information in the accounts is as up to date as the most recent transactions. Computer systems can record events in the factory almost as soon as they occur. Cost accounting information is also based on more precise measures of product costs.

With so many different kinds of companies operating today, many different cost accounting systems are used in practice. The cost accounting system used by a company depends on the nature of its products and its manufacturing activities. The variety of cost accounting systems is so extensive that it would not be possible to explain all of them even in an advanced textbook. However, most cost accounting systems are either job order or process cost accounting systems. The rest of this chapter explains job order cost accounting systems, where they are used, and how they work. We explain process cost accounting systems in the next chapter.

Job order and process cost accounting systems were developed long before the new production management concepts described earlier. Nevertheless, these cost accounting systems have proven to be flexible and adaptable to different environments. In fact, they are still used to meet the new needs created by these recent developments.

Progress Check
(Answers to Progress Checks are provided at the end of the chapter.)

19-1 **The concept that management should focus on the factors that limit or constrain the operations of a business is called:** *(a)* **Continuous improvement;** *(b)* **Just-in-time manufacturing;** *(c)* **Theory of constraints;** *(d)* **Total quality management.**

19-2 **What factors have encouraged the development of new ideas about production management?**

19-3 **What attitude pervades a company under total quality management?**

Many companies manufacture products individually designed to meet the needs of each customer. Each unique product is manufactured separately. Because the products are produced in response to special orders, their production is called **job order manufacturing.** In this type of manufacturing, the production of a unique product is called a **job.** Some items that might be produced as jobs include a special machine tool, a building, a yacht, or a piece of custom-made jewelry. All of these items are made to meet the unique demands of specific customers. When a job involves producing more than one unit of a unique product, it is often called a **job lot.** Products produced as job lots might include benches for a new church, imprinted tee shirts for a 10K race or a company picnic, and advertising signs for a chain of stores.

Although job order operations are usually described using examples of manufacturing operations, they also apply to service companies. Many, if not most, service companies meet their customers' needs by performing a unique service for each customer. Examples of such services include a CPA's audit of a client's financial statements, an interior designer's remodeling of an office, a wedding consultant's plan and supervision of a reception, and a lawyer's defense of a client in a lawsuit. Whether the setting is manufacturing or service, job order operations involve meeting the needs of customers by producing or performing unique jobs.

Like all manufacturing processes, job order manufacturing requires the use of materials, labor, and other manufacturing costs. When materials used in manufacturing can be clearly identified with a particular job, they are defined as direct materials. Similarly, labor used on a particular job is defined as direct labor. Other costs that contribute to the production of more than one job are manufacturing overhead. As you learned in Chapter 18, typical manufacturing overhead items are depreciation on factory buildings and equipment, factory supplies, supervision, maintenance, cleaning, and utilities.

In a typical job order manufacturing operation, the arrival of a customer's order for a unique product causes the manufacturer to begin working on a job. In other cases, management may decide to begin work on a job before a contract has been signed with a customer. Such jobs are said to be manufactured on speculation. Regardless of the job's source, the first step is to predict the cost of completing the job based on the design of the product. The design may be prepared by the customer or the manufacturer. This leads to negotiating the sales price and deciding whether to take on the job. Some jobs are priced on a cost-plus basis. Under this arrangement, the customer pays the manufacturer or contractor for the costs incurred on the job plus an agreed amount or rate of profit.

Next, the manufacturer schedules production of the job to fit the needs of the customer and to fit within its available production capacity. The work schedule should provide adequate facilities in the workplace, including tools, machinery, and supplies. Once the schedule is completed, the manufacturer can place orders for raw materials. Under JIT, the orders for materials call for delivery just in time to be used in production. Thereafter, production occurs as materials and labor are applied to the job.

CHARACTERISTICS OF JOB ORDER MANUFACTURING OPERATIONS

LO 2
Describe the type of manufacturing operations in which job order cost accounting systems are used.

FAST HINT
Relevant Quick Study:
To apply these concepts, work QS 19–2.

FAST HINT
Critical Thought Question:
Would a bottler of natural spring water be likely to use a job order cost accounting system?

SEQUENCE OF EVENTS IN A JOB ORDER MANUFACTURING OPERATION

Illustration 19–1   Manufacturing Activities during March 19X2, Medford Machine Tools Company

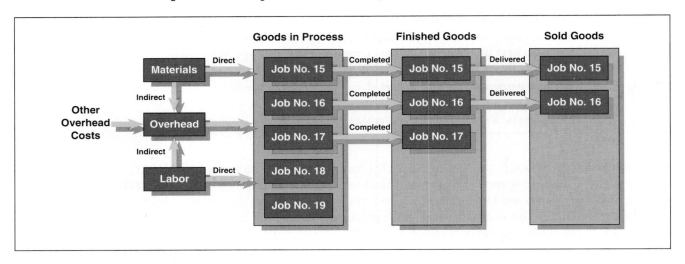

To get an overall view of job order production activity, look at Illustration 19–1. The illustration diagrams the March 19X2 production activity of Medford Machine Tools Company. Observe that materials, labor, and overhead were added to Job Nos. 15, 16, 17, 18, and 19 during the month. The company completed Job Nos. 15, 16, and 17 during the month, and delivered Job Nos. 15 and 16 to customers. At the end of the month, Job Nos. 18 and 19 remain in the goods in process inventory and Job No. 17 is in the finished goods inventory. Also notice that labor and materials are divided into their direct and indirect components. The indirect costs are added to other types of overhead, and then the total overhead cost is allocated to the jobs.

JOB ORDER OPERATIONS OF SERVICE COMPANIES

If a job consists of a service instead of a product, there generally is no lag between working on the job and delivering it to the customer. Typically, the company recognizes revenue in its financial statements as the service is performed, even though the whole job is not complete. For example, if a service job is estimated to be 60% complete at the end of a period, 60% of the revenues from the job are accrued and reported in the income statement. At the same time, the costs of the job incurred to date are reported as expenses. Thus, a service company does not report an inventory of in-process or finished services.

Progress Check

19–4   **Which of the following products is likely to involve a job order manufacturing operation?** *(a)* **Inexpensive watches;**   *(b)* **Microcomputers;**   *(c)* **Bottled soft drinks.**

19–5   **What is the difference between a job and a job lot?**

19–6   **When services are provided to customers on a job order basis, when is revenue usually recognized?**

JOB ORDER COST ACCOUNTING

LO 3

Explain how job cost sheets are used in job order cost accounting systems.

Much of the accounting information that managers of job cost operations use to plan and control production activities is not stored in general ledger accounts. Because the information includes a lot of detailed data, it is usually stored in a variety of subsidiary records controlled by general ledger accounts. Subsidiary records can store information about raw materials, overhead costs, jobs in process, and finished goods. You will learn about each of these records as you study the rest of the chapter.

Illustration 19-2 Job Cost Sheet

Medford Machine Tools — Medford, Oregon

Customer's name __Cone Lumber Company__ Job no. __15__
Address __1542 Clark Center Dr.__ City & State __Bend, Oregon__
Job description __High-speed (variable) drill press__
Date promised __March 15__ Date started __March 3__ Date completed __March 11__

Direct Materials			Direct Labor			Manufacturing Overhead		
Date	Requisition	Cost	Date	Time Ticket	Cost	Date	Rate	Cost
3/3/X2	R-4698	100.00	3/3/X2	L-3393	120.00	3/11/X2	160% of	1,600.00
3/7/X2	R-4705	225.00	3/4/X2	L-3422	150.00		Direct	
3/9/X2	R-4725	180.00	3/5/X2	L-3456	180.00		Labor	
3/10/X2	R-4777	95.00	3/8/X2	L-3479	60.00		Cost	
			3/9/X2	L-3501	90.00			
			3/10/X2	L-3535	240.00			
			3/11/X2	L-3559	160.00			
Total		600.00	Total		1,000.00	Total		1,600.00

REMARKS: Completed job on March 11 and shipped to customer on March 15. Met all specifications and requirements.

SUMMARY:
Materials 600.00
Labor 1,000.00
Overhead 1,600.00
Total cost 3,200.00

Signed: _C. Luther, Supervisor_

The primary purpose of a **job order cost accounting system** is to determine the cost of producing each job or job lot. To serve this purpose, the accounting system must include a separate record for each job. As production activity occurs, the system must capture information about the costs incurred and charge those costs to the jobs in process. The separate record maintained for each job is called a **job cost sheet.** Illustration 19–2 shows the job cost sheet for a drill press that Medford Machine Tools Company manufactured for Cone Lumber Company. The job cost sheet identifies the customer, the number assigned to the job, the product, and various dates. The costs of producing the job were recorded on the sheet as the costs were incurred. When the job was completed, the supervisor entered the date of completion, recorded any remarks, and signed the sheet.

In Illustration 19–2, note that the costs are classified as direct materials, direct labor, and overhead. The job cost sheet shows that the direct materials added to Job No. 15 on four different dates totaled $600. The seven entries for direct labor costs totaled $1,000. In addition, Medford charged overhead costs of $1,600 to the job.

During the time a job is being manufactured, its accumulated costs are included in the cost of the goods in process inventory. The collection of job cost sheets for all of the jobs in process make up a subsidiary ledger controlled by the Goods in Process Inventory account in the General Ledger. Managers use the job cost sheets to monitor the costs incurred to date and to predict and control the costs to complete each job.

When a job is finished, the job cost sheet is completed and moved from the file of jobs in process to the file of finished jobs that have not yet been delivered to customers. This latter file acts as a subsidiary ledger controlled by the Finished Goods

FAST HINT
Relevant Quick Study:
To apply these concepts, work QS 19–3.

As a Matter of Opinion

Mr. Ward received his BBA in accounting from Baylor University in 1990. As an auditor at KPMG Peat Marwick, he had clients in both the manufacturing and service industries. He currently is an operations accounting controller in the insurance group of The Associates, a wholly owned subsidiary of Ford Motor Company's financial services group.

Service firms face some of the same problems as manufacturing firms. Customers of all firms now demand better service, delivered in less time, and at a lower cost. Firms maintain their competitive edge by meeting and exceeding these expectations.

I see many parallels between manufacturing firms and service firms. Manufacturing firms have large investments in inventories and capital equipment. They seek to ensure that their production processes are efficient, quality of output is high, and costs are controlled. Service firms, however, have most of their investment in personnel, but want the services that they deliver to their customers to be provided with utmost efficiency and at reasonable costs. Success in the service industry requires excellence in every measure of efficiency.

Because their processes appear much simpler than those of manufacturing firms, service firms might appear to have uncomplicated cost or managerial accounting systems; yet, they must schedule and coordinate their resources as carefully as their manufacturing counterparts. Such firms must continually maintain and upgrade the skills of their people in order to take advantage of new opportunities.

With new opportunities constantly developing in this world of perpetual change, I am excited about the prospect of learning even more about how techniques developed for manufacturing firms can be used in service firms. In any event, firms in both sectors are challenged to be proactive, customer-oriented, and global in their strategies, because competition is *stiff*.

Timothy P. Ward

Inventory account. When a finished job is delivered to the customer, the job cost sheet is moved again to a permanent file that supports the total cost of goods sold reported in the current and prior periods.

The next sections of the chapter describe the documents used in job order cost accounting and the flow of costs through the system. We discuss materials costs, labor costs, and overhead costs in separate sections.

Progress Check

19–7 **Which of the following is a correct statement?**
  a. **The collection of job cost sheets of unfinished jobs makes up a subsidiary ledger that is controlled by the Goods in Process account.**
  b. **Job cost sheets are financial statements provided to investors.**
  c. **A separate job cost sheet is maintained in the General Ledger for each job in process.**

19–8 **What three costs are accumulated on job cost sheets?**

MATERIALS COST FLOWS AND RELATED DOCUMENTS

LO 4

Describe and record the flow of materials, labor, and overhead costs in a job order cost accounting system.

Illustration 19–3 shows the flow of materials cost data through the subsidiary records of the job cost accounting system. As items of material are received from suppliers, workers count and inspect them. They also note the quantity and cost of the items on a receiving report. This report serves as a source document for recording the receipt on a **materials ledger card** and in the general ledger accounts. In nearly all job order cost accounting systems, materials ledger cards are perpetual records that are updated each time units are purchased and each time units are issued for use in production.

As Illustration 19–3 shows, materials may be requisitioned to be used on a specific job (direct materials) or to be used as overhead (indirect materials). The cost of direct materials flows from the materials ledger card to the job cost sheet. The cost of indirect materials flows from the materials ledger card to the Indirect Materials

Illustration 19-3 Flow of Materials Costs through the Subsidiary Records

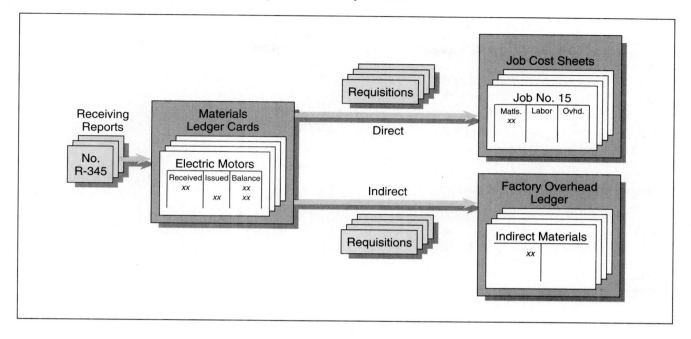

account in the Factory Overhead Ledger. (This is a subsidiary ledger controlled by the Factory Overhead account in the General Ledger.)

Illustration 19–4 shows a materials ledger card for a material used by Medford Machine Tools. Notice that the card identifies the item as a high-speed drill motor. The card also shows the item's stock number, its location in the storeroom, information about the maximum and minimum quantities that should be on hand, and the quantity to be ordered. In Illustration 19–4, note the issue of a motor that was recorded on March 7, 19X2. The job cost sheet in Illustration 19–2 shows that this motor was used in manufacturing Job No. 15.

When materials are needed in production, a production manager prepares a **materials requisition** and sends it to the materials manager. Illustration 19–5 shows the materials requisition for the high-speed drill motor for Job No. 15. Notice that the requisition shows the number of the job, the type of material, the quantity needed, and the signature of the manager authorized to make the requisition. To see how the requisition relates to the flow of costs, compare the information on Illustration 19–5 with the March 7, 19X2, entries in Illustration 19–2 and Illustration 19–4.

This entry records the use of the motor on Job No. 15:

Mar.	7	Goods in Process Inventory—Job No. 15	225.00	
		Raw Materials Inventory—M-347		225.00
		To record use of material on Job No. 15.		

This entry is posted to the general ledger accounts and to the subsidiary records. Posting to the subsidiary records includes a debit to a job cost sheet and a credit to a materials ledger card. An entry to record the use of indirect materials is the same except the debit is to Factory Overhead. In the subsidiary Factory Overhead Ledger, this entry is posted to Indirect Materials.

FAST HINT
Important Point to Remember: Indirect materials will be included within factory overhead on the job cost sheet. The procedure for assigning overhead costs to products is presented later in this chapter.

FAST HINT
Important Point to Remember: Several requisitions may be accumulated and recorded in a single journal entry. The frequency of such entries may vary depending on the job, the industry, and the internal accounting procedures.

Illustration 19–4   Raw Materials Ledger Card

Medford Machine Tools

Item _____High-speed drill motor_____   Stock no. _____M-347_____   Location in storeroom _____Bin 137_____
Maximum quantity _____5 units_____   Minimum quantity_____1 unit_____   Quantity to reorder _____2 units_____

	Received				Issued				Balance		
Date	Receiving Report Number	Units	Unit Price	Total Price	Requi-sition Number	Units	Unit Price	Total Price	Units	Unit Price	Total Price
3/4/X2	C-7117	2	225.00	450.00					1	225.00	225.00
3/7/X2									3	225.00	675.00
					R-4705	1	225.00	225.00	2	225.00	450.00

Illustration 19–5   Materials Requisition

REQUISITION NUMBER   R-4705

Job No. _____15_____   Date _____3/7/X2_____
Material Stock No. _____M-347_____   Material Description _____Electric motor_____

Quantity Requested _____1_____   Requested By _____C. Luther_____

Quantity Provided_____1_____   Date Provided _____3/7/X2_____
Filled By_____M. Bateman_____   Material Received By _____C. Luther_____
Remarks_____

Medford Machine Tools

LABOR COST FLOWS AND RELATED DOCUMENTS

LO 4

Describe and record the flow of materials, labor, and overhead costs in a job order cost accounting system.

Illustration 19–6 shows the flow of labor costs from the Factory Payroll account to the subsidiary records of the job cost accounting system. We mentioned previously that the cost flows in the subsidiary records provide the detailed information needed to manage operations.

The flow of costs in Illustration 19–6 begins with the **clock cards** used by employees to record the number of hours they work. Clock cards serve as source documents for the entries to record labor costs. Each pay period, payroll clerks use clock card data on the number of hours worked to determine total labor cost, which is then debited to the Factory Payroll account. Factory Payroll is a temporary account that holds the total payroll cost (both direct and indirect) until it is allocated to specific jobs and to overhead.

To assign labor costs to specific jobs and to overhead, the clerks must know how each employee's time at work was used and how much it cost. Source documents called **time tickets** usually capture this data. Employees fill out time tickets each day

Illustration 19–6 Flow of Labor Costs to the Subsidiary Records

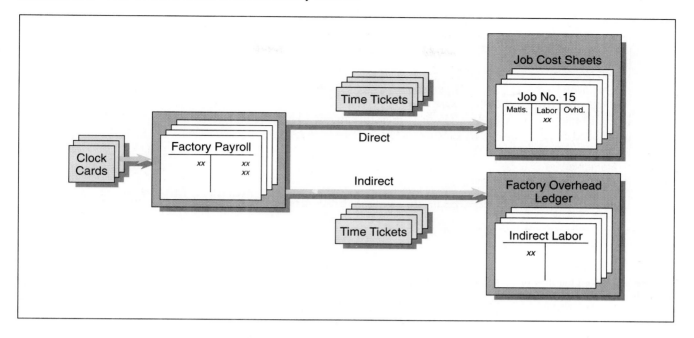

to report how much time they spent on each job. An employee who works on several jobs during a day completes a separate time ticket for each job. Tickets are also prepared for time that should be charged to overhead as indirect labor.

Illustration 19–7 shows a time ticket reporting the time a Medford Machine Tools employee spent working on Job No. 15. Note that the employee's supervisor signed the ticket to confirm its accuracy. The hourly rate and total labor cost were calculated after the time ticket reached the accounting department. To see the effect of this time ticket on the job cost sheet, look in Illustration 19–2 on page 731 for the entry dated March 8, 19X2.

When time tickets report labor used on a specific job, the cost should be recorded as direct labor. For example, this entry records the time ticket in Illustration 19–7:

FAST HINT
Critical Thought Question:
How do you suppose clerical support would be accounted for when the work cannot be easily identified with a specific job?

Mar.	8	Goods in Process Inventory—Job No. 15	60.00	
		Factory Payroll		60.00
		To record direct labor used on Job No. 15.		

The debit in this entry is posted to both the general ledger account and to the appropriate job cost sheet. An entry to record indirect labor debits Factory Overhead and credits Factory Payroll. In the subsidiary Factory Overhead Ledger, the debit in this entry is posted to the Indirect Labor account.

The cost flows diagrammed in Illustration 19–8 are associated with manufacturing overhead. Note that the four sources of overhead costs include indirect materials and indirect labor. As we already discussed, these costs are recorded in response to requisitions for indirect materials and time tickets for indirect labor. The remaining sources of overhead are vouchers that authorize payments for items such as supplies or utilities and adjusting entries for costs such as depreciation.

OVERHEAD COST FLOWS AND RELATED DOCUMENTS

Illustration 19-7 Labor Time Ticket

TIME TICKET   L-3479

Job No. _____15_____ Date _____3/8/X2_____

Employee Name _____T. Thompson_____ Employee Number _____3969_____

TIME AND RATE INFORMATION:

Start Time _____9:00_____ Finish Time _____12:00_____

Elapsed Time _____3.0_____ Hourly Rate _____$20.00_____ Total Cost _____$60.00_____

Approved By _____C. Luther_____

Remarks _____

Medford Machine Tools

LO 4

Describe and record the flow of materials, labor, and overhead costs in a job order cost accounting system.

Recall that factory overhead includes all manufacturing costs other than direct materials and direct labor. Because factory overhead usually includes many different costs, a separate account for each overhead cost is often maintained in a subsidiary Factory Overhead Ledger. This ledger is controlled by the Factory Overhead account in the General Ledger. Like the Factory Payroll account, Factory Overhead is a temporary account that accumulates costs until they are assigned (applied) to jobs.

As you learned in Chapter 18, manufacturing overhead costs are recorded with debits to the Factory Overhead account and credits to other accounts such as Cash, Accounts Payable, and Accumulated Depreciation, Equipment. In the subsidiary Factory Overhead Ledger, the debits are posted to the appropriate accounts such as Depreciation of Factory Equipment, Insurance on Factory Equipment, or Amortization of Patents.

In Illustration 19–8, observe that overhead costs flow from the Factory Overhead account to the job cost sheets. This assignment of overhead to jobs is difficult because by definition, manufacturing overhead is made up of costs not clearly associated with specific units or batches of product. In other words, the accountant cannot clearly determine that a specific dollar amount of overhead was incurred to produce one job while another dollar amount was incurred to produce another job. Nevertheless, manufacturing overhead costs are necessary if any manufacturing activity is to take place. Therefore, if the calculated total cost of a job is to include all of the costs to manufacture the job, some amount of manufacturing overhead must be included in the total.

In Chapter 18, you learned how to assign overhead to inventories and cost of goods sold by relating overhead to some other variable used in production, such as direct labor or machine hours. In that chapter, for example, total overhead cost incurred during a period was expressed as a percentage of total direct labor cost incurred. Then, overhead was applied by multiplying that percentage by the estimated amount of direct labor in each ending inventory and in cost of goods sold.

Job order cost accounting systems often use a similar procedure to assign overhead costs to jobs. However, the fact that perpetual inventory records are used means the assignment of overhead to jobs cannot wait until the end of the period. Instead, overhead must be predicted in advance and assigned to jobs by using a **predetermined overhead application rate.** To set this rate, the total overhead cost and total direct labor cost (or other variable) are estimated prior to the beginning of the period. Even though financial reports may be prepared monthly or quarterly, the estimates are usually for annual amounts. Then, the relationship between these predicted amounts is used during the period to assign overhead to jobs.

Illustration 19–8 Flow of Manufacturing Overhead Costs

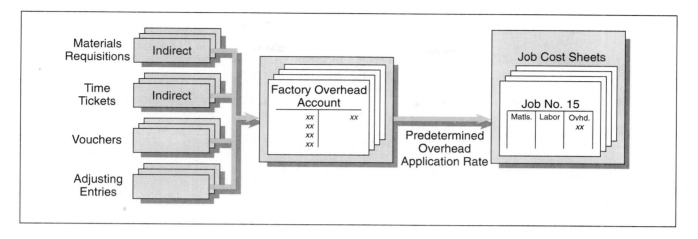

For example, assume that Medford Machine Tools assigns overhead to jobs by relating overhead to direct labor. At the beginning of 19X2, management predicted that total direct labor cost for 19X2 would be $125,000. It also predicted that total factory overhead costs would be $200,000. Based on these estimates, managers calculated the predetermined overhead application rate as 160% of direct labor cost ($200,000/$125,000).

Turn now to the job order cost sheet for Job No. 15 in Illustration 19–2 on page 731. Notice that $1,000 of direct labor was assigned to the job. Then, using the predetermined overhead application rate of 160%, $1,600 of overhead was assigned to the job. The journal entry to record this amount is:

Mar.	11	Goods in Process Inventory—Job. No. 15	1,600.00	
		Factory Overhead		1,600.00
		To assign overhead to Job No. 15.		

Because the application rate for overhead is estimated at the beginning of the period, the total amount assigned to jobs during the period usually is not equal to the total amount actually incurred. Later in the chapter, we explain how this difference is treated at the end of the period.

In the previous sections, we showed journal entries that charged Goods in Process and Job No. 15 for the cost of a direct materials requisition, for the cost of a direct labor time ticket, and for manufacturing overhead. Although separate entries for each material requisition and labor time ticket are appropriate, each item typically is not recorded with a separate entry. Instead, materials requisitions may be collected for a day or a week and recorded with a single entry that summarizes the requisitions. The same may be done with labor time tickets. When such summary entries are made, supporting schedules of the jobs to be charged and the types of materials used provide the basis for postings to the subsidiary records.

As described in the previous paragraph, summary entries are usually recorded more often than monthly. Nevertheless, to show all of the manufacturing cost flows during a period and the related entries, we continue with the example of Medford Machine Tools. Illustration 19–9 presents the costs related to all of Medford's manufacturing activities during March 19X2. Recall that Medford did not have any jobs in process at the beginning of the month. The firm applied materials, labor, and overhead to five

FAST HINT
Alternative Example:
If management predicted total direct labor costs for 19X2 to be $100,000, what would be the predetermined overhead application rate?
Answer: 200% of direct labor cost

FAST HINT
Relevant Exercise:
To apply these concepts, work Exercises 19–2 and 19–5.

FAST HINT
Relevant Exercise:
To apply these concepts, work Exercise 19–7.

SUMMARY OF ALL MANUFACTURING COST FLOWS DURING THE PERIOD

Illustration 19–9   Medford Machine Tools—Costs of All Manufacturing Activities during March 19X2

Explanation	Materials	Labor	Overhead Incurred	Overhead Assigned	Goods in Process	Finished Goods	Cost of Goods Sold
Job 15	$ 600	$1,000		$1,600			$3,200
Job 16	300	800		1,280			2,380
Job 17	500	1,100		1,760		$3,360	
Job 18	150	700		1,120	$1,970		
Job 19	250	600		960	1,810		
Total job costs	$1,800	$4,200		$6,720	$3,780	$3,360	$5,580
Indirect materials	550		$ 550				
Indirect labor		1,100	1,100				
Other overhead			$5,070				
Total costs used in production	$2,350	$5,300	$6,720				
Ending inventory	1,400						
Materials available	$3,750						
Less beginning inventory	(1,000)						
Purchases	$2,750						

Illustration 19–10   Flow of All Manufacturing Costs and End-of-Month Job Cost Sheets

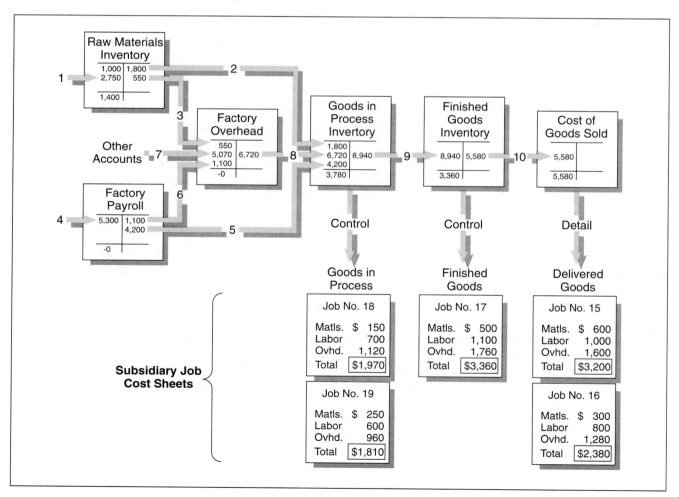

jobs during the month; workers completed Job Nos. 15 and 16 and delivered them to the customers. At the end of the month, Job No. 17 was completed but not delivered and Job Nos. 18 and 19 were still in process. In Illustration 19–9, note that raw materials were purchased for $2,750, labor costs incurred were $5,300, and overhead costs incurred were $6,720.

Illustration 19–10 shows the flow of these costs through the general ledger accounts and the resulting end-of-month status of the subsidiary records. The numbered arrows at the top of the illustration show the flows of total costs for the month. Keep in mind that each numbered cost flow represents several entries made during March. However, to review the form of those entries, we represent each cost flow with a single entry that summarizes the actual entries made during the month. The numbers of the entries correspond to the arrows in Illustration 19–10.

1.	Raw Materials Inventory	2,750.00	
	Accounts Payable		2,750.00
	Acquired materials on credit for use in the factory.		
2.	Goods in Process Inventory	1,800.00	
	Raw Materials Inventory		1,800.00
	To assign the cost of direct materials used in producing jobs.		
3.	Factory Overhead	550.00	
	Raw Materials Inventory		550.00
	To record the use of indirect materials in production.		
4.	Factory Payroll	5,300.00	
	Cash (and other accounts)		5,300.00
	To record salaries and wages of factory personnel (other accounts include various payroll liabilities).		
5.	Goods in Process Inventory	4,200.00	
	Factory Payroll		4,200.00
	To assign the cost of direct labor used in producing jobs.		
6.	Factory Overhead	1,100.00	
	Factory Payroll		1,100.00
	To record indirect labor costs as overhead.		
7.	Factory Overhead	5,070.00	
	Cash (and other accounts)		5,070.00
	To record overhead costs incurred such as insurance on factory equipment, utilities, rent of factory building, and depreciation of equipment.		
8.	Goods in Process Inventory	6,720.00	
	Factory Overhead		6,720.00
	To apply overhead costs to jobs at the rate of 160% of direct labor cost.		
9.	Finished Goods Inventory	8,940.00	
	Goods in Process Inventory		8,940.00
	To record the completed production of Job Nos. 15, 16, and 17.		
10.	Cost of Goods Sold	5,580.00	
	Finished Goods Inventory		5,580.00
	To record the sale of Job Nos. 15 and 16 to customers.		

FAST HINT
Class Discussion:
Ask students to describe the relationship between the flow of manufacturing costs through the general ledger accounts and the job cost sheets. Use Illustration 19–10 as reinforcement.

FAST HINT
Relevant Exercise:
To apply these concepts, work Exercise 19–6.

The bottom of Illustration 19–10 shows the status of the job cost sheets at the end of the month. Note that the sum of the costs assigned to the jobs in process ($1,970 + $1,810) equals the $3,780 balance in Goods in Process Inventory. Also, the costs assigned to Job No. 17 equal the $3,360 balance in Finished Goods Inventory. Finally, the sum of the costs assigned to Job Nos. 15 and 16 ($3,200 + $2,380) equals the $5,580 balance in Cost of Goods Sold.

THE MANUFACTURING STATEMENT

A manufacturing statement prepared under a job order cost accounting system appears just like one prepared under a general accounting system. Under both systems, the statement summarizes the total costs of manufacturing activities during the period. The manufacturing statement for Medford Machine Tools appears in Illustration 19–11.

Progress Check

19-9   In a job order cost accounting system, which account would be debited in recording a raw materials requisition?
        a. Raw Materials Inventory.
        b. Raw Materials Purchases.
        c. Goods in Process Inventory if for a specific job.
        d. Goods in Process Inventory if they are indirect materials.

19-10   What are materials ledger cards?

19-11   What are the purposes of clock cards and time tickets?

19-12   Which four sources of information lead to recording costs in the Factory Overhead account?

19-13   Why does a job order cost accounting system use a predetermined overhead application rate?

19-14   What events would lead to a debit to Factory Payroll? What events would lead to a credit?

ADJUSTING FOR UNDERAPPLIED AND OVERAPPLIED FACTORY OVERHEAD

LO 5

Explain how the accounts are adjusted for any overapplied or underapplied factory overhead.

In Illustration 19–10, look at the debits in the Factory Overhead account and notice that the total cost of factory overhead actually incurred during the period was $550 + $5,070 + $1,100 = $6,720. Then, notice that this $6,720 is exactly equal to the amount applied to production in entry 8. We made the overhead incurred and overhead applied equal to each other to simplify the previous discussion. However, in a real company, the amount of overhead incurred would rarely, if ever, equal the amount of overhead applied.

Recall that a job order cost accounting system uses a predetermined overhead application rate to apply factory overhead costs to jobs. Also remember that the firm calculates a predetermined overhead application rate before the accounting period begins. The rate is, in fact, an estimated relationship between future overhead costs and another variable such as future direct labor costs. After the period is over, the amounts of overhead and direct labor costs actually incurred rarely are exactly equal to the estimated amounts. Thus, the amount of overhead incurred rarely equals the amount of overhead applied.

Illustration 19-11

MEDFORD MACHINE TOOLS, INC.
Manufacturing Statement
For Month Ended March 31, 19X2

Direct materials used	$ 1,800
Direct labor	4,200
Factory overhead	6,720
Total manufacturing costs	$12,720
Add goods in process inventory, February 28, 19X2 . .	–0–
Total goods in process during the month	$12,720
Deduct goods in process inventory, March 31, 19X2 . .	(3,780)
Cost of goods manufactured	$ 8,940

Underapplied Overhead

If less overhead was applied than was actually incurred, the remaining debit balance in the Factory Overhead account at the end of a period is described as **underapplied overhead.** For example, suppose that Medford Machine Tools incurred a total overhead cost of $7,200 during March 19X2. Since the amount of overhead applied was only $6,720, the Factory Overhead account is left with a $480 debit balance, as shown here:

Factory Overhead					**Acct. No. 540**
Date		**Explanation**	**Debit**	**Credit**	**Balance**
19X2					
Mar.	31	Indirect materials cost	550		550
	31	Indirect labor cost	1,100		1,650
	31	Other overhead costs	5,550		7,200
	31	Overhead costs applied to jobs		6,720	480

(debit)

The $480 debit balance represents manufacturing costs that were not charged to jobs. As a result, the balances in Goods in Process Inventory, Finished Goods Inventory, and Cost of Goods Sold fail to include all the manufacturing costs incurred. Thus, the Factory Overhead balance should be allocated among those accounts. Ideally, the method of allocating the underapplied overhead should be consistent with the allocation method used during the period. For Medford Machine Tools, the underapplied overhead should be allocated to jobs based on direct labor.

Illustration 19-12 shows the necessary calculations. In that illustration, note that the direct labor assigned to each job is expressed as a percentage of total direct labor. Then, these percentages are multiplied by $480 to determine how much of the underapplied overhead should be allocated to each job. This adjusting entry records the allocation of the underapplied overhead:

Mar.	31	Goods in Process Inventory	149.00	
		Finished Goods Inventory	126.00	
		Cost of Goods Sold	205.00	
		Factory Overhead		480.00
		To adjust the cost of the jobs worked on in March for underapplied overhead cost.		

FAST HINT
Alternative Example:
Assume that $1,200 of direct labor was assigned to Job No. 15 and $500 was assigned to Job No. 18 in Illustration 19–12. How would this change affect the allocation of underapplied overhead?
Answer:
Job No. 15 = 28.6% of total
Job No. 18 = 11.9% of total
Allocation:

Goods in Process	$126
Finished Goods	126
Cost of Goods Sold	228
	$480

Illustration 19-12
Allocation of Underapplied
Overhead to Jobs

FAST HINT
Relevant Exercise:
To apply these concepts, work
Exercise 19–9.

Illustration 19-12
Allocation of Underapplied
Overhead to Jobs

FAST HINT
Relevant Exercise:
To apply these concepts, work
Exercise 19–9.

| Job | Direct Labor Assigned to Jobs | | Allocation of Underapplied Overhead Percentages × $480 | | |
	Dollars	Percentages	Goods in Process	Finished Goods	Cost of Goods Sold
15	$1,000	23.8%			$114
16	800	19.0			91
17	1,100	26.2		$126	
18	700	16.7	$ 80		
19	600	14.3	69		
Total	$4,200	100.0%	$149	$126	$205

Overapplied Overhead

FAST HINT
Relevant Exercise:
To apply these concepts, work
Exercise 19–8.

If the amount of overhead applied during a period exceeds the overhead incurred, the resulting credit balance in the Factory Overhead account is **overapplied overhead.** The treatment of overapplied overhead at the end of the period is the same as the treatment of underapplied overhead. In other words, whether the remaining Factory Overhead balance is a debit or credit makes no difference. It should be allocated to goods in process, finished goods, and cost of goods sold.

Underapplied and Overapplied Amounts that Are Not Material

Sometimes, the amount of underapplied or overapplied overhead is not material compared to the total manufacturing costs incurred during the period. When this is the case, many companies prefer to avoid the calculations that must be made to allocate the underapplied or overapplied amount to goods in process, finished goods, and cost of goods sold. Instead, they simply transfer the remaining Factory Overhead account balance to Cost of Goods Sold. For most companies, a large portion of the overhead cost ends up in this account anyway. If Medford Machine Tools' management had decided that the $480 of underapplied overhead was immaterial, the entry would have been:

FAST HINT
Alternative Example:
What entry would record $480
of overapplied factory overhead
if management decides it is
immaterial?
Answer:
Factory Overhead 480.00
  Cost of Goods Sold 480.00

Mar.	31	Cost of Goods Sold	480.00	
		Factory Overhead		480.00
		To adjust cost of goods sold for underapplied overhead.		

Progress Check

19-15 **A company assigns overhead at a predetermined rate of 120% of direct labor. At the end of the period, direct labor costs totaled $50,000 and overhead costs $62,000. The adjusting entry to allocate the over- or underapplied overhead would include:**
  a. **A $2,000 credit to Cost of Goods Sold if the amount is considered immaterial.**
  b. **Credits to Goods in Process Inventory, Finished Goods Inventory, and Cost of Goods Sold in proportion to direct labor incurred during the period for each category, if the amount is considered material.**
  c. **A $2,000 credit to Factory Overhead.**

19-16 **In a job order cost accounting system, why does the Factory Overhead account usually have an overapplied or underapplied balance at the end of the period?**

19-17 **At the end of a period, the Factory Overhead account has a debit balance. Does this represent overapplied or underapplied overhead?**

LO 1. **Identify five new production management concepts and explain how they affect the management of manufacturing processes.** Production management experienced important changes in the 1970s and 1980s as five new concepts began to be widely implemented. These concepts include customer orientation, total quality management (TQM), just-in-time (JIT) manufacturing, the theory of constraints (TOC), and continuous improvement. These concepts have helped production managers change the kinds of products, the attitudes of employees toward quality and improvement, and the way that they operate production facilities.

LO 2. **Describe the type of manufacturing operations in which job order cost accounting systems are used.** Job order cost accounting systems account for operations involving the manufacture of products that are individually designed to meet the needs of each customer. Job order cost accounting systems also may be used by service companies that provide a unique service for each customer.

LO 3. **Explain how job cost sheets are used in job order cost accounting systems.** In a job order cost accounting system, the costs of producing each job are accumulated on a separate job cost sheet. On a job cost sheet, the costs of direct materials, direct labor, and manufacturing overhead are accumulated separately and then added to determine the total cost of the job. Job cost sheets for the jobs in process, finished jobs, and jobs that have been sold are subsidiary records controlled by related general ledger accounts.

LO 4. **Describe and record the flow of materials, labor, and overhead costs in a job order cost accounting system.** In the subsidiary records, the costs of materials flow from receiving reports to materials ledger cards and then to job cost sheets or to the Indirect Materials account in the Factory Overhead Ledger. The costs of labor flow from clock cards to the Factory Payroll account and then to job cost sheets or to the Indirect Labor account in the Factory Overhead Ledger. Manufacturing overhead costs are accumulated in the Factory Overhead account that controls the subsidiary Factory Overhead Ledger. Then, based on a predetermined overhead application rate, overhead costs are charged to jobs.

LO 5. **Explain how the accounts are adjusted for any overapplied or underapplied factory overhead.** At the end of each period, the Factory Overhead account normally has a residual debit or credit balance. A debit balance represents underapplied overhead and a credit balance represents overapplied overhead. If this balance is material, it is allocated to Goods in Process Inventory, Finished Goods Inventory, and Cost of Goods Sold. The allocation should be based on the same variable, such as direct labor, that was used to apply overhead during the period. If the balance is not material, it is usually transferred to Cost of Goods Sold.

SUMMARY OF THE CHAPTER IN TERMS OF LEARNING OBJECTIVES

DEMONSTRATION PROBLEM

The following information describes the job order manufacturing activities of Peak Manufacturing Company for May:

Raw materials purchases	$16,000
Factory payroll cost	15,400
Overhead costs incurred:	
Indirect materials	5,000
Indirect labor	3,500
Other factory overhead	9,500

The predetermined overhead rate was 150% of the direct labor cost. These costs were allocated to the three jobs worked on during May:

	Job 401	Job 402	Job 403
Balances on April 30:			
Direct materials	$3,600		
Direct labor	1,700		
Applied overhead	2,550		
Costs during May:			
Direct materials	3,550	$3,500	$1,400
Direct labor	5,100	6,000	800
Applied overhead	?	?	?
Status on May 31	Finished (sold)	Finished (unsold)	In process

Required

1. Determine the total cost of:
   a. The April 30 inventory of jobs in process.
   b. The materials used during May.
   c. The labor used during May.
   d. The factory overhead incurred and applied during May and the amount of any over- or underapplied overhead on May 31.
   e. Each job as of May 31, the May 31 inventories of goods in process and finished goods, and the goods sold during May.

2. Present summarized journal entries for the month to record:
   a. The materials purchases (on credit), the factory payroll (paid with cash), indirect materials, indirect labor, and the other factory overhead (paid with cash).
   b. The assignment of direct materials, direct labor, and overhead costs to the Goods in Process Inventory account. (Use separate debit entries for each job.)
   c. The transfer of each completed job to the Finished Goods Inventory account.
   d. The cost of goods sold.
   e. The removal of any underapplied or overapplied overhead from the Factory Overhead account. (Assume the amount is not material.)

3. Prepare a manufacturing statement for May.

Planning the Solution

- Determine the cost of the April 30 in-process inventory by adding up the materials, labor, and applied overhead costs for Job 401.
- Calculate the cost of materials used and labor by adding up the amounts assigned to jobs and to overhead.
- Calculate the total overhead incurred by adding the amounts of the three components; calculate the amount of applied overhead by multiplying the total direct labor cost by the predetermined overhead rate; compute the underapplied or overapplied amount as the difference between the actual cost and the applied cost.
- Determine the total cost charged to each job by adding any costs incurred in April to the materials, labor, and overhead applied during May.
- Group the costs of the jobs according to their status as completed.
- Record the direct materials costs assigned to the three jobs, using a separate Goods in Process Inventory account for each job; do the same thing for the direct labor and the applied overhead.
- Transfer the costs of Jobs 401 and 402 from Goods in Process Inventory to Finished Goods Inventory.
- Record the costs of Job 401 as the cost of goods sold.
- Record the transfer of the underapplied overhead from the Factory Overhead account to the Cost of Goods Sold account.
- On the manufacturing statement, remember to include the beginning and ending in-process inventories, and to deduct the underapplied overhead.

1. Total cost of:

    a. April 30 inventory of jobs in process (Job 401):

Direct materials	$ 3,600
Direct labor	1,700
Applied overhead	2,550
Total	$ 7,850

Solution to
Demonstration
Problem

    b. Materials used during May:

Direct materials:	
Job 401	$ 3,550
Job 402	3,500
Job 403	1,400
Total direct materials	$ 8,450
Indirect materials	5,000
Total materials	$13,450

    c. Labor used during May:

Direct labor:	
Job 401	$ 5,100
Job 402	6,000
Job 403	800
Total direct labor	$11,900
Indirect labor	3,500
Total labor	$15,400

    d. Factory overhead incurred during May:

Indirect materials	$ 5,000
Indirect labor	3,500
Other factory overhead	9,500
Total actual overhead	$18,000
Overhead applied (150% × $11,900)	17,850
Underapplied overhead	$ 150

    e. Total cost of each job:

	401	402	403
From April:			
Direct materials	$ 3,600		
Direct labor	1,700		
*Applied overhead	2,550		
From May:			
Direct materials	3,550	$ 3,500	$1,400
Direct labor	5,100	6,000	800
*Applied overhead	7,650	9,000	1,200
Total costs	$24,150	$18,500	$3,400

    *Equals 150% of the direct labor cost.

Total cost of the May 31 inventory of goods in process (Job 403) = $3,400

Total cost of the May 31 inventory of finished goods (Job 402) = $18,500

Total cost of goods sold during May (Job 401) = $24,150

2. Journal entries:

a.	Raw Materials Inventory		16,000.00	
	Accounts Payable			16,000.00
	To record materials purchases.			
	Factory Payroll		15,400.00	
	Cash			15,400.00
	To record factory payroll.			
	Factory Overhead		5,000.00	
	Raw Materials Inventory			5,000.00
	To record indirect materials.			
	Factory Overhead		3,500.00	
	Factory Payroll			3,500.00
	To record indirect labor.			
	Factory Overhead		9,500.00	
	Cash			9,500.00
	To record other factory overhead.			
b.	Assignment of costs to goods in process:			
	Goods in Process Inventory (Job 401)		3,550.00	
	Goods in Process Inventory (Job 402)		3,500.00	
	Goods in Process Inventory (Job 403)		1,400.00	
	Raw Materials Inventory			8,450.00
	To assign direct materials to jobs.			
	Goods in Process Inventory (Job 401)		5,100.00	
	Goods in Process Inventory (Job 402)		6,000.00	
	Goods in Process Inventory (Job 403)		800.00	
	Factory Payroll			11,900.00
	To assign direct labor to jobs.			
	Goods in Process Inventory (Job 401)		7,650.00	
	Goods in Process Inventory (Job 402)		9,000.00	
	Goods in Process Inventory (Job 403)		1,200.00	
	Factory Overhead			17,850.00
	To apply overhead to jobs.			
c.	Finished Goods Inventory		42,650.00	
	Goods in Process Inventory (Job 401)			24,150.00
	Goods in Process Inventory (Job 402)			18,500.00
	To record completion of jobs.			
d.	Cost of Goods Sold		24,150.00	
	Finished Goods Inventory			24,150.00
	To record sale of Job 401.			
e.	Cost of Goods Sold		150.00	
	Factory Overhead			150.00
	To assign underapplied overhead.			

3.

PEAK MANUFACTURING COMPANY
Manufacturing Statement
For Month Ended May 31

Direct materials used		$ 8,450
Direct labor used		11,900
Factory overhead:		
Indirect materials	$5,000	
Indirect labor	3,500	
Other factory overhead	9,500	18,000
Total manufacturing costs		$38,350
Add goods in process, April 30		7,850
Total goods in process during the month		$46,200
Deduct goods in process, May 31		(3,400)
Deduct underapplied overhead		(150)
Cost of goods manufactured		$42,650

GLOSSARY

Clock card a source document that an employee uses to record the number of hours at work and that is used to determine the total labor cost for each pay period. p. 734

Constraint anything that prevents a company from achieving higher performance in terms of its goals. p. 726

Continuous improvement an attitude of constantly seeking ways to improve company operations, including customer service, product quality, product features, the production process, and employee interactions. p. 727

Customer orientation a management concept that encourages all managers and employees (including those in the factory) to be in tune with the wants and needs of customers; leads to flexible product designs and production processes. p. 723

Job a unique product or service that is produced to meet the demands of a particular customer. p. 729

Job cost sheet a subsidiary record in a job order cost accounting system used to record the costs of producing a job. p. 731

Job lot a group of unique products produced for a particular customer. p. 729

Job order cost accounting system a cost accounting system that is designed to determine the cost of producing each job or job lot and that accumulates manufacturing costs by job. p. 731

Job order manufacturing a type of manufacturing that produces unique products (or services) for each customer. p. 729

Just-in-time (JIT) an approach to managing inventories and production operations such that units of materials and products are obtained and provided only as they are needed. p. 724

Materials ledger card a subsidiary record of a raw materials item that records data on the quantity and cost of units

purchased, units issued for use in production, and units that remain in the raw materials inventory. p. 732.

Materials requisition a source document that production managers use to request materials for manufacturing and that is used to assign materials costs to specific jobs or to overhead. p. 733

Overapplied overhead the amount by which the overhead applied to jobs during a period with the predetermined overhead application rate exceeds the overhead incurred during the period. p. 742

Predetermined overhead application rate the rate established prior to the beginning of a period that relates estimated overhead to another variable such as estimated direct labor, and that is used to assign overhead cost to jobs. p. 736

Theory of constraints (TOC) a management concept that asserts the primary focus of managers should be to discover and then relax or overcome the factors that limit the throughput of the company's operations. p. 726

Throughput the added value (selling price minus direct costs of production) of finished products processed through the system. p. 726

Time ticket a source document that an employee uses to report how much time was spent working on a job or on overhead activities and that is used to determine the amount of direct labor to charge to the job or to determine the amount of indirect labor to charge to factory overhead. p. 734

Total Quality Management (TQM) a management concept under which all managers and employees at all stages of operations strive toward higher standards and a reduced number of defective units. p. 724

Underapplied overhead the amount by which overhead incurred during a period exceeds the overhead applied to jobs with the predetermined overhead application rate. p. 741

QUESTIONS

1. What is the essence of customer orientation?
2. What does just-in-time manufacturing try to accomplish for finished goods and raw materials inventories?
3. When managers use the theory of constraints to streamline a company's production process, what do they look for?
4. What types of information are recorded on a job cost sheet? How are job cost sheets used by management?
5. In a job order cost accounting system, what records serve as a subsidiary ledger for Goods in Process Inventory? For Finished Goods Inventory?
6. What entries are recorded when a materials manager receives a materials requisition and then issues materials for use in the factory?
7. What events cause debits to be recorded in the Factory Overhead account? What events cause credits to be recorded in the account?
8. How does the process of determining the ending goods in process in a job order cost accounting system differ from the process used in a general accounting system?
9. What method should be used to eliminate a material amount of overapplied or underapplied overhead from the Factory Overhead account?
10. Suppose that Lands' End, Inc., produces 1,000 sweaters of a particular style. Do you suppose that this production project would be accounted for as a job lot? Explain briefly.
11. Essentially each package delivered by Federal Express represents a unique job because it is taken from one specific location to another. Do you think that each package is accounted for separately using a job cost accounting system? Why?

FedEx
Federal Express

QUICK STUDY (FIVE-MINUTE EXERCISES)

QS 19–1
(LO 1)

Match each of the following new production management concepts with the phrase that best describes it by filling in the blank with the appropriate letter:

1. ____ Customer orientation
2. ____ Total quality management
3. ____ Just-in-time manufacturing
4. ____ Theory of constraints
5. ____ Continuous improvement

a. Focuses on factors that limit the operations of the business.
b. Inventory is acquired or produced only as it is needed.
c. Calls for flexible product designs that can be modified to accommodate customer choices.
d. Every manager and employee constantly looks for ways to improve company operations.
e. Focuses on quality throughout the entire production process.

QS 19–2
(LO 2)

Determine which products from the following list would most likely be manufactured as a job and which as a job lot:

1. Hats imprinted with a company logo.
2. A handcrafted table.
3. A custom-designed home.
4. A 90-foot motor yacht.
5. Little League trophies.
6. Wedding dresses for a chain of department stores.

QS 19–3
(LO 3)

The following information was found on materials requisitions and time tickets for Job 9–1005, which was completed by Beaufort Boats for Redfish Rentals. The requisitions are identified by code numbers starting with the letter *Q* and the time tickets start with *W*:

Date	Document	Amount
7/1/X4	Q–4698	$1,250
7/1/X4	W–3393	600
7/5/X4	Q–4725	1,000
7/5/X4	W–3479	450
7/10/X4	W–3559	300

Before the year started, management estimated that the overhead cost would equal 140% of the direct labor cost for each job. Determine the total cost on the job cost sheet for Job 9–1005.

During one month, a company that uses a job order cost accounting system purchased raw materials for $50,000 cash. It then used $12,000 of the raw materials indirectly as factory supplies and used $42,000 as direct materials. Prepare entries to record these transactions.

QS 19–4
(LO 4)

During one month, a company that uses a job order cost accounting system had a monthly factory payroll of $120,000, paid in cash. Of this amount, $28,000 was classified as indirect labor and the remainder as direct. Prepare entries to record these transactions.

QS 19–5
(LO 4)

Relay Company allocates overhead at a rate of 150% of direct labor cost. Actual overhead for the period was $950,000 and direct labor was $600,000. Overhead for the period has been assigned to jobs as follows:

QS 19–6
(LO 5)

Jobs completed and sold	60%
Jobs still in finished goods inventory . . .	15
Goods in process inventory	25

Assuming it is material, prepare the general journal entry to eliminate any over- or underapplied overhead.

EXERCISES

As of the end of June, the job cost sheets of Harrell Company showed that the following total costs had been accumulated on three jobs:

Exercise 19–1
Analysis of cost flows
(LO 3)

	Job 102	Job 103	Job 104
Direct materials	$15,000	$33,000	$27,000
Direct labor	9,000	13,200	21,000
Overhead	11,250	16,500	26,250

Job 102 had been started in production during May and the following costs had already been assigned to it in that month: direct materials of $6,000, direct labor of $1,800, and overhead of $2,250. Jobs 103 and 104 were started during June. Overhead cost was applied with a predetermined application rate based on direct labor cost. Only Jobs 102 and 103 were finished during June, and it is expected that Job 104 will be finished in July. No raw materials were used indirectly during June. Using this information, answer the following questions:

a. What was the cost of the raw materials requisitioned during June?

b. How much direct labor cost was incurred during June?

c. What predetermined overhead application rate was used during June?

d. How much cost was transferred to finished goods during June?

The following left column includes the names of several documents used in job order cost accounting systems. The right column presents short descriptions of the purposes of the documents. In the blank space beside each of the numbers in the right column, write the letter of the document that serves the described purpose.

Exercise 19–2
Documents used in job order cost accounting systems
(LO 4)

a. Factory Payroll account

_____ 1. Communicates to the storeroom that materials are needed to complete a job.

b. Materials ledger card

_____ 2. Shows only the total amount of time that an employee works each day.

c. Time ticket

_____ 3. Shows the amount approved for payment of an overhead cost.

d.	Voucher	____ 4.	Shows the amount of time an employee worked on a specific job.
e.	Materials requisition	____ 5.	Temporarily accumulates the cost of incurred overhead until the cost is assigned to specific jobs.
f.	Factory Overhead account	____ 6.	Temporarily accumulates labor costs incurred until they are assigned to specific jobs or to overhead.
g.	Clock card	____ 7.	Perpetual inventory record of raw materials received, used, and on hand.

Exercise 19–3
Calculating overhead
application rate; assigning
costs to jobs
(LO 3, 4)

In December 19X1, Luna Company's management established the 19X2 overhead application rate based on direct labor cost. The information used in setting the rate included the cost accountant's estimates that the company would incur $480,000 of overhead costs and $300,000 of direct labor cost during 19X2. During March of 19X2, Luna began and completed Job No. 13–56. Calculate the overhead application rate for 19X2 and use the information on the following job cost sheet to determine the total cost of the job.

JOB COST SHEET

Customer's Name _____Keiser Co._____   Job No. __13–56__
Job Description _____5 Two Page Color Monitors -- 21 inch_____

Direct Materials			Direct Labor		Overhead Costs Applied	
Date	Requisition No.	Amount	Time Ticket Number	Amount	Rate	Amount
Mar. 8	4-129	5,000.00	T-306	640.00		
11	4-142	7,050.00	T-432	1,280.00		
18	4-167	3,550.00	T-456	1,280.00		
Total						

Exercise 19–4
Analysis of costs assigned to
goods in process
(LO 4)

Angus Company uses a job order cost accounting system that charges overhead to jobs on the basis of direct labor cost. At the end of last year, the company's Goods in Process Inventory account showed the following:

Goods in Process Inventory				Account No. 121	
Date		Explanation	Debit	Credit	Balance
19X2 Dec.	31	Direct materials cost	1,500,000		1,500,000
	31	Direct labor cost	240,000		1,740,000
	31	Overhead costs	288,000		2,028,000
	31	To finished goods		1,368,000	660,000

Required

1. Determine the overhead application rate (based on direct labor cost) used by the company.

2. Only one job was in the goods in process inventory at the end of December. Its direct materials cost was $528,000. How much direct labor cost must have been assigned to it? How much overhead cost must have been assigned to it?

The Oasis Company produces special order products and uses a job order cost accounting system. The system provided the following information:

	April 30	May 31
Inventories:		
Raw materials	$39,000	$ 48,000
Goods in process	9,600	19,500
Finished goods	66,000	43,200
Information about May:		
Raw materials purchases (paid with cash) . .		$ 189,000
Factory payroll (paid with cash)		375,000
Factory overhead:		
Indirect materials		12,000
Indirect labor		75,000
Other overhead costs		100,500
Sales (received in cash)		1,140,000
Predetermined overhead application rate based on direct labor cost		62.5%

Calculate the following amounts for the month of May:

a.   Cost of direct materials used.

b.   Cost of direct labor used.

c.   Cost of goods manufactured.

d.   Cost of goods sold.

e.   Gross profit.

Using the information provided in Exercise 19–5 and your answers to the questions for that exercise, prepare general journal entries to record the following events for May:

a.   Raw materials purchases.

b.   Direct materials usage.

c.   Indirect materials usage.

d.   Factory payroll costs.

e.   Direct labor usage.

f.   Indirect labor usage.

g.   Factory overhead other than indirect materials and indirect labor (record the credit in Other Accounts).

h.   Application of overhead to goods in process.

i.   Transfer of finished jobs to the finished goods inventory.

j.   Sale and delivery of finished goods to customers.

Set up six T-accounts like those shown in Illustration 19–10. Using the information in Exercise 19–5, enter the beginning inventory balances and show the flows of manufacturing costs during May. (Use arrows like those in Illustration 19–10.)

In December 19X1, Sierra Company established its predetermined overhead application rate for jobs produced during 19X2 by using the following predictions:

Overhead costs	$900,000
Direct labor costs	750,000

At the end of 19X2, the company's records showed that actual overhead costs for the year had been $787,500. The actual direct labor cost had been assigned to jobs as follows:

Jobs completed and sold	$540,000
Jobs still in the finished goods inventory	94,500
Jobs in the goods in process inventory	40,500
Total actual direct labor cost	$675,000

Required

1. Calculate the predetermined overhead application rate for 19X2.

2. Set up a T-account for Factory Overhead and enter the overhead costs incurred and the amounts applied to jobs during the year with the predetermined rate. Determine whether overhead was overapplied or underapplied during the year.

3. Prepare the general journal entry to allocate any over- or underapplied overhead among the cost of goods sold, the ending finished goods inventory, and the goods in process inventory.

Exercise 19–9
Eliminating the end-of-period balance in Factory Overhead
(LO 5)

In December 19X1, Setter Company established its predetermined overhead application rate for jobs produced during 19X2 by using the following predictions:

Overhead costs	$900,000
Direct labor costs	600,000

At the end of 19X2, the company's records showed that actual overhead costs for the year had been $1,010,000. The actual direct labor cost had been assigned to jobs as follows:

Jobs completed and sold	$420,000
Jobs still in the finished goods inventory ..	84,000
Jobs in the goods in process inventory ...	56,000
Total actual direct labor cost	$560,000

Required

1. Calculate the predetermined overhead application rate for 19X2.

2. Set up a T-account for Factory Overhead and enter the overhead costs incurred and the amounts applied to jobs during the year with the predetermined rate. Determine whether overhead was overapplied or underapplied during the year.

3. Prepare the general journal entry to allocate any over- or underapplied overhead among the cost of goods sold, the ending finished goods inventory, and the goods in process inventory.

PROBLEMS

Problem 19–1
Recording manufacturing costs and preparing financial reports
(LO 4, 5)

The following information refers to the job order manufacturing activities of Montero Company for October:

The September 30 inventory of raw materials was $100,000. Raw materials purchases during October were $400,000. Factory payroll cost during October was $220,000. Overhead costs incurred during October were:

Indirect materials	$30,000
Indirect labor	14,000
Factory rent	20,000
Factory utilities	12,000
Factory equipment depreciation	28,000

The predetermined overhead rate was 50% of the direct labor cost. Costs allocated to the three jobs worked on during October were:

	Job 306	Job 307	Job 308
Balances on September 30:			
Direct materials	$ 14,000	$ 18,000	
Direct labor	18,000	16,000	
Applied overhead	9,000	8,000	
Costs during October:			
Direct materials	100,000	170,000	$ 80,000
Direct labor	30,000	56,000	120,000
Applied overhead	?	?	?
Status on October 31 . . .	Finished (sold)	Finished (unsold)	In process

Job 306 was sold for $380,000 cash during October.

Required

Preparation component:

1. Determine the total of each manufacturing cost incurred for October (direct labor, direct materials, allocated overhead), and the total cost assigned to each of the three jobs (including the balances from September 30).

2. Present journal entries for the month to record:

   a. The materials purchases (on credit), the factory payroll (paid with cash), and the actual overhead costs, including indirect materials and indirect labor. (The factory rent and utilities were paid with cash.)

   b. The assignment of direct materials, direct labor, and applied overhead costs to the Goods in Process Inventory.

   c. The transfer of Jobs 306 and 307 to the Finished Goods Inventory.

   d. The cost of goods sold for Job 306.

   e. The revenue from the sale of Job 306.

   f. The assignment of any underapplied or overapplied overhead to the Cost of Goods Sold account. (The amount is not material.)

3. Prepare a manufacturing statement for October (use a single line presentation for direct materials and show the details of overhead cost). Also, present a calculation of gross profit for October and show how the inventories would be presented on the October 31 balance sheet.

CHECK FIGURE:
Cost of goods manufactured, $483,000

Analysis component:

4. Assume now that the under- or overapplied overhead is material. Montero is still considering assigning all of it to cost of goods sold. Describe how this treatment will affect the financial statements for the current year and the following year.

The following trial balance of the Scobey Company was generated by the computer system on the morning of December 31, 19X2. Warren Kemp, the company's accountant, knows that something is wrong with the trial balance because it does not show any balance for goods in process inventory and it still shows balances in the Factory Payroll and Factory Overhead accounts:

Problem 19–2
Source documents, journal entries, and financial statements
(LO 3, 4, 5)

Cash	$ 48,000	
Accounts receivable	42,000	
Raw materials inventory	24,000	
Goods in process inventory	–0–	
Finished goods	9,000	
Prepaid rent	3,000	
Accounts payable		$ 10,500
Notes payable		13,500
Common stock		30,000
Retained earnings		87,000
Sales		180,000
Cost of goods sold	105,000	
Factory payroll	18,000	
Factory overhead	27,000	
Miscellaneous expenses	45,000	
Total	$321,000	$321,000

After a few moments of searching a cluttered in-box, Kemp found six source documents that needed to be processed to bring the accounting records up to date:

Materials requisition 21–3010:	$3,600 direct materials to Job 402
Materials requisition 21–3011:	$6,600 direct materials to Job 404
Materials requisition 21–3012:	$2,100 indirect materials
Labor time ticket 6052:	$6,000 direct labor to Job 402
Labor time ticket 6053:	$9,000 direct labor to Job 404
Labor time ticket 6054:	$3,000 indirect labor

Jobs 402 and 404 are the only units in process at the end of the year. The predetermined overhead application rate is 210% of direct labor cost.

Required

Preparation component:

1. Use the information on the six source documents to prepare journal entries to assign the following costs:

    a. Direct material costs to goods in process inventory.

    b. Direct labor costs to goods in process inventory.

    c. Overhead costs to goods in process inventory.

    d. Indirect material costs to the overhead account.

    e. Indirect labor costs to the overhead account.

2. Determine the new balance of the Factory Overhead account after making the entries in requirement 1. Determine whether there is any under- or overapplied overhead for the year. If so, prepare the appropriate adjusting entry to close the overhead account, assuming that the amount is not material.

3. Prepare a revised trial balance.

CHECK FIGURE:
Net income, $29,400

4. Prepare an income statement for 19X2 and a balance sheet as of December 31, 19X2.

Analysis component:

5. Assume that the $2,100 on materials requisition 21–3012 should have been direct materials charged to Job 404. Without providing specific calculations, describe what impact this error would have on Scobey's 19X2 income statement and balance sheet.

Problem 19–3
Source documents and journal entries under job order cost accounting
(LO 3, 4)

Harbison Company's predetermined overhead application rate during a recent month was 200% of direct labor. The company's activities related to manufacturing during the month were:

a. Purchased raw materials on account, $100,000.

b. Paid factory wages with cash, $84,000.

c. Paid miscellaneous factory overhead costs with cash, $11,000.

d. Materials requisitions for the month show that the following materials were used on jobs and indirectly:

Job 136	$20,000
Job 137	10,000
Job 138	22,000
Job 139	24,000
Job 140	4,000
Total direct materials	$80,000
Indirect materials	12,000
Total materials used	$92,000

e. Labor time tickets for the month show the following labor was used on jobs and indirectly:

Job 136	$ 8,000
Job 137	14,000
Job 138	18,000
Job 139	26,000
Job 140	2,000
Total direct labor	$68,000
Indirect labor	16,000
Total	$84,000

f. Overhead was applied to Jobs 136, 138, and 139.

g. Jobs 136, 138, and 139 were transferred to finished goods.

h. Jobs 136 and 138 were sold on account for a total price of $240,000.

i. Overhead costs incurred during the month were as follows. (Credit Prepaid Insurance for the expired factory insurance.)

Depreciation of factory building	$37,000
Depreciation of factory equipment	31,000
Expired factory insurance	7,000
Accrued property taxes payable	21,000

j. At the end of the month, overhead is applied to the goods in process (Jobs 137 and 140) using the predetermined rate of 200% of direct labor cost.

Required

1. Prepare general journal entries to record the events and transactions *a* through *j*.

2. Set up T-accounts for each of the following general ledger accounts, each of which started the month with a zero balance. Then, post the journal entries to these T-accounts and determine the balance of each account.

Raw Materials Inventory	Factory Payroll
Goods in Process Inventory	Factory Overhead
Finished Goods Inventory	Cost of Goods Sold

3. Prepare a job cost sheet for each job worked on during the month. Use the following simplified form of the job cost sheet:

Job No.	
Materials	$
Labor	
Overhead	
Total cost	$

4. Prepare a schedule showing the total cost of each job in process and proving that the sum of the costs equals the Goods in Process Inventory account balance. Prepare similar schedules for the finished goods inventory and the cost of goods sold.

CHECK FIGURE:
Finished goods inventory, $102,000

Problem 19–4

Allocating overhead based on predetermined overhead application rate

(LO 5)

In December 19X1, Cantu Company's accountant estimated the next year's direct labor as the cost of 40 persons, working an average of 1,900 hours each at an average wage rate of $12 per hour. The accountant also estimated the following manufacturing overhead costs for 19X2:

Indirect labor	$159,600
Factory supervision	120,000
Rent on factory building	70,000
Factory utilities	44,000
Factory insurance expired	34,000
Depreciation of factory equipment	240,000
Repairs, factory equipment	30,000
Factory supplies used	14,000
Miscellaneous production costs	18,000
Total	$729,600

At the end of 19X2, the cost records showed the company had incurred $700,000 of overhead costs. It had completed and sold five jobs with the following direct labor costs:

201	$154,000
202	130,000
203	175,000
204	220,000
205	184,000

In addition, Job 206 was in process at the end of the year and had been charged $10,000 for direct labor. The company's predetermined overhead application rate is based on direct labor cost.

Required

1. Determine:

    a. The predetermined overhead application rate for 19X2.

    b. The total overhead cost applied to each of the six jobs during 19X2.

    c. The over- or underapplied overhead at year-end.

CHECK FIGURE:
Factory overhead, $1,600 Cr.

2. Assuming that the amount of over- or underapplied overhead is not material, prepare the appropriate journal entry to close the Factory Overhead account at the end of 19X2.

Problem 19–5

Recording manufacturing transactions; subsidiary records

(LO 4, 5)

If the working papers that accompany this text are not available, do not attempt to solve this problem.

The Kaplan Company manufactures special variations of its product, a technopress, in response to special orders from its customers. On May 1, the company had no inventories of goods in process or finished goods but held the following raw materials:

Material M	120 units	@	$200	=	$24,000
Material R	80 units	@	160	=	12,800
Paint	44 units	@	72	=	3,168
Total					$39,968

On May 4, the company began working on two technopresses: Job 102 for Grobe Company and Job 103 for Reynco Company.

Required

CHECK FIGURE:
Balance in Factory Overhead, $1,536 credit, overapplied

Follow the instructions given in this list of activities and then complete the statements provided in the working papers:

a. Purchased raw materials on credit and recorded the following information from the receiving reports and invoices:

Receiving Report No. 426, Material M, 150 units at $200 each.

Receiving Report No. 427, Material R, 70 units at $160 each.

(Instructions: Record the purchases with a single general journal entry and post it to

the appropriate general ledger T-accounts, using the transaction letter to identify the entries. Also, enter the receiving report information on the materials ledger cards.)

b. Requisitioned the following raw materials for production:

Requisition No. 35, for Job 102, 80 units of Material M.

Requisition No 36, for Job 102, 60 units of Material R.

Requisition No. 37, for Job 103, 40 units of Material M.

Requisition No. 38, for Job 103, 30 units of Material R.

Requisition No. 39, for 12 units of paint.

(Instructions: Enter the amounts for the direct materials requisitions only on the materials ledger cards and the job cost sheets. Enter the indirect material amount on the raw materials ledger card and record a debit to the Indirect Materials account in the subsidiary Factory Overhead Ledger. Do not record a general journal entry at this time.)

c. Employees turned in the following time tickets for work in May:

Time tickets Nos. 1 to 10 for direct labor on Job 102, $40,000.

Time tickets Nos. 11 to 30 for direct labor on Job 103, $32,000.

Time tickets Nos. 31 to 36 for equipment repairs, $12,000.

(Instructions: Record the direct labor reported on the time tickets only on the job cost sheets and debit the indirect labor to the Indirect Labor account in the subsidiary Factory Overhead Ledger. Do not record a general journal entry at this time.)

d. Paid cash for the following items during the month:

Factory payroll, $84,000.

Miscellaneous overhead items, $36,000.

(Instructions: Record the payments with general journal entries and then post them to the general ledger accounts. Also record a debit in the Miscellaneous Overhead account in the subsidiary Factory Overhead Ledger.)

e. Finished Job 102 and transferred it to the warehouse. The company assigns overhead to each job with a predetermined overhead application rate equal to 70% of direct labor cost.

(Instructions: Enter the allocated overhead on the cost sheet for Job 102, fill in the cost summary section of the cost sheet, and then mark the cost sheet as "Finished." Next, prepare a journal entry to record the job's completion and transfer to finished goods, and then post it to the general ledger accounts.)

f. Delivered Job 102 and accepted the customer's promise to pay $290,000 within 30 days.

(Instructions: Prepare general journal entries to record the sale of Job 102 and the cost of goods sold. Post them to the general ledger accounts.)

g. Applied overhead to Job 103, based on the job's direct labor to date.

(Instructions: Enter the overhead on the job cost sheet but do not make a general journal entry at this time.)

h. Recorded the total direct and indirect materials costs as reported on all the requisitions for the month.

(Instructions: Prepare a general journal entry to record these costs, and post it to the general ledger accounts.)

i. Recorded the total direct and indirect labor costs as reported on all the time tickets for the month.

(Instructions: Prepare a general journal entry to record these costs, and post it to the general ledger accounts.)

j. Recorded the total overhead costs applied to jobs.

(Instructions: Prepare a general journal entry to record the application of these costs, and post it to the general ledger accounts.)

CRITICAL THINKING: ESSAYS, PROBLEMS, AND CASES

Analytical Essay

(LO 4, 5)

The president of Ivanhoe Company has hired you as the new accountant. He has asked you to prepare the financial statements for the year ended December 31, 19X2, based on the adjusted trial balance that follows:

IVANHOE COMPANY
Adjusted Trial Balance
December 31, 19X2

Cash	$ 51,440	
Accounts receivable	57,000	
Raw materials inventory	4,200	
Goods in process inventory	28,500	
Finished goods inventory	47,600	
Store equipment	73,780	
Accumulated depreciation, store equipment		$ 27,080
Accounts payable		25,200
Long-term notes payable		69,600
Common stock		71,600
Retained earnings		63,940
Sales		193,000
Sales returns and allowances	2,500	
Cost of goods sold	138,400	
Factory payroll	4,800	
Factory overhead	2,400	
Miscellaneous expenses	39,800	
	$450,420	$450,420

The president has informed you that this trial balance was prepared by the previous accountant and is supposedly ready to be used in preparing the statements. He has also told you that Ivanhoe uses a job order cost accounting system and assigns factory overhead using a predetermined overhead rate that relates overhead to direct labor.

After taking a brief look at the adjusted trial balance, you suspect that some items of information for the period were not processed, or were processed incorrectly, and that you need some time to research the problem. Explain the basis of your suspicions to the president and describe the nature of the entries that will probably be required to correct the adjusted trial balance.

Managerial Analysis Problems

MAP 19–1
(LO 4, 5)

Kipp Corporation's accountant was in the process of posting summary entries for the month when he became ill. In a confused state, he posted only parts of several entries. Following are selected general ledger accounts with their May 1 balances and the results of posting some parts of the summary entries for May's activities. In some cases, either the debit or the credit portion of a particular entry appears in the accounts, but one or more of the offsetting credits or debits is missing. Assume that all entries have been completely posted except for postings to the following accounts. This additional information is available:

- The company charges overhead to jobs with an overhead application rate of 125% of direct labor cost.

- The $36,000 debit in the Factory Overhead account is the sum of all overhead costs for May other than indirect materials and indirect labor.

Raw Materials Inventory		
May 1 Bal.	30,000	35,000
	48,000	

Factory Payroll	
65,000	

Goods in Process Inventory		
May 1 Bal.	10,000	100,000
Direct matl.	25,000	
Direct labor	50,000	

Cost of Goods Sold	

Finished Goods Inventory		
May 1 Bal.	12,500	94,000

Factory Overhead	
36,000	

Required

1. Copy the accounts on a sheet of paper and add the missing debits and credits. Identify the debits and credits of each entry with a code letter. (Hint: You may find it helpful to draft the entries in general journal form.)

2. Answer the following questions before considering overapplied or underapplied overhead:

   a. What is the May 31 balance of the Finished Goods account?

   b. How much factory labor cost (direct and indirect) was incurred during May?

   c. What was the cost of the goods sold for May?

   d. How much overhead was incurred during the month?

   e. How much overhead was charged to jobs during the month?

3. Was overhead overapplied or underapplied during the month? By how much?

Dynamic Company's factory was completely destroyed by an explosion and fire on April 18, 19X2. All inventories were lost and many accounting records were destroyed, although some were salvaged from the ashes, and others were available from off-site backups. In preparing to settle with the fire insurance company, Dynamic's management has asked you to help estimate the costs of the destroyed raw materials, goods in process, and finished goods. The company uses job order cost accounting and the following information is available:

MAP 19–2 (LO 3)

a. The company's December 31, 19X1, balance sheet reported these costs for the inventories: raw materials, $135,000; goods in process, $150,000; and finished goods, $180,000.

b. The cost of raw materials purchased between January 1 and April 18 was $247,500. Direct and indirect materials costing $168,000 (combined) were issued to the factory during the same period.

c. Between January 1 and April 18, factory wages totaling $600,000 were paid and charged to jobs or overhead.

d. The total debits to Factory Overhead during the period before the fire amounted to $450,000. Indirect materials represented $60,000 of this balance, and indirect labor represented $120,000.

e. The overhead application rate used by the company was 90% of direct labor cost.

f. The cost of jobs transferred to the finished goods inventory during the January 1 to April 18 period was $1,050,000.

g.   Jobs costing $937,500 were sold and delivered to customers between January 1 and April 18, 19X2.

h.   The April 18 Factory Overhead account balance should be allocated among the goods in process inventory, the finished goods inventory, and the cost of goods sold. The allocation should be made in proportion to the direct labor charged to the three groups of jobs between January 1 and April 18. The direct labor charges were:

Sold jobs	$331,200
Finished but unsold jobs	76,800
Jobs in process	72,000
Total direct labor	$480,000

Required

To determine the April 18 inventories, set up T-accounts for the following accounts and enter the appropriate balances and postings based on the available information: Raw Materials Inventory, Goods in Process Inventory, Finished Goods Inventory, Factory Payroll, Cost of Goods Sold, and Factory Overhead.

ANSWERS TO PROGRESS CHECKS

19–1   *c*

19–2   The factors include: (*a*) increased demands by customers for higher quality products, custom-designed products, and faster delivery; (*b*) increased international competition; (*c*) improvements in computers.

19–3   Under TQM, all managers and employees should strive toward higher standards in their work and in the products and services they offer to customers.

19–4   *b*

19–5   A job is a special order for a unique product. A job lot consists of a quantity of identical items.

19–6   The revenue is usually recognized as the services are provided.

19–7   *a*

19–8   The three costs are direct materials, direct labor, and manufacturing overhead.

19–9   *c*

19–10   Materials ledger cards are perpetual inventory records showing the quantities and costs of each type of raw material on hand.

19–11   A clock card is the source document for payroll. A time ticket is the source document for the amount of time spent on each job or on indirect labor tasks.

19–12   The four sources are materials requisitions, time tickets, vouchers, and adjusting entries.

19–13   Because a job order cost accounting system uses perpetual inventory records, overhead costs must be assigned to jobs before the end of the period. This requires the use of a predetermined overhead application rate.

19–14   Debits are recorded when wages and salaries of factory employees are paid or accrued. Credits are recorded when direct labor costs are assigned to jobs and when indirect labor costs are transferred to the Factory Overhead account.

19–15   *c*

19–16   Overapplied or underapplied overhead exists at the end of the period because the application of overhead is based on estimates of overhead and another variable such as direct labor. Those estimates rarely, if ever, equal the actual amounts incurred.

19–17   A debit balance represents underapplied overhead.

Process Cost Accounting

The Boeing Company is the world leader in the commercial aerospace industry. Recently, Boeing launched several strategic initiatives to enhance its competitiveness. The company believes continuous improvement can be accomplished only if it identifies specific opportunities for improvement.

To help identify such opportunities, management decided that it needed to examine cost data based on an analysis of processes and activities. This required redesigning the accounting system so that the cost information would track the flow of resources in the processes at Boeing. Managers saw this as a necessary change if they were to confidently use accounting data as an aid in targeting and measuring Boeing's movement toward its goal of continuous quality improvement.

Boeing's Propulsion Systems Division, which produces the 737 engine, was chosen as a pilot test site for the Process and Activity Analysis project, their new process cost system. The four major objectives of the new process cost system were defined as follows:

1. The new system should provide increased cost visibility, specifically when work crossed organizational boundaries.

2. The new system should identify the major cost drivers to be analyzed and predict cost behavior.

3. The new system should improve the ability to trace overhead costs.

4. The system should identify activities that add value to the end product and activities that are nonvalue-added.

LEARNING OBJECTIVES

After studying Chapter 20, you should be able to:

1. **Explain the nature of process operations and how they differ from job order operations.**
2. **Describe the process of accumulating direct materials, direct labor, and manufacturing overhead costs according to each production process and prepare entries to record the flow of costs in a process cost accounting system.**
3. **Explain how equivalent units are used in process cost accounting systems and calculate the equivalent units produced during a period.**
4. **Describe the purposes served by and be able to prepare a process cost summary.**
5. **Define or explain the words and phrases listed in the chapter glossary.**

In Chapter 19, you learned about job order cost accounting systems. Companies use these systems to account for manufacturing when each product or job consists of one unit (or a group of units) that is uniquely designed to meet the requirements of a particular customer. In other words, each unit (or group of units) is a distinct product or job that requires unique applications of material, labor, and overhead. As we explained in Chapter 19, manufacturing operations of this nature are best served by a job order cost accounting system that maintains a separate accounting record for each job and accumulates costs by job.

Not all products are manufactured in this way; some have standard designs, and one unit of product is no different from any other unit. Typically, a large number of units are produced on a more or less continuous basis, period after period. In producing this kind of product, all units pass through the same series of manufacturing steps or processes. In this chapter, you will learn how to use a process cost accounting system to account for products like this. We explain how manufacturing costs are accumulated for each process and then assigned to the units that pass through the processes.

PROCESS MANUFACTURING OPERATIONS

LO 1

Explain the nature of process manufacturing operations and how they differ from job order operations.

Many companies produce large quantities of identical products. Examples of such products are carpeting, hand tools, personal computers, furniture, skis, television sets, compact disks, building supplies (lumber, doors, paint, etc.), greeting cards, calculators, and small pleasure boats. For example, **Dell Computer Corporation** uses a process cost accounting system for a portion of its operations.

Products like these are produced in manufacturing operations that pass the products through a series of *processes*, or steps in production. Each process involves a different set of activities. For example, a manufacturing operation that produces prefabricated doors might include these four processes:

1. Cutting the wood for the door and frame.
2. Planing and sanding the wood, and fabricating the door and frame from the wood components.
3. Mounting the hardware, including the hinges, latch, and knob, and assembling the finished door and the finished frame.
4. Packaging the completed unit for shipment.

Illustration 20–1   Job order and process manufacturing operations

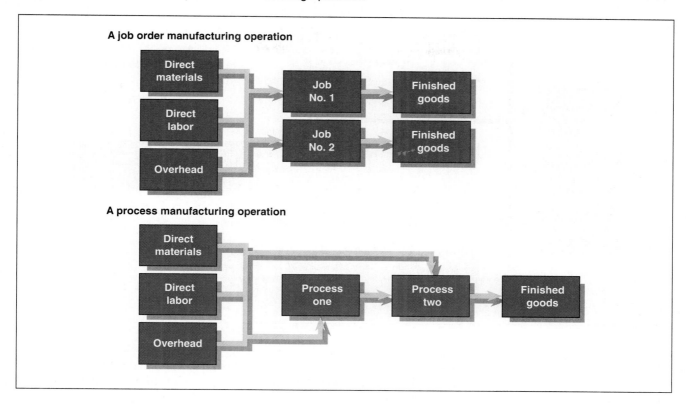

Comparing Process and Job Order Manufacturing Operations

Process and job order manufacturing operations are similar because they both combine materials, labor, and other manufacturing overhead items in the process of producing products. However, they differ in the way they are organized and managed.
Illustration 20–1 shows that direct materials, direct labor, and overhead are applied
to specific jobs in a job order operation. By comparison, a process manufacturing operation applies direct materials, direct labor, and overhead to specific manufacturing
processes. Thus, the focus of job order operations is on specific jobs while the focus
of process operations is on the series of processes used to complete the production of
the product.

FAST HINT
Additional Insight:
The manufacturing process for
prescription drugs includes: (1)
blending, (2) tablet making, (3)
tablet coating, and (4) packaging.

Organization of Process Manufacturing Operations

In a process manufacturing operation, each process is identified as a separate *production department, workstation,* or *work center.* Unlike a job order operation that
assigns each job to a manager, a process operation assigns responsibility for each
process to a manager. With the exception of the first department or process, each receives the output from the prior department as a partially processed product. Depending on the nature of the process, direct labor, manufacturing overhead, and, perhaps, additional direct materials are combined to move the product further toward
completion. Only the last department in the series produces finished goods ready for
sale to customers.

Most process manufacturing operations are more complex than the one shown in
Illustration 20–1. For example, Illustration 20–2 shows an operation in which components of a final product are manufactured in three parallel processes and then

Illustration 20-2   A Manufacturing Operation with Parallel and Sequential Processes

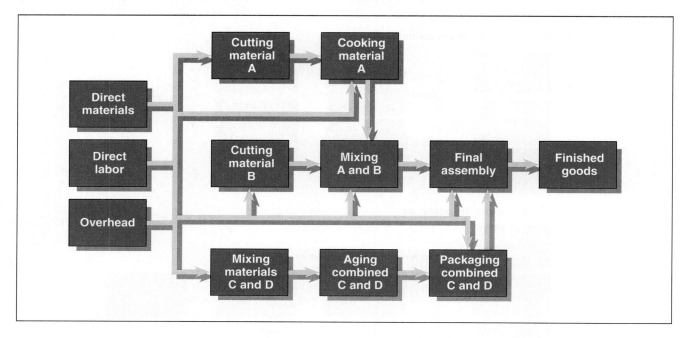

combined at different stages of production. Although this illustration may appear complex, many manufacturing operations involve hundreds of different components and related production processes.

Process Cost Accounting Systems for Service Companies

Many service companies also use process departments to perform specific tasks for consumers. For example, hospitals have radiology and physical therapy facilities with special equipment and trained employees. When patients need services, they are processed through the appropriate departments and receive the prescribed care. As another example, **AT&T Corporation** uses a system similar to process cost accounting to accumulate costs for services such as directory assistance.

Cost accounting information is needed by service providers as much as by manufacturers. Managers of service processes use information about the cost of providing services to plan future operations, to control costs, and to determine prices to charge customers. Although manufacturing operations are used in this chapter to illustrate process accounting systems, the basic techniques of process cost accounting may be applied equally well to service operations.

Delta Processing Company—A Comprehensive Case

To provide a basis for illustrating process cost accounting, consider Delta Processing Company. Delta produces a simple product called Noxall, an over-the-counter remedy for upset stomachs. Delta sells Noxall to wholesale distributors who in turn sell it to retailers. Noxall is produced in two steps. The first step uses a grinding process to pulverize large blocks of the active ingredient, called Noxalene. The second step

Illustration 20–3   Floor Plan of Delta Processing Company's Factory

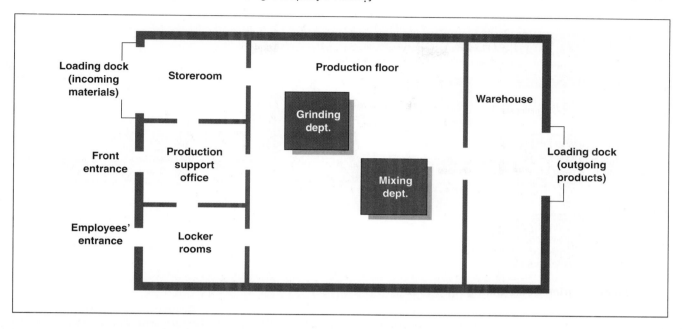

mixes this powder with flavorings and preservatives, and molds it into Noxall tablets. This process also puts the Noxall tablets into packages.

Illustration 20–3 shows a simplified floor plan of the Delta factory, which has five rooms:

- The *storeroom,* where materials are received and then distributed in response to requisitions.
- The *production support office,* which is used by administrative and maintenance employees who support manufacturing operations.
- The employees' *locker rooms,* where workers change from street clothes into uniforms before working in the factory.
- The *production floor,* which is divided into two areas for use by the grinding and mixing departments.
- The *warehouse,* where finished products are stored before being shipped to wholesalers.

Even though Delta Processing Company's product is relatively simple, the factory could have five or more managers, as shown in this diagram:

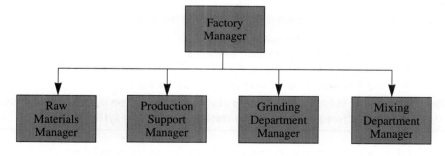

The first step in process manufacturing is the decision to produce a specific product. Management must determine the types and quantities of materials and labor needed and then schedule the work for the departments. Based on these plans, production begins.

Illustration 20–4   Process Manufacturing Operations—Delta Processing Company

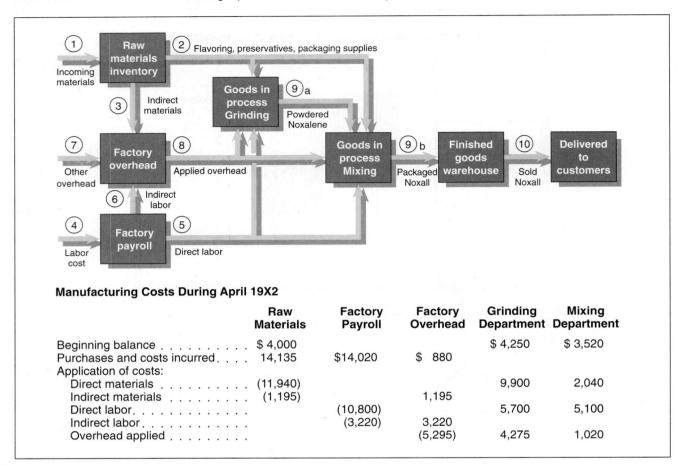

Manufacturing Costs During April 19X2

	Raw Materials	Factory Payroll	Factory Overhead	Grinding Department	Mixing Department
Beginning balance	$ 4,000			$ 4,250	$ 3,520
Purchases and costs incurred. . . .	14,135	$14,020	$ 880		
Application of costs:					
Direct materials	(11,940)			9,900	2,040
Indirect materials	(1,195)		1,195		
Direct labor.		(10,800)		5,700	5,100
Indirect labor.		(3,220)	3,220		
Overhead applied			(5,295)	4,275	1,020

The flowchart at the top of Illustration 20–4 shows the production steps for Delta Processing Company. The table at the bottom of the illustration summarizes Delta's manufacturing inventories at the beginning of April 19X2, the manufacturing costs Delta incurred during April, and the application of those costs to the grinding and mixing departments. In the following sections, we explain how Delta uses a process cost accounting system to account for these costs.

Progress Check

(Answers to Progress Checks are provided at the end of the chapter.)

20–1   **A process manufacturing operation:**
   a. **Is another name for a job order operation.**
   b. **Does not use the concepts of direct materials or direct labor.**
   c. **Assigns responsibility for each process to a manager.**

20–2   **Under what conditions is a process cost accounting system more suitable for measuring manufacturing costs than a job order cost accounting system?**

ACCUMULATING THE COSTS OF EACH MANUFACTURING PROCESS

In a job order operation, managers are responsible for planning and controlling the costs of manufacturing each job. To provide managers with relevant cost information, a job order cost accounting system accumulates the costs of each job on a separate job cost sheet. By comparison, managers in a process operation are responsible for planning and controlling the costs of each process. Thus, a **process cost accounting system** accumulates the manufacturing costs of each process. Then, the cost per unit is determined by dividing the total cost assigned to a process by the number of units that passed through the process. You learn more about calculating unit costs later in the chapter.

Direct and Indirect Costs in Process Cost Accounting

In Chapter 18, you learned that direct material and direct labor costs can be clearly associated with specific units or batches of product. Other manufacturing costs that cannot be clearly associated with specific units or batches of product are defined as manufacturing overhead. Chapter 19 explained how the concepts of direct and indirect materials and labor are used in job order cost accounting. In summary, materials and labor used on jobs are charged to the jobs as direct costs. Materials and labor that contribute to manufacturing but that are not clearly associated with specific jobs are indirect costs and are allocated to jobs as manufacturing overhead.

Process cost accounting systems also use the concepts of direct and indirect manufacturing costs. Materials and labor that are clearly associated with specific manufacturing processes are assigned to those processes as direct costs. Materials and labor that are not clearly associated with a specific process are indirect costs and are assigned to overhead.[1]

Accounting for Materials Costs

In Illustration 20–4, arrow 1 represents the arrival of materials at Delta Processing Company's factory. These materials include Noxalene, flavorings, preservatives, packaging supplies, and supplies for the production support office. Assuming that Delta uses a perpetual inventory system and makes all purchases on credit, this entry summarizes the receipts of raw materials during April:

1	Raw Materials Inventory	14,135.00	
	Accounts Payable		14,135.00
	Acquired materials on credit for use in the factory.		

The accounting department makes entries to record the receipt of materials when it receives copies of receiving reports from the storeroom.

Arrow 2 in Illustration 20–4 represents the flow of direct materials to the grinding and mixing departments, where they are used in producing Noxall. Most direct materials are physically incorporated into the finished product. However, in process cost accounting, direct materials include supplies used in a specific process because they can be clearly associated with that process.

As in a job order system, the manager of a process usually obtains material for use in the process by submitting a materials requisition to the raw materials storeroom manager. However, in some situations, materials move continuously from the raw materials inventory to a manufacturing process. For example, **Coca-Cola Bottling Co. Consolidated** uses a manufacturing process in which inventory moves through the system continuously. In these cases, a **materials consumption**

LO 2
Describe the process of accumulating direct materials, direct labor, and manufacturing overhead costs according to each production process and prepare entries to record the flow of costs in a process cost accounting system.

FAST HINT
Important Point to Remember:
Manufacturing companies typically use perpetual inventories for raw materials. The differences between accounting for perpetual and periodic inventory methods for manufacturers were discussed in Chapters 18 and 19.

FAST HINT
Critical Thought Question:
What types of supplies might be treated as direct materials costs?

FAST HINT
Critical Thought Question:
What are other examples of production processes in which inventory moves through the system continuously?

[1]Some cost classified as manufacturing overhead in a job order system may be classified as direct costs in process cost accounting. For example, depreciation on a machine used entirely by one process is a direct cost of that process. In this introductory discussion, however, all manufacturing costs other than direct materials and direct labor are treated as overhead.

report summarizes the materials used by a department during a reporting period and replaces materials requisitions.

The following entry records the use of direct materials by Delta Processing Company's two production departments during April:

2	Goods in Process Inventory—Grinding	9,900.00	
	Goods in Process Inventory—Mixing	2,040.00	
	Raw Materials Inventory		11,940.00
	To assign costs of direct materials used in the		
	grinding and mixing departments.		

Two goods in process inventory accounts allow the costs incurred by each process to be separately accumulated. Note that the entry does not increase or decrease the company's assets because it merely transfers costs from one asset account to two other asset accounts.

In Illustration 20–4, arrow 3 shows the flow of indirect materials from the storeroom to factory overhead. These materials are not clearly associated with either the grinding or the mixing departments. They are used in support of production. The production support office is called a **service department** because its activities are not directly involved in manufacturing products. By comparison, the grinding and mixing departments are called **production departments** because they produce the products.

The following entry records the cost of indirect materials used by Delta during April:

3	Factory Overhead	1,195.00	
	Raw Materials Inventory		1,195.00
	To record indirect materials used in April.		

After the entries for materials are posted, the Raw Materials Inventory account looks like this:

Raw Materials Inventory   **Account No.** 132

Date		Explanation	Debit	Credit	Balance
19X2					
Mar.	31	Beginning balance			4,000
Apr.	30	Materials purchases	14,135		18,135
	30	Direct materials usage		11,940	6,195
	30	Indirect materials usage		1,195	5,000

The April 30 balance sheet presents the balance of this account as a current asset.

Accounting for Labor Costs

Illustration 20–4 represents the factory payroll cost for Delta Processing Company with arrow 4. The total labor cost of $14,020 is paid with cash and is recorded in the Factory Payroll account with this entry:

4	Factory Payroll	14,020.00	
	Cash		14,020.00
	To record factory wages for April.		

FAST HINT
Critical Thought Question:
What types of materials might the flow of arrow 3 in Illustration 20–4 represent?
Answer: Goggles, gloves, other protective clothing, record-keeping supplies, etc.

This entry is triggered by time reports sent to the company's accountant from the two production departments and the production support office. (For simplicity, we have not identified withholdings and additional payroll taxes for the employees.)

In a process operation, the direct labor of a production department includes all labor used exclusively by that department, even if it is not applied to the product itself. For example, if a production department has a full-time manager and a full-time maintenance worker, their salaries are direct labor costs, not factory overhead.

Arrow 5 in Illustration 20–4 shows Delta's use of direct labor in the grinding and mixing departments. The following entry transfers April's direct labor costs from the Factory Payroll account to the two goods in process accounts:

5	Goods in Process Inventory—Grinding	5,700.00	
	Goods in Process Inventory—Mixing	5,100.00	
	Factory Payroll		10,800.00
	To assign costs of direct labor used in the grinding and mixing departments.		

Arrow 6 in Illustration 20–4 represents the indirect labor of Delta Processing Company. These employees provide the clerical, maintenance, and other services that help the grinding and mixing departments produce Noxall more efficiently. For example, they order materials, deliver them to the factory floor, repair equipment, operate and program computers used in production, keep payroll and other production accounting records, clean up, and move the finished goods to the warehouse. The following entry charges these indirect labor costs to factory overhead:

FAST HINT
Important Point to Remember:
A departments' indirect labor cost might include an allocated portion of the salary of a production manager who supervises two departments. Allocation of costs between departments is discussed in Chapter 21.

6	Factory Overhead	3,220.00	
	Factory Payroll		3,220.00
	To record indirect labor as overhead.		

After these entries for labor are posted, the Factory Payroll account looks like this:

Factory Payroll				Account No. 530
Date	Explanation	Debit	Credit	Balance
19X2				
Mar. 31	Beginning balance			–0–
Apr. 30	Total payroll for April	14,020		14,020
30	Direct labor costs		10,800	3,220
30	Indirect labor costs		3,220	–0–

This account is now closed and ready to receive entries for May.

FAST HINT
Critical Thought Question:
Should the factory payroll account normally have a zero balance at the end of an accounting period? Explain your answer.

Accounting for Factory Overhead

Overhead costs other than indirect materials and indirect labor are represented by arrow 7 in Illustration 20–4. These overhead items include the costs of insuring manufacturing assets, renting the factory building, using factory utilities, and depreciating the equipment. The following entry records these costs for the month of April:

FAST HINT
Relevant Exercise:
To apply these concepts, work Exercises 20–1 and 20–2.

7	Factory Overhead	880.00	
	Prepaid Insurance		80.00
	Accrued Utilities Payable		200.00
	Cash		250.00
	Accumulated Depreciation, Factory Equipment		350.00
	To record manufacturing overhead items incurred during April.		

After this entry is posted, the Factory Overhead account balance is $5,295. This total overhead cost for April includes indirect materials of $1,195, indirect labor of $3,220, and $880 of other overhead items.

Arrow 8 in Illustration 20–4 represents the application of factory overhead to the

production departments. Recall from Chapters 18 and 19 that factory overhead is applied to products or jobs by relating the overhead cost to another variable such as direct labor hours or machine hours used in production. Process cost systems also use predetermined application rates. For example, recall the discussion of the **Boeing Company** at the beginning of the chapter. Boeing chose total labor hours as the basis for allocating overhead costs to products.

In many situations, a single allocation basis (like direct labor hours) fails to provide useful allocations. As a result, management may use different rates for different production departments. For example, based on an analysis of each department's operations, Delta Processing Company applies overhead as follows:

	Predetermined Overhead Application Rate
Grinding department	75% of its direct labor cost
Mixing department	20% of its direct labor cost

The results of multiplying April's direct labor costs by these rates are:

Production Department	Direct Labor Cost	Predetermined Rate	Overhead Applied
Grinding	$5,700	75%	$4,275
Mixing	5,100	20	1,020
Total			$5,295

FAST HINT
Alternative Example:
If the grinding department uses a 70% application rate, what balance would remain in the factory overhead account after overhead has been applied to both departments?
Answer:
Overhead costs	$5,295
Overhead applied	5,010
Underapplied overhead	$ 285

Delta records these overhead applications with the following entry:

8	Goods in Process Inventory—Grinding	4,275.00	
	Goods in Process Inventory—Mixing	1,020.00	
	Factory Overhead		5,295.00
	Allocated factory overhead costs to the grinding department at 75% of direct labor cost and to the mixing department at 20% of direct labor cost.		

After posting this entry, the Factory Overhead account looks like this:

Factory Overhead				Account No. 540
Date	Explanation	Debit	Credit	Balance
19X2				
Mar. 31	Beginning balance			–0–
Apr. 30	Indirect materials	1,195		1,195
30	Indirect labor costs	3,220		4,415
30	Other overhead costs	880		5,295
30	Applied to production depts.		5,295	–0–

FAST HINT
Alternative Example:
If the calculation of applied overhead resulted in a $5,400 credit to the factory overhead account, would the account balance represent an over- or underapplied amount?
Answer: $105 overapplied

To simplify the Delta Processing Company example, the amount of overhead applied exactly equals the actual overhead incurred during April. In actual practice, however, using a predetermined overhead application rate almost certainly leaves an overapplied or underapplied balance in the Factory Overhead account. At the end of the period, this overapplied or underapplied balance should be allocated among the cost of goods sold and the goods in process and finished goods inventories. The procedures for making this allocation are the same as the ones used in Chapter 19 for job order cost accounting systems.

Progress Check

20-3   When Department X sends partially completed units to Department Y, the entry that records the transfer includes:
    a. A debit to Goods in Process Inventory—Department X.
    b. A debit to Goods in Process Inventory—Department Y.
    c. A credit to Goods in Process Inventory—Department Y.

20-4   What are the three catagories of cost incurred by both job order and process manufacturing operations?

20-5   How many Goods in Process Inventory accounts are needed in a process cost accounting system?

In the previous sections, we explained how the manufacturing costs for a period are accumulated in separate Goods in Process accounts for each manufacturing process. However, note that we have not explained the flows labeled 9_a, 9_b, and 10 in Illustration 20–4. These arrows represent the transfer of products from the grinding department to the mixing department, from the mixing department to finished goods inventory, and from finished goods inventory to cost of goods sold. To determine the costs that should be recorded for these flows, you must first determine the cost per unit of product and then apply this result to the number of units transferred.

Accounting for Beginning and Ending Goods in Process Inventories

If a manufacturing process does not have any beginning or ending goods in process inventory, the unit cost calculation is simple. The unit cost of goods transferred out of a process is:

$$\frac{\text{Total cost assigned to the process}}{\text{Total number of units started and finished during the period}}$$

CALCULATING AND USING EQUIVALENT UNITS OF PRODUCTION

LO 3

Explain how equivalent units are used in process cost accounting systems and calculate the equivalent units produced during a period.

However, if a process has a beginning or ending inventory of partially processed units, the cost assigned to the process should be allocated to all units that were worked on during the period. In other words, the denominator must be a measure of the entire production activity of the process during the period. This measure is called the **equivalent units of production.** Equivalent units of production measure the activity of a process as the number of units that would have been completed if all effort during a period had been applied to units that were started and finished.

Equivalent Units for Materials May Not Be the Same as for Direct Labor and Overhead

In many manufacturing processes, the equivalent units of production for materials is not the same as it is for labor and overhead. To see why this is true, consider the following manufacturing process:

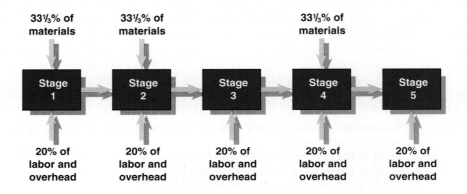

FAST HINT
Critical Thought Question:
Can you give an example of a manufacturing process in which materials are added at different stages of the production process?

This diagram shows a single production process that consists of five stages. One-third of the direct material cost is added at each of three stages 1, 2, and 4. One-fifth of the direct labor cost is added at each of the five stages. Because overhead is applied as a percentage of direct labor, one-fifth of the overhead also is added at each of the five stages.

If units have gone through Stage 1, they are one-third complete with respect to materials but only one-fifth complete with respect to labor and overhead. If they have gone through Stage 2, they are two-thirds complete with respect to materials, but only two-fifths complete with respect to labor and overhead. If they have gone through Stage 3, they are still two-thirds complete with respect to materials, but three-fifths complete with respect to labor and overhead. And, if they are through Stage 4, they are 100% complete with respect to materials but only four-fifths complete with respect to labor and overhead.

Assume that 300 units of product were started and processed through Stage 1 during a month. At the end of the month, they are one-third complete *with respect to materials.* Expressed in terms of equivalent finished units, the processing of these 300 units is equivalent to finishing 100 units; that is, $300 \times 33\frac{1}{3}\% = 100$.

Although the processing of the 300 units equals 100 equivalent units of production with respect to materials, only one-fifth of the direct labor and overhead were added to the 300 units at the end of Stage 1. Therefore, the equivalent units of production *with respect to direct labor and overhead* equals $300 \times 20\% = 60$ units.

The following table shows the information needed to calculate equivalent units of production for Delta's grinding department:

Beginning inventory:	
Units of product	30,000
Percentage of completion—direct materials . .	100%
Percentage of completion—direct labor	33⅓%
Units started during April	90,000
Units transferred from grinding to mixing	100,000
Ending inventory:	
Units of product	20,000
Percentage of completion—direct materials . .	100%
Percentage of completion—direct labor	25%

ACCOUNTING FOR DELTA PROCESSING COMPANY'S GRINDING DEPARTMENT

In calculating equivalent units, we assume that each of Delta's production departments process units on a first-in, first-out basis.[2] Thus, the 100,000 units transferred from grinding to mixing during April include the 30,000 units from the beginning inventory. The remaining 70,000 units transferred out were started during April. In the preceding table, note that a total of 90,000 units were started during April. Because 70,000 of these units were completed, 20,000 units remain unfinished at the end of the month.

Equivalent Units of Production and Cost Per Unit —Direct Materials

In the grinding department, all materials (the Noxalene blocks) are added at the beginning of the process. That is, a unit of product is 100% complete with respect to materials as soon as it is started. Therefore, the beginning goods in process inventory for April received all its materials in March and should not be assigned any additional materials cost. The units started and completed during April and the April 30 goods in process inventory received all their materials during April. Thus, with respect to materials, the grinding department's equivalent units of production are calculated as follows:

FAST HINT
Relevant Quick Study:
To apply these concepts, work QS 20–2.

GRINDING—Equivalent Units of Production (Direct Materials)

	Units of Product	Percent Added	Equivalent Units
Beginning goods in process	30,000	0%	–0–
Goods started and completed	70,000	100	70,000
Ending goods in process	20,000	100	20,000
Total units	120,000		90,000

The table in Illustration 20–4 on page 766 shows that the total direct materials cost for the grinding department was $9,900. Thus, the direct materials cost per equivalent unit is $0.11 ($9,900/90,000 units).

---

[2]We assume a FIFO flow throughout the calculations of this chapter. Weighted-average and LIFO can be used but they are less useful for measuring how effectively costs were controlled during a period.

Illustration 20-5   Use of Direct Labor during April—Grinding Department

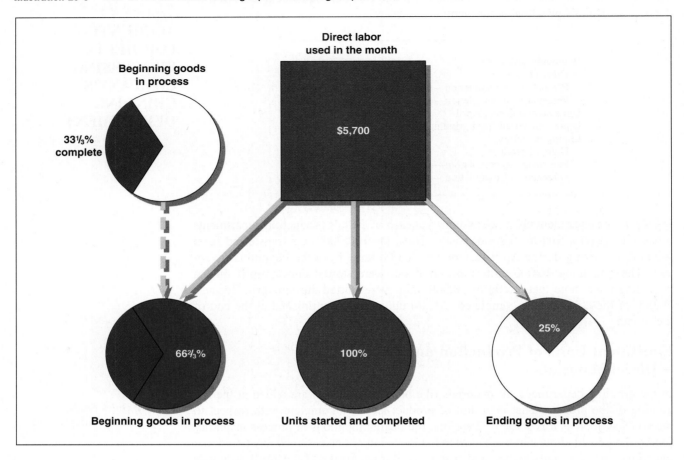

Equivalent Units of Production and Cost Per Unit— Direct Labor

Recall from Illustration 20–4 that Delta's grinding department incurred $5,700 of direct labor cost during April. In Illustration 20–5, the square represents this direct labor activity. The illustration shows how the direct labor was applied to three different groups of products.

Part of the direct labor was used to finish the beginning goods in process. In the diagram, the white portion of the upper left circle represents the unfinished portion of the 30,000 units in the beginning goods in process inventory. The lower circle on the left shows that this portion was completed during April. Direct labor also was applied to 70,000 units that were started and completed during April. In addition, the rest of the direct labor was used to start work on the 20,000 units that remain unfinished in the April 30 goods in process inventory. In Illustration 20–5, the shaded portion of the lower right circle represents the fact that they are only 25% complete.

The grinding department's total direct labor cost of $5,700 must be allocated among all units worked on during April. Therefore, we must calculate direct labor cost per unit based on the department's equivalent units of production. The following table summarizes the calculation:

GRINDING—Equivalent Units of Production (Direct Labor)

	Units of Product	Percent Added	Equivalent Units
Beginning goods in process	30,000	66⅔%	20,000
Goods started and completed	70,000	100	70,000
Ending goods in process	20,000	25	5,000
Total units	120,000		95,000

FAST HINT
Alternative Excercise:
If the ending goods in process were 20% complete, what would the equivalent units for labor and overhead be?
Answer: 94,000 units

FAST HINT
Relevant Excercise:
To apply these concepts, work Exercise 20–5.

Note that the direct labor used to finish the beginning inventory was equivalent to the labor that would be used to start and finish 20,000 units. An additional 70,000 units were started and completed during the month. Finally, the work performed on the 20,000 units in the ending inventory was equivalent to starting and finishing 5,000 units. Total equivalent units of production with respect to direct labor is 95,000 units. Because the total direct labor cost was $5,700, the cost per equivalent unit was $0.06 ($5,700/95,000).

Equivalent Units of Production and Cost Per Unit—Overhead

Earlier, we explained that Delta assigns overhead to the grinding department at the rate of 75% of the direct labor cost. As a result, the total overhead applied to the department was $4,275 ($5,700 × 75%). Because overhead is assigned on the basis of direct labor cost, the equivalent units of production is the same for overhead as for direct labor. Therefore, the overhead cost per unit is $0.045 ($4,275/95,000).

Progress Check

20-6 Equivalent units are:
　a. A measure of a production department's productivity in using direct materials, direct labor, or overhead.
　b. Units of a product produced by a foreign competitor that are similar to units produced by a domestic company.
　c. Generic units of a product similar to brand-name units of a product.

20-7 What is the meaning of a department's equivalent units of production with respect to direct labor?

20-8 A department began an accounting period with 8,000 units that were one-fourth complete, started and completed 50,000 units, and ended with 6,000 units that were one-third complete. How many equivalent units did it produce during the period?

Process Cost Summary—Grinding Department

The primary managerial accounting report for a process cost accounting system is the **process cost summary.** A separate process cost summary is prepared for each process or production department. The three primary purposes of the report are: *(a)* to help managers control their departments; *(b)* to help factory managers evaluate department managers' performance; and *(c)* to provide cost information for the financial statements. A process cost summary accomplishes these purposes by describing the costs charged to the department, the equivalent units of production achieved by the department, and the costs assigned to the output.

Illustration 20–6 shows the Delta grinding department's process cost summary for April. Notice that the summary is divided into three sections. Section 1 summarizes the total costs charged to the department, including the direct materials, direct labor, and overhead costs incurred plus the cost of the beginning goods in process inventory.

LO 4

Describe the purposes served by and be able to prepare a process cost summary.

Illustration 20–6

DELTA PROCESSING COMPANY
Process Cost Summary for the Grinding Department
For Month Ended April 30, 19X2

1

Costs Charged to the Department

Direct materials requisitioned	$ 9,900
Direct labor charged	5,700
Overhead allocated (at predetermined rate)	4,275
Total processing costs for the month	$19,875
Goods in process at the beginning of the month	4,250
Total costs to be accounted for	$24,125

2

Equivalent Unit Processing Costs

	Equivalent Units		
	Units of Product	Direct Materials	Labor and Overhead
Units processed:			
Beginning goods in process	30,000	–0–	20,000
Units started and completed	70,000	70,000	70,000
Ending goods in process	20,000	20,000	5,000
Total	120,000	90,000	95,000

Total direct materials cost for April	$9,900
Direct materials cost per equivalent unit ($9,900/90,000 units)	$0.110
Total direct labor cost for April	$5,700
Direct labor cost per equivalent unit ($5,700/95,000 units)	$0.060
Total overhead cost for April	$4,275
Overhead cost per equivalent unit ($4,275/95,000 units)	$0.045

3

Assignment of Costs to the Output of the Department

	Equivalent Units	Cost per Unit	Total Cost
Goods in process, March 31, 19X2, and completed during April:			
Costs from prior month			$ 4,250
Direct materials added (none)			–0–
Direct labor added	20,000	$0.060	1,200
Overhead applied	20,000	$0.045	900
Total costs to process			$ 6,350
Goods started and completed during April:			
Direct materials added	70,000	$0.110	$ 7,700
Direct labor added	70,000	$0.060	4,200
Overhead applied	70,000	$0.045	3,150
Total costs to process			$15,050
Total costs transferred to mixing department (unit cost = $21,400/100,000 units 5 $0.214)			$21,400
Goods in process, April 30, 19X2:			
Direct materials added	20,000	$0.110	$ 2,200
Direct labor added	5,000	$0.060	300
Overhead applied	5,000	$0.045	225
Total costs to process			$ 2,725
Total costs accounted for			$24,125

Section 2 describes the equivalent units of production achieved by the department. Equivalent units for materials and equivalent units for direct labor and overhead appear in separate columns. Section 2 also calculates the direct materials, direct labor, and overhead costs per equivalent unit.

Section 3 allocates the total costs among the products worked on during the month. Note that the costs of finishing the beginning inventory units are calculated and then added to the cost carried forward from March to get a total processing cost of $6,350 for the beginning inventory units. Next, the costs of processing 70,000 units from start to finish are calculated and added to get a total processing cost of $15,050. The $6,350 and the $15,050 are then added to determine the $21,400 total cost of goods transferred out of the department.

The next portion of section 3 calculates the $2,725 cost of partially processing the ending inventory units. Finally, all the assigned costs are added to show that the total $24,125 cost charged to the department in section 1 has been assigned to units in section 3.

FAST HINT
Critical Thought Question:
Refer to Illustration 20–6. In section 2, what is the sum of the direct material, direct labor, and overhead costs per equivalent unit for work performed in April? Why is this different from the unit cost shown in section 3 for units transferred to the next department?

FAST HINT
Relevant Excercise:
To apply these concepts, work Excercise 20–9.

Progress Check

20-9   A process cost summary for a department has three sections. What information is presented in each of them?

Transferring Goods between Departments

Arrow 9_a in Illustration 20–4 on page 766 represents the transfer of units (powdered Noxalene) from the grinding department to the mixing department. The $21,400 cost of this transfer, as calculated in section 3 of the process cost summary, is recorded with the following entry:

LO 2
Describe the process of accumulating direct materials, direct labor, and manufacturing overhead costs according to each production process and prepare entries to record the flow of costs in a process cost accounting system.

9_a.		Goods in Process Inventory—Mixing	21,400.00	
		Goods in Process Inventory—Grinding		21,400.00
		To record the transfer of partially completed goods from the grinding department to the mixing department.		

After this entry is posted, the Goods in Process Inventory account for the grinding department appears as follows:

FAST HINT
Important Point to Remember:
The balance in the general ledger Goods in Process Inventory account at the end of an accounting period should be equal to the balance shown on the Process Cost Summary for the same time period.

Goods in Process Inventory—Grinding				Account No. 133
Date	**Explanation**	**Debit**	**Credit**	**Balance**
19X2				
Mar. 31	Beginning balance			4,250
Apr. 30	Direct materials	9,900		14,150
30	Direct labor costs	5,700		19,850
30	Applied overhead	4,275		24,125
30	Transfer to mixing department		21,400	2,725

Notice that the $2,725 ending balance equals the cost assigned to these partially completed units in section 3 of the process cost summary in Illustration 20–6.

Progress Check

20-10   What effect does the transfer of a partially completed product from one production
        department to another have on the total assets of the company?

**ACCOUNTING
FOR DELTA
PROCESSING
COMPANY'S
MIXING
DEPARTMENT**

LO 3

Explain how equivalent units
are used in process cost accounting systems and calculate
the equivalent units produced
during a period.

The mixing department starts working on the Noxalene as soon as it is received from
the grinding department. Then, it gradually adds direct materials in the form of fla-
voring, preservatives, and packaging supplies. Direct labor and overhead are added at
the same rate as direct materials.

Equivalent Units of Production—Mixing Department

In the grinding department, the equivalent units of production for direct labor and
overhead were not the same as for direct materials. However, the mixing department
requires only one calculation of equivalent units of production because direct materials, direct labor, and overhead are all used at the same rate. The following table provides the data needed to calculate equivalent units of production:

Beginning inventory:	
Units of product	16,000
Percentage of completion—Direct materials, direct labor, and overhead . .	25%
Units received from grinding department	100,000
Units transferred to finished goods	101,000
Ending inventory:	
Units of product	15,000
Percentage of completion—Direct materials, direct labor, and overhead . .	33⅓%

Note that 101,000 units were transferred to finished goods during April. Based on
a first-in, first-out assumption, 16,000 of these units came from the beginning goods
in process inventory and 85,000 were started and completed during the period. Because 100,000 units were received from the grinding department during April and
85,000 of those units were completed, the ending goods in process inventory contains
15,000 units. The following table calculates the department's equivalent units of production during April:

**MIXING—Equivalent Units of Production (Direct Materials, Direct
Labor, and Overhead)**

	Units of Product	Percent Added	Equivalent Units
Beginning goods in process	16,000	75%	12,000
Goods started and completed	85,000	100	85,000
Ending goods in process	15,000	33⅓	5,000
Total units	116,000		102,000

Process Cost Summary—Mixing Department

LO 4

Describe the purposes served by
and be able to prepare a process
cost summary.

Illustration 20–7 shows the process cost summary for the mixing department. Notice
that the costs charged to the department in section 1 include $21,400 transferred in
from the grinding department. Section 2 shows the equivalent units of production for
the direct materials, direct labor, and overhead added by the mixing department. Section 2 also calculates the costs per equivalent unit added during the mixing process.

Illustration 20-7

DELTA PROCESSING COMPANY
Process Cost Summary for the Mixing Department
For Month Ended April 30, 19X2

1

Costs Charged to the Department

Direct materials requisitioned	$ 2,040
Direct labor charged	5,100
Overhead allocated (at predetermined rate)	1,020
Total processing costs for the month	$ 8,160
Goods in process at the beginning of the month	3,520
Costs transferred in from the grinding department (100,000 units at $0.214 each)	21,400
Total costs to be accounted for	$33,080

2

Equivalent Unit Processing Costs

	Units of Product	Equivalent Units of Production
Units processed:		
Beginning goods in process	16,000	12,000
Units started and completed	85,000	85,000
Ending goods in process	15,000	5,000
Total	116,000	102,000

Total direct materials cost for April	$ 2,040
Direct materials cost per equivalent unit ($2,040/102,000 units)	$ 0.020
Total direct labor cost for April	$ 5,100
Labor cost per equivalent unit ($5,100/102,000 units)	$ 0.050
Total overhead cost for April	$ 1,020
Overhead cost per equivalent unit ($1,020/102,000 units)	$ 0.010

3

Assignment of Costs to the Output of the Department

	Equivalent Units	Cost per Unit	Total Cost
Goods in process, March 31, 19X2, and completed during April:			
Costs from prior month			$ 3,520
Direct materials added	12,000	$0.020	240
Direct labor added	12,000	$0.050	600
Overhead applied	12,000	$0.010	120
Total costs to process			$ 4,480
Goods started and completed during April:			
Costs transferred in (85,000 × $0.214)			$18,190
Direct materials added	85,000	$0.020	1,700
Direct labor added	85,000	$0.050	4,250
Overhead applied	85,000	$0.010	850
Total costs to process			$24,990
Total costs transferred to finished goods			
(unit cost 5 $29,470/101,000 units = $0.2918)			$29,470
Goods in process, April 30, 19X2:			
Costs transferred in (15,000 × $0.214)			$ 3,210
Direct materials added	5,000	$0.020	100
Direct labor added	5,000	$0.050	250
Overhead applied	5,000	$0.010	50
Total costs to process			$ 3,610
Total costs accounted for			$33,080

Section 3 shows how the costs charged to the department are assigned to the output of the department. The $29,470 cost of the units transferred to finished goods is cal-culated as the combined cost of the beginning units in process and the started and completed units.

Because all Noxalene received from the grinding department enters production at the beginning of the mixing process, the beginning goods in process inventory is 100% complete with respect to Noxalene. None of the Noxalene transferred in during April was used to finish the beginning inventory units. Therefore, the $21,400 cost trans-ferred in during April relates to the 100,000 units that the mixing department started to process during April. In section 3 of Illustration 20–7, notice that $18,190 of the $21,400 was assigned to the 85,000 units started and finished during April (85,000 × $0.214). The remaining $3,210 was assigned to the 15,000 units in the ending in-ventory (15,000 × $0.214).

Progress Check

20-11   The waxing department's total processing costs for a month were $262,500. To com-plete its beginning goods in process, the department added 20,000 equivalent units of materials, labor, and overhead. The department started and completed 70,000 units during the month and had 15,000 equivalent units remaining in process at the end of the month. Costs transferred in from the sanding department during the month totaled $300,000, of which 25% related to units the waxing department did not finish during the period. On the waxing department's process cost summary, what should be reported as the total costs to process the goods started and completed?

TRANSFERRING COSTS TO FINISHED GOODS INVENTORY AND TO COST OF GOODS SOLD

LO 2

Describe the process of accumu-lating direct materials, direct la-bor, and manufacturing over-head costs according to each production process and prepare entries to record the flow of costs in a processing cost ac-counting system.

Arrow 9$_b$ in Illustration 20–4 on page 766 represents the transfer of finished products from the mixing department to the Finished Goods Inventory. The process cost sum-mary for the mixing department shows that 101,000 units of packaged Noxall were assigned a cost of $29,470. The following entry records the transfer:

9$_b$.	Finished Goods Inventory	29,470.00	
	Goods in Process Inventory—Mixing		29,470.00
	To record the transfer of completed units of Noxall out of production.		

After this entry is posted, the mixing department's Goods in Process Inventory ac-count appears as follows:

Goods in Process Inventory—Mixing				Account No. 134	
Date		Explanation	Debit	Credit	Balance
19X2					
Mar.	31	Beginning balance			3,520
Apr.	30	Direct materials	2,040		5,560
	30	Direct labor costs	5,100		10,660
	30	Applied overhead	1,020		11,680
	30	Transfer from grinding department	21,400		33,080
	30	Transfer to warehouse		29,470	3,610

The ending balance equals the cost assigned to the partially completed units in section 3 of Illustration 20–7.

Assume that Delta Processing Company sold 106,000 units of Noxall during April. The beginning inventory of finished goods consisted of 23,000 units with a cost of $6,440. The remaining 83,000 units sold came from the 101,000 that were completed during April. Thus, the ending finished goods inventory amounted to 18,000 units. Notice in section 3 of Illustration 20–7 that the total manufacturing cost per unit finished during April was $0.2918 ($29,470/101,000). Thus, cost of goods sold during April was:

23,000 units from the beginning inventory	$ 6,440
83,000 units manufactured during April (83,000 × $0.2918) . .	24,219
Total cost of goods sold	$30,659

The following entry records the cost of goods sold for the month:

10		Cost of Goods Sold	30,659.00	
		Finished Goods Inventory		30,659.00
		To record cost of goods sold during April.		

After this entry is posted, the Finished Goods Inventory account appears as follows:

	Finished Goods Inventory			**Account No.** 135
Date	**Explanation**	**Debit**	**Credit**	**Balance**
19X2				
Mar. 31	Beginning balance			6,440
Apr. 30	Transfer from mixing department	29,470		35,910
30	Cost of goods sold		30,659	5,251

Summary of Delta Processing Company's Manufacturing Cost Flows

Illustration 20–8 summarizes the flows of Delta Processing Company's manufacturing costs during April. Previous sections of the chapter explained each of these flows and showed the entries to record them. The flow of costs through the accounts reflects the flow of manufacturing activities and products in the factory.

You learned about several new production management concepts in Chapter 19. Adopting these concepts brings about changes in some process manufacturing operations. For example, management concerns with throughput and just-in-time manufacturing have caused boundary lines between departments to become less distinct. In some cases, higher quality and better efficiency are obtained by reorganizing the production processes. For example, instead of producing both doors and cabinets in a series of departments, a separate work center for each product may be established within one department. When this rearrangement occurs, the process cost accounting system must be modified to accumulate the costs of each work center.

When a company adopts just-in-time (JIT) manufacturing techniques, the

NEW PRODUCTION MANAGEMENT CONCEPTS AND PROCESS MANUFACTURING SYSTEMS

Illustration 20-8 Flows of Costs through Delta Processing Company for April 19X2

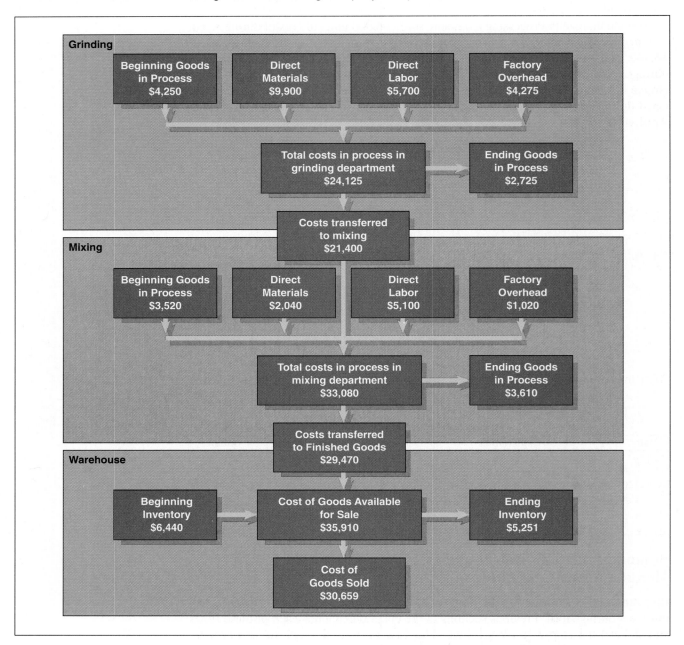

inventories described in this chapter may virtually disappear. For example, if raw materials are not ordered or received until they are needed, a Raw Materials Inventory account may not be necessary. Instead, the materials cost is immediately debited to the Goods in Process Inventory account. Similarly, a Finished Goods Inventory account may not be needed. Instead, the cost of the finished goods can be debited directly to the Cost of Goods Sold account instead of the Finished Goods Inventory account.

When a company uses the theory of constraints to increase throughput, the cost accounting system should help the managers locate bottlenecks. For example, the presence of a bottleneck may be signaled by the existence of large upstream or downstream inventories. Based on their analysis of inventories, managers may be able to pinpoint the bottleneck and manage it to improve efficiency.

In Chapter 21, you will learn about *activity-based costing*, which uses several factors to allocate overhead. The **Boeing Company's** new cost system, described at the beginning of the chapter, was based on process and activity analysis. Each process was analyzed to determine the various activities or tasks that were necessary to complete the process. Then, costs were assigned based on the total labor dollars needed to perform each task. Total costs needed for each task were projected  based on how many times the task needed to be performed and tasks were ranked from highest cost to lowest. High-cost activities often provided the best opportunities for process improvements.

In many manufacturing operations, activity-based costing is used because direct labor is not a meaningful basis for allocating costs. For example, automated factories often reduce the amount of direct labor to less than 10% of a product's total cost. When direct labor cost is this small, it is not likely to be closely correlated with overhead. Therefore, allocations of overhead based on direct labor cost are not useful in these circumstances. Instead, other factors lead to more useful information.

Progress Check

20-12   A company successfully uses just-in-time manufacturing and essentially eliminates its goods in process inventories. How does this affect its calculations of equivalent units of production?

SUMMARY OF THE CHAPTER IN TERMS OF LEARNING OBJECTIVES

LO 1. Explain the nature of process operations and how they differ from job order operations. Process operations produce large quantities of identical products or services by passing them through a series of processes or steps in production. Like job order operations, they combine direct materials, direct labor, and overhead in the manufacturing operation. Unlike job order operations that assign the responsibility for each job to a manager, process operations assign the responsibility for each process to a manager. Thus, the primary focus is on the series of processes used to complete the production of products.

LO 2. Describe the process of accumulating direct materials, direct labor, and manufacturing overhead costs according to each production process and prepare entries to record the flow of costs in a process cost accounting system. A process cost accounting system uses a separate goods in process inventory account for each process and accumulates manufacturing costs in these accounts. As units of product are transferred from one manufacturing process to the next, the accumulated cost of those units is transferred from one goods in process account to the next. As units complete the last manufacturing process and are eventually sold, their accumulated cost is transferred to Finished Goods Inventory and finally to Cost of Goods Sold.

LO 3. Explain how equivalent units are used in process cost accounting systems and calculate the equivalent units produced during a period. Equivalent units of production measure the productivity of a process with respect to its use of direct materials or direct labor or overhead. To calculate equivalent units, determine the number of units that would have been finished if all of the direct materials (or direct labor or overhead) had been used to manufacture units that were started and completed during the period. The costs incurred by a process are divided by its equivalent units of production to determine cost per unit.

LO 4. Describe the purposes served by and be able to prepare a process cost summary. A process cost summary is a managerial accounting report that summarizes the activity of a production process or department during a period. A process cost summary is divided into three sections. The first section shows the costs charged to the department. These include the cost of the beginning goods in process, the cost transferred in from a preceding department during the period, and the costs of direct materials, direct labor, and overhead added by the department. The second section shows the equivalent units of output produced during the period and the costs per equivalent unit. The third section uses the equivalent units and the unit costs to allocate the total cost from the first section among the products worked on during the period.

DEMONSTRATION PROBLEM

The Pennsylvania Company produces a product by passing it through a molding process and then through an assembly process. Information related to manufacturing activities during July follows:

Raw materials:

Beginning inventory	$100,000
Raw materials purchased on credit	300,000
Direct materials used in molding	(190,000)
Direct materials used in assembling	(88,600)
Indirect materials used	(51,400)
Ending inventory	$ 70,000

Factory payroll:

Direct labor used in molding	$ 42,000
Direct labor used in assembling	55,375
Indirect labor used	50,625
Total payroll cost (paid with cash)	$148,000

Factory overhead incurred:

Indirect materials used	$ 51,400
Indirect labor used	50,625
Other overhead costs	71,725
Total factory overhead incurred	$173,750

Factory overhead applied:

Molding (150% of direct labor)	$ 63,000
Assembling (200% of direct labor)	110,750
Total factory overhead applied	$173,750

Molding department:

Beginning goods in process inventory (units)	5,000
Percentage completed—materials	100%
Percentage completed—labor and overhead	60%
Units started and completed	17,000
Ending goods in process inventory (units)	8,000
Percentage completed—materials	100%
Percentage completed—labor and overhead	25%
Costs:	
Beginning in process inventory	$ 53,000
Direct materials added	190,000
Direct labor added	42,000
Overhead applied (150% of direct labor)	63,000
Total costs	$348,000

Assembling department:

Beginning goods in process inventory	$154,800
Ending goods in process inventory	108,325

Finished goods inventory:

Beginning inventory	$ 96,400
Cost transferred in from assembling	578,400
Cost of goods sold	(506,100)
Ending inventory	$168,700

Required

1. Compute the equivalent units of production for the molding department for July, and determine the costs per equivalent unit for direct materials, direct labor, and overhead.
2. Compute the cost of the units transferred from molding to assembling during the month and the cost of the ending goods in process inventory for the molding department.
3. Prepare summary journal entries to record the events of July.

- Calculate the molding department's equivalent units of production and cost per unit with respect to direct materials.
- Calculate the molding department's equivalent units of production with respect to direct labor and overhead and determine the cost per unit for each.
- Compute the total cost of the goods transferred to the assembly department by using the equivalent units and unit costs to determine: *(a)* the cost of the beginning in-process inventory; *(b)* the materials, labor, and overhead costs added to the beginning in-process inventory; and *(c)* the materials, labor, and overhead costs added to the units that were started and completed in the month.
- Use the information to record entries for *(a)* raw materials purchases, *(b)* direct materials usage, *(c)* indirect materials usage, *(d)* factory payroll costs, *(e)* direct labor usage, *(f)* indirect labor usage, *(g)* other overhead costs (credit Other Accounts), *(h)* application of overhead to the two departments, *(i)* transferring partially completed goods from molding to assembling, *(j)* transferring finished goods out of assembling, and *(k)* the cost of goods sold.

Planning the Solution

Solution to Demonstration Problem

1. Equivalent units of production—direct materials:

	Units of Product	Percent Added	Equivalent Units
Beginning goods in process	5,000	0%	–0–
Goods started and completed	17,000	100	17,000
Ending goods in process	8,000	100	8,000
Total units	30,000		25,000

Materials cost per equivalent unit = $190,000/25,000 = $7.60 per unit
Equivalent units of production—direct labor and overhead:

	Units of Product	Percent Added	Equivalent Units
Beginning goods in process	5,000	40%	2,000
Goods started and completed	17,000	100	17,000
Ending goods in process	8,000	25	2,000
Total units	30,000		21,000

Labor cost per equivalent unit = $42,000/21,000 = $2.00 per unit
Overhead cost per equivalent unit = $63,000/21,000 = $3.00 per unit

2. Cost of units transferred from molding to assembling during the month:

	Equivalent Units	Cost per Unit	Total Cost
Beginning goods in process:			
Costs from prior month			$ 53,000
Direct materials added	–0–	$7.60	–0–
Direct labor added	2,000	2.00	4,000
Overhead applied	2,000	3.00	6,000
Total cost to process			$ 63,000
Units started and completed:			
Direct materials added	17,000	$7.60	$129,200
Direct labor added	17,000	2.00	34,000
Overhead applied	17,000	3.00	51,000
Total cost to process			$214,200
Cost of transferred units			$277,200

3.   Summary general journal entries for July:

Raw materials purchases:

	Raw Materials Inventory	300,000.00	
	Accounts Payable		300,000.00

Direct materials usage:

	Goods in Process Inventory—Molding	190,000.00	
	Goods in Process Inventory—Assembling	88,600.00	
	Raw Materials Inventory		278,600.00

Indirect materials usage:

	Factory Overhead	51,400.00	
	Raw Materials Inventory		51,400.00

Factory payroll costs:

	Factory Payroll	148,000.00	
	Cash		148,000.00

Direct labor usage:

	Goods in Process Inventory—Molding	42,000.00	
	Goods in Process Inventory—Assembling	55,375.00	
	Factory Payroll		97,375.00

Indirect labor usage:

	Factory Overhead	50,625.00	
	Factory Payroll		50,625.00

Other overhead costs:

| | | Factory Overhead . . . . | 71,725.00 | |
| | | Other Accounts . . . . | | 71,725.00 |

Application of overhead:

		Goods in Process Inventory—Molding	63,000.00	
		Goods in Process Inventory—Assembling	110,750.00	
		Factory Overhead		173,750.00

Transferring partially completed goods from molding to assembling:

| | | Goods in Process Inventory—Assembling . . . . | 277,200.00 | |
| | | Goods in Process Inventory—Molding . . . . | | 277,200.00 |

Transferring finished goods:

| | | Finished Goods Inventory . . . . | 578,400.00 | |
| | | Goods in Process Inventory—Assembling . . . . | | 578,400.00 |

Cost of goods sold:

| | | Cost of Goods Sold . . . . | 506,100.00 | |
| | | Finished Goods Inventory . . . . | | 506,100.00 |

GLOSSARY

Equivalent units of production a measure of the productivity of a process with respect to its use of direct materials or direct labor or overhead; expresses the activity of a process as the number of units that would have been processed during a period if all effort had been applied to units that were started and finished during the period. p. 772

Materials consumption report a document that shows the raw materials issued to a department during a period and that substitutes for materials requisitions. p. 767–768

Process cost accounting system a system of accounting in which the costs of each process are accumulated separately and then assigned to the units of product that passed through the process. p. 766

Process cost summary a managerial accounting report that describes the costs charged to a department, the equivalent units of production by the department, and how the costs were assigned to the output. p. 775

Production department an organizational unit of a factory that has the responsibility for partially manufacturing or producing a product. p. 768

Service department an organizational unit of a factory that has the responsibility for providing support for the work of the production departments. p. 768

QUESTIONS

1. Can services be delivered by process operations? Give an example.

2. What procedure is used to assign service departments' costs to production departments?

3. Why is it possible for direct labor in a process manufacturing operation to include the labor of employees who do not work specifically on products?

4. What purposes are served by a process cost summary?

5. A manufacturing company produces a single product by processing it first through a mixing department and next through a cutting department. What accounts do direct labor costs flow through in this company's process cost system?

6. After all labor costs for a period are allocated, what balance should remain in the Factory Payroll account?

7. Is it possible to have underapplied or overapplied overhead costs in a process cost accounting system?

8. Explain why equivalent units of production for direct labor and overhead may be the same and why they may differ from equivalent units for direct materials.

9. The Walt Disney Company has two major segments: motion pictures and amusement parks. What types of cost accounting systems are likely to be used in accounting for the activities in these segments? Why?

10. Suppose that Lands' End, Inc., produces work shirts through a multiple process production line. Starting with cutting the fabric, what are some of the processes that might be included in manufacturing the shirts?

QUICK STUDY (Five-Minute Exercises)

QS 20–1
(LO 1)

For each of the following, indicate whether it is most likely to be produced in a process operation or a job-order operation:

a.	Door hinges.	*f.*	Folding chairs.
b.	Wall clocks.	*g.*	Custom-tailored suits.
c.	Cut flower arrangements.	*h.*	Sport shirts.
d.	Bolts and nuts.	*i.*	Concrete swimming pools.
e.	House paint.	*j.*	Pianos.

QS 20–2
(LO 2)

Texton Company manufactures a product requiring two processes: cutting and sewing. During August, partially completed units with a cost of $297,500 were transferred from cutting to sewing. The sewing department requisitioned $58,200 of direct materials and incurred direct labor of $96,000. Overhead is applied to the sewing department at 100% of direct labor. Units with a cost of $102,400 were completed and transferred to finished goods. Prepare the journal entries to record the August activities of the sewing department.

QS 20–3
(LO 3)

The following information pertains to units processed in the binding department of Lowe Printing Company during March:

	Units of Product	Percent of Labor Added
Goods in process	150,000	25%
Goods started and completed	340,000	100
Ending goods in process	120,000	40

Calculate the total equivalent units of production with respect to labor for March.

QS 20–4
(LO 4)

The following information for a company's assembly department describes its manufacturing operations for one month:

Costs charged to the department:

Total processing costs	$105,000
Goods in process at the beginning of the month	10,000
Cost transferred from prior department (32,000 units at $3.25 each)	104,000
Total costs to be accounted for	$219,000

Equivalent units produced during the month for direct materials, direct labor, and overhead:

Beginning in process inventory	4,000
Units started and completed	24,000
Ending in process inventory	2,000
Total units	30,000

The units transferred to the assembly department were immediately placed in production, with the result that none of their $104,000 cost was added to the beginning in process inventory. Their cost was divided between the units started and completed and the units in the ending goods in process inventory. What is the total cost of the units transferred from the assembly department to finished goods during the month?

EXERCISES

Match each of the following items with the appropriate description of its purpose:

a. Materials consumption report

b. Process cost summary

c. Goods in Process Inventory— Department A

d. Raw Materials Inventory account

e. Materials requisition

f. Finished Goods Inventory account

g. Factory Overhead account

_____ 1. Holds costs of finished products until sold to customers.

_____ 2. Holds costs for indirect materials, indirect labor, and other similar costs until assigned to production departments.

_____ 3. Describes the direct materials used in a production department.

_____ 4. Notifies the materials manager that materials should be sent to a production department.

_____ 5. Holds costs of materials until they are used in production departments or as factory overhead.

_____ 6. Holds costs of direct materials, direct labor, and applied overhead until products are transferred from Department A.

_____ 7. A periodic report that describes the activity and output of a production department.

Exercise 20–1
Documents used in process cost accounting systems
(LO 2)

The Apex Company manufactures products with two processes: sanding and painting. Prepare entries to record the following activities for January:

a. Purchased raw materials on credit at a cost of $30,000.

b. Used direct materials with costs of $9,000 in the sanding department and $15,000 in the painting department.

c. Used indirect materials with a cost of $10,500.

d. Incurred total labor cost of $75,000, all of which was paid in cash.

Exercise 20–2
Journal entries in a process cost accounting system
(LO 2)

e. Used direct labor with costs of $30,000 in the sanding department and $24,000 in the painting department.

f. Used indirect labor with a cost of $21,000.

g. Incurred other overhead costs of $24,000 (credit Cash).

h. Applied overhead at the rates of 125% of direct labor in the sanding department and 75% of direct labor in the painting department.

i. Transferred partially completed products with a cost of $69,900 from the sanding department to the painting department.

j. Transferred completed products with a cost of $135,000 from the painting department to the finished goods inventory.

k. Sold products on credit for $291,000. Their accumulated cost was $141,000.

Exercise 20–3
Interpreting journal entries in a process cost accounting system
(LO 2)

The following journal entries were recorded by the Sasser Company's process cost accounting system. The company produces its products by passing them through a cutting department and a molding department. Overhead is applied to production departments based on the direct labor cost during the period. Provide a brief explanation of the event recorded by each entry.

a.	Factory Overhead	5,000.00	
	Other Accounts		5,000.00
b.	Finished Goods Inventory	44,000.00	
	Goods in Process Inventory—Molding		44,000.00
c.	Factory Payroll	16,000.00	
	Cash		16,000.00
d.	Raw Materials Inventory	26,000.00	
	Accounts Payable		26,000.00
e.	Goods in Process Inventory—Cutting	12,000.00	
	Goods in Process Inventory—Molding	9,000.00	
	Raw Materials Inventory		21,000.00
f.	Goods in Process Inventory—Cutting	8,000.00	
	Goods in Process Inventory—Molding	5,000.00	
	Factory Payroll		13,000.00
g.	Accounts Receivable	125,000.00	
	Sales		125,000.00
	Cost of Goods Sold	50,000.00	
	Finished Goods Inventory		50,000.00
h.	Goods in Process Inventory—Molding	30,000.00	
	Goods in Process Inventory—Cutting		30,000.00
i.	Factory Overhead	3,000.00	
	Factory Payroll		3,000.00
j.	Goods in Process Inventory—Cutting	6,000.00	
	Goods in Process Inventory—Molding	7,000.00	
	Factory Overhead		13,000.00
k.	Factory Overhead	5,000.00	
	Raw Materials Inventory		5,000.00

Exercise 20–4
Recording cost flows in a process cost system
(LO 2)

Babic Company manufactures a product by processing it through the shredding department and then through the bagging department. The following information describes the manufacturing operations for April:

	Shredding Department	Bagging Department
Direct materials used	$ 240,000	$360,000
Direct labor used	45,000	75,000
Predetermined overhead application rate (based		
on direct labor)	120%	200%
Goods transferred from shredding to bagging	$(345,000)	$345,000
Goods transferred from bagging to finished goods		(603,000)

In addition, sales for the month totaled $900,000 on credit and cost of goods sold was $642,000.

Required

Prepare summary general journal entries to record the April activities.

During a recent month, a production department in a process manufacturing system completed a number of units of product and transferred them to finished goods. Of these units, 50,000 were in process in the department at the beginning of the month and 220,000 were started and completed during the month. The beginning inventory units were 70% complete with respect to materials and 80% complete with respect to labor when the month began. At the end of the month, 66,000 additional units were in process in the department and were 40% complete with respect to materials and 10% complete with respect to labor.

Exercise 20–5
Calculating equivalent units
(LO 3)

Required

Calculate *(a)* the number of physical units transferred to finished goods and *(b)* the number of equivalent units with respect to materials and with respect to labor produced in the department during the month.

The production department described in Exercise 20–5 had $653,500 of direct materials and $496,860 of direct labor cost charged to it during the month. Calculate the direct materials cost and the direct labor cost per equivalent unit in the department and allocate the costs among the units in the goods in process inventories and the units started and completed during the month.

Exercise 20–6
Assigning costs to inventories in a process cost system
(LO 3, 4)

A production department in a process manufacturing system completed 250,000 units of product and transferred them to finished goods during a recent week. Of these units, 75,000 were in process at the beginning of the week. The other 175,000 units were started and completed during the week. At the end of the period, 50,000 units were in process.

Exercise 20–7
Calculating equivalent units
(LO 3)

Required

Calculate the department's equivalent units of production with respect to direct materials under each of the following unrelated assumptions:

a. All direct materials are added to the products when processing begins.

b. The direct materials are added to the products evenly throughout the process. The beginning goods in process inventory was 50% complete and the ending goods in process inventory was 70% complete.

c. One-half the direct materials are added to the products when the process begins and the other half is added when the process is 75% complete as to direct labor. The beginning goods in process inventory was 40% complete as to direct labor and the ending goods in process inventory was 60% complete as to direct labor.

The following flowchart shows the production activity of the punching and bending departments of the Laker Company for August. Use the amounts shown on the flowchart to calculate the missing numbers identified by question marks.

Exercise 20–8
Completing a flowchart for a process system
(LO 2)

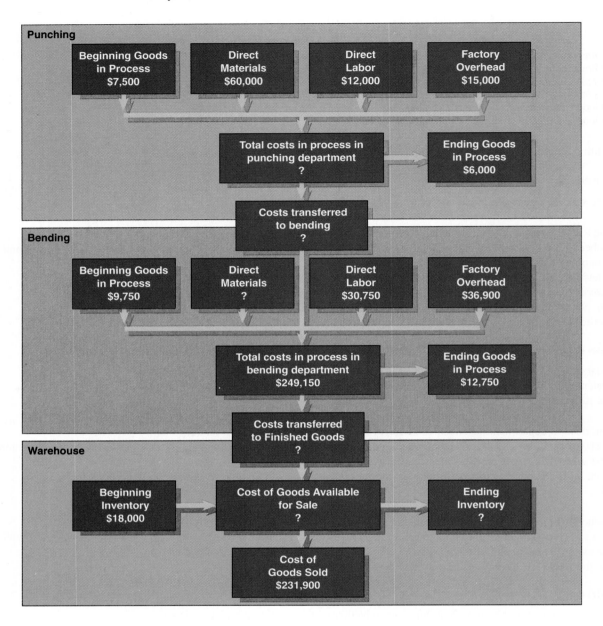

Exercise 20-9
Completing a process cost
summary
(LO 4)

The following partially completed process cost summary describes the July activities of the slicing department of the Serranos Company. The output of the slicing department is sent to the canning department, which sends the finished goods to the warehouse for shipping. A partially completed process cost summary for the slicing department follows:

Costs Charged to the Department

Direct materials requisitioned	$124,000
Direct labor charged	39,000
Overhead allocated (at 150% predetermined rate)	58,500
Total processing costs for the month	$221,500
Goods in process at the beginning of the month	18,000
Total costs to be accounted for	$239,500

Equivalent Unit Processing Costs

	Units of Product	Equivalent Units Direct Materials	Equivalent Units Labor and Overhead
Beginning goods in process	1,600	800	1,200
Units started and completed	10,000	10,000	10,000
Ending goods in process	2,400	1,600	1,800
Total	14,000	12,400	13,000

Prepare the process cost summary for the slicing department by completing the Equivalent Unit Processing Costs section and the Assignment of Costs to the Output of the Department section.

PROBLEMS

The Homestyle Company manufactures blankets by passing the products through a weaving department and a sewing department. This information is known about its inventories for May:

Problem 20–1
Measuring production costs and preparing journal entries
(LO 2, 3)

	Beginning Inventory	Ending Inventory
Raw materials	$ 120,000	$ 105,000
Goods in process—Weaving	300,000	330,000
Goods in process—Sewing	570,000	705,000
Finished goods	1,266,000	1,206,000

The following information describes the company's activities during May:

Raw materials purchases (on credit)	$ 420,000
Factory payroll cost (paid with cash)	1,200,000
Other overhead cost (credit Other Accounts)	156,000
Materials used:	
Direct—Weaving	240,000
Direct—Sewing	75,000
Indirect	120,000
Labor used:	
Direct—Weaving	600,000
Direct—Sewing	180,000
Indirect	420,000
Overhead rates as a percentage of direct labor:	
Weaving	80%
Sewing	120%
Sales (on credit)	$2,625,000

Required

1. Compute (a) the cost of products transferred from weaving to sewing, (b) the cost of products transferred from sewing to finished goods, and (c) the cost of goods sold.

2. Prepare summary general journal entries to record the activities during May.

CHECK FIGURE:
Cost of goods sold, $1,686,000

Problem 20–2
Calculating costs per equivalent unit and allocating costs to products
(LO 3)

CHECK FIGURE:
Direct labor cost per equivalent unit, $1.60

The Peppard Company passes its product through several departments, the last of which is the carving department. Direct labor is added evenly throughout the process in this department. One-fourth of direct materials are added at the beginning of the process and the remaining three-fourths is added when the process is 50% complete with respect to direct labor. During November, 475,000 units of product were transferred to finished goods from the carving department. Of these units, 100,000 units were 40% complete with respect to labor at the beginning of the period and 375,000 were started and completed during the period. At the end of November, the goods in process inventory consisted of 225,000 units that were 30% complete with respect to labor.

The carving department's direct labor cost for November was $804,000 and direct materials cost was $455,625.

Required

Preparation component:

1. Determine the carving department's equivalent units of production with respect to direct labor and with respect to direct materials.
2. Calculate the direct labor cost and the direct materials cost per equivalent unit.
3. Calculate the amount of direct labor cost and the amount of the direct materials cost assigned to the beginning goods in process inventory, to the units started and completed, and to the ending goods in process inventory.

Analysis component:

4. Peppard sells and ships all units to customers as soon as they are completed. Assume that an error was made in determining the percentage of completion for the units in ending inventory. Instead of being 30% complete with respect to labor, they were actually 60% complete. Write a brief essay describing how this error would affect Peppard's November financial statements.

Problem 20–3
Journal entries in a process cost accounting system and using equivalent units
(LO 2, 3)

The Walden Company produces large quantities of a product that goes through two processes—spinning and cutting. These facts are known about the factory's activities for March:

Raw materials:	
Beginning inventory	$ 32,000
Raw materials purchased (on credit)	221,120
Direct materials used in spinning	(160,000)
Direct materials used in cutting	(37,120)
Indirect materials used	(40,560)
Ending inventory	$ 15,440
Factory payroll:	
Direct labor used in spinning	$ 68,000
Direct labor used in cutting	55,680
Indirect labor used	36,320
Total payroll cost (paid with cash)	$160,000
Factory overhead incurred:	
Indirect materials used	$ 40,560
Indirect labor used	36,320
Other overhead costs	91,640
Total factory overhead incurred	$168,520
Factory overhead applied:	
Spinning (125% of direct labor)	$ 85,000
Cutting (150% of direct labor)	83,520
Total factory overhead applied	$168,520

The following facts are known about the inventory in the spinning department:

Units:

Beginning in process inventory	4,000
Started and completed	12,000
Ending in process inventory	8,000

Percentage completed:

Beginning in process inventory

Materials	100%
Labor and overhead	25%

Ending in process inventory

Materials	100%
Labor and overhead	25%

Costs:

Beginning in process inventory	$ 41,000
Direct materials added	160,000
Direct labor added	68,000
Overhead applied (125% of direct labor)	85,000
Total costs	$354,000
Transferred out to cutting department	(272,000)
Ending in process inventory	$ 82,000

These facts are known about the goods in process inventories for the cutting department:

Beginning in process inventory	$174,000
Ending in process inventory	177,120

These facts are known about the finished goods:

Beginning inventory	$148,400
Cost transferred in from cutting	445,200
Cost of goods sold	(530,000)
Ending inventory	$ 63,600

During the month, 10,000 units of finished goods were sold for cash at the price of $120 each.

Required

Preparation component:

1. Prepare entries to record the activities of March.
2. Calculate the equivalent units of production for the spinning department for March, and calculate the costs per equivalent unit for direct materials, direct labor, and overhead.
3. Calculate the cost of the ending goods in process inventory for the spinning department.

CHECK FIGURE:
Cost per equivalent unit: materials, $8.00; labor, $4.00; overhead, $5.00

Analysis component:

4. Walden provides incentives to managers of the processing departments by paying monthly bonuses based on their success in controlling costs per equivalent unit of production. Assume that the spinning department underestimated the percentage of completion for the units in ending inventory, with the result that the equivalent units of production in ending inventory for March were understated. What impact would this error have on the bonuses paid to the manager of the spinning department and the manager of the cutting department? What impact, if any would this error have on April bonuses?

Problem 20–4
Preparing a process cost summary
(LO 3, 4)

Praxair Company produces its product by passing it through a single processing department. Direct materials, direct labor, and overhead are added to the product evenly throughout the process. The company uses month-long reporting periods for its process cost accounting system.

The Goods in Process Inventory account appears as follows after posting entries for direct materials, direct labor, and overhead costs during October:

		Goods in Process Inventory			Acct. No. 133
Date		**Explanation**	**Debit**	**Credit**	**Balance**
Oct.	1	Beginning balance			40,800
	31	Direct materials	92,250		133,050
	31	Direct labor costs	307,500		440,550
	31	Applied overhead	123,000		563,550

During October, the company finished and transferred 150,000 units of the product to finished goods. Of these units, 30,000 were in process at the beginning of the month and 120,000 were started and completed during the month. The beginning goods in process inventory was 40% complete. At the end of the month, the goods in process inventory consisted of 22,500 units that were 70% complete.

Required

1. Calculate the number of equivalent units of production for October.

2. Prepare the department's process cost summary for October.

3. Prepare an entry to transfer the cost of the completed units to finished goods inventory.

CHECK FIGURE:
Total cost transferred to finished goods, $510,000

Problem 20–5
Preparing a process cost summary
(LO 3, 4)

Manchaca Company manufactures a single product in one department. All direct materials are added at the beginning of the manufacturing process. Direct labor and overhead are added evenly throughout the process. The company uses month-long reporting periods for its process cost accounting system.

During May, the company completed and transferred 22,200 units of product to the finished goods inventory. The beginning goods in process inventory consisted of 3,000 units that were 100% complete with respect to direct materials and 40% complete with respect to direct labor and overhead. The other 19,200 completed units were started during the month. In addition, 2,400 units were in process at the end of the month. They were 100% complete with respect to direct materials and 75% complete with respect to direct labor and overhead.

After posting the entries to record direct materials, direct labor, and overhead during May, the company's Goods in Process Inventory account appears as follows:

		Goods in Process Inventory			Acct. No. 133
Date		**Explanation**	**Debit**	**Credit**	**Balance**
May	1	Beginning balance			181,320
	31	Direct materials	496,800		678,120
	31	Direct labor costs	1,185,600		1,863,720
	31	Applied overhead	948,480		2,812,200

Required

1. Calculate the department's equivalent units of production for May.

2. Prepare the department's process cost summary for May.

3. Prepare the entry to transfer the cost of the completed units to finished goods inventory.

CHECK FIGURE:
Total cost transferred to finished goods, $2,588,520

CRITICAL THINKING: ESSAYS, PROBLEMS, AND CASES

The Empire Company uses a process cost accounting system for its manufacturing operation that passes products through the smelting and the turning departments. The predetermined overhead application rates are 100% of direct labor cost for the smelting department and 180% of the direct labor cost for the turning department. In a recent month, the following costs were reported:

Analytical Essay

(LO 2, 3, 4)

	Smelting	Turning
Direct materials	$100,000	$162,500
Direct labor	37,500	55,000
Factory overhead applied	37,500	99,000
Totals	$175,000	$316,500

Because both departments have very short processing times, there are no beginning or ending goods in process inventories. There is no finished goods inventory because units of product are sold and delivered to customers as soon as they are completed.

Assume that two employees who worked in the turning department incorrectly coded their time sheets. As a result, the smelting department's reported direct labor cost incorrectly includes $6,250 that should have been charged to the turning department.

Required

Write a brief essay explaining the effects of the error on the company's financial statements and process cost summaries.

Managerial Analysis Problems

A processing department of the Bidden Company started October with 125,000 units in its goods in process inventory, each of which was 80% complete. During October, an additional 1,100,000 units were started in the department. A total of 1,125,000 units were completed and transferred to finished goods. If October's production was measured as 1,060,000 equivalent units, how many units of product were in process at the end of the month and what was their stage of completion?

MAP 20–1

(LO 3)

IBM's most significant activity is manufacturing many different kinds of computers, including small personal computers that are highly standardized and large custom-designed mainframe computers. The company also produces various kinds of software, including custom programs written to meet specific customers' needs. In addition, IBM provides repair services for both small and large computers.

For each of the following activities, indicate the type of cost accounting system most likely to be used by IBM. Provide a brief statement justifying your answers.

MAP 20–2

(LO 1)

a. Manufacturing personal computers.

b. Manufacturing custom-designed mainframe computer systems.

c. Producing custom-designed software for specific customers.

d. Providing repair services.

COMPREHENSIVE PROBLEM

Dessau Company
(Review of Chapters 2, 5, 9, 18, 20)

The Dessau Company produces a product by sending it through two processes, one of which takes place in Department One and the other in Department Two. All of Department One's output is transferred to Department Two. In addition to the goods in process inventories in Departments One and Two, Dessau maintains inventories of raw materials and finished goods. Dessau uses raw materials as direct materials in Departments One and Two and as indirect materials. Its factory payroll costs include direct labor for each department and indirect labor.

Required

In this problem, you are to maintain certain records and produce various measures of the inventories to reflect the events of July. Round all calculations of unit costs to the nearest penny and all other dollar amounts to the nearest whole dollar. To begin, set up the following general ledger accounts and enter their June 30 balances:

Raw Materials Inventory	$ 64,000
Goods in Process Inventory—Department One	128,440
Goods in Process Inventory—Department Two	50,000
Finished Goods Inventory	220,000
Sales	–0–
Cost of Goods Sold	–0–
Factory Payroll	–0–
Factory Overhead	–0–

1. Prepare entries to record the following events that occurred in July:

   a. Purchased raw materials for $200,000 cash (use a perpetual inventory system).

   b. Used raw materials as follows:

Department One	$72,000
Department Two	89,600
Indirect materials	42,000

   c. Incurred factory payroll cost of $360,000, paid with cash (ignore income and other taxes).

   d. Assigned factory payroll costs as follows:

Department One	$200,000
Department Two	100,000
Indirect labor	60,000

   e. Incurred additional factory overhead costs of $48,000, paid in cash.

   f. Allocated factory overhead to Departments One and Two as a percentage of the direct labor costs. (To make this entry, you must first compute the overhead allocation rate using direct labor and overhead costs incurred during July.)

2. Information about the units of product on hand or worked on during July follows:

	Department One	Department Two
Units in beginning inventory	500	1,000
Percent completed with respect to:		
Materials	50%	40%
Labor and overhead	40%	62%
Units started and finished in July	2,000	1,800
Percent completed with respect to:		
Materials	100%	100%
Labor and overhead	100%	100%
Units in ending inventory	1,000	1,600
Percent completed with respect to:		
Materials	15%	25%
Labor and overhead	20%	20%

Use this information and the facts from part 1 to make the following calculations:

a. Equivalent units of production in Department One and the per unit costs for labor, materials, and overhead.

b. Equivalent units of production in Department Two and the per unit costs for labor, materials, and overhead.

3. Using the results from requirement 2 and previously given information, make the following calculations, and prepare general journal entries to record:

g. Total cost of units transferred from Department One to Department Two during July.

h. Total cost of units transferred from Department Two to finished goods during July.

i. Sale of finished goods that cost $531,400 for $1,250,000 cash.

4. Post the journal entries from parts 1 and 3 to the ledger accounts that you set up at the beginning of the problem.

5. Compute the amount of gross profit from the sales in July.

ANSWERS TO PROGRESS CHECKS

20–1 c

20–2 When a company produces large quantities of identical products, a process cost accounting system is more suitable.

20–3 b

20–4 The costs are direct materials, direct labor, and manufacturing overhead.

20–5 One Goods in Process Inventory account is needed for each production department.

20–6 a

20–7 Equivalent units with respect to direct labor is the number of units that would have been produced if all of the labor had been used on units that were started and finished during the period.

20–8

	Units of Product	Percent Added	Equivalent Units
Beginning inventory	8,000	75%	6,000
Units started and finished	50,000	100	50,000
Ending inventory	6,000	33⅓	2,000
Equivalent units			58,000

20–9 The first section shows the costs charged to the department. The sectionP describes the equivalent units produced by the department. The third section shows how the total costs are assigned to units worked on during the period.

20–10 The transfer decreases one Goods in Process Inventory account and increases another. Therefore, the transfer has no effect on total assets

20–11 Equivalent unit processing cost:

$$\frac{\$262,500}{20,000 + 70,000 + 15,000} = \$2.50$$

Goods started and completed:	
Costs transferred in	$225,000
Total costs added (70,000 × $2.50)	175,000
Total costs to process	$400,000

12–12 If goods-in-process inventories are eliminated, equivalent units of production is the number of units started and completed during the period.

Cost Allocation and Activity-Based Costing

Kent Moore Cabinets is the largest producer of custom cabinets in Texas. Charles Rhinehart, its vice president and controller was concerned about the company's problem with custom cabinets built to incorrect specifications. Accurate building specifications are necessary so the cabinets fit the space allowed. Rhinehart had decided to track the costs of returning, reworking, and redelivering the cabinets in a separate expense account. He discovered that this expense amounted to 4.5% of sales.

A mistake in cabinet specifications was seldom discovered until the cabinets were installed. Cabinets that were the wrong size had to be returned, reworked, and then reinstalled. Kent Moore used an outside contractor to deliver and install the cabinets and paid twice for cabinets that had to be reworked.

Manufacturing was frustrated whenever Rhinehart brought up the high cost of reworking cabinets because they had built the cabinets according to the drawings submitted by sales. The causes of the problem were either measurement errors by sales personnel or changes by builders after orders were placed. Sales personnel ignored Rhinehart because they had taken orders based on original house plans from their customers. Also, their focus was maintaining sales. They believed their time was best used by selling more cabinets.

Rhinehart decided to use theory of constraints problem-solving tools to identify the core problem and develop a method to motivate salespersons to take responsibility for accurate cabinet measurements.

LEARNING OBJECTIVES

After studying Chapter 21, you should be able to:

1. **Explain why businesses are divided into subunits or departments and explain the difference between cost centers and profit centers.**

2. **Describe the difference between direct and indirect expenses of departments, the bases used to allocate indirect expenses, and the procedures used in the allocation process.**

3. **Prepare reports that measure the performance of a profit center and describe the factors that should be considered in eliminating an unprofitable department.**

4. **Explain the concept of controllable costs and describe the problems associated with allocating joint costs between products.**

5. **Describe activity-based costing and its advantages for generating useful information for management.**

6. **Define or explain the words and phrases listed in the chapter glossary.**

The three preceding chapters have focused on measuring the costs of products manufactured in factories, with some emphasis on using the results in published financial statements. This chapter shifts our focus to managerial accounting reports that can be used in directing a company's activities. In particular, it explains how and why management divides companies into departments. This chapter also describes how to allocate manufacturing costs shared by more than one product to those products and the allocation of the indirect costs of shared items such as utilities, advertising, and rent. Finally, the chapter describes activity-based cost accounting. Your understanding of these cost allocation procedures and assumptions is important if you are to use management accounting data.

DEPARTMENTAL ACCOUNTING

LO 1

Explain why businesses are divided into subunits or departments and explain the difference between cost centers and profit centers.

FAST HINT
Important Point to Remember:
The purpose of responsibility accounting is to improve performance by avoiding pitfalls and capitalizing on opportunities.

Managerial accounting information about subunits of a business is very useful for managers of both large and small companies. In fact, when they get to be too large to be managed effectively as a single unit, almost all businesses are divided into subunits or departments. For example, the discussion of process cost accounting in Chapter 20 showed you how many manufacturing systems are subdivided into departments so that they can be more easily managed.

Managerial accounting for the departments of a business has two primary goals. The first is to provide information that management can use to evaluate the profitability or cost effectiveness of each department's activities. This goal is met by **departmental accounting systems.** The second goal is to assign costs and expenses to the particular managers who are responsible for controlling those costs and expenses. This information is then used to control those costs and to evaluate the performance of those managers. This information is provided by **responsibility accounting systems.** Departmental and responsibility accounting systems are closely related and share much of the same information.

CREATING DEPARTMENTS WITHIN A BUSINESS

Most businesses are sufficiently large and complex to be divided into subunits or departments. When a business is departmentalized, usually each department is placed under the direction of a manager. As the business grows larger, management may divide a department into new departments. This division is needed so that the responsibilities for the activities of a unit do not overwhelm the manager's ability to oversee and control the unit effectively. Where possible, the company also establishes departments to take full advantage of the specialized skills of particular managers.

Basis for Departmentalization

Chapter 20 described the two most basic categories of departments: *production departments* and *service departments*. In a factory, production departments engage directly in manufacturing. Factory departments are usually organized to put each manufacturing process under the direction of a single manager. The process is identified by the activities that it carries out or the products or components that it manufactures.

In a store, production departments make sales directly to customers. In this setting, management usually organizes departments around the goods that each of them sells. That is, each *selling department* has the task of selling one or more lines of merchandise.

In either a factory or a store, service departments help manufacturing or selling departments by providing support services. Examples of these services include advertising, purchasing, payroll processing, human resource management, and corporate-level management. The service departments assist or otherwise perform services for the production departments. Service departments do not directly manufacture products or produce revenues through sales. However, their activities are important for the profitability of each production department and the entire company.

USING INFORMATION TO EVALUATE DEPARTMENTS

When a business is divided into departments, company managers need to know how well each department is performing. Therefore, the accounting system must supply information about the resources used and outputs achieved by each department. This evaluation requires the system to measure and accumulate revenue and expense information for each department wherever possible. Because of its potential usefulness to competitors, this information is not distributed to the public. Instead, information about departments is prepared exclusively for internal managers to help them control operations, appraise performance, allocate resources, and take corrective actions. For example, if one of several departments is particularly profitable, management may decide to expand its operations. Or, if a department is showing poor results, information about its revenues, costs, and expenses may suggest useful changes.

More and more companies are emphasizing customer satisfaction as the number one responsibility of every operating department. This has led to changes in the measures needed to be reported in responsibility accounting systems. Increasingly, financial measurements are being supplemented with quality and customer satisfaction indexes. For example, **Motorola, Inc.,** uses two key measures: the number of defective parts per million parts produced and the percentage of orders delivered on time to customers.

The kind of financial information used to evaluate a department depends on whether it is a **profit center** or a **cost center.** A profit center incurs costs and also generates revenues. The selling departments of a business are often evaluated as profit centers. A cost center is a department that incurs costs or expenses without directly generating revenues. For example, the manufacturing departments of a factory and service departments such as accounting, advertising, and purchasing are cost centers.

In a similar manner, evaluating the performance of individual managers depends on whether they are responsible for profit centers or cost centers. Managers of profit

FAST HINT
Additional Insight:
While it obviously is an invaluable first step, simply knowing which areas are profitable isn't sufficient to guarantee success. To improve its profitability, Sears, Roebuck & Co. eliminated its catalog division.

FAST HINT
Relevant Quick Study:
To apply these concepts, work QS 21-1

centers are judged on their ability to generate revenues in excess of the department's expenses. Managers of cost centers are judged on their ability to control costs by keeping them within a satisfactory range. In the **Kent Moore Cabinets** example at the beginning of the chapter, the controller understood that he could not evaluate the performance of the manufacturing group by including the costs they could not control. The costs of reworking cabinets that did not fit were caused by another department.

OBTAINING INFORMATION ABOUT DEPARTMENTS

Different companies use various methods to generate information about their departments. To a considerable extent, the needed information depends on the focus and philosophy of management. For example, **Hewlett-Packard Company's** statement of corporate objectives indicates that the reason for the company's existence is to satisfy real customer needs. The challenge is to establish management responsibility accounting systems that provide relevant feedback for evaluating performance in terms of corporate objectives such as this.

The methods of gathering information about departments depend on the extent to which they use computers and sophisticated cash registers.

FAST HINT
Additional Insight:
Some retailers use a computerized point-of-sales system that captures sales data and creates the necessary documents to both release inventory from the warehouse and order additional merchandise. Wal-Mart Stores' computerized sales system not only collects data for internal purposes but also is used by Procter & Gamble to plan its production and delivery schedule of products sold to Wal-Mart.

Computerized Systems

Sophisticated cash registers allow the managers of a merchandising company to accumulate information about each department's sales and sales returns. In a networked system, the registers transfer this information directly to the store's computer. Many cash registers are capable of actually doing much more than accumulating sales information for each department. They also print relevant information on the sales ticket given to the customer, total the ticket, and initiate entries to record credit sales in the customer's account. If information about the sold goods is recorded at the register by a scanner or a keyboard, the system can produce detailed daily departmental summaries of the items sold and those that remain in the company's inventory.

Using Separate Accounts for Each Department

Sophisticated systems allow businesses to easily determine total sales and sales returns for each department on a daily basis. More clerical effort is needed for less sophisticated systems that do not connect the registers to a computer. In these systems, the totals are usually accumulated by one of two methods: A business may provide separate Sales and Sales Returns accounts in its general ledger for each department. Alternatively, the business may produce a *supplementary spreadsheet analysis* of departmental sales and sales returns. These methods can also accumulate information about purchases and purchases returns for the departments.

If a business uses special journals and has separate Sales, Sales Returns, Purchases, and Purchases Returns accounts for each selling department, its special journals should have separate columns for routine transactions by departments. For example, Illustration 21–1 shows a sales journal used to record information for each selling department. The amounts to be debited to the customers' accounts are entered in the Accounts Receivable Debit column and posted to these accounts daily. Less frequently, perhaps

Illustration 21-1   A Departmentalized Sales Journal

					Departmental Sales		
				Accounts			
		Invoice	P	Receivable	Dept. 1	Dept. 2	Dept. 3
Date	Account Debited	Number	R	Debit	Credit	Credit	Credit
Oct. 1	Walter Marshfield	737		145.23	90.15	55.08	
1	Thomas Higgins	738		85.90		40.30	45.60
—	—	—		—	—	—	—
—	—	—		—	—	—	—
—	—	—		—	—	—	—
Total				10,400.85	4,056.75	4,292.10	2,052.00

The table heading *Sales Journal* spans the columns, and *Departmental Sales* spans Dept. 1 Credit, Dept. 2 Credit, and Dept. 3 Credit.

Illustration 21-2   Departmental Sales Spreadsheet

Date	Men's Wear Dept.	Boys' Wear Dept.	Shoe Dept.	Leather Goods Dept.	Women's Wear Dept.	Total Sales
May 1	957.15	775.06	615.00	575.25	927.18	3,849.64
2	898.55	736.27	545.80	410.20	887.27	3,478.09
—	—	—	—	—	—	—
—	—	—	—	—	—	—
—	—	—	—	—	—	—
Total	24,124.10	19,647.29	15,090.40	12,810.85	23,587.85	95,260.49

monthly, this column's total is posted to the Accounts Receivable controlling account. The amounts sold to the customer from each department are entered in the last three columns. The totals of these columns are posted to the ledger accounts at least monthly.

Departmental Sales Spreadsheet Analyses

If separate accounts are not maintained in the general ledger for each department, a business can develop departmental information by using a supplemental spreadsheet analysis. In applying this approach, the firm records sales, sales returns, purchases, and purchases returns as if the business is not departmentalized. Then, the company's accountant identifies each department's transactions and enters the amounts on a spreadsheet.

For example, after recording sales in its usual manner, the system may find daily total sales for each department and then enter the daily totals on a sales spreadsheet like the one in Illustration 21–2. At the end of a month or other period, the column totals of the spreadsheet show sales by departments, and the combined total of all the columns should equal the balance of the Sales account.

When a store uses a spreadsheet analysis of department sales, it may use separate spreadsheets to accumulate sales, sales returns, purchases, and purchases returns. At the end of the period, the several spreadsheets show the store's sales, sales returns, purchases, and purchases returns by departments. If each department counts its inventory, it can also calculate its gross profit.

FAST HINT
Important Point to Remember:
Computer spreadsheet programs are useful for creating forms like the departmental sales spreadsheet shown in Illustration 21–2. These programs are also useful for allocating expenses, as discussed later in this chapter.

FAST HINT
Additional Insight:
Link Wood Products, a manufacturer of wood lawn and garden products, records each invoice in a column for each department on a computer spreadsheet. The summarized daily total is then accumulated in another spreadsheet to obtain monthly sales information.

Accumulating information and computing the gross profit for each selling department in a departmentalized business is not difficult. However, some companies do not even attempt to measure the net income generated by each department because of the complexities of allocating expenses among departments. Nonetheless, this information can be very useful and many companies do gather it.

Progress Check
(Answers to Progress Checks are provided at the end of the chapter.)

21-1   What is the difference between departmental accounting systems and responsibility accounting systems?

21-2   Service departments: *(a)* Manufacture products; *(b)* Make sales directly to customers; *(c)* Produce revenues; *(d)* Assist production departments.

21-3   Explain the difference between a cost center and a profit center, and give an example of each.

21-4   A company that develops departmental information by using supplemental sales analysis spreadsheets would probably:
   a. Have a sophisticated computerized cash register system.
   b. Use separate spreadsheets to accumulate sales, sales returns, purchases, and purchases returns.
   c. Provide separate Sales accounts for each department in its general ledger.

ALLOCATING EXPENSES AMONG DEPARTMENTS

LO 2
Describe the difference between direct and indirect expenses of departments, the bases used to allocate indirect expenses, and the procedures used in the allocation process.

FAST HINT
Class Discussion:
Utility expense has elements of both fixed and variable costs. Ask students for other examples of expenses that contain both fixed and variable elements.

FAST HINT
Class Discussion:
Ask students to identify two situations in which supplies would be handled as a direct expense rather than an indirect expense.

If a business attempts to measure departmental net income, its management must solve some special managerial accounting problems. The problems involve allocating the company's expenses among its selling departments.

Direct Expenses Do Not Require Allocation

A company's **direct expenses** are easily traced to a specific department because they are incurred for the sole benefit of that department. For example, the salary of an employee who works in only one department is a direct expense of that department.

Notice that the concept of direct expense is very similar to the concept of direct cost that was first introduced in Chapter 18. There, we used the term *direct cost* in the context of a manufacturing operation where all manufacturing costs are product costs rather than period costs (expenses). In nonmanufacturing departments, costs are charged to expense as they are incurred. In these situations, the term *direct expense* is used instead of *direct cost.*

Allocating Indirect Expenses

A company's expenses also include **indirect expenses.** Indirect expenses (like indirect costs) are incurred for the joint benefit of more than one department. For example, if two or more departments share a single building, they jointly enjoy the benefits of the expenses of renting, heating, and lighting the building. These expenses are indirect because they cannot be easily traced to any specific department. However, if there is a need for managerial accounting information about the income produced by each department, the indirect expenses should be allocated among the departments that benefited from them. If so, each indirect expense should be allocated on a basis that fairly approximates the relative benefit received by each department. However, measuring the benefit each department receives from an indirect expense is usually difficult or impossible. Even after a reasonable allocation basis is chosen, considerable doubt often exists regarding the share to be charged to each department.

To illustrate how an indirect expense can be allocated, assume that a jewelry store purchases janitorial services from an outside firm. The management then decides to allocate the cost among the store's three departments according to the floor space that each occupies. The cost of janitorial services for a recent month is $300. This table shows the square feet of floor space occupied by each department, computes the percentage of the total square feet, and then allocates this $300 cost among them by using those percentages:

Department	Square Feet	Percentage of Total	Allocated Cost
Jewelry	1,000	25.0%	$ 75
Watch repair	600	15.0	45
China and silver	2,400	60.0	180
Total	4,000	100.0%	$300

The table shows that the jewelry department occupies 25% of the floor space in the store. Thus, it is likely that 25% of the janitorial services are applied to cleaning its space. Therefore, 25% of the total $300 cost is assigned to the jewelry department. When the allocation process is completed, these and other allocated costs are deducted from the gross profits generated by each department to determine the net income that each produced.

You can apply the concepts of *direct* and *indirect costs* or *expenses* in a variety of situations. In general, you can easily associate direct costs or expenses with a *cost object*. In this chapter, the relevant cost object is a department. However, other cost objects may be relevant for other decisions. In general accounting systems for manufacturing operations (Chapter 18) and job order cost systems (Chapter 19), the cost object is a job or a group of products. In process cost systems (Chapter 20), the cost object is a process.

One consideration in allocating costs is to motivate managers and employees toward some desired behavior. Therefore, a cost incurred in one department might be allocated to another department because the latter department caused the cost and can control it. Consider the example presented at the beginning of the chapter regarding **Kent Moore Cabinets.** The controller captured the costs of reworking, delivering, and reinstalling defective cabinets in separate accounts. Then, he removed the costs from manufacturing accounts and allocated them to the individual salespersons who serviced the customers receiving defective cabinets. This reassigned the costs from manufacturing to those who could best control them.

Bases for Allocating Indirect Expenses

The following paragraphs describe some bases that are often used to allocate common indirect expenses among departments. There are no hard-and-fast rules about which basis is most useful for a given expense. Such rules are not appropriate because an expense allocation often involves several factors and the relative importance of the factors varies from situation to situation. Judgment is required, and people may not agree on the most useful basis for allocating an indirect expense.

Wages and Salaries. Employees' wages may be either a direct or an indirect expense. If their time is spent entirely in one department, their wages are a direct expense of that department. But, if the employees work in more than one department, their wages are an indirect expense to be allocated among the benefited departments. In general, an employee's contribution to a department depends on the hours worked

FAST HINT

Critical Thought Question:
What might be a reasonable basis for allocating the cost of operating a hospital cafeteria to the various departments?

in the department. Thus, a reasonable basis for allocating employees' wages is the relative amount of time they spend in each department.

A supervisory employee may supervise more than one department. In such cases, the time spent in each department can be a useful basis for allocating the supervisor's salary. However, a supervisor is frequently on the move, and it may not be practical to record the time spent in each department. Therefore, some companies allocate supervisory salaries to the departments on the basis of the number of employees in each department. This basis is reasonable if the supervisor's primary task is managing people. Others make the allocation on the basis of the sales achieved in the supervised departments. This basis is reasonable if the supervisor's relative contributions to the departments are reflected by their levels of selling activity.

Rent, Depreciation, and Related Building Expenses. Rent expense for a building is reasonably allocated to departments on the basis of the amount of the floor space occupied by each department. However, some floor space may be more valuable than other space because of its location. If so, the allocation method should charge some departments with more expense per square foot than other departments. For example, ground floor retail space is usually more valuable than basement or upper-floor space because all customers must pass the departments near the entrance while fewer of them go beyond the first floor. Because there are no precise measures of floor space values, however, it may be helpful to base the allocation on other data, including statistics about customer traffic and opinions of real estate leasing experts. In any case, all allocations of rent ultimately depend on management's judgment.

If the company owns the building, depreciation, taxes, insurance, and similar expenses usually are allocated like rent expense.

Advertising. When a store effectively advertises a department's products, people come into the store to buy them. Of course, a customer may buy unadvertised products during the same visit. Thus, advertising products for some departments may help the sales of all departments. Accordingly, many stores treat advertising as an indirect expense in their departmental income statements. A common technique allocates this cost on the basis of each department's proportion of total sales. For example, a department that has 10% of the store's total sales will be assigned 10% of the advertising expense.

Other stores try to be more precise in their allocations and analyze each advertisement to determine the column inches of newspaper space or minutes of TV or radio time devoted to the products of a department. Then, each department is charged with the actual costs of producing and publishing the advertisements. However, management must consider whether this precision creates sufficient added usefulness to justify the effort.

Equipment Depreciation. To account for each department's equipment depreciation expense, a company should keep sufficiently detailed records to show which departments use specific assets. Depreciation on equipment used only in one department is a direct expense of that department. Depreciation for an asset used by more than one department is an indirect expense to be allocated among all of them. In these cases, the relative number of hours that the equipment is used by the departments is a reasonable basis for allocating depreciation to them.

Utilities Expenses. Firms usually allocate utilities expenses (such as for heating and lighting) on the basis of floor space occupied by departments. This practice should be based on an observation that the amount of heat and the number of lights, their wattage, and the extent of their use are uniform throughout the business. Should there be significant differences in these factors among the departments, further analysis

FAST HINT
Relevant Quick Study:
To apply these concepts, work QS 21–2

FAST HINT
Additional Insight:
Manufacturers often allocate electricity cost to departments on the basis of the horsepower of the equipment located in each department.

and a separate allocation may produce more useful information. Again, there is a trade-off between the usefulness of the more precise information and the effort of getting it.

Service Departments. To manufacture products and make sales, production departments must have services provided by such departments as the general office, personnel, payroll, advertising, and purchasing departments. Because service departments do not produce revenues, companies evaluate them as cost centers. To assist these evaluations, the departmental accounting system can accumulate and report costs incurred directly by each service department. If the service departments' evaluations are based on all costs, the departmental accounting system should allocate indirect costs to each department that benefits from them.

By definition, a service department supports the activities of other departments. Therefore, when any production department's effectiveness is assessed, managers should consider the cost of any benefits it receives from service departments. *Thus, after the costs of operating service departments have been compiled, they should be allocated to the production (or selling) departments.* In effect, the costs of service departments are shared indirect expenses of production departments. If management wants to evaluate selling departments as profit centers using net income instead of gross profit, service department costs should be allocated to them. The following list shows some commonly used bases for allocating service department costs to production and selling departments:

Service Departments	Commonly Used Expense Allocation Bases
General office	Number of employees or sales in each department
Personnel	Number of employees in each department
Payroll	Number of employees in each department
Advertising	Sales or amounts of advertising charged directly to each department
Purchasing	Dollar amounts of purchases or number of purchase orders processed
Cleaning and maintenance	Square feet of floor space occupied

Each profit center must be assigned its full expenses to produce a complete income statement. These costs include direct expenses and indirect expenses shared with other departments. As we just described, it may be useful to compile the full amount of expenses incurred in the service departments and then assign them to the production departments. To illustrate, suppose that the Alphamax Hardware Store has five departments. Two of them (general office and purchasing) are service departments and the other three (hardware, housewares, and appliances) are selling departments. There are three stages in allocating costs to the selling departments.

The first stage assigns *direct* expenses to each service and selling department, as follows:

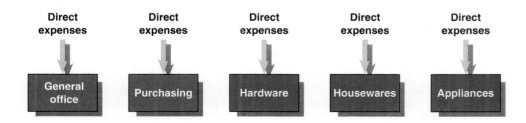

The direct expenses include salaries and other expenses that each department incurs but does not share with any other department. This information is accumulated in departmental expense accounts maintained in the accounting system.

The second step allocates the *indirect* expenses among all five departments according to the allocation base used for each expense. This process is represented as follows:

**Indirect
Expenses**

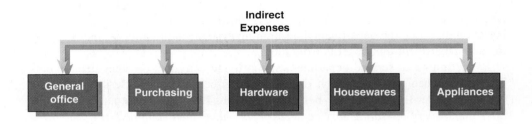

The indirect expenses include the items discussed earlier, such as depreciation, rent, and supervisory costs. These indirect costs are recorded in general expense accounts, and the allocation is accomplished with a *departmental expense allocation spreadsheet* like the one in Illustration 21–3.

The third step allocates the *service department expenses* of the general office and purchasing departments to the three sales departments. The following chart represents this process:

General office expenses

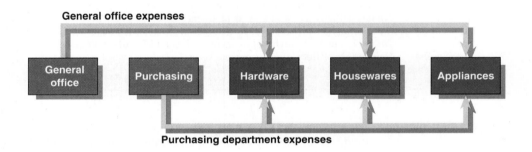

Purchasing department expenses

FAST HINT
Important Point to Remember:
Complex situations may require
allocating service department
costs among service departments before allocating them to
production departments. This
step-wise process is discussed in
advanced accounting courses.

The expenses are allocated by using one of the bases listed previously. The calculations are made on a spreadsheet like the one shown in Illustration 21–3.[1]

Notice that the first column in Illustration 21–3 lists the direct and indirect expense categories. The lower section of the first column lists the names of the service departments. The allocation bases are in the second column, and the total expense amounts are in the third.

The first stage of the allocation assigns the three direct expenses (salaries, equipment depreciation, and supplies) to the five departments. The second stage allocates the four indirect expenses (rent, utilities, advertising, and insurance) using the listed allocation bases.

---

[1]In some circumstances, a company may allocate costs of a service department to other service departments because they use its services. For example, the costs of the payroll office benefit all service and production departments, with the possible result that some of its costs could be assigned to all of them. In this book, virtually all the examples and assignment materials allocate service cost only to production departments.

Illustration 21-3 A Departmental Expense Allocation Spreadsheet

ALPHAMAX HARDWARE STORE
Departmental Expense Allocations
For Year Ended December 31, 19X1

			Allocation of Expenses to Departments				
	Allocation Bases	**Expense Account Balance**	**General Office Dept.**	**Pur-chasing Dept.**	**Hard-ware Dept.**	**House-wares Dept.**	**Appli-ances Dept.**
Direct expenses:							
Salaries expense	Payroll records	51,900	13,300	8,200	15,600	7,000	7,800
Depreciation on equipment . .	Depreciation records	1,500	500	300	400	100	200
Supplies expense	Requisitions	900	200	100	300	200	100
Indirect expenses:							
Rent expense	Amount and value of space . .	12,000	600	600	4,860	3,240	2,700
Utilities expense	Floor space	2,400	300	300	810	540	450
Advertising expense	Sales	1,000			500	300	200
Insurance expense	Value of insured assets	2,500	400	200	900	600	400
Total department expenses	. . . .	72,200	15,300	9,700	23,370	11,980	11,850
Service department expenses:							
General office department . .	Sales		15,300		7,650	4,590	3,060
Purchasing department	Purchase orders			9,700	3,880	2,630	3,190
Total expenses allocated to selling departments	. . . .	72,200			34,900	19,200	18,100

For example, consider the allocation of the rent expense. The five departments occupy the following square feet of space:

General office	1,500
Purchasing	1,500
Hardware	4,050
Housewares	2,700
Appliances	2,250
Total	12,000

Even though the two service departments occupy 25% of the total space (3,000 sq. feet/12,000 sq. feet), they are located in the rear of the building, which has a lower value than the space in the front occupied by the selling departments. Management estimates that the space in the rear produces only $1,200 of the total rent expense of $12,000. This table allocates the $1,200 rent expense between the two departments in proportion to their square footage:

Department	Square Feet	Percentage of Total	Allocated Cost
General office	1,500	50.0%	$ 600
Purchasing	1,500	50.0	600
Total	3,000	100.0%	$1,200

FAST HINT
Relevant Exercise:
To apply these concepts, work Exercise 21–2.

FAST HINT
Alternative Example:
How would the rent expense be allocated if the general office occupied 2,000 square feet and the purchasing department occupied 1,000 square feet?
Answer: General office, $800; Purchasing, $400.

Illustration 21-4

ALPHAMAX HARDWARE STORE
Departmental Income Statement
For Year Ended December 31, 19X1

	Hardware Department	Housewares Department	Appliances Department	Combined
Sales	$119,500	$71,700	$47,800	$239,000
Cost of goods sold	73,800	43,800	30,200	147,800
Gross profit on sales	$ 45,700	$27,900	$17,600	$ 91,200
Operating expenses:				
Salaries expense	$ 15,600	$ 7,000	$ 7,800	$ 30,400
Depreciation expense, equipment	400	100	200	700
Supplies expense	300	200	100	600
Rent expense	4,860	3,240	2,700	10,800
Utilities expense	810	540	450	1,800
Advertising expense	500	300	200	1,000
Insurance expense	900	600	400	1,900
Share of general office expenses	7,650	4,590	3,060	15,300
Share of purchasing expenses	3,880	2,630	3,190	9,700
Total operating expenses	$ 34,900	$19,200	$18,100	$ 72,200
Net income (loss)	$ 10,800	$ 8,700	$ (500)	$ 19,000
Analysis:				
Gross profit as percent of sales	38.2%	38.9%	36.8%	38.2%

FAST HINT
Alternative Example:
If the $15,300 general office department expenses in Illustration 21–4 were allocated equally among the departments, what would be the revised net income for the hardware department and for the combined company?
Answer: Hardware department net income, $13,350; Combined net income, $19,000.

Then, the next table allocates the remaining $10,800 of rental cost among the three selling departments:

Department	Square Feet	Percentage of Total	Allocated Cost
Hardware	4,050	45.0%	$ 4,860
Housewares	2,700	30.0	3,240
Appliances	2,250	25.0	2,700
Total	9,000	100.0%	$10,800

More simply, the square footage occupied by the five departments is used for allocating the utilities expense of $2,400:

Department	Square Feet	Percentage of Total	Allocated Cost
General office	1,500	12.50%	$ 300
Purchasing	1,500	12.50	300
Hardware	4,050	33.75	810
Housewares	2,700	22.50	540
Appliances	2,250	18.75	450
Total	12,000	100.00%	$2,400

Examine the rows in Illustration 21–3 for the rent and utilities expenses to see that they show the amounts from these tables. For simplicity, the details of the other allocations are not shown.

Notice that each of the four indirect expenses is allocated to all five departments, except for the advertising expense. Because the advertising expense is allocated on the basis of sales and the service departments do not have any sales, it is allocated to only the three selling departments.

The third stage allocates the total expenses of the two service departments to the three selling departments. The allocations are accomplished with the listed allocation bases.

When the spreadsheet is completed, the amounts in the departmental columns can be used to prepare the departmental income statements that appear in Illustration 21–4.

FAST HINT
Important Point to Remember: Employee morale usually suffers when policies or procedures are perceived as unfair. Therefore, it may be worthwhile to exert the additional effort to design and explain an appropriate method of allocating service department costs.

Progress Check

21–5 If a company has two sales departments (shoes and hats) and two service departments (payroll and advertising), which of the following statements is correct?
   a. Wages incurred in the payroll department are direct expenses of the shoe department.
   b. Wages incurred in the payroll department are indirect expenses of the sales departments.
   c. Advertising department expenses should be allocated to the other three departments.

21–6 Which of the following bases could be used to allocate the wages and salaries of supervisors among production departments?
   a. Hours spent in each department.
   b. Number of employees in each department.
   c. Sales achieved in each department.
   d. Any of the above, depending on which seems most relevant.

21–7 What are the three steps in allocating expenses to profit centers?

Measures of departmental net incomes like those in Illustration 21–4 do not necessarily provide a valid basis for evaluating each department's performance, especially if the indirect expenses are a large portion of total expenses. The weakness exists in these situations because the net income numbers are greatly affected by the somewhat arbitrary assumptions and decisions involved in allocating indirect expenses. This limitation of departmental net income numbers can be overcome by evaluating departmental performance on the basis of their **departmental contributions to overhead.** A department's contribution to overhead is the amount by which its revenues exceed its *direct* costs and expenses.[2]

Illustration 21–5 shows the departmental contributions to overhead for Alphamax Company. Using the information in Illustrations 21–4 and 21–5, we can now perform a more complete evaluation of the profitability of the three sales departments. Compare the performance of the appliance department as described in the two reports. Illustration 21–4 shows a net loss of $500 resulting from the department's operations. On the other hand, Illustration 21–5 shows a positive contribution to overhead of $9,500, which is 19.9% of sales. Although the contribution of the appliance department is not as large as those of the other departments, a $9,500 contribution to overhead appears much better than a $500 loss.

When a department shows poor performance by reporting a net loss or a low contribution to overhead, management may consider eliminating it. However, in considering this action, neither the net income figure nor the contribution to overhead provides sufficient information for the decision. In fact, the department's **escapable**

DEPARTMENTAL CONTRIBUTIONS TO OVERHEAD

LO 3
Prepare reports that measure the performance of a profit center and describe the factors that should be considered in eliminating an unprofitable department.

ELIMINATING AN UNPROFITABLE DEPARTMENT

---

[2] The department's contribution is said to be to overhead because of the old practice of considering all indirect expenses to be "overhead." Thus, the excess of a department's revenues over its expenses represents a contribution toward paying the company's total overhead.

Illustration 21-5

ALPHAMAX HARDWARE STORE
Income Statement Showing Departmental Contributions to Overhead
For Year Ended December 31, 19X1

	Hardware Department	Housewares Department	Appliances Department	Combined
Sales	$119,500	$71,700	$47,800	$239,000
Cost of goods sold	73,800	43,800	30,200	147,800
Gross profit on sales	$ 45,700	$27,900	$17,600	$ 91,200
Direct expenses:				
Salaries expense	$ 15,600	$ 7,000	$ 7,800	$ 30,400
Depreciation expense, equipment	400	100	200	700
Supplies expense	300	200	100	600
Total direct expenses	$ 16,300	$ 7,300	$ 8,100	$ 31,700
Departmental contributions to overhead	$ 29,400	$20,600	$ 9,500	$ 59,500
Indirect expenses:				
Rent expense				$ 10,800
Utilities expense				1,800
Advertising expense				1,000
Insurance expense				1,900
General office department expense				15,300
Purchasing department expense				9,700
Total indirect expenses				$ 40,500
Net income				$ 19,000
Contribution percentages	24.6%	28.7%	19.9%	24.9%

FAST HINT
Important Point to Remember:
The net income in Illustration 21–4 and Illustration 21–5 is the same. The method of presenting indirect expenses in Illustration 21–5 does not change total net income but does identify each department's contribution to net income.

expenses and **inescapable expenses** must be considered. Escapable expenses (sometimes called *avoidable expenses*) are the expenses that would not be incurred if the department were eliminated. Inescapable expenses (sometimes called *unavoidable expenses*) are the expenses that would continue even if the department were eliminated. For example, the management of Alphamax Company is considering whether to eliminate its appliances department. An analysis of the various operating expenses for the whole company and the department shows that the expenses assigned to the appliances department fall into these categories:

FAST HINT
Relevant Exercise:
To apply these concepts, work Exercise 21–6

	Total Expenses	Escapable Expenses	Inescapable Expenses
Cost of goods sold	$30,200	$30,200	
Direct expenses:			
Salaries expense	7,800	7,800	
Depreciation expense, equipment	200		$ 200
Supplies expense	100	100	
Indirect expenses:			
Rent expense	2,700		2,700
Utilities expense	450		450
Advertising expense	200	200	
Insurance expense	400	300	100
Service department costs:			
Share of office department expenses	3,060	2,200	860
Share of purchasing expenses	3,190	1,000	2,190
Total	$48,300	$41,800	$6,500

FAST HINT
Critical Thought Question:
Why is insurance classified as both escapable and inescapable in this table?

This analysis shows that Alphamax would avoid total expenses of $41,800 if it eliminated the appliances department. But, the department's sales are $47,800, which means that the company will lose $6,000 of income if it eliminates the department. *As a general rule, a department can be considered a candidate for elimination if its revenues are less than its escapable expenses.* In effect, the escapable expenses are the costs of obtaining the department's revenues. When the escapable expenses are greater than the revenues, the company is better off if it eliminates the department.

In considering the elimination of an unprofitable department, you also need to determine whether its presence increases the revenues of other departments. Even though one department is unprofitable on its own, it may still contribute to the sales and profits of other departments by bringing in more customers. In this case, a department might be continued even when its revenues are less than its escapable expenses. On the other hand, even a profitable department might be discontinued if its space, assets, and staff can be more profitably used by expanding an existing department or by creating a completely new one.

From this discussion, you should understand that the decision to keep or eliminate a department requires a more complex analysis than simply looking at the bottom line of a departmental income statement or another managerial accounting report. Even though these reports provide useful information, they are only the starting point for the decision.

FAST HINT
Class Discussion:
Give an example of a department that might be used by companies to attract customers even though it might incur a loss.

Progress Check

21-8 **On an income statement showing departmental and combined contributions to overhead:**
a. **Indirect expenses are subtracted from each department's revenues.**
b. **Only direct costs and expenses are subtracted from each department's revenues.**
c. **Net income is shown for each department.**

21-9 **What is the difference between escapable and inescapable expenses?**

21-10 **As a general rule, a department can be considered a candidate for elimination if:**
a. **Its revenues are less than its escapable expenses.**
b. **It has a net loss.**
c. **Its inescapable expenses are greater than its revenues.**

Management can use *departmental accounting* reports of net income and contributions to overhead in assessing whether a department should remain in the company. However, are these numbers useful for assessing how well a department *manager* has performed? In these situations, neither a department's net income nor its contribution to overhead may be very useful because many expenses that enter into them are beyond the control of the manager. Instead, the performance of a manager should be evaluated with information provided in *responsibility accounting* reports that describe the department's activities in terms of **controllable costs.** A cost is controllable if the manager has the power to determine or at least strongly influence the amounts incurred. An **uncontrollable cost** is not within the manager's control or influence.

CONTROLLABLE COSTS AND EXPENSES

LO 4

Explain the concept of controllable costs and describe the problems associated with allocating joint costs between products.

Controllable Costs and Direct Costs

You should understand that controllable costs are not necessarily the same as direct costs. Direct costs are easily traced to a specific department, but their amounts may or may not be under the control of the department's manager. For example, department managers often have little or no control over the amount of depreciation expense because they cannot do anything to affect the amount of equipment assigned to their departments. Also, managers usually have no control over their own salaries. On the other hand, department managers can control or influence the cost of goods sold and the supplies used in the department.

When controllable costs are used to judge managers' performances, managers should rely on data that describes the departments' outputs and their controllable costs and expenses. A manager's performance should be judged by comparing the current period's results with planned levels and the results of prior periods.

Circumstances that Make Costs Controllable or Uncontrollable

Controllable and uncontrollable costs must be identified with a particular manager and a definite time period. Without defining these two reference points, it is not possible to know whether a cost is controllable or uncontrollable. For example, the cost of property insurance may not be controllable at the department manager's level, but it is subject to control by the executive responsible for obtaining the company's insurance coverage. Likewise, this executive may not have any control over expenses resulting from insurance policies already in force. But, when a policy eventually expires, the executive is free to renegotiate the replacement policy and thus gain some control or influence over the cost in the long run. Thus, all costs are controllable at some level of management if the time period is sufficiently long.

RESPONSIBILITY ACCOUNTING

The concept of controllable costs and expenses provides the basis for a responsibility accounting system. In a responsibility accounting system, managers are responsible for the costs and expenses that fall under their control. Prior to each reporting period, the company develops plans that specify the expected costs or expenses under the control of each manager. Those plans are called **responsibility accounting budgets.** To enlist the cooperation of each manager and to be sure that the budgets establish reasonable goals, the managers should be closely involved in preparing their budgets.

The responsibility accounting system accumulates costs and expenses to include in timely reports to the managers about the costs for which they are responsible. These reports are called **performance reports.** They compare actual costs and expenses to the budgeted amounts. Managers use performance reports to focus their attention on specific actual costs that differ from the budgeted amounts. With this information in hand, they can decide what corrective action to take.

Higher management levels also use performance reports to evaluate the effectiveness of lower-level managers in controlling costs and keeping them within budgeted amounts. To achieve proper motivation, managers should not be evaluated using costs that they do not control. Chapter 24 gives further consideration to the nature and use of performance reports.

A responsibility accounting system should reflect the fact that control over costs and expenses belongs to several levels of management. For example, consider the organization chart in Illustration 21–6. In the chart, the lines connecting the various managerial positions represent channels of authority. Thus, while the three department managers are responsible for the controllable costs and expenses incurred in their departments, those same costs are subject to the general control of the western plant manager. And, the western plant's costs are subject to the control of the vice president of production, the president, and ultimately the board of directors.

At the lowest levels, managers have only limited responsibilities and relatively little control over costs. As a result, performance reports for this management level should cover only a few controllable costs. Responsibilities and control broaden at higher levels in the company. Reports to higher-level managers are therefore broader and cover a wider range of costs. However, reports to managers at these levels normally do not contain all the details reported to their subordinates. Instead, the details reported to lower-level managers are normally summarized on the reports to their superiors. The details are summarized for two reasons: (1) lower-level managers are pri-

FAST HINT
Relevant Exercise:
To apply these concepts, work Exercise 21–7.

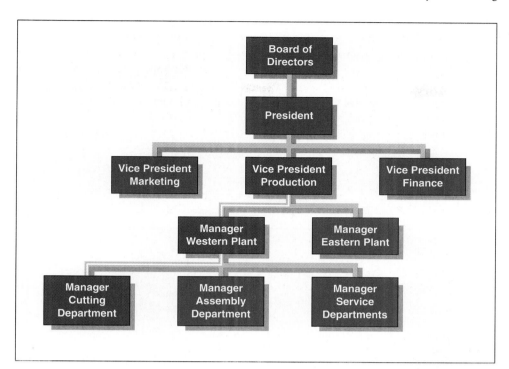

Illustration 21-6
Levels of Organizational
Responsibility

marily responsible for the costs described by the details and (2) reports with too many details can obscure more important points. When reports to higher-level managers are too detailed, they may draw attention from the broader, more important issues confronting the company.

Illustration 21–7 presents summarized performance reports for the three management levels highlighted in Illustration 21–6. Observe in Illustration 21–7 that costs under the control of the cutting department manager are totaled and included among the controllable costs of the Western plant manager. Also, the costs under the control of the plant manager are totaled and included among the controllable costs of the vice president for production. In this manner, a responsibility accounting system provides relevant information for each management level.

Before going on, we need to acknowledge that computers have caused our ability to produce vast amounts of information to far outstrip our ability to use the information. Good managers need to select relevant data for planning and controlling the area under their responsibility. A good responsibility accounting system reflects this need and makes every effort to get the right information to the right person at the right time. The right person is the person who can control the cost and the right time is before the cost gets out of control.

Consider again the opening discussion of **Kent Moore Cabinets.** Charles Rhinehart's ultimate solution was to change the basis for calculating the commissions paid to salespersons. Sales revenues were reduced by the raw materials, direct labor, delivery, and reinstallation costs of reworking cabinets. He combined the concepts of cost allocation, controllable costs and responsibility accounting to motivate salespersons to control the cost of errors. Because salespersons were now rewarded on sales net of the cost of the controllable errors, their behavior changed. They verified the specifications before submitting the cabinet drawings to be built. This resulted in a reduction of the costs and a net income increase of more than 20%.

Illustration 21-7
Responsibility Accounting
Performance Reports

Vice president, production

Controllable Costs	For July		
	Budgeted Amount	Actual Amount	Over (Under) Budget
Salaries, plant managers	$ 80,000	$ 80,000	$　　–0–
Quality control costs	21,000	22,400	1,400
Office costs	29,500	28,800	(700)
Western plant	276,700	279,500	2,800
Eastern plant	390,000	380,600	(9,400)
Total	$797,200	$791,300	$(5,900)

Manager, western plant

Controllable Costs	For July		
	Budgeted Amount	Actual Amount	Over (Under) Budget
Salaries, department managers	$ 75,000	$ 78,000	$3,000
Depreciation	10,600	10,600	–0–
Insurance	6,800	6,300	(500)
Cutting department	79,600	79,900	300
Assembly department	61,500	60,200	(1,300)
Service department 1	24,300	24,700	400
Service department 2	18,900	19,800	900
Total	$276,700	$279,500	$2,800

FAST HINT
Critical Thought Question:
In Illustration 21–7, if the actual amount charged to the manager, western plant, for service department 2 were $17,000 instead of $19,800, the total of the actual expenses and budgeted expense would be equal. Would an analysis of the controllable expenses for the western plant still be useful? Explain.

Manager, cutting department

Controllable Costs	For July		
	Budgeted Amount	Actual Amount	Over (Under) Budget
Raw materials	$26,500	$25,900	$ (600)
Direct labor	32,000	33,500	1,500
Indirect labor	7,200	7,000	(200)
Supplies	4,000	3,900	(100)
Other controllable costs	9,900	9,600	(300)
Total	$79,600	$79,900	$　300

JOINT COSTS

FAST HINT
Relevant Quick Study:
To apply these concepts, work QS 21–4.

Most manufacturing processes involve **joint costs.** A joint cost is a single cost incurred in producing or purchasing two or more essentially different products. A joint cost is somewhat similar to an indirect expense in the sense that it is shared among more than one cost object. For example, a petroleum refining company incurs a joint cost when it buys crude oil that it breaks apart to produce different grades of gasoline, lubricating oil, kerosene, paraffin, ethylene, and a variety of other products. Likewise, a sawmill incurs joint costs when it buys a log and cuts it into boards classified as Clear, Select Structural, No. 1 Common, No. 2 Common, No. 3 Common, as well as other types of lumber and by-products.

When a joint cost is incurred, a question arises as to whether its amount should be allocated to the different products produced from it. Because the allocation of a joint cost is always arbitrary, the best answer is to avoid allocating the cost to the products

Illustration 21–8
Allocating a Joint Cost on a
Physical Basis

Grade of Lumber	Board Feet Produced	Percentage of Total	Allocated Cost	Selling Price	Gross Profit
Structural	10,000	10.0%	$ 3,000	$12,000	$ 9,000
No. 1 Common	30,000	30.0	9,000	18,000	9,000
No. 2 Common	40,000	40.0	12,000	16,000	4,000
No. 3 Common	20,000	20.0	6,000	4,000	(2,000)
Total	100,000	100.0%	$30,000	$50,000	$20,000

whenever possible. Many managerial decisions, such as whether to continue buying logs and cutting lumber, should be based on unallocated cost information.

When GAAP financial statements are prepared, however, the full joint cost must be assigned to specific products. Thus, the financial accountant faces the problem of deciding how to allocate the joint cost among the products that result from incurring the cost. For example, if some products are sold and others remain in inventory, allocating the joint cost allows the accountant to assign costs to the cost of goods sold and the ending inventory.

A joint cost could be allocated on some physical basis, such as the ratio of pounds, cubic feet, or gallons of each joint product to the total pounds, cubic feet, or gallons of all joint products flowing from the cost. However, this method is not usually applied because the resulting cost allocations do not reflect the relative market values acquired with the joint cost or produced from the joint cost. For example, certain parts of a log are more valuable than others because of the products that can be produced from them. A simple physical basis for allocating the joint cost would not reflect the extra value flowing into some products or the inferior value flowing into others. In turn, a physical basis could cause the sale of some joint products to appear more profitable than others. Some joint products may even be reported as selling at a loss while others show a profit.

As an example of using a physical measure to allocate a joint cost, suppose that a sawmill bought logs for $30,000. When cut, the logs produced 100,000 board feet of lumber in the grades and amounts shown in Illustration 21–8. Observe that the logs produced 20,000 board feet of No. 3 Common lumber, which is 20% of the total lumber produced from the logs. Under the physical allocation, the No. 3 Common lumber would be assigned 20% of the $30,000 cost of the logs, or $6,000 ($30,000 × 20%). Because this low-grade lumber can be sold for only $4,000, this allocation would cause a $2,000 loss to be reported from its production and sale.

The disadvantage of the physical allocation approach is that it does not reflect the fact that some portions of the raw materials (such as logs) are more valuable than others. For example, the portion of a log used to produce Structural grade lumber is worth more than the portion used to produce No. 3 Common lumber.

A better approach allocates the joint cost in proportion to the value of the output produced by the process at the point of separation. Illustration 21–9 demonstrates this approach to allocation. Here, the percentages of the total cost allocated to each grade are determined by the ratio of each grade's selling price to the total selling price of $50,000. Thus, for example, the Structural grade lumber receives 24% of the total cost ($12,000/$50,000) instead of the 10% portion based on the physical measure. And, the No. 3 Common lumber receives only 8% of the total cost, or $2,400, which is materially less than the $6,000 assigned to it with the physical basis. Notice that one outcome of the value-based allocation is that *every* grade produces exactly the same 40% gross profit on its selling price. This 40% rate also equals the gross profit rate from selling all the lumber made from the $30,000 logs for a combined price of $50,000.

Illustration 21-9
Allocating a Joint Cost on a
Value Basis

FAST HINT
Alternative Example:
Refer to Illustration 21–9. If the
selling price of structural lumber is changed to $10,000, what
would be the revised ratio of the
market value of No. 1 common
to the total?
Answer: $18,000/$48,000 =
37.5%

Grade of Lumber	Selling Price	Percent of Total	Allocated Cost	Gross Profit
Structural	$12,000	24.0%	$ 7,200	$ 4,800
No. 1 Common	18,000	36.0	10,800	7,200
No. 2 Common	16,000	32.0	9,600	6,400
No. 3 Common	4,000	8.0	2,400	1,600
Total	$50,000	100.0%	$30,000	$20,000

Progress Check

21-11 Would departmental net income and contribution to overhead be useful when assessing the performance of a department manager? Explain why.

21-12 Performance reports that are used to evaluate managers should:
a. Include data about controllable expenses.
b. Compare actual results with planned levels.
c. Both a and b are correct.

21-13 A company produces three products: B1, B2, and B3. The joint cost incurred during the current month for these products is $180,000. The following data relate to this month's production:

Product	Units Produced	Unit Sales Price
B1	96,000	$3.00
B2	64,000	6.00
B3	32,000	9.00

The amount of joint cost that should be allocated to B3 is: (a) $30,000; (b) $54,000; (c) $90,000.

ACTIVITY-BASED COSTING

LO 5

Describe activity-based costing and its advantages for generating useful information for management's use.

In reading the preceding section, you may have recognized that the factory overhead costs in job order and process cost accounting systems are shared indirect costs. Factory overhead is an indirect cost because it cannot be clearly associated with specific jobs, processes, or products. Factory overhead is also a shared cost, or common cost, because it is incurred in producing more than one product. In earlier chapters, we allocated this shared cost primarily in proportion to the direct labor cost incurred for a job or a process.

From the discussion in this chapter and the previous two or three chapters, you should have gained the insight that overhead cost is really too complex to be explained as the result of the variation of only one factor such as direct labor.[3] In reality, indirect costs are produced by many different factors. **Activity-based costing** attempts to deal with this complexity by doing a better job of allocating costs to the users of overhead activities.

Inappropriate allocations can distort unit costs. To simplify our examples, we usually limit the number of products or departments to two or three items. When the number of products (and/or departments) increases, the possibility of improperly

---

[3]Because technological advances keep increasing the extent of automated manufacturing, direct labor cost generally has declined as a percentage of total production cost. In some companies, direct labor cost is such a small part of total cost that it is treated as overhead.

Illustration 21-10   Activity-Based Cost Accounting—General Situation

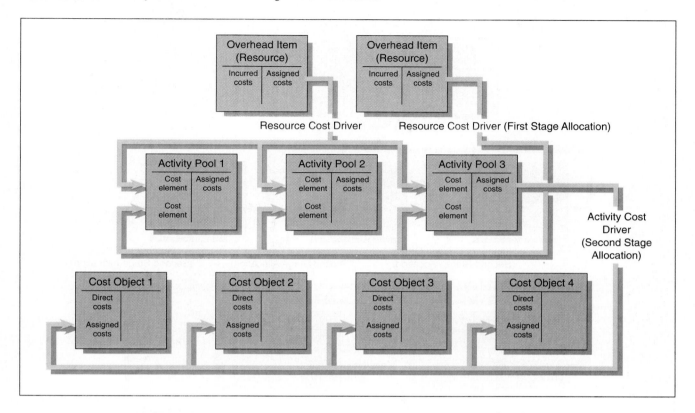

assigning costs increases. In realistic situations, traditional ways of allocating over-head costs on the basis of direct labor often distort unit costs.

The idea of using activities to allocate costs certainly is not new. Recently, though, many firms have been attracted by the potential benefits of activity-based costing. Robert Kaplan of Harvard University and Robin Cooper, formerly with Harvard University, are the primary developers of the latest variation of activity-based costing (ABC). In a series of articles, they have documented the improper accumulation, allocation, and use of traditional cost data.[4]

Illustrations 21–10 and 21–11 show the type of allocations represented by activity-based costing. Illustration 21–10 depicts a general case and includes standard ABC terminology.

Starting at the top of Illustration 21–10, the costs of separate overhead items or *resources* are collected in separate temporary accounts. Then, the cost of each resource is allocated among the **activity cost pools.** Each activity cost pool is a temporary account that accumulates the costs a company incurs to support an identified activity. The basis selected to allocate the cost of a resource to activity cost pools is called a **cost driver.** Ideally, the cost driver selected is the factor that caused the resource to be consumed by the identified activities.

The costs accumulated in each activity cost pool include direct costs of the activity as well as indirect costs that are assigned using the allocation methods illustrated earlier in this chapter. In Illustration 21–10, each **cost element** represents the cost of a resource consumed by an activity and assigned to an activity cost pool. Since both direct and indirect costs are assigned in this *first stage* of ABC, it corresponds to the

---

[4]You especially might be interested in reading "Does Your Company Need a New Cost System?" by Robin Cooper, *Harvard Business Review,* Spring 1987.

Illustration 21-11   Activity-Based Cost Accounting—Specific Example

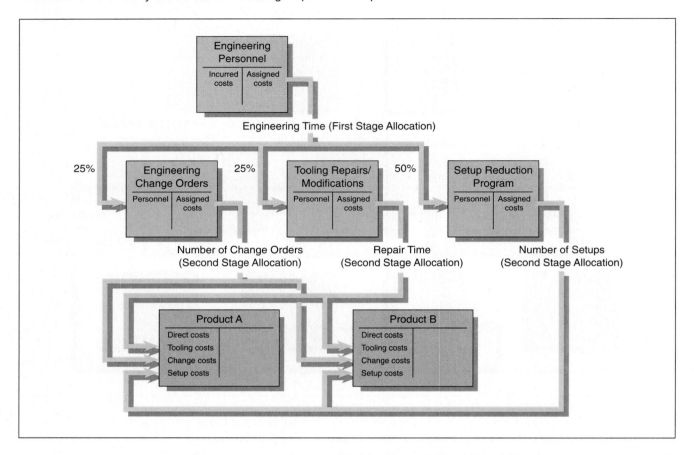

first and second stages that we discussed in the *"Procedures for Allocating Costs and Expenses"* section of this chapter.

In practice, an activity cost pool account is handled in the same way as a manufacturing overhead account. After all activity costs have been accumulated in an activity cost pool account, consumers of the activity, termed *cost objects,* are assigned a portion of the total activity cost using an appropriate cost driver or allocation base. This allocation is the *second stage* of ABC. A cost object can be a product, a department, a process, a job, or any other item of interest.

Illustration 21–11 shows the assignment of a specific overhead item, Engineering department personnel costs, to three activity cost pools—Engineering Change Orders, Tooling Repairs/Modifications, and Setup Reduction Program. The cost driver for the first stage allocation of the resource to the activity pools is engineering time spent in each activity. In this example, 25% of the engineering personnel's time is spent on engineering change orders that modify the production process, 25% on tooling repairs or modifications, and 50% on reducing the total time required to get equipment ready to run the next job (setup reduction program).

The total costs of each activity cost pool are then assigned to the final cost objects, Products A and B. The activity cost driver or allocation base for the Engineering Change Orders pool is the estimated number of change orders for each product. The activity cost driver for the Tooling Repairs/Modifications pool is the estimated time spent on machinery used by each product. The Setup Reduction Program activity pool in Illustration 21–11 is assigned using the estimated number of setup reductions associated with each product.

As Illustrations 21–10 and 21–11 show, ABC assigns costs first to activities and then from activities to users of the activities. For example, all factory overhead is first assigned to the activity requiring the expenditure, such as the processing of engineering change orders. Second, it is assigned to the products or cost objects using the activity. Realize that one activity cost pool may be allocated to another activity cost pool or pools before it reaches a final cost object.

To illustrate the impact on unit cost of ABC's emphasis on selecting appropriate cost drivers, the following information relates to a company's purchasing department and other general company activity:

Purchasing department

Direct costs	$90,000
Indirect administrative and service costs	$15,000
Purchase orders originated	35,000 orders
Unique part numbers handled	29,000 part numbers

Other Activity	Direct Labor Cost	Unique Part Numbers	Purchase Orders	Total Units Produced
Principal product A	$ 700,000	650	18,000	20,000
Principal product B	400,000	1,200	12,000	10,000
Other products	100,000	27,150	5,000	15,000
Totals	$1,200,000	29,000	35,000	45,000

In this example, purchasing (the purchasing department) is the activity cost pool. The first stage of cost assignment (assigning direct and indirect costs to the activity pool) has already been accomplished. Following the practice of most manufacturing companies, purchasing department costs traditionally are included in a general overhead account that is allocated on the basis of direct labor. If this practice is followed, the traditional overhead rate due entirely to purchasing is $0.0875 and the partial unit product costs are as shown in the next table.

Traditional allocation

Purchasing department overhead rate: $105,000/$1,200,000 = $0.0875 per direct labor dollar or, 8.75% of direct labor cost

	Unit Costs		
	Product A	**Product B**	**Other Products**
$\dfrac{\$0.0875 \times \$700,000}{20,000 \text{ units}}$	$3.0625		
$\dfrac{\$0.0875 \times \$400,000}{10,000 \text{ units}}$		$3.5000	
$\dfrac{\$0.0875 \times \$100,000}{15,000 \text{ units}}$			$0.5833

After completing a study, the company decides that the work of the purchasing department is driven (increased) primarily by the number of unique part numbers that must be ordered. Therefore, the purchasing department overhead, under an activity-based system, should be allocated on the basis of part numbers. Product unit costs under ABC are shown in the next table.

Activity-based allocation

Purchasing department overhead rate: $105,000/29,000 = $3.621 per part

	Unit Costs		
	Product A	**Product B**	**Other Products**
$\dfrac{\$3.621 \times 650 \text{ part numbers}}{20,000 \text{ units}}$	$0.1177		
$\dfrac{\$3.621 \times 1,200 \text{ part numbers}}{10,000 \text{ units}}$		$0.4345	
$\dfrac{\$3.621 \times 27,150 \text{ part numbers}}{15,000 \text{ units}}$			$6.5540

FAST HINT
Relevant Quick Study:
To apply these concepts, work QS 21–5.

The change in unit costs for Products A and B and the other products is substantial when using ABC compared to the usual traditional approach. The following table shows that the ABC unit costs of Products A and B decreased almost 100%. The percentage increase in unit costs of the other products, though, is more than 1,000%.

	Change in Unit Costs		
	Product A	**Product B**	**Other Products**
Absolute increase (decrease) with ABC	($2.9448)	($3.0655)	$5.9707
Percentage increase (decrease)	(96.2%)	(87.6%)	1,023.6%

The main differences between traditional allocation methods and ABC involve how many cost drivers are used and how many allocations companies make. Traditional cost systems commonly accumulate overhead in one overhead account (or a small number of overhead accounts). Companies typically assign these overhead costs to departments using a single allocation base such as direct labor. Service department costs may be allocated to production departments separately. Once all indirect costs are accumulated at the departmental level, accounting personnel assign departmental costs to the units or products produced by the department.

Under ABC, the costs of resources (which may include service departments) are assigned to activities that use the resources. Each resource may have a unique cost driver (allocation base). The firm uses this driver (base) to assign the total cost of the resource to various production-related activities (pools) consuming the resource. Then, the firm selects an appropriate cost driver (allocation base) for each activity pool. The

firm uses this cost driver to assign the accumulated activity costs to the cost objects (such as products or departments) that benefited from the activity. For a typical firm, an ABC system may involve 6 to 12 (or more) times as many allocations as a traditional cost system.

Perkin-Elmer Corporation, a maker of analytical instruments in Norwalk, Connecticut, recently installed an activity-based cost system. John Bennett, the corporate controller, indicated that at first they tried to analyze too many cost drivers. Then, they established cross-functional teams and were able to identify the most important cost drivers in each area of the company.

Illustration 21-12 Costs and Cost Drivers in Activity-Based Costing

Cost	Cost Driver
Materials purchasing	Number of purchase orders received from a department
Materials handling	Number of materials requisitions received from a department or for a job
Personnel processing	Number of employees hired or laid off
Equipment depreciation	Number of products produced or hours of use
Quality inspection costs	Number of units inspected
Indirect labor for setting up equipment for production	Number of setups required by a department
Engineering costs for product modifications	Number of modifications (engineering change orders) initiated for a product

The actual allocation procedures for ABC are similar to the practices used in this chapter for allocating indirect costs among departments and for allocating service department costs to production departments. Under ABC, a service department is termed a resource and its costs are allocated to activity cost pools rather than to production departments. Of course, a cost pool can be a production department.

Some examples of indirect cost pools and their cost drivers are listed in Illustration 21–12. The accounting system uses these cost drivers to assign activity costs to cost objects and, ultimately, to products produced.

ABC is especially effective in situations where many different kinds of products are manufactured in the same department or departments. For example, some products produced in a department might be simple, while others are more complex. The more complex products are likely to require more assistance from certain service departments, such as engineering, maintenance, and materials handling. However, if the same amount of direct labor is applied to the complex and simple products, a traditional overhead allocation system assigns the same overhead cost to them, despite their differences. With the more detailed approach of ABC, the more complex products are assigned a greater portion of the overhead cost. As a result, pricing and other kinds of decisions may be affected. In addition, production department managers can more usefully focus on managing the activities that drive overhead cost instead of merely trying to reduce allocated overhead cost by reducing direct labor cost. Even with ABC, however, a company's managers cannot focus solely on activities. The contribution of an activity to the entire production process must be kept firmly in mind.

Another benefit of ABC is that it causes management to pay closer attention to all the activities that take place in the business. If overhead costs are grouped together in a single account, it is possible that attention will not be directed to controlling any of them individually. But when ABC is implemented, it requires managers to look very closely at each item. In turn, the system encourages them to manage each cost more carefully to increase the benefit obtained for each dollar spent. In addition, this analysis encourages managers to cooperate because it allows them to see how their efforts are interrelated. When these things occur, the company is said to have implemented *activity-based management*. In effect, implementing activity-based costing can bring about many improvements in a company that reach far beyond cost accounting information.

Progress Check

21-14   **What is a cost driver?**

21-15   **When activity-based costing is implemented rather than traditional allocation methods:**
a. **Managers must identify cost drivers for various components of overhead cost.**
b. **Individual cost items in service departments are allocated to products manufactured or sold in production or selling departments.**
c. **Managers can direct their attention to the activities that drive overhead cost.**
d. **All of the above.**

SUMMARY OF THE CHAPTER IN TERMS OF LEARNING OBJECTIVES

LO 1.   Explain why businesses are divided into subunits or departments and explain the difference between cost centers and profit centers. Businesses are divided into departments whenever they become too large to be effectively managed as a single unit. Production departments either manufacture products in a factory or sell products in a store. Service departments support the activities of these production departments. Departmental accounting systems provide information for evaluating departments' performances and responsibility accounting systems provide information for evaluating the performance of department managers. Departments are evaluated as cost centers if they incur costs but do not generate revenues. Departments are evaluated as profit centers if they generate revenues.

LO 2.   Describe the difference between direct and indirect expenses of departments, the bases used to allocate indirect expenses, and the procedures used in the allocation process. Direct expenses are easily traced to a specific department because they are incurred for the sole benefit of one department. Indirect expenses, on the other hand, benefit more than one department. If departmental net incomes are measured, indirect expenses are allocated to the departments on some reasonable basis. The allocation basis selected for an indirect expense is a matter of judgment but should reflect the relative benefit the departments receive from the expense.

LO 3.   Prepare reports that measure the performance of a profit center and describe the factors that should be considered in eliminating an unprofitable department. Departmental income statements can be used to evaluate the profitability of the departments that generate revenues. But, if indirect expenses are large and difficult to allocate, the departments should be evaluated on the basis of their contributions to overhead. In general, an unprofitable department should not be eliminated if its revenues exceed its escapable expenses. However, a decision to eliminate a department should also consider how it affects the performance of the other departments as well as alternative uses of the space, assets, and staff.

LO 4.   Explain the concept of controllable costs and describe the problems associated with allocating joint costs between products. A controllable cost must be identified with a specific level of management and a specific time period. The total expenses of operating a department often include items that are not controllable by the department manager. To be useful, performance reports produced by a responsibility accounting system for evaluating departmental managers should include only the expenses (and revenues) controllable by the managers.

A joint cost is a single cost incurred in producing or purchasing two or more different products. When income statements are prepared, joint costs should be allocated to the resulting joint products based on the relative market value of the joint products at the point of separation.

LO 5. Describe activity-based costing and its advantages for generating useful information for management. Activity-based costing is a system for assigning overhead costs to products and departments in accordance with cost drivers. ABC differs from traditional cost accounting systems that allocate overhead in proportion to a single allocation base, such as direct labor hours. The main purpose of ABC is to gain more understanding about the costs of producing different products. Beyond providing this information, a major advantage of ABC is that it forces managers to analyze and then control individual overhead cost items instead of merely lumping them together in a single unmanageable group.

DEMONSTRATION PROBLEM

Use the following information to prepare departmental income statements for Hacker's Haven, a computer store. The store has five departments. Three of them are selling departments (hardware, software, and repairs), and two are service departments (general office and purchasing).

Some accounting information about the five departments' activities for 19X1 follows:

	General Office	Purchasing	Hardware	Software	Repairs
Sales	—	—	$960,000	$600,000	$840,000
Cost of goods sold	—	—	500,000	300,000	200,000
Direct expenses:					
Payroll	$60,000	$45,000	80,000	25,000	325,000
Depreciation	6,000	7,200	33,000	4,200	9,600
Supplies	15,000	10,000	10,000	2,000	25,000

In addition, several indirect expenses are incurred in the departments. In preparing an income statement, these indirect expenses are allocated among the five departments. Then, the expenses of the two service departments are allocated to the three production departments. The total amounts and the allocation bases for each expense are as follows:

Type of Indirect Expense	Total Cost	Allocation Basis
Rent	$150,000	Square footage occupied
Utilities	50,000	Square footage occupied
Advertising	125,000	Dollars of sales
Insurance	30,000	Value of assets insured
Service departments:		
General office	?	Number of employees
Purchasing	?	Dollars of cost of goods sold

The following information is needed for the allocations:

Department	Square Feet	Sales	Insured Assets	Employees	Cost of Goods Sold
General office	500		$ 60,000		
Purchasing	500		72,000		
Hardware	4,000	$ 960,000	330,000	5	$500,000
Software	3,000	600,000	42,000	5	300,000
Repairs	2,000	840,000	96,000	10	200,000
Total	10,000	$2,400,000	$600,000	20	$1,000,000

Required

1. Complete a departmental expense allocation worksheet for Hacker's Haven.
2. Prepare a departmental income statement reporting net income for each selling department and for all selling departments combined.

Planning the Solution

- Set up and complete four schedules to allocate the indirect expenses for rent, utilities, advertising, and insurance.
- Allocate the departments' indirect expenses with a six-column worksheet like the one in Illustration 21–3. Enter the given amounts of the direct expenses for each department. Then enter the allocated amounts of the indirect expenses that were just calculated.
- Complete two schedules for allocating the general office and purchasing department costs to the three selling departments. Enter these amounts on the worksheet and determine the total expenses allocated to the three selling departments.
- Prepare a four-column departmental income statement like the one in Illustration 21–4. Show sales, cost of goods sold, the gross profit from sales, the individual direct and indirect expenses, and the net income for each of the three selling departments and for the entire company.

Solution to Demonstration Problem

Allocations of indirect expenses among the five departments:

Rent	Square Feet	Percentage of Total	Allocated Cost
General office	500	5.0%	$ 7,500
Purchasing	500	5.0	7,500
Hardware	4,000	40.0	60,000
Software	3,000	30.0	45,000
Repairs	2,000	20.0	30,000
Total	10,000	100.0%	$150,000

Utilities	Square Feet	Percentage of Total	Allocated Cost
General office	500	5.0%	$ 2,500
Purchasing	500	5.0	2,500
Hardware	4,000	40.0	20,000
Software	3,000	30.0	15,000
Repairs	2,000	20.0	10,000
Total	10,000	100.0%	$50,000

Advertising	Sales Dollars	Percentage of Total	Allocated Cost
Hardware	$ 960,000	40.0%	$ 50,000
Software	600,000	25.0	31,250
Repairs	840,000	35.0	43,750
Total	$2,400,000	100.0%	$125,000

Insurance	Assets Insured	Percentage of Total	Allocated Cost
General office	$ 60,000	10.0%	$ 3,000
Purchasing	72,000	12.0	3,600
Hardware	330,000	55.0	16,500
Software	42,000	7.0	2,100
Repairs	96,000	16.0	4,800
Total	$600,000	100.0%	$30,000

Departmental Expense Allocation Spreadsheet
For Year Ended December 31, 19X1

Expense	Allocation Bases	Expense Account Balance	General Office	Purchasing	Hardware Dept.	Software Dept.	Repairs Dept.
Direct expenses:							
Payroll		$ 535,000	$60,000	$45,000	$ 80,000	$ 25,000	$325,000
Depreciation		60,000	6,000	7,200	33,000	4,200	9,600
Supplies		62,000	15,000	10,000	10,000	2,000	25,000
Indirect expenses:							
Rent	Square ft.	150,000	7,500	7,500	60,000	45,000	30,000
Utilities	Square ft.	50,000	2,500	2,500	20,000	15,000	10,000
Advertising	Sales	125,000	—	—	50,000	31,250	43,750
Insurance	Assets	30,000	3,000	3,600	16,500	2,100	4,800
Total		$1,012,000	$94,000	$75,800	$269,500	$124,550	$448,150
Service dept. expenses:							
General office	Employees		$94,000		23,500	23,500	47,000
Purchasing	Goods sold			$75,800	37,900	22,740	15,160
Total expenses allocated to selling departments		$1,012,000			$330,900	$170,790	$510,310

Allocations of service department expenses among the three selling departments:

General Office

	Employees	Percent of Total	Allocated Cost
Hardware	5	25.0%	$23,500
Software	5	25.0	23,500
Repairs	10	50.0	47,000
Total	20	100.0%	$94,000

Purchasing

	Cost of Goods Sold	Percent of Total	Allocated Cost
Hardware	$ 500,000	50.0%	$37,900
Software	300,000	30.0	22,740
Repairs	200,000	20.0	15,160
Total	$1,000,000	100.0%	$75,800

HACKER'S HAVEN COMPUTER STORE
Departmental Income Statement
For Year Ended December 31, 19X1

	Hardware	Software	Repairs	Combined
Sales	$960,000	$600,000	$840,000	$2,400,000
Cost of goods sold	500,000	300,000	200,000	1,000,000
Gross profit	$460,000	$300,000	$640,000	$1,400,000
Expenses:				
Payroll	$ 80,000	$ 25,000	$325,000	$ 430,000
Depreciation	33,000	4,200	9,600	46,800
Supplies	10,000	2,000	25,000	37,000
Rent	60,000	45,000	30,000	135,000
Utilities	20,000	15,000	10,000	45,000
Advertising	50,000	31,250	43,750	125,000
Insurance	16,500	2,100	4,800	23,400
General office	23,500	23,500	47,000	94,000
Purchasing	37,900	22,740	15,160	75,800
Total expenses	$330,900	$170,790	$510,310	$1,012,000
Net income	$129,100	$129,210	$129,690	$ 388,000

GLOSSARY

Activity-based costing a system of assigning costs to departments and products on the basis of a variety of activities instead of only one. p. 820

Activity cost pool a temporary account that accumulates the costs a company incurs to support an identified activity. p. 821

Controllable costs costs with amounts that the manager has the power to determine or at least strongly influence. p. 815

Cost center a department that incurs costs (or expenses) without directly generating revenues. p. 803

Cost driver a basis for allocating the cost of a resource to an activity cost pool or allocating the cost of an activity cost pool to a cost object. p. 821

Cost element the cost of a resource consumed by an activity and assigned to an activity cost pool. p. 821

Departmental accounting system an accounting system that provides information that management can use to evaluate the profitability or cost effectiveness of a department's activities. p. 802

Departmental contribution to overhead the amount by which a department's revenues exceed its direct costs and expenses. p. 813

Direct expenses expenses that are easily traced and assigned to a specific department because they are incurred for the sole benefit of that department. p. 806

Escapable expenses expenses that would not be incurred if a department were eliminated. p. 813

Indirect expenses expenses that are not easily associated with a specific department; they are incurred for the benefit of more than one department. p. 806

Inescapable expenses expenses that will continue even if a department is eliminated. p. 814

Joint cost a single cost incurred in producing or purchasing two or more essentially different products. p. 818

Performance report a responsibility accounting report that compares actual costs and expenses for a department with the budgeted amounts. p. 816

Profit center a unit of a business that not only incurs costs but also generates revenues. p. 803

Responsibility accounting budget a plan that specifies the expected costs and expenses under the control of a manager. p. 816

Responsibility accounting system an accounting system that provides information that management can use to evaluate the performance of a department's manager. p. 802

Uncontrollable costs costs that the manager does not have the power to determine or at least strongly influence. p. 815

QUESTIONS

1. Why are businesses divided into departments?

2. What is the difference between production departments and service departments?

3. Is it possible to evaluate the profitability of a cost center? Why?

4. How is a departmental sales analysis spreadsheet used in determining sales by departments?

5. What is the difference between direct and indirect expenses?

6. Suggest a reasonable basis for allocating each of the following indirect expenses to departments: *(a)* salary of a supervisor who manages several departments, *(b)* rent, *(c)* heat, *(d)* electricity used for lighting, *(e)* janitorial services, *(f)* advertising, *(g)* expired insurance on equipment, and *(h)* property taxes on equipment.

7. How is a department's contribution to overhead measured?

8. What are controllable costs?

9. Why should managers be closely involved in preparing their responsibility accounting budgets?

10. In responsibility accounting, who is the right person to be given timely reports and statistics for a specific cost?

11. What is a joint cost? How are joint costs usually allocated among the products produced from them?

12. What is activity-based costing?

13. Lands' End receives telephone orders for merchandise presented in different catalogs sent to different groups of customers. Why would it be useful to *(a)* collect information from customers that identifies the particular catalog they are ordering from, and *(b)* treat each catalog as a profit center?

14. Federal Express flies packages from drop off points to Memphis, sorts them there in a central facility, and then delivers them the next morning to their destinations. In evaluating the profitability of a manager of a field office (such as Fresno, California), would it be useful to allocate any of the central sorting facility costs to that manager's performance report?

QUICK STUDY (Five-Minute Exercises)

In each of the blanks next to the following terms, place the identifying letter of the description that best matches each term:

**QS 21–1
(LO 1)**

Terms:

——— Cost center
——— Departmental accounting system
——— Production department
——— Profit center
——— Responsibility accounting system
——— Service department

Descriptions:

a. Provides information used to evaluate the performance of a department.

b. Provides information used to evaluate the performance of a department manager.

c. Does not directly manufacture products, but contributes to the profitability of the entire company.

d. Engages directly in manufacturing or in making sales directly to customers.

e. Incurs costs without directly generating revenues.

f. Incurs costs but also generates revenues.

For each of the following types of indirect and service department expenses, name one possible allocation basis that could be used to distribute it to the departments indicated:

**QS 21–2
(LO 2)**

a. Advertising expense to the selling departments:

———————————————————————————————

b. Electric utility expense to all departments:

———————————————————————————————

c. Purchasing department expenses to the production departments:

———————————————————————————————

d. General office department expenses to the production departments:

———————————————————————————————

Using the following information, calculate each department's contribution to overhead (both in dollars and as a percentage). Which department contributes the highest dollar amount to total overhead? Which department's contribution percentage is the highest?

**QS 21–3
(LO 3)**

	Dept. L	Dept. M	Dept. N
Sales	$53,000	$170,000	$84,000
Cost of goods sold	34,185	103,700	49,560
Gross profit	18,815	66,300	34,440
Total direct expenses	6,360	37,060	8,736
Contribution to overhead	$	$	$
Contribution percentage	%	%	%

A 5,010 square foot commercial building was purchased for $325,000. An additional $50,000 was spent to split the space into two separate rental units and to get it ready to rent. Unit A, which has the desirable location on the corner and contains 1,670 square feet, will be rented out for $1.00 per square foot. Unit B contains 3,340 square feet and will be rented out for $0.75 per square foot. How much of the joint cost should be assigned to Unit B?

**QS 21–4
(LO 4)**

The following is taken from the May financial reports of a factory with two production departments:

**QS 21–5
(LO 5)**

	Direct Labor	Hours of Machine Use
Department 1	$ 9,400	600
Department 2	6,600	1,000
Totals	$16,000	1,600

Factory overhead:	
Rent and utilities	$ 6,100
Indirect labor	2,700
General office expense	1,700
Equipment depreciation	1,500
Supplies	900
Total overhead	$12,900

Calculate the total amount of overhead cost that would be allocated to Department 1 for May if activity-based costing is used. Assume the cost driver for indirect labor and supplies is direct labor and the cost driver for the remaining overhead items is hours of machine use.

EXERCISES

Exercise 21–1

Departmental expense allocations

(LO 2)

Pembroke Corporation has four departments: materials, personnel, manufacturing, and packaging. In a recent month, the four departments incurred three shared indirect costs. The amounts of these expenses and the bases used to allocate them are:

Expense	Cost	Allocation Base
Supervision	$ 75,000	Number of employees
Utilities	60,000	Square feet occupied
Insurance	16,500	Value of assets in use
Total expenses	$151,500	

These quantities are to be used in allocating the costs for the month:

Department	Employees	Square Feet	Assets Value
Materials	9	9,000	$ 12,000
Personnel	3	1,500	2,400
Manufacturing	33	15,000	75,600
Packaging	15	4,500	30,000
Total	60	30,000	$120,000

Using this information, prepare allocations of each of the three indirect expenses among the four departments. Then, prepare a table that shows the total expenses assigned to the four departments.

Exercise 21–2

Allocating rent expense to departments

(LO 2)

The Home Decorating Store pays $128,000 rent every year for its two-story building. The space in the building is occupied by five departments as follows:

Paint department	1,390 square feet of first-floor space
Flooring department	3,410 square feet of first-floor space
Window department	2,040 square feet of second-floor space
Wallpaper department	960 square feet of second-floor space
Accessory department	1,800 square feet of second-floor space

The company allocates 65% of the total rent expense to the first floor and 35% to the second floor. It then allocates the rent expense for each floor to the departments on that floor on the basis of the space occupied. Determine the rent to be allocated to each department. (Round all percentages to the nearest one-tenth and all dollar amounts to the nearest whole dollar.)

The following partially completed lower section of a departmental allocation spreadsheet is being prepared for Early Bird Bookstore. At this stage it shows only the amounts of direct and indirect expenses that have been allocated to the five departments:

Exercise 21–3
Allocating service department expenses to production departments
(LO 2)

Expense	Allocation Bases	Expense Account Balance	Adver-tising Dept.	Purchas-ing Dept.	Book Dept.	Magazine Dept.	Newspaper Dept.
Total		$654,000	$22,000	$30,000	$425,000	$86,000	$91,000
Service dept. expenses:							
Advertising	Sales		?		?	?	?
Purchasing	Purchase orders			?	?	?	
Total expenses allocated to selling departments			?		?	?	?

Complete the spreadsheet by allocating the two service departments' expenses to the three selling departments. These amounts were known about the allocation bases for the three selling departments:

	Sales	Purchase Orders
Books	$ 896,000	212
Magazines	288,000	156
Newspapers	416,000	132
Total	$1,600,000	500

Eliza Short works in both the jewelry department and the hosiery department of Fine's Department Store. Short assists customers in both departments and also straightens and stocks the merchandise in both departments as needed. The store allocates Short's annual wages of $19,200 between the two departments based on a sample of the time worked in the two departments. The sample was obtained from a diary that Short kept of hours worked in a randomly chosen week. The diary showed that the following hours were spent in these activities:

Exercise 21–4
Allocating indirect payroll expense to departments
(LO 2)

Selling in the jewelry department	32
Straightening and rearranging merchandise in the jewelry department	3
Selling in the hosiery department	7
Straightening and stocking merchandise in the hosiery department	6
Idle time spent waiting for a customer to enter one of the selling departments . .	2

Required

Prepare calculations to allocate Short's wages between the departments. Round all percentages to the nearest tenth of a percent and all dollar amounts to the nearest whole dollar.

The Wheel Shop has two service departments (advertising and administrative), and two sales departments (motorcycles and clothing). During 19X1, the departments had the following direct expenses:

Exercise 21–5
Departmental expense allocation spreadsheet
(LO 2)

Advertising department	$ 10,560
Administrative department	12,740
Motorcycle department	101,600
Clothing department	11,900

The departments occupy the following square feet of floor space:

Advertising department	544
Administrative department	576
Motorcycle department	3,168
Clothing department	2,112

The advertising department developed and distributed 50 ad pieces during the year. Of these, 38 promoted motorcycles and 12 promoted clothing. The store sold $251,000 of merchandise during the year. Of this amount, $203,310 was from the motorcycle department while the remainder was from the clothing department.

Required

Prepare an expense allocation sheet for the Wheel Shop that assigns the direct expenses to all four departments and the year's $64,000 of utilities expense to the four departments on the basis of floor space occupied. In addition, allocate the advertising department expenses on the basis of the number of ads placed and the administrative department expenses based on the amount of sales. Provide supplemental schedules showing how you computed the expense allocations. (Round all percentages to the nearest one-tenth and all dollar amounts to the nearest whole dollar.)

Exercise 21–6
Income effects of eliminating departments
(LO 3)

Fulmore Company's management expects the next year to produce the following net incomes for its five departments:

	Dept. A	Dept. C	Dept. F	Dept. P	Dept. T
Sales	$ 35,000	$56,000	$42,000	$ 28,000	$63,000
Expenses:					
Escapable	$ 36,400	$22,400	$14,000	$ 37,800	$ 9,800
Inescapable	12,600	4,200	29,400	9,800	51,800
Total	$ 49,000	$26,600	$43,400	$ 47,600	$61,600
Net income (loss)	$(14,000)	$29,400	$ (1,400)	$(19,600)	$ 1,400

Required

Prepare a combined income statement for the company under each of the following conditions:

a. Management does not eliminate any departments.

b. Management eliminates those departments expected to show net losses.

c. Management eliminates only those departments not expected to increase the company's net income (or reduce its net loss).

Exercise 21–7
Evaluating managerial performance
(LO 4)

Helen Dobie manages the stereo service department of a large department store. This is the 19X1 income statement for the department:

Revenues:		
Sales of parts	$ 72,000	
Sales of services	105,000	$177,000
Costs and expenses:		
Building depreciation	$ 9,300	
Cost of parts sold	30,000	
Income taxes allocated to department . .	8,700	
Interest on long-term debt	7,500	
Manager's salary	12,000	
Payroll taxes	8,100	
Supplies	15,900	
Utilities	14,400	
Wages (hourly)	6,000	
Total costs and expenses		111,900
Department net income		$ 65,100

Analyze the items on the income statement to identify those that clearly should be included on a performance report used to evaluate Dobie's performance. List them and explain why you have chosen them. Then, list and explain the items that should clearly be excluded. Finally, list the items that are not clearly included or excluded and explain why they fall in that category.

Capital Properties just completed developing a subdivision that includes 200 home sites. The 170 lots in the Canyon section are below a ridge and do not have views of the neighboring canyons and hills, while the 30 lots in the Hilltop section offer unobstructed views. The Canyon lots are expected to sell for $25,000 each, while the Hilltop lots are expected to sell for $60,000 each. The developer acquired the land for $1,500,000 and spent another $2,500,000 on street and utilities improvements. Assign the joint land and improvement costs to the lots and determine the average cost per lot. (Round all percentages to the nearest one-tenth and all dollar amounts to the nearest whole dollar.)

Exercise 21–8
Assigning joint real estate costs
(LO 4)

Tasty Seafood Company purchases lobsters and processes them into tails and flakes. It then sells the lobster tails for $21.00 per pound and sells the flakes for $14.00 per pound. On average, 100 pounds of lobster can be processed into 52 pounds of tails and 22 pounds of flakes, with 26 pounds of waste.

Assume that 1,200 pounds of lobster are purchased for $4.50 per pound. The lobsters are then processed with an additional labor cost of $600. No materials or labor costs are assigned to the waste. If 548 pounds of tails are sold and 162 pounds of flakes are sold, what is the allocated cost of the sold items and the cost of the remaining inventory?

Exercise 21–9
Assigning joint product costs
(LO 4)

The Tenuto Company manufactures two products, hinges and fasteners, on the same production line. Last month, the company experienced the following costs and results:

Exercise 21–10
Activity-based costing
(LO 5)

	Hinges	Fasteners	Total
Direct materials	$ 9,500	$21,600	$ 31,100
Direct labor	6,100	11,900	18,000
Overhead (300% of labor)	18,300	35,700	54,000
Total cost	$33,900	$69,200	$103,100
Quantity produced	10,500	14,100	
Average cost per unit	$3.23	$4.91	

Several of the managers have approached the cost accounting department for help in understanding activity-based costing. Their specific request is that ABC be applied to the production results to see whether the average cost per unit is significantly changed. This additional information is extracted from the production records for the month:

- The overhead cost for supervision was $2,160. The cost driver for supervision is direct labor cost.

- The overhead cost for machinery depreciation was $28,840. The cost driver for this cost is hours of use. The machinery was used 300 hours for hinges and 700 hours for fasteners.

- The overhead cost for preparing the line to manufacture products was $23,000. The line was set up 31 times to produce different kinds of hinges and 94 times to produce different kinds of fasteners.

Required

Use this information to:

a. Assign the overhead cost to the products using activity-based costing.

b. Determine the average cost per unit of the two products using direct materials, direct labor, and overhead allocated under ABC.

PROBLEMS

Toy Time, Inc., has several departments that occupy both floors of a building. The departmental accounting system has a single account in the ledger called Building Occupancy Cost. These types and amounts of costs were recorded in this account for last year:

Problem 21–1
Allocation of building occupancy costs
(LO 2)

Depreciation, building	$18,000
Interest, building mortgage	27,000
Taxes, building and land	8,000
Heating expense	2,500
Lighting expense	3,000
Cleaning expense	5,500
Total	$64,000

The building has 2,000 square feet on each floor. For simplicity, the bookkeeper merely divided the $64,000 occupancy cost by 4,000 square feet to find an average cost of $16.00 per square foot. Then, each department was charged with a building occupancy cost equal to this rate times the number of square feet that it occupies.

Joan French manages a first-floor department that occupies 600 square feet and Leo Perry manages a second-floor department that occupies 800 square feet of floor space. In discussing the departmental reports, they have questioned whether using the same rate per square foot for all departments makes sense because the first-floor space has a greater value. Looking further into the issue, the two managers checked a recent real estate study of average rental costs for similar space. The amounts do not include costs for heating, lighting, and cleaning. They found that ground-floor space is worth $30.00 per square foot while second-floor space is worth only $18.00.

Required

Use the preceding information to:

1. Allocate the occupancy cost to the two departments by the bookkeeper's method.

2. Allocate the occupancy cost to the two departments in proportion to the relative market values of the space, except for the heating, lighting, and cleaning costs, which should be allocated on an equal basis per square foot occupied. Round costs per square foot to the nearest cent.

CHECK FIGURE:
2. Total occupancy cost to French, $11,586

Problem 21–2
Departmental income statement
(LO 3)

Great Walls, Inc., began operating in January 19X1 with two selling departments and one office department. The 19X1 departmental net incomes are:

GREAT WALLS, INC.
Departmental Income Statement
For Year Ended December 31, 19X1

	Clocks	Mirrors	Combined
Sales	$122,500	$52,500	$175,000
Cost of goods sold	60,000	32,000	92,000
Gross profit from sales	$ 62,500	$20,500	$ 83,000
Direct expenses:			
Sales salaries	$ 20,000	$ 7,000	$ 27,000
Advertising	1,200	500	1,700
Store supplies used	900	400	1,300
Depreciation of equipment	1,500	300	1,800
Total direct expenses	$ 23,600	$ 8,200	$ 31,800
Allocated expenses:			
Rent expense	$ 7,020	$ 3,780	$ 10,800
Utilities expense	2,600	1,400	4,000
Share of office department expenses . .	10,500	4,500	15,000
Total allocated expenses	$ 20,120	$ 9,680	$ 29,800
Total expenses	$ 43,720	$17,880	$ 61,600
Net income	$ 18,780	$ 2,620	$ 21,400

Starting in January 19X2, Great Walls plans to open a third department that will sell paintings. Management predicts that the new department will produce $35,000 in sales with a 55% gross profit margin and that it will require the following direct expenses: sales salaries, $8,000; advertising, $800; store supplies, $500; and equipment depreciation, $200.

Since opening, the store has rented space in a building. It will be possible to fit the new department into the same overall space by taking some square footage from the other two departments. When the new painting department is opened, it will fill one-fifth of the space presently used by the clock department and one-sixth of the space used by the mirror department. Management does not predict any increase in utilities costs, which are allocated among the departments in proportion to occupied space.

The company allocates its office department expenses among the selling departments in proportion to their sales. It expects the painting department to increase office department expenses by $7,000.

Because the painting department will bring new customers into the store, management expects sales in the clock and mirror departments to increase by 7%. Those departments' gross profit percentages are not expected to change. No changes are expected in their direct expenses, except for store supplies used, which will increase in proportion to sales.

Required

Prepare a departmental income statement that shows the company's predicted results of operations for 19X2 with three selling departments. (Round all percentages to the nearest one-tenth and all dollar amounts to the nearest whole dollar.)

CHECK FIGURE:
Forecasted combined net income, $29,815

Save-All Pharmacy has three selling departments (drugs, cosmetics, and miscellaneous) and two service departments (general office and purchasing). After the end of the year, the following information was available for preparing financial statements and internal reports:

Problem 21–3
Departmental expense allocation spreadsheet
(LO 2, 3)

	Drugs	Cosmetics	Misc.
Sales	$300,000	$180,000	$120,000
Purchases	185,000	70,000	85,000
January 1 (beginning) inventory	25,000	9,000	12,000
December 31 (ending) inventory	55,000	7,000	19,000

Save-All classifies salaries, supplies used, and depreciation as direct expenses of the departments. Payroll, requisition, and plant asset records showed these amounts of direct expenses for the year:

	Salaries	Supplies Used	Depreciation
General office department	$18,000	$800	$1,700
Purchasing department	13,000	700	1,200
Drug department	37,000	900	3,500
Cosmetic department	17,000	350	600
Miscellaneous department	14,000	250	1,000

The store incurred the following amounts of indirect expenses:

Rent expense	$6,000
Advertising expense	4,800
Expired insurance	3,000
Utilities expense	9,000
Custodial expense	7,200

In preparing financial statements and internal reports, Save-All Pharmacy allocates the indirect expenses among the departments as follows:

a. Rent expense is first allocated between the selling and service departments on the basis of the value of floor space. The general office and purchasing departments occupy space in the rear of the store that is not as valuable as space in the front. Thus, only $700 of the total rent is allocated to these two departments. This amount is allocated between them in proportion to the space they occupy. The remaining rent is divided among the three selling departments in proportion to the space they occupy. The five departments occupy these amounts of space:

General office department	. . . .	1,650 square feet
Purchasing department	. . . . . .	1,350 square feet
Drug department	. . . .	4,800 square feet
Cosmetic department	. . . .	4,200 square feet
Miscellaneous department	. . . .	3,000 square feet

b.   Advertising expense is allocated among the selling departments on the basis of sales.

c.   Insurance expense is allocated in proportion to the insured value of the equipment in the five departments. The insured values of the equipment in the departments are:

General office department	. . . .	$10,500
Purchasing department	. . . .	7,500
Drug department	. . . .	22,000
Cosmetic department	. . . .	4,000
Miscellaneous department	. . . . .	6,000

d.   Utilities and custodial care expenses are assigned to the departments on the basis of floor space occupied.

Save-All then allocates its general office department expenses among its three selling departments on the basis of their dollars of sales, and it allocates purchasing department expenses on the basis of the dollars of purchases.

Required

1.   Prepare allocation schedules for the shared indirect expenses.

2.   Prepare a departmental expense allocation spreadsheet for the company. Show the allocation tables for the costs of the service departments. (Round all percents to the nearest one-tenth and all dollar amounts to the nearest whole dollar.)

3.   Prepare a departmental income statement showing sales, cost of goods sold, expenses, and net income by department and for the entire store.

4.   Prepare a departmental income statement that displays each selling department's contribution to overhead.

CHECK FIGURE:
4. Drug department contribution to overhead, $103,600

Problem 21–4
Analysis of escapable and inescapable expenses
(LO 3)

The management of Fontana Company is trying to decide whether to eliminate Department 200, which has produced losses or low profits for several years. The company's 19X1 departmental income statement shows the following results:

FONTANA COMPANY
Income Statement
For Year Ended December 31, 19X1

	Dept. 100	Dept. 200	Combined
Sales	$436,000	$290,000	$726,000
Cost of goods sold	262,000	207,000	469,000
Gross profit from sales	$174,000	$ 83,000	$257,000
Operating expenses:			
Direct expenses:			
Advertising	$ 17,000	$ 12,000	$ 29,000
Store supplies used	4,000	3,800	7,800
Depreciation of store equipment	5,000	3,300	8,300
Total direct expenses	$ 26,000	$ 19,100	$ 45,100
Allocated expenses:			
Sales salaries	$ 65,000	$ 39,000	$104,000
Rent expense	9,440	4,720	14,160
Bad debts expense	9,900	8,100	18,000
Office salary	18,720	12,480	31,200
Insurance expense	2,000	1,100	3,100
Miscellaneous office expenses	2,400	1,600	4,000
Total allocated expenses	$107,460	$ 67,000	$174,460
Total expenses	$133,460	$ 86,100	$219,560
Net income (loss)	$ 40,540	$ (3,100)	$ 37,440

In analyzing the decision to eliminate Department 200, the management has looked at the following items of information:

a.   The company has one office worker who earns $600 per week or $31,200 per year and four sales clerks who each earn $500 per week or $26,000 per year.

b.   Currently, the full salaries of two sales clerks are charged to Department 100. The full salary of one sales clerk is charged to Department 200. Because the fourth clerk works half-time in both departments, her salary is divided evenly between the two departments.

c.   The sales salaries and the office salary currently assigned to Department 200 would be avoided if the department were eliminated. However, management prefers another plan. Two sales clerks have indicated that they will be quitting soon. Management thinks that their work can be done by the other two clerks if the one office worker works in sales half-time. The office worker's schedule will allow this shift of duties if Department 200 is eliminated. If this change is implemented, half the office worker's salary would be reported as sales salaries and half would be reported as office salary.

d.   The store building is rented under a long-term lease that cannot be changed. Therefore, the space presently occupied by Department 200 will have to be used by the current Department 100. The equipment used by Department 200 will be used by the current Department 100.

e.   Closing Department 200 will eliminate its expenses for advertising, bad debts, and store supplies. It will also eliminate 70% of the insurance expense allocated to the department for coverage on its merchandise inventory. In addition, 25% of the miscellaneous office expenses presently allocated to Department 200 will be eliminated.

Required

Preparation component:

1.   Prepare a three-column schedule that lists (a) the company's total expenses (including cost of goods sold), (b) the expenses that would be eliminated by closing Department 200, and (c) the expenses that will continue.

2.   Prepare a forecasted income statement for the company reflecting the elimination under the assumption that sales and the gross profit will not be affected. The statement should also reflect the reassignment of the office worker to one-half time as a sales clerk.

CHECK FIGURE:
2. Forecasted net income without Department 200, $31,510

Analysis component:

3.   Prepare a reconciliation of the company's combined net income with the forecasted net income assuming Department 200 is eliminated. Also compare Department 200's revenues and its escapable expenses and explain why you think the department should or should not be eliminated.

Vi Symanski, the manager of Royal Manufacturing Company's Indiana plant, is responsible for all costs of the plant's operation other than her own salary. The plant has two production departments and one service department. The camper and trailer departments manufacture different products and have their own managers. The office department provides services equally to the two production departments. Symanski manages the office department. A budget is prepared for each production department and the office department. The responsibility accounting system must assemble the information to present budgeted and actual costs in performance reports for each of the production department managers and the plant manager.

Problem 21–5
Responsibility accounting performance reports
(LO 4)

Each performance report includes only those costs that the particular manager can control. The production department managers control the costs of raw materials, wages, supplies used, and equipment depreciation. The plant manager is responsible for the department managers' salaries, utilities, building rent, office salaries other than her own, other office costs, plus all the costs controlled by the two production department managers.

The annual departmental budgets and cost accumulations for the two production departments were as follows:

	Budget			Actual		
	Campers	**Trailers**	**Combined**	**Campers**	**Trailers**	**Combined**
Raw materials	$154,000	$255,000	$ 409,000	$159,400	$246,500	$ 405,900
Wages	99,000	191,000	290,000	102,300	193,700	296,000
Department manager salary	40,000	44,000	84,000	40,000	45,100	85,100
Supplies used	34,000	83,000	117,000	31,900	84,600	116,500
Equipment depreciation	58,000	110,000	168,000	58,000	110,000	168,000
Utilities	2,800	4,200	7,000	2,500	3,800	6,300
Building rent	4,800	7,200	12,000	4,800	7,200	12,000
Office department costs	54,000	54,000	108,000	52,000	52,000	104,000
Total	$446,600	$748,400	$1,195,000	$450,900	$742,900	$1,193,800

Office department budget and actual costs consisted of the following:

	Budget	Actual
Plant manager salary	$ 57,000	$ 57,100
Other office salaries	29,000	27,700
Other office costs	22,000	19,200
Total	$108,000	$104,000

Required

Prepare responsibility accounting performance reports that list the costs controlled by the following managers:

1. Manager of the camper department.

2. Manager of the trailer department.

3. Manager of the Indiana plant.

In each report, include the budgeted and actual costs and show the amount that each actual cost is over or under the budgeted amount.

CHECK FIGURE:
3. Indiana plant controllable costs, $1,300 under budget

Problem 21–6
Allocating joint costs
(LO 4)

Jack Tandy's orchards produced a good crop of peaches in 19X1. After preparing the following income statement, Tandy concluded that he should have given the No. 3 peaches to charity and saved a lot of money and trouble.

JACK TANDY ORCHARDS
Income from Peaches
For Year Ended December 31, 19X1

	No. 1	No. 2	No. 3	Combined
Sales (by grade):				
No. 1: 300,000 lbs. @ $1.25	$375,000			
No. 2: 300,000 lbs. @ $0.55		$165,000		
No. 3: 700,000 lbs. @ $0.30			$210,000	
Total sales				$750,000
Costs:				
Tree pruning and care @ $0.20/lb.	$ 60,000	$ 60,000	$140,000	$260,000
Picking, sorting, and grading @ $0.12/lb. . .	36,000	36,000	84,000	156,000
Delivery @ $0.03/lb.	9,000	9,000	21,000	39,000
Total costs	$105,000	$105,000	$245,000	$455,000
Net income (loss)	$270,000	$ 60,000	$(35,000)	$295,000

In preparing the statement, Tandy allocated the joint costs among the grades as an equal amount per pound. Records about the delivery cost show that $30,000 of the $39,000 was the cost of crating the No. 1 and No. 2 peaches and hauling them to the buyer. The remaining

$9,000 of delivery cost was the cost of crating the No. 3 peaches and hauling them to the cannery where they were used to make preserves.

Required

Preparation component:

1. Prepare allocation schedules showing how the costs would be allocated on the basis of the relative sales values of the three grades. Separate the delivery cost into the amounts directly identifiable to the grades. Then, allocate any shared delivery cost on the basis of the relative sales values of the grades. (Round all percentages to the nearest one-tenth and all dollar amounts to the nearest whole dollar.)

2. Using your answers to requirement 1, prepare an income statement that shows the results of producing and delivering the peaches.

Analysis component:

3. Do you think the delivery cost is a true joint cost? Explain your answer.

CHECK FIGURES:
2. Net income from No. 1 peaches, $146,180

CRITICAL THINKING: ESSAYS, PROBLEMS, AND CASES

Consolidated Technologies, Inc., is a national chain with more than 100 stores located all over the country. The manager of each store receives a salary as well as a bonus equal to a percentage of the store's net profit for the reporting period. The following net income calculation appeared on the Boston store manager's performance report for a recent three-month period:

Analytical Essay

(LO 4)

Sales	$1,500,000
Cost of goods sold	(900,000)
Wages expense	(282,000)
Utilities expense	(18,000)
Home office expense	(45,000)
Net income	$ 255,000
Manager's bonus (5%)	$ 12,750

In previous periods, the bonus percentage had been 5% but the performance report had not included any charges for the home office expense. The home office expense is now assigned to every store as a percentage of its sales.

Required

1. Describe a valid reason for including a charge for the expenses of operating the home office in a performance report for store managers.

2. Describe the main disadvantages of imposing a new charge for the home office based on a percentage of the sales achieved by a store manager.

3. Suggest an alternative approach that offers more advantages than the one being used by Consolidated Technologies, Inc.

Tops Discount Market is considering the possibility of closing down its floral department, which has been experiencing declining performance over several years. Information from the department's most recent annual income report shows these results:

Management Decision Case

(LO 3)

Sales	$600,000
Expenses:	
Direct escapable	315,000
Indirect escapable	190,000
Direct inescapable	60,000
Indirect inescapable	95,000

Required

1. What is the floral department's net income (loss)?

2. What is the floral department's contribution to overhead?

3. What is the excess of the floral department's revenues over its escapable expenses?

4. Assuming that eliminating the floral department will not reduce sales in other departments, should it be closed down?

5. A marketing manager has proposed replacing the floral department with a deli department. The proposal includes these forecasted amounts:

Sales	$700,000
Expenses:	
Direct escapable	230,000
Indirect escapable	405,000
Direct inescapable	20,000
Indirect inescapable	30,000

Taking this alternative into consideration, should the floral department be eliminated? Explain your answer.

Business Communications Case

(LO 3)

Bessel Corporation retails two models of large tractors used by farmers and ranchers. The company's operations produced these results in the year that just ended:

	T550	T850
Units sold	600	500
Selling price per unit	$15,000	$22,000
Cost per unit	$10,000	$14,000
Sales commission per unit	$300	$440
Indirect selling and administrative expenses per unit	$712.50	$1,045.00

The total indirect selling and administrative expenses were $950,000. They were allocated to the models on the basis of their relative sales. The T550 model produced $9,000,000 of revenue and the T850 model produced $11,000,000. Thus, the T550 model was assigned 45% of the $950,000 of indirect expenses, or $427,500. Then, this amount was divided by the number of units to get $712.50 per unit. The same calculations produced the $1,045.00 per unit indirect cost for the T850 model.

Bessel's vice president of operations, Dean Matz, is in the process of selecting among three management strategies for the next quarter. The three alternatives are: (1) do no special advertising, in which case sales of each model will continue at present levels; (2) increase the sales of the T550 model by a special advertising effort; or (3) increase the sales of the T850 model by a special advertising effort. Because the demand for tractors is stable, an increase in the unit sales of one model will cause an equal decrease in unit sales of the other model. By spending $50,000 on advertising for the T550, the company can sell 100 additional units of the T550 and lose 100 units of sales of the T850. Or, the opposite effect will occur if the company advertises the T850 model.

On February 19, Matz asks you to compare the three alternative strategies on the basis of contribution to overhead and net income. You are to report your findings to him in a memo the next day. You should recommend the best action for Bessel and support your recommendation with income statements for each alternative. (Assume that the indirect expenses do not change.)

CONCEPT TESTER

Test your understanding of the concepts introduced in this chapter by completing the following crossword puzzle:

Across Clues

4. 2 words; costs the amount of which the manager can determine or strongly influence.

5. 2 words; a basis for allocating a cost in an activity-based cost system.

6. 2 words; expenses that are incurred for the benefit of more than one department.

7. 2 words; expenses incurred for the sole benefit of one department.

Down Clues

1. 2 words; a single cost incurred in producing two or more different products.

2. 2 words; a business unit that incurs costs and also generates revenues.

3. 2 words; a report that compares actual costs and expenses with budgeted amounts.

4. 2 words; a business unit that incurs costs or expenses without directly generating revenues.

ANSWERS TO PROGRESS CHECKS

21–1 Departmental accounting systems provide information used to evaluate the performance of departments. Responsibility accounting systems provide information used to evaluate the performance of department managers.

21–2 *d*

21–3 A cost center incurs costs without directly generating revenues, like a manufacturing or service department. A profit center incurs costs but also generates revenues, like a selling department.

21–4 *b*

21–5 *b*

21–6 *d*

21–7 1. Assign the direct expenses to each department.
2. Allocate indirect expenses to all departments.
3. Allocate the service department expenses to the production departments.

21–8 *b*

21–9 Escapable expenses will be avoided if a department is eliminated, and inescapable expenses will continue even after the department is eliminated.

21–10 *a*

21–11 No, because many of the expenses that enter into these calculations are beyond the control of the manager, and managers should not be evaluated using costs they do not control.

21–12 *c*

21–13 *b*

21–14 A cost driver is a factor that affects the amount of a component of overhead cost. In activity-based costing, cost drivers are the allocation bases used to assign overhead costs to products and processes.

21–15 *d*

Cost-Volume-Profit Analysis

The marketing manager and the controller for WonderSeal, Inc., a North Carolina producer of caulks and sealants, met to sort out the issues related to a new sales proposal.[1] The company had been approached about supplying a line of private-label caulks for a major paint distributor.

WonderSeal's current sales volume was roughly 15% of the national market. It had attained this position by having consistently high-quality products and a reputation for customer service. The company's caulk was number one in the south and was slowly gaining brand recognition on a national level.

In discussing the new proposal, the marketing manager noted that the private label sales would nearly double WonderSeal's volume. The paint distributor currently did not carry WonderSeal's caulks so the sales would not affect the company's existing market. Furthermore, the new business would not require advertising or a salesperson to service the account. Given these factors, the marketing manager proposed a price below current branded product pricing. It covered the current inventory cost plus a 15% gross profit.

The controller listened and proposed meeting at the end of the week to set the price. The controller explained that the current inventory product cost was an average of the current costs to manufacture at the present volume. He wanted to make certain the costs in the decision included any and all real cost increases or decreases. This would require using cost-volume-profit analysis to evaluate the impact of the proposed private label business on profits.

---

[1]WonderSeal, Inc., is a fictitious name used at the request of the real company.

LEARNING OBJECTIVES

After studying Chapter 22, you should be able to:

1. **Describe different types of cost behavior in relation to sales volume.**
2. **State the assumptions used in cost-volume-profit analysis and explain how they limit the usefulness of the analysis.**
3. **Prepare and interpret a scatter diagram of past costs and sales volume.**
4. **Calculate a break-even point for a single product company and present its costs and revenues in a graph.**
5. **Describe several applications of cost-volume-profit analysis.**
6. **Calculate the break-even point for a multiproduct company by constructing a composite sales unit.**
7. **Define or explain the words and phrases listed in the chapter glossary.**

This chapter explains different kinds of costs and shows how they are affected by changes in the operating volume of a business. By studying the chapter, you will learn to analyze the costs and revenues of a business so that you can describe how different operating strategies affect its profit or loss. Managers use this kind of analysis to forecast what will happen if changes are made in costs, sales volume, selling prices, or product mix. They then use the forecasts to select the best strategy for the future.

For example, **Compaq Computer Corporation** got its start through venture capital money. Rod Canion, Jim Harris, and Bill Murto had all been senior managers at Texas Instruments, and they had a well-formulated plan to take on IBM with a technologically superior product. Start-up capital of $20 million was raised based on a solid cost-volume-profit projection showing break-even volumes attainable within the first year following product development. Compaq established a dealer network within one year of exhibiting its first prototype and first year sales totaled more than $100 million.[2]

QUESTIONS ADDRESSED BY COST-VOLUME-PROFIT ANALYSIS

FAST HINT
Important Point to Remember:
Budgeting is another aspect of planning. Budgeting is described in Chapter 23.

FAST HINT
Important Point to Remember:
The what-if capabilities of computer spreadsheets make them important and effective tools for analyzing alternative strategies.

The first phase in managing a company's future is planning its activities and other events. The first step in the planning phase is predicting the volume of activity, the costs to be incurred, revenues to be received, and profits to be earned. An important tool that helps managers carry out this first step in the planning phase is **cost-volume-profit analysis (CVP).** CVP helps managers predict how income will be affected by changes in costs and sales levels. In its most basic form, CVP involves determining the sales level at which a company neither earns a profit nor incurs a loss, or, in other words, the point at which it is said to break even. For this reason, this most basic form of cost-volume-profit analysis is sometimes called *break-even analysis.* However, managers use other applications of the analysis to answer questions like these:

- What sales volume is needed to earn a desired net income?
- How much net income will be earned if unit selling prices are reduced and sales volume is increased?
- How much net income will be earned if we install a new machine that reduces labor costs?
- How much net income will be earned if we change the sales mix of our products?

---

[2]Ravi Venkatesan, "Bootstrap Finance: The Art of Startup," *Harvard Business Review,* November–December 1992.

When the technique is expanded to answer these additional questions, the phrase *cost-volume-profit analysis* is more descriptive than break-even analysis.

Conventional cost-volume-profit analysis requires management to classify all costs as either *fixed* or *variable*. Some costs are definitely fixed in nature while others are definitely variable. However, when you examine various costs, you will find that some are neither completely fixed nor completely variable.

Fixed Costs

The amount of a **fixed cost** incurred each period remains unchanged even when production volume varies from period to period. For example, $5,000 rent paid for a factory building remains the same each month, whether the factory operates with a single eight-hour shift or around the clock with three shifts. Furthermore, the rent cost is the same each month at any level of output from zero on up to the full production capacity of the plant. Although the total fixed cost remains constant as the level of production changes, the fixed cost per unit of product decreases as volume increases. For example, if 20 units are produced in a month, the average factory building rent cost per unit is $250. When production increases to 100 units per month, the average cost per unit decreases to $50. And, the average cost decreases to $10 per unit if production increases to 500 units per month. Other examples of fixed costs include depreciation, property taxes, office salaries, and many other service department costs. In effect, fixed costs are incurred to create productive and marketing capacity for a particular period of time.

When production volume and costs are presented on a graph, units of product are usually plotted on the horizontal axis, and dollars of cost are plotted on the vertical axis. Fixed costs are represented as a horizontal line because the total amount remains constant at all levels of production. The graph in Illustration 22–1 represents this behavior. Note that the fixed costs remain at $32,000 at all production levels up to the factory's monthly capacity of 2,000 units of output.

Variable Costs

The total amount of a **variable cost** changes in proportion to changes in volume. For example, the direct material cost of a product is a variable cost. If one unit of product requires materials that cost $20, total materials costs are $200 when 10 units of product are manufactured, $400 for 20 units, $600 for 30 units, and so on. Notice that the variable cost per unit produced remains constant while the total amount of variable cost changes in direct proportion to changes in the level of production. Other variable costs include direct labor (if workers are paid for completed units), some overhead costs, selling commissions, and shipping costs. Variable costs are plotted on a graph of cost and volume as a straight line that starts at the zero cost level. It also has an upward (positive) slope. That is, the line rises as the production volume increases. Notice that the variable cost line for this example of $20 per unit appears in Illustration 22–1. In effect, variable costs are incurred in using the productive and marketing capacity created by the fixed costs.

Total Cost

In simple cases, the total cost to be incurred equals the sum of the fixed costs and the variable costs. The upper line in Illustration 22–1 represents the total cost. It originates on the vertical axis at the $32,000 fixed cost point. Thus, at the zero level of output, the total cost equals only the fixed costs. Then, the total cost increases as the activity level increases. The amount of the increase equals the variable cost per unit for each additional unit produced. (The slope of the total cost line equals the slope of

COST BEHAVIOR

LO 1

Describe different types of cost behavior in relation to sales volume.

FAST HINT
Critical Thought Question:
If production decreases, what happens to the total fixed costs? What happens to the per-unit fixed costs?

FAST HINT
Critical Thought Question:
If production decreases, what happens to the total variable costs? What happens to the per-unit variable costs?

FAST HINT
Important Point to Remember:
Fixed costs are constant in total, but vary per unit. Variable costs vary in total, but are fixed per unit. Many students have difficulty with this concept; therefore, the concept should be repeated often.

Illustration 22-1   Relationships of Fixed Costs, Variable Costs, and Total Costs to Volume

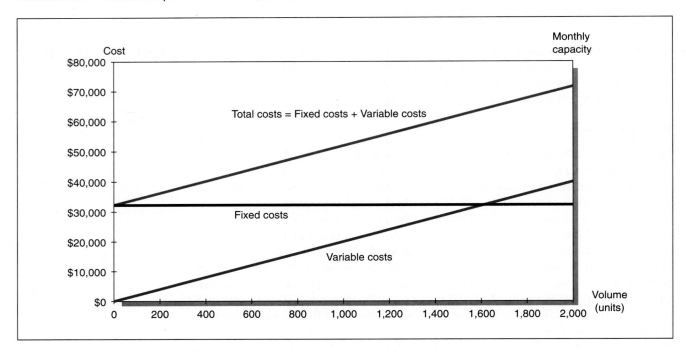

the variable cost line, which also equals the variable cost per unit.) The total cost reaches its maximum level at the limit of the productive capacity for the planned period.

Step-Variable Costs and Semivariable Costs

In real situations, many costs are neither completely fixed nor completely variable. For example, some costs go up in steps, such as the salaries of production supervisors. Their salaries are fixed for a particular production volume from zero up to the maximum that can be completed on one shift. When an additional shift is added to increase production, additional supervisors must be hired, and the total cost for supervisory salaries goes up by a lump-sum amount. Total supervisory salaries then remain fixed at this new level until a third shift is added, in which case the cost increases by another lump sum. Costs that show this behavior are **step-variable costs.** They are also called *step-wise costs* or *stair-step costs.* A step-variable cost is represented graphically in Illustration 22–2. Notice how it is flat within a narrow range. Then it jumps up to the next higher level and stays there over another range. In a conventional CVP analysis, a step-variable cost must be treated as either a fixed cost or a variable cost. The specific treatment depends on the cost's behavior in the expected range of operations.

Other costs may be semivariable or *nonlinear* in nature. **Semivariable costs** increase as volume increases but not at a constant rate like pure variable costs. These costs change with production-level changes but not proportionately. Thus, they must be plotted on a graph as a curved line. Illustration 22–2 represents a semivariable cost as the curved line beginning at zero when production is zero and increasing at different rates, with its highest rate as the sales volume approaches the maximum capacity for the month.

An example of a semivariable cost is total direct labor cost when workers are paid by the hour. At low levels of production, adding more workers allows each of them to specialize by doing the same task over and over again instead of doing several different tasks. Thus, the whole crew becomes more efficient and able to produce additional units for lower costs. Eventually, however, a point of diminishing returns is reached and adding more workers begins to create inefficiencies. For example, work-

Illustration 22-2 Step-Variable Costs, Semivariable Costs, and the Relevant Range

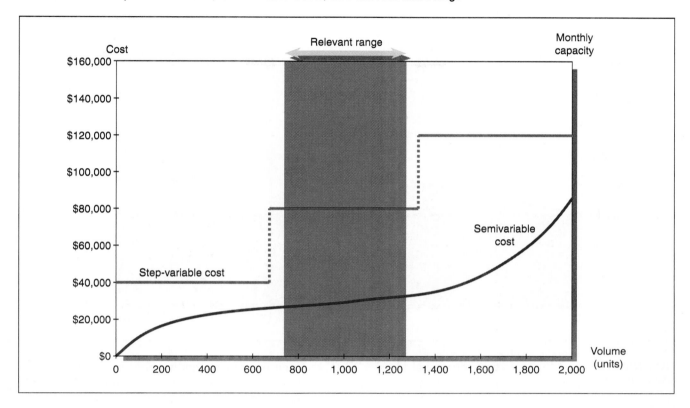

ers may have to spend more time and effort in merely communicating with each other or coordinating their efforts. As a result, adding more workers increases output but the labor cost per unit increases and the total labor cost goes up with a steeper slope. Note these effects in Illustration 22–2 where the semivariable cost curve starts at zero, rises, flattens out, and then increases at a faster rate as the volume approaches the productive capacity for the month.

Mixed Costs. Other costs act like a combination of a fixed and a variable cost. These costs are called **mixed costs.** For example, the compensation cost for sales representatives can include a fixed monthly salary and a variable commission based on sales. Illustration 22–3 presents a graph of a mixed cost. Like a fixed cost, it is greater than zero even when volume is at zero. Then, unlike a fixed cost, it increases steadily in proportion to the increase in volume.

In a CVP analysis, the simplest way to include mixed costs is to divide them into their fixed and variable components. Notice that Illustration 22–3 identifies these two components of the mixed cost. Then, the fixed component is added to other fixed costs for the planning period and the variable component is added to the other variable costs.

Recall the discussion of **WonderSeal, Inc.,** at the beginning of the chapter. In analyzing the private-label sales order, the controller's first course of action was to separate all manufacturing and selling costs into variable and fixed categories. After reviewing the way costs behaved at Wonder-Seal, the controller concluded that only raw materials and sales commissions were truly variable costs. Direct labor could be added only in eight-hour shifts and was categorized as a step-variable

Illustration 22-3 A Mixed Cost and Its Components

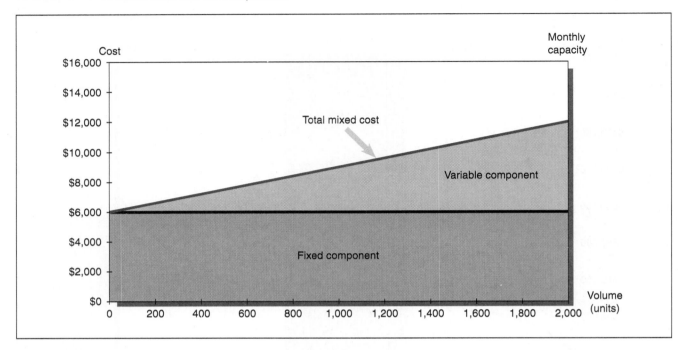

cost for several reasons. First, caulking is a process and requires sequential steps to produce and does not allow the building of work-in-process inventory buffers. Second, caulking cannot be stored longer than six months and the very large increase in volume could not be satisfied by working overtime. All other manufacturing costs were categorized as fixed costs.

Progress Check

22-1 Which of the following statements is typically true?
  a. Variable cost per unit increases as volume increases.
  b. Fixed cost per unit decreases as volume increases.
  c. A semivariable cost includes both fixed and variable elements.

22-2 Describe the behavior of a fixed cost.

22-3 If a raw material cost per unit remains constant (fixed), why is it called a variable cost?

ASSUMPTIONS USED IN COST-VOLUME-PROFIT ANALYSIS

LO 2

State the assumptions used in cost-volume-profit analysis and explain how they limit the usefulness of the analysis.

Cost-volume-profit analysis is based on relationships that can be expressed as straight lines similar to those in Illustration 22–1. Thus, users of CVP classify all costs as either fixed or variable. In addition, they treat revenues as variable, with all units of a product being sold at the same unit price. Once they classify the costs and revenues in this manner, they can use the data to answer a variety of questions. However, the usefulness of the answers to those questions depends on the validity of at least these three basic assumptions:

1. The actual selling price per unit must remain constant for all units sold during the planning period.

2. For costs classified as variable, the actual costs per unit of output must remain constant.

3. For costs classified as fixed, the total amount must remain constant over the volumes projected for the planning period.

Even though these assumptions are not always realistic, they do not necessarily limit the usefulness of CVP as a first step in forecasting the effects of a plan.

Relationship between Production Output and Sales Volume

So far in this discussion, we have defined variable costs and fixed costs in terms of the level of *output produced*. However, CVP typically describes the planning period's level of activity in terms of *sales volume* rather than output. This sales volume can be described as either the number of units sold or the dollars of sales.

To simplify the analysis, we assume that the level of production will be the same as the level of sales. Thus, we do not have to be concerned with costs that would flow into the inventory instead of being sold or with costs that would flow into cost of goods sold from the prior period's inventory. This simplifying assumption is justified because CVP provides only a tentative plan that does not include the details of inventory management.

Working with the Assumptions

If the expected events are consistent with the previous assumptions, costs and revenues for the planning period can be represented in a graph by straight lines. However, the behavior of actual individual costs and revenues often is not perfectly consistent with these assumptions. If the expected cost and revenue behavior is significantly inconsistent with the assumptions, the results of a CVP analysis are not very useful. However, there are several reasons why we can perform useful analyses while using these assumptions.

Aggregating Costs May Offset Deviations. Although individual components of total variable costs may not be perfectly variable, aggregating the many components may allow their individual deviations to offset each other. In other words, the assumption of variable behavior may be satisfied with respect to total variable costs even though it is not satisfied by individual variable cost items. Similarly, the assumption that fixed costs are constant may be satisfied for total fixed costs even though individual fixed cost items may not be perfectly consistent with the assumption.

Relevant Range of Operations. Revenues, variable costs, and fixed costs also can be reasonably represented as straight lines in a graph if the assumptions are intended to apply only over a **relevant range of operations.** The relevant range of operations is the normal operating range for the business. Except for unusually difficult or prosperous times, management typically plans for operating within a range of volume that is neither close to zero nor approaching full capacity. Thus, the relevant range for planning excludes extremely high and low operating levels that are not likely to be encountered. Assuming that a specific cost is fixed or variable is more apt to be valid when operations remain within the relevant range.

As shown in Illustration 22–2, a semivariable cost can be treated as perfectly variable if the relevant range encompasses the volumes in which it has a relatively constant slope. Beyond the limits of the relevant range, none of the costs may behave as we expect within the range. However, these deviations are not a matter of concern when plans involve operating within the relevant range.

Cost-Volume-Profit Analysis Is Not Precise. As a practical matter, CVP yields approximate first answers to questions about costs, volumes, and profits. These first answers do not have to be precise because the analysis makes only initial predictions about the future. As long as managers understand that the answers are nothing more than approximations, cost-volume-profit analysis can be a useful tool for starting the planning process.

Consider again the discussion of **WonderSeal, Inc.,** at the beginning of the chapter and the controller's decision to use CVP. Although WonderSeal's variable costs  per unit appeared to be stable, the proposed private-label volume was well beyond the current relevant range of WonderSeal's production capacity. The company was already at capacity during peak months and the current location could not be expanded. After including the new fixed costs necessary to expand the capacity, WonderSeal established a tentative price to recover all relevant costs and contribute 15% to overhead and operating income.

However, the CVP analysis was only the starting point. Other qualitative factors had to be considered. The large capital outlay for a second manufacturing facility would increase fixed costs substantially. These fixed costs would highly leverage the company and make it vulnerable in a business downturn. Fixed costs do not go away if volume does. In addition, the private label sales to the paint distributor would represent 45% of WonderSeal's business and the company could end up being a captive supplier. This would make it vulnerable to pressure for future price concessions.

Progress Check

22–4   **Using conventional CVP, a mixed cost should be**
   a. **Disregarded**
   b. **Treated as a fixed cost**
   c. **Separated into fixed and variable components.**

22–5   **What are the three basic assumptions used in CVP?**

IDENTIFYING COST BEHAVIOR

LO 3

Prepare and interpret a scatter diagram of past costs and sales volume.

Identifying the behavior of a company's costs requires a careful examination of experience and, to a certain extent, management's judgment in interpreting that data. Initially, individual costs should be analyzed and classified as fixed or variable based on the manager's understanding of how each cost is likely to behave in the relevant range. Some costs can be classified easily at this stage. For example, raw material costs for a manufacturer or cost of goods sold for a merchandiser are clearly variable. Monthly expenses for rent or administrative salaries are clearly fixed.

Scatter Diagrams. If a cost is not obviously fixed or variable, an analysis of past cost behavior can be useful. One helpful technique for analyzing past behavior is to display data about past costs on a **scatter diagram** like the one in Illustration 22–4. In preparing a scatter diagram, volume in dollars or units is plotted on the horizontal axis and cost is plotted on the vertical axis. Thus, the cost and volume for each operating period appear as a single point on the diagram.

Illustration 22–4 shows a scatter diagram of a company's total costs and sales for each of 12 months. Each point represents the total costs incurred and the sales volume for a specific month. As an example, note the point labeled May. That month's sales were $25,000 and its total costs were $25,000.

FAST HINT
Relevant Exercise:
To apply these concepts, work Exercise 22–4.

Estimated Line of Cost Behavior. Illustration 22–4 includes a line drawn among the scattered points. This line is the **estimated line of cost behavior.** It is drawn to identify the past relationship between total cost and sales volume. If the factors that shaped this line in the past are still in effect, management can use it to predict future cost levels at different sales volumes. Three alternative methods can be used to derive this line.

Illustration 22–4 A Scatter Diagram with an Estimated Line of Cost Behavior

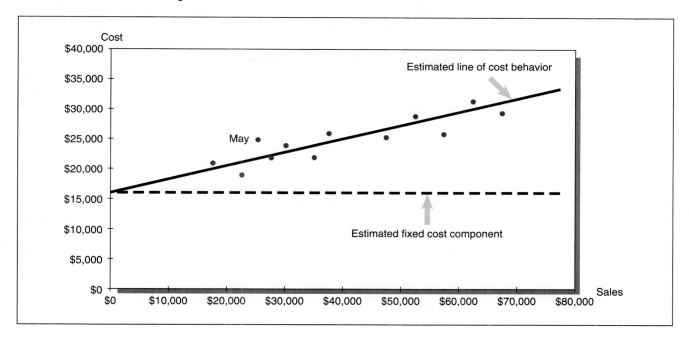

First, the **high-low method** is a simple way to draw the estimated line of behavior. However, its results are likely to be imprecise. To apply this method, you merely connect the two points in the diagram representing the highest and the lowest total cost. The obvious deficiency of the high-low method is that it totally ignores all the available cost and sales volume points except the highest and lowest. The outcome is likely to be imprecise because it is based on the most extreme points rather than more typical conditions that are more likely to occur in future periods.

A second simple but potentially more useful approach is to visually assess the scattered points and draw a line through them that appears to represent the relationship between cost and volume. Like the high-low method, this approach can be satisfactory for quick and rough estimates.

Third, a more sophisticated method of identifying cost behavior is also commonly used. The statistical method of **least-squares regression** requires calculations that can be readily accomplished with spreadsheet or statistical applications computer programs. The result of applying this technique is a line that best fits the actual cost and sales volume experience of the company.[3] The techniques for producing least-squares regressions are covered in statistics courses and their uses in accounting situations are described in more advanced cost accounting courses.

Notice that the actual monthly sales volumes plotted in Illustration 22–4 range from approximately $17,500 to $67,500. In all likelihood, this range represents the relevant range for the company. If the estimated line of cost behavior is extended too far beyond this range in either direction, it is less likely to be useful for predicting future costs. Also, notice that the line intercepts the vertical axis at $16,000. As shown in the diagram, you can use this amount as the fixed costs for a month, as long as the sales volume is within the relevant range.

FAST HINT
Alternative Example:
In Illustration 22–4, if sales in a given month are projected to be $40,000, what is the predicted cost for that month?
Answer: Approximately $25,000

---

[3]The method is called *least-squares* because the line minimizes the sum of the squared distances between each point and the line.

Variable costs per dollar of sales are represented in Illustration 22–4 by the slope of the estimated line of cost behavior. The slope of any straight line is found by comparing any two points that lie on the line. To estimate variable cost per sales dollar, divide the change in total cost between the two points (the vertical distance) by the change in dollar sales volume between those two points (the horizontal distance).

For example, in Illustration 22–4, we can select the two points where the sales volume equals zero and $40,000. At these points, the costs were $16,000 and $25,000. Therefore, calculate the slope as follows:

$$\frac{\text{Change in cost}}{\text{Change in sales}} = \frac{\$25,000 - \$16,000}{\$40,000 - \$ -0-} = \frac{\$9,000}{\$40,000} = \$0.225 \text{ per sales dollar}$$

If you analyze a company's past costs, you might be able to use these statistical techniques to predict fixed and variable costs without analyzing each individual cost component. However, you may have greater confidence in the predictions if you classify individual cost components and then test your results against past observations. To test the classifications, you can prepare scatter diagrams and estimated lines of cost behavior for individual cost items, total variable costs, total fixed costs, and total costs.

Progress Check

22–6 Which of the following would yield the most precise estimated line of cost behavior?
a. High-low method.
b. Least-squares method.
c. Scatter diagram.

22–7 What is the primary weakness of the high-low method?

FINDING THE BREAK-EVEN POINT

LO 4

Calculate a break-even point for a single product company and present its costs and revenues in a graph.

FAST HINT
Additional Insight:
Even though a company operates at a level in excess of its break-even point, its management may decide to stop operating because it is not earning a reasonable return on its investment.

FAST HINT
Relevant Quick Study:
To apply these concepts, work QS 22–4 and QS 22–5.

The **break-even point** is the unique sales level at which a company neither earns a profit nor incurs a loss. The break-even point can be expressed either in units of product or in dollars of sales. For example, assume that Carson Company sells a single product for $100 per unit and incurs $70 of variable costs per unit sold. The fixed costs are $24,000 per month and the monthly capacity is 1,800 units of product. Therefore, the company breaks even for a month when it sells 800 units, which provides a sales volume of $80,000. You can determine this break-even point as follows:

1. Each unit sold at $100 recovers $70 of variable costs and contributes $30 toward the fixed costs.
2. Sales of 800 units contribute exactly $24,000 toward the fixed costs, which are fully recovered at this volume.
3. When 800 units are sold at $100 each, the total sales volume is $80,000.

The amount by which the sales price per unit exceeds variable costs per unit is a product's **contribution margin per unit.** In effect, the contribution margin per unit is the amount that the sale of one unit contributes toward recovering the fixed costs and profit.

The contribution margin for a product also can be expressed as a percentage of its sales price. This percentage is called the product's **contribution rate.** For the Carson Company, the contribution rate of its product is 30% ($30/$100).

The contribution margin per unit can be used to calculate the break-even point in units of product. And, the contribution rate can be used to calculate a break-even point in dollars. These formulas are:

Illustration 22–5
Derivation of Break-Even
Formulas

Let: S = sales in units R = revenue per unit
             F = fixed costs per month V = variable cost per unit
             $S \times R$ = dollar sales $S \times V$ = total variable cost

Then: Contribution margin per unit = $R - V$
At break-even: Sales = Fixed Costs + Variable Costs
               $(S \times R) = F + (S \times V)$
               $(S \times R) - (S \times V) = F$
               $S \times (R - V) = F$
               $S = F/(R - V)$
               $S = F/\text{Contribution margin per unit}$

And: Contribution rate = $(R - V)/R$
At break-even: $S = F/(R - V)$
               $S \times R = (F \times R)/(R - V)$
               $S \times R = F \times [R/(R - V)]$
               $S \times R = F/[(R - V)/R]$
               $S \times R = F/\text{Contribution rate}$

Illustration 22–6
Income Statement at a
Break-Even Sales Level

CARSON COMPANY
Forecasted Income Statement

Sales (800 units @ $100 each)		$80,000
Costs:		
Fixed costs	$24,000	
Variable costs (800 units @ $70 each) . . .	56,000	80,000
Net income		$ –0–

FAST HINT
Alternative Example:
What will be the net income if
sales in Illustration 22–6 are
799 units? 801 units?
Answer: $30 loss; $30 profit

$$\text{Break-even point in units} = \frac{\text{Fixed costs}}{\text{Contribution margin per unit}}$$

$$\text{Break-even point in dollars} = \frac{\text{Fixed costs}}{\text{Contribution rate}}$$

For those readers interested in the mathematics, Illustration 22–5 presents the derivations of these formulas.

Inserting Carson Company's fixed costs and contribution rate in the second formula gives this result:

$$\text{Break-even point in dollars} = \frac{\$24,000}{30\%} = \$80,000$$

In this example, the solution comes out evenly. In other circumstances, carry the contribution rate out to several decimal places to avoid rounding errors when calculating the break-even point in dollars. The calculated break-even point in units may include a fraction of a unit, such as 520.25 units. In solving the exercises and problems, round the result normally, even though the company would not actually break even at a rounded-down volume (520 units, in this case). The practice of always rounding up (to 521 units) is sometimes encouraged, but doing so assumes a precision that cannot be justified because of the predictions used in the calculation.

To verify that Carson Company's break-even point equals $80,000 and 800 units, prepare a simple income statement similar to the one in Illustration 22–6. It shows that the $80,000 revenue from the sales of 800 units exactly equals the sum of the fixed and variable costs.

FAST HINT
Critical Thought Question:
The break-even point changes as
the elements of the equation
change. What effect would the
purchase of new production
equipment have on the break-
even point?

DRAWING A CVP CHART

Illustration 22–7 is a graphic representation of the cost-volume-profit relationships for Carson Company for a month. This type of presentation is a **CVP chart.** It is also called a *break-even graph* or *break-even chart.* Notice that the horizontal axis represents the number of units sold and the vertical axis represents dollars of sales and costs. In accordance with the simplifying assumptions used in basic analyses, straight lines depict costs and revenues on the graph. To prepare a CVP chart like the one in Illustration 22–7, complete the following steps:

1. Plot the amount of fixed costs on the vertical axis. If you wish, draw a horizontal line at this level to show that fixed costs remain unchanged regardless of sales volume. So that you can see this effect, Illustration 22–7 includes this line. However, the fixed cost line is not essential to the analysis and is usually omitted.

2. Draw a line to represent total costs (variable costs plus fixed costs). For any sales level on the graph, the line shows the sum of the fixed costs and the variable costs for that level. This line starts at the fixed costs level on the vertical axis because total costs equal the fixed costs at the zero sales level. The slope of the total cost line equals the variable cost per unit. To draw the line, compute the total costs for any sales level, and connect this point with the vertical axis intercept. Do not extend this line beyond the productive capacity for the planning period.

3. Draw a sales line starting at the origin (zero units and zero dollars of sales). The slope of this line equals the selling price per unit. To draw the line, compute the total revenues for any sales level, and connect this point with the origin. Do not extend this line beyond the productive capacity for the planning period. The total revenue will be at its maximum level at maximum capacity. It is likely that the relevant range will be near the middle of the graph.[4]

FAST HINT

Alternative Example:
In Illustration 22–7, the sales line intersects the total cost line at 800 units. At what point would the two lines intersect if the selling price were increased by 20% to $120 per unit?
Answer: $24,000/$50 = 480 units

As you examine Illustration 22–7, observe that the total cost line and the sales line intersect at 800 units of product. This intersection is the break-even point because the total sales revenue of $80,000 equals the $80,000 sum of the fixed and variable costs.

On either side of the break-even point, the vertical distance between the sales line and the total cost line at any specific sales volume measures the profit or loss expected at that volume. At volume levels to the left of the break-even point, this vertical distance is the amount of the loss because the total cost line is above the total sales line. And, at volume levels to the right of the break-even point, the vertical distance represents the amount of profit because the total sales line is above the total cost line.

Progress Check

22–8   **Fixed cost divided by the contribution rate yields the:**
a. **Break-even point in dollars.**
b. **Contribution margin per unit.**
c. **Break-even point in units.**

22–9   **A company sells a product for $90 per unit with variable costs of $54 per unit. What is the contribution rate?**

22–10   **Refer to 22–9. If fixed costs for the period are $90,000, what is the break-even point in dollars?**

FINDING THE INCOME FROM AN EXPECTED SALES LEVEL

LO 5

Describe several applications of cost-volume-profit analysis.

Cost-volume-profit analysis can be used to develop preliminary answers to a variety of planning questions. Generally, the first question that managers need to answer is, "How much income will we have from our expected level of sales?" CVP provides information for answering this question by including four factors in this equation:

---

[4]These instructions are provided to guide you through a manual drafting process. The graph can also be drawn with computer assistance, including spreadsheet programs that can convert numeric data to graphs.

Illustration 22-7 Cost-Volume-Profit Chart

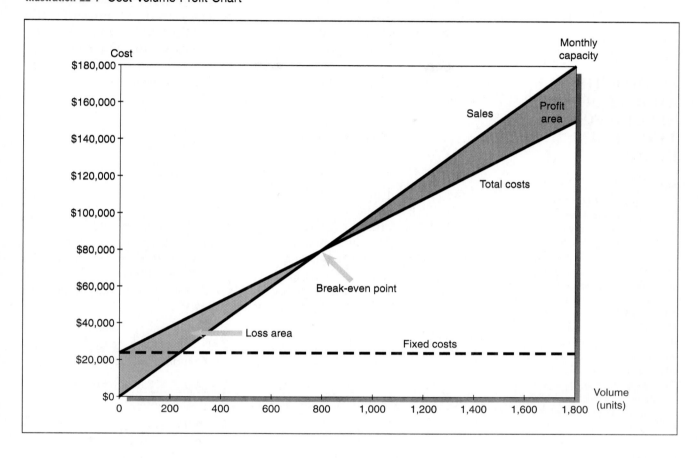

$$\text{Profit} = \text{Sales} - (\text{Fixed costs} + \text{Variable costs})$$

or

$$\text{Profit} = \text{Sales} - \text{Fixed costs} - \text{Variable costs}$$

You can use this equation to calculate the profit from an expected sales level. For example, assume that the management of Carson Company expects to sell 1,500 units of its product. How much profit will result if the monthly sales reach this level? At this volume, revenues would be $150,000 (1,500 units × $100). Carson Company's fixed costs are $24,000 per month. The variable costs per unit are $70 per unit, and total variable costs for 1,500 units of product are $105,000 ($70 × 1,500 units). By substituting these amounts in the equation, we can calculate the profit this way:

$$\begin{aligned} \text{Profit} &= \$150,000 - \$24,000 - \$105,000 \\ &= \$150,000 - \$129,000 \\ &= \$21,000 \end{aligned}$$

Notice that the $21,000 profit does not include the effects of income taxes. If the management of Carson Company wants to find the amount of after-tax income from selling 1,500 units, they must apply the appropriate tax rates to the $21,000. If the tax rate is 25%, the equation becomes:

$$\begin{aligned} \text{Net income} &= \$21,000 - (25\% \times \$21,000) \\ &= \$21,000 - \$5,250 \\ &= \$15,750 \end{aligned}$$

Then, the management must go on to determine whether this profit is an adequate return on the assets invested in providing the operating capacity. Management also should consider whether total dollars of sales can be increased by raising or lowering prices. CVP is a good tool for addressing these kinds of what-if questions.

FINDING THE AMOUNT OF SALES NEEDED FOR A TARGET NET INCOME

CVP can also be used to find the sales level needed to produce a target net income. The formula is:

$$\text{Dollar sales} = \frac{\text{Fixed costs} + \text{Target net income} + \text{Income taxes}}{\text{Contribution rate}}$$

FAST HINT
Critical Thought Question:
If any item in the numerator of the dollar sales formula increases, what happens to the dollar sales amount? If the denominator increases, what happens to the dollar sales amount?

FAST HINT
Critical Thought Question:
If a company reacts to a 10% increase in variable costs by increasing its selling price by 10%, does its break-even point in dollars of sales change? What about its break-even point in units?

FAST HINT
Critical Thought Question:
If a company's income tax rate increases from 30 to 35%, what effect does that have on the company's break-even point?

FAST HINT
Relevant Exercise:
To apply these concepts, work Exercise 22–8.

For those interested in the underlying mathematics, Illustration 22–8 presents the derivation of the formula.

To illustrate the formula's use, recall that Carson Company has monthly fixed costs of $24,000 and a 30% contribution rate. Now, assume that the management has set a target monthly income of $18,000 after considering income taxes at the rate of 25%. At this rate, the before-tax income needs to be $24,000 [$18,000/(1 − .25)] and the tax is $6,000. Under these assumptions, $160,000 of sales are necessary to produce a $18,000 net income. Calculate this amount as follows:

$$\text{Dollar sales at target income level} = \frac{\text{Fixed costs} + \text{Net income} + \text{Income taxes}}{\text{Contribution rate}}$$

$$= \frac{\$24,000 + \$18,000 + \$6,000}{30\%}$$

$$= \frac{\$48,000}{30\%} = \$160,000$$

You can also use this formula with the contribution margin as the denominator. If so, the result is the number of units that must be sold to reach the target income level. This calculation applies to the Carson Company's situation:

$$\text{Unit sales at target income level} = \frac{\text{Fixed costs} + \text{Net income} + \text{Income taxes}}{\text{Contribution margin}}$$

$$= \frac{\$24,000 + \$18,000 + \$6,000}{\$30}$$

$$= \frac{\$48,000}{\$30} = 1,600 \text{ units}$$

These two calculations have equivalent answers because sales of 1,600 units at $100 per unit will yield $160,000 of revenue.

The next step in the planning process is to determine whether the company can sell 1,600 units at the assumed price. If not, other alternatives need to be examined.

FINDING THE MARGIN OF SAFETY

The excess of expected sales over the sales at the break-even point is a company's **margin of safety.** This difference is called the margin of safety because it is the amount that sales could drop before the company will incur a loss. The margin of safety can be expressed in units of product, in dollars, or even as a percentage of the predicted level of sales. For example, if Carson Company's expected sales are $100,000, the margin of safety is $20,000 over the break-even sales of $80,000. As a percentage, the margin of safety is 20% of the expected sales:

Illustration 22-8
Derivation of Target Income
Formula

Let: S = sales in units R = revenue per unit
       F = fixed costs per month V = variable cost per unit
       N = target net income T = income taxes
       $S \times R$ = dollar sales $S \times V$ = total variable cost

And: Contribution rate = $(R - V)/R$

Then: $N = (S \times R) - F - (S \times V) - T$
       $(S \times R) - (S \times V) = F + N + T$
       $S \times (R - V) = F + N + T$
       $S = (F + N + T)/(R - V)$
       $S \times R = [(F + N + T) \times R]/(R - V)$
       $S \times R = (F + N + T) \times [R/(R - V)]$
       $S \times R = (F + N + T)/[(R - V)/R]$
       $S \times R = (F + N + T)/\text{Contribution rate}$

$$\text{Margin of safety} = \frac{\text{Expected sales} - \text{Break-even sales}}{\text{Expected sales}}$$

or

$$= \frac{\$100,000 - \$80,000}{\$100,000} = 20\%$$

Then, management should assess whether this margin of safety is adequate in light of the variability of sales volumes that might be expected in the future.

FINDING THE ANSWERS TO OTHER QUESTIONS

FAST HINT
Relevant Exercise:
To apply these concepts, work Exercise 22–9.

In planning business operations, managers often consider a variety of strategies. These possible strategies often affect the costs and revenues of the business. Cost-volume-profit analysis is useful for helping managers complete preliminary evaluations of likely effects of new strategies. For example, managers may want to know what would happen if they reduced the selling price of the product to increase sales. Or, managers might want to know what would happen to profits if they installed a new automated machine that would increase fixed costs while reducing variable costs. If the managers can describe how the change would affect the company's fixed costs, variable costs, selling price, and volume, they can use CVP to predict the resulting profit.

To illustrate the possible effect of a change, assume that the manager of Carson Company is thinking about buying a new machine that would increase the monthly fixed costs from $24,000 to $30,000. If the purchase is made, the machine will reduce variable costs from $70 per unit to $60 per unit. Because the product's selling price will remain unchanged at $100, the contribution margin and the contribution rate will both increase. The new contribution margin will be $40 per unit ($100 − $60) and the new contribution rate will be 40% of the selling price ($40/$100). The manager wants to know what the break-even point will be if the machine is bought.

If the machine is purchased, the company's new break-even point in dollars will be:

$$\text{New break-even point in dollars} = \frac{\text{New fixed costs}}{\text{New contribution rate}}$$

$$= \frac{\$30,000}{40\%} = \$75,000$$

The new fixed costs and the new contribution rate can also be used to determine the expected income at a given sales level, to find the sales level needed to earn a target net income, or to answer other questions management may raise before purchasing the new machine.

Progress Check

22–11 A company has fixed costs of $50,000 and a 25% contribution rate. How many dollars of sales would be necessary for the company to achieve a net income of $120,000 if the tax rate is 20%?
  a. $800,000
  b. $680,000
  c. $600,000.

22–12 If the contribution rate decreases from 50 to 25%, what can be said about unit sales needed to achieve a target income level?

22–13 What is a company's margin of safety?

MULTIPRODUCT BREAK-EVEN POINT

LO 6

Calculate the break-even point for a multiproduct company by constructing a composite sales unit.

Up to this point, we have considered only those situations in which the company produces a single product because the basic model requires this simplicity. However, it is possible to modify the basic model for use when a company produces and sells several products in a fairly consistent ratio. A company that sells more than one product can estimate the break-even point by using a *composite unit* composed of specific numbers of units of each product in proportion to their expected **sales mix.** The sales mix is the ratio of the volumes of the various products. Then, CVP analyses treat the composite unit as though it is a single product.

To illustrate the use of a composite unit, assume that Denson Company sells three products: A, B, and C. Management wants to estimate the company's break-even point for the next month. Unit selling prices for the three products are:

Product A $5
Product B 8
Product C 4

Because the sales mix is the ratio of 4 units of A to 2 units of B to 1 unit of C (more conveniently expressed as 4:2:1), the selling price of a composite unit consisting of the three products is calculated as follows:

4 units of Product A @ $5 per unit	$20
2 units of Product B @ $8 per unit	16
1 unit of Product C @ $4 per unit	4
Selling price of a composite unit	$40

The company's fixed costs are $48,000 per month and the variable costs of the three products are:

Product A	$3.25
Product B	4.50
Product C	2.00

Thus, the variable costs of a composite unit of the products are:

4 units of Product A @ $3.25 per unit	$13
2 units of Product B @ $4.50 per unit	9
1 unit of Product C @ $2.00 per unit	2
Variable costs of a composite unit	$24

After the variable costs and selling price of a composite unit of the company's products are found, the Denson Company can calculate the contribution margin for a composite unit by subtracting the variable costs of a composite unit from its selling price:

FAST HINT
Relevant Exercise:
To apply these concepts, work Exercise 22–13.

$$\text{Contribution margin per composite unit} = \text{Selling price} - \text{Variable costs}$$
$$= \$40 - \$24 = \$16$$

The management then uses the $16 contribution margin to determine the company's break-even point in composite units. The break-even point is found as follows:

$$\text{Break-even point in composite units} = \frac{\text{Fixed costs}}{\text{Contribution margin per composite unit}}$$
$$= \frac{\$48,000}{\$16}$$
$$= 3,000 \text{ composite units}$$

According to this calculation, Denson Company breaks even when it sells 3,000 composite units of its products. To determine how many units of each product must be sold to break even, the number of units of each product in the composite unit is multiplied by 3,000:

Product A:	4	×	3,000	12,000 units
Product B:	2	×	3,000	6,000 units
Product C:	1	×	3,000	3,000 units

The schedule in Illustration 22–9 verifies these results by showing the company's revenues and costs at the break-even point.

Illustration 22-9

DENSON COMPANY
Forecasted Product Income Statement
at the Break-Even Point

	Product A	Product B	Product C	Combined
Sales:				
Product A (12,000 @ $5)	$60,000			
Product B (6,000 @ $8)		$48,000		
Product C (3,000 @ $4)			$12,000	
Total revenues				$120,000
Variable costs:				
Product A (12,000 @ $3.25)	39,000			
Product B (6,000 @ $4.50)		27,000		
Product C (3,000 @ $2.00)			6,000	
6,000				
Total variable costs				72,000
Contribution margin	$21,000	$21,000	$ 6,000	$ 48,000
Fixed costs				48,000
Net income				$ –0–

A cost-volume-profit analysis based on composite units can be used to answer a variety of planning questions. Once a product mix is established, all answers are based on the assumption that it remains constant at all sales levels, just like the other factors in the analysis. And, like the other factors, the sales mix can be varied to see what would happen under alternative strategies.

EVALUATING THE USEFULNESS OF COST-VOLUME-PROFIT ANALYSES

Cost-volume-profit analysis is useful when management begins the planning process and needs to predict the results of alternative strategies for selling prices, fixed costs, variable costs, sales volume, and product mix. But, you should keep two points in mind before using the results of CVP. First, the data in the analysis are predictions of future conditions. Therefore, the output of the analysis can be no better than the quality of those predictions. Second, the CVP analysis presented in this chapter is based on assumptions that the selling price will remain constant, that fixed costs are truly fixed, and that variable costs are truly variable. These assumptions do not always correspond to reality. Therefore, the results of the analyses are rough approximations at best. If you keep these limits in mind, CVP can be useful for starting to plan the activities of a business.

More complex CVP analyses can be designed to reflect such things as nonlinear revenue and cost behaviors. These analyses are described in more advanced managerial accounting courses.

Progress Check

22-14   The sales mix of a company's two products, X and Y, is 2:1. Unit price and variable cost data are:

	X	Y
Unit sales price	$5	$4
Unit variable cost . . .	2	2

What is the contribution margin per composite unit? *(a)* $5; *(b)* $10; *(c)* $8.

22-15   What additional assumption about sales mix must be made in doing a conventional CVP analysis in a company that produces and sells more than one product?

LO 1. Describe different types of cost behavior in relation to sales volume. A cost's behavior is described in terms of how its amount changes in relation to production and sales volume changes. As volume increases, total fixed costs remain unchanged. Total variable costs change in direct proportion to volume changes. Step-variable costs remain constant over a small volume range, increase by a lump-sum, then remain constant over another volume range, and so on. Semivariable costs change in a nonlinear relationship to volume changes. Mixed costs display the effects of fixed and variable components.

LO 2. State the assumptions used in cost-volume-profit analysis and explain how they limit the usefulness of the analysis. Conventional cost-volume-profit analysis is based on assumptions that the selling price of the single product remains constant and that variable and fixed costs behave consistently with those classifications. These assumptions are not likely to hold at volume levels outside the relevant range of operations of the business. If the assumptions do not lead to valid predictions of future costs, the CVP will not be helpful.

LO 3. Prepare and interpret a scatter diagram of past costs and sales volume. A scatter diagram is a graph that plots points representing the actual cost and sales volume for a number of past periods. To predict future costs, an estimated line of cost behavior is drawn through the points. This line can be fitted to the points by the high-low method, a visual approximation, or a least-squares regression. The vertical intercept approximates the fixed costs and the slope approximates the variable cost per unit.

LO 4. Calculate a break-even point for a single product company and present its costs and revenues in a graph. A company's break-even point for a period is the sales volume at which total revenues equal the total costs. To calculate a break-even point in terms of units, divide total fixed costs by the contribution margin per unit. To calculate a break-even point in terms of sales dollars, divide total fixed costs by the contribution rate.

LO 5. Describe several applications of cost-volume-profit analysis. Cost-volume-profit analysis can be used to develop initial predictions of what would happen under alternative strategies concerning sales volume, selling prices, variable costs, or fixed costs.

LO 6. Calculate the break-even point for a multiproduct company by constructing a composite sales unit. CVP can be applied to a multiproduct company by expressing the predicted sales volume in terms of composite units of product.

SUMMARY OF THE CHAPTER IN TERMS OF LEARNING OBJECTIVES

DEMONSTRATION PROBLEM

The Tate Manufacturing Co. produces and sells a single product on a simple production line. The fixed costs of operating the business have averaged about $150,000 per month, and the variable costs have been about $5 per unit. All the manufactured product can be sold at $8 per unit and the fixed costs provide a production capacity of up to 100,000 units per month.

Required

1. Use formulas to calculate the following:
    a. Contribution margin per unit.
    b. Break-even point in terms of the number of units produced and sold.
    c. Amount of profit at 30,000 units per month (ignore income taxes).
    d. Amount of profit at 85,000 units per month (ignore income taxes).
    e. Quantity of units to be produced and sold to provide $45,000 of after-tax profits, assuming an income tax rate of 25%.

2. Draw a CVP chart for the company, showing units of output on the horizontal axis. Identify the break-even point and the amount of pre-tax profit when the level of production is 75,000 units. (Omit the fixed cost line.)

3. Use formulas to calculate the following:
    a. Contribution rate.
    b. Break-even point in terms of sales dollars.
    c. Amount of profit at $250,000 of sales per month (ignore income taxes).
    d. Amount of profit at $600,000 of sales per month (ignore income taxes).
    e. Dollars of sales needed to provide $45,000 of after-tax profits, assuming an income tax rate of 25%.

Planning the Solution

- Find the formulas in the chapter for the required items concerning volumes expressed in units and solve them using the original data given in the problem.
- Draw a CVP chart that reflects the facts given in the problem. The horizontal axis should plot the volume in units up to 100,000, and the vertical axis should plot the total dollars up to $800,000. Plot the total cost line as upward-sloping, starting at the fixed cost level ($150,000) on the vertical axis and increasing until it reaches $650,000 at the maximum volume of 100,000 units. Verify that the break-even point (where the two lines cross) equals the amount you computed in Part 1.
- Find the formulas in the chapter for the required items concerning volumes expressed in units and solve them using the original data given in the problem.

Solution to Demonstration Problem

1.
a. $$\text{Contribution margin per unit} = \text{Selling price per unit} - \text{Variable cost per unit}$$
    $$= \$8 - \$5 = \$3$$

b. $$\text{Break-even point in units} = \frac{\text{Fixed costs}}{\text{Contribution margin per unit}}$$
    $$= \frac{\$150,000}{\$3} = 50,000 \text{ units}$$

c. $$\text{Profit at 30,000 unit sales} = (\text{Units} \times \text{Contribution margin per unit}) - \text{Fixed costs}$$
    $$= (30,000 \times \$3) - \$150,000 = -\$60,000 \text{ (a loss)}$$

d. $$\text{Profit at 85,000 unit sales} = (\text{Units} \times \text{Contribution margin per unit}) - \text{Fixed costs}$$
    $$= (85,000 \times \$3) - \$150,000 = \$105,000 \text{ profit}$$

e. $$\text{Pre-tax profit} = \$45,000/75\% = \$60,000$$
    $$\text{Income taxes} = \$60,000 \times 25\% = \$15,000$$
    $$\text{Units needed for \$45,000 profit} = \frac{\text{Fixed costs} + \text{Net income} + \text{Income taxes}}{\text{Contribution margin per unit}}$$
    $$= \frac{\$150,000 + \$45,000 + \$15,000}{\$3} = 70,000 \text{ units}$$

2. CVP chart:

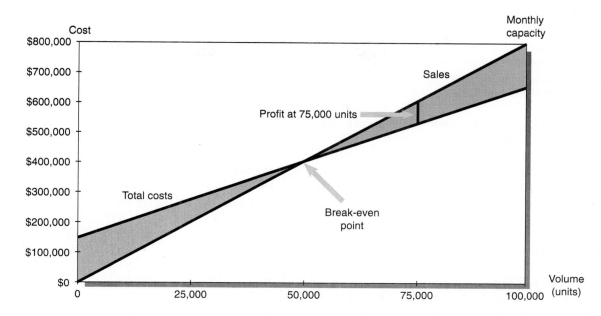

3.

a. Contribution rate $= \dfrac{\text{Contribution margin per unit}}{\text{Selling price per unit}} = \dfrac{\$3}{\$8} = .375$, or 37.5%

b. Break-even point in dollars $= \dfrac{\text{Fixed costs}}{\text{Contribution rate}} = \dfrac{\$150,000}{37.5\%} = \$400,000$

c. Profit at sales of $250,000
= (Sales × Contribution rate) − Fixed costs
= ($250,000 × 37.5%) − $150,000
= − $56,250 (a loss)

d. Profit at sales of $600,000
= (Sales × Contribution rate) − Fixed costs
= ($600,000 × 37.5%) − $150,000
= $75,000 profit

e. Dollars of sales to have $45,000 profits $= \dfrac{\text{Fixed costs + Net income + Income taxes}}{\text{Contribution rate}}$

$= \dfrac{\$150,000 + \$45,000 + \$15,000}{37.5\%} = \$560,000$

GLOSSARY

Break-even point the unique sales level at which a company neither earns a profit nor incurs a loss. p. 854

Contribution margin per unit the amount that the sale of one unit contributes toward recovering fixed costs and profit. p. 854

Contribution rate the contribution margin per unit expressed as a percentage of the product's selling price. p. 854

Cost-volume-profit analysis the first step in the planning phase of operating a business; the analysis predicts the effects of changes in costs and sales level on the income of a business. p. 846

CVP chart a graph that plots volumes on the horizontal axis and costs and revenues on the vertical axis. p. 856

Estimated line of cost behavior a line on a scatter diagram that is intended to reflect the past relationship between cost and volume. p. 852

Fixed cost a cost that remains unchanged in total amount even when production volume varies from period to period. p. 847

High-low method a simple way to draw an estimated line of cost behavior by connecting the highest and lowest costs on a scatter diagram with a straight line. p. 853

Least-squares regression a statistical method for deriving an estimated line of cost behavior that is more precise than the high-low method. p. 853

Margin of safety the excess of expected sales over the sales at the break-even point. p. 858

Mixed cost a cost that can be separated into fixed and variable components. p. 849

Relevant range of operations a business's normal operating range; excludes extremely high and low volumes that are not likely to be encountered. p. 851

Sales mix the ratio of the sales volumes of the various products sold by a company. p. 860

Scatter diagram a graph used to analyze past cost behaviors by displaying costs and volumes for each period as points on the diagram. p. 852

Semivariable cost a cost that changes with volume but not at a constant rate. p. 848

Step-variable cost a cost that remains constant over limited ranges of volumes but increases by a lump sum when volume increases beyond maximum amounts. p. 848

Variable cost a cost that changes in proportion to changes in production volume. p. 847

QUESTIONS

1. Why is cost-volume-profit analysis used?
2. When volume increases, do fixed costs per unit increase or decrease? Why? What happens to the amount of variable costs per unit?
3. What is a variable cost? Identify two variable costs.
4. How do step-variable costs and semivariable costs differ?
5. In performing a conventional CVP analysis for a manufacturing company, what simplifying assumption is usually made about the volume of production and the volume of sales?
6. What two factors tend to justify classifying all costs as either fixed or variable even though individual costs might not behave perfectly consistently with these classifications?
7. How does assuming a relevant range affect cost-volume-profit analysis?
8. How can a scatter diagram be used in identifying the behavior of a company's costs?
9. Assume that a straight line on a CVP chart intersects the vertical axis at the level of fixed costs and has a positive slope, such that it rises with each additional unit of vol-

ume by the amount of the variable costs per unit. What would this line represent?
10. Why are fixed costs depicted as a horizontal line on a CVP chart?
11. Two similar companies each have sales of $100,000 and total costs of $80,000 for a month. Company A's total costs include $20,000 of variable costs and $60,000 of fixed costs. If Company B's total costs include $60,000 of variable costs and $20,000 of fixed costs, which company will enjoy a greater profit if sales double?
12. Consider the process of preparing sandwiches for sale during the lunch rush hour at a McDonald's store. Identify some of the variable and fixed costs associated with that process.
13. Federal Express flies packages from drop off points to Memphis, sorts them there in a central facility, and then delivers them the next morning to their destinations. Is it likely that some flights produce more costs than revenues?

QUICK STUDY (Five-Minute Exercises)

Following are three series of costs measured at various volume levels. Examine each series and identify which is fixed, variable, and step-variable.

QS 22–1
(LO 1)

Volume (Units)	Series 1	Series 2	Series 3
0	$–0–	$450	$ 800
100	800	450	800
200	1,600	450	800
300	2,400	450	1,600
400	3,200	450	1,600
500	4,000	450	2,400
600	4,800	450	2,400

For each of the following, determine whether it would best be described as a fixed, variable, or mixed cost:

QS 22–2
(LO 1)

a. Taxes on factory building.

b. Shipping expense.

c. Wages of an assembly-line worker paid on the basis of acceptable units produced.

d. Factory supervisor's salary.

e. Maintenance of factory machinery.

f. Rubber used in manufacture of tennis shoes.

Which of the following is one of the assumptions that underlie cost-volume-profit analyses?

QS 22–3
(LO 2)

a. The actual selling price per unit must change in proportion to the number of units sold during the planning period.

b. For costs classified as variable, the actual costs per unit of output must remain constant.

c. For costs classified as fixed, the actual costs per unit of output must remain constant.

The following scatter diagram reflects past maintenance hours and corresponding maintenance costs:

QS 22–4
(LO 3)

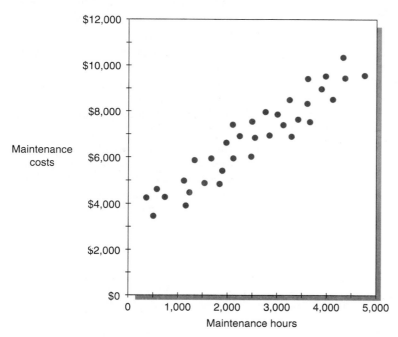

Draw an estimated line of cost behavior and determine the fixed and variable components of maintenance costs.

**QS 22–5
(LO 4)**

Hatfield Company manufactures and sells a product for $50 per unit. Fixed costs for the period total $225,000 and variable costs are $30 per unit. Determine the *(a)* contribution margin per unit and *(b)* the break-even point in units.

**QS 22–6
(LO 4)**

Refer to QS 22–5. Determine the *(a)* contribution rate and *(b)* the break-even point in dollars.

**QS 22–7
(LO 5)**

Refer to QS 22–5. Assume that Hatfield Company is subject to a combined federal and state income tax rate of 40%. Calculate the units of product that must be sold to earn after-tax income of $630,000.

**QS 22–8
(LO 6)**

Luna Company manufactures and sells two products, toasters and mixers, in the ratio of 5:3. Fixed costs are $835,125 and the contribution margin per composite unit is $85. What is the number of mixers that will be sold at the break-even point?

EXERCISES

**Exercise 22–1
Identifying categories of cost behavior
(LO 1)**

The left column presents the names of several categories of costs. The right column presents short definitions of those costs. In the blank space beside each of the numbers in the right column, write the letter of the cost described by the definition.

a.   Fixed cost
b.   Mixed cost
c.   Variable cost
d.   Semivariable cost
e.   Step-variable cost
f.   Total cost

_____ 1.   This cost is the combined amount of all the other costs.

_____ 2.   This cost increases in direct proportion to increases in volume because its amount is constant for each unit produced.

_____ 3.   This cost increases when volume increases, but the increase is not constant for each unit produced.

_____ 4.   This cost remains the same over all volume levels within the productive capacity for the planning period.

_____ 5.   This cost has a component that remains the same over all volume levels and another component that increases in direct proportion to increases in volume.

_____ 6.   This cost remains constant over a limited range of volume that is less than the total productive capacity; when it reaches the end of its limited range, it increases by a lump sum and remains at that level until another limited range is exceeded.

The following five graphs represent various cost behaviors:

Exercise 22–2
Recognizing cost behavior graphs
(LO 1)

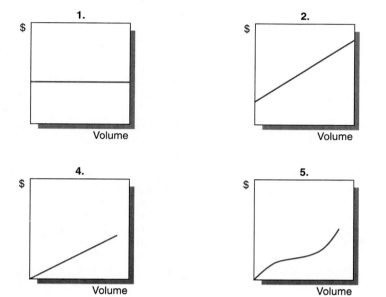

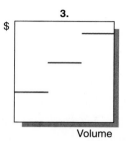

Required

a. Identify the type of cost behavior that each graph represents.

b. For each of the following items, identify the graph that best illustrates the cost behavior described:

1. Plant security requires one guard per 20 factory workers.

2. An addition of hourly paid workers that provides substantial gains in efficiency as a few workers are added, but gradually smaller gains in efficiency as more workers are added.

3. Insurance on factory machinery.

4. Commissions to salespersons.

5. Factory utilities that include the standard monthly charge plus usage.

Following are five series of costs measured at various volume levels. Examine each series and identify which is fixed, variable, mixed, semivariable, and step-variable:

Exercise 22–3
Recognizing cost behavior patterns
(LO 1)

Volume (Units)	Series A	Series B	Series C	Series D	Series E
0	$ –0–	$3,200	$ –0–	$2,000	$4,200
400	6,000	3,700	3,200	2,000	4,200
800	6,600	4,200	6,400	2,000	4,200
1,200	7,200	4,700	9,600	4,000	4,200
1,600	7,800	5,200	12,800	4,000	4,200
2,000	9,600	5,700	16,000	6,000	4,200
2,400	13,500	6,200	19,200	6,000	4,200

Exercise 22–4
Scatter diagram and cost behavior—six data points
(LO 3)

A company's accounting system provides the following information about its monthly sales volume and the amount of a specific cost in those months:

Month	Sales	Cost
1	$15,000	$8,100
2	10,500	5,500
3	10,500	7,000
4	7,500	5,500
5	9,000	6,000
6	12,500	6,500

Use this data to prepare a scatter diagram. Then, draw an estimated line of cost behavior and determine whether the cost appears to be variable, fixed, or mixed.

Exercise 22–5
Scatter diagram and cost behavior—15 data points
(LO 3)

Use the following information about monthly sales volume and the amount of a specific cost to prepare a scatter diagram. Then, draw a cost line that reflects the behavior displayed by this cost. Finally, determine whether the cost is variable, semivariable, step-variable, fixed, or mixed.

Period	Sales	Cost	Period	Sales	Cost
1	$38,000	$29,500	9	$29,000	$19,500
2	40,000	28,000	10	16,500	12,000
3	10,500	11,500	11 ...	12,500	12,250
4	20,500	20,000	12	36,000	27,500
5	24,500	19,500	13	14,000	13,000
6	31,500	27,500	14	22,000	20,500
7	34,000	29,500	15	19,000	13,250
8	27,500	21,500			

Exercise 22–6
Calculating contribution margin and rate
(LO 4)

Kappa Company manufactures a single product that sells for $84 per unit. The total variable costs of the product are $63 per unit and the company's annual fixed costs are $315,000. Use these data to calculate the company's:

a. Contribution margin.

b. Contribution rate.

c. Break-even point in units.

d. Break-even point in dollars of sales.

Exercise 22–7
Calculating additional sales necessary to break even
(LO 5)

Prepare an income statement for Kappa Company's operations (from Exercise 22–6) showing sales, variable costs, and fixed costs at the break-even point. If Kappa's fixed costs were to increase by $45,000, what amount of sales (in dollars) would be needed to break even?

Exercise 22–8
Calculating sales required to obtain desired income
(LO 5)

The management of Kappa Company (in Exercise 22–6) wants to earn an annual after-tax income of $360,000. The company is subject to a combined federal and state income tax rate of 40%. Calculate:

a. The units of product that must be sold to earn the target after-tax net income.

b. The dollars of sales that must be reached to earn the target after-tax net income.

Exercise 22–9
Estimating the income result from increased volume
(LO 5)

In looking ahead, the sales manager of Kappa Company (in Exercise 22–6) predicts that the annual sales of the company's product will soon reach 51,000 units even though the price will increase to $120 per unit. According to the production manager, the variable costs are expected to increase to $84 per unit but fixed costs will remain at $315,000. The company's tax adviser expects that the combined federal and state income tax rate will still be 40%. What amounts of before-tax and after-tax income can the company expect to earn from selling units at this expected level with these expected costs?

Driskill Company expects to sell 80,000 units of its product next year, which should produce total revenues of $12 million. Management predicts that the pre-tax net income for the year will be $2,400,000 and that the contribution margin per unit will be $40. Using this information, compute *(a)* the total expected variable costs and *(b)* the total expected fixed costs for next year.

Exercise 22–10
Calculating total variable and fixed costs
(LO 5)

In predicting the events of the upcoming quarter, the management of the Techno Company thinks that it will incur a total of $375,000 of variable costs and $600,000 of fixed costs while earning a pre-tax income of $150,000. The management predicts that the contribution margin per unit will be $75. Using this information, determine *(a)* the total expected dollar sales for the quarter and *(b)* the number of units expected to be sold in the quarter.

Exercise 22–11
Calculating unit and dollar sales using contribution margin
(LO 5)

The management of the Waterloo Company predicts that it will incur fixed costs of $600,000 next year and that the pre-tax income will be $240,000. The expected contribution rate is 75%. Use this information to compute the amounts of *(a)* total dollar sales and *(b)* total variable costs.

Exercise 22–12
Calculating sales and variable costs using contribution rate
(LO 5)

The AA Hardware Company sells windows and doors in the ratio of 10:3 (10 windows for every 3 doors). The selling price of each window is $70 and the selling price of each door is $450. The variable cost of a window is $40 and the variable cost of a door is $290. Next year's fixed costs are expected to be $975,000. Use this information to determine:

Exercise 22–13
CVP analysis using composite units
(LO 6)

a. The selling price of a composite unit of these products.

b. The variable costs per composite unit.

c. The break-even point in composite units.

d. The number of units of each product that will be sold at the break-even point.

PROBLEMS

The accounting system of the Jubilee Company collected the following monthly total sales and cost data about its operating activities for the past year:

Problem 22–1
Scatter diagram with estimated line of cost behavior
(LO 3)

Period	Sales	Total Cost
1	$250,000	$170,000
2	190,000	130,000
3	234,000	200,000
4	210,000	160,000
5	300,000	230,000
6	210,000	170,000
7	270,000	200,000
8	250,000	190,000
9	170,000	130,000
10	200,000	180,000
11	180,000	140,000
12	170,000	150,000

The management of the company wants to use this historical data to predict future fixed and variable costs.

Required

1. Prepare a scatter diagram with sales volume plotted on the horizontal axis (scale this axis in $40,000 intervals) and with total cost plotted on the vertical axis (scale this axis in $40,000 intervals). Then, plot the sales and cost data for Jubilee.

2. Develop an estimated line of cost behavior by a visual inspection and draw it on the scatter diagram. (Assume a linear relationship, which means that you should draw a straight line on the graph.)

3. Based on the estimated line of cost behavior and the assumption that the future will be like the past, predict the amount of monthly fixed costs for Jubilee. Also, predict future variable cost per sales dollar.

4. Use the estimated line of cost behavior to predict future total costs when the sales volume is $200,000 and $280,000.

Problem 22–2
Completing CVP analyses, including a chart
(LO 4)

Grove Company manufactures and markets a number of products. Management is considering the future of Product A, which has not been as profitable as planned. Because this product is manufactured and marketed independently from the other products, its total costs can be precisely measured. The plan for the next year calls for a selling price of $480 per unit. The fixed costs for the year are expected to be $300,000, up to the maximum capacity of 2,500 units. The forecasted variable costs are $180 per unit.

Required

1. Predict the break-even point for Product A in terms of (a) units and (b) dollars of sales.

2. Prepare a CVP chart for Product A. Use 2,500 as the maximum number of units on the graph and $1,200,000 as the maximum number of dollars.

3. Prepare an income statement showing sales, fixed costs, and variable costs for Product A at the break-even point.

4. Determine the sales volume in dollars that the company must achieve to earn a $231,000 income from Product A, after income taxes are assessed at 30%.

5. Determine the after-tax income that the company would earn from sales of $1,200,000.

Problem 22–3
CVP chart and income statements to confirm projections
(LO 4, 5)

In 19X2, Kidder Company sold 15,000 units of its only product and incurred a $84,000 loss (ignoring income taxes), as follows:

KIDDER COMPANY
Income Statement
For Year Ended December 31, 19X2

Sales		$ 750,000
Costs:		
Fixed	$384,000	
Variable	450,000	834,000
Net loss		$ (84,000)

During a planning session for 19X3's activities, the production manager has pointed out that variable costs can be reduced 50% by installing a machine that automates several operations presently being done by hand. To obtain these savings, the company must increase its annual fixed costs by $120,000. The maximum capacity of the system would be 30,000 units per year.

Required

1. Calculate 19X2's break-even point in terms of dollars.

2. Calculate the dollar break-even point for 19X3 under the assumption that the new machine is installed.

3. Prepare a CVP chart for 19X3 under the assumption that the new machine is installed.

4. Prepare a forecasted income statement for 19X3 that shows the expected results with the new machine installed. Assume that there will be no change in the selling price and no change in the number of units sold. The combined federal and state income tax rate is 30%.

5. Calculate the sales level required to earn $147,000 of after-tax income in 19X3 with the new machine installed and with no change in the selling price. Prepare a forecasted income statement that shows the results at this sales level.

Last year, Kirby Company sold 35,000 units of product at $16 per unit. Manufacturing and selling the product required $120,000 of fixed manufacturing costs and $180,000 of fixed selling and administrative expenses. Last year's variable costs and expenses per unit were:

Material	$4.00
Direct labor (paid on the basis of completed units) ..	3.00
Variable manufacturing overhead costs	0.40
Variable selling and administrative expenses	0.20

Problem 22–4
Analyzing the effects of price and volume changes on profits
(LO 5)

A new raw material has recently become available that is both easier to work with and cheaper than the old material. Management has already established that the company will switch to the new material because material costs can be decreased by 60% and direct labor costs can be decreased by 40%. The new material will not affect the product's quality or marketability. The next set of decisions concerns the marketing strategy to be used. Because the factory's output is creeping up to its annual capacity of 40,000 units, some consideration is being given to increasing the selling price to reduce the number of units sold. At this point, two strategies have been identified. Under Plan 1, the company will keep the price at the current level and sell the same volume as last year. This plan increases profits because of the materials change. Under Plan 2, the product's price will be increased by 25%, but unit sales volume will fall only 10%. Under both Plan 1 and Plan 2, all of the fixed costs and variable costs (per unit) will be exactly the same.

Required

1. Calculate the break-even point in dollars for Plan 1 and Plan 2.

2. Prepare CVP charts for both Plan 1 and Plan 2.

3. Prepare side-by-side condensed forecasted income statements showing the anticipated results of Plan 1 and Plan 2. The statements should show sales, total fixed costs, total variable costs and expenses, income before taxes, income taxes (30% rate), and net income.

CHECK FIGURE:
Net income under Plan 2, $142,800

OMR Company produces and sells two products, A and B. These products are manufactured in separate factories and marketed through completely different channels. Thus, they do not have any shared costs. Last year, OMR sold 50,000 units of each product. The following income statement describes the financial results:

Problem 22–5
Break-even analysis comparing different cost structures
(LO 5)

	Product A	Product B
Sales	$800,000	$800,000
Costs:		
Fixed costs	$100,000	$560,000
Variable costs	560,000	100,000
Total costs	$660,000	$660,000
Income before taxes	$140,000	$140,000
Income taxes (32% rate)	44,800	44,800
Net income	$ 95,200	$ 95,200

Required

Preparation component:

1. Calculate the break-even point in dollars for each product.

2. Prepare a CVP chart for each product. Use 80,000 as the annual capacity.

3. Assume that the company expects the sales of each product to decline to 33,000 units in the upcoming year, even though the price will remain unchanged. Prepare a forecasted income statement that shows the expected profits from the two products. Follow the format of the preceding statement and assume that any loss before taxes results in a tax savings.

4. Assume that the company expects the sales of each product to increase to 64,000 units in the upcoming year, even though the price will remain unchanged. Prepare a forecasted income statement that shows the expected profits from the two products. Follow the format of the preceding statement.

CHECK FIGURE:
After-tax income, Product B, $228,480

Analysis component:

5. If sales were to greatly decrease, which of these products would experience the greater loss? Why?

6. Describe some factors that might have created the different cost structures for these two products.

Problem 22–6
Break-even analysis with composite units
(LO 6)

Peabody Company manufactures and sells three products, Red, White, and Blue. Their individual selling prices are:

Red	$50.00 per unit
White	$75.00 per unit
Blue	$125.00 per unit

The variable costs of manufacturing and selling the products have been:

Red	$30.00 per unit
White	$50.00 per unit
Blue	$75.00 per unit

Their sales mix is a ratio of 5:4:2, and the annual fixed costs shared by all three products are $120,000. One particular item of raw materials is used in manufacturing all three products. Management has learned that a new material is just as good and cheaper. The new material would reduce the variable costs as follows: Red by $5.00, White by $6.25, and Blue by $10. But, the new material requires new equipment, which will increase annual fixed costs by $9,500.

Required

1. Assuming that the company continues to use the old material, determine the company's break-even point in dollars and units of each product that would be sold at the break-even point.

CHECK FIGURE:
New plan break-even point, 350 composite units

2. Assuming that the company decides to use the new material, determine the company's new break-even point in dollars and units of each product that would be sold at the 873 break-even point.

CRITICAL THINKING: ESSAYS, PROBLEMS, AND CASES

Managerial Decision Cases

MDC 22–1
(LO 4, 5)

Infotex Corporation produces a computer chip. Last year, the company's plant operated at a level near its capacity with the results shown in the following condensed income statement:

Sales (20,000 units)	$2,000,000
Cost of goods manufactured and sold (fixed, $400,000; variable, $720,000)	1,120,000
Gross profit	$ 880,000
Selling and administrative expenses (fixed, $200,000; variable, $160,000)	360,000
Income before taxes	$ 520,000

Tycon Company has offered Infotex a two-year contract whereby it will buy 12,000 chips each year for $80 each. Tycon would export these chips overseas and these sales would not reduce domestic sales. To produce that many additional chips, the company's plant would have to be expanded, with the result that all fixed manufacturing costs would be doubled. Variable manufacturing costs per unit would be the same in the new plant as in the old plant. The expansion would not affect either fixed or variable selling and administrative expenses.

Required

The manager is not sure whether Infotex should enter into the contract and has asked for your help in identifying information to help decide whether to accept the offer. Present your advice, based on the following information:

1. The predicted income before taxes for each year under the contract, assuming that there is no change in domestic sales.

2. A comparison of break-even sales levels in dollars before and after the plan addition. Because management is concerned about what happens after the contract expires, compute the break-even point assuming no export sales.

3. The predicted income before taxes after the plant expansion but assuming no contract sales, and assuming that domestic sales continue at the current level.

Tasti-snax sells three products: chips, pretzels, and nuts. Last year's sales mix for the three products was in the ratio of 5:3:2, with combined sales of all products totaling 3 million cases. Chips sell for $12.50 per case and have a 40% contribution rate. Pretzels sell for $16 per case and have a 25% contribution rate, and nuts sell for $20 per case and have a 35% contribution rate. The fixed costs of manufacturing and selling the products amount to $450,000. The company estimates that next year's combined sales of the three products will again be 3 million cases.

The sales manager has suggested slanting the company's advertising and sales efforts toward pretzels and nuts during the coming year, with no increases in cost. This will change the sales mix of the three products to the ratio of 4:3:3.

MDC 22–2
(LO 4, 5, 6)

Required

Explain why the company should change its sales mix as suggested. Support your answer with figures.

Premier Company operated at near capacity during the last year and its management expects a 40% increase in this year's unit sales. As a result, the management is trying to decide how to provide adequate capacity for this year. The search for a solution has ended up with two alternatives. In both cases, the selling price would remain at last year's level to discourage competitors from entering the market. The first alternative would keep fixed costs constant but would increase variable costs for all units to 55% of the product's selling price. The second alternative would increase fixed costs over current levels by 20% but would not affect variable costs as a percent of sales.

MDC 22–3
(LO 5)

Last year's income statement for Premier provided the following summarized information:

Sales	$3,600,000
Costs:	
Variable costs	(1,440,000)
Fixed costs	(1,500,000)
Pretax income	$ 660,000

Required

Which alternative do you recommend? Support your recommendation with any relevant data.

Read the ethics case on page 860. What do you think that the accountant should do? Who would gain from manipulating the predicted figures? Who would lose? What would happen if the project was accepted and then turned out to be a disaster?

Ethical Issues Case

CONCEPT TESTER

Test your understanding of the concepts introduced in this chapter by completing the following crossword puzzle:

Across Clues

3. Two words; a cost that changes with volume but not at a constant rate.
4. Two words; the ratio of the sales volumes of the various products sold by a company.
6. Three words; the unique sales level at which a company neither earns a profit nor incurs a loss.
7. Two words; a cost that can be separated into fixed and variable components.
8. Two words; the contribution margin per unit expressed as a percentage of selling price.

Down Clues

1. Two words; a cost that changes in proportion to changes in production volume.
2. Three words; the excess of expected sales over the sales at the break-even point.
3. Two words; a graph that displays costs and volumes for each period as points on the diagram.
5. Two words; a cost that remains unchanged in total amount even when sales volume changes.

ANSWERS TO PROGRESS CHECKS

22–1   *b*

22–2   A fixed cost remains unchanged in total amount regardless of production levels.

22–3   The cost of raw materials is a variable cost because the total cost changes in proportion to volume changes.

22–4   *c*

22–5   The three basic assumptions are (1) that the actual selling price per unit remains constant for all units sold during the planning period; (2) that for costs classified as variable, the actual costs per unit of output will remain constant; and (3) that for costs classified as fixed, the total amount will remain constant over the volumes projected for the planning period.

22–6   *b*

22–7   The high-low method ignores all of the cost/volume data points except the high and low extremes.

22–8   *a*

22–9   ($90 − $54)/$90 = 40%

22–10 $90,000/40% = $225,000

22–11   *a* Before-tax income = $120,000/(1 − .20) = $150,000

$$\frac{\$50,000 + \$120,000 + (\$150,000 \times 20\%)}{25\%} = \$800,000$$

22–12   If the contribution rate decreases by 50%, unit sales would have to double.

22–13   The margin of safety is the excess of the predicted sales level over its break-even sales level.

22–14   *c*   Selling price of a composite unit:

2 units of X @ $5 per unit	$10
1 unit of Y @ $4 per unit	4
Selling price of a composite unit	$14

Variable costs of a composite unit:

2 units of X @ $2 per unit	$ 4
1 unit of Y @ $2 per unit	2
Variable costs of a composite unit	$ 6

Contribution margin per composite unit . .	$ 8

22–15   It must be assumed that the sales mix remains unchanged at all sales levels in the relevant range.

The Master Budget: A Formal Plan for the Business

The Renton Coil Spring Company is one of the largest producers of titanium coil springs. It has supplied the domestic and international aviation industry since the beginning of the commercial jet age with coils and springs, both steel and titanium.

When weight, corrosion, and volume constraints are considerations, titanium offers greater efficiency than steel, at a fraction of the weight. Renton Coil Spring's titanium coil springs are used in the NASA space shuttles; in the moon buggy; and in McDonnell Douglas, Aerobus, and Boeing aircraft.

Chuck Pepka, owner and president, described the importance of the company's budget planning process as follows:

In 1992, we were very aerospace dependent. We knew we were vulnerable to any downturn in the aerospace industry. We used our budget process to project the anticipated downturn in aircraft demand and analyzed the effect on our cash flow. The starting point was to identify and project our current customer sales needs for 1992. The outcome I was interested in was the cash flow. After reviewing the budget for 1992, it was apparent an immediate change in plan and action were essential if we were to remain a healthy company.

LEARNING OBJECTIVES

After studying Chapter 23, you should be able to:

1. Explain the importance of budgeting and describe its benefits.
2. Describe the components of a master budget and list the sequence of steps in preparing a master budget.
3. Prepare each component of a master budget and explain the importance of each budget to the overall budgeting process.
4. Integrate the component budgets into budgeted financial statements.
5. Define or explain the words and phrases listed in the chapter glossary.

Once management has used cost-volume-profit analysis to select an operating strategy for the upcoming period, it must turn that strategy into specific plans. These plans are usually compiled in a master budget. The budgeting process serves several purposes, including motivation and communication. The budget also coordinates the activities of all parts

of the company toward its objectives. And, the budget later serves as a standard for evaluating actual results and performance. In this chapter, you will learn how to prepare a master budget as the formal plan for the future activities of a company. This kind of planning was critical to the success of **Renton Coil Spring Company.** If you ever go into business for yourself, your ability to prepare this kind of formal plan will help you achieve success.

THE IMPORTANCE OF BUDGETING

LO 1

Explain the importance of budgeting and describe its benefits.

If a business is to accomplish the variety of objectives expected of it, management must carefully plan its activities for future weeks, months, and years. Then, managers should monitor and control the activities so that they conform to the plan. In many situations, particularly in a continuous improvement environment, management will find it useful to replace the original version of the plan with a new one that reflects new information. This revised plan then serves as the basis for controlling the company's activities.

Budgeting is the process of planning future business actions and expressing them as formal plans. The **budget** is the formal statement of the company's future plans. Because the economic or financial aspects of the business are the primary relevant factors involved in management decisions, budgets are usually expressed in monetary terms.

BENEFITS FROM BUDGETING

All business managers should engage in planning because it is absolutely necessary if business activities are to succeed in the long run. Managers who plan carefully and formalize plans with a complete budgeting process can expect to obtain the benefits described in the following paragraphs.

Budgeting Promotes Study, Research, and a Focus on the Future

When management plans the future with the care and attention to detail needed for preparing the budget, the process involves thorough study and research. This process should not only lead to the best conceivable plans but also instill in the managers the good habit of making careful analyses before reaching decisions. In effect, a careful budgeting process tends to promote good decision making.

In addition, the relevant items for a budgetary analysis are concerned with the future. Thus, the budgeting process focuses management's attention on future events and the opportunities available to the business. The pressures of daily operating problems often divert management's attention and take precedence over planning. If so, the company can be left without carefully considered objectives. A good budgeting system counteracts this tendency by formalizing the planning process. Budgeting makes planning an explicit management responsibility.

Budgeting Provides a Basis for Evaluating Performance

The control function requires management to evaluate business operations in comparison to norms or objectives. Then, using these evaluations, management can implement appropriate corrective actions. In evaluating operations, they can compare actual results against these two alternative norms or objectives: (1) past performance or (2) expected performance as described in the budget.

Although past performance is occasionally used as the basis of evaluation, budgeted performance is potentially superior for determining whether actual results are acceptable or show a need for corrective action. Past performance is often inferior as a standard for evaluation because it fails to take into account changes that may affect current activities. For example, a firm achieved past sales under economic conditions that may be dramatically different from those shaping current sales results. Changes in overall economic conditions, shifts in competitive advantages within the industry, new product developments, increased or decreased advertising commitments, and other factors all tend to reduce the usefulness of comparisons between past results and recent performance.

On the other hand, managers develop budgeted performance levels after careful research that attempts to anticipate such broad factors and take their effects into account. Thus, budgets provide the benefit of a superior basis for evaluating performance. In turn, management has a more effective control system.

FAST HINT
Important Point to Remember:
Managers can evaluate performance by preparing reports that compare actual results to the budgeted plans. Performance reports are described in Chapter 24.

Budgeting Is a Source of Motivation

Because budgeting provides standards for evaluating actual performance, the budget and how it is used can significantly affect the attitudes of the employees who are evaluated. If management is not careful, the budgeting process can have a negative effect on employees' attitudes. For example, budgeted levels of performance must be realistic to avoid discouraging employees. Also, the personnel who will be evaluated should be consulted and involved in preparing the budget to increase their commitment to meeting it. In addition, evaluations of performance must allow the affected employees to explain the reasons for apparent performance deficiencies. After all, the managerial accounting reports may not tell the complete story.

In summary, these three guidelines are important:

1. The employees who will be affected by a budget should be consulted when the budget is prepared.
2. The objectives reflected in a budget should be obtainable.
3. The subsequent evaluations of performance should be made carefully with opportunities to explain apparent deficiencies.

When these guidelines are followed, budgeting can be a strongly positive motivating force in the organization. Budgeted performance levels can provide goals that individuals strive to attain or even exceed as they fulfill their responsibilities to the organization.

Budgeting Is a Means of Coordinating Business Activities

When a business is large enough to be organized into departments, an important management task is to be sure that the departments' activities all contribute to meeting the overall goals of the company. This task requires careful coordination. Budgeting provides a way to achieve this coordination.

When a budget is prepared, each department's objectives are determined in advance. Carefully designed objectives can lead each department to contribute to achieving overall goals for the company. For example, managers can budget a production department to produce approximately the number of units the selling department is expected to sell. Then, they can budget the purchasing department to buy raw materials on the basis of budgeted production. Also, they can budget the hiring activities of the personnel department to consider the budgeted production levels. In this way, the budgeting process coordinates the activities of various departments to meet the company's overall goals.

Budgeting Is a Means of Communicating Plans and Instructions

In a very small business, the manager can adequately explain business plans directly to the employees. For example, the manager can communicate specific operating plans to the employees with frequent conversations. However, conversations can create uncertainty and confusion if they are not supported by documents that clearly state the plans. Further, such conversations are inadequate for all but the smallest companies. It is better to use a written budget that informs employees throughout the organization about management's broad plans for the business. The budget also communicates management's specific plans for actions to be taken by responsible employees during the budget period.

THE BUDGET COMMITTEE

To achieve the best results, the task of preparing a budget should not be the sole responsibility of any one department. Similarly, the budget generally should not be simply handed down as top management's final word. Rather, budget figures and budget estimates often are more useful if they are developed through a *bottom up* process. For example, the sales department should have a hand in preparing sales estimates. Likewise, the production department should have initial responsibility for preparing its own expense budget. Otherwise, sales representatives and production employees may believe that the budget figures are meaningless because they may think that they were prepared by people who know little, if anything, about sales and production problems and needs.

Although budgets usually should be developed by this bottom up process, the budgeting system also requires central guidance to keep matters in balance. This guidance can be supplied by a budget committee of department heads and other high-level executives responsible for seeing that budgeted amounts are realistic and coordinated. If a department submits initial budget figures that do not reflect efficient performance, the budget committee should return them to the department with explanatory comments on how to improve them. Then, the originating department must either adjust its proposals or explain why they should be accepted. Communication between the originating department and the budget committee should continue as needed to ensure that both parties accept the budget as reasonable, attainable, and desirable.

The concept of continuous improvement may apply to budgeting as well as production. **Amoco Corporation** recently streamlined its monthly budget reporting package from a one-inch-thick stack of monthly control reports to a tidy, two-page flash report on monthly earnings and key production statistics. "Those reports were our Bible. There's less of an attitude that finance's job is to control. People really have come to see that our job is to help attain business objectives," says John Carl, Amoco corporate controller. The key to the efficiency gain was the integration of the new budgeting and cost allocation processes with Amoco's strategic planning process.[1]

FAST HINT
Critical Thought Question:
In a large organization with many divisions, developing an annual budget through a bottom up process may involve hundreds of employees and take many weeks to complete. What factors might interfere with the usefulness of the resulting budget?

THE BUDGET PERIOD

For convenience, budget periods usually coincide with accounting periods. Thus, most companies prepare at least an annual budget. In addition to their annual budgets, many companies prepare long-range budgets that set forth major objectives for periods of 3, 5, or even 10 years in advance. Long-range budgets should plan the accomplishment of long-range objectives. These budgets are particularly important in planning major expenditures for plant and equipment. Additionally, long-range budgets are useful for deciding whether to finance major projects by issuing bonds, issuing stock, or retaining cash generated by operating activities.

The annual budget for a business reflects the objectives that have been adopted for the next year. To provide more specific guidance, the annual budget usually is broken down into quarterly or monthly budgets. Short-term budgets like these are useful because they allow management to promptly evaluate actual performance and take corrective action. Once they know quarterly or monthly results, managers can compare them to budgeted amounts in a report similar to Illustration 23–1. Notice that the report shows the actual results, the budgeted results, and any difference (called a *variance*). Management can use the third column of variances to quickly identify potential areas for improvement.

Many businesses follow the practice of **continuous budgeting** by preparing **rolling budgets.** As each monthly or quarterly budget period goes by, these firms revise their entire set of budgets, adding new monthly or quarterly budgets to replace the ones that have lapsed. Thus, at any point in time, monthly or quarterly budgets are available for the next 12 months or four quarters. Illustration 23–2 represents the five rolling budgets that would be prepared starting in December 19X1. The first one covers the next four quarters through December 19X2. Then, in March 19X2, the company would prepare another rolling budget for the next four quarters through March 19X3. The same process would be repeated every three months. As a result, management is continuously planning ahead. Also notice that any particular quarter's

---

[1]Stephen Barr, "Grinding It Out," *CFO Magazine,* Vol. 11, no. 1 (January 1995).

Illustration 23–1
Comparing Actual
Performance with Budgeted
Performance

FAST HINT
Critical Thought Question:
Assume that you are the accountant who must explain variances to top management.
Which variances in Illustration
23–1 would you research
and why?

CONSOLIDATED STORES, INC.
Income Statement with Variations from Budget
For Month Ended April 30, 19X2

	Actual	Budget	Variance
Sales	$63,500	$60,000	$ +3,500
Less: Sales returns and allowances	1,800	1,700	+100
Sales discounts	1,200	1,150	+50
Net sales	$60,500	$57,150	$ +3,350
Cost of goods sold:			
Merchandise inventory, April 1, 19X2	$42,000	$44,000	$ −2,000
Purchases, net	39,100	38,000	+1,100
Transportation-in	1,250	1,200	+50
Goods available for sale	$82,350	$83,200	$ −850
Merchandise inventory, April 30, 19X2	41,000	44,100	−3,100
Cost of goods sold	$41,350	$39,100	$ +2,250
Gross profit	$19,150	$18,050	$ +1,100
Operating expenses:			
Selling expenses:			
Sales salaries	$ 6,250	$ 6,000	$ +250
Advertising	900	800	+100
Store supplies	550	500	+50
Depreciation, store equipment	1,600	1,600	
Total selling expenses	$ 9,300	$ 8,900	$ +400
General and administrative expenses:			
Office salaries	$ 2,000	$ 2,000	
Office supplies used	165	150	$ +15
Rent	1,100	1,100	
Insurance........................	200	200	
Depreciation, office equipment	100	100	
Total general and administrative expenses ..	$ 3,565	$ 3,550	$ +15
Total operating expenses	$12,865	$12,450	$ +415
Income from operations	$ 6,285	$ 5,600	$ +685

budget is drawn up four times using the most recent information available. For example, Illustration 23–2 shows that the budget for the fourth quarter of 19X2 would
be prepared in December 19X1, and in March, June, and September of 19X2. In contrast, when continuous budgeting is not used, the fourth-quarter budget will be nine
months old when it is finally implemented. In a rapidly changing environment, this
plan could easily be out of date.

THE MASTER BUDGET

When a company formalizes a comprehensive or overall plan for the future, the resulting budget is a **master budget.** As an overall plan, the master budget includes
specific plans for expected sales, the units of product to be produced, the merchandise (or materials) to be purchased, the expenses to be incurred, the long-term assets
to be purchased, and the amounts of cash to be borrowed or loans to be repaid. The
planned activities of each subunit of the business should be presented separately within
the master budget.

To include definite plans for all activities, a master budget contains several subbudgets. The subbudgets connect with each other, or *articulate,* to form the overall
coordinated plan for the business. Thus, the master budget typically includes budgets
for sales, purchases, production, various expenses, capital expenditures, and cash.
Also, managers may express the expected financial results of the planned activities
in a budgeted income statement for the budget period and a budgeted balance sheet
as of the end of the budget period.

Illustration 23-2   Rolling Budgets

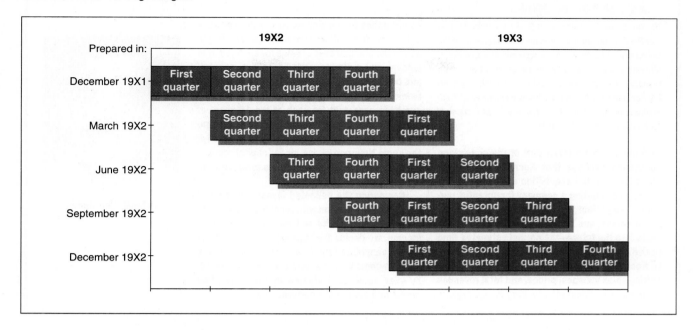

Progress Check
(Answers to the Progress Checks are provided at the end of the chapter.)

23–1   **What are the major benefits of budgeting?**

23–2   **What is a master budget?**

23–3   **What is the responsibility of the budget committee?**

23–4   **What is the usual time period covered by a budget?**

23–5   **What are rolling budgets?**

PREPARING THE MASTER BUDGET

LO 2

Describe the components of a master budget and list the sequence of steps in preparing a master budget.

In general, the number and types of budgets included in the master budget depend on the size and complexity of the business. At a minimum, a master budget should include the following items:

1. Operating budgets.
    a. *Sales budget.*
    b. For merchandising companies: *merchandise purchases budget* (describing the number of units to be purchased).
    c. For manufacturing companies:
        (1) *Production budget* (describing the number of units to be produced).
        (2) *Manufacturing budget* (describing the planned manufacturing costs).
    d. *Selling expense budget.*
    e. *General and administrative expense budget.*
2. *Capital expenditures budget* (describing the budgeted expenditures for new plant and equipment).
3. Financial budgets.
    a. *Cash budget* (describing the budgeted cash receipts and disbursements).
    b. *Budgeted income statement.*
    c. *Budgeted balance sheet.*

In addition to these budgets, managers may include supporting calculations and schedules in the master budget.

Management cannot prepare some budgets until other budgets are complete. For example, the merchandise purchases budget cannot be prepared until the sales budget is available because the number of units to be purchased depends on how many units are expected to be sold. As a result, you must prepare the budgets within the master budget in the following sequence, which is represented as flowcharts in Illustration 23–3:

First: The *sales budget* must be prepared first because the amount of sales determines the level of activity in all parts of the company.

Second: The other *operating budgets* are prepared next. For merchandising companies, the budgets for merchandise purchases, selling expenses, and general and administrative expenses can be prepared in any sequence. For manufacturing companies, the production budget must be prepared before the manufacturing budget because the number of units to be produced clearly shapes the quantities of materials, direct labor, and overhead to be budgeted. The budgets for selling expenses and general and administrative expenses also can be prepared at this stage.

Third: The *capital expenditures budget* is prepared next, but only if capital expenditures are anticipated during the budget period.

Fourth: Based on the information provided in the preceding budgets, the *cash budget* is prepared.

Fifth: The *budgeted income statement* is prepared next. It shows the budgeted revenues and expenses for the budget period.

Sixth: The *budgeted balance sheet* is prepared last. It shows the budgeted assets, liabilities, and equity as of the last day of the budget period.

At any stage, the process may reveal undesirable outcomes, with the result that changes must be introduced into prior budgets and the previous steps must be repeated. For

Illustration 23-3 Sequence of Budgeting Steps

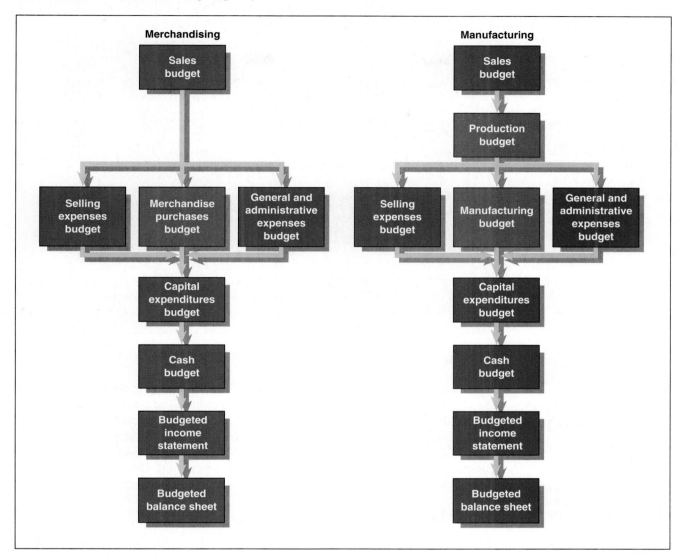

example, an early version of the cash budget may show that an inadequate amount of cash would be generated under the existing plan unless cash outlays are reduced. Or, a preliminary budgeted balance sheet may indicate that too much debt would result from an ambitious capital expenditures budget. In either case, revised plans may be needed.

Progress Check

23-6 **A master budget:**
   a. Always includes a manufacturing budget that specifies the number of units to be produced.
   b. Is prepared with a process that starts with the operating budgets and continues with the capital expenditures budget, the cash budget, and the budgeted financial statements.
   c. Is prepared with a process that ends with the budgeted income statement.

23-7 **What are the three primary categories of budgets in the master budget?**

NORTHERN COMPANY
Balance Sheet
September 30, 19X2
Assets

Cash		$ 20,000
Accounts receivable		42,000
Inventory (9,000 units @ $6)		54,000
Equipment*	$200,000	
Less accumulated depreciation	(36,000)	164,000
Total assets		$280,000

Liabilities and Stockholders' Equity

Liabilities:		
Accounts payable	$ 58,200	
Income taxes payable (due October 31, 19X2) . .	20,000	
Note payable to bank	10,000	$ 88,200
Stockholders' equity:		
Common stock	$150,000	
Retained earnings	41,800	191,800
Total liabilities and stockholders' equity		$280,000

*The equipment is being depreciated on a straight-line basis over 10 years. Predicted
salvage value is $20,000.

ILLUSTRATING THE PREPARATION OF THE MASTER BUDGET

This section of the chapter explains the procedures used to prepare the master budget for Northern Company, a retailer of a single product. The company's master budget includes operating, capital expenditure, and cash budgets for each month in a quarter. It also includes a budgeted income statement for each quarter and a budgeted balance sheet as of the last day of each quarter. On the following pages, Northern Company budgets are prepared for October, November, and December 19X2. Illustration 23–4 presents the beginning balance sheet for this budgeting period.

Preparing a Sales Budget

The first step in preparing the master budget is the development of the **sales budget.** This plan shows the units of goods to be sold and the revenue to be derived from the sales. The sales budget is the starting point in the budgeting process because the plans for most departments are related to sales. The sales budget should emerge from a careful analysis of forecasted economic and market conditions, plant capacity, proposed selling expenses (such as advertising), and predictions of unit sales. Because people normally feel a greater commitment to goals they have had a hand in setting, the sales personnel of a company are usually asked to develop predictions of sales for each territory and department. Another advantage of using this participatory approach to budgeting is that it applies the knowledge and experience of those people actually engaged in the activity. The final sales budget is based on these predictions after the budget committee has considered the forecasted business conditions, selling expenses, and other factors.

During September 19X2, Northern Company sold 7,000 units of product at $10 per unit. After obtaining predictions from sales personnel and considering the market conditions affecting Northern Company's product, the sales budget in Illustration 23–5 is established. Because the purchasing department must base December 19X2 purchases on estimated sales for January 19X3, the sales budget is expanded to include January 19X3, as well as the three months in the fourth quarter.

Illustration 23–5
Sales Budget Showing
Planned Unit Sales and
Dollar Sales

NORTHERN COMPANY
Monthly Sales Budget
October 19X2–January 19X3

	Budgeted Unit Sales	Budgeted Unit Price	Budgeted Total Sales
September 19X2 (actual)	7,000	$10	$ 70,000
October 19X2	10,000	10	100,000
November 19X2	8,000	10	80,000
December 19X2	14,000	10	140,000
January 19X3	9,000	10	90,000

The sales budget in Illustration 23–5 is more detailed than simple projections of total sales. Specifically, it contains forecasts of both unit sales and unit prices. Some companies prepare a sales budget expressed only in total sales dollars. In practice, most sales budgets are more detailed because they must show units and unit prices for many different products, classified by sales representative, by department, and by territory.

In our beginning chapter story, the **Renton Coil Spring Company** was preparing a new market plan. Previously they had classified their sales budget by product mix, steel and titanium. Then, management expanded the classifications to product mix by type of industry. They used the planning process to identify industries other than aerospace that could benefit from the high tensile strength and lightweight properties of titanium coil springs. One of the industries identified and  successfully marketed was NASCAR race car parts. In race cars, both strength and weight are important enough to justify the expense of titanium coil springs. By using the budgeting planning process, Renton Coil Springs was able to project the effects of the aerospace downturn and plan a successful strategy to replace lost volume. Not only did the company remain healthy, over the next two years it was actually able to increase titanium coil spring sales from 30 to 50% of their product mix. The majority of the growth came from outside the aerospace industry.

Preparing a Merchandise Purchases Budget

A variety of sophisticated techniques help management make inventory purchasing decisions. These techniques all recognize that the number of units to be added to inventory depends on the budgeted sales volume. Whether a company manufactures or purchases the product it sells, budgeted future sales volume is the primary factor to consider in most inventory management decisions.

Just-in-Time Inventory Systems. The managers of *just-in-time* inventory systems use sales budgets for very short periods (covering perhaps as few as one or two days) to order just enough merchandise or materials to satisfy the immediate sales demand. As a result, the level of inventory on hand is held to a minimum (including zero in ideal situations). A just-in-time system minimizes the costs of maintaining an inventory. However, just-in-time systems are practical only if customers are content to order in advance or if managers can determine short-term sales demand with very little error. Also, suppliers must be able and willing to ship small quantities regularly and promptly.

Safety Stock Inventory Systems. The market conditions and manufacturing processes for many products do not allow a just-in-time system to be used. Instead, many companies keep enough inventory on hand to reduce the risk of running out. This practice requires sufficient purchases to satisfy the budgeted sales amounts and to maintain an additional quantity of inventory as a **safety stock.** The safety stock provides protection against lost sales caused by unfulfilled demands from customers or delays in shipments from suppliers.

Merchandise Purchases Budget. Companies usually express a **merchandise purchases budget** in both units and dollars. This table shows the general formula for compiling a purchases budget:

	Units
Budgeted ending inventory	7,200
Add budgeted sales	10,000
Required units of available merchandise	17,200
Deduct the beginning inventory	(9,000)
Inventory to be purchased	8,200

In equation form, the formula can be expressed as:

$$
\begin{array}{c}
\text{Inventory} \\
\text{to be} \\
\text{purchased}
\end{array}
=
\begin{array}{c}
\text{Budgeted} \\
\text{ending} \\
\text{inventory}
\end{array}
+
\begin{array}{c}
\text{Budgeted} \\
\text{sales for} \\
\text{the period}
\end{array}
-
\begin{array}{c}
\text{Budgeted} \\
\text{beginning} \\
\text{inventory}
\end{array}
$$

If the calculation is expressed in units and only one product is involved, the number of dollars of inventory to be purchased can be budgeted simply by multiplying the units to be purchased by the cost per unit.

After considering the cost of maintaining an inventory and the risk associated with a temporary inventory shortage, Northern Company has decided that the number of units in its inventory at the end of each month should equal 90% of the next month's predicted sales. In other words, the inventory at the end of October should equal 90% of the budgeted November sales, the November ending inventory should equal 90% of the expected December sales, and so on. Also, the company's suppliers have indicated that the September 19X2 per unit cost of $6 should remain unchanged through January 19X3. Based on these factors and on the fact that 9,000 units were on hand at September 30 (see Illustration 23–4), the company prepared the merchandise purchases budget in Illustration 23–6.

The first three lines of Northern Company's merchandise purchases budget determine the required ending inventories. Then, budgeted unit sales are added to the desired ending inventory and the beginning inventory is subtracted to determine the budgeted number of units to be purchased. Finally, the last lines calculate the budgeted cost of the purchases by multiplying the units to be purchased by the predicted cost per unit.

Recall from the previous discussion that some budgeting systems describe only the total dollars of budgeted sales. Likewise, a system may state a merchandise purchases budget only in terms of the total cost of merchandise to be purchased without stating the number of units to be purchased. When this practice is used, however, you must assume a constant relationship between sales and cost of goods sold. For example, Northern Company expects the cost of goods sold to equal 60% of sales. (Note that the budgeted sales price is $10 and the budgeted unit cost is $6.) Thus, its cost of goods sold could be budgeted in dollars on the basis of budgeted sales without re-

NORTHERN COMPANY
Merchandise Purchases Budget
October, November, and December 19X2

	October	November	December
Next month's budgeted sales (units)	8,000	14,000	9,000
Ratio of inventory to future sales	× 90%	× 90%	× 90%
Budgeted ending inventory (units)	7,200	12,600	8,100
Add budgeted sales for the month (units) . . .	10,000	8,000	14,000
Required units of available merchandise . . .	17,200	20,600	22,100
Deduct beginning inventory (units)	(9,000)	(7,200)	(12,600)
Number of units to be purchased	8,200	13,400	9,500
Budgeted cost per unit	$ 6	$ 6	$ 6
Budgeted cost of merchandise purchases . . .	$49,200	$80,400	$57,000

Illustration 23–6

FAST HINT
Alternative Example:
If the ending inventory in Illustration 23–6 is required to equal only 80% of the next month's predicted sales, how many units must be purchased each month?
Answer:
Budgeted ending inventory:
  October   6,400 units
  November   11,200 units
  December   7,200 units
Required purchases:
  October   7,400 units
  November   12,800 units
  December   10,000 units

quiring information on the number of units involved. However, it still would be necessary to consider the effects of the beginning and ending inventories in determining the amounts to be purchased.

Preparing Production Budgets and Manufacturing Budgets

Because Northern Company does not manufacture its product, its budget for acquiring goods to be sold is a *merchandise purchases budget,* as shown in Illustration 23–6. A manufacturing company must prepare a **production budget** instead of a merchandise purchases budget. A production budget shows the number of units to be produced each month. Production budgets are similar to merchandise purchases budgets except that the number of units to be purchased each month (as shown in Illustration 23–6) would be replaced by the number of units to be manufactured each month. Also, a production budget does not show costs because it is always expressed entirely in units of product. The budgeted production costs (for materials, direct labor, and overhead) are shown in the **manufacturing budget,** which is based on the production volume in the production budget.

A manufacturing budget shows the budgeted costs for raw materials, direct labor, and manufacturing overhead. In many companies, the manufacturing budget actually consists of three subbudgets: a raw materials purchases budget, a direct labor budget, and an overhead budget. These budgets show the total cost of goods to be manufactured during the budget period.

Preparing a Selling Expense Budget

The initial responsibility for preparing a **selling expense budget** typically belongs to the vice president of marketing or an equivalent sales manager. This budget is a plan listing the types and amounts of selling expenses expected during the budget period. Typically, the sales budget is prepared and then the selling expense budget is created to provide sufficient selling expenses to meet those sales goals. Thus, predictions of selling expenses are based on both the tentative sales budget and on the experience of previous periods adjusted for expected changes.

After some or all of the master budget is tentatively prepared, management may decide that the projected sales volume is inadequate. If so, subsequent adjustments in the sales budget may require corresponding adjustments in the selling expense budget.

Illustration 23-7

NORTHERN COMPANY				
Selling Expense Budget				
October, November, and December 19X2				
	October	November	December	Total
Budgeted sales	$100,000	$80,000	$140,000	$320,000
Sales commission percentage . .	× 10%	× 10%	× 10%	× 10%
Sales commissions	$ 10,000	$ 8,000	$ 14,000	$ 32,000
Salary for sales manager	2,000	2,000	2,000	6,000
Total selling expenses	$ 12,000	$10,000	$ 16,000	$ 38,000

FAST HINT
Critical Thought Question:
If sales commissions in Illustration 23–7 were increased, what budgets would be affected?

Northern Company's selling expenses consist of commissions paid to sales personnel and a $2,000 monthly salary paid to the sales manager. Sales commissions equal 10% of total sales and are paid during the month the sales are made. No advertising expenses are budgeted for this particular quarter. Illustration 23–7 shows the selling expense budget for Northern Company.

Preparing a General and Administrative Expense Budget

The office manager usually has the responsibility for preparing the initial proposal for the **general and administrative expense budget.** This budget is a plan that shows the predicted operating expenses that are not included in the selling expenses budget. The amounts of variable general and administrative expenses depend on budgeted sales volume. However, many of these expenses are fixed and do not vary in proportion to changes in sales volume.

Although interest expense and income tax expense are often classified as general and administrative expenses in published income statements, they generally cannot be planned at this stage of the budgeting process. The prediction of interest expense must follow the preparation of the cash budget that determines if any loans are needed. The predicted income tax expense depends on the amount of pre-tax income on the budgeted income statement. In addition, interest and income taxes are usually beyond the control of the office manager. As a result, they should not be used in evaluating that person's performance in comparison to the budget.

General and administrative expenses for Northern Company include administrative salaries of $54,000 per year, or $4,500 per month. The salaries are paid each month when they are earned. Using the facts described in Illustration 23–4, the depreciation on the company's equipment is $18,000 per year [($200,000 − $20,000)/10 years], or $1,500 per month ($18,000/12 months). Illustration 23–8 shows the budget for these expenses.

Preparing a Capital Expenditures Budget

The next step is preparing the **capital expenditures budget.** This budget lists dollar amounts to be received from disposing of equipment and to be spent on purchasing additional equipment if the proposed production program is carried out. Because production capacity is limited by the company's plant and equipment, this budget is usually affected by long-range plans for the business instead of short-term sales budgets for the next year or quarter. Nevertheless, the process of preparing a sales or manufacturing budget may reveal that the company needs more capacity and that additional equipment must be purchased.

NORTHERN COMPANY General and Administrative Expense Budget October, November, and December 19X2				
	October	November	December	Total
Administrative salaries	$4,500	$4,500	$4,500	$13,500
Depreciation of equipment	1,500	1,500	1,500	4,500
Total general and administrative expenses	$6,000	$6,000	$6,000	$18,000

Illustration 23–8

FAST HINT
Alternative Example:
In Illustration 23–8, how would a rental agreement of $5,000 per month + 1% of sales affect the general and administrative expense budget? (Budgeted sales are presented in Illustration 23–5.)
Answer:
Rent expense:

October	$ 6,000
November	5,800
December	6,400
Total	$18,200

Total general and administrative expenses:

October	$12,000
November	11,800
December	12,400
Total	$36,200

The process of evaluating and planning capital expenditures is called *capital budgeting*. Because capital expenditures often involve long-run commitments of large amounts, planning those expenditures is an important responsibility of higher levels of management. Typically, capital expenditures involve large dollar amounts that have a major effect on the predicted cash flows and perhaps on the company's need for debt or equity financing. Accordingly, the capital expenditures budget may be closely tied to management's evaluation of the company's ability to service more debt. You will learn more about capital budgeting in Chapter 25.

Northern Company does not anticipate any disposals of equipment through December 19X2. However, management plans to acquire additional equipment for $25,000 cash near the end of December 19X2. Because of the limited capital expenditures, no separate budget for them is presented here. However, the cash budget in Illustration 23–9 includes this amount.

Preparing a Cash Budget

After developing tentative budgets for sales, merchandise purchases, expenses, and capital expenditures, the next step is preparing the **cash budget.** This budget shows the expected cash inflows and outflows during the budget period. The cash budget is especially helpful in maintaining a cash balance adequate to meet the company's obligations. Thus, by preparing a cash budget, management can prearrange loans to cover any anticipated cash shortages well before they are needed. On the other hand, the cash budget also helps management avoid having a cash balance that is too large. Too much cash is undesirable because it earns a relatively low rate of return, if any. For these reasons, a company that prepares a cash budget usually has better control over its cash balances.

For example, **Ford Motor Company's** debt roughly doubled between 1989 and 1990 to more than $7.4 billion. As the company borrowed heavily to fund product development programs and acquisitions, the company's treasurer was responsible for matching cash inflows from operations with debt financing to ensure that Ford could fund its current operations and debt repayment. Ford also required capital to invest in future long-term strategic decisions.[2] Managing cash flows of this magnitude demanded extremely careful and detailed budgeting by Ford's cash management team.

[2]Larry Marion, "The Corporate Ivy League," *CFO Magazine,* Vol. 7, no. 10 (October 1991).

NORTHERN COMPANY
Cash Budget
October, November, and December 19X2

	October	November	December
Beginning cash balance	$ 20,000	$ 20,000	$ 22,272
Cash receipts from customers	82,000	92,000	104,000
Total cash available	$102,000	$112,000	$126,272
Cash disbursements:			
Payments for merchandise	$ 58,200	$ 49,200	$ 80,400
Sales commissions (Illustration 23–7)	10,000	8,000	14,000
Salaries:			
Sales (Illustration 23–7)	2,000	2,000	2,000
Administrative (Illustration 23–8)	4,500	4,500	4,500
Accrued income taxes payable (Illustration 23–4)	20,000		
Dividends ($150,000 × 2%)		3,000	
Interest on bank loan:			
October ($10,000 × 1%)	100		
November ($22,800 × 1%)		228	
Purchase of equipment			25,000
Total cash disbursements	$ 94,800	$ 66,928	$125,900
Preliminary balance	$ 7,200	$ 45,072	$ 372
Additional loan from bank	12,800		19,628
Repayment of loan from bank		(22,800)	
Ending cash balance	$ 20,000	$ 22,272	$ 20,000
Loan balance, end of month	$ 22,800	$ –0–	$ 19,628

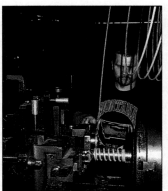

For another example, refer again to discussion of **Renton Coil Spring Company** at the beginning of the chapter. Chuck Pepka's major interest in the budget results were cash flow projections. Renton Coil Spring attained its dominance in the titanium coil spring market because of innovative technology in the engineering of titanium coil springs and its development of a superior computer-based spring design package. The company produces parts for highly technical industries; to remain a market leader it must have sufficient cash resources to continuously plan and fund research and development in both manufacturing technology and engineering design. You can understand Pepka's concern that the current cash flow be sufficient for current investment in the business as a means of ensuring future profitability.

In preparing the cash budget, the accountant adds expected receipts to the beginning cash balance and deducts expected expenditures. If the expected cash balance is inadequate, the required additional cash appears in the budget as a planned increase from short-term loans. If the tentative ending balance exceeds the minimum, the excess should be applied to repaying the loans or to acquiring temporary investments.

Much of the information needed for preparing the cash budget can be obtained directly from the previously prepared operating and capital expenditures budgets. However, further investigation and additional calculations may be necessary to determine the amounts to be included.

Illustration 23–9 shows the cash budget for Northern Company. In the illustration, October's beginning cash balance was obtained from the September 30, 19X2, balance sheet in Illustration 23–4.

Budgeted sales of Northern Company were shown in Illustration 23–5. An analysis of past sales records indicates that 40% of Northern Company's sales are for cash. The remaining 60% are credit sales and these customers can be expected to pay in full during the month after the sales. The budgeted cash receipts from customers are calculated as follows:

FAST HINT
Critical Thought Question:
Is it realistic for a company to expect to collect 100% of its credit sales? Why or why not?

	September	October	November	December
Sales	$70,000	$100,000	$80,000	$140,000
Ending accounts				
receivable (60%)	$42,000	$ 60,000	$48,000	$ 84,000
Cash receipts from:				
Cash sales (40%)		$ 40,000	$32,000	$ 56,000
Collections of prior				
month's receivables		42,000	60,000	48,000
Total cash receipts		$ 82,000	$92,000	$104,000

The calculation shows that October's budgeted cash receipts consist of $40,000 from expected cash sales ($100,000 × 40%) plus the anticipated collection of $42,000 of accounts receivable from the end of September. Also note that each month's total cash receipts are listed on the second line of Illustration 23–9.

Northern Company's purchases of merchandise are entirely on account, and full payments are made during the month following the purchases. Thus, in Illustration 23–9, the cash disbursements for purchases are obtained from the September 30, 19X2, balance sheet (Illustration 23–4) and from the merchandise purchases budget (Illustration 23–6) as follows:

October payments (September 30 balance)	$58,200
November payments (October purchases)	49,200
December payments (November purchases)	80,400

Because sales commissions and all salaries are paid monthly, the budgeted cash disbursements for these expenses come from the selling expense budget (Illustration 23–7) and the general and administrative expense budget (Illustration 23–8). Notice that the cash budget is not affected by the depreciation expense in the general and administrative expenses budget.

As indicated in the September 30, 19X2, balance sheet (Illustration 23–4), accrued income taxes are due and payable in October. The cash budget in Illustration 23–9 shows this $20,000 expected expenditure in that month. Predicted income tax expense for the quarter ending December 31 is 40% of net income and is due in January 19X3. This amount appears in the budgeted income statement as income tax expense. The same amount appears on the budgeted balance sheet as the income tax liability.

During the second month of each quarter, Northern Company pays a cash dividend equal to 2% of the par value of the common stock. The cash budget in Illustration 23–9 shows a November payment of $3,000 for this planned disbursement.

Northern Company has an agreement with the bank that grants additional loans to the company at the end of each month if needed to maintain a minimum cash balance of $20,000. Interest is paid at the end of each month at the rate of 1% of the beginning balance of the loans. And, if the cash balance exceeds $20,000 at the end of a month, the firm uses the excess to repay any outstanding loans. The interest payments in Illustration 23–9 equal 1% of the prior month's ending loan balance. For

FAST HINT
Critical Thought Question:
Give two reasons for maintaining a minimum cash balance when the budget shows the extra cash will not be needed.

Illustration 23–10

NORTHERN COMPANY
Budgeted Income Statement
For Three Months Ended December 31, 19X2

Sales (Illustration 23–5, 32,000 units @ $10)		$320,000
Cost of goods sold (32,000 units @ $6)		192,000
Gross profit		$128,000
Operating expenses:		
Sales commissions (Illustration 23–7)	$32,000	
Sales salaries (Illustration 23–7)	6,000	
Administrative salaries (Illustration 23–8)	13,500	
Depreciation on equipment (Illustration 23–8)	4,500	
Interest expense (Illustration 23–9)	328	(56,328)
Net income before income taxes		$ 71,672
Income tax expense ($71,672 × 40%)		(28,669)
Net income		$ 43,003

October, this expenditure is 1% of the $10,000 balance in the balance sheet in Illustration 23–4. For November, the company expects to pay interest of $228, which is 1% of the $22,800 expected loan balance as of October 31. No interest is scheduled for December because the company anticipates repaying the loans in full at the end of November.

Illustration 23–9 shows that the October 31 preliminary balance (before any loan-related activity) falls to $7,200, which is less than the $20,000 minimum. Thus, Northern Company expects to bring the balance up to the minimum by borrowing $12,800 through another short-term note. At the end of November, the budget shows a preliminary cash balance of $45,072 before any loan activity. As a result, the company expects to repay the $22,800 loan. Note, however, that the equipment purchase budgeted for December will again draw the preliminary cash balance to only $372, which is well below the $20,000 minimum. Thus, the company expects to borrow $19,628 in that month to get back up to the minimum ending balance.

FAST HINT
Relevant Exercise:
To apply these concepts, work Exercises 23–2 and 23–3.

Progress Check

23-8 In preparing monthly budgets for the third quarter, Lakeway Company budgeted 120 unit sales for July and 140 unit sales for August. The June 30 finished goods inventory consists of 50 units and management wants each month's ending inventory to be 60% of the next month's sales. How many units of product should the production budget for the third quarter call for producing in July?
   a. 84
   b. 120
   c. 154
   d. 204.

23-9 What is the difference between operating budgets for merchandising and manufacturing companies?

23-10 How does a just-in-time inventory system differ from a safety stock system?

Preparing a Budgeted Income Statement

LO 4

Integrate the component budgets into budgeted financial statements.

The next-to-last step in preparing a master budget is summarizing the effects of the various plans in the **budgeted income statement.** The budgeted income statement is a managerial accounting report that presents predicted amounts of the company's revenues and expenses for the budget period. The information needed for preparing a budgeted income statement comes primarily from the previously prepared budgets and the research that was conducted in the process of preparing them.

For many companies, the volume of information summarized in the budgeted income statement and the budgeted balance sheet is so large that the managerial accountants use work sheets to accumulate the budgeted transactions and classify them by their effects on the income statement and the balance sheet. In this example, the Northern Company has only a few expected transactions and account balances. Thus, the budgeted financial statements can be prepared by analyzing the other budgets and by using information from the related discussions. Northern Company's budgeted income statement is shown in Illustration 23–10. Notice that it is now possible to predict the amount of income tax expense for the quarter as 40% of the budgeted pre-tax net income.

Preparing a Budgeted Balance Sheet

The final step in preparing the master budget is the compilation of the **budgeted balance sheet.** This managerial accounting report presents predicted amounts of the company's assets, liabilities, and stockholders' equity as of the end of the budget period.

As previously mentioned, the Northern Company has only a few transactions and account balances. Thus, its budgeted balance sheet, which appears in Illustration 23–11, can be prepared by analyzing the other budgets and using information in the related discussions of those budgets. The sources of the amounts shown in the budgeted balance sheet are as follows:

Item	Amount	Explanation
Cash	$ 20,000	Ending balance for December from the cash budget in Illustration 23–9.
Accounts receivable	$ 84,000	60% of $140,000 sales budgeted for December from the sales budget in Illustration 23–5.
Inventory	$ 48,600	8,100 units in budgeted December ending inventory at the budgeted cost of $6 per unit (from the purchases budget in Illustration 23–6).
Equipment	$225,000	September 30 balance of $200,000 from the beginning balance sheet in Illustration 23–4 plus $25,000 cost of new equipment from the cash budget in Illustration 23–9.
Accumulated depreciation	$ 40,500	September 30 balance of $36,000 from the beginning balance sheet in Illustration 23–4 plus $4,500 expense from the general and administrative expense budget in Illustration 23–8.
Accounts payable	$ 57,000	Budgeted cost of merchandise purchases for December from the purchases budget in Illustration 23–6.
Income taxes payable	$ 28,669	Budgeted income tax expense from the budgeted income statement for the fourth quarter in Illustration 23–10.
Bank loan payable	$ 19,628	Budgeted December 31 balance from the cash budget in Illustration 23–9.
Common stock	$150,000	Unchanged from the beginning balance sheet in Illustration 23–4.
Retained earnings	$ 81,803	September 30 balance of $41,800 from the beginning balance sheet in Illustration 23–4 plus budgeted net income of $43,003 from the budgeted income statement in Illustration 23–10 minus budgeted cash dividends of $3,000 from the cash budget in Illustration 23–9.

An eight-column work sheet can be used to prepare the budgeted income statement and budgeted balance sheet. The first two columns of the work sheet show the

Illustration 23–11

NORTHERN COMPANY		
Budgeted Balance Sheet		
December 31, 19X2		
Assets		
Cash		$ 20,000
Accounts receivable		84,000
Inventory (8,100 units @ $6)		48,600
Equipment	$225,000	
Less accumulated depreciation	(40,500)	184,500
Total assets		$337,100
Liabilities and Stockholders' Equity		
Liabilities:		
Accounts payable	$ 57,000	
Income taxes payable	28,669	
Bank loan payable	19,628	$105,297
Stockholders' equity:		
Common stock	$150,000	
Retained earnings	81,803	231,803
Total liabilities and stockholders' equity		$337,100

FAST HINT
Important Point to Remember:
Similar procedures are followed
to develop a work sheet whether
actual or budgeted amounts are
used. The preparation of financial statements from a work
sheet was described in Chapters
4 and 5.

post-closing trial balance as of the last day of the period prior to the budget period. Next, the budgeted transactions and adjustments are entered in the second pair of work sheet columns in the same manner as end-of-period adjustments are entered on an ordinary work sheet. For example, if the budget calls for credit sales of $250,000, the title of the Sales account is entered on the work sheet in the Account Titles column. Then, the Sales account is credited and Accounts Receivable is debited for $250,000 in the second pair of money columns. After all budgeted transactions and adjustments are entered on the work sheet, the post-closing trial balance amounts in the first pair of money columns are combined with the budget amounts in the second pair of columns and sorted to the proper Income Statement and Balance Sheet columns of the work sheet. Finally, the balances in these columns are used to prepare the budgeted income statement and balance sheet.

Progress Check

23–11   In preparing a budgeted balance sheet:
   a. Plant and equipment can be determined by analyzing the capital expenditures budget and the balance sheet from the beginning of the budget period.
   b. Liabilities can be determined by analyzing the general and administrative expense budget.
   c. Retained earnings can be determined from information contained in the cash budget and the balance sheet from the beginning of the budget period.

23–12   What sequence is followed in preparing the budgets that comprise the master budget?

SUMMARY OF THE CHAPTER IN TERMS OF LEARNING OBJECTIVES

LO 1. Explain the importance of budgeting and describe its benefits. Planning is a management responsibility of critical importance to business success, and budgeting is the process used by management to formalize its plans. Budgeting promotes study and research by management and focuses its attention on the future. Budgeting also provides a basis for evaluating performance, serves as a source of motivation, is a means of coordinating business activities, and communicates management's plans and instructions to the company's employees.

LO 2. Describe the components of a master budget and list the sequence of steps in preparing a master budget. A master budget is a formal overall plan for a business that consists of specific plans for business operations, capital expenditures, and the financial results of those activities. The budgeting process begins with preparing a sales budget. Based on the expected sales volume, merchandising companies can budget merchandise purchases, selling expenses, and administrative expenses. Manufacturing companies also must budget production quantities, raw materials purchases, direct labor costs, and overhead. Next, the capital expenditures budget is prepared, followed by the cash budget, and the budgeted financial statements.

LO 3. Prepare each component of a master budget and explain the importance of each budget to the overall budgeting process. In the process of preparing a master budget, each component budget is designed to provide guidance for the persons responsible for the activities covered by that budget. The budgets show how much revenue is to be received from sales and how much expense is to be incurred. The budgets are designed to reflect the fact that the activities of one area (such as manufacturing) will support the activities of the others (such as marketing). As a result, the various components of the business are directed to pursue activities that are consistent with and supportive of the overall objectives of the business.

LO 4. Integrate the component budgets into budgeted financial statements. The operating budgets, the capital expenditures budget, and the cash budget, along with their supporting calculations and the balance sheet prior to the first budget period, contain the information needed to prepare a budgeted income statement for the budget period and a budgeted balance sheet as of the end of the budget period. A small company can prepare these budgeted financial statements by extracting the necessary information from the budgets, related calculations, and beginning balance sheet. The budgeted financial statements show the expected financial consequences of the planned activities described in the budgets.

The management of Daredevil Company has asked you to prepare a master budget for the company from the following information. The budget is to cover the months of April, May, and June of 19X2.

DEMONSTRATION PROBLEM

DAREDEVIL COMPANY
Balance Sheet
March 31, 19X2

Assets

Cash	$ 50,000	
Accounts receivable	175,000	
Inventory	126,000	
Total current assets		$351,000
Equipment	$480,000	
Accumulated depreciation	(90,000)	390,000
Total assets		$741,000

Liabilities and Stockholders' Equity

Accounts payable	$156,000	
Short-term notes payable	12,000	
Total current liabilities		$168,000
Long-term note payable		200,000
Total liabilities		$368,000
Common stock	$235,000	
Retained earnings	138,000	
Total stockholders' equity		373,000
Total liabilities and stockholders' equity		$741,000

a. Actual unit sales for March were 10,000 units. Each month's sales are expected to exceed the prior month's results by 5%. The selling price of the product is $25 per unit.

b. The company's policy calls for the ending inventory of a given month to equal 80% of the next month's expected unit sales. The March 31 inventory was 8,400 units, which was in compliance with the policy.

c. Sales representatives' commissions are 12.5% and are paid in the month of the sales. The sales manager's salary will be $3,500 in April and $4,000 thereafter.

d. The general and administrative expenses include administrative salaries of $8,000 per month, depreciation of $5,000 per month, and 0.9% monthly interest on the long-term note payable.

e. Thirty percent of the company's sales are expected to be for cash and the remaining 70% will be on credit. Receivables are collected in full in the month following the sale (none is collected in the month of the sale).

f. All purchases of merchandise are on credit, and no payables arise from any other transactions. The purchases of one month are fully paid in the next month. The purchase price is $15 per unit.

g. The minimum ending cash balance for all months is $50,000. If necessary, the company will borrow enough cash to reach the minimum. The resulting short-term note will require an interest payment of 1% at the end of each month. If the ending cash balance exceeds the minimum, the excess will be applied to repaying the short-term notes payable.

h. Dividends of $100,000 are to be declared and paid in May.

i. No cash payments for income taxes are to be made during the second quarter. Income taxes will be assessed at 35% in the quarter.

j. Equipment purchases of $55,000 are scheduled for June.

Required

Prepare the following budgets and other financial information:

1. The sales budget, including sales for July.
2. The purchases budget, the budgeted cost of goods sold for each month and the quarter, and the cost of the June 30 budgeted inventory.
3. The selling expense budget.
4. The general and administrative expense budget.
5. The expected cash receipts from customers and the expected June 30 balance of accounts receivable.
6. The expected cash payments for purchases and the expected June 30 balance of accounts payable.
7. The cash budget.
8. The budgeted income statement.
9. The budgeted statement of retained earnings.
10. The budgeted balance sheet.

Planning the Solution

*   The sales budget shows the expected sales for each month in the quarter. Start by multiplying March sales by 105%, and do the same thing for the remaining months. July's sales are needed for the purchases budget. To complete the budget, multiply the expected unit sales by the selling price of $25 per unit.

*   Use these results and the 80% inventory policy to budget the size of the ending inventory for April, May, and June. Then, add the budgeted sales to these numbers, and subtract the actual or expected beginning inventory for each month. The result will be the number of units to be purchased in each month. Multiply these numbers by the per unit cost of $15. Find the budgeted cost of goods sold by multiplying the unit sales in each month by the $15 cost per unit. And, find the cost of the June 30 ending inventory by multiplying the units expected to be on hand at that date by the $15 cost per unit.

*   The selling expense budget has only two items. Find the amount of the sales representatives' commissions by multiplying the expected dollar sales in each month by the

12.5% commission rate. Then, add the sales manager's salary of $3,500 in April and $4,000 in May and June.

- The general and administrative expense budget should show three items. Administrative salaries are fixed at $8,000 per month and depreciation is to be $5,000 per month. Budget the monthly interest expense on the long-term note by multiplying its $200,000 balance by the 0.9% monthly interest rate.

- Determine the amounts of cash sales in each month by multiplying the budgeted sales by 30%. Add to this amount the credit sales of the prior month, which you can compute as 70% of the prior month's sales. April's cash receipts from collecting receivables will equal the March 31 balance of $175,000. The expected June 30 accounts receivable balance equals 70% of June's total budgeted sales.

- Determine expected cash payments on accounts payable for each month by making them equal to the merchandise purchases in the prior month. The payments for April equal the March 31 balance of accounts payable shown on the beginning balance sheet. The June 30 balance of accounts payable equals merchandise purchases for June.

- Prepare the cash budget by combining the given information and the amounts of cash receipts and payments on account that you just calculated. Complete the cash budget for each month by either borrowing enough to raise the preliminary balance up to the minimum or paying off the short-term note as much as the balance will allow without falling below the minimum. Also show the ending balance of the short-term note in the budget.

- Prepare the budgeted income statement by combining the budgeted items for all three months. Determine the income before income taxes and multiply it by the 35% rate to find the quarter's income tax expense.

- The budgeted statement of retained earnings should show the March 31 balance plus the quarter's net income minus the quarter's dividends.

- The budgeted balance sheet includes updated balances for all the items that appear in the beginning balance sheet and an additional liability for unpaid income taxes. The amounts for all asset, liability, and equity accounts can be found either in the budgets and schedules or by adding amounts found there to the beginning balances.

Solution to Demonstration Problem

1. The sales budget:

	April	May	June	July
Prior month's sales	10,000	10,500	11,025	11,576
Plus 5% growth	500	525	551	579
Projected unit sales	10,500	11,025	11,576	12,155

	April	May	June	Quarter
Projected unit sales	10,500	11,025	11,576	
Selling price per unit	× $25	× $25	× $25	
Projected sales revenue	$262,500	$275,625	$289,400	$827,525

2. The purchases budget:

	April	May	June	Quarter
Next month's unit sales	11,025	11,576	12,155	
Ending inventory percentage	× 80%	× 80%	× 80%	
Desired ending inventory	8,820	9,261	9,724	
This month's unit sales	10,500	11,025	11,576	
Units to be available	19,320	20,286	21,300	
Beginning inventory	(8,400)	(8,820)	(9,261)	
Units to be purchased	10,920	11,466	12,039	
Budgeted cost per unit	$15	$15	$15	
Projected purchases	$163,800	$171,990	$180,585	$516,375

Budgeted cost of goods sold:

	April	May	June	Quarter
This month's unit sales	10,500	11,025	11,576	
Budgeted cost per unit	× $15	× $15	× $15	
Projected cost of goods sold	$157,500	$165,375	$173,640	$496,515
Budgeted inventory for June 30:				
Units			9,724	
Cost per unit			× $15	
Total			$145,860	

3. Selling expense budget:

	April	May	June	Quarter
Budgeted sales	$262,500	$275,625	$289,400	$827,525
Commission percentage	× 12.5%	× 12.5%	× 12.5%	× 12.5%
Sales commissions	$ 32,813	$ 34,453	$ 36,175	$103,441
Manager's salary	3,500	4,000	4,000	11,500
Projected selling expenses	$ 36,313	$ 38,453	$ 40,175	$114,941

4. General and administrative expense budget:

	April	May	June	Quarter
Administrative salaries	$ 8,000	$ 8,000	$ 8,000	$24,000
Depreciation	5,000	5,000	5,000	15,000
Interest on long-term note				
payable (0.9% × $200,000)	1,800	1,800	1,800	5,400
Projected expenses	$14,800	$14,800	$14,800	$44,400

5. Expected cash receipts from customers:

	April	May	June	Quarter
Budgeted sales	$262,500	$275,625	$289,400	
Ending accounts receivable (70%) . .	$183,750	$192,938	$202,580	
Cash receipts:				
Cash sales (30%)	$ 78,750	$ 82,687	$ 86,820	$248,257
Collections of prior				
month's receivables	175,000	183,750	192,938	551,688
Total cash to be collected	$253,750	$266,437	$279,758	$799,945

6. Expected cash payments to suppliers:

	April	May	June	Quarter
Cash payments (equal to prior				
month's purchases)	$156,000	$163,800	$171,990	$491,790
Expected June 30 balance of				
accounts payable				
(June purchases)			$180,585	

7. Cash budget:

	April	May	June
Beginning cash balance	$ 50,000	$ 89,517	$ 50,000
Cash received from customers	253,750	266,437	279,758
Total cash available	$303,750	$355,954	$329,758
Cash payments:			
Payments for merchandise	$156,000	$163,800	$171,990
Sales commissions	32,813	34,453	36,175
Salaries:			
Sales	3,500	4,000	4,000
Administrative	8,000	8,000	8,000
Interest on long-term note	1,800	1,800	1,800
Dividends		100,000	

	April	May	June
Equipment purchase			55,000
Interest on short-term notes:			
April ($12,000 × 1.0%)	120		
June ($6,099 × 1.0%)			61
Total	$202,233	$312,053	$277,026
Preliminary balance	$101,517	$ 43,901	$ 52,732
Additional loan		6,099	
Loan repayment	(12,000)		(2,732)
Ending cash balance	$ 89,517	$ 50,000	$ 50,000
Ending short-term notes	$ –0–	$ 6,099	$ 3,367

8.

DAREDEVIL COMPANY
Budgeted Income Statement
Quarter Ended June 30, 19X2

Sales		$827,525	*(part 1)*
Cost of goods sold		(496,515)	*(part 2)*
Gross profit		$331,010	
Operating expenses:			
Sales commissions	$103,441		*(part 3)*
Sales salaries	11,500		*(part 3)*
Administrative salaries	24,000		*(part 4)*
Depreciation	15,000		*(part 4)*
Interest on long-term note	5,400		*(part 4)*
Interest on short-term notes	181		*(part 7)*
Total operating expenses		(159,522)	
Income before income taxes		$171,488	
Income taxes (35%)		(60,021)	
Net income		$111,467	

9.

DAREDEVIL COMPANY
Budgeted Statement of Retained Earnings
For the Quarter Ended June 30, 19X2

Beginning retained earnings	$138,000	*(given)*
Net income	111,467	*(income statement)*
Total	$249,467	
Dividends	(100,000)	*(given)*
Ending retained earnings	$149,467	

10.

DAREDEVIL COMPANY
Budgeted Balance Sheet
June 30, 19X2

Cash	$ 50,000		*(part 7)*
Accounts receivable	202,580		*(part 5)*
Inventory	145,860		*(part 2)*
Total current assets		$398,440	
Equipment	$535,000		*(given plus purchase)*
Accumulated depreciation	(105,000)	430,000	*(given plus expense)*
Total assets		$828,440	
Accounts payable	$180,585		*(part 6)*
Short-term notes payable	3,367		*(part 7)*
Estimated income taxes payable	60,021		*(income statement)*
Total current liabilities		$243,973	
Long-term note payable		200,000	*(given)*
Total liabilities		$443,973	
Common stock	$235,000		*(given)*
Retained earnings	149,467		*(retained earnings*
Total stockholders' equity		384,467	*statement)*
Total liabilities and equity		$828,440	

GLOSSARY

Budget a formal statement of future plans, usually expressed in monetary terms. p. 880

Budgeted balance sheet a managerial accounting report that presents predicted amounts of the company's assets, liabilities, and stockholders' equity as of the end of the budget period. p. 897

Budgeted income statement a managerial accounting report that presents predicted amounts of the company's revenues and expenses for the budget period. p. 896

Budgeting the process of planning future business actions and expressing them as formal plans. p. 880

Capital expenditures budget a plan that lists dollar amounts to be received from disposing of equipment and dollar amounts to be spent on purchasing additional equipment if the proposed production program is carried out. p. 892

Cash budget a plan that shows the expected cash inflows and outflows during the budget period, including receipts from loans needed to maintain a minimum cash balance and repayments of such loans. p. 893

Continuous budgeting the practice of preparing budgets for each of several future periods and revising those budgets as each period is completed; as one period is completed, a new budget is added, with the result that the budget always covers the same number of future periods. p. 883

General and administrative expense budget a plan that lists the types and amounts of general and administrative expenses expected during the budget period. p. 892

Manufacturing budget a plan that shows the predicted costs for materials, direct labor, and overhead costs to be incurred in manufacturing the units in the production budget. p. 891

Master budget a comprehensive or overall formal plan for a business that includes specific plans for expected sales, the units of product to be produced, the merchandise (or materials) to be purchased, the expense to be incurred, the long-term assets to be purchased, and the amounts of cash to be borrowed or loans to be repaid, as well as a budgeted income statement and balance sheet. p. 884

Merchandise purchases budget a plan that states the units or costs of merchandise to be purchased by a merchandising company during the budget period. p. 890

Production budget a plan that states the number of units to be manufactured during each future period covered by the budget, based on the budgeted sales for the period and the levels of inventory needed to support future sales. p. 891

Rolling budgets the set of periodic budgets that are prepared and periodically revised in the practice of continuous budgeting. p. 883

Safety stock a quantity of merchandise or materials over the minimum needed to satisfy budgeted demand; provides protection against lost sales caused by unfulfilled demands from customers or delays in shipments from suppliers. p. 890

Sales budget a plan showing the units of goods to be sold and the revenue to be derived from the sales; the starting point in the budgeting process because the plans for most departments are related to sales. p. 888

Selling expense budget a plan that lists the types and amounts of selling expenses expected during the budget period. p. 891

QUESTIONS

1. How does budgeting help managers control a business?
2. How does budgeting tend to promote good decision making?
3. What two alternative norms or objectives can be used to evaluate actual performance? Which of the two is generally more useful?
4. What is the benefit of continuous budgeting?
5. Why should each department participate in preparing its own budget?
6. How does budgeting help management coordinate business activities?
7. What is a sales budget? A selling expense budget? A capital expenditures budget?
8. What is the difference between a production budget and a manufacturing budget?

9. What is a cash budget? Why do operating budgets and the capital expenditures budget need to be prepared before the cash budget?
10. Federal Express has managers in its local branches and in its headquarters in Memphis. What kinds of capital expenditures would these different kinds of managers plan?

11. Because of the nature of the business, do you think that the management of a local McDonald's store would do much long-term budgeting?

QUICK STUDY (Five-Minute Exercises)

What are three guidelines that should be followed if budgeting is to serve effectively as a source of motivation?

QS 23–1
(LO 1)

Which of the following comprise the master budget:

QS 23–2
(LO 2)

a. Sales budget, operating budgets, financial budgets.

b. Operating budgets, budgeted income statement, budgeted balance sheet.

c. Sales budget, capital expenditures budget, financial budgets.

d. Operating budgets, financial budgets, capital expenditures budget.

The July sales budget of the Penrose Company calls for sales of $325,000. The store expects to begin July with a $50,000 inventory and to end the month with a $55,000 inventory. The cost of goods sold is typically about 70% of sales. Determine the cost of goods that should be purchased during July.

QS 23–3
(LO 3)

Use the following information to prepare a cash budget for the Fuller Company. The budget should show expected cash receipts and disbursements for the month of March and the balance expected on March 31.

QS 23–4
(LO 3)

a. Beginning cash balance on March 1, $62,000.

b. Cash receipts from sales, $328,000.

c. Budgeted cash payments for purchases, $110,200.

d. Budgeted cash disbursements for salaries, $73,400.

e. Other budgeted cash expenses, $55,000.

f. Repayment of bank loan, $30,000.

Wyatt Company manufactures Product X and has a policy that requires ending inventory to equal 40% of the next month's sales. Wyatt estimates that October's ending inventory will consist of 122,000 units. Sales for November and December are estimated to be 340,000 and 405,000, respectively. Calculate the number of units of Product X to be produced that would appear on Wyatt's production budget for November.

QS 23–5
(LO 3)

Dumont Company anticipates sales for April and May of $420,000 and $398,000, respectively. Cash sales are normally 60% of total sales. Of the credit sales, 10% are collected in the same month as the sale, 70% are collected during the first month after the sale, and the remaining 20% is collected in the second month. Determine the amount of accounts receivable that should be reported on Dumont's budgeted balance sheet as of May 31.

QS 23–6
(LO 4)

EXERCISES

Bogart Company manufactures a single product. The management predicts that the ending inventory for the first quarter will include 160,000 units. The following unit sales of the product are expected during the rest of the year:

Exercise 23–1
Production budget for two quarters
(LO 3)

Second quarter	280,000
Third quarter	400,000
Fourth quarter	600,000

Management's policy calls for the ending inventory of a quarter to equal 60% of the next quarter's budgeted sales.

Required

Prepare a production budget showing the units of product that should be manufactured during the year's second and third quarters.

Exercise 23–2
Cash budget for three months
(LO 3)

Keller Company budgeted the following cash receipts and cash disbursements from operations for the first quarter of the next year:

	Receipts	Disbursements
January	$435,000	$416,400
February	525,000	467,580
March	600,000	631,500

According to a credit agreement with the company's bank, Keller promises to have a minimum cash balance of $30,000 at the end of each month. In return, the bank has agreed that the company can borrow up to $150,000 with interest of 12% per year, paid on the last day of each month. The interest is calculated on the beginning balance of the loan for the month. The company is expected to have a cash balance of $30,000 and a loan balance of $60,000 on January 1.

Required

Prepare monthly cash budgets for the first quarter.

Exercise 23–3
Cash budget from transaction data
(LO 3)

Use the following information to prepare a cash budget for the Brock Company. The budget should show expected cash receipts and disbursements for the month of March and the balance expected on March 31.

a. Beginning cash balance on March 1: $50,000.

b. Cash receipts from sales: 30% are collected in the month of sale, 50% in the next month, 18% in the second month, and 2% are uncollectible. The following actual and budgeted amounts of sales are known:

January (actual)	$1,720,000
February (actual)	1,200,000
March (budgeted)	1,400,000

c. Payments on purchases: 60% in the month of purchase and 40% in the month following purchase. The following actual and budgeted amounts of merchandise purchases are known:

February (actual)	$430,000
March (budgeted)	600,000

d. Budgeted cash disbursements for salaries in March: $211,000.

e. Budgeted depreciation expense for March: $12,000.

f. Other cash expenses budgeted for March: $150,000.

g. Accrued income taxes due in March: $80,000.

h. Bank loan interest due in March: $6,600.

Exercise 23–4
Budgeted income statement and balance sheet
(LO 4)

Based on the information provided in Exercise 23–3 and the additional information that follows, prepare a budgeted income statement for the month of March and a budgeted balance sheet for March 31:

a. Cost of goods sold is 44% of sales.

b. The inventory at the end of April was $80,000.

c. Salaries payable on February 28 were $50,000 and are expected to be $40,000 on March 31.

d. The Equipment account has a balance of $1,600,000. On February 28, accumulated depreciation was $280,000.

e. The $6,600 cash payment of interest represents the 1% monthly expense on a bank loan of $660,000.

f. Income taxes payable on February 28 were $80,000, and the income tax rate applicable to the company is 30%.

g. The 2% of sales that prove to be uncollectible are debited to Bad Debts Expense and credited to the Allowance for Doubtful Accounts during the month of sale. Specific accounts that prove to be uncollectible are written off at the end of the second month after the sale.

h. The only other balance sheet accounts are Common Stock, which has a balance of $600,000, and Retained Earnings, which has a balance of $1,013,600 on February 28.

Hudson Company prepared monthly budgets for the current year. The budgets planned for a June inventory of 15,000 units. The company follows a policy of ending each month with merchandise inventory on hand equal to a specified percentage of the budgeted sales for the following month. Budgeted sales and merchandise purchases for three months were as follows:

Exercise 23–5
Merchandise purchases budget for three months·
(LO 3)

	Sales (Units)	Purchases (Units)
April	120,000	138,000
May	210,000	204,000
June	180,000	159,000

Based on this information, calculate the following amounts:

a. The percentage relationship between a month's ending inventory and sales budgeted for the following month.

b. The units budgeted to be sold in July.

c. The units budgeted for April's beginning inventory.

Then, show how the company compiled the merchandise purchases budgets for April, May, and June.

Roche Company's cost of goods sold is consistently 40% of sales. The company plans to have a merchandise inventory at the beginning of each month with a cost equal to 30% of that month's budgeted cost of goods sold. All merchandise is purchased on credit, and 50% of the purchases made during a month are paid in that month. Another 35% is paid for during the first month after purchase, and the remaining 15% is paid for during the second month after purchase.

Exercise 23–6
Calculations of budgeted cash payments
(LO 3)

Use the following sales budgets to calculate the expected cash payments to be made during October:

August	$250,000
September	200,000
October	300,000
November	350,000

Valvano Company purchases its merchandise on credit. It has recently budgeted the following accounts payable balances and merchandise inventory balances:

Exercise 23–7
Budgeting monthly cost of goods sold
(LO 3)

	Accounts Payable	Merchandise Inventory
January 31	$160,000	$400,000
February 28	200,000	480,000
March 31	176,000	448,000
April 30	228,000	396,000

Cash payments on accounts payable during each month are expected to be:

January	$1,340,000
February	1,540,000
March	1,300,000
April	1,580,000

a. Calculate the budgeted amounts of purchases for February, March, and April.

b. Calculate the budgeted amounts of cost of goods sold for February, March, and April.

Exercise 23–8
Budgeting accounts payable balances
(LO 3)

Thornton Company, a merchandising company, budgets its monthly cost of goods sold to equal 70% of sales. The inventory policy calls for a beginning inventory in each month equal to 25% of the budgeted cost of goods sold for that month.

All purchases are on credit, and 20% of the purchases in any month are paid for during the same month. Another 50% is paid during the first month after purchase, and the remaining 30% is paid in the second month after purchase. The following sales budgets have been established:

July	$600,000
August	480,000
September	540,000
October	480,000
November	420,000

a. Calculate the budgeted purchases for July, August, September, and October.

b. Calculate the budgeted payments on accounts payable for September and October.

c. Calculate the budgeted ending balances of accounts payable for September and October.

PROBLEMS

Problem 23–1
Production budget and materials purchases budget
(LO 3)

Sportworld Company produces water skis. Each ski requires two pounds of carbon fiber. The company's management predicts that there will be 6,000 units of the product and 12,000 pounds of the carbon fiber on June 30 of the current year, and that 100,000 units of the product will be sold during the next quarter. Because the peak selling season will be over, management wants to end the third quarter with only 4,000 finished skis and 5,000 pounds of carbon fiber in the materials inventory. Carbon fiber can be purchased for approximately $6.00 per pound.

CHECK FIGURE:
Cost of carbon fiber purchases, $1,134,000

Required

Prepare a third-quarter production budget and a third-quarter carbon fiber purchases budget for the company (include the dollar cost of the purchases).

Problem 23–2
Production budget and merchandise purchases budget
(LO 3)

Barton Corporation retails three products that it buys ready for sale. The company's February 28 inventories are:

Product A	14,700 units
Product B	68,700 units
Product C	35,700 units

The company's management has realized that excessive inventories have accumulated for all three products. As a result, the managers have created a new policy that the ending inventory in any month should equal 25% of the expected unit sales for the following month.

Expected sales in units for March, April, May, and June are as follows:

	Budgeted Sales in Units			
	March	**April**	**May**	**June**
Product A	15,000	21,000	27,000	33,000
Product B	66,000	90,000	114,000	78,000
Product C	36,000	30,000	24,000	18,000

Required

Preparation component:

CHECK FIGURE:
Product A purchases for May, 28,500 units

Prepare separate purchases budgets (in units) for each of the three products covering March, April, and May.

Analysis component:

Your answer to the preparation component of this problem should reflect much smaller purchases of all three products in March compared to April and May. What factor caused these smaller purchases to be planned? Suggest some conditions in the business that would cause this factor to affect Barton like it apparently has.

During the last week of August, the owner of the Keller Company approached the bank for a $70,000 loan to be made on September 1 and repaid on November 30 with annual interest of 12%. The owner planned to increase the store's inventory by $60,000 during September and needed the loan to pay for the merchandise in October and November. The bank's loan officer needed more information about Keller's ability to repay the loan and asked the owner to forecast the store's November 30 cash position.

Problem 23–3
Monthly cash budgets
(LO 3)

On September 1, Keller was expected to have a $3,000 cash balance, $120,000 of accounts receivable, and $100,000 of accounts payable. Its budgeted sales, purchases, and cash expenditures for the coming three months are as follows:

	September	October	November
Sales	$200,000	$300,000	$360,000
Merchandise purchases	230,000	160,000	200,000
Payroll	16,000	17,000	18,000
Rent	6,000	6,000	6,000
Other cash expenses	64,000	8,000	7,000
Repayment of bank loan			70,000
Interest on the loan			2,100

The budgeted September purchases include the inventory increase. All sales are on account. The company's regular past experience shows that 25% is collected in the month of the sale, 45% is collected in the month following the sale, 20% in the second month, 9% in the third, and the remainder is not collected. Applying these percentages to the September 1 accounts receivable balance shows that $81,000 of the $120,000 will be collected during September, $36,000 during October, and $16,200 during November. All merchandise is purchased on credit. Eighty percent of the balance is paid in the month following a purchase and the remaining 20% is paid in the second month. The $100,000 of accounts payable at the end of August will be paid as follows: $80,000 in September and $20,000 in October.

Required

Prepare cash budgets for September, October, and November for the Keller Company. Provide additional supplemental schedules as needed.

CHECK FIGURE:
Budgeted total disbursements for November, $277,100

Monarch Company has a cash balance of $60,000 on June 1. The company's product sells for $125 per unit. Actual and projected sales are:

Problem 23–4
Cash budgets with supporting schedules
(LO 3)

	Units	Dollars
April (actual)	8,000	$1,000,000
May (actual)	4,000	500,000
June (budgeted)	12,000	1,500,000
July (budgeted)	6,000	750,000
August (budgeted)	7,600	950,000

All the sales are on credit. Recent experience shows that 20% of the revenues are collected in the month of the sale, 30% in the next month after the sale, 48% in the second month after the sale, and 2% prove to be uncollectible.

The purchase price of the product is $100 per unit. All purchases are payable within 12 days. Thus, 60% of the purchases made in a month are paid in that month and the other 40% are paid in the next month. Monarch's management has a policy of maintaining an ending monthly inventory of 25% of the next month's unit sales plus a safety stock of 100 units. The March 31 and May 31 actual inventory levels were consistent with this policy.

Cash selling and administrative expenses for the year are $1,200,000, and are paid evenly throughout the year.

The company's minimum cash balance for the end of a month is $60,000. This minimum is maintained, if necessary, by borrowing cash from the bank. If the balance goes over $60,000, the company repays as much of the loan as it can without going below the minimum. This loan carries an annual 9% interest rate. On May 31, the balance of the loan was $32,000.

Required

Preparation component:

1. Prepare a schedule that shows how much cash will be collected in June and July from the credit customers.

2. Prepare a schedule that shows the budgeted ending inventories for April, May, June, and July.

3. Prepare a schedule showing the purchases budgets for the product for May, June, and July. Present the calculation in terms of units and then show the dollar amount of purchases for each month.

4. Prepare a schedule showing the cash to be paid out during June and July for product purchases.

CHECK FIGURE:
Budgeted ending loan balance for July, $136,782

5. Prepare monthly cash budgets for June and July, including any loan activity and interest expense. Also, show the loan balance at the end of each month.

Analysis component:

6. Refer to your answer to part 5. Note that Monarch's cash budget indicates that the company will need to borrow over $40,000 in June and over $60,000 in July. Suggest some reasons why knowing this information in May would be helpful to Monarch's management.

Problem 23–5
Preparation and analysis of budgeted income statements
(LO 4)

Perkins Company buys one kind of merchandise at $64 per unit and sells it at $120 per unit. The company's sales representatives receive an 8% commission on each sale. The December income statement shows the following information:

PERKINS COMPANY
Income Statement
For Month Ended December 31

Sales	$1,200,000
Cost of goods sold	640,000
Gross profit	$ 560,000
Expenses:	
Sales commissions	$ 96,000
Advertising	160,000
Store rent	24,000
Administrative salaries	40,000
Depreciation	50,000
Other	12,000
Total	$ 382,000
Net income	$ 178,000

The company's management believes that the December results would be repeated during January, February, and March without any changes in strategy. However, some changes are being considered. Management believes that unit sales will increase at a rate of 10% each month during the next quarter (including January) if the item's selling price is reduced to $112 per unit and if advertising expenses are increased by 25% and remain at that level for all three months. Even if these changes are made, the purchase price will remain at $64 per unit. Under this plan, the sales representatives would continue to earn an 8% commission and the remaining expenses would remain unchanged.

Required

Using a three-column format, prepare budgeted income statements for January, February, and March, that show the expected results of implementing the proposed changes. Based on the information in the budgeted income statements, recommend whether management should implement the plan.

CHECK FIGURE:
Budgeted net income for February, $146,384

Problem 23–6
Preparing a complete master budget
(LO 2, 3, 4)

Shortly before the end of 19X2, the management of Burke Corporation prepared the following budgeted balance sheet for December 31, 19X2:

BURKE CORPORATION
Budgeted Balance Sheet
As of December 31, 19X2

Cash		$ 36,000
Accounts receivable		525,000
Inventory		150,000
Total current assets		$ 711,000
Equipment	$540,000	
Accumulated depreciation	67,500	472,500
Total		$1,183,500
Accounts payable	$360,000	
Loan from bank	15,000	
Taxes payable (due March 15, 19X3)	90,000	
Total liabilities		$ 465,000
Common stock	$472,500	
Retained earnings	246,000	
Total stockholders' equity		718,500
Total		$1,183,500

In anticipation of preparing a master budget for January, February, and March 19X3, management has gathered the following information:

a. Burke's single product is purchased for $30 per unit and resold for $45 per unit. The expected inventory level on December 31 (5,000 units) is greater than management's desired level for 19X3 of 25% of the next month's expected sales (in units). Budgeted sales are:

January	6,000 units
February	8,000
March	10,000
April	9,000

b. Cash sales are 25% of total sales and credit sales are 75% of total sales. Of the credit sales, 60% are collected in the first month after the sale and 40% in the second month after the sale. Sixty percent of the December 31, 19X2, balance of accounts receivable will be collected during January and 40% will be collected during February.

c. Merchandise purchased by the company is paid for as follows: 20% in the month after purchase, and 80% in the second month after purchase. Twenty percent of the Accounts Payable balance on December 31, 19X2, will be paid during January, and 80% will be paid during February.

d. Sales commissions of 20% of sales are paid each month. Additional sales salaries are $90,000 per year.

e. General and administrative salaries are $144,000 per year. Repair expenses equal $3,000 per month and are paid in cash.

f. The equipment shown in the December 31, 19X2, balance sheet was purchased in January 19X2. It is being depreciated over eight years under the straight-line method with no salvage value. The following new purchases of equipment are planned in the coming quarter:

January	$72,000
February	96,000
March	28,800

This equipment also will be depreciated with the straight-line method over eight years, with no salvage value. A full month's depreciation is taken for the month in which the equipment is purchased.

g. The company plans to acquire some land at the end of March at a cost of $150,000. The purchase price will be paid with cash on the last day of the month.

h. Burke has a working arrangement with the bank to obtain additional loans as needed. The interest rate is 12% per year, and the interest is paid at the end of each month based on the beginning balance. Partial or full payments on these loans can be made on the last day of the month. Burke has agreed to maintain a minimum ending cash balance of $36,000 in every month.

i. The income tax rate applicable to the company is 40%. However, income taxes on the first quarter's income will not be paid until April 15.

Required

Prepare a master budget for the first quarter of 19X3. It should include the following component budgets:

1. Monthly sales budgets (showing both budgeted unit sales and dollar sales).
2. Monthly merchandise purchases budgets.
3. Monthly selling expense budgets.
4. Monthly general and administrative expense budgets.
5. Monthly capital expenditures budgets.
6. Monthly cash budgets.
7. Budgeted income statement for the first quarter.
8. Budgeted balance sheet as of March 31, 19X3.

CHECK FIGURE:
Budgeted net income for quarter, $32,955

Provide as many supplemental schedules as you need. Round all amounts to the nearest dollar.

CRITICAL THINKING: ESSAYS, PROBLEMS, AND CASES

Managerial Analysis Case

(LO 3)

Pace Tire Company produces bicycle tires that require 6 pounds of rubber per unit. The owner of the company is negotiating with the bank for approval to obtain loans as they are needed. An important item in the discussion has been the question of how much cash will be required to pay for purchases of rubber.

Pace purchases its rubber on account, and the resulting payables are paid in cash as follows: 40% during the month after purchase and 60% during the second month after purchase.

The company plans to manufacture enough tires to maintain an ending monthly inventory equal to 30% of the next month's sales. Sufficient rubber is to be purchased each month to maintain an ending monthly inventory equal to 20% of the next month's production requirements.

During the coming months, budgeted unit sales are as follows:

June	80,000
July	120,000
August	150,000
September	50,000

The following data are available on May 31:

Tires on hand	30,000
Pounds of rubber on hand	132,000
Accounts Payable	
Due in June	$600,000
Due in July	900,000

Recent prices of rubber have varied substantially and the owner speculates that the price could range from $2 to $6 per pound during the next few months. You are asked to assist the owner by predicting the cash payments to be made in the months of June, July, and August. Prepare separate predictions based on a low price of $2 and a high price of $6.

The Tanner Corporation has budgeted the following monthly sales volumes:

February	280,000
March	240,000
April	200,000
May	250,000

Managerial Analysis Problem

(LO 3)

The company's inventory policy is to maintain an ending monthly finished goods inventory of 20% of the next month's budgeted sales plus a safety stock of 10,000 units. The February 1 inventory was 52,000 units.

An analysis of Tanner's manufacturing costs shows:

Material cost	$ 5.00 per unit
Direct labor cost	$ 2.00 per unit
Variable overhead cost	$11.00 per unit
Fixed overhead costs	$820,000 per month

Required

Prepare production budgets and manufacturing budgets for the months of February, March, and April. The manufacturing budgets should show the total manufacturing costs expected in each of the three months.

Examine the ethics case that appears on page 882. What specific factor in the first situation makes the accounting clerk's action unethical? In the second situation, the executive's activity concerning his stock seems to be prompted by his resignation and his need for cash. Do you think that these considerations change the ethics of the situation?

Ethical Issues Essay

CONCEPT TESTER

Test your understanding of the concepts introduced in this chapter by completing the following crossword puzzle:

Across Clues

3. Two words; the practice of preparing budgets and revising them as each period goes by.
4. Two words; a quantity of inventory over the minimum needed to satisfy budgeted demand.
6. Two words; the set of budgets prepared and revised in the practice of continuous budgeting.
7. Two words; a plan showing the units to be sold and the revenue to be derived from sales.
8. The process of planning future business actions and expressing them as formal plans.
9. Two words; a plan that states the number of units to be produced during each budget period.

Down Clues

1. A formal statement of future plans, usually expressed in monetary terms.
2. Two words; a comprehensive or overall formal plan for a business.
5. Two words; a plan that shows the expected cash inflows and outflows.

ANSWERS TO PROGRESS CHECKS

23–1 The major benefits include: (1) promoting a focus on the future; (2) providing a basis for evaluating performance; (3) providing a source of motivation; (4) coordinating the departments of a business; (5) communicating plans and instructions.

23–2 A master budget is a comprehensive or overall plan for a business.

23–3 The budget committee's responsibility is to provide central guidance to ensure that budget figures are realistic and coordinated.

23–4 Budget periods usually coincide with accounting periods and therefore cover a month, quarter, or a year. Budgets also can be prepared to cover a long-range period, such as five years.

23–5 Rolling budgets are budgets that are periodically revised in the process of continuous budgeting.

23–6 *b*

23–7 The master budget includes operating budgets, the capital expenditures budget, and financial budgets.

23–8 *c* $(.60 \times 140) + 120 - 50 = 154$

23–9 Merchandising companies prepare merchandise purchases budgets while manufacturing companies prepare production and manufacturing budgets.

23–10 With a just-in-time system, the level of inventory is kept to a minimum and orders for merchandise or materials are intended to meet immediate sales demand. A safety stock system maintains an inventory that is large enough to meet sales demands plus an amount to satisfy unexpected sales demands and an amount to cover delayed shipments from suppliers.

23–11 *a*

23–12 (1) Sales budget, (2) Other operating budgets, (3) Capital expenditures budget, (4) Cash budget, (5) Budgeted income statement, (6) Budgeted balance sheet.

Flexible Budgets and Standard Costs

*R*ecall the discussion of Renton Coil Spring Company in Chapter 23. Renton Coil Spring supplies parts for Boeing airplanes. When the Boeing Company sells an airplane, its customers are guaranteed one-day service on spare parts needed to repair any Boeing airplane grounded due to a broken part. Boeing's commitment is an important selling point and is formally known as the Airplane on Ground (AOG) program. Parts ordered for this program are given special priority.

In the past two years, Boeing has focused on reducing inventories and has explored numerous methods of ensuring it has the parts available to support AOG at a minimum inventory dollar investment. This has increased pressure on suppliers for shorter turn around times for parts ordered. It has also resulted in smaller order sizes and increased the number of orders for less than five parts. Because each part is unique to Boeing airplanes, production of the parts by Renton Coil Spring requires a unique setup of the machinery needed to produce the parts. For most of the orders, the setup time required is longer than the cycle time to run the parts and is essentially the same whether producing 1 part or 10. As a result, an order of 1 part is assigned a cost equal to the run time for 10 parts. The only real variable cost is the raw materials. The cost for 1 part is $410 while 10 units cost $500, or $50 per unit.

Boeing's purchasing manager reviewed the large variation in unit prices and called Chuck Pepka, Renton Coil Spring's owner, for an explanation. Pepka promised to review the invoices and respond. Later that day, Pepka and his controller were reviewing the cost assignment to the parts. Clearly the invoices reflected the actual costs associated with producing the parts but what would be the best way to explain to Boeing that a part could cost $50 or $410?

LEARNING OBJECTIVES

After studying Chapter 24, you should be able to:

1. **Describe the differences between and relative advantages of fixed budgets and flexible budgets and be able to prepare a flexible budget.**

2. **State what standard costs represent, how they are determined, and how they are used by management to evaluate performance.**

3. **Calculate material, labor, and overhead variances, and describe what each variance indicates about the performance of a company.**

4. **Explain how standard cost accounting information is useful for the technique of management by exception.**

5. **Prepare journal entries to record standard costs and to account for price and quantity variances.**

6. **Define or explain the words and phrases listed in the chapter glossary.**

In Chapter 23, you learned that budgeting organizes and formalizes management's planning activities. You also learned that budgets can provide a basis for evaluating actual performance. In this chapter, we look more closely at how budgets can be used to evaluate performance. These evaluations are important for controlling business operations. By studying this chapter, you will learn another way that managerial accounting contributes to fulfilling management's control responsibility.

FIXED BUDGETS AND PERFORMANCE REPORTS

You learned in Chapter 23 that the initial step in preparing a master budget is predicting sales volume for the budget period. Then, all other budgets in the master budget are based on this specific prediction of sales volume. In effect, the budgeted amount of each cost is based on the assumption that a specific (or *fixed*) amount of sales will take place. A budget based on a single predicted amount of sales or production volume is called a **fixed budget** or a *static budget*. The total amount of each cost in a fixed budget does not reflect the possibility that the actual sales or production volume may be different from the fixed budgeted amount.

Remember from Chapter 23 that one benefit of a budget is that it provides a useful basis for analyzing the success of actual results. Information useful for this analysis is often presented as a comparison in a **performance report** like the one in Illustration 24–1. This particular report compares actual results for the Orlando Company for November 19X2 with the results expected under a fixed budget for 10,000 units of product. (In this example, the production volume equals sales volume so that the amount of inventory does not change.) Notice that the performance report designates the differences between budgeted and actual performance as *variances*. You should also note the letters *F* and *U* beside the numbers in the third column of the performance report. Their meanings are:

F = Favorable variance—compared to the budget, the actual cost or revenue contributes to a *higher* income.

U = Unfavorable variance—compared to the budget, the actual cost or revenue contributes to a *lower* income.

This convention is followed throughout the chapter.

In evaluating Orlando Company's operations, management is likely to ask a variety of questions, including these:

- Why is actual income from operations $13,400 higher than the budgeted amount?

- Are the amounts paid for each expense item too high?

FAST HINT
Critical Thought Question:
Why does a favorable sales variance in Illustration 24–1 lead to so many unfavorable variances?

Illustration 24-1

A Performance Report Based on a Fixed Budget

ORLANDO COMPANY
Performance Report
For Month Ended November 30, 19X2

	Fixed Budget	Actual Performance	Variances
Sales: In units	10,000	12,000	
In dollars	$100,000	$125,000	$25,000 F
Cost of goods sold:			
Direct materials	$ 10,000	$ 13,000	$ 3,000 U
Direct labor	15,000	20,000	5,000 U
Overhead:			
Factory supplies	2,000	2,100	100 U
Utilities	3,000	4,000	1,000 U
Depreciation of machinery	8,000	8,000	
Supervisory salaries	11,000	11,000	
Selling expenses:			
Sales commissions	9,000	10,800	1,800 U
Shipping expenses	4,000	4,300	300 U
General and administrative expenses:			
Office supplies	5,000	5,200	200 U
Insurance expense	1,000	1,200	200 U
Depreciation of office equipment	7,000	7,000	
Administrative salaries	13,000	13,000	
Total expenses	$ 88,000	$ 99,600	$11,600 U
Income from operations	$ 12,000	$ 25,400	$13,400 F

F = Favorable variance
U = Unfavorable variance

- Is the manufacturing department using too much direct material?
- Is the manufacturing department using too much direct labor?

In fact, the performance report in Illustration 24–1 provides little help in answering these questions because the actual sales volume was 2,000 units higher than budgeted. The manager might assume that this higher level caused total dollar sales and many of the expenses to be higher, but other factors also could have influenced their amounts. This fixed budget performance report has limited usefulness because it fails to show whether actual costs were out of line for the actual sales volume. The report really does not provide management much useful information beyond the simple fact that the sales volume was 2,000 units higher than expected.

FLEXIBLE BUDGETS

To help management answer questions like the previous ones, many companies prepare **flexible budgets,** also called *variable budgets.* Unlike the planning budgets described in Chapter 23, flexible budgets are prepared after a specific period's activities are completed. Their primary purpose is to help managers evaluate past performance instead of helping them plan future events. In contrast to fixed budgets based on one expected amount of budgeted sales or production, flexible budgets are prepared to describe the amounts of revenue and expense that should have occurred at the actual level of output. Flexible budgets are more useful for evaluations because they reflect the fact that different levels of activity produce different amounts of cost.

LO 1

Describe the differences between and relative advantages of fixed budgets and flexible budgets and be able to prepare a flexible budget.

As a result, comparisons of actual results with budgeted performance are more likely to direct management to the reasons why the actual results differed from what should have happened.

PREPARING A FLEXIBLE BUDGET

Flexible budgeting is designed to reveal the effects of volume on the level of costs. To prepare a flexible budget, management depends on the distinctions between fixed and variable costs used in the cost-volume-profit analyses described in Chapter 22. Remember from Chapter 22 that the variable cost per unit of activity remains constant. Thus, the total amount of a variable cost changes in direct proportion to a change in the level of activity. On the other hand, the total amount of a fixed cost remains unchanged regardless of changes in the level of activity within the relevant (or normal) operating range of activity.[1]

In generating the numbers used in a flexible budget, the accountant expresses each variable cost as a constant amount per unit of sales (or as a percentage of a sales dollar). In contrast, the budgeted amount of each fixed cost is expressed as the total amount expected to occur at any sales volume.

Illustration 24–2 shows a set of possible flexible budgets for Orlando Company for November 19X2. Notice that seven of the expenses are classified as variable costs. The remaining five expenses are fixed costs. These classifications result from management's investigation of each of the company's expenses. (You should avoid drawing general rules from these examples. These particular expense categories are not always the same for every company. For example, depending on the nature of the company's operations, office supplies expense may be fixed or variable with respect to sales. In the present example, the company's management concluded that the office supplies cost is variable.)

The flexible budgets in Illustration 24–2 list sales and then the variable costs. They show the total variable costs and then subtract the total from sales. As you learned in Chapter 22, this difference between sales and variable costs equals the contribution margin. The budgets then list the expected amounts of fixed costs and present the expected income from operations before income taxes.

In Illustration 24–2, the first and second columns show the flexible budget amounts applied to any volume of sales within the relevant range. The other columns illustrate the flexible budgets that would be generated by applying these amounts to three selected sales volumes. For example, the first flexible budget (for 10,000 units) shows the same amounts that appeared in Illustration 24–1. The numbers are the same because that volume was assumed when the company prepared the fixed budget for November.

Remember that Orlando Company's actual sales volume for November was 12,000 units. This level was 2,000 units more than the 10,000 units originally forecasted in the master budget. To find the difference in expected costs for these two levels, compare the flexible budget for 10,000 units in the third column of Illustration 24–2 with the flexible budget for 12,000 units in the fourth column.

To identify opportunities for improving performance, the company's managers should compare the actual income of $25,400 (from Illustration 24–1) with the $22,400 income expected at the actual sales volume of 12,000 units. Thus, the total variance in income to be explained and understood is only $3,000 instead of the $13,400 variance identified in Illustration 24–1. After receiving the flexible budget based on November's actual volume, management's next step is to determine what caused this $3,000 difference. A flexible budget performance report provides useful guidance for answering this question.

---

[1]In Chapter 22, we acknowledged that some costs are neither strictly variable nor strictly fixed. In the present discussion, we continue using the assumption that all costs can be reasonably classified as either variable or fixed within the relevant range.

ORLANDO COMPANY Possible Flexible Budgets For Month Ended November 30, 19X2					
	Flexible Budget		Flexible Budget for Unit Sales of 10,000	Flexible Budget for Unit Sales of 12,000	Flexible Budget for Unit Sales of 14,000
	Variable Amount per Unit	Total Fixed Cost			
Sales	$10.00		$100,000	$120,000	$140,000
Variable costs:					
Direct materials	$ 1.00		$ 10,000	$ 12,000	$ 14,000
Direct labor	1.50		15,000	18,000	21,000
Factory supplies	0.20		2,000	2,400	2,800
Utilities	0.30		3,000	3,600	4,200
Sales commissions	0.90		9,000	10,800	12,600
Shipping expenses	0.40		4,000	4,800	5,600
Office supplies	0.50		5,000	6,000	7,000
Total variable costs	$ 4.80		$ 48,000	$ 57,600	$ 67,200
Contribution margin	$ 5.20		$ 52,000	$ 62,400	$ 72,800
Fixed costs:					
Depreciation, machinery		$ 8,000	$8,000	$ 8,000	$ 8,000
Supervisory salaries		11,000	11,000	11,000	11,000
Insurance expense		1,000	1,000	1,000	1,000
Depreciation, office equipment		7,000	7,000	7,000	7,000
Administrative salaries		13,000	13,000	13,000	13,000
Total fixed costs		$40,000	$ 40,000	$ 40,000	$ 40,000
Income from operations			$ 12,000	$ 22,400	$ 32,800

Illustration 24–2
A Set of Flexible Budgets

FAST HINT
Alternative Example:
What would be the expected income from operations for unit sales of 11,000 in Illustration 24–2? For unit sales of 13,000? *Answer:* $17,200 for unit sales of 11,000 and $27,600 for unit sales of 13,000.

Continuing the story at the beginning of the chapter: The controller for **Renton Coil Spring Company** decided to apply the concept of flexible budgeting to explain to the **Boeing Company** the unit cost difference when ordering 1 unit rather than 10 units. He used the following flexible budget format separating the variable cost components from the fixed cost components:

Volume (units per order)	1	10
Raw materials cost	$ 10	$100
Set up and labor time cost	400	400
Total order cost	410	500
Unit cost	410	50

A **flexible budget performance report** helps management analyze the difference between actual performance and budgeted performance based on the actual sales volume (or other level of activity). The report should direct management's attention toward those particular costs or revenues with actual amounts that differ substantially from the budgeted amounts.

Illustration 24–3 shows the flexible budget performance report for Orlando Company for November. The managerial accountant prepared this report after the actual volume was known to be 12,000 units. Observe that Illustration 24–3 shows a $5,000 favorable variance in total dollar sales. Because the actual and budgeted volumes are both 12,000 units, the $5,000 sales variance must have resulted solely from a selling

FLEXIBLE BUDGET PERFORMANCE REPORT

FAST HINT
Relevant Quick Study:
To apply these concepts, work QS 24–1.

price that was higher than expected. Further analysis of the facts surrounding this $5,000 sales variance produces these results:

Actual average price per unit	$125,000/12,000 = $10.4167
Budgeted price per unit	$120,000/12,000 = 10.0000
Favorable sales variance per unit	$5,000/12,000 = $ 0.4167

Management would use this information to assess whether the decision to increase the selling price met its goals. Then, they would consider which pricing strategy to use in the future.

FAST HINT
Critical Thought Question:
Do you think the pricing strategy of Illustration 24–3 should be continued? Why?

The other variances in Illustration 24–3 should direct management's attention to areas where corrective actions could help them control Orlando Company's operations. Each variance can be analyzed like the previous sales variance. That is, think of each expense as the joint result of using a given number of units of the expense item and paying a specific price per unit. According to this approach, a variance in Illustration 24–3 can be created in part by a difference between the actual price per unit and the budgeted price per unit. That part is a **price variance.** And, a variance also can be created in part by a difference between the actual number of units used and the budgeted number of units expected to be used. That part is a **quantity variance.** You learn more about this technique of **variance analysis** in the following section on standard costs.

Progress Check
(Answers to Progress Checks are provided at the end of the chapter.)

24–1   A flexible budget:
    a. Shows fixed costs as constant amounts of cost per unit of activity.
    b. Shows variable costs as constant amounts of cost per unit of activity.
    c. Is prepared based on one expected amount of budgeted sales or production.

24–2   What is the initial step in preparing a flexible budget?

24–3   What is the difference between a fixed and a flexible budget?

24–4   What is the contribution margin?

STANDARD COSTS

LO 2

State what standard costs represent, how they are determined, and how they are used by management to evaluate performance.

In Chapters 19 and 20, you learned about job order and process cost accounting systems. You should recall that many different variations of these two basic types of systems are used in practice. One important variation is a standard cost accounting system.

The costs described in Chapters 19 and 20 are **historical costs** because they are the dollar amounts paid by the business in past transactions. These historical (or actual) costs provide useful information for some purposes. However, management needs a basis of comparison to decide whether the amounts of the historical costs are reasonable or excessive.

Standard costs offer a useful basis for these evaluations. They are the costs that should be incurred under normal conditions to produce a specific product or component or to perform a specific service. Standard costs are established through personnel, engineering, and accounting studies of past experience and other data. Then, management uses standard costs to assess the reasonableness of the actual costs incurred

Illustration 24–3

ORLANDO COMPANY
Flexible Budget Performance Report
For Month Ended November 30, 19X2

	Flexible Budget	Actual Results	Variances
Sales (12,000 units)	$120,000	$125,000	$5,000 *F*
Variable costs:			
Direct materials	$ 12,000	$ 13,000	$1,000 *U*
Direct labor	18,000	20,000	2,000 *U*
Factory supplies	2,400	2,100	300 *F*
Utilities	3,600	4,000	400 *U*
Sales commissions	10,800	10,800	
Shipping expenses	4,800	4,300	500 *F*
Office supplies	6,000	5,200	800 *F*
Total variable costs	$ 57,600	$ 59,400	$1,800 *U*
Contribution margin	$ 62,400	$ 65,600	$3,200 *F*
Fixed costs:			
Depreciation of machinery	$ 8,000	$ 8,000	
Supervisory salaries	11,000	11,000	
Insurance expense	1,000	1,200	$ 200 *U*
Depreciation of office equipment	7,000	7,000	
Administrative salaries	13,000	13,000	
Total fixed costs	$ 40,000	$ 40,200	$ 200 *U*
Income from operations	$ 22,400	$ 25,400	$3,000 *F*

F = Favorable variance
U = Unfavorable variance

FAST HINT
Important Point to Remember: Because standard costs are budgeted amounts, they can be used to prepare both fixed budgets (Chapter 23) and flexible budgets (Chapter 24).

when producing the product or service during the past period. When actual costs vary from standard, management can use that information to help them identify possible problems and corrective actions.

Standard costs are the budgeted amounts. They are used in preparing budgets because they should be incurred under normal conditions. Thus, terms such as *standard material cost, standard labor cost,* and *standard overhead cost* refer to the amounts budgeted for direct materials, direct labor, and overhead in normal circumstances.

Managerial accountants, engineers, personnel administrators, and other managers combine their efforts to set the amounts of standard costs. To identify standard direct labor costs, management can conduct time and motion studies for each labor operation in the process of manufacturing a product or providing a service. From these studies, management can learn the best way to perform the operation and set the standard labor time required for the operation under normal conditions. In a similar manner, standards for materials are determined by investigating the quantity, grade, and cost of each material used. Detailed studies of machines and other productive equipment also help the company achieve greater efficiency and learn what standard overhead costs should be.

Regardless of the care exercised in setting standard costs and in revising them as conditions change, actual costs frequently differ from standard costs. These differences may result from more than one factor. For example, the actual quantity of material used may differ from standard and the price paid per unit of material also may differ from standard. Similar quantity and price differences from standard amounts can occur for labor. That is, the actual labor time and the actual labor price may vary from what was expected. Later in the chapter, you learn about factors that may cause actual overhead cost to differ from standard.

SETTING THE AMOUNTS OF STANDARD COSTS

FAST HINT
Critical Thought Question: What factors might be considered when deciding whether to revise standard costs?

VARIANCES

LO 3

Calculate material, labor, and overhead variances, and describe what each variance indicates about the performance of a company.

The differences between actual and standard costs are called **cost variances.** As you have learned, variances can be favorable or unfavorable. A variance from standard cost is considered favorable if the actual cost is less than the standard cost, and it is considered unfavorable if the actual cost is more than the standard cost.[2]

When a cost variance occurs, management should examine the circumstances to determine the factors that created it. By doing so, management should be able to identify those responsible for the variance and help them correct the problem. For example, assume that the standard material cost for producing 2,000 units of a product is $8,000, but that material costing $9,000 was actually used. The $1,000 unfavorable variance may have resulted from paying a price for the material that was higher than the standard price. Alternatively, the process may have used a greater quantity of material than standard. Or, there may have been some combination of these factors.

The purchasing department is usually responsible for the price paid for a material. Therefore, responsibility for explaining the problem rests with the purchasing manager if the variance was caused by a price higher than standard. On the other hand, the production department is usually responsible for the amount of material used. Thus, the production department manager is responsible for explaining the problem if the process used more than the standard amount of materials.

However, the production department may have used more than the standard amount of material because its quality did not meet specifications, with the result that more waste was created. Then, the purchasing manager is responsible for explaining why the inferior materials were acquired. On the other hand, the production manager is responsible for explaining what happened if the analysis shows that the waste was caused by inefficiencies.

In summary, the cost variances trigger questions. These questions call for answers that, in turn, should lead to changes designed to correct the problem and eliminate the variances for the next reporting period. A performance report may identify the existence of the problem, but it can do no more than point the direction for further investigation of what can be done to improve future results. The diagram in Illustration 24–4 shows the flow of events in this management cycle.

A major manufacturing trend of the 90s is the concept of strategic partnerships. R. D. Garwood, manufacturing consultant and author of *Shifting Paradigms— Reshaping the Future of Industry,* defines the ideal as a joint effort by the supplier and the manufacturing customer to improve the quality and the delivery to the consumer of the end product. This partnership requires trust, communication, and sharing in the financial rewards. The concept is based on the idea that there really is no sale for either partner until the product is delivered to the end user. "In practice," Garwood says, "manufacturer–vendor partnerships frequently fall short of the ideal primarily because

---

[2]Rules are seldom as simple as they seem. For example, if management spends less than the budgeted amount on maintenance or insurance, the performance report would identify the difference as a favorable variance. However, cutting these expenses could lead to major losses in the long run if the machinery wears out prematurely or the insurance coverage proves to be inadequate.

Illustration 24-4   The Variance Analysis Cycle

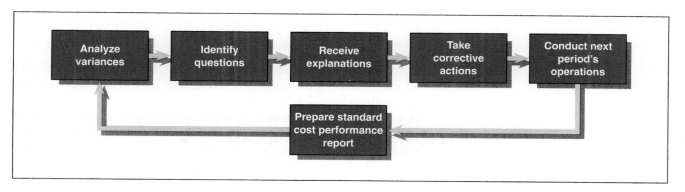

the compensation system focuses on the purchase price variance. This requires multiple suppliers and a mentality of least cost versus total benefit."[3]

Isolating Material and Labor Variances

You can break down a cost variance into components that provide more information about the factors that caused it to occur. The total materials cost or labor cost can be expressed as the following equation:

$$\text{Actual Cost} = \text{Actual Quantity} \times \text{Actual Price}$$
$$AC = AQ \times AP$$

Also, the standard cost that should have been incurred can be expressed in this formula:

$$\text{Standard Cost} = \text{Standard Quantity} \times \text{Standard Price}$$
$$SC = SQ \times SP$$

The difference between actual cost and standard cost is the cost variance, stated as:

$$\text{Cost Variance} = \text{Actual Cost} - \text{Standard Cost}$$
$$CV = AC - SC$$

We explained earlier that two factors create a cost variance: (1) a difference between the actual quantity and the standard quantity and (2) a difference between the actual price and the standard price. To assess the effects of these two factors, we can express the cost variance as the sum of the quantity variance and the price variance. The quantity variance can be calculated with this formula:

$$\text{Quantity Variance} = (\text{Actual Quantity} - \text{Standard Quantity}) \times \text{Standard Price}$$
$$QV = (AQ - SQ) \times SP$$

This amount represents the additional cost incurred because the actual quantity *(AQ)* was greater than the expected standard quantity *(SQ)*. Or, if the variance is favorable, it shows how much was saved by reducing the quantity to less than the standard amount.

---

[3]Lawrence Henry, "Marriages of Convenience," *CFO Magazine, Vol.* 7, no. 7 (July 1991).

The price variance is calculated as follows:

$$\text{Price Variance} = (\text{Actual Price} - \text{Standard Price}) \times \text{Actual Quantity}$$

$$\text{PV} = (\text{AP} - \text{SP}) \times \text{AQ}$$

This variance shows how much additional cost was incurred because the actual price was higher than standard. Or, if the variance is favorable, it shows how much the company saved by negotiating a lower price.

To illustrate cost variances, the following discussion is based on the example of the Green Company. For this example, assume that the company has established the following standard quantities for materials and labor, and these standard costs per unit for Product Z:

Direct materials (1 lb. per unit at $1 per lb.) ..	$1.00
Direct labor (1 hr. per unit at $6 per hr.)	6.00
Overhead ($2 per standard direct labor hour) ..	2.00
Total standard cost per unit	$9.00

Material Variances

During May, Green Company started and completed 3,500 units of Product Z, and used 3,600 pounds of direct materials that cost $1.05 per pound. Thus, the total material cost was $3,780. Under these facts, the actual and standard direct material costs for the 3,500 units and the direct material cost variance are:

Actual cost	3,600 lbs. @ $1.05 per lb. = $3,780
Standard cost	3,500 lbs. @ $1.00 per lb. = 3,500
Direct material cost variance (unfavorable) ..	= $ 280

Initially, it is apparent that the total variance is the combined result of using more materials than planned and buying those materials at a higher price than was anticipated.

Using the equations presented earlier, the actual cost also can be calculated as follows:

$$\text{AC} = \text{AQ} \times \text{AP}$$
$$= 3,600 \times \$1.05$$
$$= \$3,780$$

The standard cost for the 3,500 units can be calculated as follows:

$$\text{SC} = \text{SQ} \times \text{SP}$$
$$= 3,500 \times \$1.00$$
$$= \$3,500$$

Therefore, the direct material cost variance is:

$$\text{CV} = \text{AC} - \text{SC}$$
$$= \$3,780 - \$3,500$$
$$= \$280 \text{ (unfavorable)}$$

FAST HINT
Relevant Quick Study:
To apply these concepts, work
QS 24–2.

Regardless of how the information is presented, the actual direct material cost for these units is $280 greater than the standard cost. We can get dollar measures of the contributions of the factors that created this unfavorable variance by calculating a direct material quantity variance and a direct material price variance. These calculations are presented in the following table:

FAST HINT
Class Discussion:
Ask students to give examples
of a manufacturing situation in
which a favorable price variance
for a raw material might be the
cause of an unfavorable quantity
variance.

Quantity Variance:			
Actual units at standard price	3,600 lbs. @ $1.00 =	$3,600	
Standard units at standard price	3,500 lbs. @ $1.00 =	3,500	
Variance (unfavorable)	100 lbs. @ $1.00 =		$100
Price Variance:			
Actual units at actual price	3,600 lbs. @ $1.05 =	$3,780	
Actual units at standard price	3,600 lbs. @ $1.00 =	3,600	
Variance (unfavorable)	3,600 lbs. @ $0.05 =		180
Direct material cost variance (unfavorable) . .			$280

The formulas also can be used to calculate the variances in this table. Thus, the quantity variance can be calculated like this:

$$QV = (AQ - SQ) \times SP$$
$$= (3,600 - 3,500) \times \$1.00$$
$$= \$100 \text{ (unfavorable)}$$

FAST HINT
Alternative Example:
Calculate the direct material
quantity variance and the direct
material price variance if the
actual price is $0.85 per unit.

And, the price variance can be computed with this formula:

$$PV = (AP - SP) \times AQ$$
$$= (\$1.05 - \$1.00) \times 3,600$$
$$= \$180 \text{ (unfavorable)}$$

Regardless of how it is presented, the analysis shows that $100 of the excess direct material cost resulted from using 100 more pounds than standard, and $180 resulted from a unit purchase price that was $0.05 above standard. With this information, management can go to the responsible individuals for explanations. The excess usage of 100 pounds should be explained by the manager of the production department and the higher price of $1.05 needs to be explained by the manager of the purchasing department.

FAST HINT
Critical Thought Question:
Describe at least two factors
that might have caused the $100
unfavorable material quantity
variance and the $180 unfavorable material price variance.

In evaluating price variances, managers must recognize that a favorable price variance may indicate a problem with product quality. For example, **Redhook Ale,** the largest micro brewery in the Pacific Northwest, could save 10 to 15% by buying six-row barley malt instead of the better two-row from Washington's Yakima valley. "But," said David Mikelson, Redhook's chief financial officer, "why gamble? We don't cut costs when it comes to the taste and quality of our ale." Purchasing at Redhook is measured on the quality of the raw materials as well as the purchase price variance. Redhook's stand on quality is having an impact. Sales have increased more than 35% per year for five years while gross margin also increased.[4]

---

[4]Chris Barnett, "Just the Right Brew," *CFO Magazine,* Vol. 6, no. 6 (June 1992).

Labor Variances

The labor cost for a specific product or service depends on the number of hours worked (the quantity) and the wage rate paid to the employees (the price). Therefore, when actual amounts for a task differ from standard, the labor cost variance may be divided into a quantity variance and a price variance, just like the material cost variance.

For example, the direct labor standard for 3,500 units of Product Z is one hour per unit, or 3,500 hours at $6 per hour. If 3,400 hours at $6.30 per hour were actually used to complete the units, the actual and standard labor costs for these units are:

Actual cost	3,400 hrs. @ $6.30 per hr. = $21,420
Standard cost	3,500 hrs. @ $6.00 per hr. = 21,000
Direct labor cost variance (unfavorable) . .	$ 420

The actual cost is only $420 over the standard but computing the quantity and price variances reveals the following additional data:

Quantity Variance:		
Actual hours at standard price	3,400 hrs. @ $6.00 = $20,400	
Standard hours at standard price	3,500 hrs. @ $6.00 = 21,000	
Variance (favorable)	(100) hrs. @ $6.00 =	$ (600)
Price Variance:		
Actual hours at actual price	3,400 hrs. @ $6.30 = $21,420	
Actual hours at standard price	3,400 hrs. @ $6.00 = 20,400	
Variance (unfavorable)	3,400 hrs. @ $0.30 =	1,020
Direct labor cost variance (unfavorable) . .		$ 420

FAST HINT

Class Discussion:

Ask students to give specific examples of a service business in which a favorable price variance for labor might be the cause of an unfavorable quantity variance.

FAST HINT

Alternative Example:

Calculate the labor quantity variance and the labor price variance if 3,700 actual hours were used at the actual price of $5.50 per hour.

Answer: $1,200 unfavorable labor quantity variance and $1,850 favorable labor price variance.

FAST HINT

Critical Thought Question:

Explain the possible relationship between the variances identified in the preceding alternative example. If you were the production manager, what factors would you consider in deciding whether to recommend changes?

FAST HINT

Relevant Exercise:

To apply these concepts, work Exercise 24–6.

The information in this table can also be computed with the formulas. Thus, the quantity variance can be calculated as follows:

$$QV = (AQ - SQ) \times SP$$
$$= (3,400 - 3,500) \times \$6.00$$
$$= -\$600 \text{ (favorable)}$$

And, the price variance can be determined with this formula:

$$PV = (AP - SP) \times AQ$$
$$= (\$6.30 - \$6.00) \times 3,400$$
$$= \$1,020 \text{ (unfavorable)}$$

The analysis shows that a favorable quantity variance of $600 resulted from using 100 fewer direct labor hours than standard for the units produced. However, this favorable variance was more than offset by a wage rate that was $0.30 more than standard. Thus, the production manager should explain how the labor hours were reduced. (If the experience can be repeated and transferred to other departments, the savings can be multiplied.) And, the personnel administrator should explain why the wage rate was higher than expected.

One possible explanation of the factors that led to these labor variances might lie in the fact that the factory or department has workers of various skill levels. If so, it is the responsibility of the production manager to assign each task to workers with the skill level appropriate for getting it done. In this case, an investigation might show that higher skilled workers were used to produce the 3,500 units of Product Z. As a result, fewer labor hours were required for the work. However, the wage rate paid to the workers was higher than standard because of their greater skills. In Green Company's situation, the effect of this strategy was a higher than standard total cost. Thus, steps should be taken to change the strategy in the future.

When standard costs are used, the predetermined overhead rate assigns standard overhead costs to the goods or services produced during the period. The rate may be based on the relationship between standard overhead and standard labor cost, standard labor hours, standard machine hours, or some other measure of production. For example, Green Company charges its Product Z with $2 of standard overhead cost per standard direct labor hour. Because the direct labor standard for Product Z is one hour per unit, the 3,500 units manufactured in May were charged with $7,000 of standard overhead costs.

Before going on, recall that only 3,400 actual direct labor hours were used in producing these units. But, overhead costs are assigned to the units on the basis of standard labor hours, not on the basis of actual labor hours. Standard labor hours are used because the total amount of overhead charged to all units produced should equal the total expected overhead cost for the period. Thus, the total overhead costs should be assigned to the products even though less than the standard amount of labor was used in producing them. In other words, the allocated costs should not vary from the expected amount simply because the amount of direct labor used was different from expected.

Establishing Overhead Standards

Standard overhead costs, like other standard costs, are the amounts expected to occur at the projected level of operation for the planned period. Unlike direct materials and direct labor, however, overhead includes both variable and fixed cost components. As a result, the average overhead cost per unit changes as the projected volume changes. Because standard costs are budgeted costs, they must be established before the reporting period begins. Therefore, standard overhead costs are average per unit costs, based on the projected volume of output.

To establish the standard overhead cost rate for a future period, management uses the same cost structure that will be used to construct a flexible budget after the period is completed. This cost structure identifies the different overhead cost components and classifies them as variable or fixed. To produce the standard overhead rate, management must select a specific volume and predict the total overhead cost. Then, they divide this total by the allocation base to produce the standard rate. In many cases, the allocation base is the standard direct labor hours expected to be used to produce the projected volume.

Illustration 24–5 presents the overhead cost structure used in developing flexible budgets for the Green Company. It also establishes the predetermined standard overhead rate for May before the month begins. The first column lists the per unit amounts of the variable costs and the monthly amounts of fixed costs. The next four columns show the total costs expected to occur at four possible levels of output. Notice that the overhead cost per unit gets smaller as the volume increases. This result occurs because the fixed costs remain constant for the month.

In setting the standard overhead cost for May, management selects an expected volume. As indicated in Illustration 24–5, the managers of the Green Company chose the 80% level for a volume of 4,000 units. At this volume, they budgeted $8,000 for the total overhead for May. This total cost produces a $2 per unit average overhead cost. And, because the company has a standard of one direct labor hour for each unit, the predetermined standard overhead application rate for May is $2 per standard direct labor hour.

ASSIGNING STANDARD OVERHEAD COSTS TO PRODUCTS AND SERVICES

FAST HINT
Important Point to Remember:
The type of overhead costs incurred should be considered when choosing the basis for assigning overhead costs to products. Predetermined overhead rates were explained in Chapter 19.

FAST HINT
Important Point to Remember:
As explained in Chapter 22, variable costs per unit remain constant, but fixed costs per unit change inversely with changes in volume. Thus, the fixed cost per unit causes the average overhead cost per unit to change inversely with changes in volume.

Illustration 24–5

GREEN COMPANY
Possible Total Overhead Costs
For Month Ended May 31, 19X2

	Flexible Budget Amounts	Possible Production Levels (Percent of Monthly Capacity)			
		70%	80%	90%	100%
Production in units	1 unit	3,500	4,000	4,500	5,000
Factory overhead:					
Variable costs (per unit):					
Indirect labor	$0.40	$1,400	$1,600	$1,800	$2,000
Indirect materials	0.30	1,050	1,200	1,350	1,500
Power and lights	0.20	700	800	900	1,000
Maintenance	0.10	350	400	450	500
Totals	$1.00	$3,500	$4,000	$4,500	$5,000
Fixed costs (per month):					
Building rent	$1,000	$1,000	$1,000	$1,000	$1,000
Depreciation, machinery	1,200	1,200	1,200	1,200	1,200
Supervisory salaries	1,800	1,800	1,800	1,800	1,800
Totals	$4,000	$4,000	$4,000	$4,000	$4,000
Total factory overhead		$7,500	$8,000	$8,500	$9,000
Standard direct labor hours	1 hr./unit	3,500	4,000	4,500	5,000
Predetermined overhead rate per standard direct labor hour		$2.143	$2.000	$1.889	$1.800

When selecting the expected operating level for the plant, management must consider a number of factors. Theoretically, the level could be set as high as 100% of capacity, but it is almost always set at a lower level. Some factors that can cause the expected operating level to be less than full capacity include difficulties in scheduling work, equipment that is unavailable because of maintenance, and insufficient demand for the product. In addition, a good long-run management practice calls for having some plant capacity in excess of current operating needs to allow for future growth. Because of a combination of these factors, the management of the Green Company determined that the expected production level for May would be at 80% of capacity, or 4,000 units.

OVERHEAD VARIANCES

When standard costs are used, the cost accounting system applies overhead to production on the basis of the predetermined standard overhead cost rate. Then, at the end of a cost period, the difference between the total overhead cost applied to products and the total overhead cost actually incurred is called the **overhead cost variance.** Calculate this variance as follows:

Overhead Cost Variance = Actual Overhead Incurred − Standard Overhead Applied

OCV   =   AOI   −   SOA

To help management identify the factors that created the overhead cost variance, the managerial accountant can divide it into two components.[5] First, the *actual* production volume during the period may be different than the *expected* production volume used to establish the standard overhead application rate. In this case, the amount of

---

[5]It is also possible to divide the total overhead variance into three components. This three-way analysis of overhead variance is left for more advanced cost accounting courses.

overhead assigned to the product during the month is based on an assumed level of production that did not occur. Second, the *actual* overhead costs may differ from the *expected* amounts for the actual volume. In other words, two factors may cause the total difference between the allocated cost and the actual cost: (1) an inaccurate prediction of the volume of operation, and (2) actual costs that do not match the expected amounts. To describe the effects of these two factors, the total overhead cost variance is the sum of the volume variance and the controllable variance.

Volume Variance

The **volume variance** is the difference between two dollar amounts of overhead cost. The first amount equals the total overhead cost that would have been expected if the actual operating volume had been accurately predicted. The second number is the overhead cost allocated to the month's products using the predetermined standard overhead rate. Thus, the volume variance can be described with this formula:

$$\text{Volume Variance} = \begin{array}{c}\text{Overhead Budgeted at} \\ \text{the Actual Production} \\ \text{Volume Achieved}\end{array} - \text{Standard Overhead Applied}$$

$$\text{VV} = \text{OB} - \text{SOA}$$

FAST HINT
Critical Thought Question:
Is it possible to have a volume variance of zero? Explain your answer.

For example, the Green Company actually operated at 70% of capacity during May even though the expected production volume was 80% of capacity when the predetermined overhead application rate was set. From the facts shown in Illustration 24–5, we can see that the company would have budgeted only $7,500 of overhead at this volume instead of $8,000. If this volume had been predicted, the standard overhead rate would have been $2.143 per hour instead of $2.00 per hour. But, the company did produce only 3,500 units of Product Z and did assign overhead to those units at the predetermined standard rate of $2 per direct labor hour. In light of these facts, the company's volume variance for May is:

Volume Variance:

Budgeted overhead at 3,500 units	$7,500
Standard overhead applied to products (3,500 standard labor hours at the $2 per hour standard rate)	7,000
Variance (unfavorable)	$ 500

The table shows the same result as this equation:

$$\text{VV} = \text{OB} - \text{SOA}$$
$$= \$7,500 - \$7,000$$
$$= \$500 \text{ (unfavorable)}$$

In summary, the company expected to assign $8,000 of overhead to 4,000 units during May but actually assigned only $7,000 of overhead to 3,500 units.

To understand this volume variance more completely, examine the detailed amounts in Illustration 24–5 for the possible volumes of 70% and 80% of capacity. Observe that the company can subdivide the $2 per hour overhead rate at the 80% level into $1 per hour for variable overhead and $1 per hour for fixed overhead only at that level. Thus, when the $2 overhead rate was applied to the 3,500 units produced at the actual 70% level, the $1 fixed cost portion of the rate fell short by $500 in allocating the total budgeted fixed overhead cost of $4,000.

Illustration 24–6   The Overhead Volume Variance

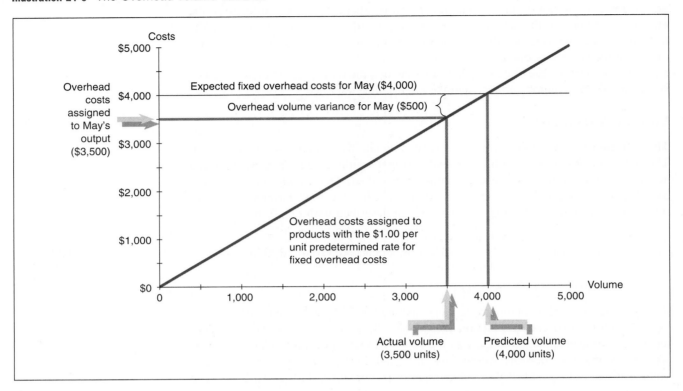

This result is shown graphically in Illustration 24–6. In the graph, the upward slop-ing line represents the amount of fixed overhead costs expected to be applied to the units produced in May. The horizontal line represents the $4,000 of total fixed costs expected for May. These two lines intersect at the planned operating volume of 4,000 units. At the 3,500 unit volume, the application line falls $500 below the budgeted overhead line. This shortfall is the volume variance.

An unfavorable volume variance simply reflects the fact that the plant did not reach its expected operating level. In every case, management would already know this re-sult, and the variance would not convey any new information. However, management still needs to answer the question of why the volume was not up to the expected level. The primary purpose of the volume variance comes from the fact that it eliminates that portion of the total variance caused by failing to meet the expected level. This allows management to focus on controlling overhead costs.

Controllable Variance

The **controllable variance** is the difference between overhead costs actually incurred and the overhead budgeted to occur at the actual operating level. This variance is cal-culated as follows:

$$\text{Controllable Variance} = \text{Actual Overhead Incurred} - \text{Overhead Budgeted at the Actual Production Volume Achieved}$$

$$\text{CV} = \text{AOI} - \text{OB}$$

For this example, the Green Company incurred $7,650 of total actual overhead cost in May. The budgeted overhead cost for this level (70% of capacity) is $7,500, as

Illustration 24-7

GREEN COMPANY
Factory Overhead Variance Report
For Month Ended May 31, 19X2

Volume Variance:

Expected production level	80% of capacity	
Production level achieved	70% of capacity	
Volume variance	$500 (unfavorable)	

Controllable Variance:

	Flexible Budget	Actual Results	Variances
Variable overhead costs:			
Indirect labor	$1,400	$1,525	$125 *U*
Indirect materials	1,050	1,025	25 *F*
Power and lights	700	750	50 *U*
Maintenance	350	350	
Total variable costs	$3,500	$3,650	$150 *U*
Fixed overhead costs:			
Building rent	$1,000	$1,000	
Depreciation, machinery	1,200	1,200	
Supervisory salaries	1,800	1,800	
Total fixed costs	$4,000	$4,000	
Total overhead costs	$7,500	$7,650	$150 *U*

F = Favorable variance
U = Unfavorable variance

shown in Illustration 24–5. The controllable overhead variance for May is the difference between these two numbers:

Controllable Variance:

Actual overhead incurred	$7,650
Overhead budgeted at operating level achieved . .	7,500
Variance (unfavorable)	$ 150

The calculation can also be made with this formula:

$$CV = AOI - OB$$
$$= \$7,650 - \$7,500$$
$$= \$150 \text{ (unfavorable)}$$

The controllable overhead variance shows how well management controlled the total overhead cost (particularly the variable components) at the actual operating level. Management exceeded the budget by $150 at the actual 70% level.

A complete overhead variance report provides managers with more detailed information about the specific overhead costs and how they differed from the budgeted amounts. In Illustration 24–7, the May overhead variance report for Green Company shows that the fixed costs and maintenance cost occurred as expected. However, the costs for indirect labor and power and lights were higher than expected at the actual volume. And, the indirect materials cost was slightly less than the expected amount.

FAST HINT
Relevant Quick Study:
To apply these concepts, work QS 24–4.

Combining the Volume and Controllable Variances

The total overhead variance was measured earlier at $650. This amount equals the sum of the volume and controllable variances:

$$\text{Overhead Cost Variance} = \text{Volume Variance} + \text{Controllable Variance}$$

$$\text{OCV} \quad = \quad \text{VV} \quad + \quad \text{CV}$$

You can also combine the volume and controllable variances as shown in this table:

Volume Variance:			
Overhead budgeted at operating level achieved		$7,500	
Standard overhead applied to production (3,500 standard hours at $2 per hour)		7,000	
Variance (unfavorable)			$500
Controllable Variance:			
Actual overhead incurred		$7,650	
Overhead budgeted at actual operating level		7,500	
Variance (unfavorable)			150
Overhead Cost Variance—Actual overhead incurred in excess of overhead charged to production—(unfavorable)			$650

Progress Check

24-6 The following information is available for York Company:

Actual hours worked per unit	2.5
Standard direct labor hours per unit	2.0
Actual production (units)	2,500
Budgeted production (units)	3,000
Actual price per hour	$3.10
Standard cost per hour	$3.00

The direct labor quantity variance is: *(a)* $3,750 U; *(b)* $3,750 F; *(c)* $3,875 U; *(d)* $3,875 F.

24-7 Refer to Progress Check 24-6. The direct labor price variance is: *(a)* $500 U; *(b)* $500 F; *(c)* $625 F; *(d)* $625 U.

24-8 What is a cost variance?

24-9 If the material quantity variance is favorable and the material price variance is unfavorable, can the total material cost variance be favorable?

24-10 Under what conditions is the overhead volume variance considered to be favorable?

USING STANDARD COSTS TO CONTROL A BUSINESS

LO 4

Explain how standard cost accounting information is useful for the technique of management by exception.

To control business activities, top management must be able to influence the actions of the lower-level managers responsible for the company's revenues, costs, and expenses. After a budget is prepared and standard costs are established, management should take appropriate action to gain control when actual costs differ from the standard or budgeted amounts.

Reports like the ones in this chapter call management's attention to variances from business plans and other standards. When managers use these reports to focus on problem areas, the budgeting process contributes to the control function. As a matter of efficiency in using the budget performance reports, management should practice the analytical technique known as **management by exception.** Under this approach, managers focus on the most significant variances and give less attention to the areas where performance is close enough to the standard to be satisfactory. In effect, management concentrates on the exceptional or irregular situations and defers dealing with areas showing actual results that are reasonably close to the plan.

As a Matter of Ethics

You are an internal auditor looking into your company's procedures for comparing actual results with budgeted amounts. You notice that for several years running, one manager (who has managed several different departments over the years) always spends exactly what is budgeted for discretionary supplies and small items of equipment.

Looking into the records further, you find that 25 to 35% of the annual budget for these items has been spent by this manager in November and December, right before the end of the budget year. An interview with the manager reveals that he always spends what is budgeted, whether or not the supplies and equipment are really needed. He offers three reasons to justify his actions. First,

he doesn't want his budget to be cut back and thinks it will be if he doesn't spend all that he is allocated. Second, the company's practice of following management by exception calls attention to big deviations from the budget, and he would just as soon avoid that kind of attention. Third, he feels that the practice doesn't hurt anyone because the money was budgeted to be spent.

Although there is some logic in the manager's actions and explanation, you wonder whether you should comment on this matter in your report. You also wonder what recommendations, if any, you should offer.

Managers of many companies use standard costs and variance analysis only for manufacturing costs. In these cases, the master budget includes selling and general and administrative expenses, but subsequent control over these expenses is not based on standard costs and variances. However, managers of other companies recognize that standard costs and variances can help them control their nonmanufacturing expenses. In addition, companies that provide services to customers (instead of products) can use standard costs. The previous uses of variances can be easily adapted to these nonmanufacturing situations.

USING STANDARD COSTS FOR SERVICE AND OTHER NON-MANUFACTURING ACTIVITIES

FAST HINT
Additional Insight:
Hospitals use standard costs to help them control their expenses. Standard costs can be used as a basis for budgeting throughout a hospital.

Progress Check

24-11 To use management by exception with standard costs:
a. A company must record standard costs in its accounts.
b. Variances from flexible budget amounts should be calculated to allow management to focus its attention on significant differences between actual and budgeted performance.
c. Only variances for direct materials and direct labor should be analyzed.

As shown in this chapter, companies use standard costs in management reports. Most standard cost systems also record the costs and the variances in the accounts. This practice simplifies record-keeping and helps the managerial accountant prepare the reports more easily. You do not need a detailed knowledge of standard cost accounting practices to be able to understand standard costs and how they are used. However, you should know how to interpret accounts in which standard costs and variances have been recorded. The following entries briefly illustrate the process for Green Company's standard costs and variances for May.

The first entry records the standard materials cost incurred in May in the Goods in Process Inventory account. This part of the entry should be familiar from your prior study of cost accounting. Notice that the amount of the debit equals the standard cost ($3,500) instead of the actual cost ($3,780). The entry credits Raw Materials Inventory for the actual cost. The difference between the standard and actual costs is recorded with debits to two separate materials variance accounts. Both the material quantity variance and material price variance are recorded as debits because they represent additional costs greater than the standard cost. This treatment also reflects the fact that they are unfavorable because they represent higher costs and lower net income.

STANDARD COSTS IN THE ACCOUNTS

LO 5
Prepare journal entries to record standard costs and to account for price and quantity variances.

May	31	Goods in Process Inventory	3,500.00	
		Direct Material Quantity Variance	100.00	
		Direct Material Price Variance	180.00	
		Raw Materials Inventory		3,780.00
		To charge production for the standard quantity of materials used (3,500 pounds) at the standard price ($1 per pound) and to record the direct material quantity and price variances.		

The next entry debits the Goods in Process Inventory account for the standard labor cost of the goods manufactured during May ($21,000) instead of the actual cost ($21,420). The actual cost is recorded with a credit to the Factory Payroll account. The difference between the standard and actual costs is explained by two variances. The direct labor price variance is unfavorable and is debited to an account with that name. The direct labor quantity variance, which was favorable, is credited.

May	31	Goods in Process Inventory	21,000.00	
		Direct Labor Price Variance	1,020.00	320.00
		Direct Labor Quantity Variance		600.00
		Factory Payroll		21,420.00
		To charge production with 3,500 standard hours of direct labor at the standard $6 per hour rate and to record the direct labor quantity and price variances.		

The direct labor quantity variance is favorable because it represents a lower cost and a higher net income.

The next entry assigns the standard predetermined overhead to the cost of the goods manufactured during the period. It debits the predetermined amount ($7,000) to the Goods in Process Inventory account instead of the actual cost ($7,650). To account for the difference, the entry includes a debit of $500 to the Volume Variance account and a $150 debit to the Controllable Variance account.

May	31	Goods in Process Inventory	7,000.00	
		Volume Variance	500.00	
		Controllable Variance	150.00	
		Factory Overhead		7,650.00
		To apply overhead at the standard rate of $2 per standard direct labor hour (3,500 hours) and to record overhead variances.		

FAST HINT
Relevant Exercise:
To apply these concepts, work Exercise 24–9.

The balances of these six separate variance accounts accumulate until the end of the accounting period. Thus, unfavorable variances of some months offset against favorable variances of others. Then, because these amounts represent the results of events during the year, their balances must be closed at the end of the year. Because their balances represent differences between actual and standard costs, they must be added to or subtracted from the manufacturing costs recorded during the year. By doing so, the recorded manufacturing costs equal the actual costs incurred during the year. The company must use these actual amounts in external financial statements prepared in accordance with generally accepted accounting principles. If the variances are material, they need to be added to or subtracted from the balances of the Goods in Process Inventory, the Finished Goods Inventory, and the Cost of Goods Sold accounts. If the amounts are immaterial, they are typically added to or subtracted from the balance of the Cost of Goods Sold account.[6]

Progress Check

24-12   Carlo Company uses a standard cost system. Prepare the journal entry that records these material variances:

Direct material cost actually incurred	$73,200
Direct material quantity variance (favorable) . .	3,800
Direct material price variance (unfavorable) . .	1,300

24-13   If standard manufacturing costs are recorded in the accounts, how are the recorded variances treated at the end of an accounting period?

SUMMARY OF THE CHAPTER IN TERMS OF LEARNING OBJECTIVES

LO 1.   Describe the differences between and relative advantages of fixed budgets and flexible budgets and be able to prepare a flexible budget. A fixed budget shows the revenues, costs, and expenses expected to occur at the specified production and sales volume. Therefore, if the actual production and sales volume is at some other level, the amounts in the fixed budget do not provide a reasonable basis for evaluating actual performance. A flexible budget expresses variable costs in per unit terms so that it can be used to develop budgeted amounts for any production and sales volume within the relevant range. As a result, managers calculate budgeted amounts after a period for the volume that actually occurred. This budget is more useful in evaluating the actual performance.

LO 2.   State what standard costs represent, how they are determined, and how they are used by management to evaluate performance. Standard costs are the normal costs that should be incurred to produce a product or perform a service. As such, they are the amounts that should be budgeted ahead of time and used in evaluations. Standard costs should be based on a careful examination of the processes used to produce a product or perform a service and the quantities and prices that should be incurred in carrying out those processes. On a performance report, these standard costs (which are really flexible budget amounts) are compared to actual costs and the differences are presented as variances. The variances suggest areas for management attention and possible corrective action.

LO 3.   Calculate material, labor, and overhead variances, and describe what each variance indicates about the performance of a company. Material and labor cost variances are the differences between the actual costs incurred and the budgeted costs. These total cost variances can be broken into quantity variances and price variances to direct management's attention to the actions of the lower-level managers responsible for quantities used or prices paid. The overhead cost variance is the difference between actual overhead incurred and overhead applied to the output produced in the period. This total variance can be broken into a volume variance and a controllable variance. The volume variance occurs because the standard overhead application rate is applied to an actual volume that differs from the expected or budgeted volume. The controllable variance is the difference between actual overhead incurred and the overhead that should have been incurred at the actual volume achieved during the period.

---

[6]This process is similar to the one demonstrated in Chapter 19 for eliminating an underapplied or overapplied balance in the Factory Overhead account.

LO 4. Explain how standard cost accounting information is useful for the technique of management by exception. Standard cost accounting provides management with information about costs that differ from budgeted amounts. Performance reports disclose the costs or areas of operations that have significant variances from normal or budgeted amounts. This disclosure of differences from expected levels allows managers to devote their attention to the exceptions and pay less attention to areas in which operations are proceeding normally.

LO 5. Prepare journal entries to record standard costs and to account for price and quantity variances. When a company records standard costs in its accounts, the standard costs of materials, labor, and overhead are debited to the Goods in Process Inventory account. Based on an analysis of the material, labor, and overhead costs, each quantity variance, price variance, volume variance, and controllable variance is recorded in a separate account. At the end of the period, if the variances are material, they are allocated among the balances of the Goods in Process Inventory, Finished Goods Inventory, and Cost of Goods Sold accounts. If they are not material, they may be simply debited or credited to the Cost of Goods Sold account.

DEMONSTRATION PROBLEM

The Gregory Company provides the following information about its budgeted and actual results for April 19X2. Although the expected volume for April was 25,000 units produced and sold, the company actually produced and sold 27,000 units.

Budget data—25,000 units (asterisks identify factory overhead items):

Selling price	$5.00 per unit
Variable costs (per unit of output):	
Direct materials	1.24 per unit
Direct labor	1.50 per unit
*Factory supplies	0.25 per unit
*Utilities	0.50 per unit
Selling costs	0.40 per unit
Fixed costs (per month):	
*Depreciation of machinery	$3,750
*Depreciation of building	2,500
General liability insurance	1,200
Property taxes on office equipment	500
Other administrative expense	750

Actual results during April—27,000 units produced:

Selling price (per unit of output)	$5.23 per unit
Variable costs (per unit of output):	
Direct materials	1.12 per unit
Direct labor	1.40 per unit
*Factory supplies	0.37 per unit
*Utilities	0.60 per unit
Selling costs	0.34 per unit
Fixed costs (per month):	
*Depreciation of machinery	$3,710
*Depreciation of building	2,500
General liability insurance	1,250
Property taxes on office equipment	485
Other administrative expense	900

Standard manufacturing costs based on expected output of 25,000 units:

	Per Unit of Output	Quantity to Be Used	Total Cost
Direct materials, 4 oz. @ $0.31/oz.	$1.24/unit	100,000 oz.	$31,000
Direct labor, 0.25 hrs. @ $6.00/hr.	1.50/unit	6,250 hrs.	37,500
Overhead	1.00/unit		25,000

Actual costs incurred to produce 27,000 units:

	Per Unit of Output	Quantity Used	Total Cost
Direct materials, 4 oz. @ $0.28/oz.	$1.12/unit	108,000 oz.	$30,240
Direct labor, 0.20 hrs. @ $7.00/hr.	1.40/unit	5,400 hrs.	37,800
Overhead	1.20/unit		32,400

If standards had been based on an expected output of 27,000 units, standard manufacturing costs would have been:

	Per Unit of Output	Quantity to Be Used	Total Cost
Direct materials, 4 oz. @ $0.31/oz.	$1.24/unit	108,000 oz.	$33,480
Direct labor, 0.25 hrs. @ $6.00/hr.	1.50/unit	6,750 hrs.	40,500
Overhead			26,500

Required

1. Develop possible flexible budgets for April showing expected revenues, costs, and income under assumptions of 20,000, 25,000, and 30,000 units of output made and sold.

2. Prepare a performance report that contrasts the actual results with the amounts that would have been budgeted if the actual volume had been expected.

3. Present variance analyses for direct materials, direct labor, and manufacturing overhead.

- Prepare a table showing the expected results at the three specified possible levels of output. Compute the variable costs by multiplying the per unit variable costs by the expected volumes. Include fixed costs at the given amounts. Combine the amounts in the table to show the total variable costs, the total contribution margin, total fixed costs, and income from operations.

- Prepare another table that shows the actual results and the amounts that should have been incurred at 27,000 units. Show any differences in the third column, and label them with either an F for favorable if they increase income or a U for unfavorable if they decrease income.

- Using the table format from the chapter, compute these total variances and the individual variances:

  - Total materials variance (including the direct materials quantity variance and the direct materials price variance).

  - Total direct labor variance (including the direct labor quantity variance and the direct labor price variance).

  - Total overhead variance (including the overhead volume variance and the overhead controllable variance).

Planning the Solution

Solution to Demonstration Problem

1. Flexible budgets:

	20,000 Units	25,000 Units	30,000 Units
Sales	$100,000	$125,000	$150,000
Variable costs:			
Direct materials	$ 24,800	$ 31,000	$ 37,200
Direct labor	30,000	37,500	45,000
Factory supplies	5,000	6,250	7,500
Utilities	10,000	12,500	15,000
Selling costs	8,000	10,000	12,000
Total variable costs	$ 77,800	$ 97,250	$116,700
Contribution margin	$ 22,200	$ 27,750	$ 33,300
Fixed costs:			
Depreciation of machinery	$ 3,750	$ 3,750	$ 3,750
Depreciation of building	2,500	2,500	2,500
General liability insurance	1,200	1,200	1,200
Property taxes on office equipment	500	500	500
Other administrative expense	750	750	750
Total fixed costs	$ 8,700	$ 8,700	$ 8,700
Income from operations	$ 13,500	$ 19,050	$ 24,600

2.

THE GREGORY COMPANY
Flexible Budget Performance Report
For Month of April 19X2

	Flexible Budget	Actual Results	Variance
Sales (27,000 units)	$135,000	$141,210	$ 6,210 F
Variable costs:			
Direct materials	$ 33,480	$ 30,240	$ 3,240 F
Direct labor	40,500	37,800	2,700 F
Factory supplies	6,750	9,990	3,240 U
Utilities	13,500	16,200	2,700 U
Selling costs	10,800	9,180	1,620 F
Total variable costs	$105,030	$103,410	$ 1,620 F
Contribution margin	$ 29,970	$ 37,800	$ 7,830 F
Fixed costs:			
Depreciation of machinery	$ 3,750	$ 3,710	$ 40 F
Depreciation of building	2,500	2,500	
General liability insurance	1,200	1,250	50 U
Property taxes on office equipment	500	485	15 F
Other administrative expense	750	900	150 U
Total fixed costs	$ 8,700	$ 8,845	$ 145 U
Income from operations	$ 21,270	$ 28,955	$ 7,685 F

F = Favorable variance
U = Unfavorable variance

3.   Variance analyses of manufacturing costs:

Material variances:

Actual cost	108,000 oz. @ $0.28	$30,240
Standard cost	108,000 oz. @ $0.31	33,480
Direct material cost variance (favorable)		$ (3,240)

Quantity variance:

Actual units at standard price	108,000 oz. @ $0.31	$33,480
Standard units at standard price	108,000 oz. @ $0.31	33,480
Variance (none)		$ –0–

Price variance:

Actual units at actual price	108,000 oz. @ $0.28	$30,240
Actual units at standard price	108,000 oz. @ $0.31	33,480
Variance (favorable)	108,000 oz. @ ($0.03)	(3,240)
Direct material cost variance (favorable)		$ (3,240)

Labor variances:

Actual cost	5,400 hrs. @ $7.00	$37,800
Standard cost	6,750 hrs. @ $6.00	40,500
Direct labor cost variance (favorable)		$ 2,700

Quantity variance:

Actual hours at standard price	5,400 hrs. @ $6.00	$32,400
Standard hours at standard price	6,750 hrs. @ $6.00	40,500
Variance (favorable)	(1,350) hrs. @ $6.00	$ (8,100)

Price variance:

Actual hours at actual price	5,400 hrs. @ $7.00	$37,800
Actual hours at standard price	5,400 hrs. @ $6.00	32,400
Variance (unfavorable)	5,400 hrs. @ $1.00	5,400
Direct labor cost variance (favorable)		$ (2,700)

Overhead variances:

Total overhead cost incurred	27,000 units @ $1.20	$32,400
Total overhead applied	27,000 units @ $1.00	27,000
Overhead cost variance (unfavorable)		$ 5,400

Volume variance:

Budgeted overhead at 27,000 units	$26,500
Standard overhead applied to production	
(27,000 units @ $1.00 per unit rate)	27,000
Variance (favorable)	$ (500)

Controllable variance:

Actual overhead incurred	$32,400
Overhead budgeted at operating level achieved	26,500
Variance (unfavorable)	5,900
Total overhead variance (unfavorable)	$ 5,400

GLOSSARY

Controllable variance   the difference between the overhead costs that were actually incurred and the overhead budgeted at the actual operating level. p. 932

Cost variance   the difference between the actual incurred cost and the standard amount. p. 924

Fixed budget   a planning budget based on a single predicted amount of sales or production volume; unsuitable for evaluations if the actual volume differs from the predicted volume. p. 918

Flexible budget   a budget prepared after an operating period is complete in order to help managers evaluate past performance; uses fixed and variable costs in determining total costs. p. 919

Flexible budget performance report   an internal report that helps management analyze the difference between actual performance and budgeted performance based on the actual sales volume (or other level of activity); presents the differences between actual and budgeted amounts as variances. p. 921

Historical costs   dollar amounts paid by the business in past transactions. p. 922

Management by exception   an analytical technique used by management to focus on the most significant variances and give less attention to the areas where performance is satisfactory. p. 934

Overhead cost variance the difference between the actual overhead incurred during a period and the standard overhead applied to products. p. 930

Performance report an internal report that compares actual cost and revenue amounts with budgeted amounts and identifies the differences between them as favorable or unfavorable variances. p. 918

Price variance a difference between actual and budgeted revenue or cost caused by the difference between the actual price per unit and the budgeted price per unit. p. 922

Quantity variance the difference between actual and budgeted revenue or cost caused by the difference between the actual number of units sold or used and the budgeted number of units. p. 922

Standard costs the costs that should be incurred under normal conditions to produce a specific product (or component) or to perform a specific service. p. 922

Variance analysis a process of examining the differences between actual and budgeted revenues or costs and describing them in terms of the amounts that resulted from price and quantity differences. p. 922

Volume variance the difference between the total overhead cost that would have been expected if the actual operating volume had been accurately predicted and the amount of overhead cost that was allocated to products using the predetermined standard overhead rate. p. 931

QUESTIONS

1. What limits the usefulness of fixed budget performance reports?

2. In what sense can a variable cost be considered to be constant?

3. What type of analysis does a flexible budget performance report help management make?

4. What is a price variance? What is a quantity variance?

5. What is the purpose of using standard costs?

6. What department is usually responsible for a direct material price variance? What department is usually responsible for a direct material quantity variance?

7. What is the predetermined standard overhead rate? How is it created?

8. In a two-way analysis of the overhead variance, what is the volume variance?

9. In a two-way analysis of the overhead variance, what is the controllable variance and what creates it?

10. If a company is budgeted to operate at 80% of capacity and actually operates at 84% of capacity, what effect will the 4% excess have on the controllable variance?

11. If a company's overhead costs consisted of only variable costs and the actual sales volume was 5% lower than the budgeted sales volume, what kind of volume variance would the company experience?

12. What is the relationship among standard costs, variance analysis, and management by exception?

13. Suppose that Federal Express has a standard fuel cost for a particular flight from an outlying location into its sorting facility in Memphis. List several factors that might cause the actual cost incurred to vary from the standard.

14. Would a flexible budget be useful for a movie-making project conducted by The Walt Disney Company? Would a flexible budget be useful for one of its amusement parks?

QUICK STUDY (Five-Minute Exercises)

QS 24–1
(LO 1)

Milestone Company showed the following results for May:

Sales (150,000 units)	$1,275,000
Variable costs	712,500
Fixed costs	275,400

For this level of production, sales were budgeted to be $1,350,000, variable costs, $750,000, and fixed costs, $275,400.

Prepare a flexible budget performance report for May.

QS 24–2
(LO 2, 3)

Clawson Company's output for the period required a standard direct material cost of $150,000. During the period, the direct material variances included a favorable price variance of $9,000 and a favorable quantity variance of $3,705. What was the actual total direct materials cost for the period?

Neely Company's output for the period had an unfavorable direct labor price variance of $26,220 and an unfavorable direct labor quantity variance of $7,108. The goods produced during the period required a standard direct labor cost of $342,200. What was the actual total direct labor cost incurred during the period?

QS 24–3
(LO 2, 3)

Hammond Company's output for the period had a favorable overhead volume variance of $30,000 and an unfavorable overhead controllable variance of $50,400. Standard overhead charged to production during the period amounted to $225,000. What was the actual total overhead cost incurred during the period?

QS 24–4
(LO 2, 3)

During a recent period, Holloway Company's manufacturing operations experienced a favorable price variance of $12,000 on its direct materials usage. The actual price per pound of material was $77.00 while the standard price was $77.80. How many pounds of material were used during the period?

QS 24–5
(LO 2, 3)

Explain the concept of management by exception and the reason why standard costs assist managers in applying this concept.

QS 24–6
(LO 5)

Refer to the information presented in QS 24–4. Hammond records standard costs in its accounts. Prepare the journal entry to charge overhead costs to the Goods in Process Inventory account and to record the variances.

QS 24–7
(LO 5)

EXERCISES

A company manufactures and sells bicycles. It normally operates eight hours a day, five days per week. On the basis of this general information, classify each of the following costs as fixed or variable. If certain facts would affect your choice, describe at least one reason that would cause you to change your conclusion.

Exercise 24–1
Classifying costs as fixed or variable
(LO 1)

a. Management salaries.
b. Direct labor.
c. Screws.
d. Repair expense for power tools.
e. Wheels.
f. Incoming shipping expenses.

g. Natural gas used for heating.
h. Depreciation on power tools.
i. Insurance on property.
j. Pension cost.
k. Office supplies.

Stockton Company prepared the following fixed budget for the first quarter of 19X2:

Exercise 24–2
Preparing a flexible budget
(LO 1)

Sales (10,000 units)		$2,000,000
Cost of goods sold:		
Direct materials	$640,000	
Direct labor	340,000	
Production supplies	264,000	
Plant manager's salary	30,000	(1,274,000)
Gross profit		$ 726,000
Selling expenses:		
Sales commissions	$160,000	
Packaging	210,000	
Advertising	100,000	(470,000)
Administrative expenses:		
Administrative salaries	$ 60,000	
Depreciation, office equipment	30,000	
Insurance	18,000	
Office rent	12,000	(120,000)
Income from operations		$ 136,000

Following the format of Illustration 24–2, prepare a schedule that shows the amounts of the variable costs per unit and the fixed costs per quarter and three possible flexible budgets for sales volumes of 7,500, 10,000, and 12,500 units.

Exercise 24–3
Analysis of fixed budget performance report
(LO 1)

Shank Company's fixed budget performance report for a recent month shows this information:

	Fixed Budget	Actual Results	Variance
Unit sales	8,400	10,800	
Sales	$693,000	$891,000	$198,000 F
Expenses	480,000	586,200	106,200 U
Income from operations	$213,000	$304,800	$ 91,800 F

The budgeted expenses of $480,000 included $420,000 of variable expenses and $60,000 of fixed expenses. The actual expenses included $57,000 of fixed expenses.

Prepare a flexible budget performance report that shows any variances between the budgeted results and the actual results. (List the fixed and variable expenses separately.)

Exercise 24–4
Analysis of fixed budget performance report
(LO 1)

Bolado Company's fixed budget performance report for a recent month shows this information:

	Fixed Budget	Actual Results	Variance
Unit sales	6,000	4,800	
Sales	$480,000	$422,400	$57,600 U
Expenses	440,000	394,000	46,000 F
Income from operations	$ 40,000	$ 28,400	$11,600 U

The budgeted expenses of $440,000 included $300,000 of variable expenses and $140,000 of fixed expenses. The actual expenses included $130,000 of fixed expenses.

Prepare a flexible budget performance report that shows any variances between the budgeted results and the actual results. (List the fixed and variable expenses separately.)

Exercise 24–5
Direct material variances
(LO 2, 3)

Rafferty Company has just finished making 6,000 bookshelves using 93,000 board feet of wood that cost $567,300. The company's direct material standards for one bookshelf are 15 board feet of wood at $6.50 per board foot.

Required

Measure the direct material variances incurred in manufacturing these bookshelves.

Exercise 24–6
Direct labor variances
(LO 2, 3)

After evaluating Longhorn Company's manufacturing process, management decided to establish standards of 1.2 hours of direct labor per unit of product, and $12.00 per hour for the labor rate.

During October, the company used 4,650 hours of direct labor at a total cost of $56,265 to produce 4,000 units of product. In November, the company used 6,060 hours of direct labor at a total cost of $74,235 to produce 5,000 units of product.

Calculate the quantity variance, the price variance, and the total direct labor cost variance for each of these two months.

Exercise 24–7
Calculating volume and controllable variances
(LO 3)

Cypress Company expected to operate last month at 80% of its productive capacity of 50,000 units per month. At this planned level, the company expected to use 40,000 standard hours of direct labor. The overhead is allocated to products using a predetermined standard rate based on direct labor hours. At the 80% level of operation, the total budgeted cost includes $100,000 of fixed overhead cost and $124,000 of variable overhead cost.

During the month, the company actually incurred $199,300 of overhead while producing 38,400 units of product. Find the overhead volume variance, the overhead controllable variance, and the total overhead variance.

Darwin Company established the following standard costs for one unit of its product for a recent month:

Direct material (20 lbs. @ $2.50 per lb.)	$ 50.00
Direct labor (15 hrs. @ $8.00 per hr.)	120.00
Factory overhead (15 hrs. @ $3.00 per hr.)	45.00
Standard cost	$215.00

The $3 overhead rate per direct labor hour is based on an expected operating level equal to 75% of the factory's capacity of 50,000 units per month. The following monthly flexible budget information applies to the situation:

	Operating Levels		
	70%	75%	80%
Budgeted output (units)	35,000	37,500	40,000
Budgeted labor (standard hours)	525,000	562,500	600,000
Budgeted overhead:			
Variable overhead	$1,312,500	$1,406,250	$1,500,000
Fixed overhead	281,250	281,250	281,250
Total overhead	$1,593,750	$1,687,500	$1,781,250

During the past month, the company operated at 70% of capacity and incurred the following actual overhead costs:

Variable overhead costs	$1,267,500
Fixed overhead costs	285,000
Total overhead costs	$1,552,500

Required

1. Show how the company calculated the predetermined overhead application rate of $3 per hour.

2. Calculate the overhead volume variance, the overhead controllable variance, and the total overhead variance.

Refer to the facts in Exercise 24–5 in working this exercise.

Rafferty Company records standard costs in its accounts. Thus, it records its material variances in separate accounts when it assigns raw materials costs to the Goods in Process Inventory account.

Exercise 24–9
Recording material variances
in the accounts
(LO 5)

Required

1. Show the general journal entry that would be made to charge the direct materials costs to the Goods in Process Inventory account and to record the material variances in their accounts.

2. Assume that the material variances created by the facts in Exercise 24–5 were the only variances accumulated in the accounting period and that they are not considered material. Show the adjusting journal entry that would be made to close the variance accounts at the end of the period.

PROBLEMS

Danka Company's master budget for 19X2 included the following budgeted income statement. It was based on an expected production and sales volume of 20,000 units.

Problem 24–1
Preparing and using
a flexible budget
(LO 1)

DANKA COMPANY
Fixed Budget
For Year Ended December 31, 19X2

Sales		$3,080,000
Cost of goods sold:		
Direct materials	$1,180,000	
Direct labor	260,000	
Machinery repairs (variable cost)	57,200	
Depreciation of plant (annual)	240,000	
Utilities (variable cost is 25%)	200,000	
Supervisory salaries	140,000	(2,077,200)
Gross profit		$1,002,800
Selling expenses:		
Packaging	$ 60,000	
Shipping	116,000	
Sales salary (a fixed annual amount)	180,000	(356,000)
General and administrative expenses:		
Insurance expense	$ 80,800	
Salaries	241,600	
Rent expense	108,400	(430,800)
Income from operations		$ 216,000

Required

CHECK FIGURE:
Budgeted income at 24,000
units, $487,360

1. Classify the items in the fixed budget as variable or fixed and determine their amounts per unit or for the year, as appropriate.

2. Prepare one schedule showing two possible flexible budgets for the company for sales and production volumes of 18,000 and 24,000 units.

3. A consultant has suggested that business conditions are improving. One possible effect could be a sales volume of approximately 28,000 units. The president of the company is confident that this volume is within the relevant range of existing capacity. How much would operating income increase over the 19X2 budgeted amount if this level could be reached without having to increase capacity?

4. The consultant's report also describes the possibility of an unfavorable change, in which case production and sales volume for 19X2 could fall to 14,000 units. How much income from operations would occur if the volume falls to this level?

Problem 24–2
Flexible budget performance report
(LO 1)

Refer to the facts in Problem 24–1 in working this problem. Danka Company's actual statement of income for 19X2 follows:

DANKA COMPANY
Statement of Income from Operations
For Year Ended December 31, 19X2

Sales (24,000 units)		$3,840,000
Cost of goods sold:		
Direct materials	$1,400,000	
Direct labor	360,000	
Machinery repairs (variable cost)	46,400	
Depreciation of plant (annual)	240,000	
Utilities (fixed cost is $154,000)	218,000	
Supervisory salaries	150,000	(2,414,400)
Gross profit		$1,425,600
Selling expenses:		
Packaging	$ 84,000	
Shipping	124,000	
Sales salary (annual)	182,000	(390,000)
General and administrative expenses:		
Insurance expense	$ 104,000	
Salaries	232,000	
Rent expense	108,000	(444,000)
Income from operations		$ 591,600

Required

Preparation component:

1. Using the flexible budget prepared for Problem 24–1, present a flexible budget performance report for 19X2.

Analysis component:

2. Explain the sales variance and the direct materials variance.

Luna Company established the following standard unit costs for its single product:

Direct material (32 lbs. @ $3.50 per lb.)	$112.00
Direct labor (8 hrs. @ $7.00 per hr.)	56.00
Factory overhead (8 hrs. @ $9.00 per hr.)	72.00
Total standard cost	$240.00

The overhead rate was based on an expectation that the operating volume would equal 80% of the productive capacity of 60,000 units per quarter. The following additional flexible budget information is available:

	Operating Levels		
	70%	**80%**	**90%**
Production in units	42,000	48,000	54,000
Standard direct labor hours	336,000	384,000	432,000
Budgeted overhead:			
Fixed factory overhead	$2,000,000	$2,000,000	$2,000,000
Variable factory overhead	1,274,000	1,456,000	1,638,000

During a recent quarter, the company actually operated at 70% of capacity and produced 42,000 units of product. These units were assigned the following standard costs:

Direct material (1,344,000 lbs. @ $3.50 per lb.)	$ 4,704,000
Direct labor (336,000 hrs. @ $7.00 per hr.)	2,352,000
Factory overhead (336,000 hrs. @ $9.00 per hr.)	3,024,000
Total standard cost	$10,080,000

Actual costs incurred during the quarter were:

Direct material (1,360,000 lbs. @ $ 3.25)	$ 4,420,000
Direct labor (352,000 hrs. @ $6.75)	2,376,000
Fixed factory overhead costs	1,960,000
Variable factory overhead costs	1,300,000
Total actual costs	$10,056,000

Required

1. Compute the total direct material cost variance and the price and quantity variances.
2. Compute the total direct labor cost variance and the price and quantity variances.
3. Compute the total overhead cost variance and the volume and controllable variances.

Mila Company has established the following standard costs per unit for the product it manufactures:

Direct material (10 lbs. @ $3.00 per lb.)	$30.00
Direct labor (4 hrs. @ $6.00 per hr.)	24.00
Overhead (4 hrs. @ $2.50 per hr.)	10.00
Total standard cost	$64.00

The overhead rate was based on an expectation that the operating volume would equal 80% of the productive capacity of 10,000 units per month. The following additional flexible budget information is available:

	Operating Levels		
	70%	80%	90%
Production in units	7,000	8,000	9,000
Standard direct labor hours	28,000	32,000	36,000
Budgeted overhead:			
Variable costs:			
Indirect materials	$ 8,750	$10,000	$11,250
Indirect labor	14,000	16,000	18,000
Power	3,500	4,000	4,500
Maintenance	1,750	2,000	2,250
Total variable costs	$28,000	$32,000	$36,000
Fixed costs:			
Rent of factory building ...	$12,000	$12,000	$12,000
Depreciation, machinery ...	20,000	20,000	20,000
Taxes and insurance	2,400	2,400	2,400
Supervisory salaries	13,600	13,600	13,600
Total fixed costs	$48,000	$48,000	$48,000
Total overhead costs	$76,000	$80,000	$84,000

During August, the company operated at 90% of capacity and produced 9,000 units. The following actual costs were incurred:

Direct material (92,000 lbs. @ $2.95 per lb.) ..		$271,400
Direct labor (37,600 hrs. @ $6.05 per hr.)		227,480
Overhead costs:		
Indirect materials	$10,000	
Indirect labor	16,000	
Power	4,500	
Maintenance	3,000	
Rent of factory building	12,000	
Depreciation, machinery	19,200	
Taxes and insurance	3,000	
Supervisory salaries	14,000	81,700
Total costs		$580,580

Required

1. Compute the direct material variances, including the quantity and price variances.

2. Compute the direct labor variances, including the quantity and price variances.

3. Prepare a factory overhead variance report that shows the total volume and controllable variances.

4. Prepare a detailed factory overhead variance report (like Illustration 24–7) that shows the variances for the individual items of overhead.

CHECK FIGURE:
Total overhead controllable variance, $2,300 favorable

Problem 24–5
Flexible budget, variance analysis, and report for overhead costs
(LO 1, 2, 3, 4)

The Randall Company has established the following standard costs for one unit of its product:

Direct material (48 kgs. @ $4.00 per kg.)	$192.00
Direct labor (12 hrs. @ $9.00 per hr.)	108.00
Overhead (12 hrs. @ $4.50 per hr.)	54.00
Total standard cost	$354.00

The predetermined overhead application rate ($4.50 per direct labor hour) is based on an expected volume of 50% of the factory's capacity of 10,000 units per month. Thus, the expected monthly output is 5,000 units. Following are the company's budgeted overhead costs for one month at the 50% level:

RANDALL COMPANY
Monthly Factory Overhead Budget (at 50% of capacity)

Variable costs:

Indirect materials	$40,000	
Indirect labor	80,000	
Power	20,000	
Repairs and maintenance	30,000	
Total variable costs		$ 170,000

Fixed costs:

Depreciation, building	$20,000	
Depreciation, machinery	30,000	
Taxes and insurance	10,000	
Supervision	40,000	
Total fixed costs		100,000
Total overhead costs		$ 270,000

The company incurred the following actual costs when it unexpectedly operated at 40% of capacity during May:

Direct material (196,000 kgs. @ $4.00)		$ 784,000
Direct labor (46,000 hrs. @ $9.15)		420,900
Overhead costs:		
Indirect materials	$30,000	
Indirect labor	66,000	
Power	15,600	
Repairs and maintenance	21,000	
Depreciation, building	20,000	
Depreciation, machinery	30,000	
Taxes and insurance	9,600	
Supervision	39,600	231,800
Total costs		$1,436,700

Required

1. Classify the items in the overhead budget as variable or fixed and determine their amounts per unit or for the month, as appropriate.

2. Prepare a set of possible flexible overhead budgets for May showing the amounts of each variable and fixed cost at the 40%, 50%, and 60% levels.

3. Compute the direct material variances, including the quantity and price variances.

4. Compute the direct labor variances, including the quantity and price variances.

5. Prepare a factory overhead variance report that shows the total volume and controllable variances.

6. Prepare a detailed factory overhead variance report (like Illustration 24–7) that shows the variances for the individual items of overhead.

CHECK FIGURE:
Overhead volume variance, $20,000 unfavorable

Patton Company's standard cost accounting system recorded the following information concerning its operations during September:

Problem 24–6
Recording material, labor, and overhead variances
(LO 4, 5)

Standard direct material cost	$125,000
Direct material quantity variance (favorable) ..	5,250
Direct material price variance (unfavorable) ..	1,100
Actual direct labor cost	62,500
Direct labor quantity variance (unfavorable) ..	7,500
Direct labor price variance (favorable)	800
Actual overhead cost	249,000
Volume variance (favorable)	11,000
Controllable variance (unfavorable)	8,800

CHECK FIGURE:
Goods in Process Inventory (for overhead), $251,200

Required

Preparation component:

1. Prepare general journal entries dated April 30 to record the company's costs and variances for the month.

Analysis component:

2. Identify areas that would attract the attention of a manager who uses management by exception and explain what action the manager should take.

CRITICAL THINKING: ESSAYS, PROBLEMS, AND CASES

Analytical Essays

AE 24–1
(LO 1)

The Kempf Company recently prepared a fixed budget for the coming year based on an expected volume of 200,000 units. At this volume, the fixed costs were expected to be $300,000 and the variable costs also were expected to be $300,000.

Required

1. What amount would be expected for the fixed, variable, and total costs at 100,000 units? At 400,000 units?

2. Explain why the amount of total expected costs at 100,000 units is not 25% of the amount of total expected costs at 400,000 units.

3. Suppose that the company could reduce fixed costs by 25% while increasing variable costs by 50%. What would be the expected amounts of fixed, variable, and total costs at 100,000 units? At 200,000 units? At 400,000 units?

4. Explain why knowledge of the fixed and variable nature of a company's costs is essential for preparing useful plans for the future and useful evaluations of the past.

AE 24–2
(LO 1)

In Exercise 24–3, Shank Company's fixed budget analysis shows a favorable variance for sales, an unfavorable variance for expenses, and a favorable variance for income from operations.

However, the flexible budget analysis prepared in solving the exercise shows no variance for sales, a favorable variance for expenses, and a much smaller favorable variance for income from operations.

Explain why the analyses produce such different outcomes.

Managerial Analysis Problems

MAP 24–1
(LO 2, 3)

In preparing its budget for June, Jasco Company's management planned to sell spices for $30 a rack. Each rack was expected to require 2 pounds of special spices that the company planned to purchase for $9.00 per pound. The racks were expected to be produced at the rate of five per direct labor hour, and the company expected to hire workers for $4.50 per hour. Each rack was to be packaged in a crate, which the company planned to buy at $1 each.

For volumes ranging between 6,000 and 12,000 racks, the management expected to incur these fixed expenses in June:

Administrative and sales salaries	$20,000
Depreciation	12,000
Utilities	4,200
Insurance	3,520

During June, Jasco actually produced and sold 8,000 spice racks at $32.50 each. It used 16,200 pounds of spices, which had been purchased at $9.60 per pound. Workers were paid $4.40 per hour and worked 1,500 hours to produce the racks. The company used 8,050 crates, which it actually purchased for $1.20 each. All the fixed expenses occurred as planned.

Although these facts are available to the company's managers, they have not yet been able to clearly evaluate the operating performance of the company's separate activities. They can see that the actual operating income differed from the expected amount but have not established how much of that amount was contributed by the different activities. They have asked you to describe how the differences between the actual and expected amounts affected the company's performance. Do what you can to help them.

The Springdale Company manufactures a product with a seasonal demand and a short shelf life. As a result, the product cannot be accumulated in advance of its sale, and the numbers of units manufactured in different quarters vary a great deal.

MAP 24–2
(LO 2)

The company's cost accounting system operates on a quarterly cycle, and adds actual costs to the Goods in Process Inventory. In turn, these costs flow into the Cost of Goods Sold account for each quarter or into the Finished Goods Inventory account. At the end of last year, which reflected a typical set of seasonal variations, this summarized cost report was prepared for the company manager:

SPRINGDALE COMPANY
Quarterly Reports of Average Product Costs
For Year Ended December 31

	First Quarter	Second Quarter	Third Quarter	Fourth Quarter
Direct materials	$264,000	$1,046,400	$2,187,500	$ 791,100
Direct labor	94,500	384,000	812,500	297,000
Variable overhead costs	146,700	600,000	1,262,500	445,500
Fixed overhead costs	400,000	400,000	400,000	400,000
Total costs	$905,200	$2,430,400	$4,662,500	$1,933,600
Units of output	7,500	30,000	62,500	22,500
Average cost per unit	$120.69	$81.01	$74.60	$85.94

Because of some difficulty in interpreting the report, the manager has asked you to explain why the average cost per unit varies so much among quarters. The manager also has asked you to suggest any improvements in the cost accounting system that could lead to more useful information. The manager believes that quarterly reports are needed for a timely response to apparent control problems, so your suggestion should include a schedule showing how last year's material, labor, and overhead costs per unit would have been reported under your suggestion.

Nancy Bode has been employed by Stripling Company for 15 years, with the last 4 in one of the assembly departments. About a year ago, Bode was made the department manager and has achieved a strong performance in that position. Since the promotion, internal complaints and employee turnover and absenteeism have declined, while output has increased and employee morale has soared. During the past two months, the department has been operating at less than its standard costs, which hasn't happened for five or six years.

Managerial Decision Case

(LO 2, 3)

Recently, Roger Conant, one of Bode's crew, suggested that the company modify the department's machinery to make it more versatile and automatic. The modifications would cost $50,000 and would have an eight-year life and no salvage value. They should increase the rate of production by 10%, reduce maintenance costs $2,000 per year, and reduce the size of the crew by one person. The wages of the least senior person in the department are about $22,000 per year.

Upon receiving the suggestion, Bode's response was, "I appreciate the suggestion, but let's forget it for now. We have been doing real well in meeting our standards, and the company doesn't need the extra capacity right now. Besides, the job market is tough, and whoever we let go could be on unemployment for a long time. I think our team's relationships are real strong, and I don't want to have to pick somebody to lay off. We just can't do anything as drastic as this and keep up the head of steam that we have going for us."

Does your analysis of the recommendation lead you to agree with Bode's initial response? Is it advantageous for decisions like these to be made at the department level, or should they be handled at a higher level in the company? Is there an appropriate way for Conant to pass this suggestion to a manager at a level higher than Bode?

Ethical Issues Essay

Examine the ethics case on page 935. Evaluate the reasons given by the department manager for his behavior in ordering supplies in the pattern described in the case. Do these actions seem ethical to you? As the internal auditor, what would you do next?

ANSWERS TO PROGRESS CHECKS

24–1 *b*

24–2 The first step is classifying each cost as variable or fixed.

24–3 A fixed budget is prepared using an expected volume of sales or production, and a flexible budget compares actual costs with the costs that should have been incurred at the actual volume.

24–4 It is the difference between sales and variable costs.

24–5 *c*

24–6 *a* Total actual hours: $2,500 \times 2.5 = 6,250$
Total standard hours: $2,500 \times 2.0 = 5,000$
$QV = (6,250 - 5,000) \times \$3.00 = \$3,750$ U

24–7 *d* $PV = (\$3.10 - \$3.00) \times 6,250 = \$625$ U

24–8 It is the difference between actual cost and standard cost.

24–9 Yes, if the material quantity variance is greater than the material price variance.

24–10 The overhead volume variance is favorable when the actual operating level is larger than the expected level.

24–11 *b*

24–12

Goods in Process Inventory	75,700.00	
Direct Material Price Variance	1,300.00	
Direct Material Quantity Variance		3,800.00
Raw Materials Inventory		73,200.00

24–13 If the variances are material, they should be prorated among the Goods in Process Inventory, Finished Goods Inventory, and Cost of Goods Sold accounts. If they are not material, they can be closed to Cost of Goods Sold.

Capital Budgeting and Other Managerial Decisions

Several years ago, Greg Cass, vice president of finance for the Olympic Homecare Products Division of the Clorox Company, was excited. E.I. duPont deNemours & Company had just announced its intention to sell its Lucite paint line. Olympic Homecare Products had been actively looking for acquisition targets to compliment its exterior stain products. Olympic had considered creating an exterior/interior paint line. However, the opportunity to acquire Lucite paint had immediate advantages over starting up an entirely new paint line with the Olympic name. Acquiring Lucite from DuPont would allow immediate access to proven formulas for a quality paint. Lucite not only provided a positive consumer awareness on a national level but also had a customer distribution base already in place.

DuPont had requested that interested parties submit dollar bids based on acquiring the paint formulas, the Lucite logo and trademark, and the existing customer list. The sale would not include any fixed assets. Olympic assembled an acquisition team from finance, marketing, and manufacturing to examine the opportunity and create a bid proposal. The purchase price would need to represent the current value of Lucite paint based on the predicted increases in future earnings the Clorox Company would receive if the purchase took place. This required making assumptions regarding the advertising costs necessary to retain or capture a new market share, the industry growth rate, the stability of market prices and raw material costs, changes in support and manufacturing staff, and capital asset purchases necessary to produce and support the product. The project looked formidable, and the team had less than two months.

LEARNING OBJECTIVES

After studying Chapter 25, you should be able to:

1. **Explain the importance of capital budgeting, calculate the expected payback period of an investment, and describe its limitations.**

2. **Calculate the expected average rate of return on an investment and describe its limitations.**

3. **Calculate the net present value of the cash flows from a proposed investment, and describe the procedures used in this method and its advantages and disadvantages.**

4. **Explain how information about incremental costs affects decisions about accepting or rejecting additional volume and about making or buying a component of a product.**

5. **Describe the importance of sunk costs, out-of-pocket costs, opportunity costs, and contribution margins for decisions such as the choice between scrapping or re-working defective units, selling a product or processing it further, or selecting a sales mix.**

6. **Define or explain the words and phrases listed in the chapter glossary.**

Business decisions involve choosing between alternative courses of action. Although many factors can affect these decisions, the analysis typically begins by looking for the alternative that offers the highest return on the investment or the greatest reduction in costs. Some decisions are based on little more than an intuitive understanding of the situation because the available information is too limited to allow a more systematic approach. In other circumstances, intangible factors such as convenience, prestige, and environmental considerations are more important than strictly quantitative factors. Even in these situations, you can reach a more sound decision if you can describe the consequences of alternative choices in quantitative terms. This chapter examines several systematic methods of analysis that can help managers to make decisions.

CAPITAL BUDGETING

LO 1

Explain the importance of capital budgeting, calculate the expected payback period of an investment, and describe its limitations.

FAST HINT
Additional Insight:
The nature of capital spending has changed with the business environment. Budgets for information technology increased from 27.2% of corporate capital spending in 1980 to an estimated 35.2% in 1991. White-collar productivity is expected to continue to rise as information technology is applied more effectively.

Chapter 23 described the capital expenditures budget, which is management's plan for acquiring and selling plant assets. The process of analyzing alternative investments and deciding which assets to acquire or sell is called **capital budgeting.** The plans may involve buying such things as a new machine, a new building, or a whole new project. In all cases, a fundamental goal for implementing the decision is to earn a satisfactory return on the investment. Capital budgeting decisions require careful analysis because they are generally the most difficult and risky decisions that management faces. The decisions are difficult because they are usually based on predictions of numerous events that might occur well into the future. At best, these predictions are highly tentative and potentially undependable. A capital budgeting decision is risky because (1) the outcome is highly uncertain, (2) large amounts of money are usually involved, (3) the investment involves a long-term commitment, and (4) the decision may be difficult or impossible to reverse, no matter how poor it turns out to be.

The practice of capital budgeting involves a wide range of decisions. As a result, managers have developed a variety of techniques for helping them make these decisions. Despite this variety, essentially all of these techniques involve predicting the cash inflows and outflows of each proposed investment, assessing the advantages of those flows, and then choosing the investments to be made. In this chapter, we consider three widely recognized methods for comparing alternative investments. These methods call for calculating the *payback period*, the *rate of return on average investment*, and the *net present value*.

	Expected Net Income	Expected Cash Flows
Annual sales of new product	$30,000	$30,000
Deduct annual expenses:		
Cost of materials, labor, and overhead (other than depreciation)	(15,500)	(15,500)
Depreciation	(2,000)	
Additional selling and administrative expenses ..	(9,500)	(9,500)
Annual pre-tax income	$ 3,000	
Income taxes (30%)	(900)	(900)
Annual net income	$ 2,100	
Annual net cash flow		$ 4,100

Illustration 25–1
Expected Net Income and Net Cash Flow from an Investment

PAYBACK PERIOD

Any investment project, whether it involves a machine or some other long-term asset, produces cash inflows and requires cash outflows. The difference between these inflows and outflows in a period is the *net cash flow*. The **payback period** for an investment is the time expected to pass before the net cash flows return the investment's initial cost. In general, managers prefer assets with shorter payback periods to reduce the risk that the investment might not be profitable over the long run. As a result of acquiring assets with short payback periods, the company is less vulnerable to inaccurate long-term predictions of future cash flows.

For example, assume that the Murray Company is considering several capital investments. One involves purchasing a machine to be used in manufacturing a new product. The machine would cost $16,000 and is expected to have an eight-year life with no salvage value. Management also predicts that the machine will produce 10,000 units of product each year and that the product will be sold for $3 per unit. Illustration 25–1 shows the expected annual revenues and expenses (including depreciation and income taxes) from the asset. The illustration also shows the cash flows the asset is expected to generate each year in its life.

Illustration 25–1 calculates the cash flows from the investment by subtracting the expected cash outflows from the expected cash inflows. The second column simply excludes noncash items (in this case, depreciation is the only noncash item). An alternative approach adjusts the projected net income for revenue and expense items that do not involve cash flows. For this example, the $4,100 annual net cash flow equals the net income of $2,100 plus the $2,000 depreciation.

The payback period for an investment is calculated as follows:

$$\text{Payback period} = \frac{\text{Cost of Asset}}{\text{Annual Net Cash Flow}}$$

This ratio shows how long it will take the investment project to generate enough net cash flow to return (or pay back) the cash initially invested to buy it. The calculation for this example is as follows:

$$\text{Payback period} = \frac{\$16,000}{\$4,100} = 3.9 \text{ years}$$

Because of the uncertainty associated with the predicted annual net cash flows, the result of 3.9 years is rounded to only one decimal place. Carrying it any further would not add any meaning or usefulness to the result. The cash flows are expected to occur over as many as eight future years. Predictions like these are not dependable enough to justify more precise calculations and carrying the decimals further would suggest an inappropriate degree of accuracy. In light of this uncertainty, we might even question carrying the calculation to one decimal place. Perhaps the most appropriate interpretation of the statistic is to say that the payback period appears to be approximately four years long.[1]

Calculating Payback Periods When Cash Flows Are Not Uniform

The previous example assumed net cash flows were $4,100 each and every year. The payback period can also be calculated when the predicted cash flows vary from year to year. Instead of taking a ratio, it is necessary to find the cumulative total of the net cash inflows.

For example, assume that an investment costing $15,000 is expected to produce the following net cash flows over the next four years:

	Annual Net Cash Flows
Year 1	$3,000
Year 2	4,000
Year 3	5,000
Year 4	6,000

The net cash flows accumulate as shown in the second column of this schedule:

	Annual Net Cash Flows	Cumulative Net Cash Flows
Year 1	$3,000	$ 3,000
Year 2	4,000	7,000
Year 3	5,000	12,000
Year 4	6,000	18,000

The cumulative net cash flows are $12,000 at the end of year 3 and $18,000 at the end of year 4. Thus, the expected payback period for the $15,000 investment is somewhere between three and four years. The project is expected to pay back $12,000 of the $15,000 investment during the first three years. If the cash flows occur evenly throughout each year, the remaining $3,000 will be paid back around the middle of year 4. Thus, the payback period is about 3.5 years.

Recall from the beginning of the chapter the decision by the Olympic Homecare Products Division of the **Clorox Company** to consider acquiring Lucite paint from **DuPont.** Olympic's finance group put together a seven-year forecast of cash flows that would result from the acquisition. Revenue was projected to grow annually based on an assumed increasing market share and stable prices for the current mix of products. Projected cash outflows reflected a substantially increased advertising budget that marketing estimated would be necessary to increase the market share and sales revenue. Projected outflows assumed stable raw material costs with

---

[1] This caution in interpreting the results is suitable for all calculations involving predictions. Managers and managerial accountants need to avoid a spurious accuracy that looks reasonable but that is not justified by the potential imprecision of the predictions.

modest increases in plant, administrative, and sales costs. The assumption was that the Lucite products could be sold and administered by Olympic's existing sales and administration staff. These cash flows were compared with the estimated net cash flows from investing in a start-up paint line and entering the market with no existing market share. In the rest of the analysis, the comparison of the two alternatives was used to set a ceiling on the investment that could be paid for the Lucite brand.

Evaluating the Payback Period as a Method of Comparing Investments

A short payback period is desirable because the more quickly cash is received, the more quickly it is available for other uses. Furthermore, a short payback period also means the invested funds are at risk for a shorter time. This short period improves the company's ability to respond to unanticipated changes. In effect, a short payback period reduces the company's risk of having to hold an unprofitable investment.

The payback period should never be the only consideration in evaluating investments because it ignores at least two important factors. First, it fails to reflect differences in the timing of net cash flows within the payback period. In the previous example, the net cash flows in the first four years were $3,000, $4,000, $5,000, and $6,000. If another asset had predicted cash flows of $9,000, $3,000, $2,000, and $2,000 in the four years, its payback period would also be 3.5 years. However, the second pattern would be more desirable because it would provide more cash more quickly.

Second, the payback period is deficient because it ignores *all* cash flows after the period. For example, one investment may pay back its cost in 3 years but stop producing cash after another year, while a second investment would require 5 years to pay back its cost but continue to produce net cash flows for another 15 years. Anyone considering only the payback period would mistakenly choose the first investment.

FAST HINT
Important Point to Remember:
The time value of money causes us to prefer the second pattern of cash flows. The time value of money was described in Chapter 12 and is discussed later in this chapter under the net present value method of analysis.

FAST HINT
Relevant Quick Study:
To apply these concepts, work QS 25–2.

Progress Check *(Answers to Progress Checks are provided at the end of the chapter.)*

25-1   **Capital budgeting is:**
   a. **Concerned with analyzing alternative sources of capital, including debt and preferred stock.**
   b. **An essential activity for all companies as they consider what assets to acquire.**
   c. **Best accomplished by intuitive assessments of the value of assets and their potential usefulness to the company.**

25-2   **Why are capital budgeting decisions often difficult to make?**

25-3   **Select Corporation is considering the purchase of a new piece of equipment that costs $75,000. Annual net cash flows to be produced by this investment are $30,000, $25,000, $15,000, $10,000, and $5,000. The payback period is:** *(a)* **4 years;** *(b)* **3.5 years;** *(c)* **3 years.**

25-4   **If depreciation is an expense, why is it added to net income from an investment to calculate the net cash flow from the investment?**

25-5   **If two investments have the same payback period, are they equally desirable? Explain your answer.**

To overcome these disadvantages of the payback period as a capital budgeting tool, it is possible to use the **rate of return on average investment** for an asset or a project. This approach takes into consideration all cash flows from the investment. In addition, it provides a more appropriate way to compare and rank alternatives that have differing life spans. This rate is calculated by dividing the after-tax net income from the project by the average investment in the project. Despite its superiority over the payback period, the rate of return on the average investment has its own limitations, which we discuss later.

RATE OF RETURN ON AVERAGE INVESTMENT

LO 2
Calculate the expected average rate of return on an investment and describe its limitations

Illustration 25–2
Calculating Average
Investment When Net Cash
Flows Are Received Evenly
Throughout Each Year

	Beginning Book Value	Annual Depreciation	Ending Book Value	Average Book Value
Year 1	$16,000	$ 2,000	$14,000	$15,000
Year 2	14,000	2,000	12,000	13,000
Year 3	12,000	2,000	10,000	11,000
Year 4	10,000	2,000	8,000	9,000
Year 5	8,000	2,000	6,000	7,000
Year 6	6,000	2,000	4,000	5,000
Year 7	4,000	2,000	2,000	3,000
Year 8	2,000	2,000	0	1,000
Total		$16,000		

Rate of Return When Net Cash Flows Are Received Evenly throughout the Year

In calculating the average investment to use in finding the rate, management must make an assumption about the timing of the cash flows that represent the recovery of the asset's annual depreciation. In most cases, net cash flows are received evenly throughout the year. If this pattern can be assumed, the average investment for each year should be calculated as the average of its beginning and ending book values. If the Murray Company's $16,000 machine is depreciated $2,000 each year, the average amount invested in the machine for each year can be calculated as shown in Illustration 25–2. The average for any year is the average of the beginning and ending book values.

To perform this analysis, we need the average book value during the asset's entire life. The amount can be found by taking the average of the eight yearly averages. This approach is necessary if an accelerated depreciation method is used. If we use straight-line depreciation, we can find the average book value for the eight years as the sum of the beginning and ending book values divided by 2:

$$\text{Average investment} = \frac{\text{Beginning book value} + \text{Ending book value}}{2}$$

$$= \frac{\$16,000 + \$ \text{-0-}}{2}$$

$$= \$8,000$$

This example is simplified by the assumption that the machine has no salvage value. If the machine had a salvage value, the average investment would be calculated as (Original cost + Salvage value)/2.

After the average investment is determined, the rate of return on average investment can be calculated. This step divides the estimated annual after-tax net income by the average investment. In equation form, the calculation appears as follows:

$$\text{Return on average investment} = \frac{\text{Annual after-tax net income}}{\text{Average investment}}$$

Because the Murray Company expects an after-tax annual net income of $2,100, the expected rate of return (rounded to the nearest percentage) is:

FAST HINT
Relevant Exercise:
To apply these concepts, work
Exercise 25–4.

$$\text{Return on average investment} = \frac{\$2,100}{\$8,000} = 26\%$$

Average Investment When the Net Cash Flows Are Received at Year-End

In some cases, the revenue from an investment is not spread evenly over each year but is received in a lump sum near the end of each year. For example, a financial investment might pay interest in a lump sum at the end of the year. Or, a building's owner might receive a year's annual rent near the end of a year. In analyzing these cases, depreciation can be considered to be recovered near the end of the year. Thus, the asset's book value equals the beginning balance during the entire year, up until the very end. As a result, the average investment during the year is the asset's beginning book value. As applied to the example in Illustration 25–2, an assumption of year-end flows produces the following calculation of the average investment:

$$\text{Average investment} = \frac{\text{First year's book value} + \text{Final year's book value}}{2}$$

$$= \frac{\$16,000 + \$2,000}{2}$$

$$= \$9,000$$

If the machine had a salvage value, the book value at the beginning of (and throughout) the final year would equal the salvage value plus the final year's depreciation expense.

With this $9,000 average investment, the return on average investment for the Murray Company's asset is calculated as follows:

$$\text{Return on average investment} = \frac{\$2,100}{\$9,000} = 23\%$$

The result is a lower rate of return because the average investment is higher by $1,000.

Evaluating the Return on Average Investment

At this point, the question should arise whether 26% (or 23%) is a satisfactory rate of return. On the surface, 26% appears better than a lower rate, such as 10 or 15%. However, this conclusion is valid only if the alternatives have similar lives and involve similar levels of risk. And, other available investment alternatives might yield even higher returns. In other words, an investment's return can be considered to be satisfactory or unsatisfactory only when it is related to returns from other investments with similar lives and risk. When average investment returns are used to select between capital investments, the one with the least risk, the shortest payback period, and the highest return for the longest time is often identified as the best.

Perhaps because the rate of return on average investment is relatively easy to calculate, it has long been used in evaluating investment opportunities. However, its usefulness is limited because the measure of the amount invested is based on a systematic prediction of the asset's values in the future. Depreciation methods were created to allocate costs among years, not to predict market values of the assets. The usefulness is also limited when the asset's net incomes are expected to vary from year to year because the rate's calculation must be based on the *average* annual net income. Two investments with the same average annual net income are not equivalent if one is expected to have higher amounts in the early years and lower amounts in the later years. The rate of return on average investment fails to distinguish between these two investments. Because of these deficiencies, a comparison of *net present values* generally offers a better method of selecting the preferred investment.

FAST HINT
Additional Insight:
Use of return on average investment has decreased. Between 1980 and 1988, its use for all decisions decreased by more than 50%. For high technology capital budget decisions, its use declined by 75%.

FAST HINT
Relevant Quick Study:
To apply these concepts, work QS 25–3.

Illustration 25-3
Net Present Value Analysis of Future Cash Inflows from a Proposed Investment

	Net Cash Flows	Present Value of $1 at 12%	Present Value of Net Cash Flows
Year 1	$ 4,100	0.8929	$ 3,661
Year 2	4,100	0.7972	3,269
Year 3	4,100	0.7118	2,918
Year 4	4,100	0.6355	2,606
Year 5	4,100	0.5674	2,326
Year 6	4,100	0.5066	2,077
Year 7	4,100	0.4523	1,854
Year 8	4,100	0.4039	1,656
Total	$32,800		$20,367
Amount to be invested			(16,000)
Net present value of investment			$ 4,367

Progress Check

25-6 The following data relate to a machinery purchase that the Westwood Company is considering:

Cost	$180,000
Salvage value	15,000
Annual income	40,000

The expected rate of return on average investment, assuming that the net cash flows from the investment are received evenly throughout the year (ignore income taxes) is: (a) 22%; (b) 41%; (c) 21%.

25-7 Is a 15% return on the average investment in a machine a good rate?

NET PRESENT VALUES

LO 3

Calculate the net present value of the cash flows from a proposed investment, and describe the procedures used in this method and its advantages and disadvantages.

FAST HINT
Additional Insight:
Use of present value techniques for all types of capital budgeting decisions has increased dramatically. For high technology projects, 75% of firms surveyed in 1988 stated that discounting is their primary decision evaluation technique.

To use net present values, you need a good understanding of the concepts of discounting. We explain these concepts in Chapter 12, beginning on page 457. Review that discussion before going on if you do not fully understand these concepts. An expanded explanation of discounting is presented in Appendix E. In addition, you can use the present value tables in Appendix E, to solve several of the problems at the end of this chapter.

When a business invests in a new plant asset, it expects that asset to produce a stream of future net cash flows. Normally, a business should not acquire the asset unless its expected cash flows are sufficient to provide a satisfactory return on that investment and recover the amount initially invested. For example, assume that the cash flows from the Murray Company's investment will be received at the end of each year. Will the asset provide a satisfactory return while recovering the amount of the investment? If the company considers a 12% compounded annual return to be satisfactory, we can answer this question with the calculations shown in Illustration 25–3. The table shows the calculation of the **net present value** of the investment, which is an estimate of the asset's value to the company. The net present value is calculated by discounting the future cash flows from the investment at a satisfactory rate and then subtracting the initial cost of the investment.

The Murray Company must invest $16,000 to purchase the machine described in Illustration 25–3. The company expects to sell the machine's output and receive net cash flows of $4,100 each year for the next eight years. The first column of Illustration 25–3 shows the amounts of the annual cash flows. The table values in the second column are based on the assumption that the net cash flows are received at the end of each year. (To simplify the discussion of net present values and the related problems at the end of the chapter, we assume that the net cash flows are received at the end of the year. More complex calculations are presented in advanced accounting and finance courses.)

The annual net cash flows in the first column of Illustration 25–3 are multiplied by the table values in the second column to determine the present values in the third column. In the lower section of the illustration, the asset's $16,000 initial cost is deducted from the $20,367 total present value of the future cash inflows. Notice that the total present value exceeds the amount to be invested by $4,367. Therefore, this machine is expected to recover its cost, provide a 12% compounded return, and generate another $4,367. The analysis can also be summarized by saying that the value of the future cash flows to the Murray Company exceeds their $16,000 cost by $4,367.[2]

Generally, when the expected cash flows from an asset are discounted at a satisfactory rate and have a *positive* net present value, the asset should be acquired. Also, when comparing several investment opportunities of about the same cost and the same risk, the one with the highest positive net present value is preferred.

Simplifying the Calculation

The calculation in Illustration 25–3 uses the separate present values of $1 at 12% for each of the eight years. Each year's cash flow is multiplied by the present value of $1 at 12% for that number of years to determine its present value. Then, the present values of the eight cash flows are added to determine their total. The calculation can be simplified in two different ways because the annual cash flows are the same size. One simplification adds the eight yearly present values of $1 at 12% to get a total of 4.9676. Then, this amount is multiplied by the annual cash flow of $4,100 to get the $20,367 total present value of the cash flows.

An even simpler calculation is based on Table E–3, which shows the present value of $1 to be received periodically for a number of periods. (A series of equal payments is called an *annuity.*) In this case, $4,100 is expected to be received annually for eight years. To determine the present value of these annual receipts discounted at 12%, go down the 12% column of Table E–3 to the amount on the eighth line. The table value is 4.9676. Then, the present value of the eight annual $4,100 receipts is $20,367 (4.9676 × $4,100).

The easiest way to simplify the calculation is to use a handheld calculator with compound interest functions. You can also find the answers by using a spreadsheet program on a personal computer. Of course, the actual technique that you use does not matter, as long as the calculation is properly made.

Unequal Future Cash Flows

Net present value analysis can also be used when cash flows are not uniform. For example, assume that a company can choose only one capital investment from among Projects A, B, and C. Each would have a cost of $12,000. The future cash flows are shown in the first column of the tables for each asset in Illustration 25–4.

All three projects in Illustration 25–4 are expected to produce the same total cash flows of $15,000. However, Project A is expected to produce equal amounts each year, Project B is expected to produce a greater amount in the first year, and Project C is expected to produce a greater amount in the third year. Therefore, if the present

---

[2] Another calculation shows that the *internal rate of return* for this investment is 19.4% per year, well in excess of the 12% minimum rate specified by the company's management. This calculation finds the discount rate that makes the present value of the net cash inflows equal the $16,000 cost of the investment. Notice that this rate differs from the rate of return on average investment for this asset. The difference arises from the fact that the two calculations use different bases for the amount invested and received each year.

Illustration 25–4

Comparing Net Present Values of Projects When the Timing and Amounts of the Future Cash Flows Are Different

	Net Cash Flows	Present Value of $1 at 10%	Present Value of Net Cash Flows
Project A:			
Year 1	$ 5,000	0.9091	$ 4,546
Year 2	5,000	0.8264	4,132
Year 3	5,000	0.7513	3,757
Total	$15,000		$12,435
Amount to be invested			(12,000)
Net present value of investment			$ 435
Project B:			
Year 1	$ 8,000	0.9091	$ 7,273
Year 2	5,000	0.8264	4,132
Year 3	2,000	0.7513	1,503
Total	$15,000		$12,908
Amount to be invested			(12,000)
Net present value of investment			$ 908
Project C:			
Year 1	$ 1,000	0.9091	$ 909
Year 2	5,000	0.8264	4,132
Year 3	9,000	0.7513	6,762
Total	$15,000		$11,803
Amount to be invested			(12,000)
Net present value of investment			$ (197)

FAST HINT
Critical Thought Question:
Would the rankings of Projects A, B, and C change with the use of different discount rates as long as the same rate is used for all three projects? (When would it be appropriate to use different discount rates for the three projects?)

FAST HINT
Alternative Example:
If 12% is the minimum required rate of return in Illustration 25–4, which project appears to be the best investment alternative?
Answer: Project B is still the best investment. Net present value:
Project A, $ 10
Project B,   553
Project C, (715)

values of the cash flows are found at the 10% rate used in the illustration, the projects will not produce the same net present values.[3]

Project A has a $435 positive net present value. Project B has a higher positive net present value of $908 because it brings in more cash more quickly. However, Project C has a $197 *negative* net present value because it has a small cash flow in the first year and a large one in the third year. If a minimum 10% return is required, Project C should be rejected because the investment's net present value indicates it will not earn at that rate. Furthermore, if only one project can be accepted, Project B appears to be the best investment because its cash flows have the highest net present value.

Considering the Effects of Salvage Value and Accelerated Depreciation

We assumed that the $16,000 machine in the Murray Company example would have no salvage value at the end of its useful life. In many cases, a machine or other asset is expected to have a salvage value. If so, this amount is an additional cash flow that will be received at the end of the final year in the asset's life.

Recall the story of the **Clorox Company's** acquisition of Lucite paint. The acquisition analysis used the series of cash flows previously mentioned and assumed the ability to sell the paint brand at 12 times earnings at the end of seven years. In the analysis, this sales price was the salvage value.

---

[3] The amounts in Illustration 25–4 are rounded to the nearest whole dollar. However, it is likely that this much precision is spurious accuracy because future cash flows and their present values are always based on predictions.

The Murray Company example computed depreciation using the straight-line method. In practice, however, accelerated depreciation is often used for income tax reporting. Accelerated depreciation produces larger depreciation deductions in the early years of an asset's life and smaller deductions in the later years. This pattern results in smaller income tax payments in the early years and larger payments in later years.

Accelerated depreciation does not change the basic nature of a present value analysis, but it can change the result. Using accelerated depreciation for tax reporting affects the net present value of the asset's cash flows because it produces larger net cash inflows in the early years of the asset's life and smaller ones in later years. Because early cash flows are more valuable than later ones, being able to use accelerated depreciation for tax reporting always makes an investment more desirable.

FAST HINT
Important Point to Remember:
Chapter 10 on plant and equipment describes income tax depreciation methods.

Selecting the Earnings Rate

Top management should select the earnings rate to be used for evaluating capital investments. Although financial formulas can aid this selection, the choice of a satisfactory minimum rate is largely subjective. Management may do something as simple as deciding that many investment opportunities can be found that will earn, say, a 10% compounded return. This rate then becomes the minimum. The company should refuse to make an investment at less than this rate if it has average risk.

The required earnings rate should always be higher than the rate at which money can be borrowed because the return on an investment must cover the interest and provide an additional profit to reward the company for its risk. For example, if money can be borrowed at around 10%, a required after-tax return of 15% may be acceptable in industrial companies with average risk. A lower rate may be suitable for public utilities with lower risks, while a higher rate is needed for other companies facing unusually high risks.

FAST HINT
Critical Thought Question:
How could management evaluate the risk associated with a particular investment?

In analyzing the Lucite paint acquisition, the Clorox Company used an 18% required return on investment. Based on this rate, the bid price was accepted by DuPont and Lucite paint became a branded product of the Olympic Homecare Products Division of Clorox.

However, any model that is based on assumptions about the future is only as good as the assumptions. Two years after the Lucite acquisition, it became apparent that the assumptions that drove the model failed to take into account the inherent differences in customer and distribution bases between the Olympic Division and Lucite paint. This resulted in much higher administrative, delivery, and sales costs than anticipated. Furthermore, the assumed increase in market share failed to develop. In fact, the Lucite brand continued to suffer market deterioration, as it had under DuPont's ownership, despite the high rate of spending on advertising and marketing. After continued disappointing results, the Olympic Division and its Lucite brand were sold six years later to Pittsburgh Paints at considerably less than the original purchase price.

FAST HINT
Relevant Quick Study:
To apply these concepts, work QS 25–4.

Progress Check

25-8 **Casco Bay Company can invest in only one of two projects. Each project requires a $20,000 investment and is expected to generate end-of-period cash flows as follows:**

	Annual Cash Flows	
	Project A	Project B
Year 1	$12,000	$ 4,500
Year 2	8,500	8,500
Year 3	4,000	13,000
	$24,500	$26,000

Assuming a discount rate of 10%, which project has the greater net present value?

25-9   Two investment alternatives are expected to generate annual cash flows that have the same net present value, assuming the same discount rate is applied to each. Based on this information, can you conclude that the two alternatives are equally desirable?

25-10   When two investment alternatives have the same total expected cash flows but differ in the timing of those flows, which method of evaluating those investments is superior?
a. Rate of return on average investment.
b. Net present value.

OTHER MANAGERIAL DECISIONS

This section describes six general categories of decisions that managers must make in many different situations. The objective of the discussions is to show you which costs and other financial factors are relevant to those decisions. The descriptions also show you how to structure an analysis to reach a decision more easily.

REPLACING PLANT ASSETS

New and better machines are continuously coming on the market. As a result, managers must frequently decide whether to replace an existing machine with a new and better one. In many cases, an existing machine is in good physical condition and is still producing the company's product. However, a new machine should be considered if it can do the job with a large savings in operating costs. In this situation, management must decide whether the after-tax savings in operating costs justify the investment.

The decision analysis should compare the cash savings with the cash outflows needed to obtain the new machine, net of any cash inflow from selling the old one. The net present value method is the best way to analyze these predicted cash flows.

Finding the amount of after-tax cash effects of replacing an existing machine may be complicated by the fact that the annual tax depreciation on the new machine could be based on the book value of the old machine plus the cash paid. This complexity arises only if the old asset is given in exchange for the new one (see Chapter 10). Because other complications can also arise, a complete discussion of these decisions is left to more advanced managerial accounting courses.

ACCEPTING ADDITIONAL BUSINESS

LO 4

Explain how information about incremental costs affects decisions about accepting or rejecting additional volume and about making or buying a component of a product.

We have seen in prior chapters that the measures of costs provided by cost accounting systems are average historical costs. Although useful in product pricing and in controlling operations, historical costs are not necessarily relevant to decisions about accepting additional business. Instead, the relevant costs are the additional costs, generally called the **incremental costs** or *differential costs*. The incremental costs are incurred only if the company accepts the additional volume.

For example, assume that a company operates at its normal level, which is 80% of full capacity. The company produces and sells approximately 100,000 units of product annually, with the following average and total costs:

As a Matter of Ethics

Several months ago, Colfax Corporation's top management adopted new policies to control equipment purchases. According to the new policy, any proposal for a purchase in excess of $5,000 must be submitted for a careful review and capital budgeting analysis. When preparing a proposal, the manager must include predictions of future cash flows that are expected to result from the equipment purchase. These predictions are appraised by a central financial analysis group and modified as necessary. This group has the authority to approve or disapprove the proposal based on an analysis of its merits and the availability of funds.

Gary Waters, one of Colfax's middle-level managers, has recently decided that his group can perform more efficiently and effectively with a major upgrade of its personal computer network. The upgrade will require several new computers, large capacity hard disks, additional internal memory, a new network controller, software, and various other items. All items can be delivered quickly, and the benefits are expected to be realized within a short time.

Although the total cost of the items Waters wants to purchase is approximately $25,000, he is thinking about planning the purchase in a way that will avoid the hassle of preparing a lengthy proposal. No single component costs more than $5,000, and if he prepares six or seven purchase orders, all of the proposed items could be purchased without exceeding $5,000 for any one order.

You are a close friend of Waters, and he asks your opinion. He says that the new equipment would definitely improve profits. It would take a lot of effort to develop suitable predictions of cash flows, and the financial analysis group's decision will probably take two months. By that time, Waters is confident that he could receive the equipment, add it to the network, and start getting the job done.

What is your advice to your friend?

	Per Unit	Total
Sales (100,000 units)	$10.00	$1,000,000
Direct materials	$ 3.50	$ 350,000
Direct labor	2.20	220,000
Factory overhead	1.10	110,000
Selling expenses	1.40	140,000
Administrative expenses	0.80	80,000
Total expenses	$ 9.00	$ 900,000
Operating income	$ 1.00	$ 100,000

The marketing department reports it has found a customer who wants to buy and export the company's product to another country. This customer has offered to buy 10,000 units of product at the lower than average price of $8.50 per unit. The price reduction is being considered because this potential sale is several times larger than any previous sale made by the company. Because the units will be exported, the new business will not affect domestic sales. To determine whether this order should be accepted or rejected, management needs to know whether net income will increase if the offer is accepted. The following analysis shows that if management simply relied on the per unit average costs, the sale would be rejected:

	Per Unit	Total
Sales (10,000 units)	$ 8.50	$85,000
Direct materials	$ 3.50	$35,000
Direct labor	2.20	22,000
Factory overhead	1.10	11,000
Selling expenses	1.40	14,000
Administrative expenses	0.80	8,000
Total expenses	$ 9.00	$90,000
Operating loss	$(0.50)	$ (5,000)

The sale appears to generate a loss. However, average costs are not relevant to this decision.

Illustration 25–5
The Effects of Accepting
Additional Business

FAST HINT
Critical Thought Question:
Illustration 25–5 presents only
quantitative information. Suggest some qualitative factors
that should be considered when
deciding whether to accept this
project.

	Present Business	Additional Business	Combined
Sales	$1,000,000	$85,000	$1,085,000
Direct materials	$ 350,000	$35,000	$ 385,000
Direct labor	220,000	22,000	242,000
Factory overhead	110,000	5,000	115,000
Selling expenses	140,000	2,000	142,000
Administrative expense	80,000	1,000	81,000
Total expenses	$ 900,000	$65,000	$ 965,000
Operating income	$ 100,000	$20,000	$ 120,000

Instead, the *incremental* costs are relevant for deciding whether to accept the new business. Therefore, before making the decision, the costs of the new business must be analyzed more closely. Assume that the analysis reveals the following information:

* Manufacturing 10,000 additional units of product would require additional direct materials of $3.50 per unit and additional direct labor of $2.20 per unit (just like the units already being produced).

* The 10,000 units can be manufactured with only $5,000 of incremental factory overhead costs for power, packaging, and indirect labor for handling materials.

* Incremental commissions and other selling expenses resulting from the sale would be only $2,000.

* Incremental administrative expenses of $1,000 for clerical efforts would be needed.

Based on this added information, Illustration 25–5 shows how the additional business would affect the company's net income.

The analysis in the illustration suggests that the additional business should be accepted. The additional business would provide $85,000 of revenue while creating only $65,000 of additional costs. When this analysis is made, it shows that accepting the additional business at $8.50 per unit should generate $20,000 of additional pre-tax income. In fact, the company would have more income at any price more than $6.50 per unit.

Incremental costs of additional volume always are relevant, but they may greatly exceed the relatively small amounts in this example. The incremental costs were small because the additional volume was within the existing available capacity of the factory. If the additional volume requires the company to expand its capacity by obtaining more equipment, more space, or more supervisory personnel, the incremental costs could easily exceed the incremental revenue.

Another factor relevant to a decision to accept additional volume is the effect on existing sales. In the example, all the new units are to be sold elsewhere without affecting domestic sales. However, if the order would cause existing sales to decline, that fact would need to be included in the analysis.

And, if the future cash flows are to be received over several time periods, their net present value should be calculated and used in making the analysis for management.

In summary, the key point is that management should not use the average costs generated by a cost accounting system, especially allocated overhead. Instead, the managerial accounting system needs to provide information about the incremental costs that will be incurred only if the additional business is accepted.

FAST HINT
Relevant Exercise:
To apply these concepts, work
Exercise 25–8.

Incremental costs also are relevant when deciding about making or buying a particular component of a product. For example, assume that a manufacturer has excess productive capacity. The idle machines can be used to manufacture Part 417, a component of the company's product. This component is presently purchased and delivered to the plant at a cost of $1.20 per unit. The manufacturer estimates that making Part 417 would cost $0.45 for direct materials, $0.50 for direct labor, and an undetermined amount of factory overhead. At this point, we need to figure out how much overhead should be added to these costs to provide useful information for the decision. If the normal predetermined overhead application rate is 100% of direct labor cost, we might say that the overhead cost is $0.50 per unit. If so, the total cost would be $1.45, and we would decide that the company would be better off to buy the part at $1.20 each.

The prior section shows that only the incremental overhead costs are relevant and that we should ignore the normal predetermined overhead rate. The incremental overhead costs might include, for example, power for operating the machines, supplies, cleanup, materials handling, and quality control. If these incremental overhead costs are less than $0.25 per unit, the total cost of making the component would be less than $1.20. If so, the manufacturer may be justified in manufacturing the part in the short run. If the decision to make the part would require the company to incur major incremental fixed costs to expand its capacity, the cost of making the part could increase to the point that buying it would be more economical.

As we saw, any amount of overhead less than $0.25 per unit results in a total cost for Part 417 that is less than the $1.20 purchase price. Nevertheless, in deciding whether to make or buy the part, the manufacturer should consider other factors, including such things as quality, timeliness of delivery (especially in a just-in-time setting), the reactions of customers and suppliers, and other intangible items. When these additional factors are considered, small cost differences may not matter.

Again, a key point is that the full average cost provided by a cost accounting system is not likely to be relevant to this decision. Instead, only the incremental costs must be considered.

MAKE OR BUY DECISIONS

FAST HINT
Relevant Quick Study:
To apply these concepts, work QS 25–5.

Progress Check

25-11   Kaspar Company has just received a special order for 200 units of its product. To be able to stamp the buyer's name on each unit, Brown must incur an additional fixed cost of $400 above its normal manufacturing costs. Without the order, the company would be operating at 75% of capacity. At this level, it would produce 7,500 units of product and incur the following costs:

Direct materials	$37,500
Direct labor	60,000
Factory overhead (30% variable)	20,000
Selling expenses (60% variable)	25,000

This order will not affect Kaspar's normal unit sales and will not increase fixed overhead and selling costs. Also, variable selling expenses on the special order will be reduced to one-half the normal amount. The price per unit Kaspar will need to earn $1,000 on the order is: *(a)* $14.80; *(b)* $15.80; *(c)* $19.80; *(d)* $20.80; *(e)* $21.80.

25-12   What are the incremental costs of accepting an additional volume of business?

Additional categories of costs related to managerial decisions include *sunk costs, out-of-pocket costs,* and *opportunity costs.*

A **sunk cost** arises from a past decision. It is considered sunk in the sense that it cannot be avoided or changed in any way. As a result, sunk costs are irrelevant to decisions. For example, the historical cost of a machine is a sunk cost. Nothing done in

OTHER COST CONCEPTS

LO 5
Describe the importance of sunk costs, out-of-pocket costs, opportunity costs, and contribution margins for decisions such as the choice between scrapping or reworking defective units, selling a product or processing it further, or selecting a sales mix.

FAST HINT
Critical Thought Question:
Is depreciation a sunk cost if it is based on a systematic allocation of original cost? Would it be a sunk cost if it were based on a loss in market value expected to occur when the asset is used? Explain.

FAST HINT
Critical Thought Question:
Depreciation and amortization are allocations of the original cost of plant and equipment and intangible assets. Are they out-of-pocket costs? Explain your answer.

the future can change that cost. Instead, we need to consider the current market value of the machine in any decision about what to do with it in the future.

An **out-of-pocket cost** requires a current outlay of cash. Costs for materials, labor, supplies, and utilities are examples of out-of-pocket costs. Generally, out-of-pocket costs are incurred or avoided as a result of management's decisions. Thus, they are relevant to those decisions. Most *allocated* costs, especially fixed overhead costs such as depreciation and amortization, are not out-of-pocket costs.

The costs discussed previously result from expenditures to obtain goods or services. In addition, the concept of cost should be broadened to include **opportunity costs.** These costs are the potential benefits lost by choosing an alternative course of action. For example, if a student must turn down a job to attend summer school, the $3,000 salary that is not received must be considered part of the cost of going to school. As another example, suppose that a company decides to make a component instead of buying it. By choosing to do so, the company gives up the benefit that could be obtained by using the productive capacity for another activity. If the capacity cannot be used, there is no opportunity cost. On the other hand, if the capacity can be used to produce net cash flows of $100,000, that amount is the opportunity cost that must be considered in the make-or-buy decision. In retailing, the commitment of shelf space to one class of merchandise (such as snacks) means that the space is not available for another type of merchandise (such as cereal). In deciding whether to try selling more snacks, management's analysis should include an opportunity cost equal to the lost profits from not being able to sell the cereal.

Opportunity costs are not entered in the accounting records. However, they always are relevant to decisions involving rejected opportunities. As an example of a situation in which both sunk costs and opportunity costs must be identified, we next turn to decisions between scrapping or reworking defective units of product.

SCRAPPING OR REWORKING DEFECTIVE UNITS

Any costs incurred in manufacturing units of product that do not meet quality standards are sunk costs. They have been incurred and cannot be changed. Thus, they are irrelevant and should not enter into a decision between selling the units as scrap or reworking them so that they meet the quality standards. For example, assume that a company has 10,000 defective units of product that cost $1 per unit to manufacture. The units can be sold as they are for $0.40 each, or they can be reworked for $0.80 per unit, after which they can be sold for their full price of $1.50 per unit. Should the company rework the units or should it sell them as scrap?

Note that the original manufacturing costs of $1 per unit are sunk and *completely* irrelevant to the decision. Based on the given information, the comparative returns from scrapping or reworking the units are summarized as follows:

	Scrap	Rework
Sales of defective units	$4,000	$15,000
Less cost to rework		(8,000)
Net return	$4,000	$ 7,000

Reworking is a better tactic as long as it does not interfere with normal operations. However, suppose that reworking the defective units would cause the company to be unable to manufacture 10,000 new units with an incremental cost of $1 per unit. If they can be sold for $1.50 per unit, the comparative returns should be analyzed as follows:

	Scrap	Rework
Sales of defective units	$ 4,000	$15,000
Sales of new units	15,000	
Less cost to rework the old units		(8,000)
Less cost to manufacture the new units ...	(10,000)	
Net return from using capacity	$ 9,000	$ 7,000

If the defective units are scrapped, the plant's limited capacity can be used to manufacture new units that will be sold for a net profit of $5,000. This tactic produces a $9,000 total return from selling the new and scrapping the defective units. Obviously, this outcome is better than the $7,000 net return generated by using the productive capacity to rework the defective units.

This situation can also be analyzed using an opportunity cost. If reworking the defective units requires the company to give up manufacturing the new units, the company incurs the opportunity cost of the lost $5,000 net return from making and selling new units. This opportunity cost is the difference between the $15,000 revenue from selling the new units and their $10,000 manufacturing costs. The following analysis shows how the opportunity cost should be included:

	Scrap	Rework
Sale of defective units	$4,000	$15,000
Less cost to rework the old units		(8,000)
Less opportunity cost (return lost by		
not manufacturing the new units) ...		(5,000)
Net return from using capacity	$4,000	$ 2,000

Observe that the two analyses lead to the same conclusion. Either way, there is a $2,000 difference in favor of scrapping the defective units. But, this result is different from the first analysis that showed a $3,000 advantage for reworking the units. That analysis was incomplete because it omitted the $5,000 opportunity cost.

Sunk costs, out-of-pocket costs, and opportunity costs also enter into a sound analysis of a decision between selling partially completed products as they are or processing them further. If the completed products are processed further, the company will be able to sell them to customers.

For example, suppose that the Monarch Company has 40,000 units of partially finished product (called Product Q). These units cost $0.75 per unit to manufacture, for a total cost of $30,000. The 40,000 units can be sold to another manufacturer as a raw material for $50,000. Alternatively, Monarch Company can process them further and turn them into finished products X, Y, and Z at an incremental cost of $2 per unit. The additional processing will produce the following numbers of each product, which can be sold at the indicated unit prices:

Product	Price	Units	Revenue
X	$4.00	10,000	$ 40,000
Y	6.00	22,000	132,000
Z	8.00	6,000	48,000
Spoilage	0.00	2,000	-0-
Total		40,000	$220,000

PROCESS OR SELL

FAST HINT
Relevant Exercise:
To apply these concepts, work Exercise 25–10.

Revenue if processed further		$220,000
Less:		
Additional costs of processing (40,000 @ $2) . .	$80,000	
Opportunity cost (lost sales of Product Q)	50,000	
Total cost of processing		130,000
Net advantage of additional processing		$ 90,000

The company's management must determine whether the additional revenue from selling these finished products exceeds the cost of finishing them. Illustration 25–6 shows the analysis that should be completed.

Observe that the revenue that would be received by selling Product Q is an opportunity cost of doing additional processing on the units. Also notice that the $30,000 manufacturing cost for the 40,000 units of Product Q does not appear in Illustration 25–6. This cost is the same regardless of which alternative is chosen. Therefore, it is sunk and irrelevant to the decision.

Another way to analyze this decision is to compare the incremental revenue from further processing with the incremental cost of the additional work. This table shows the relevant calculations:

Revenue if processed further	$220,000
Revenue if sold as is	50,000
Incremental revenue	$170,000
Incremental cost of processing	80,000
Incremental advantage	$ 90,000

This analysis leads to the same conclusion that the company is better off incurring the cost to produce Products X, Y, and Z because the additional revenue generated by selling them is greater than the additional cost.

SELECTING A SALES MIX

When a company sells a variety of products, some are likely to be more profitable than others. If so, management may be wise to concentrate its sales efforts on the more profitable products. However, if production facilities or other factors are limited, an increase in the production and sale of one product may require the company to reduce the production and sale of others. In this situation, management must identify the most profitable combination (or *sales mix*) of the products and concentrate on selling the products in this combination.

To identify the best sales mix for its products, management must know the contribution margin of each product. In addition, management must know about the facilities required to produce the products and any limits or *constraints* on these facilities and the markets for the products. For example, assume that the Keystone Company produces and sells two products, A and B. The same machines are used to produce both products, which have the following selling prices and variable costs per units:

	Product A	Product B
Selling price	$5.00	$7.50
Variable costs	3.50	5.50
Contribution margin	$1.50	$2.00

The variable costs are included in the analysis because they are the incremental costs of producing the products within the existing capacity of 100,000 machine hours per month.

If both products use one machine hour per unit and there is an unlimited market for Product B, the Keystone Company should produce as much of Product B as it possibly can because of its larger contribution margin per unit. At full capacity, the company would generate $200,000 of contribution margin.

Alternatively, suppose that Product A uses one machine hour per unit while Product B requires two machine hours for each unit. If the market for Product A is unlimited, the company should commit all of its efforts to this product because it produces $1.50 of contribution margin per machine hour while Product B produces only $1 per machine hour. This calculation is as follows:

	Product A	Product B
Selling price	$5.00	$7.50
Variable costs	3.50	5.50
Contribution margin	$1.50	$2.00
Machine hours per unit	1.0	2.0
Contribution margin per machine hour	$1.50	$1.00

Thus, by using the entire capacity of 100,000 machine hours to produce 100,000 units of Product A, the Keystone Company can generate $150,000 of contribution margin. If the entire 100,000 hours were used to produce 50,000 units of Product B, the company would generate a contribution margin of only $100,000. Thus, when a company has no excess capacity, only the most profitable product should be manufactured.

But, the need for a mix of different products arises if market demand is not sufficient to allow the company to sell all that it can produce with its capacity. To see how this need arises, assume that the Keystone Company can sell no more than 80,000 units of Product A, even though it can produce as many as 100,000 units. Given this market constraint, the company should produce no more than 80,000 units of Product A. This level will leave another 20,000 machine hours of capacity available for manufacturing Product B. Therefore, the company should use the spare capacity to produce 10,000 units of Product B. This sales mix will maximize the company's contribution margin at $140,000 for the time period.[4]

FAST HINT
Alternative Example:
Assume that Product B's variable costs per unit increased to $6.00 and Product A's variable costs per unit decreased to $3.00. If the same machine hours per unit were used, which product line should Keystone Company emphasize? Why? *Answer:* Product A because its contribution margin of $2.00 per machine hour is higher than Product B's contribution margin of $0.75 per machine hour.

FAST HINT
Relevant Quick Study:
To apply these concepts, work QS 25–6.

Progress Check

25-13 Jimbo, Inc., incurs a joint cost of $1,000 in producing its four products. The selling prices in the following list are for partially and fully processed products. Also shown are the additional costs that would be incurred in finishing the partially processed units:

Product	Unfinished Selling Price	Finished Selling Price	Additional Processing Costs
Alpha	$300	$600	$150
Beta	450	900	300
Gamma	275	425	125
Delta	150	210	75

Which of these products should not be processed further? (a) Alpha; (b) Beta; (c) Gamma; (d) Delta.

25-14 Under what conditions is a sunk cost relevant to decision making?

[4]A mathematical technique called *linear programming* is especially useful for finding the optimal sales mix of a large number of products subject to many different market and production constraints.

LO 1. Explain the importance of capital budgeting, calculate the expected payback period of an investment, and describe its limitations. Capital budgeting is the process of analyzing alternative investments and deciding which assets to acquire or sell. Generally, capital budgeting involves predicting the cash flows to be received from alternative possibilities, evaluating their merits, and then choosing which ones should be pursued.

One method of comparing possible investments calculates and compares their payback periods. This period is an estimate of the time that can be expected to pass before the cumulative net cash inflow from the investment equals its initial cost. The payback period analysis is limited because it fails to reflect the riskiness of the cash flows, differences in the timing of cash flows within the payback period, and all cash flows that occur after the payback period.

LO 2. Calculate the expected average rate of return on an investment and describe its limitations. A project's expected rate of return on the average investment is calculated by dividing the periodic after-tax net income by the average investment in the project. When the net cash flows are received evenly throughout each period, the average investment is calculated as the average of the investment's initial book value and its salvage value. If the net cash flows are expected to be received at the end of each year, the average investment is calculated as the average of the investment's initial book value and its book value at the beginning of the last year in its life. One major limitation of rate of return on average investment is its dependence on predictions of future value derived from depreciation methods. It also fails to reflect year to year variations in expected net incomes.

LO 3. Calculate the net present value of the cash flows from a proposed investment, and describe the procedures used in this method and its advantages and disadvantages. The net present value of an investment is determined by predicting the future cash flows that it is expected to generate, discounting them at a rate that represents an acceptable return, and then subtracting the initial cost of the investment from the sum of the present values. This technique can deal with any pattern of expected cash flows and applies a superior concept of return on investment. However, it is limited by the subjectivity inherent in predicting future cash flows and in selecting the discount rate.

LO 4. Explain how information about incremental costs affects decisions about accepting or rejecting additional volume and about making or buying a component of a product. In deciding whether to produce and sell additional units of product, the relevant factors are the incremental costs and revenues from the additional volume. Costs that will not change as a result of the decision are irrelevant and must not be considered. Incremental costs and revenues are also relevant to a decision between making or buying a component of a product.

LO 5. Describe the importance of sunk costs, out-of-pocket costs, opportunity costs, and contribution margins for decisions such as the choice between scrapping or reworking defective units, selling a product or processing it further, or selecting a sales mix. Sunk costs cannot be avoided because they result from past decisions. Out-of-pocket costs require current outlays of cash. Opportunity costs are potential benefits that are lost as a result of choosing a particular course of action. Because sunk costs have already been incurred, they are not relevant to any decision, including the choice between scrapping or reworking defective units. Out-of-pocket costs that change as a result of choosing an alternative are incremental and relevant to the choice between alternatives. Also, when one course of action precludes taking an alternative, the lost benefits of the rejected alternative should be included among the costs of taking the chosen course of action. These costs apply in decisions between selling a partially completed product or processing it further. The contribution margins of the products must be compared in selecting the sales mix.

Determine the appropriate action in each of the following decision situations:

DEMONSTRATION PROBLEM

a. The Eagleview Company has been operating at 80% of its 100,000 unit per year capacity for manufacturing its product. A chain store has offered to buy an additional 10,000 units at $22 each and sell them in an area where Eagleview currently has no outlet. Consider the following facts:

	Per Unit	Total
Costs at 80% of capacity:		
Direct materials	$ 8.00	$ 640,000
Direct labor	7.00	560,000
Total (fixed and variable) overhead	12.50	1,000,000
Totals	$27.50	$2,200,000

In producing the 10,000 additional units, fixed overhead costs would remain at their present level but incremental variable overhead costs of $3.00 per unit would be incurred. Should the company accept or reject this order?

b. The Foothills Company uses Part JR345 in manufacturing its products. In the past, it has always purchased this part from a supplier for $40 each. It recently upgraded its own manufacturing capabilities and has enough excess capacity (including trained workers) to begin manufacturing Part JR345 instead of buying it. The bookkeeper has prepared the following projection of the cost of making the part, assuming that overhead should be allocated to the part with the normal predetermined application rate of 200% of the direct labor cost:

Direct materials	$11.00
Direct labor	15.00
Total fixed and variable overhead	
(200% of direct labor cost)	30.00
Total	$56.00

The company's accountant reviewed these calculations and determined that the volume of output of the part will not require any incremental fixed overhead cost. Incremental variable overhead cost will be $17 per unit. Should the company make or buy this part?

c. Georgetown Company's manufacturing process causes a relatively large number of defective parts to be produced. The defective parts can be *(1)* sold for scrap, *(2)* melted down to recover the metal for reuse, or *(3)* reworked and otherwise repaired. If defective parts are reworked, the output of other good units is reduced because there is no excess capacity. In fact, each unit reworked means that one new unit cannot be produced. The following information is available about 500 defective parts currently on hand:

Proceeds of selling as scrap	$2,500
Additional cost of melting down all	
defective parts	$ 400
Cost of metal purchases that can be avoided	
by using recycled metal	$4,800
Cost to rework 500 defective parts:	
Direct materials	$ -0-
Direct labor	1,500
Incremental overhead	1,750
Cost to produce 500 new parts:	
Direct materials	$6,000
Direct labor	5,000
Incremental overhead	3,200

Should the company melt down the parts, sell them as scrap, or rework them?

Planning the Solution

- Determine whether the Eagleview Company should accept the additional business by finding the incremental costs of materials, labor, and overhead that will be incurred if the order is accepted. Leave out those fixed costs that will not be increased by the order. If the incremental revenue will exceed the incremental cost, accept the order.

- Determine whether the Foothills Company should make or buy the component by finding the incremental cost of making each unit. If the incremental cost exceeds the purchase price, the component should be purchased.

- Determine whether the Georgetown Company should sell the defective parts, melt them down and recycle the metal, or rework them. To compare the three choices, examine all costs incurred and disposal proceeds received in going from the current condition of having 500 defective units to the condition of having 500 new units. For the scrapping tactic, include the costs of producing 500 brand new units and subtract the $2,500 proceeds from selling the old ones. For the melting tactic, include the costs of melting the defective units, add the net cost of new materials in excess over those obtained from recycling, and add the direct labor and overhead costs. For the reworking tactic, merely add the costs of direct labor and incremental overhead. Then, select the alternative that has the lowest cost. Notice that the cost assigned to the 500 defective units is sunk and not considered in choosing among the three alternatives.

Solution to Demonstration Problem

a. This decision concerns accepting additional business. Because the unit costs seem to be $27.50, it appears as if the offer to sell for $22.00 should be rejected. However, the $27.50 cost includes some fixed costs. When the analysis includes only the incremental costs, the per unit cost is reduced as follows:

Direct materials	$ 8.00
Direct labor	7.00
Variable overhead	3.00
Total incremental cost	$18.00

Therefore, the offer should be accepted because it will produce $4.00 of additional profit per unit, which is a total profit of $40,000 for the 10,000 units.

b. This is a make or buy decision. The bookkeeper's analysis is faulty because it includes the nonincremental overhead of $13 per unit. When only the incremental overhead of $17 is included, the unit cost of manufacturing the part is:

Direct materials	$11.00
Direct labor	15.00
Variable overhead	17.00
Total incremental cost	$43.00

Therefore, it would be better to continue buying the part for $40 instead of making it for $43. (This analysis shows that it is possible to reach the right decision even though the information is incorrect.)

c. This is a scrap or rework decision. The goal is to identify the alternative that produces the greatest benefit to the company. To compare the alternatives on an equal basis, determine the net cost of obtaining 500 marketable units. The comparison is as follows:

	Sell as Is	Melt and Recycle	Rework Old Units
Incremental cost to produce 500 marketable units:			
Direct material:			
Cost of new materials	$ 6,000	$6,000	
Value of recycled metal		(4,800)	
Net materials cost		$1,200	
Melting costs		400	
Total direct material cost . . .	$ 6,000	$1,600	
Direct labor	5,000	5,000	$1,500
Incremental overhead	3,200	3,200	1,750
Total cost to produce 500 marketable units	$14,200	$9,800	$3,250
Less proceeds of selling defective units as scrap	(2,500)		
Net cost	$11,700	$9,800	$3,250

The incremental cost of obtaining 500 marketable parts is smallest if the defective parts are reworked.

GLOSSARY

Capital budgeting the process of analyzing alternative investments and deciding which assets to acquire or sell. p. 954

Incremental cost an additional cost incurred only if a particular action is taken. p. 964

Net present value an estimate of an asset's value to the company; calculated by discounting the future cash flows from the investment at a satisfactory rate and then subtracting the initial cost of the investment. p. 960

Opportunity cost the potential benefits of one alternative that are lost by choosing another. p. 968

Out-of-pocket cost a cost that requires a current outlay of cash; usually an incremental cost. p. 968

Payback period the time expected to pass before the net cash flows from an investment return its initial cost. p. 955

Rate of return on average investment a rate used to evaluate the acceptability of an investment; equals the after-tax periodic income divided by the average investment in the asset. p. 957

Sunk cost a cost that cannot be avoided or changed in any way because it arises from a past decision; irrelevant to future decisions. p. 967

QUESTIONS

1. What is capital budgeting? Why are capital budgeting decisions risky?

2. The predicted net cash flows from an investment may be calculated and expressed directly or indirectly. What is the difference between these two presentations?

3. Why is an investment more attractive if it has a short payback period?

4. What is the average amount invested in a machine during its life if it costs $132,000 and has a predicted five-year life with a $27,000 salvage value? Assume that the net income is received evenly throughout each year.

5. What is your answer to Question 4, assuming that the net income is received near the end of each year?

6. Why is the present value of $100 that you expect to receive one year from now less than $100? What is the present value of $100 that you expect to receive one year from now, discounted at 12%?

7. If the present value of the expected net cash flows from a machine, discounted at 12%, exceeds the amount to be invested, what can you say about the expected rate of return on the investment? What can you say about the expected rate of return if the present value of the net cash flows, discounted at 12%, is less than the amount of the investment?

8. Why is the value of an investment increased by using accelerated depreciation (instead of straight-line) for income tax reporting?

9. A company manufactures and sells 250,000 units of product at $50 per unit in domestic markets. The product costs $30 per unit to manufacture. Can you describe a situation under which the company may be willing to sell an additional 25,000 units of the product in an international market at $24 per unit?

10. What is an out-of-pocket cost? What is an opportunity cost? Are opportunity costs recorded in the accounting records?

11. Any costs that have been incurred in manufacturing a product are sunk costs. Why are sunk costs irrelevant in

deciding whether to sell the product in its present condition or to make it into a new product through additional processing?

12. Identify the incremental costs incurred by Federal Express for one additional package that is dropped off by the sender at a local office and delivered as one of a number of other packages to the headquarters of a major corporation. How might the company's pricing policies reflect these incremental costs?

QUICK STUDY (Five-Minute Exercises)

QS 25–1
(LO 1)

Blaylock Company is considering investment X that requires an immediate payment of $12,000 and provides an expected cash return of $4,800 annually for four years. What is the payback period?

QS 25–2
(LO 1)

Maddock Company is considering two alternative investments: Investment A has a payback period of 2.5 years and Investment B has a payback period of 3.25 years. Why might Maddock analyze the two alternatives and choose B over A?

QS 25–3
(LO 2)

Jake Company is considering two investments, each of which is expected to generate an average net income after taxes of $5,000 for three years. Each investment costs $30,000 and has no salvage value. The cash flows from investment M are received evenly throughout the year and the cash flows from investment N are received at the end of each year. Calculate the rate of return on each investment.

QS 25–4
(LO 3)

If Fox Company invests $60,000 now, it can expect to receive $11,000 at the end of each year for seven years plus $6,000 at the end of the seventh year. What is the net present value of the investment, assuming Fox demands an 8% return on the investment?

QS 25–5
(LO 4)

Gaff Company incurs the following per unit costs related to one of the products it currently manufactures and sells for $8 per unit: The per unit costs and expenses assigned to the product amount to $6. Instead of manufacturing and selling this product, Gaff can purchase a similar product for $5 and sell it for $7. If this is done, unit sales would remain unchanged and $4.50 of the costs assigned to the product would be eliminated. Should Gaff continue to manufacture the product or purchase the alternative product?

QS 25–6
(LO 5)

Nance Company can sell all the units of products X and Y that it produces but has limited production capacity. It can produce two units of X per hour or four units of Y per hour and has 6,000 production hours available. Product X has a contribution margin of $4 and Product Y has a contribution margin of $3. What is the most profitable sales mix for Nance Company?

EXERCISES

Calculate the payback periods for these two unrelated investments:

Exercise 25–1
Payback period,
 uniform cash flows
(LO 2)

a. A new automatic control system for an existing machine is expected to cost $125,000 and have a useful life of nine years. The system should save $60,000 (after 30% taxes) each year, after deducting straight-line depreciation on the system. The predicted salvage value of the system is $12,500.

b. A machine costs $250,000, has a $10,000 salvage value, is expected to last five years, and will generate net income of $52,000 per year after straight-line depreciation and after 40% income taxes.

The Arrow Company is considering the purchase of an asset for $120,000. The asset is expected to produce the following net cash flows:

Exercise 25–2
Payback period, unequal annual
net cash inflows
(LO 2)

	Net Cash Inflows
Year 1	$ 30,000
Year 2	37,500
Year 3	45,000
Year 4	60,000
Year 5	9,000
Total	$181,500

The cash flows would occur evenly throughout each year. Calculate the payback period for this investment.

A machine can be purchased for $240,000 and used for five years to generate these net incomes:

Exercise 25–3
Payback period from income
statement data
(LO 2)

Year 1	$ 34,000
Year 2	67,200
Year 3	100,400
Year 4	133,600
Year 5	166,800

In projecting the expected net incomes, double-declining balance depreciation was deducted, based on a five-year life and a salvage value of $22,000. Present calculations to show the payback period for the machine. Ignore income taxes.

Asset X is expected to cost $750,000. Management also predicts that it will have a 10-year service life and a $120,000 salvage value. Asset Y is expected to cost $360,000. Management predicts that the asset will have a four-year service life and no salvage value. Straight-line depreciation would be used for these assets.

Exercise 25–4
Calculating average investment
(LO 3)

   Calculate the average investment in each asset under the assumptions that the income from using them is to be received (a) evenly throughout each year and (b) at the end of each year.

Roya Company is considering the purchase of equipment that would allow the company to add a new product to its line. The equipment is expected to cost $160,000 with an eight-year life and no salvage value. It will be depreciated on a straight-line basis. The company expects to sell 96,000 units of the equipment's product each year. However, the product is very specialized and can be sold only during the holiday season at the end of each year. As a result, all sales and cash flows will occur during the last 30 days of the year. Expected annual net income is as follows:

Exercise 25–5
Payback and return on
average investment
(LO 2, 3)

Sales		$124,800
Costs:		
Materials, labor, and overhead (except for depreciation on the new equipment)	$ 81,600	
Depreciation on the new equipment	20,000	
Selling and administrative expenses	12,000	
Total expenses		$113,600
Operating income		$ 11,200
Income taxes (30%)		3,360
Net income		$ 7,840

Required

Calculate (a) the payback period and (b) the return on average investment for this equipment.

Exercise 25–6
Net present value of an investment
(LO 3)

After evaluating the risk of the investment described in Exercise 25–5, the Roya Company concludes that it must earn at least a 4% compounded return on the investment in the equipment. Use this rate to determine the net present value of the investment in the equipment.

Exercise 25–7
Net present values of investments
(LO 4)

The Mega Company can invest in each of three projects, A, B, and C. Each project would require an initial investment of $190,000 and would produce the following annual cash flows:

	A	B	C
Year 1	$ 20,000	$ 80,000	$180,000
Year 2	80,000	80,000	40,000
Year 3	140,000	80,000	20,000
Total	$240,000	$240,000	$240,000

Required

Under the assumption that the company requires a 12% compounded return from its investments, use net present values to determine which project or projects should be acquired.

Exercise 25–8
Analysis of an offer for additional volume
(LO 5)

Lanier Company expects to sell 100,000 units of its product during the next period with the following results:

Sales		$3,000,000
Costs and expenses:		
Direct materials	$ 320,000	
Direct labor	800,000	
Factory overhead	220,000	
Selling expenses	300,000	
Administrative expenses	514,000	
Total costs and expenses		$2,154,000
Net income		$ 846,000

The company has an opportunity to sell 30,000 additional units at a price of $20 per unit. The additional sales would not affect the regular sales. Direct material and direct labor unit costs would be the same for the additional units as they are for the regular units. However, the additional volume would create these incremental effects on costs:

• Total factory overhead would increase by 15%.
• Total administrative expenses would increase by $86,000.

Prepare an appropriate analysis to determine whether the company should accept or reject the offer to sell the additional units at the reduced price.

Exercise 25–9
Analysis of a make or buy decision
(LO 5)

Devoe Company currently manufactures a part at a cost of $2.30 per unit. This cost is based on a normal production rate of 100,000 units per year. The variable costs are $1.74 per unit, fixed costs related only to the part are $36,000 per year, and allocated fixed costs are $60,000 per year. These allocated costs would continue whether the company makes or buys the part. Devoe is considering buying the part from a supplier that has quoted a price of $2.50 per unit. This price would be guaranteed for a three-year period.

Should the company continue to manufacture the part or should it purchase the part from the outside supplier? Support your answer with an analysis.

The Newton Company has 15,000 units of Product A that were manufactured for a total cost of $30 per unit. The 15,000 units can be sold at this stage for $975,000. Alternatively, they can receive further processing at a total additional cost of $222,000 and be converted into 4,500 units of Product B and 10,500 units of Product C. Product B can be sold for $100 per unit and Product C can be sold for $64 per unit.

Exercise 25–10
Analysis of whether to do additional processing on a product
(LO 6)

Required

Prepare an analysis that shows whether the units of Product A should be processed further.

The Persimmons Company owns a machine that can produce two different products. Product 1 can be produced at the rate of two units per hour and Product 2 can be produced at the rate of five units per hour. The capacity of the machine is 2,200 hours per year. The highly specialized products are sold to a single customer who has agreed to buy all of the company's output up to a maximum of 3,750 units of Product 1 and 2,000 units of Product 2. Selling prices and variable costs per unit to produce the products are:

Exercise 25–11
Analysis of best sales mix
(LO 5)

	Product 1	Product 2
Selling price	$12.50	$7.50
Variable costs	3.75	4.50

Required

Determine the most profitable sales mix for the company and calculate the contribution margin that results from that sales mix.

PROBLEMS

The Heartland Company is planning to add a new product to its line. To assemble this product, the company would have to buy a new machine at a cost of $250,000. The asset is expected to have a four-year life and a $20,000 salvage value. This additional information is available:

Problem 25–1
Payback, return on investment, and net present value
(LO 2, 3, 4)

Expected annual sales of new product	$1,187,500
Expected costs:	
Direct materials	312,500
Direct labor	437,500
Factory overhead excluding depreciation on new machine	202,500
Selling and administrative expenses	100,000
State and federal income taxes	40%

All sales are for cash and all costs are out-of-pocket, except the depreciation on the new machine.

Required

1. Calculate the amount of straight-line depreciation that would be taken in each year of the asset's life.

2. Determine the amounts of net income and cash flow expected in each year of the asset's life.

3. Calculate the payback period on the investment in the new machine, assuming that the cash flows occur evenly throughout each year.

4. Calculate the rate of return on the average investment in the new machine, assuming that the net income occurs at the end of each year.

5. Calculate the net present value of the investment with a discount rate of 7%, assuming that all cash flows occur at the end of each year. (Be sure to include the salvage value as a cash flow in the last year of the asset's life.)

Problem 25–2
Payback, return on investment, and net present value
(LO 2, 3, 4)

The Hendrix Company has the opportunity to invest in one of two projects. Project Y requires an investment of $144,000 for new machinery having a four-year life and no salvage value. Project Z requires an investment of $144,000 for new machinery having a three-year life and no salvage value. The two projects would produce the following predicted annual results:

	Project Y	Project Z
Sales	$180,000	$150,000
Expenses:		
Direct materials	$ 24,000	$ 18,000
Direct labor	37,500	27,000
Factory overhead including depreciation	81,000	78,000
Selling and administrative expenses	18,000	18,000
Total expenses	$160,500	$141,000
Operating income	$ 19,500	$ 9,000
Income taxes (25%)	4,875	2,250
Net income	$ 14,625	$ 6,750

Assume that the company uses straight-line depreciation and that the cash flows occur at the end of the year.

Required

Preparation component:

1. Find the annual cash flows expected for the two projects.
2. Find the payback period expected for the two projects.

3. Find the rate of return on average investment expected for the two projects.
4. Find the net present value of the investment for the two projects, using 8% as the discount rate.

Analysis component:

5. Select the project that you would recommend to management and explain your choice.

Problem 25–3
Income results of added sales
(LO 5)

ColorKing Company manufactures markers that it sells to wholesalers at $4 per package. The company manufactures and sells approximately 300,000 packages of markers each year, and normal costs for the production and sale of this quantity are as follows:

Direct materials	$384,000
Direct labor	96,000
Factory overhead	288,000
Selling expenses	120,000
Administrative expenses	80,000
Total	$968,000

A wholesaler has offered to buy 50,000 packages of markers for $3.44 each. These markers would be marketed under the wholesaler's name and would not affect ColorKing's sales through its normal channels.

A study of the costs of the new business reveals the following information:

- Direct material costs are 100% variable.
- The per unit direct labor costs for the additional units would be 50% greater than normal because their production would require overtime pay at one-and-one-half times the usual labor rate.
- One-fourth of the normal annual overhead costs are fixed at any production level from 250,000 to 400,000 units. The remaining three-fourths of the annual overhead cost is variable with volume.
- There will be no additional selling costs if the new business is accepted.
- Accepting the new business would increase administrative expenses by a fixed amount of $4,000.

Required

Prepare a three-column comparative income statement that shows:

1. The operating income for one year without the special order.
2. The operating income that would be received from the new business.
3. The combined results for one year from normal business and the new business.

CHECK FIGURE:
Combined operating income,
$276,000

The McMorris Corporation is considering a project that would require a $30,000 investment in an asset with no salvage value. The project would produce $12,000 of income before depreciation at the end of each year for six years. The company's income tax rate is 40%. In compiling its tax return and computing its income tax payments, the company can choose between these two alternative depreciation schedules:

Problem 25–4
Calculating cash flows and net present values with alternative tax depreciation methods
(LO 4)

	Straight-Line Depreciation Schedule	MACRS Depreciation Schedule
Year 1	$ 3,000	$ 6,000
Year 2	6,000	9,600
Year 3	6,000	5,760
Year 4	6,000	3,456
Year 5	6,000	3,456
Year 6	3,000	1,728
Total	$30,000	$30,000

Required

Preparation component:

1. Produce a five-column table that shows these items for each of the six years: *(a)* income before depreciation, *(b)* straight-line depreciation expense, *(c)* taxable income, *(d)* income taxes, and *(e)* net cash flow. The net cash flow equals the amount of income before depreciation minus the income taxes.

2. Produce a five-column table that shows these items for each of the six years: *(a)* income before depreciation, *(b)* MACRS depreciation expense, *(c)* taxable income, *(d)* income taxes, and *(e)* net cash flow. The net cash flow equals the amount of income before depreciation minus the income taxes.

3. Calculate the net present value of the investment if straight-line depreciation is used. Use 10% as the discount rate.

4. Calculate the net present value of the investment if MACRS depreciation is used. Use 10% as the discount rate.

CHECK FIGURE:
Net present value of investment
(MACRS), $10,635

Analysis component:

5. Explain why the MACRS depreciation method increases the net present value of this project.

Problem 25–5
Results of alternative
sales mixes
(LO 6)

The Duffy Company is capable of producing two products, X and Y, with the same machine in its factory. These facts are known:

	Product X	Product Y
Selling price	$50.00	$100.00
Variable costs	20.00	45.00
Contribution	$30.00	$ 55.00
Machine hours to produce 1 unit	0.4	1.0
Maximum unit sales per month	500	250

The company presently operates the machine for a single eight-hour shift for 22 working days each month. The management is thinking about operating the machine for two shifts, which will increase the machine's availability by another eight hours per day for 22 days per month. This change would require additional fixed costs of $2,500 per month.

Required

1. Determine the contribution margin per machine hour that each product generates.

2. How many units of X and Y should the company produce if it continues to operate with only one shift? How much total contribution margin is produced each month with this mix?

CHECK FIGURE:

Units of Y to be produced,
152 units

3. If the company adds another shift, how many units of X and Y should the company produce? How much total contribution margin would be produced each month with this mix? Should the company add the new shift?

4. Suppose that the company determines it can also increase the maximum sales of Product X to 750 units per month by spending $5,000 per month in marketing efforts. Should the company pursue this tactic together with the double shift?

CRITICAL THINKING: ESSAYS, PROBLEMS, AND CASES

Analytical Essay

(LO 5)

The Select Company manufactures gadgets by carving them out of solid 100-pound blocks of raw material. Each block costs $120, and the one gadget from a block can be sold for $200. For many years, the scrap was simply dumped in a large waste pile and eventually biodegraded harmlessly. This wasted material represents about 20% of the total weight of the block.

Several years ago, another company developed a product that could be made from this waste. At that time, Select and the other company negotiated an arrangement. Select would bag the waste in 20-pound sacks, and the other company would pick them up at Select's factory and pay $20 per bag for them. At the time of entering into the arrangement, the Select bookkeeper had produced an analysis of the costs and concluded that the price of $2 per pound produced a profit of $0.10 per pound. Although this seemed like a small amount, it was better than nothing, and nothing was all that the company was receiving before. The analysis assigned material cost to the waste as follows:

Item	Selling Price	Percent of Total	Allocated Cost	Cost per Unit
Gadget	$200	83.3%	$100.00	$100 per gadget
Waste	20	16.7	20.00	$1.00 per lb.
Total	$220	100.0%	$120.00	

The labor cost of putting the waste into the bags was determined to be $0.40 per pound. Then, overhead was assigned at the normal rate of 125% of the labor cost. As a result, the total cost per pound was determined to be:

Material	$1.00
Labor	0.40
Overhead	0.50
Total cost	$1.90

The incremental overhead for the packaging activity was $0.08 per pound, and the remaining $0.42 happened with or without the packaging activity.

A new offer was recently received from a competitor of the company that had been hauling away the bagged waste. This company offered to simply pay $1.20 per pound and pick it up at the plant in bulk. The Select Company convened a management committee to consider this offer. Sales of gadgets had been high and a lot of waste was being produced. Any additional profit from selling it was considered important.

The senior bookkeeper prepared for the meeting by checking the files for the prior analysis. He concluded that the new arrangement would increase the profit to $0.20 per pound, which is the excess of the $1.20 selling price over the raw material cost of $1.00. The junior bookkeeper prepared another analysis that allocated the cost of the raw material differently because the selling prices would change. Here are the results of the allocation:

Item	Selling Price	Percent of Total	Allocated Cost	Cost per Unit
Gadget	$200	89.3%	$107.16	$107.15 per gadget
Waste	24	10.7	12.84	$0.642 per lb.
Total	$224	100.0%	$120.00	

Thus, this bookkeeper concluded that the new deal would create a profit of nearly $0.56 per pound, which greatly exceeds the present $0.10 per pound.

The marketing manager found the exercise amusing because the waste product used to be simply thrown away. He figured the profit would have to be at least $1.20 per pound anyway it was looked at.

In the meeting, the company's controller and president heard the opinions of the other three. When the president appeared to be leaning toward accepting the new offer, the controller quietly said, "The profit on this new deal doesn't come anywhere near the profit on the old one. We would be making a mistake to change now under these terms." The president quickly regained composure, agreed with the controller, and the meeting adjourned.

Who was right? Was this decision sound? Explain what you think and support your position with an analysis of the numbers.

Managerial Analysis Problem

(LO 2, 3, 4, 6)

Kansas Livestock Company operates several feedlots, one of which is located at Newton. The Newton feedlot no longer produces a profit because of its distance from sources of feed, relatively high transportation costs, and a lack of modern facilities. As a result, management is considering the possibility of constructing a new feedlot in Madison.

The new feedlot would be close to a feed source and near meatpackers. If the Madison lot were to be built, the Newton lot would be closed down. The company president favors making the move for several reasons, but several directors have asked for more detailed information before approving the decision. Their main concern is that abandoning the Newton lot would create a large loss.

You were asked to analyze the proposal and to provide information to help the directors decide whether to support the president's desire to move to Madison. You have developed the data described in the following paragraphs:

Loss from abandoning the Newton lot. The land and facilities of the Newton lot have a $1 million book value. Virtually none of the machinery or other assets can be sold, and the land is not suitable for any other use without prohibitive reclamation costs. Based on the price predicted by the company's real estate consultant, only $100,000 cash would be received through the sale of the land and the facilities, after considering income taxes. The $900,000 loss from this sale is standing between the directors and their support for the president.

Investment in the new lot. The new Madison feedlot would have an upfront total cost of $5 million. In addition to being closer to feed sources and cattle buyers, this feedlot would double the capacity of the Newton lot. Management estimates that 100,000 head of cattle could be handled every year.

Comparative costs. At their full capacity volumes of 50,000 and 100,000 head, the costs per head at the old lot and the predicted costs per head at the new lot are:

	Newton Lot	Madison Lot
Variable, feed, labor, and operating costs (all are out-of-pocket costs) . .	$88	$72
Depreciation (fixed cost)	2	5
Total costs per head	$90	$77

The higher per head depreciation cost for the new Madison lot arises primarily from the higher total cost, even though it will be able to handle a larger volume.

Analyze the alternatives using net present values and make a recommendation. Present any pertinent schedules needed to produce the data used in your analysis.

To make the problem manageable, assume that both feedlots can operate for 10 years. The revenue per head would be the same at the two feedlots. Despite operating at full capacity, the Newton lot has only been breaking even, which means that the revenue per head is equal to the cost per head just shown. The corporation is subject to a 30% income tax rate. It will not be possible to operate both the Newton and Madison lots. As a reflection of the high risk that they perceive, the directors want to have at least a 15% return on any investment that the company would make in the new Madison feedlot.

Ethical Issues Essay   Examine the ethics case on page 965. What do you think is the right advice to give this manager? Is there anything that might move the proposal through the system more quickly?

ANSWERS TO PROGRESS CHECKS

25–1 *b*

25–2 They usually are based on predictions of events that might occur well into the future.

25–3 *b*

25–4 Depreciation expense is subtracted from revenues in calculating net income. However, it does not use cash and should be added back to net income to calculate net cash flows.

25–5 Not necessarily. One investment may continue to generate cash flows beyond the payback period for a longer time than the other. Also, the timing of their cash flows within the payback period may differ.

25–6 *b* Average investment = ($180,000 + $15,000)/2 = $97,500
Return on average investment = $40,000/$97,500 = 41%

25–7 It cannot be determined without comparing it to the returns expected from alternative investments with similar risk.

25–8 Project A

		Project A		Project B	
Year	Present Value of $1 at 10%	Net Cash Flows	Present Value of Net Cash Flows	Net Cash Flows	Present Value of Net Cash Flows
1	.9091	$12,000	$10,909	$ 4,500	$ 4,091
2	.8264	8,500	7,024	8,500	7,024
3	.7513	4,000	3,005	13,000	9,767
Total		$24,500	$20,938	$26,000	$20,882
Amount to be invested			(20,000)		(20,000)
Net present value of investment			$ 938		$ 882

25–9   No, the information is too limited to draw that conclusion. One investment may have more risk than the other.

25–10   Net present value.

25–11   Variable costs per unit for special order:

Direct materials ($37,500/7,500)	$ 5.00
Direct labor ($60,000/7,500)	8.00
Variable factory overhead [(.30 × $20,000)/7,500]	.80
Variable selling expenses [(.60 × $25,000 × .5)/7,500] . .	1.00
Total	$14.80

Cost to produce special order:
   (200 × $14.80) + $400 = $3,360
Required price per unit:
   ($3,360 + $1,000)/200 = $21.80

25–12   They are the additional costs that will result from accepting the additional business.

25–13   *d*

25–14   It is never relevant because it results from a past decision.

Payroll Reports, Records, and Procedures

After studying Appendix C, you should be able to:

1. Describe an employer's payroll reports and records, and the procedures used to calculate tax withholdings and issue checks to employees.
2. Define or explain the terms and phrases listed in the appendix glossary.

A typical feature of many small businesses that get into financial trouble is that they have failed to file required payroll reports. Understanding the importance of following appropriate payroll procedures and keeping adequate payroll records is essential to business success.

Payroll expenses involve liabilities to individual employees, to federal and state governments, and usually to other organizations such as insurance companies. In addition to paying these liabilities, employers are required to prepare and submit a variety of reports that explain how the payments were determined.

PAYROLL REPORTS

LO 1

Describe an employer's payroll reports and records, and the procedures used to calculate tax withholdings and issue checks to employees.

Reporting FICA Taxes and Income Tax Withholdings to the Federal Government

According to the Federal Insurance Contributions Act, each employer must file an Employer's Quarterly Federal Tax Return within one month after the end of each calendar quarter. (An example of this tax information return, known as Form 941, is shown in Illustration C–1.)

In Illustration C–1, notice that on line 2 of Form 941, an employer reports the total payments of wages subject to income tax withholding. The amount of income tax withheld is reported on lines 3 and 5. The combined amount of the employees' and employer's FICA (Social Security) taxes is reported on line 6a where it says, "Taxable social security wages" $34,370.50 × 12.4% = Tax, $4,261.94. The 12.4% is the sum of the (1995) 6.2% tax withheld from the employees' wages for the quarter plus the 6.2% tax levied on the employer. The combined amount of the employees' and employer's Medicare wages is reported on line 7. Total FICA taxes (Social Security plus Medicare) are reported on lines 8 and 10, and then are added to the total income taxes withheld. Finally, the total of the amounts deposited in a **federal depository bank** during the quarter is subtracted to determine if a balance remains to be paid. Federal depository banks are authorized to accept deposits of amounts payable to the federal government.

Deposit requirements depend on the amount of tax owed. If the sum of the FICA taxes plus the employees' income taxes is less than $500 for a quarter, the taxes may be paid when the Form 941 is filed. Companies with larger payrolls may have to pay monthly or semiweekly. If the taxes are $100,000 or more at the end of any day, they must be paid by the end of the next banking day.

Illustration C–1 Employer's Quarterly Report of Federal Taxes Withheld

Form **941** (Rev. April 1994) Department of the Treasury Internal Revenue Service (O)	**Employer's Quarterly Federal Tax Return** ► See separate instructions for information on completing this return. **Please type or print.**

4141

OMB No. 1545-0029

Enter state code for state in which deposits made ► [:] (see page 2 of instructions).

Name (as distinguished from trade name)

Trade name, if any
Graphic Planners, Inc.

Address (number and street)
907 Falcon Trail

Date quarter ended
Sept. 30, 1995

Employer identification number
74-1633163

City, state, and ZIP code
Austin, TX 78746

T	
FF	
FD	
FP	
I	
T	

If address is different from prior return, check here ►

IRS Use

1 1 1 1 1 1 1 1 1 1   2   3 3 3 3 3   4 4 4

5 5 5   6   7   8 8 8 8 8   9 9 9   10 10 10 10 10 10 10 10 10

If you do not have to file returns in the future, check here ► [ ]   and enter date final wages paid ►

If you are a seasonal employer, see **Seasonal employers** on page 2 and check here (see instructions) ► [ ]

1	Number of employees (except household) employed in the pay period that includes March 12th ►		
2	Total wages and tips subject to withholding, plus other compensation	**2**	34,370 50
3	Total income tax withheld from wages, tips, and sick pay	**3**	3,820 20
4	Adjustment of withheld income tax for preceding quarters of calendar year	**4**	
5	Adjusted total of income tax withheld (line 3 as adjusted by line 4—see instructions) . . .	**5**	3,820 20
6a	Taxable social security wages . . . . $ 34,370 50 × 12.4% (.124) =	**6a**	4,261 94
b	Taxable social security tips . . . . . . $ × 12.4% (.124) =	**6b**	
7	Taxable Medicare wages and tips . . . . . $ 34,370 50 × 2.9% (.029) =	**7**	996 74
8	Total social security and Medicare taxes (add lines 6a, 6b, and 7). Check here if wages are not subject to social security and/or Medicare tax . . . . ► [ ]	**8**	5,258 68
9	Adjustment of social security and Medicare taxes (see instructions for required explanation) Sick Pay $ _____ ± Fractions of Cents $ _____ ± Other $ _____ =	**9**	
10	Adjusted total of social security and Medicare taxes (line 8 as adjusted by line 9—see instructions)	**10**	5,258 68
11	**Total taxes** (add lines 5 and 10)	**11**	9,078 88
12	Advance earned income credit (EIC) payments made to employees, if any	**12**	
13	Net taxes (subtract line 12 from line 11). **This should equal line 17, column (d) below** (or line D of Schedule B (Form 941))	**13**	9,078 88
14	Total deposits for quarter, including overpayment applied from a prior quarter	**14**	9,078 88
15	**Balance due** (subtract line 14 from line 13). Pay to Internal Revenue Service	**15**	-0-
16	**Overpayment,** if line 14 is more than line 13, enter excess here ► $ _____ and check if to be: [ ] Applied to next return **OR** [ ] Refunded.		

• **All filers:** If line 13 is less than $500, you need not complete line 17 or Schedule B.

• **Semiweekly depositors:** Complete Schedule B and check here . . . . ► [ ]

• **Monthly depositors:** Complete line 17, columns (a) through (d) and check here . . . . ► [x]

17	**Monthly Summary of Federal Tax Liability.**			
	(a) First month liability	**(b)** Second month liability	**(c)** Third month liability	**(d)** Total liability for quarter
	3,026.29	3,026.29	3,026.30	9,078.88

Sign Here   Under penalties of perjury, I declare that I have examined this return, including accompanying schedules and statements, and to the best of my knowledge and belief, it is true, correct, and complete.

Signature ►   Print Your Name and Title ► **President**   Date ►**Oct. 25, 1995**

For Paperwork Reduction Act Notice, see page 1 of separate instructions.   Cat. No. 17001Z   Form **941** (Rev. 4-94)

*U.S. Government Printing Office: 1995 — 387-095/00360

Illustration C–2 Reporting an Employee's Annual Wages and Taxes

a Control number		OMB No. 1545-0008		
b Employer's identification number 74-1633163		**1** Wages, tips, other compensation 24,560.60		**2** Federal income tax withheld 2,460.00
c Employer's name, address, and ZIP code Graphic Planners, Inc 907 Falcon Trail Austin, TX 78746		**3** Social security wages 24,560.60		**4** Social security tax withheld 1,522.76
		5 Medicare wages and tips 24,560.60		**6** Medicare tax withheld 356.13
		7 Social security tips		**8** Allocated tips
d Employee's social security number 302-02-0222		**9** Advance EIC payment		**10** Dependent care benefits
e Employee's name, address, and ZIP code Charles Robert Lusk 1310 East 5th Street Austin, TX 78711		**11** Nonqualified plans		**12** Benefits included in box 1
		13 See Instrs. for box 13		**14** Other
		15 Statutory employee ☐ Deceased ☐ Pension plan ☐ Legal rep. ☐ 942 emp. ☐ Subtotal ☐ Deferred compensation ☐		
16 State Employer's state I.D. No.	**17** State wages, tips, etc.	**18** State income tax	**19** Locality name	**20** Local wages, tips, etc. **21** Local income tax

Department of the Treasury—Internal Revenue Service

Form **W-2** **Wage and Tax Statement** **1994**

Copy B To Be Filed With Employee's FEDERAL Tax Return

This information is being furnished to the Internal Revenue Service.

Reporting FUTA Taxes and SUTA Taxes

An employer's federal unemployment taxes are reported on an annual basis. The report is filed on an Annual Federal Unemployment Tax Return, Form 940. It must be mailed on or before January 31 following the end of each tax year. (Ten additional days are allowed for filing if all required tax deposits are made on a timely basis and the full amount of the tax is paid on or before January 31.) Payments of FUTA taxes are made quarterly to a federal depository bank if the total amount due exceeds $100. If $100 or less is due, the taxes are remitted annually with the Form 940.

Requirements for the payment and reporting of state unemployment taxes vary depending on the laws of the state. A requirement of quarterly payments and quarterly reports is typical.

Reporting Wages to Employees

Employers are required to provide each employee an annual report of the employee's wages subject to FICA and federal income taxes and the amounts of such taxes withheld. The report, a Wage and Tax Statement or Form W-2, must be given to the

Illustration C–3 A Payroll Register

														Payroll Week Ended
		Daily Time									Earnings			
Employees	Clock Card No.	M	T	W	T	F	S	S	Total Hours	O.T. Hours	Regular Pay Rate	Regular Pay	O.T. Premium Pay	Gross Pay
Robert Austin	114	8	8	8	8	8			40		10.00	400.00		400.00
Judy Cross	102	8	8	8	8	8			40		15.00	600.00		600.00
John Cruz	108	0	8	8	8	8	8		40		14.00	560.00		560.00
Kay Keife	109	8	8	8	8	8	8		48	8	14.00	672.00	56.00	728.00
Lee Miller	112	8	8	8	8	0			32		14.00	448.00		448.00
Dale Sears	103	8	8	8	8	8	4		44	4	15.00	660.00	30.00	690.00
Totals												3,340.00	86.00	3,426.00

employee before January 31 following the year covered by the report. (Illustration C–2 shows an example of a Form W-2.)

Copies of the W-2 Forms must also be sent to the Social Security Administration, which posts to each employee's Social Security account the amount of the employee's wages subject to FICA tax and the FICA tax withheld. These posted amounts become the basis for determining the employee's retirement and survivors' benefits. The Social Security Administration also transmits to the Internal Revenue Service the amount of each employee's wages subject to federal income tax and the amount of such tax withheld.

PAYROLL RECORDS MAINTAINED BY EMPLOYERS

In addition to reports and payment of taxes, all employers must maintain certain payroll records. These generally include a **Payroll Register** for each pay period showing the pay period dates and the hours worked, gross pay, deductions, and net pay of each employee. An individual earnings record for each employee is also required.

The Payroll Register

Illustration C–3 shows a typical Payroll Register for a weekly pay period. Note that the columns under the heading Daily Time show the hours worked each day by each employee. If hours worked include overtime hours, these are entered in the column headed O.T. Hours.

The Regular Pay Rate column shows the hourly pay rate of each employee. Total hours worked multiplied by the regular pay rate equals regular pay. Overtime hours multiplied by the overtime premium rate equals overtime premium pay. Note that the overtime premium rate in this case is 50%. If employers are engaged in interstate commerce, federal law sets the minimum wage and overtime rate that must be paid to employees. In 1995, the minimum wage was $4.25 per hour. Also, the minimum overtime premium was 50% of the regular rate for hours worked in excess of 40 during any week. In other words, workers must earn at least 150% of their regular rate for hours in excess of 40 per week.

In Illustration C–3, notice the separate columns for each type of payroll deduction and for the expense accounts to which the payroll cost should be charged. As a result, the Payroll Register contains all of the data necessary to record the payroll in the General Journal.

March 23, 19__										
Deductions							**Payment**		**Distribution**	
FICA Taxes		Federal			Total					
Medi-care	Social Security	Income Taxes	Hosp. Ins.	Union Dues	Deduc-tions		Net Pay	Check No.	Sales Salaries	Office Salaries
5.80	24.80	37.00	40.00		107.60		292.40	893		400.00
8.70	37.20	93.00	56.00	10.00	204.90		395.10	894	600.00	
8.12	34.72	82.00	56.00	10.00	190.84		369.16	895	560.00	
10.56	45.14	127.00	56.00	10.00	248.70		479.30	896	728.00	
6.50	27.78	53.00	56.00	10.00	153.28		294.72	897	448.00	
10.00	42.78	118.00	56.00		226.78		463.22	898		690.00
49.68	212.42	510.00	320.00	40.00	1,132.10		2,293.90		2,336.00	1,090.00

Employee's Individual Earnings Record

An **Employee's Individual Earnings Record,** as shown in Illustration C–4, provides a full year's summary of an employee's working time, gross earnings, deductions, and net pay. In addition, it accumulates information that indicates when an employee's earnings have reached the tax-exempt points for FICA and state and federal unemployment taxes. It also supplies the data the employer needs to prepare the Wage and Tax Statement, Form W-2. The payroll information on an Employee's Individual Earnings Record is taken from the Payroll Register.

CALCULATING FEDERAL INCOME TAX WITHHOLDINGS

The amount of tax to be withheld from each employee's wages is determined by the amount of the wages earned and the number of the employee's personal **withholding allowances.** Each employee indicates the number of withholding allowances claimed on a withholding allowance certificate (Form W-4) and gives it to the employer. As the number of withholding allowances claimed increases, the amount of income tax to be withheld decreases.

Most employers use a **wage bracket withholding table** similar to the one shown in Illustration C–5 to determine the federal income taxes to be withheld from each employee's gross pay. The illustrated table is for single employees who are paid weekly. Different tables are provided for married employees and for biweekly, semi-monthly, and monthly pay periods.

When using the tables to determine the federal income tax to be withheld from an employee's gross wages, locate the employee's wage bracket in the first two columns of the appropriate withholding table. Then, find the amount to be withheld by looking in the withholding allowance column appropriate for the employee.

PAYING THE EMPLOYEES

In a company that has few employees, employees are paid with checks drawn on the regular bank account. A business with many employees normally uses a special **payroll bank account** to pay its employees. When such an account is used, one check for the total payroll is drawn on the regular bank account and deposited in the special payroll bank account. The entry to record this transaction is:

Mar.	23	Accrued Payroll Payable	2,293.90	
		Cash		2,293.90
		Transfer of cash to payroll bank account.		

Illustration C–4 Employee's Individual Earnings Record

Employee's Name	Robert Austin	S.S. Acct. No.	307-03-2195	Employee No.	114

Home Address: 111 South Greenwood   Notify in Case of Emergency: Margaret Austin   Phone No.: 964-9834

Employed: June 7, 1980   Date of Termination: ____   Reason: ____

Date of Birth: June 6, 1962   Date Becomes 65: June 6, 2027   Male (X) Female ( )   Married (X) Single ( )   Number of Exemptions: 1   Pay Rate: $10.00

Occupation: Clerk   Place: Office

Date		Time Lost		Time Worked			O.T. Prem. Pay	Gross Pay	FICA Taxes		Fed. Income Taxes	Hosp. Ins.	Total Deduc-tions	Net Pay	Check No.	Cumu-lative Pay
Per. Ends	Paid	Hrs.	Rea-son	Total	O.T. Hours	Reg. Pay			Medi-care	Soc. Secur-ity						
1/5	1/5			40		400.00		400.00	5.80	24.80	50.00	40.00	120.60	279.40	173	400.00
1/12	1/12			40		400.00		400.00	5.80	24.80	50.00	40.00	120.60	279.40	201	800.00
1/19	1/19			40		400.00		400.00	5.80	24.80	50.00	40.00	120.60	279.40	243	1,200.00
1/26	1/26	4	Sick	36		360.00		360.00	5.22	22.32	43.00	40.00	110.54	249.46	295	1,560.00
2/2	2/2			40		400.00		400.00	5.80	24.80	50.00	40.00	120.60	279.40	339	1,960.00
2/9	2/9			40		400.00		400.00	5.80	24.80	50.00	40.00	120.60	279.40	354	2,360.00
2/16	2/16			40		400.00		400.00	5.80	24.80	50.00	40.00	120.60	279.40	397	2,760.00
2/23	2/23			40		400.00		400.00	5.80	24.80	50.00	40.00	120.60	279.40	446	3,160.00
3/23	3/23			40		400.00		400.00	5.80	24.80	50.00	40.00	120.60	279.40	893	4,760.00

Then, individual payroll checks are drawn on the payroll bank account. Because only one check for the payroll total is drawn on the regular bank account each payday, use of a special payroll bank account simplifies internal control, especially the reconciliation of the regular bank account.

When companies use a payroll bank account, they often add a Check Number column to the Payroll Register. In this column, they enter the number of each employee's check. For example, look at Illustration C–3 and notice that check 893 was issued to Robert Austin. With this additional column, the Payroll Register serves as a permanent supplementary record of the wages earned by and paid to employees.

Progress Check

C–1 Which of the following steps must be completed when a company uses a special payroll bank account?
a. Record the information shown on the Payroll Register with a general journal entry.
b. Write a check to the payroll bank account for the total amount of the payroll and record it with a debit to Accrued Payroll Payable and a credit to Cash.
c. Deposit a check for the total amount of the payroll in the payroll bank account.
d. Write individual payroll checks to be drawn on the payroll bank account.
e. All of the above.

C–2 What determines the amount that must be deducted from an employee's wages for federal income taxes?

C–3 What amount of income tax should be withheld from the salary of a single employee who has three withholding allowances and earned $675 in a week? (Use the wage bracket withholding table in Illustration C–5 to find the answer.)

Illustration C–5 A Wage Bracket Withholding Table

SINGLE Persons—WEEKLY Payroll Period
(For Wages Paid in 1995)

If the wages are—		And the number of withholding allowances claimed is—										
At least	But less than	0	1	2	3	4	5	6	7	8	9	10
		The amount of income tax to be withheld is—										
$600	$610	100	87	73	62	54	47	40	33	26	18	11
610	620	103	89	76	63	56	49	41	34	27	20	13
620	630	106	92	79	65	57	50	43	36	29	21	14
630	640	108	95	82	68	59	52	44	37	30	23	16
640	650	111	98	84	71	60	53	46	39	32	24	17
650	660	114	101	87	74	62	55	47	40	33	26	19
660	670	117	103	90	76	63	56	49	42	35	27	20
670	680	120	106	93	79	66	58	50	43	36	29	22
680	690	122	109	96	82	69	59	52	45	38	30	23
690	700	125	112	98	85	71	61	53	46	39	32	25
700	710	128	115	101	88	74	62	55	48	41	33	26
710	720	131	117	104	90	77	64	56	49	42	35	28
720	730	134	120	107	93	80	66	58	51	44	36	29
730	740	136	123	110	96	83	69	59	52	45	38	31
740	750	139	126	112	99	85	72	61	54	47	39	32
750	760	142	129	115	102	88	75	62	55	48	41	34
760	770	145	131	118	104	91	78	64	57	50	42	35
770	780	148	134	121	107	94	80	67	58	51	44	37
780	790	150	137	124	110	97	83	70	60	53	45	38
790	800	153	140	126	113	99	86	72	61	54	47	40
800	810	156	143	129	116	102	89	75	63	56	48	41
810	820	159	145	132	118	105	92	78	65	57	50	43
820	830	162	148	135	121	108	94	81	67	59	51	44
830	840	164	151	138	124	111	97	84	70	60	53	46
840	850	167	154	140	127	113	100	86	73	62	54	47
850	860	170	157	143	130	116	103	89	76	63	56	49
860	870	173	159	146	132	119	106	92	79	65	57	50
870	880	176	162	149	135	122	108	95	81	68	59	52
880	890	178	165	152	138	125	111	98	84	71	60	53
890	900	181	168	154	141	127	114	100	87	74	62	55

SUMMARY OF THE APPENDIX IN TERMS OF LEARNING OBJECTIVE

LO 1. Describe an employer's payroll reports and records, and the procedures used to calculate tax withholdings and issue checks to employees. Employers report FICA taxes and federal income tax withholdings quarterly on Form 941. FUTA taxes are reported annually on Form 940. Annual earnings and deduction information are reported to each employee and to the federal government on Form W-2. An employer's payroll records include a Payroll Register for each pay period and an Employee's Individual Earnings Record for each employee.

Federal income tax withholdings depend on the employee's earnings and the number of withholding allowances claimed by the employee. Various wage bracket withholding tables are available for pay periods of different lengths and for several classes of employees such as single or married.

Employers with a large number of employees often use a separate payroll bank account. When this is done, the payment of employees is recorded with a single credit to Cash. This entry records the transfer of cash from the regular checking account to the payroll checking account.

GLOSSARY

Employee's Individual Earnings Record a record of an employee's hours worked, gross pay, deductions, net pay, and certain personal information about the employee. p. AP–5

Federal depository bank a bank authorized to accept deposits of amounts payable to the federal government. p. AP–1

Payroll bank account a special bank account a company uses solely for the purpose of paying employees, by depositing in the account each pay period an amount equal to the total employees' net pay and drawing the employees' payroll checks on that account. p. AP–5

Payroll Register a record for a pay period that shows the pay period dates and the hours worked, gross pay, deductions, and net pay of each employee. p. AP–4

Wage bracket withholding table a table that shows the amounts of income tax to be withheld from employees' wages at various levels of earnings. p. AP–5

Withholding allowance a number that is used to reduce the amount of federal income tax withheld from an employee's pay. p. AP–5

EXERCISE

Exercise C–1
Calculating gross and net pay
(LO 1)

Nancy Bode, an unmarried employee of a company subject to the Fair Labor Standards Act, worked 48 hours during the week ended January 12. Her pay rate is $16 per hour, and her wages are subject to no deductions other than FICA and federal income taxes. She claims two withholding allowances. Calculate her regular pay, overtime premium pay, gross pay, FICA tax deduction at an assumed rate of 6.2% for the Social Security portion and 1.45% for the Medicare portion, income tax deduction (use the wage bracket withholding table of Illustration C–5), total deductions, and net pay.

PROBLEMS

Problem C–1
General journal entries for
payroll transactions
(LO 1)

Vaughn Company has 10 employees, each of whom earns $2,600 per month and is paid on the last day of each month. All 10 have been employed continuously at this amount since January 1. Vaughn uses a payroll bank account and special payroll checks to pay its employees. On March 1, the following accounts and balances appeared in its ledger:

a. FICA Taxes Payable, $3,978. (The balance of this account represents the liability for both the employer's and employees' FICA taxes for the February payroll only.)
b. Employees' Federal Income Taxes Payable, $3,900 (liability for February only).
c. Federal Unemployment Taxes Payable, $416 (liability for January and February together).
d. State Unemployment Taxes Payable, $2,080 (liability for January and February together).

During March and April, the company had the following payroll transactions:

Mar. 15   Issued check payable to Union Bank, a federal depository bank authorized to accept employers' payments of FICA taxes and employee income tax withholdings. The $7,878 check was in payment of the February FICA and employee income taxes.

     31   Prepared general journal entries to record the March Payroll Record, which had the following column totals, and to transfer the funds from the regular bank account to the payroll bank account:

Office Salaries	Shop Wages	Gross Pay	FICA Taxes	Federal Income Taxes	Total Deductions	Net Pay
$10,400	$15,600	$26,000	$1,989	$3,900	$5,889	$20,111

     31   Issued checks payable to each employee in payment of the March payroll.

Mar. 31   Prepared a general journal entry to record the employer's payroll taxes resulting from the March payroll. The company has a merit rating that reduces its state unemployment tax rate to 4.0% of the first $7,000 paid each employee. The federal rate is 0.8%.

Apr. 15   Issued check payable to Union Bank in payment of the March FICA and employee income taxes.

15   Issued check to the State Tax Commission for the January, February, and March state unemployment taxes. Mailed the check along with the second quarter tax return to the State Tax Commission.

30   Issued check payable to Union Bank. The check was in payment of the employer's federal unemployment taxes for the second quarter of the year.

30   Mailed Form 941 to the IRS, reporting the FICA taxes and the employees' federal income tax withholdings for the second quarter.

Required

Prepare general journal entries to record the transactions.

ANSWERS TO PROGRESS CHECKS

C–1 *e*

C–2 An employee's gross earnings and the number of withholding allowances the employee claims determine the amount that must be deducted for federal income taxes.

C–3 $79

Accounting Principles, the FASB's Conceptual Framework, and Alternative Valuation Methods

LEARNING OBJECTIVES

After studying Appendix D, you should be able to:

1. **Explain the difference between descriptive concepts and prescriptive concepts, and the difference between bottom-up and top-down approaches to the development of accounting concepts.**

2. **Describe the major components in the FASB's conceptual framework.**

3. **Explain why conventional financial statements fail to adequately account for price changes.**

4. **Use a price index to restate historical cost/nominal dollar costs into constant purchasing power amounts and to calculate purchasing power gains and losses.**

5. **Explain the current cost approach to valuation, including its effects on the income statement and balance sheet.**

6. **Explain the current selling price approach to valuation.**

7. **Define or explain the words and phrases listed in the appendix glossary.**

Accounting principles or concepts are not laws of nature. They are broad ideas developed as a way of *describing* current accounting practices and *prescribing* new and improved practices. In studying Appendix D, you will learn about some new accounting concepts that the FASB developed in an effort to guide future changes and improvements in accounting. You also will learn about some major alternatives to the historical cost measurements reported in conventional financial statements. Studying these alternatives will help you understand the nature of the information that is contained in conventional statements. In addition, it will help you grasp the meaning of new reporting practices that may occur in future years.

ACCOUNTING PRINCIPLES AND THE FASB'S CONCEPTUAL FRAMEWORK

DESCRIPTIVE AND PRESCRIPTIVE ACCOUNTING CONCEPTS

To fully understand the importance of financial accounting concepts or principles, you must realize that they serve two purposes. First, they provide general descriptions of existing accounting practices. In doing this, concepts and principles serve as guidelines that help you learn about accounting. Thus, after learning how the concepts or principles are applied in a few situations, you develop the ability to apply them in different situations. This is easier and more effective than memorizing a very long list of specific practices.

Second, these concepts or principles help accountants analyze unfamiliar situations and develop procedures to account for those situations. This purpose is especially important for the Financial Accounting Standards Board (FASB), which is charged with developing uniform practices for financial reporting in the United States and with improving the quality of such reporting.

In prior chapters, we defined and illustrated several important accounting principles. These principles, which follow, describe in general terms the practices currently used by accountants.

(LO 1)

Explain the difference between descriptive concepts and prescriptive concepts, and the difference between bottom-up and top-down approaches to the development of accounting concepts.

Generally Accepted Principles

Business entity principle	Full-disclosure principle	Objectivity principle
Conservatism principle	Going-concern principle	Revenue recognition
Consistency principle	Matching principle	principle
Cost principle	Materiality principle	Time period principle

To help you learn accounting, we introduced these principles in Chapter 1 (p. 25) and have referred to them frequently in later chapters. Although these ideas are labeled *principles,* in this discussion we use the term *concepts* to include both these principles as well as other general rules developed by the FASB. The FASB also uses the word *concepts* in this general manner.

The preceding concepts are useful for teaching and learning about accounting practice and are helpful for dealing with some unfamiliar transactions. As business practices have evolved in recent years, however, these concepts have become less useful as guides for accountants to follow in dealing with new and different types of transactions. This problem has occurred because the concepts are intended to provide general descriptions of current accounting practices. In other words, they describe what accountants currently do; they do not necessarily describe what accountants should do. Also, since these concepts do not identify weaknesses in accounting practices, they do not lead to major changes or improvements in accounting practices.

Because the FASB is charged with improving financial reporting, its first members decided that a new set of concepts should be developed. They also decided that the new set of concepts should not merely *describe* what was being done under current practice. Instead, the new concepts should *prescribe* what ought to be done to make things better. The project to develop a new set of prescriptive concepts was initiated in 1973 and quickly became known as the FASB's *conceptual framework project.*

However, before we examine the concepts developed by the FASB, we need to look more closely at the differences between descriptive and prescriptive uses of accounting concepts.

THE PROCESSES OF DEVELOPING DESCRIPTIVE AND PRESCRIPTIVE ACCOUNTING CONCEPTS

Sets of concepts differ in how they are developed and used. In general, when concepts are intended to describe current practice, they are developed by looking at accepted specific practices and then making some general rules to encompass them. This bottom-up approach is diagrammed in Illustration D–1 that shows the arrows going from the practices to the concepts. The outcome of the process is a set of general rules that summarize practice and that can be used for education and for solving some new problems. For example, this approach leads to the concept that asset purchases are recorded at cost. However, these kinds of concepts often fail to show how new problems should be solved. To continue the example, the concept that assets are recorded at cost does not provide much direct guidance for situations in which assets have no cost because they are donated to a company by a local government. Further, because

Illustration D-1 A Bottom-Up
Process of Developing
Descriptive Accounting
Concepts

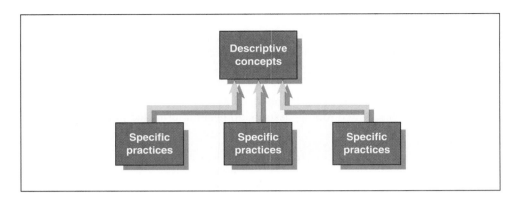

these concepts are based on the presumption that current practices are adequate, they do not lead to the development of new and improved accounting methods. To continue the example, the concept that assets are initially recorded at cost does not encourage asking the question of whether they should always be carried at that amount.

In contrast, if concepts are intended to *prescribe* improvements in accounting practices, they are likely to be designed by a top-down approach (Illustration D–2). Note that the top-down approach starts with broad accounting objectives. The process then generates broad concepts about the types of information that should be reported. Finally, these concepts should lead to specific practices that ought to be used. The advantage of this approach is that the concepts are good for solving new problems and evaluating old answers; its disadvantage is that the concepts may not be very descriptive of current practice. In fact, the suggested practices may not be in current use.

Since the FASB uses accounting concepts to prescribe accounting practices, the Board used a top-down approach to develop its conceptual framework. The Board's concepts are not necessarily more correct than the previously developed concepts. However, the new concepts are intended to provide better guidelines for developing new and improved accounting practices. The Board has stated that it will use them as a basis for its future actions and already has used them to justify important changes in financial reporting.

Progress Check

D–1   **The FASB's conceptual framework is intended to:**
  a. **Provide a historical analysis of accounting practice.**
  b. **Describe current accounting practice.**
  c. **Provide concepts that are prescriptive of what should be done in accounting practice.**

D–2   **What is the starting point in a top-down approach to developing accounting concepts?**

D–3   **What is the starting point in a bottom-up approach to developing accounting concepts?**

THE FASB'S CONCEPTUAL FRAMEWORK

(LO 2)

Describe the major components in the FASB's conceptual framework.

The FASB's approach to developing its conceptual framework is diagrammed in Illustration D–3. Between 1978 and 1985, the Board issued six *Statements of Financial Accounting Concepts (SFAC)*. These concepts statements are not the same as the FASB's *Statements of Financial Accounting Standards (SFAS)*. The *SFAS*s are authoritative statements of generally accepted accounting principles that must be followed. The *SFAC*s are guidelines the Board uses in developing new standards. Accountants are not required to follow the *SFAC*s in practice.

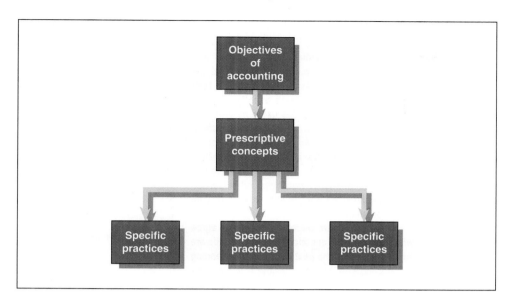

Illustration D-2 A Top-Down Process of Developing Prescriptive Accounting Concepts

The Objectives of Financial Reporting

The FASB's first *Statement of Financial Accounting Concepts (SFAC 1)* identified the broad objectives of financial reporting (Illustration D–3). The first and most general objective stated in *SFAC 1* is to "provide information that is useful to present and potential investors and creditors and other users in making rational investment, credit, and similar decisions."[1] From this beginning point in *SFAC 1,* the Board expressed other more specific objectives. These objectives recognize (1) that financial reporting should help users predict future cash flows, and (2) that information about a company's resources and obligations is useful in making such predictions. All the concepts in the conceptual framework are intended to be consistent with these general objectives. Of course, present accounting practice already provides information about a company's resources and obligations. Thus, although the conceptual framework is intended to be prescriptive of new and improved practices, the concepts in the framework also are descriptive of many current practices.

The Qualities of Useful Information

Illustration D–3 shows that the next step in the conceptual framework project was to identify the qualities (or qualitative characteristics) that financial information should have if it is to be useful in decision making. The Board discussed the fact that information can be useful only if it is understandable to users. However, the users are assumed to have the training, experience, and motivation to analyze financial reports. With this decision, the Board indicated that financial reporting should not try to meet the needs of unsophisticated or other casual report users.

In *SFAC 2,* the FASB said that information is useful if it is (1) relevant, (2) reliable, and (3) comparable. Information is *relevant* if it can make a difference in a decision. Information has this quality when it helps users predict the future or evaluate the past, and when it is received in time to affect their decisions.

---

[1]FASB, *Statement of Financial Accounting Concepts No. 1,* "Objectives of Financial Reporting by Business Enterprises" (Norwalk, CT, 1978), par. 34.

As a Matter of Opinion

Mr. Beresford graduated from the University of Southern California in 1961 with a B.A. degree in accounting. After working 10 years in the Los Angeles office of Ernst & Ernst (now Ernst & Young), he was assigned to that firm's national office and made a partner. In 1987, he was appointed to the Financial Accounting Standards Board and named as its chairman. In 1991, he was reappointed for a second term, which will expire in 1997. Among his honors is the designation as the Beta Alpha Psi "Accountant of the Year" for 1986.

When the conceptual framework was being created, some thought that it would provide immediate answers for standard-setting issues. However, it could never do that all by itself. Rather, the framework is a tool that helps the FASB do its job.

Because getting to right answers depends on asking the right questions, I've come to realize that perhaps the most critical part of the standard-setting process is identifying and stating the issues properly. That's exactly what the conceptual framework helps us do by providing us with common objectives and terms. In effect, the conceptual framework brings discipline to those who participate in the standard-setting process. This discipline helps the Board to ask the right questions. It also helps other participants comment on our projects in a more consistent manner.

Although all Board members might not agree which answer to a question is best, the odds are much higher that the best answer will be among the alternatives that we consider if we ask the right questions. As a result, we are more likely to ultimately adopt the best answer.

Dennis R. Beresford, C.P.A.

Information is *reliable* if users can depend on it to be free from bias and error. Reliable information is verifiable and faithfully represents what is supposed to be described. In addition, users can depend on information only if it is neutral. This means that the rules used to produce information should not be designed to lead users to accept or reject any specific decision alternative.

Information is *comparable* if users can use it to identify differences and similarities between companies. Comparability is possible only if companies follow uniform practices. However, even if all companies uniformly follow the same practices, comparable reports do not result if the practices are not appropriate. For example, comparable information would not be provided if all companies were to ignore the useful lives of their assets and depreciate all assets over two years.

Comparability also requires consistency (see Chapter 9, page 350), which means that a company should not change its accounting practices unless the change is justified as a reporting improvement. Another important concept discussed in *SFAC 2* is materiality (see Chapter 8, page 320).

Elements of Financial Statements

Illustration D–3 shows that another important step in developing the conceptual framework was to determine the elements of financial statements. This involved defining the categories of information that should be contained in financial reports. The Board's discussion of financial statement elements includes definitions of important elements such as assets, liabilities, equity, revenues, expenses, gains, and losses. In earlier chapters, we referred to many of these definitions when we explained various accounting procedures. The Board's pronouncement on financial statement elements was first published in 1980 as *SFAC 3*. In 1985, *SFAC 3* was replaced by *SFAC 6,* which modified the discussion of financial statement elements to include several elements for not-for-profit accounting entities.[2]

---

[2]Among the six *Statements of Financial Accounting Concepts* issued by the FASB, one *(SFAC 4)* is directed toward accounting by not-for-profit organizations. Although *SFAC 4* is important, it is beyond the scope of this course.

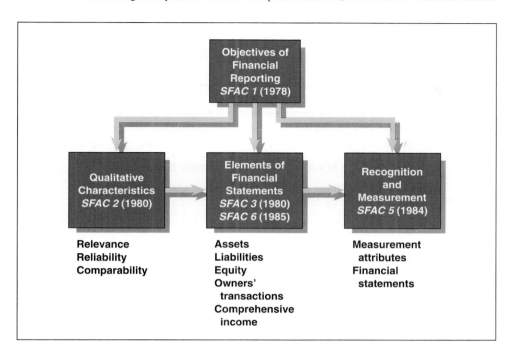

Recognition and Measurement

In *SFAC 5,* "Recognition and Measurement in Financial Statements of Business Enterprises," the FASB established concepts for deciding (1) when items should be presented (or recognized) in the financial statements, and (2) how to assign numbers to (or measure) those items. In general, the Board concluded that items should be recognized in the financial statements if they meet the following criteria:

- *Definitions.* The item meets the definition of an element of financial statements.
- *Measurability.* It has a relevant attribute measurable with sufficient reliability.
- *Relevance.* The information about it is capable of making a difference in user decisions.
- *Reliability.* The information is representationally faithful, verifiable, and neutral.

The question of how items should be measured raises the fundamental question of whether financial statements should be based on cost or on value. Since this question is quite controversial, the Board's discussion of this issue is more descriptive of current practice than it is prescriptive of new measurement methods.

In *SFAC 5,* the Board stated that a full set of financial statements should show:

1. Financial position at the end of the period.
2. Earnings for the period. (This concept is very similar to the concept of net income used in current practice.)
3. Comprehensive income for the period. (This new concept is broader than earnings and includes all changes in owner's equity other than those that resulted from transactions with the owners. Some changes in asset values are included in this concept but are excluded from earnings.)
4. Cash flows during the period.
5. Investments by and distributions to owners during the period.

We should note that *SFAC 5* was the first official pronouncement to call for the presentation of a statement of cash flows. The statement of cash flows is now required under *SFAS 95*, which was issued two years after *SFAC 5*.

Progress Check

D–4 That a business should be consistent from year to year in its accounting practices most directly relates to the FASB's concept that information reported in financial statements should be: *(a)* Relevant; *(b)* Material; *(c)* Reliable; *(d)* Comparable.

D–5 Which characteristics of accounting information make it reliable?

D–6 What is the meaning of the phrase *elements of financial statements?*

ALTERNATIVE ACCOUNTING VALUATION SYSTEMS

CONVENTIONAL FINANCIAL STATEMENTS FAIL TO ACCOUNT FOR PRICE CHANGES

(LO 3)

Explain why conventional financial statements fail to adequately account for price changes.

All accountants agree that conventional financial statements provide useful information for making economic decisions. However, many accountants also believe that conventional financial statements fail to adequately account for the impact of changing prices. Sometimes, this makes the statements misleading. That is, the statements may imply certain facts that are inconsistent with the real state of affairs. As a result, the information in the statements may lead decision makers to make decisions inconsistent with their objectives.

Failure to Account for Price Changes on the Balance Sheet

In what ways do conventional financial statements fail to account for changing prices? The general problem is that transactions are recorded in the historical number of dollars paid. Usually, these amounts are not adjusted even though subsequent price changes may dramatically change the value of the purchased items.[3] For example, Old Company purchased 10 acres of land for $25,000. Then, at the end of each accounting period, Old Company presented a balance sheet showing "Land . . . $25,000." Six years later, after price increases of 97%, New Company purchased 10 acres of land that was next to and nearly identical to Old Company's land. New Company paid $49,250 for the land. Comparing the conventional balance sheets of the two companies reveals the following balances:

	Old Company	New Company
Land	$25,000	$49,250

Without knowing the details that led to these balances, a statement reader is likely to conclude that either New Company has more land than Old Company or that New Company's land is more valuable. In reality, both companies own 10 acres that are of equal value. The entire difference between the prices paid by the two companies is explained by the 97% price increase between the two purchase dates. That is, $25,000 × 1.97 = $49,250.

---

[3]An exception to this general rule is the reporting of certain investments in debt and equity securities at their fair (market) values. This exception is explained in Chapters 8 and 11.

Failure to Account for Price Changes on the Income Statement

The failure of conventional financial statements to adequately account for changing prices also shows up in the income statement. For example, assume that in the previous example, the companies purchased machines instead of land. Also, assume that the machines of Old Company and New Company are identical except for age; both are being depreciated on a straight-line basis over a 10-year period with no salvage value. As a result, the annual income statements of the two companies show the following:

	Old Company	New Company
Depreciation expense, machinery	$2,500	$4,925

Although assets of equal value are being depreciated, the income statements show depreciation expense for New Company that is 97% higher than Old Company's. This is inconsistent with the fact that both companies own identical machines affected by the same depreciation factors. Furthermore, although Old Company appears more profitable, it must pay more income taxes due to the apparent extra profits. Also, if Old Company's selling prices are linked to its costs, it may not recover the full replacement cost of its machinery through the sale of its products.

There are three basic alternatives to the historical cost measurements presented in conventional financial statements without adjustment for changing prices. These alternatives are:

1. Historical costs adjusted for changes in the general price level.
2. Current replacement cost valuations.
3. Current selling price valuations.

We discuss each of these in the remaining sections of Appendix D.

VALUATION ALTERNATIVES TO CONVENTIONAL MEASUREMENTS OF COST

Progress Check

D-7 The following selected information is from the conventional balance sheets of A Company and B Company:

	A Company	B Company
Cash	$ 24,000	$ 40,000
Equipment, net	96,000	102,200
Land	130,000	157,800
Total assets	$250,000	$300,000

Based on this information, which of the following statements is true?
a. Company B's assets are worth $50,000 more than Company A's assets.
b. If Company A and Company B own identical tracts of land, Company B must have purchased its land at a later date than Company A.
c. The relative values of Company A's and Company B's assets cannot be determined from this conventional balance sheet information.

Illustration D-4   Expressing Costs in Constant Purchasing Power

Year Cost Was Incurred	Monetary Units Expended (a)	Price Index Factor for Adjustment to 19X2 Dollars (b)	Historical Cost Stated in 19X2 Dollars (a × b = c)	Price Index Factor for Adjustment to 19X7 Dollars (d)	Historical Cost Stated in 19X7 Dollars (c × d)
19X1	$1,000	100/92.5 = 1.08108	$1,081	168/100 = 1.68000	$1,816*
19X2	1,500		1,500	168/100 = 1.68000	2,520
Total cost	$2,500		$2,581		$4,336

*An alternative calculation is $1,000 × (168.0/92.5) = $1,816.

ADJUSTING HISTORICAL COSTS FOR GENERAL PRICE LEVEL CHANGES

(LO 4)

Use a price index to restate historical cost/nominal dollar costs into constant purchasing power amounts and to calculate purchasing power gains and losses.

One alternative to conventional financial statements is to restate dollar amounts of cost incurred in earlier years for changes in the general price level. In other words, a specific dollar amount of cost in a previous year can be restated as the number of dollars that would have been expended if the cost had been paid with dollars that have the current amount of purchasing power.

For example, assume the following general price index for December of 19X1 through 19X7:

Year	Price Index
19X1	92.5
19X2	100.0
19X3	109.5
19X4	123.7
19X5	135.0
19X6	150.0
19X7	168.0

Then, assume that a firm purchased assets for $1,000 in December 19X1 and for $1,500 in December 19X2. The 19X1 cost of $1,000 correctly states the number of monetary units (dollars) expended in 19X1. Also, the 19X2 cost of $1,500 correctly states the number of monetary units expended in 19X2. However, in a very important way, the 19X1 monetary units do not mean the same thing as the 19X2 monetary units. A dollar (one monetary unit) in 19X1 represents a different amount of purchasing power than a dollar in 19X2. Both of these dollars represent different amounts of purchasing power than a dollar in 19X7.

To communicate the total amount of purchasing power given up for the assets, the historical number of monetary units must be restated in dollars with the same amount of purchasing power. For example, the total amount of cost incurred during 19X1 and 19X2 may be stated in the purchasing power of 19X2 dollars, or stated in the purchasing power of 19X7 dollars. These calculations are presented in Illustration D–4.

Conventional financial statements disclose revenues, expenses, assets, liabilities, and owners' equity in the historical monetary units exchanged when the transactions occurred. As such, they are sometimes called **historical cost/nominal dollar financial statements.** This emphasizes the difference between conventional statements and historical cost/constant purchasing power statements. **Historical cost/constant purchasing power accounting** uses a general price index to restate the dollar amounts on conventional financial statements into amounts that represent current general purchasing power.

The same principles for determining depreciation expense, cost of goods sold, accruals of revenue, and so forth, apply to both historical cost/nominal dollar statements and historical cost/constant purchasing power statements. The same generally accepted accounting principles apply to both. The only difference between the two is that constant purchasing power statements reflect adjustments for general price level changes and nominal dollar statements do not.

The Impact of General Price Changes on Monetary Items

Some assets and liabilities are defined as monetary items. **Monetary assets** represent money or claims to receive a fixed amount of money. **Monetary liabilities** are obligations that are fixed in terms of the amount owed. The number of dollars to be received or paid does not change even though the purchasing power of the dollar may change. Examples of monetary items include cash, accounts receivable, accounts payable, and notes payable.

Because the amount of money that will be received or paid is fixed, a monetary item is not adjusted for general price level changes on a historical cost/constant purchasing power balance sheet. For example, assume that $800 in cash was owned at the end of 19X2. Regardless of how the price level has changed since the cash was acquired, the amount to be reported on the December 31, 19X2, historical cost/constant purchasing power balance sheet is $800.

Although monetary items are not adjusted on the balance sheet, they do involve special risks. When the general price level changes, monetary items create **purchasing power gains and losses.** Owning monetary assets during a period of inflation results in a loss of purchasing power. Owing monetary liabilities during a period of inflation results in a gain of purchasing power. During a period of deflation, the effects are just the opposite. Monetary assets result in purchasing power gains and monetary liabilities result in purchasing power losses.

For example, assume that a company has a cash balance of $800 on December 31, 19X2, which resulted from the following:

Cash balance, December 31, 19X1	$ 200
Cash receipts, assumed to have been received uniformly throughout the year	1,500
Cash disbursements, assumed to have been made uniformly throughout the year	(900)
Cash balance, December 31, 19X2	$ 800

Also assume that the general price index was 150.0 at the end of 19X1; that it averaged 160.0 throughout 19X3; and was 168.0 at the end of that year. As the price level increased throughout 19X2, the purchasing power of the cash declined. To calculate the loss during the year, the beginning cash balance and each receipt or disbursement must be adjusted for price changes to the end of the year. Then, the adjusted balance is compared with the actual balance to determine the loss. The calculation is as follows:

	Nominal Dollar Amounts	Price Index Factor for Restatement to December 31, 19X2	Restated to December 31, 19X2	Gain or (Loss)
Beginning balance	$ 200	168.0/150.0 = 1.12000	$ 224	
Receipts	1,500	168.0/160.0 = 1.05000	1,575	
Disbursements	(900)	168.0/160.0 = 1.05000	(945)	
Ending balance, adjusted			$ 854	
Ending balance, actual	$ 800		(800)	
Purchasing power loss				$(54)

Stated in terms of general purchasing power at year-end, the beginning cash balance plus receipts less disbursements was $854. Since the company has only $800 on hand, the $54 difference is a loss of general purchasing power.

In the preceding calculation, note that we adjusted the receipts and disbursements from the *average* price level during the year (160.0) to the ending price level (168.0). Because we assumed the receipts and disbursements occurred uniformly throughout the year, we used the average price level to approximate the price level at the time each receipt and disbursement took place. If receipts and disbursements do not occur uniformly, then we must separately adjust each receipt and each disbursement from the price level at the time of the receipt or disbursement to the price level at year-end.

The calculation of purchasing power gains and losses that result from owing monetary liabilities is the same as it is for monetary assets. Assume, for example, that a note payable for $300 was outstanding on December 31, 19X1, when the price index was 150.0. On April 5, 19X2, when the price index was 157.0, a $700 increase in the note resulted in a $1,000 balance that remained outstanding throughout the rest of 19X2. On December 31, 19X2, the price index was 168.0. On the historical cost/constant purchasing power balance sheet for December 31, 19X2, the note payable is reported at $1,000. The purchasing power gain or loss during 19X2 is calculated as follows:

	Nominal Dollar Amounts	Price Index Factor for Restatement to December 31, 19X2	Restated to December 31, 19X2	Gain or (Loss)
Beginning balance	$ 300	168.0/150.0 = 1.120	$ 336	
April 5 increase	700	168.0/157.0 = 1.070	749	
Ending balance, adjusted			$ 1,085	
Ending balance, actual	$1,000		(1,000)	
Purchasing power gain				$85

Stated in terms of general purchasing power at year-end, the amount borrowed was $1,085. Since the company can pay the note with $1,000, the $85 difference is a gain in general purchasing power earned by the firm.

To determine a company's total purchasing power gain or loss during a year, the accountant must analyze each monetary asset and each monetary liability. The final gain or loss is then described as the *purchasing power gain (or loss) on net monetary items owned or owed.*

The Impact of General Price Changes on Nonmonetary Items

Nonmonetary items include stockholders' equity and all assets and liabilities that are not fixed in terms of the number of monetary units to be received or paid. Land, equipment, intangible assets, and many product warranty liabilities are examples of non-

Illustration D–5 Reporting the Effects of Price Changes on Monetary and Nonmonetary Items

Financial Statement Item	When the General Price Level Rises (Inflation)		When the General Price Level Falls (Deflation)	
	Balance Sheet Adjustment Required	Income Statement Gain or Loss	Balance Sheet Adjustment Required	Income Statement Gain or Loss
Monetary assets	No	Loss	No	Gain
Nonmonetary assets	Yes	None	Yes	None
Monetary liabilities	No	Gain	No	Loss
Nonmonetary equities and liabilities	Yes	None	Yes	None

monetary items. The prices of **nonmonetary assets** tend to increase or decrease over time as the general price level increases or decreases. Similarly, the amounts needed to satisfy **nonmonetary liabilities** tend to change with changes in the general price level.

To reflect these changes on historical cost/constant purchasing power balance sheets, nonmonetary items are adjusted for price level changes that occur after the items were acquired. For example, assume that $500 was invested in land (a nonmonetary asset) at the end of 19X1, and the investment was still held at the end of 19X7. During this time, the general price index increased from 92.5 to 168.0. The historical cost/constant purchasing power balance sheets would disclose the following amounts:

Asset	December 31, 19X1, Historical Cost/Constant Purchasing Power Balance Sheet (a)	Price Index Factor for Adjustment to December 31, 19X7 (b)	December 31, 19X7, Historical Cost/Constant Purchasing Power Balance Sheet (a × b)
Land	$500	168.0/92.5 = 1.81622	$908

The $908 shown as the investment in land at the end of 19X7 reflects the same amount of general purchasing power as $500 at the end of 19X1. Thus, no change in general purchasing power is recognized from holding the land.

Illustration D–5 summarizes the impact of general price level changes on monetary and nonmonetary items. The illustration shows which items require adjustments to prepare a historical cost/constant purchasing power balance sheet. It also shows which items generate purchasing power gains and losses that are recognized on a constant purchasing power income statement.

Progress Check

D–8 Foster Company purchased 150 acres of land for $100,000 in 19X1 when the general price index was 125.0. In December 19X4, the general price index was 150.0. What amount should be reported for the land on the 19X4 historical cost/constant purchasing power balance sheet?

D–9 Refer to D–8. Should any purchasing power gain or loss pertaining to the land be reported on the 19X4 historical cost/constant purchasing power income statement?

CURRENT COST VALUATIONS

(LO 5)

Explain the current cost approach to valuation, including its effects on the income statement and balance sheet.

As we said before, all prices do not change at the same rate. In fact, when the general price level is rising, some specific prices may be falling. If this were not so, and if all prices changed at the same rate, then historical cost/constant purchasing power accounting would report current values on the financial statements.

For example, suppose that a company purchased land for $50,000 on January 1, 19X1, when the general price index was 135.0. Then, the price level increased until December 19X2, when the price index was 168.0. A December 31, 19X2, historical cost/constant purchasing power balance sheet for this company would report the land at $50,000 \times 168.0/135.0 = $62,222. If all prices increased at the same rate during that period, the market value of the land would have increased from $50,000 to $62,222, and the company's historical cost/constant purchasing power balance sheet would coincidentally disclose the land at its current value.

Because all prices do not change at the same rate, however, the current value of the land may differ substantially from the historical cost/constant dollar amount of $62,222. For example, assume that the company had the land appraised and determined that its current value on December 31, 19X2, was $80,000. The difference between the original purchase price of $50,000 and the current value of $80,000 is explained as follows:

Unrealized holding gain	$80,000 − $62,222 = $17,778
Adjustment for general price level increase	$62,222 − $50,000 = $12,222
Total change	$80,000 − $50,000 = $30,000

In this case, the historical cost/constant purchasing power balance sheet would report land at $62,222, which is $17,778 ($80,000 − $62,222) less than its current value. This illustrates an important fact about historical cost/constant purchasing power accounting; it does not attempt to report current value. Rather, historical cost/constant purchasing power accounting restates original transaction prices into equivalent amounts of current, *general* purchasing power. The balance sheets display current values only if current, *specific* purchasing power is the basis of valuation.

Current Costs on the Income Statement

When the current cost approach to accounting is used, the reported amount of each expense, or **current cost,** is the number of dollars that would have been needed at the time the expense was incurred to acquire the consumed resources. For example, assume that the annual sales of a company included an item sold in May for $1,500. The item had been acquired on January 1 for $500. Also, suppose that in May, at the time of the sale, the cost to replace this item was $700. Then, the annual current cost income statement would show sales of $1,500 less cost of goods sold of $700. In other words, when an asset is acquired and then held for a time before it expires, the historical cost of the asset usually is different from its current cost at the time it expires. Current cost accounting measures the amount of expense as the cost to replace the asset at the time the asset expires or is sold.

The result of measuring expenses in current costs is that revenue is matched with the current (at the time of the sale) cost of the resources used to earn the revenue. Thus, operating profit is not greater than zero unless revenues are large enough to replace all of the resources consumed in the process of producing those revenues. Those who argue for current costs believe that operating profit measured in this fashion provides an improved basis for evaluating the effectiveness of operating activities.

Current Costs on the Balance Sheet

On the balance sheet, current cost accounting reports assets at the amounts that would have to be paid to purchase them as of the balance sheet date. Liabilities are reported at the amounts that would have to be paid to satisfy the liabilities as of the balance sheet date. Note that this valuation basis is similar to historical cost/constant purchasing power accounting in that a distinction exists between monetary and nonmonetary assets and liabilities. Monetary assets and liabilities are fixed in amount regardless of price changes. Therefore, monetary items are not adjusted for price changes. All of the nonmonetary items, however, must be evaluated at each balance sheet date to determine the best estimate of current cost.

For a moment, think about the large variety of assets reported on balance sheets. Given that there are so many different assets, you should not be surprised that accountants have difficulty obtaining reliable estimates of current costs. In some cases, they use price indexes that relate to specific categories of assets. Such specific price indexes may provide the most reliable source of current cost information. In other cases, when an asset is not new and has been partially depreciated, accountants may estimate its current cost by determining the cost to acquire a similar but new asset. Depreciation on the old asset is then based on the current cost of the new asset. Clearly, the accountant's professional judgment is an important factor in developing current cost data.

Progress Check

D-10 **On a balance sheet prepared under the current cost approach to accounting:**
   a. Monetary items are not adjusted for price changes.
   b. Nonmonetary items are restated to reflect general price level changes.
   c. Monetary items are restated to reflect general price level changes.

D-11 **Describe the meaning of *operating profit* under a current cost accounting system.**

CURRENT SELLING PRICE VALUATIONS

(LO 6)

Explain the current selling price approach to valuation.

In the previous discussion, you learned that conventional financial statements generally report historical costs in nominal dollars. That is, adjustments usually are not made for price changes. We also explained how accountants use a general price level index to adjust the nominal dollar amounts to measure the historical costs in terms of a constant purchasing power. Next, we discussed the alternative of reporting current (replacement) costs in the financial statements.

The final alternative to be considered is the reporting of assets (and liabilities) at current selling prices. On the balance sheet, this means assets would be reported at the amounts that would be received if the assets were sold. Similarly, liabilities would be reported at the amounts that would have to be paid to settle or eliminate the liabilities. The financial press describes this selling price approach to valuation as mark-to-market accounting.

The argument for reporting the current selling prices of assets is based on the idea that the alternative to owning an asset is to sell it. Thus, the sacrifice a business makes to hold an asset is the amount it would receive if the asset were sold. Further, the benefit derived from owing a liability is the amount the business avoids paying by not eliminating the liability. If these current selling prices are reported on the balance sheet, the stockholders' equity represents the net amount of cash that would be realized by liquidating the business. This net liquidation value is the amount that could be invested in other projects if the business were liquidated. Therefore, one can argue that net liquidation value is the most relevant basis for evaluating whether the income the company earns is enough to justify remaining in business.

Some proponents of the current selling price approach believe that it should be applied to assets but not to liabilities. Others argue that it applies equally well to both. Still others believe that it should be applied only to assets held for sale. They would not apply it to assets held for use in the business.

A related issue is whether to report the adjustments to selling price as gains and losses in the income statement. Some businesses, especially banks, argue that reporting such gains or losses causes excessive fluctuations in their reported net incomes. As an alternative to reporting the gains or losses on the income statement, they may be shown in stockholders' equity on the balance sheet as "unrealized gains and losses."

As Chapters 8 and 11 explain, a very recent pronouncement by the FASB *(SFAS 115)* requires companies to use the selling price approach to valuation for some assets. Investments in trading securities are reported at their fair (market) values, with the related changes in fair values reported on the income statement. Investments in securities available for sale are also reported at their fair values, but the related changes in fair values are not reported on the income statement. Instead, they are reported as part of stockholders' equity.

Progress Check

D-12   **If current selling price valuations were used to account for the assets and liabilities of a business:**
   a. **Gains and losses from changing market values would not be recorded.**
   b. **Losses from changing market values would be recorded but not gains.**
   c. **The accounting system might be described as mark-to-market accounting.**

D-13   **What is meant by the current selling price valuation of a liability?**

SUMMARY OF APPENDIX D IN TERMS OF LEARNING OBJECTIVES

LO 1. Explain the difference between descriptive concepts and prescriptive concepts, and the difference between bottom-up and top-down approaches to the development of accounting concepts. Some accounting concepts provide general descriptions of current accounting practices and are most useful in learning about accounting. Other accounting concepts prescribe the practices accountants should follow. These prescriptive concepts are most useful in developing accounting procedures for new types of transactions and making improvements in accounting practice. A bottom-up approach to developing concepts begins by examining the practices currently in use. Then, concepts are developed that provide general descriptions of those practices. In contrast, a top-down approach begins by stating the objectives of accounting. From these objectives, concepts are developed that prescribe the types of accounting practices accountants should follow.

LO 2. Describe the major components in the FASB's conceptual framework. The FASB's conceptual framework begins with *SFAC 1* by stating the broad objectives of financial reporting. Next, *SFAC 2* identifies the qualitative characteristics accounting information should possess. The elements contained in financial reports are defined in *SFAC 6* and the recognition and measurement criteria to be used are identified in *SFAC 5*.

LO 3. Explain why conventional financial statements fail to adequately account for price changes. Conventional financial statements report transactions in terms of the historical number of dollars received or paid. Therefore, the statements are not adjusted to reflect general price level changes or changes in the specific prices of the items reported.

LO 4. Use a price index to restate historical cost/nominal dollar costs into constant purchasing power amounts and to calculate purchasing power gains and losses. To restate a historical cost/nominal dollar cost in constant purchasing power terms, multiply the nominal dollar cost by a factor that represents the change in the general price level since the cost was incurred. On the balance sheet, monetary assets and liabilities should not be adjusted for changes in prices. However, purchasing power gains or losses result from holding monetary assets and owing monetary liabilities during a period of general price changes.

LO 5. Explain the current cost approach to valuation, including its effects on the income statement and balance sheet. Current costs on the balance sheet are the dollar amounts that would be spent to purchase the assets at the balance sheet date. On the income statement, current costs are the dollar amounts that would be necessary to acquire the consumed assets on the date they were consumed.

LO 6. Explain the current selling price approach to valuation. Reporting current selling prices of assets and liabilities is supported by those who believe the balance sheet should show the net cost of not selling the assets and settling the liabilities. Some argue for applying selling price valuations to all assets and liabilities, or to marketable investments and marketable liabilities only, or to assets only. The related gains and losses may be reported on the income statement, but some would show them as unrealized stockholders' equity items on the balance sheet. The FASB's newly issued *SFAS 114* requires companies to use the selling price approach in reporting certain securities investments.

GLOSSARY

Current cost in general, the cost that would be required to acquire (or replace) an asset or service at the present time. On the income statement, the number of dollars that would be required, at the time the expense is incurred, to acquire the resources consumed. On the balance sheet, the amounts that would have to be paid to replace the assets or satisfy the liabilities as of the balance sheet date. p. AP–22

Historical cost/constant purchasing power accounting an accounting system that adjusts historical cost/nominal dollar financial statements for changes in the general purchasing power of the dollar. p. AP–19

Historical cost/nominal dollar financial statements conventional financial statements that disclose revenues, expenses, assets, liabilities, and owners' equity in terms of the historical monetary units exchanged at the time the transactions occurred. p. AP–18

Monetary assets money or claims to receive a fixed amount of money; the number of dollars to be received does not change regardless of changes in the purchasing power of the dollar. p. AP–19

Monetary liabilities fixed amounts that are owed; the number of dollars to be paid does not change regardless of changes in the general price level. p. AP–19

Nonmonetary assets assets that are not claims to a fixed number of monetary units, the prices of which therefore tend to fluctuate with changes in the general price level. p. AP–21

Nonmonetary liabilities obligations that are not fixed in terms of the number of monetary units needed to satisfy them, and that therefore tend to fluctuate in amount with changes in the general price level. p. AP–21

Purchasing power gains or losses the gains or losses that result from holding monetary assets and/or owing monetary liabilities during a period in which the general price level changes. p. AP–19

QUESTIONS

1. Can a concept be used descriptively and prescriptively?

2. Explain the difference between the FASB's Statements of Financial Accounting Concepts and the Statements of Financial Accounting Standards.

3. Which three qualitative characteristics of accounting information did the FASB identify as being necessary if the information is to be useful?

4. What is implied by saying that financial information should have the qualitative characteristic of relevance?

5. What are the four criteria an item should satisfy to be recognized in the financial statements?

6. Some people argue that conventional financial statements fail to adequately account for inflation. What general problem with conventional financial statements generates this argument?

7. What is the fundamental difference in the adjustments made under current cost accounting and under historical cost/constant purchasing power accounting?

8. What are historical cost/nominal dollar financial statements?

9. What is the difference between monetary and nonmonetary assets?

EXERCISES

Exercise D–1
Adjusting costs for historical cost/constant purchasing power statements
(LO 5)

A company's plant and equipment consisted of land purchased in late 19X1 for $460,000, machinery purchased in late 19X3 for $154,000, and a building purchased in late 19X5 for $210,000. Values of the general price index for December of 19X1 through 19X8 are as follows:

19X1	100.0	19X5	128.0
19X2	106.5	19X6	139.0
19X3	111.0	19X7	144.0
19X4	121.3	19X8	153.0

Required

1. Assuming the preceding price index adequately represents end-of-year price levels, calculate the amount of each asset's cost that would be shown on a historical cost/constant purchasing power balance sheet for *(a)* December 31, 19X7, and *(b)* December 31, 19X8. Ignore any accumulated depreciation. Round calculations to three decimals.

2. Would the historical cost/constant purchasing power income statement for 19X8 disclose any purchasing power gain or loss as a consequence of holding these assets? If so, how much?

Exercise D–2
Classifying monetary and nonmonetary items
(LO 5, 6)

Determine whether the following are monetary or nonmonetary items:

1. Notes payable.
2. Merchandise inventory.
3. Copyrights.
4. Savings accounts.
5. Common stock.
6. Product warranties liability.
7. Wages payable.
8. Contributed capital in excess of par value, common stock.
9. Accounts receivable.
10. Goodwill.
11. Prepaid insurance.
12. Computer equipment.
13. Retained earnings.
14. Prepaid rent.

Exercise D–3
Calculating amounts for current cost statements
(LO 6)

A company purchased land in 19X1 at a cost of $730,000 and in 19X2 at a cost of $357,000. What is the current cost of these land purchases in *(a)* 19X3 and *(b)* 19X4, given the following specific price index for land costs?

19X1	104.0
19X2	100.0
19X3	109.2
19X4	117.0

Exercise D–4
Calculating general purchasing power gain or loss
(LO 5)

Calculate the general purchasing power gain or loss in 19X2 given the following information (round calculations to three decimals):

Time Period	Price Index
December 19X1	95.6
Average during 19X2	100.2
December 19X2	105.0

a. The cash balance on December 31, 19X1, was $74,000. During 19X2, cash sales occurred uniformly throughout the year and amounted to $452,000. Payments of expenses also occurred evenly throughout the year and amounted to $315,000. Accounts payable of $22,500 were paid in December.

b. Accounts payable amounted to $52,000 on December 31, 19X1. Additional accounts payable amounting to $97,000 were recorded evenly throughout 19X2. The only payment of accounts during the year was $22,500 in late December.

PROBLEMS

Garson Company purchased machinery for $330,000 on December 31, 19X1. It expected the equipment to last five years and to have no salvage value; straight-line depreciation was to be used. It sold the equipment on December 31, 19X5, for $82,000. End-of-year general price index numbers were as follows:

19X1	106.0
19X2	110.1
19X3	117.0
19X4	122.3
19X5	128.9

Problem D–1
Adjusting costs to historical cost/constant purchasing power amounts
(LO 5)

Required

(Round answers to the nearest whole dollar.)

1. What should be presented for the machinery and accumulated depreciation on a historical cost/constant purchasing power balance sheet dated December 31, 19X4? Hint: Depreciation is the total amount of cost that has been allocated to expense. Therefore, the price index number that is used to adjust the nominal dollar cost of the asset should also be used to adjust the nominal dollar amount of depreciation.

2. How much depreciation expense should be shown on the historical cost/constant purchasing power income statement for 19X4?

3. How much depreciation expense should be shown on the historical cost/constant purchasing power income statement for 19X5?

4. How much gain on the sale of the machinery should be reported on the historical cost/nominal dollar income statement for 19X5?

5. After adjusting the machinery's cost and accumulated depreciation to the end-of-19X5 price level, how much gain in (loss of) purchasing power was realized on the sale of the machinery?

Parker Company had three monetary items during 19X2: cash, accounts receivable, and accounts payable. The changes in these accounts during the year were as follows:

Problem D–2
Calculating purchasing power gain or loss
(LO 5)

Cash:
Beginning balance.	$ 90,500
Cash proceeds from sale of building (in May 19X2)	51,200
Cash receipts from customers (spread evenly throughout the year)	359,400
Payments of accounts payable (spread evenly throughout the year)	(274,700)
Dividends declared and paid in July 19X2	(44,000)
Payments of other cash expenses during August 19X2	(77,800)
Ending balance	$104,600

Accounts receivable:	
Beginning balance	$ 92,800
Sales to customers (spread evenly throughout the year)	375,600
Cash receipts from customers (spread evenly throughout the year)	(359,400)
Ending balance	$109,000
Accounts payable:	
Beginning balance	$115,000
Merchandise purchases (spread evenly throughout the year)	231,600
Special purchase December 31, 19X2	47,500
Payments of accounts payable (spread evenly throughout the year)	(274,700)
Ending balance	$119,400

General price index numbers at the end of 19X1 and during 19X2 are as follows:

December 19X1	196.4
January 19X2	202.1
May 19X2	211.0
July 19X2	214.1
August 19X2	215.6
December 19X2	217.0
Average for 19X2	214.8

Required

Calculate the general purchasing power gain or loss experienced by Parker Company in 19X2. Round all amounts to the nearest whole dollar.

Problem D–3

Historical cost/nominal dollars, historical cost/constant purchasing power, and current costs

(LO 4, 5, 6)

Longhorn Corporation purchased a tract of land for $574,000 in 19X1, when the general price index was 127.4. At the same time, a price index for land values in the area of Longhorn's tract was 133.1. In 19X2, when the general price index was 134.6 and the specific price index for land was 142.5, Longhorn bought another tract of land for $296,000. In late 19X7, the general price index is 157.2 and the price index for land values is 174.0.

Required

Preparation Component:

1. In preparing a balance sheet at the end of 19X7, show the amount that should be reported for land based on:

   a. Historical cost/nominal dollars.

   b. Historical cost/constant purchasing power.

   c. Current costs.

   (Round all amounts to the nearest whole dollar.)

Analysis Component:

2. In Longhorn's December 19X7 meeting of the board of directors, one director insists that Longhorn has earned a gain in purchasing power as a result of owning the land. A second director argues that there could not have been a purchasing power gain or loss since land is a nonmonetary asset. Which director do you think is correct? Explain your answer.

CRITICAL THINKING: ESSAYS, PROBLEMS, AND CASES

Write a brief essay that explains the difference between descriptive and prescriptive concepts and that explains why the FASB's conceptual framework is designed to be prescriptive. Also discuss the question of whether specific concepts can be both descriptive and prescriptive.

Analytical Essay

(LO 1, 2, 3)

ANSWERS TO PROGRESS CHECKS

D–1 *c*

D–2 A top-down approach to developing accounting concepts begins by identifying appropriate objectives of accounting reports.

D–3 A bottom-up approach to developing accounting starts by examining existing accounting practices and determining the general features that characterize those procedures.

D–4 *d*

D–5 To have the qualitative characteristic of being reliable, accounting information should be free from bias and error, should be verifiable, should faithfully represent what is supposed to be described, and should be neutral.

D–6 The elements of financial statements are the objects and events that financial statements should describe, for example, assets, liabilities, revenues, and expenses.

D–7 *c*

D–8 $100,000 \times (150/125) = 120,000$

D–9 No. Land is a nonmonetary asset and therefore no purchasing power gain or loss is generated.

D–10 *a*

D–11 Operating profit is measured as revenues less the current (at the time of sale) cost of the resources that were used to earn those revenues.

D–12 *c*

D–13 The current selling price of a liability is the amount that would have to be paid to settle or eliminate the liability.

Present and Future Values: An Expansion

After studying Appendix E, you should be able to:

1. **Explain what is meant by the present value of a single amount and the present value of an annuity, and be able to use tables to solve present value problems.**

2. **Explain what is meant by the future value of a single amount and the future value of an annuity, and be able to use tables to solve future value problems.**

The concept of present value is introduced and applied to accounting problems in Chapters 12 and 15. This appendix supplements those presentations with additional discussion, more complete tables, and additional homework exercises. In studying this appendix, you also learn about the concept of future value.

PRESENT VALUE OF A SINGLE AMOUNT

LO 1

Explain what is meant by the present value of a single amount and the present value of an annuity, and be able to use tables to solve present value problems.

The present value of a single amount to be received or paid at some future date may be expressed as:

$$p = \frac{f}{(1 + i)^n}$$

where

p = Present value
f = Future value
i = Rate of interest per period
n = Number of periods

For example, assume that $2.20 is to be received one period from now. It would be useful to know how much must be invested now, for one period, at an interest rate of 10% to provide $2.20. We can calculate that amount with this formula:

$$p = \frac{f}{(1 + i)^n} = \frac{\$2.20}{(1 + .10)^1} = \$2.00$$

Alternatively, we can use the formula to find how much must be invested for two periods at 10% to provide $2.42:

$$p = \frac{f}{(1 + i)^n} = \frac{\$2.42}{(1 + .10)^2} = \$2.00$$

Note that the number of periods (n) does not have to be expressed in years. Any period of time such as a day, a month, a quarter, or a year may be used. However, whatever period is used, the interest rate (i) must be compounded for the same period. Thus, if a problem expresses n in months, and i equals 12% per year, then 1% of the amount invested at the beginning of each month is earned during that month and added to the investment. Thus, the interest is compounded monthly.

A present value table shows present values for a variety of interest rates (i) and a variety of numbers of periods (n). Each present value is based on the assumption that the future value (f) is 1. The following formula is used to construct a table of present values of a single future amount:

$$p = \frac{1}{(1 + i)^n}$$

Table E–1 on page AP–36 is a table of present values of a single future amount and often is called a *present value of 1* table.

Progress Check

E-1   **Lamar Company is considering an investment that will yield $70,000 after six years. If Lamar requires an 8% return, how much should it be willing to pay for the investment?**

The following formula for the present value of a single amount can be modified to become the formula for the future value of a single amount with a simple step:

$$p = \frac{f}{(1 + i)^n}$$

By multiplying both sides of the equation by $(1 + i)^n$, the result is:

$$f = p \times (1 + i)^n$$

For example, we can use this formula to determine that $2.00 invested for one period at an interest rate of 10% will increase to a future value of $2.20:

$$f = p \times (1 + i)^n$$
$$= \$2.00 \times (1 + .10)^1$$
$$= \$2.20$$

Alternatively, assume that $2.00 will remain invested for three periods at 10%. The $2.662 amount that will be received after three periods is calculated with the formula as follows:

$$f = p \times (1 + i)^n$$
$$= \$2.00 \times (1 + .10)^3$$
$$= \$2.662$$

A future value table shows future values for a variety of interest rates (i) and a variety of numbers of periods (n). Each future value is based on the assumption that the present value (p) is 1. Thus, the formula used to construct a table of future values of a single amount is:

$$f = (1 + i)^n$$

Table E–2 on page AP–37 is a table of future values of a single amount and often is called a *future value of 1* table.

In Table E–2, look at the row where $n = 0$ and observe that the future value is 1 for all interest rates because no interest is earned.

Observe that a table showing the present values of 1 and a table showing the future values of 1 contain exactly the same information because both tables are based on the same equation:

$$p = \frac{f}{(1 + i)^n}$$

This equation is nothing more than a reformulation of:

$$f = p \times (1 + i)^n$$

FUTURE VALUE OF A SINGLE AMOUNT

LO 2
Explain what is meant by the future value of a single amount and the future value of an annuity, and be able to use tables to solve future value problems.

Both tables reflect the same four variables, p, f, i, and n. Therefore, any problem that can be solved with one of the two tables can also be solved with the other table.

For example, suppose that a person invests $100 for five years and expects to earn 12% per year. How much should the person receive after five years? To solve the problem using Table E–2, find the future value of 1, five periods from now, compounded at 12%. In the table, $f = 1.7623$. Thus, the amount to be accumulated over five years is $176.23 ($100 × 1.7623).

Table E–1 shows that the present value of 1, discounted five periods at 12% is 0.5674. Recall that the relationship between present value and future value may be expressed as:

$$p = \frac{f}{(1 + i)^n}$$

This formula can be restated as:

$$p = f \times \frac{1}{(1 + i)^n}$$

In turn, it can be restated as:

$$f = \frac{p}{\dfrac{1}{(1 + i)^n}}$$

Because we know from Table E–1 that $1/(1 + i)^n$ equals 0.5674, the future value of $100 invested for five periods at 12% is:

$$f = \frac{\$100}{0.5674} = \$176.24$$

In summary, the future value can be found two ways. First, we can multiply the amount invested by the future value found in Table E–2. Second, we can divide the amount invested by the present value found in Table E–1. As you can see in this problem, immaterial differences can occur between these two methods through rounding.

Progress Check

E–2 On May 9, Cindy Huber was notified that she had won $150,000 in a sweepstakes. She decided to deposit the money in a savings account that yields an 8% annual rate of interest and plans on quitting her job when the account equals $299,850. How many years will it be before Cindy is able to quit working? *(a)* 2; *(b)* 8; *(c)* 9.

PRESENT VALUE OF AN ANNUITY

LO 1

Explain what is meant by the present value of a single amount and the present value of an annuity, and be able to use tables to solve present value problems.

An annuity is a series of equal payments occurring at equal intervals, such as three annual payments of $100 each. The present value of an annuity is defined as the present value of the payments one period prior to the first payment. Graphically, this annuity and its present value (p) may be represented as follows:

One way to calculate the present value of this annuity finds the present value of each payment with the formula and adds them together. For this example, assuming an interest rate of 15%, the calculation is:

$$p = \frac{\$100}{(1 + .15)^1} + \frac{\$100}{(1 + .15)^2} + \frac{\$100}{(1 + .15)^3} = \$228.32$$

Another way calculates the present value of the annuity by using Table E–1 to compute the present value of each payment then taking their sum:

First payment:	$p = \$100 \times 0.8696 =$	$ 86.96
Second payment:	$p = \$100 \times 0.7561 =$	75.61
Third payment:	$p = \$100 \times 0.6575 =$	65.75
Total:		$p = \$228.32$

We can also use Table E–1 to solve the problem by first adding the table values for the three payments and then multiplying this sum by the $100 amount of each payment:

From Table E–1: $i = 15\%, n = 1, p = $ 0.8696
$i = 15\%, n = 2, p = $ 0.7561
$i = 15\%, n = 3, p = $ 0.6575
2.2832
$2.2832 \times \$100 = \$228.32$

An easier way to solve the problem uses a different table that shows the present values of annuities like Table E–3 on page AP–38, which often is called a *present value of an annuity of 1* table. Look in Table E–3 on the row where $n = 3$ and $i = 15\%$ and observe that the present value is 2.2832. Thus, the present value of an annuity of 1 for three periods, discounted at 15%, is 2.2832.

Although a formula is used to construct a table showing the present values of an annuity, you can construct one by adding the amounts in a present value of 1 table.[1] Examine Table E–1 and Table E–3 to confirm that the following numbers were drawn from those tables:

From Table E–1		From Table E–3	
$i = 8\%, n = 1$	0.9259		
$i = 8\%, n = 2$	0.8573		
$i = 8\%, n = 3$	0.7938		
$i = 8\%, n = 4$	0.7350		
Total	3.3120	$i = 8\%, n = 4$	3.3121

The minor difference in the results occurs only because the numbers in the tables have been rounded.

In addition to the preceding methods, you can use preprogrammed business calculators and spreadsheet computer programs to find the present value of annuities.

Progress Check

E-3 **Smith & Company is considering an investment that would pay $10,000 every six months for three years. The first payment would be received in six months. If Smith & Company requires an annual return of 8%, they should be willing to invest no more than:** *(a)* **$25,771;** *(b)* **$46,229;** *(c)* **$52,421.**

---

[1]The formula for the present value of an annuity of 1 is:

$$p = \frac{1 - \frac{1}{(1 + i)^n}}{i}$$

FUTURE VALUE OF AN ANNUITY

LO 2

Explain what is meant by the future value of a single amount and the future value of an annuity, and be able to use tables to solve problems that involve future values.

Just as an annuity has a present value, it also has a future value. The future value of an annuity is the accumulated value of the annuity payments and interest as of the date of the final payment. Consider the earlier annuity of three annual payments of $100. These are the points in time at which the present value (p) and the future value (f) occur:

$$
\begin{array}{cccc}
& \$100 & \$100 & \$100 \\
\circ \!\!-\!\!-\!\!-\!\!-\!\!-\!\!\circ\!\!-\!\!-\!\!-\!\!-\!\!\circ\!\!-\!\!-\!\!-\!\!-\!\!\circ \\
p & & & f
\end{array}
$$

Note that the first payment is made two periods prior to the point at which the future value is determined. Therefore, for the first payment, $n = 2$. For the second payment, $n = 1$. Since the third payment occurs on the future value date, $n = 0$.

One way to calculate the future value of this annuity uses the formula to find the future value of each payment and adds them together. Assuming an interest rate of 15%, the calculation is:

$$f = \$100 \times (1 + .15)^2 + \$100 \times (1 + .15)^1 + \$100 \times (1 + .15)^0 = \$347.25$$

Another way calculates the future value of the annuity by using Table E–2 to find the sum of the future values of each payment:

First payment:	$f = \$100 \times 1.3225 =$	$132.25
Second payment:	$f = \$100 \times 1.1500 =$	115.00
Third payment:	$f = \$100 \times 1.0000 =$	100.00
Total:		$f = \underline{\underline{\$347.25}}$

A third approach adds the future values of three payments of 1 and multiplies the sum by $100:

From Table E–2:	$i = 15\%, n = 2, f =$ 1.3225
	$i = 15\%, n = 1, f =$ 1.1500
	$i = 15\%, n = 0, f =$ 1.0000
	Sum = 3.4725

Future value = $3.4725 \times \$100 = \underline{\underline{\$347.25}}$

A fourth and easier way to solve the problem uses a table that shows the future values of annuities, often called a *future value of an annuity of 1* table. Table E–4 on page AP–39 is such a table. Note in Table E–4 that when $n = 1$, the future values are equal to 1 ($f = 1$) for all rates of interest because the annuity consists of only one payment and the future value is determined on the date of the payment. Thus, the future value equals the payment.

Although a formula is used to construct a table showing the future values of an annuity of 1, you can construct one by adding together the amount in a future value of 1 table like Table E–2.[2] Examine Table E–2 and Table E–4 to confirm that the following numbers were drawn from those tables:

From Table E–2		From Table E–4	
$i = 8\%, n = 0$	1.0000		
$i = 8\%, n = 1$	1.0800		
$i = 8\%, n = 2$	1.1664		
$i = 8\%, n = 3$	1.2597		
Total	4.5061	$i = 8\%, n = 4$	4.5061

---

[2]The formula for the future value of an annuity of 1 is:

$$f = \frac{(1 + i)^n - 1}{i}$$

Minor differences may occur because the numbers in the tables have been rounded.

You can also use business calculators and spreadsheet computer programs to find the future values of annuities.

Observe that the future value in Table E–2 is 1.0000 when $n = 0$ but the future value in Table E–4 is 1.0000 when $n = 1$. Why does this apparent contradiction arise? When $n = 0$ in Table E–2, the future value is determined on the date that the single payment occurs. Thus, no interest is earned and the future value equals the payment. However, Table E–4 describes annuities with equal payments occurring each period. When $n = 1$, the annuity has only one payment, and its future value also equals 1 on the date of its final and only payment.

Progress Check

E-4 **Syntel Company invests $45,000 per year for five years at 12%. Calculate the value of the investment at the end of five years.**

LO 1. Explain what is meant by the present value of a single amount and the present value of an annuity, and be able to use tables to solve present value problems. The present value of a single amount to be received at a future date is the amount that could be invested now at the specified interest rate to yield that future value. The present value of an annuity is the amount that could be invested now at the specified interest rate to yield that series of equal periodic payments. Present value tables and business calculators simplify calculating present values.

LO 2. Explain what is meant by the future value of a single amount and the future value of an annuity, and be able to use tables to solve future value problems. The future value of a single amount invested at a specified rate of interest is the amount that would accumulate at a future date. The future value of an annuity to be invested at a specified rate of interest is the amount that would accumulate at the date of the final equal periodic payment. Future value tables and business calculators simplify calculating future values.

SUMMARY OF THE APPENDIX IN TERMS OF LEARNING OBJECTIVES

Table E-1   Present Value of 1 Due in *n* Periods

							Rate					
Periods	**1%**	**2%**	**3%**	**4%**	**5%**	**6%**	**7%**	**8%**	**9%**	**10%**	**12%**	**15%**
1	0.9901	0.9804	0.9709	0.9615	0.9524	0.9434	0.9346	0.9259	0.9174	0.9091	0.8929	0.8696
2	0.9803	0.9612	0.9426	0.9246	0.9070	0.8900	0.8734	0.8573	0.8417	0.8264	0.7972	0.7561
3	0.9706	0.9423	0.9151	0.8890	0.8638	0.8396	0.8163	0.7938	0.7722	0.7513	0.7118	0.6575
4	0.9610	0.9238	0.8885	0.8548	0.8227	0.7921	0.7629	0.7350	0.7084	0.6830	0.6355	0.5718
5	0.9515	0.9057	0.8626	0.8219	0.7835	0.7473	0.7130	0.6806	0.6499	0.6209	0.5674	0.4972
6	0.9420	0.8880	0.8375	0.7903	0.7462	0.7050	0.6663	0.6302	0.5963	0.5645	0.5066	0.4323
7	0.9327	0.8706	0.8131	0.7599	0.7107	0.6651	0.6227	0.5835	0.5470	0.5132	0.4523	0.3759
8	0.9235	0.8535	0.7894	0.7307	0.6768	0.6274	0.5820	0.5403	0.5019	0.4665	0.4039	0.3269
9	0.9143	0.8368	0.7664	0.7026	0.6446	0.5919	0.5439	0.5002	0.4604	0.4241	0.3606	0.2843
10	0.9053	0.8203	0.7441	0.6756	0.6139	0.5584	0.5083	0.4632	0.4224	0.3855	0.3220	0.2472
11	0.8963	0.8043	0.7224	0.6496	0.5847	0.5268	0.4751	0.4289	0.3875	0.3505	0.2875	0.2149
12	0.8874	0.7885	0.7014	0.6246	0.5568	0.4970	0.4440	0.3971	0.3555	0.3186	0.2567	0.1869
13	0.8787	0.7730	0.6810	0.6006	0.5303	0.4688	0.4150	0.3677	0.3262	0.2897	0.2292	0.1625
14	0.8700	0.7579	0.6611	0.5775	0.5051	0.4423	0.3878	0.3405	0.2992	0.2633	0.2046	0.1413
15	0.8613	0.7430	0.6419	0.5553	0.4810	0.4173	0.3624	0.3152	0.2745	0.2394	0.1827	0.1229
16	0.8528	0.7284	0.6232	0.5339	0.4581	0.3936	0.3387	0.2919	0.2519	0.2176	0.1631	0.1069
17	0.8444	0.7142	0.6050	0.5134	0.4363	0.3714	0.3166	0.2703	0.2311	0.1978	0.1456	0.0929
18	0.8360	0.7002	0.5874	0.4936	0.4155	0.3503	0.2959	0.2502	0.2120	0.1799	0.1300	0.0808
19	0.8277	0.6864	0.5703	0.4746	0.3957	0.3305	0.2765	0.2317	0.1945	0.1635	0.1161	0.0703
20	0.8195	0.6730	0.5537	0.4564	0.3769	0.3118	0.2584	0.2145	0.1784	0.1486	0.1037	0.0611
25	0.7798	0.6095	0.4776	0.3751	0.2953	0.2330	0.1842	0.1460	0.1160	0.0923	0.0588	0.0304
30	0.7419	0.5521	0.4120	0.3083	0.2314	0.1741	0.1314	0.0994	0.0754	0.0573	0.0334	0.0151
35	0.7059	0.5000	0.3554	0.2534	0.1813	0.1301	0.0937	0.0676	0.0490	0.0356	0.0189	0.0075
40	0.6717	0.4529	0.3066	0.2083	0.1420	0.0972	0.0668	0.0460	0.0318	0.0221	0.0107	0.0037

Table E-2 Future Value of 1 Due in *n* Periods

						Rate						
Periods	**1%**	**2%**	**3%**	**4%**	**5%**	**6%**	**7%**	**8%**	**9%**	**10%**	**12%**	**15%**
0	1.0000	1.0000	1.0000	1.0000	1.0000	1.0000	1.0000	1.0000	1.0000	1.0000	1.0000	1.0000
1	1.0100	1.0200	1.0300	1.0400	1.0500	1.0600	1.0700	1.0800	1.0900	1.1000	1.1200	1.1500
2	1.0201	1.0404	1.0609	1.0816	1.1025	1.1236	1.1449	1.1664	1.1881	1.2100	1.2544	1.3225
3	1.0303	1.0612	1.0927	1.1249	1.1576	1.1910	1.2250	1.2597	1.2950	1.3310	1.4049	1.5209
4	1.0406	1.0824	1.1255	1.1699	1.2155	1.2625	1.3108	1.3605	1.4116	1.4641	1.5735	1.7490
5	1.0510	1.1041	1.1593	1.2167	1.2763	1.3382	1.4026	1.4693	1.5386	1.6105	1.7623	2.0114
6	1.0615	1.1262	1.1941	1.2653	1.3401	1.4185	1.5007	1.5869	1.6771	1.7716	1.9738	2.3131
7	1.0721	1.1487	1.2299	1.3159	1.4071	1.5036	1.6058	1.7138	1.8280	1.9487	2.2107	2.6600
8	1.0829	1.1717	1.2668	1.3686	1.4775	1.5938	1.7182	1.8509	1.9926	2.1436	2.4760	3.0590
9	1.0937	1.1951	1.3048	1.4233	1.5513	1.6895	1.8385	1.9990	2.1719	2.3579	2.7731	3.5179
10	1.1046	1.2190	1.3439	1.4802	1.6289	1.7908	1.9672	2.1589	2.3674	2.5937	3.1058	4.0456
11	1.1157	1.2434	1.3842	1.5395	1.7103	1.8983	2.1049	2.3316	2.5804	2.8531	3.4785	4.6524
12	1.1268	1.2682	1.4258	1.6010	1.7959	2.0122	2.2522	2.5182	2.8127	3.1384	3.8960	5.3503
13	1.1381	1.2936	1.4685	1.6651	1.8856	2.1329	2.4098	2.7196	3.0658	3.4523	4.3635	6.1528
14	1.1495	1.3195	1.5126	1.7317	1.9799	2.2609	2.5785	2.9372	3.3417	3.7975	4.8871	7.0757
15	1.1610	1.3459	1.5580	1.8009	2.0789	2.3966	2.7590	3.1722	3.6425	4.1772	5.4736	8.1371
16	1.1726	1.3728	1.6047	1.8730	2.1829	2.5404	2.9522	3.4259	3.9703	4.5950	6.1304	9.3576
17	1.1843	1.4002	1.6528	1.9479	2.2920	2.6928	3.1588	3.7000	4.3276	5.0545	6.8660	10.7613
18	1.1961	1.4282	1.7024	2.0258	2.4066	2.8543	3.3799	3.9960	4.7171	5.5599	7.6900	12.3755
19	1.2081	1.4568	1.7535	2.1068	2.5270	3.0256	3.6165	4.3157	5.1417	6.1159	8.6128	14.2318
20	1.2202	1.4859	1.8061	2.1911	2.6533	3.2071	3.8697	4.6610	5.6044	6.7275	9.6463	16.3665
25	1.2824	1.6406	2.0938	2.6658	3.3864	4.2919	5.4274	6.8485	8.6231	10.8347	17.0001	32.9190
30	1.3478	1.8114	2.4273	3.2434	4.3219	5.7435	7.6123	10.0627	13.2677	17.4494	29.9599	66.2118
35	1.4166	1.9999	2.8139	3.9461	5.5160	7.6861	10.6766	14.7853	20.4140	28.1024	52.7996	133.176
40	1.4889	2.2080	3.2620	4.8010	7.0400	10.2857	14.9745	21.7245	31.4094	45.2593	93.0510	267.864

Table E-3   Present Value of an Annuity of 1 per Period

Periods	1%	2%	3%	4%	5%	6%	7%	8%	9%	10%	12%	15%
1	0.9901	0.9804	0.9709	0.9615	0.9524	0.9434	0.9346	0.9259	0.9174	0.9091	0.8929	0.8696
2	1.9704	1.9416	1.9135	1.8861	1.8594	1.8334	1.8080	1.7833	1.7591	1.7355	1.6901	1.6257
3	2.9410	2.8839	2.8286	2.7751	2.7232	2.6730	2.6243	2.5771	2.5313	2.4869	2.4018	2.2832
4	3.9020	3.8077	3.7171	3.6299	3.5460	3.4651	3.3872	3.3121	3.2397	3.1699	3.0373	2.8550
5	4.8534	4.7135	4.5797	4.4518	4.3295	4.2124	4.1002	3.9927	3.8897	3.7908	3.6048	3.3522
6	5.7955	5.6014	5.4172	5.2421	5.0757	4.9173	4.7665	4.6229	4.4859	4.3553	4.1114	3.7845
7	6.7282	6.4720	6.2303	6.0021	5.7864	5.5824	5.3893	5.2064	5.0330	4.8684	4.5638	4.1604
8	7.6517	7.3255	7.0197	6.7327	6.4632	6.2098	5.9713	5.7466	5.5348	5.3349	4.9676	4.4873
9	8.5660	8.1622	7.7861	7.4353	7.1078	6.8017	6.5152	6.2469	5.9952	5.7590	5.3282	4.7716
10	9.4713	8.9826	8.5302	8.1109	7.7217	7.3601	7.0236	6.7101	6.4177	6.1446	5.6502	5.0188
11	10.3676	9.7868	9.2526	8.7605	8.3064	7.8869	7.4987	7.1390	6.8052	6.4951	5.9377	5.2337
12	11.2551	10.5753	9.9540	9.3851	8.8633	8.3838	7.9427	7.5361	7.1607	6.8137	6.1944	5.4206
13	12.1337	11.3484	10.6350	9.9856	9.3936	8.8527	8.3577	7.9038	7.4869	7.1034	6.4235	5.5831
14	13.0037	12.1062	11.2961	10.5631	9.8986	9.2950	8.7455	8.2442	7.7862	7.3667	6.6282	5.7245
15	13.8651	12.8493	11.9379	11.1184	10.3797	9.7122	9.1079	8.5595	8.0607	7.6061	6.8109	5.8474
16	14.7179	13.5777	12.5611	11.6523	10.8378	10.1059	9.4466	8.8514	8.3126	7.8237	6.9740	5.9542
17	15.5623	14.2919	13.1661	12.1657	11.2741	10.4773	9.7632	9.1216	8.5436	8.0216	7.1196	6.0472
18	16.3983	14.9920	13.7535	12.6593	11.6896	10.8276	10.0591	9.3719	8.7556	8.2014	7.2497	6.1280
19	17.2260	15.6785	14.3238	13.1339	12.0853	11.1581	10.3356	9.6036	8.9501	8.3649	7.3658	6.1982
20	18.0456	16.3514	14.8775	13.5903	12.4622	11.4699	10.5940	9.8181	9.1285	8.5136	7.4694	6.2593
25	22.0232	19.5235	17.4131	15.6221	14.0939	12.7834	11.6536	10.6748	9.8226	9.0770	7.8431	6.4641
30	25.8077	22.3965	19.6004	17.2920	15.3725	13.7648	12.4090	11.2578	10.2737	9.4269	8.0552	6.5660
35	29.4086	24.9986	21.4872	18.6646	16.3742	14.4982	12.9477	11.6546	10.5668	9.6442	8.1755	6.6166
40	32.8347	27.3555	23.1148	19.7928	17.1591	15.0463	13.3317	11.9246	10.7574	9.7791	8.2438	6.6418

Table E-4 Future Value of an Annuity of 1 per Period

Periods	1%	2%	3%	4%	5%	6%	7%	8%	9%	10%	12%	15%
1	1.0000	1.0000	1.0000	1.0000	1.0000	1.0000	1.0000	1.0000	1.0000	1.0000	1.0000	1.0000
2	2.0100	2.0200	2.0300	2.0400	2.0500	2.0600	2.0700	2.0800	2.0900	2.1000	2.1200	2.1500
3	3.0301	3.0604	3.0909	3.1216	3.1525	3.1836	3.2149	3.2464	3.2781	3.3100	3.3744	3.4725
4	4.0604	4.1216	4.1836	4.2465	4.3101	4.3746	4.4399	4.5061	4.5731	4.6410	4.7793	4.9934
5	5.1010	5.2040	5.3901	5.4163	5.5256	5.6371	5.7507	5.8666	5.9847	6.1051	6.3528	6.7424
6	6.1520	6.3081	6.4684	6.6330	6.8019	6.9753	7.1533	7.3359	7.5233	7.7156	8.1152	8.7537
7	7.2135	7.4343	7.6625	7.8983	8.1420	8.3938	8.6540	8.9228	9.2004	9.4872	10.0890	11.0668
8	8.2857	8.5830	8.8923	9.2142	9.5491	9.8975	10.2598	10.6366	11.0285	11.4359	12.2997	13.7268
9	9.3685	9.7546	10.1591	10.5828	11.0266	11.4913	11.9780	12.4876	13.0210	13.5795	14.7757	16.7858
10	10.4622	10.9497	11.4639	12.0061	12.5779	13.1808	13.8164	14.4866	15.1929	15.9374	17.5487	20.3037
11	11.5668	12.1687	12.8078	13.4864	14.2068	14.9716	15.7836	16.6455	17.5603	18.5312	20.6546	24.3493
12	12.6825	13.4121	14.1920	15.0258	15.9171	16.8699	17.8885	18.9771	20.1407	21.3843	24.1331	29.0017
13	13.8093	14.6803	15.6178	16.6268	17.7130	18.8821	20.1406	21.4953	22.9534	24.5227	28.0291	34.3519
14	14.9474	15.9739	17.0863	18.2919	19.5986	21.0151	22.5505	24.2149	26.0192	27.9750	32.3926	40.5047
15	16.0969	17.2934	18.5989	20.0236	21.5786	23.2760	25.1290	27.1521	29.3609	31.7725	37.2797	47.5804
16	17.2579	18.6393	20.1569	21.8245	23.6575	25.6725	27.8881	30.3243	33.0034	35.9497	42.7533	55.7175
17	18.4304	20.0121	21.7616	23.6975	25.8404	28.2129	30.8402	33.7502	36.9737	40.5447	48.8837	65.0751
18	19.6147	21.4123	23.4144	25.6454	28.1324	30.9057	33.9990	37.4502	41.3013	45.5992	55.7497	75.8364
19	20.8109	22.8406	25.1169	27.6712	30.5390	33.7600	37.3790	41.4463	46.0185	51.1591	63.4397	88.2118
20	22.0190	24.2974	26.8704	29.7781	33.0660	36.7856	40.9955	45.7620	51.1601	57.2750	72.0524	102.444
25	28.2432	32.0303	36.4593	41.6459	47.7271	54.8645	63.2490	73.1059	84.7009	98.3471	133.334	212.793
30	34.7849	40.5681	47.5754	56.0849	66.4388	79.0582	94.4608	113.283	136.308	164.494	241.333	434.745
35	41.6603	49.9945	60.4621	73.6522	90.3203	111.435	138.237	172.317	215.711	271.024	431.663	881.170
40	48.8864	60.4020	75.4013	95.0255	120.800	154.762	199.635	259.057	337.882	442.593	767.091	1,779.09

EXERCISES

Jasper Company is considering an investment which, if paid for immediately, is expected to return $172,500 five years hence. If Jasper demands a 9% return, how much will it be willing to pay for this investment?

Exercise E–1
Present value of an amount
(LO 1)

LCV Company invested $529,000 in a project expected to earn a 12% annual rate of return. The earnings will be reinvested in the project each year until the entire investment is liquidated 10 years hence. What will the cash proceeds be when the project is liquidated?

Exercise E–2
Future value of an amount
(LO 2)

Cornblue Distributing is considering a contract that will return $200,400 annually at the end of each year for six years. If Cornblue demands an annual return of 7% and pays for the investment immediately, how much should it be willing to pay?

Exercise E–3
Present value of an annuity
(LO 1)

Sarah Oliver is planning to begin an individual retirement program in which she will invest $1,200 annually at the end of each year. Oliver plans to retire after making 30 annual investments in a program that earns a return of 10%. What will be the value of the program on the date of the last investment?

Exercise E–4
Future value of an annuity
(LO 2)

Kevin Smith has been offered the possibility of investing $0.3152 for 15 years, after which he will be paid $1. What annual rate of interest will Smith earn? (Use Table E–1 to find the answer.)

Exercise E–5
Interest rate on an investment
(LO 1)

Laura Veralli has been offered the possibility of investing $0.5268. The investment will earn 6% per year and will return Veralli $1 at the end of the investment. How many years must Veralli wait to receive the $1? (Use Table E–1 to find the answer.)

Exercise E–6
Number of periods of an investment
(LO 1)

Tom Albertson expects to invest $1 at 15% and, at the end of the investment, receive $66.2118. How many years will elapse before Albertson receives the payment? (Use Table E–2 to find the answer.)

Exercise E–7
Number of periods of an investment
(LO 2)

Ed Teller expects to invest $1 for 35 years, after which he will receive $20.4140. What rate of interest will Teller earn? (Use Table E–2 to find the answer.)

Exercise E–8
Interest rate on an investment
(LO 2)

Helen Fanshawe expects an immediate investment of $9.3936 to return $1 annually for 13 years, with the first payment to be received in one year. What rate of interest will Fanshawe earn? (Use Table E–3 to find the answer.)

Exercise E–9
Interest rate on an investment
(LO 1)

Ken Priggin expects an investment of $7.6061 to return $1 annually for several years. If Priggin is to earn a return of 10%, how many annual payments must he receive? (Use Table E–3 to find the answer.)

Exercise E–10
Number of periods of an investment
(LO 1)

Steve Church expects to invest $1 annually for 40 years and have an accumulated value of $95.0255 on the date of the last investment. If this occurs, what rate of interest will Church earn? (Use Table E–4 to find the answer.)

Exercise E–11
Interest rate on an investment
(LO 2)

Bitsy Brennon expects to invest $1 annually in a fund that will earn 8%. How many annual investments must Brennon make to accumulate $45.7620 on the date of the last investment? (Use Table E–4 to find the answer.)

Exercise E–12
Number of periods of an investment
(LO 2)

Bill Lenehan financed a new automobile by paying $3,100 cash and agreeing to make 20 monthly payments of $450 each, the first payment to be made one month after the purchase. The loan was said to bear interest at an annual rate of 12%. What was the cost of the automobile?

Exercise E–13
Present value of an annuity
(LO 1)

Stephanie Powell deposited $4,900 in a savings account that earns interest at an annual rate of 8%, compounded quarterly. The $4,900 plus earned interest must remain in the account 10 years before it can be withdrawn. How much money will be in the account at the end of the 10 years?

Exercise E–14
Future value of an amount
(LO 2)

Sally Sayer plans to have $90 withheld from her monthly paycheck and deposited in a savings account that earns 12% annually, compounded monthly. If Sayer continues with her plan for 2½ years, how much will be accumulated in the account on the date of the last deposit?

Exercise E–15
Future value of an annuity
(LO 2)

Stellar Company plans to issue 12%, 15-year, $500,000 par value bonds payable that pay interest semiannually on June 30 and December 31. The bonds are dated December 31, 19X1, and are to be issued on that date. If the market rate of interest for the bonds is 10% on the date of issue, what will be the cash proceeds from the bond issue?

Exercise E–16
Present value of bonds
(LO 1)

Travis Company has decided to establish a fund that will be used 10 years hence to replace an aging productive facility. The company makes an initial contribution of $150,000 to the fund and plans to make quarterly contributions of $60,000 beginning in three months. The fund is expected to earn 12%, compounded quarterly. What will be the value of the fund 10 years hence?

Exercise E–17
Future value of an amount plus an annuity
(LO 2)

McCoy Company expects to earn 10% per year on an investment that will pay $756,400 six years hence. Use Table E–2 to calculate the present value of the investment.

Exercise E–18
Present value of an amount
(LO 1)

Comet Company invests $216,000 at 7% per year for nine years. Use Table E–1 to calculate the future value of the investment nine years hence.

Exercise E–19
Future value of an amount
(LO 2)

ANSWERS TO PROGRESS CHECKS

E–1 $70,000 × 0.6302 = $44,114

E–2   c $299,850/$150,000 = 1.9990
         Table E–2 shows this value for nine years at 8%.

E–3   c $10,000 × 5.2421 = $52,421

E–4 $45,000 × 6.3528 = $285,876

Financial Statements and Related Disclosures from Apple Computer Inc.'s 1993 Annual Report

Eleven-Year Financial History

	1993	1992	1991	1990
Results of Operations				
Net sales:				
Domestic	$ 4,387,674	$ 3,885,042	$ 3,484,533	$ 3,241,061
International	3,589,280	3,201,500	2,824,316	2,317,374
Total net sales	7,976,954	7,086,542	6,308,849	5,558,435
Costs and expenses:				
Cost of sales	5,248,834	3,991,337	3,314,118	2,606,223
Research and development (R&D)	664,564	602,135	583,046	478,019
Selling, general and administrative (SG&A)	1,632,362	1,687,262	1,740,293	1,728,508
Restructuring costs and other	320,856	—	224,043	33,673
	7,866,616	6,280,734	5,861,500	4,846,423
Operating income	110,338	805,808	447,349	712,012
Interest and other income, net	29,321	49,634	52,395	66,505
Income before income taxes	139,659	855,442	499,744	778,517
Provision for income taxes	53,070	325,069	189,903	303,622
Net income	$ 86,589	$ 530,373	$ 309,841	$ 474,895
Earnings per common and common equivalent share	$ 0.73	$ 4.33	$ 2.58	$ 3.77
Common and common equivalent shares used in the calculations of earnings per share	119,125	122,490	120,283	125,813
Financial Position				
Cash, cash equivalents, and short-term investments	$ 892,303	$ 1,435,500	$ 892,719	$ 997,091
Accounts receivable, net	$ 1,381,946	$ 1,087,185	$ 907,159	$ 761,868
Inventories	$ 1,506,638	$ 580,097	$ 671,655	$ 355,473
Net property, plant, and equipment	$ 659,546	$ 462,221	$ 447,978	$ 398,165
Total assets	$ 5,171,412	$ 4,223,693	$ 3,493,597	$ 2,975,707
Current liabilities	$ 2,515,202	$ 1,425,520	$ 1,217,051	$ 1,027,055
Deferred income taxes	$ 629,832	$ 610,803	$ 509,870	$ 501,832
Shareholders' equity	$ 2,026,378	$ 2,187,370	$ 1,766,676	$ 1,446,820
Cash dividends declared per common share	$ 0.48	$ 0.48	$ 0.48	$ 0.44
Other Data (Unaudited)				
Regular employees	11,963	12,166	12,386	12,307
Temporary employees and contractors	2,975	2,632	2,046	2,221
International net sales as a percentage of total net sales	45%	45%	45%	42%
Gross margin as a percentage of net sales	34%	44%	47%	53%
R&D as a percentage of net sales	8%	8%	9%	9%
SG&A as a percentage of net sales	20%	24%	28%	31%
Operating income as a percentage of net sales	1%	11%	7%	13%
Return on net sales	1%	7%	5%	9%
Return on average total assets	2%	14%	10%	17%
Return on average shareholders' equity	4%	27%	19%	32%
Price range per common share	$ 65–$24¼	$ 69⅞–$43¼	$ 72¾–$25	$ 49½–$28¼

The number of shares and per share amounts for fiscal years 1983 through 1986 have been adjusted to reflect the two-for-one stock split effected on May 15, 1987.

Net income for fiscal year 1989 includes a pretax gain of approximately $79 million ($48 million, or $0.37 per share, after taxes) from the Company's sale of its common stock of Adobe Systems Incorporated.

Certain prior year amounts have been reclassified to conform to the current year presentation.

(In thousands, except employee, percentage, and per share data)

1989	1988	1987	1986	1985	1984	1983
$ 3,401,462	$ 2,766,328	$ 1,940,369	$ 1,411,812	$ 1,490,396	$ 1,187,839	$ 764,416
1,882,551	1,305,045	720,699	490,086	427,884	328,037	218,353
5,284,013	4,071,373	2,661,068	1,901,898	1,918,280	1,515,876	982,769
2,694,823	1,990,879	1,296,220	891,112	1,117,864	878,586	505,765
420,083	272,512	191,554	127,758	72,526	71,136	60,040
1,534,794	1,187,644	801,856	609,497	588,156	480,303	290,845
—	—	—	—	36,966	—	—
4,649,700	3,451,035	2,289,630	1,628,367	1,815,512	1,430,025	856,650
634,313	620,338	371,438	273,531	102,768	85,851	126,119
110,009	35,823	38,930	36,187	17,277	23,334	20,003
744,322	656,161	410,368	309,718	120,045	109,185	146,122
290,289	255,903	192,872	155,755	58,822	45,130	69,408
$ 454,033	$ 400,258	$ 217,496	$ 153,963	$ 61,223	$ 64,055	$ 76,714
$ 3.53	$ 3.08	$ 1.65	$ 1.20	$ 0.49	$ 0.53	$ 0.64
128,669	129,900	131,615	128,630	123,790	121,774	119,734
$ 808,950	$ 545,717	$ 565,094	$ 576,215	$ 337,013	$ 114,888	$ 143,284
$ 792,824	$ 638,816	$ 405,637	$ 263,126	$ 220,157	$ 258,238	$ 136,420
$ 475,377	$ 461,470	$ 225,753	$ 108,680	$ 166,951	$ 264,619	$ 142,457
$ 334,227	$ 207,357	$ 130,434	$ 107,315	$ 90,446	$ 75,868	$ 67,050
$ 2,743,899	$ 2,082,086	$ 1,477,931	$ 1,160,128	$ 936,177	$ 788,786	$ 556,579
$ 895,243	$ 827,093	$ 478,678	$ 328,535	$ 295,425	$ 255,184	$ 130,094
$ 362,910	$ 251,568	$ 162,765	$ 137,506	$ 90,265	$ 69,037	$ 48,584
$ 1,485,746	$ 1,003,425	$ 836,488	$ 694,087	$ 550,487	$ 464,565	$ 377,901
$ 0.40	$ 0.32	$ 0.12	—	—	—	—
12,068	9,536	6,236	4,950	4,326	5,382	4,645
2,449	1,300	992	636	325	—	—
36%	32%	27%	26%	22%	22%	22%
49%	51%	51%	53%	42%	42%	49%
8%	7%	7%	7%	4%	5%	6%
29%	29%	30%	32%	31%	32%	30%
12%	15%	14%	14%	5%	6%	13%
9%	10%	8%	8%	3%	4%	8%
19%	22%	16%	15%	7%	10%	17%
36%	44%	28%	25%	12%	15%	24%
$ 49⅝–$33¾	$ 59¼–$28	$ 57½–$16¼	$ 19 7/16–$7½	$ 15 5/16–$7¼	$ 16 9/16–$8⅞	$ 31 5/16–$9 1/16

Selected Quarterly Financial Information (Unaudited)

(Tabular amounts in thousands, except per share amounts)

	Fourth Quarter	Third Quarter	Second Quarter	First Quarter
1993				
Net sales	$ 2,140,789	$ 1,861,979	$ 1,973,894	$ 2,000,292
Gross margin	$ 550,428	$ 606,004	$ 760,763	$ 810,925
Net income (loss)	$ 2,664	$ (188,316)	$ 110,900	$ 161,341
Earnings (loss) per common and common equivalent share	$ 0.02	$ (1.63)	$ 0.92	$ 1.33
Cash dividends declared per common share	$ 0.12	$ 0.12	$ 0.12	$ 0.12
Price range per common share	$ 40⅛–$24¼	$ 58¾–$39⅝	$ 65–$52¾	$ 60⅝–$43⅜
1992				
Net sales	$ 1,767,734	$ 1,740,171	$ 1,716,025	$ 1,862,612
Gross margin	$ 755,068	$ 771,327	$ 755,529	$ 813,281
Net income	$ 97,612	$ 131,665	$ 135,078	$ 166,018
Earnings per common and common equivalent share	$ 0.81	$ 1.07	$ 1.09	$ 1.36
Cash dividends declared per common share	$ 0.12	$ 0.12	$ 0.12	$ 0.12
Price range per common share	$ 49½–$43¼	$ 62¾–$44¼	$ 69⅞–$56⅜	$ 55–$47¾

At September 24, 1993, there were 34,034 shareholders of record.

The Company began declaring quarterly cash dividends on its common stock in April 1987. The dividend policy is determined quarterly by the Board of Directors and is dependent on the Company's earnings, capital requirements, financial condition, and other factors.

The price range per common share represents the highest and lowest closing prices for the Company's common stock on the NASDAQ National Market System during each quarter.

Net loss for the third quarter of 1993 and net income for fiscal year 1993 include a restructuring charge of $321 million ($199 million, or $1.72 per share, after taxes).

Management's Discussion and Analysis
of Financial Condition and Results of Operations

The following discussion should be read in conjunction with the consolidated financial statements and notes thereto. All information is based on the Company's fiscal calendar.

(Tabular information: Dollars in millions, except per share amounts)

Results of Operations

	1993	Change	1992	Change	1991
Net sales	$ 7,977	13%	$ 7,087	12%	$ 6,309
Gross margin	$ 2,728	–12%	$ 3,095	3%	$ 2,995
Percentage of net sales	34.2%		43.7%		47.5%
Operating expenses (excluding restructuring costs and other)	$ 2,297	—	$ 2,289	–1%	$ 2,323
Percentage of net sales	28.8%		32.3%		36.8%
Restructuring costs and other	$ 321	—	—	—	$ 224
Percentage of net sales	4.0%		—		3.6%
Net income	$ 87	–84%	$ 530	71%	$ 310
Earnings per share	$ 0.73	–83%	$ 4.33	68%	$ 2.58

Net Sales

The net sales growth in 1993 over 1992 reflected strong unit sales of the Company's Apple Macintosh computers, including the Macintosh Color Classic,® the Macintosh LC III, and the Macintosh Centris™ line (which has recently been consolidated with the Macintosh Quadra line), all of which were introduced in 1993. Additions to the PowerBook line of notebook computers and the Performa line of Macintosh computers also contributed to net sales growth. This growth was partially offset by declining unit sales of certain of the Company's more established products and older product versions. Total Macintosh computer unit sales increased 32% over the prior year, compared with a 20% increase from 1991 to 1992. The average aggregate revenue per unit declined 15% in 1993 compared with 1992, primarily as a result of pricing actions undertaken by the Company in response to continuing industrywide pricing pressures. Going forward, the Company anticipates continued industrywide competitive pricing and promotional actions.

Growth in net sales in 1992 over 1991 reflected strong unit sales of the Macintosh Classic II, Macintosh LC II, PowerBook, and Macintosh Quadra computers, all of which were introduced in 1992. This growth was partially offset by declining unit sales of certain of the Company's more established products and older product versions. The average aggregate revenue per unit increased slightly in 1992 when compared with 1991, primarily as a result of a shift in product mix toward the Company's PowerBook and Macintosh Quadra computers, offset somewhat by pricing and promotional actions undertaken by the Company in 1992.

In 1993, domestic net sales increased 13% over the prior year, compared with an increase of 11% in 1992 over 1991. International net sales grew 12% from 1992 to 1993, representing a slight decrease in growth rate compared with 13% growth from 1991 to 1992. In 1992, growth in international net sales slowed to 13%, compared with 22% growth from 1990 to 1991. International net sales represented 45% of net sales in 1993, 1992, and 1991.

During the fourth quarter of 1993, the Company expanded its midrange and high-end computer offerings with the introduction of the Macintosh Centris 660AV (later renamed the Macintosh Quadra 660AV) and Macintosh Quadra 840AV, respectively, which combine communications and computing capabilities by incorporating telecommunications, video, and speech technologies. On July 30, 1993, the Company introduced its first personal digital assistant (PDA) product, the Newton MessagePad. The Company also introduced the AudioVision™ 14 Display, which integrates audio and video capabilities, and several new system software products.

In addition to the products introduced in the fourth quarter, on October 21, 1993, the Company introduced several products that extend its entry-level, midrange, and notebook computer offerings. The new products include five entry-level Macintosh computers, the Macintosh Performa 460 and 470 series, the Performa 550, the Macintosh LC 475, and the Macintosh Quadra 605; two midrange computers, the Macintosh Quadra 610 and 650; and two notebook computers, the PowerBook Duo 250 and 270c. The Company also introduced the LaserWriter Select™ 360 and the LaserWriter® Pro 810, two new printers that focus on the needs of small and large workgroups, respectively. It is anticipated that a significant portion of the Company's future revenues will come from these and future new products. However, there can be no assurance that these new products will receive favorable market acceptance, and the Company cannot determine the ultimate effect these products will have on its sales or results of operations.

Gross Margin

Gross margin as a percentage of net sales in 1993 continued to decline from 1992 and 1991 levels. The gross margin percentage declined to 34.2% in 1993 from 43.7% in 1992, and during the fourth quarter of 1993 was 25.7% of net sales, compared with 42.7% in the fourth quarter of 1992. The downward trend in gross margin as a percentage of net sales was primarily a result of pricing and promotional actions undertaken by the Company in response to industrywide competitive pricing pressures and higher levels of inventory for certain products. Inventory valuation reserves recorded against certain products also contributed to the decline in gross margin as a percentage of net sales. Inventory levels increased sequentially each quarter during 1993 in support of an expanded product line and distribution channels and anticipated higher sales volumes. These higher levels of inventory, in turn, reduced the Company's liquidity position and resulted in increased levels of short-term borrowings under the Company's commercial paper program and from certain banks. The Company has commenced a number of measures that it expects will result in improved management of inventory over the course of 1994. Although the Company believes that these measures will result in improved inventory management and liquidity during 1994, there can be no assurance that these measures will be successful or that

further inventory reserves will not be necessary in future periods.

The Company's results of operations were minimally affected by changes in foreign currency exchange rates in 1993 compared with 1992. The Company's operating strategy and pricing take into account changes in exchange rates over time; however, the Company's results of operations can be significantly affected in the short term by fluctuations in foreign currency exchange rates.

The decline in gross margin as a percentage of net sales from 47.5% in 1991 to 43.7% in 1992 was primarily the result of industrywide competitive pressures and associated pricing and promotional actions, partially offset by a shift in product mix toward the Company's PowerBook and Macintosh Quadra products. The Company's results of operations were minimally affected by changes in foreign currency exchange rates in 1992 compared with 1991.

The Company anticipates that gross margins for its personal computers will remain under pressure and below historic levels due to a variety of factors, including continued pricing pressures, increased competition, and advances in technology. In response to these factors, the Company has implemented various pricing and promotional actions, and as a result, expects continued lower gross margins as a percentage of net sales in 1994 compared with 1993.

Operating Expenses	1993	Change	1992	Change	1991
Research and development	$ 665	10%	$ 602	3%	$ 583
Percentage of net sales	8.3%		8.5%		9.2%

Research and development expenditures increased in amount during 1993 and 1992 compared with 1992 and 1991, respectively, reflecting net additions to the Company's engineering staff and related costs as the Company continues to invest in the development of new products and technologies, and in the enhancement of existing products in the areas of hardware and peripherals, system software, and networking and communications. Research and development expenditures, as a percentage of net sales, have continued to decrease since 1991 as a result of revenue growth during 1992 and 1993, coupled with the Company's continuing

efforts to focus its research and development project spending. The Company believes that continued investments in research and development are critical to its future growth and competitive position in the marketplace, and are directly related to continued, timely development of new and enhanced products. The Company anticipates that research and development expenditures in 1994 will decrease slightly in amount and as a percentage of net sales as the Company continues its efforts to manage operating expense growth relative to gross margin levels.

	1993	Change	1992	Change	1991
Selling, general and administrative	$ 1,632	–3%	$ 1,687	–3%	$ 1,740
Percentage of net sales	20.5%		23.8%		27.6%

Selling, general and administrative expenses decreased in amount and as a percentage of net sales in 1993 and 1992 compared with 1992 and 1991, respectively. These decreases reflect the Company's ongoing efforts to manage operating expense growth relative to gross margin levels.

General and administrative expenses decreased in 1993 compared with 1992, primarily because of reduced employee-related expenses resulting from the restructuring actions taken in the third quarter of 1993. This decrease in general and administrative expenses was offset slightly by an increase in sales and marketing expenses as a result of increases in product marketing and advertising programs related to new product introductions and efforts to increase product demand.

In 1992, selling expenses decreased in amount and as a percentage of net sales compared with 1991, primarily because of reduced sales programs and marketing expenditures, as well as lower employee-related costs. Revenue growth also contributed to the decrease in selling expenses as a percentage of net sales. General and administrative expenses also decreased in amount and as a percentage of net sales in 1992 compared with 1991,

primarily as a result of lower legal and employee-related costs. The decrease was offset slightly by an increase in bad debt expense resulting from generally weak worldwide economic conditions.

The Company will continue to face the challenge of managing growth in selling, general and administrative expenses relative to gross margin levels, particularly in light of the Company's expectation of continued pressure on gross margins as a percentage of net sales and continued weak economic conditions worldwide. The Company's objective is to reduce selling, general and administrative expenses as a percentage of net sales in 1994 compared with 1993.

	1993	Change	1992	Change	1991
Restructuring costs and other	$ 321	—	—	—	$ 224
Percentage of net sales	4.0%		—		3.6%

In the third quarter of 1993, the Company initiated a plan to restructure its operations worldwide in order to address the competitive conditions in the personal computer industry, including the increased market demand for lower-priced products. In connection with this plan, the Company recorded a $321 million charge to operating expenses ($199 million, or $1.72 per share, after taxes). The restructuring costs included $162 million of estimated employee-related expenses and $159 million of estimated facilities, equipment, and other expenses associated with the consolidation of operations and the relocation and termination of operations and employees.

The Company's 1993 restructuring plan consists of a series of actions, the majority of which have been initiated. The remaining actions are expected to be initiated during 1994. Spending associated with certain actions is expected to extend beyond the initiation of those actions. For example, lease payments under noncancelable leases generally extend beyond the closing of the facilities. A portion of the employee-related actions was implemented in the fourth quarter of 1993. Although plans are in place to carry out the remaining actions, some plans may be refined as

the Company continues to identify the best means of achieving reductions in its cost structure. The Company believes that the restructuring actions are necessary in light of competitive pressures on its gross margins as a percentage of net sales and in light of generally weak economic conditions worldwide. While no assurances can be given that the restructuring actions will be successful or that similar actions will not be required in the future, the Company has already realized some cost-reduction benefits in the fourth quarter of 1993, and expects to realize further benefits in the future.

In 1991, the Company recorded a $197.5 million charge to operating expenses under a plan to restructure its operations worldwide. The Company believed that the restructuring actions were necessary in light of its continued expectation of lower gross margins as a percentage of net sales and in light of generally weak economic conditions worldwide. Also in 1991, the Company recorded a reserve in the amount of $26.5 million in connection with certain trademark litigation filed against it by Apple Corps Ltd. and Apple Corps S.A. in 1989, which amount was paid in settlement of such litigation in 1992.

Interest and Other Income, Net	1993	Change	1992	Change	1991
Interest and other income, net	$ 29	–41%	$ 50	–5%	$ 52

Interest and other income, net, decreased in amount in 1993 compared with 1992 because of lower interest rates, lower cash balances, expenses associated with certain financing transactions, lower gains on the sale of certain of the Company's venture capital investments, an increase in the cost of hedging certain foreign currency exposures, and an increase in interest expense due to higher commercial paper borrowing levels. This decrease was partially offset by a payment received from the Internal Revenue

Service reflecting interest earned on an income tax refund, and gains realized on foreign exchange and interest rate hedges.

Interest and other income, net, decreased slightly in amount in 1992 compared with 1991 because of lower interest rates and an increase in the cost of hedging certain foreign currency exposures. This decrease was partially offset by a gain on the sale of certain of the Company's venture capital investments, gains realized on interest rate hedges, and larger interest-earning portfolio balances.

Provision for Income Taxes	1993	Change	1992	Change	1991
Provision for income taxes	$ 53	–84%	$ 325	71%	$ 190
Effective tax rate	38%		38%		38%

The Company's effective tax rate remained unchanged in 1993, 1992, and 1991. For additional information regarding income taxes, refer to pages 25 and 26 of the Notes to Consolidated Financial Statements.

Factors That May Affect Future Results

The Company's future operating results may be affected by a number of factors, including the Company's ability to increase market share in its personal computer business while expanding its new businesses and product offerings into other markets; broaden industry acceptance of the Newton PDA product, including effectively licensing Newton technology and marketing the related products and services; realize the anticipated cost-reduction benefits associated with its restructuring plan initiated in the third quarter of 1993; develop, manufacture, and sell its products profitably; reduce existing inventory levels; and manage future inventory levels effectively. The Company's future operating results may also be affected by uncertainties relative to global economic conditions; the strength of its distribution channels; industry factors; and the availability and cost of components.

During calendar year 1994, the Company plans to introduce several Macintosh computers based on a new PowerPC Reduced Instruction Set Computing (RISC) microprocessor. Accordingly, the Company's results of operations could be adversely affected if it is unable to successfully transition over time its line of Macintosh personal computers and servers from the Motorola 68000 series of microprocessors to the PowerPC RISC microprocessor. The success of this transition will depend on the Company's ability to continue the sales momentum of products based on Motorola 68000 processors through the introduction of the PowerPC RISC-based products, to successfully manage inventory levels between both product lines, to gain market acceptance of the new RISC-based products, and to coordinate the timely development and distribution of new versions of commonly used software products specifically designed for the PowerPC RISC-based products.

The personal computer industry is highly volatile and continues to be characterized by dynamic customer demand patterns, rapid technological advances, frequent introduction of new products and product enhancements, and industrywide competition resulting in aggressive pricing practices and downward pressure on gross margins. The Company's operating results could be adversely affected should the Company be unable to accurately anticipate customer demand; introduce new products on a timely basis; manage lead times required to obtain components in order to be more responsive to short-term shifts in customer demand patterns; offer customers the latest competitive technologies while effectively managing the impact on inventory levels and the potential for customer confusion created by product proliferation; effectively manage the impact on the Company of industrywide pricing pressures; or effectively implement and manage the competitive risk associated with certain of the Company's collaboration agreements with other companies, such as the agreements with International Business Machines Corporation (IBM). The Company's results of operations could also be adversely affected, and additional inventory valuation reserves could result, if anticipated sales unit growth projections for new and current product offerings are not realized.

A large portion of the Company's revenues in recent years has come from its international operations. As a result, the Company's operations and financial results could be significantly affected by international factors, such as changes in foreign currency exchange rates or weak economic conditions in foreign markets in which the Company distributes its products. The Company's operating strategy and pricing take into account changes in exchange rates over time; however, the Company's results of operations can be significantly affected in the short term by fluctuations in foreign currency exchange rates.

In July, August, and October 1993, the Company introduced the Newton MessagePad and several new Macintosh products that extend its notebook, low-end, midrange, and high-end offerings. In addition, the Company introduced several new or enhanced peripheral products. The success of these new products is dependent on a number of factors, including market acceptance, the Company's ability to manage the risks associated with product transitions, and the Company's ability to reduce existing inventory levels and manage future inventory levels in line with anticipated product demand and to manufacture the products in appropriate quantities to meet anticipated demand. Accordingly, the Company cannot determine the ultimate effect that these new products will have on its sales or results of operations.

The Company's products include certain components, such as Motorola microprocessors and monochrome active-matrix displays manufactured by Hosiden Corporation, that are currently available only from single sources. Any availability limitations, interruptions in supplies, or price increases of these and other components could adversely affect the Company's business and financial results.

The majority of the Company's research and development activities, its corporate headquarters, and other critical business operations are located near major earthquake faults. Operating results could be materially adversely affected in the event of a major earthquake.

A number of uncertainties also exist regarding the marketing and distribution of the Company's products. The Company's primary means of distribution is through third-party computer resellers and various education and consumer channels. Although the Company has in place certain policies to limit concentrations of credit risk, business and financial results could be adversely affected in the event that the generally weak financial condition of third-party computer resellers worsens. In addition, the Company is continuing its expansion into new distribution channels, such as mass-merchandise stores, consumer electronics outlets, and computer superstores, in response to changing industry practices

and customer preferences. At this time, the Company cannot determine the ultimate effect of these or other future distribution expansion efforts on its future operating results.

Because of the foregoing factors, as well as other factors affecting the Company's operating results, past financial performance should not be considered to be a reliable indicator of future performance, and investors should not use historical trends to anticipate results or trends in future periods. In addition, the Company's participation in a highly dynamic industry often results in significant volatility of the Company's common stock price.

Liquidity and Capital Resources	1993	1992	1991
Cash, cash equivalents, and short-term investments	$ 892	$ 1,436	$ 893
Working capital	$ 1,823	$ 2,133	$ 1,647
Cash generated by (used for) operations	$ (662)	$ 921	$ 189
Cash used for investment activities, excluding short-term investments	$ 228	$ 264	$ 276
Cash generated by (used for) financing activities	$ 347	$ (114)	$ (18)

More cash was used for operations in 1993 compared with 1992, primarily because of a significant increase in inventory levels; decreases in net income, income taxes payable, and other current liabilities; and an increase in accounts receivable levels. Cash used for operations was offset slightly by increases in accrued restructuring costs and accounts payable.

Inventory increased substantially during 1993 as a result of higher levels of purchased parts, work in process, and finished goods inventory in support of an expanded product line and distribution channels and anticipated higher sales volumes. The Company expects that during the course of 1994, inventory levels will decline from fourth quarter 1993 levels, as the Company has identified measures intended to reduce inventory levels. These measures include promotional and pricing actions, increased emphasis on designing in commonality of parts among products, increased use of manufacturing-on-demand techniques based on product orders rather than forecasts, and greater rationalization of product offerings. Although the Company believes that these measures will result in improved inventory management and liquidity during 1994, there can be no assurance that these measures will be successful or that further inventory reserves will not be necessary in the future. The decrease in net income resulted primarily from a reduction in gross margins and the restructuring charge included in operating expenses for the third quarter. The reduction in earnings also contributed to the decrease in income taxes payable. Other current liabilities decreased as the Company continued to manage operating expense levels. The increase in accounts receivable corresponded with the higher sales levels achieved in 1993, coupled with slower collections resulting from economic pressures in the reseller industry, and the Company's expansion into consumer channels, where payment terms are

generally longer. These uses of cash were offset slightly by increases in accrued restructuring costs as a result of the Company's plan to restructure its operations worldwide and increases in accounts payable, reflecting the higher level of inventory purchases.

In 1992, net cash generated by operations increased compared with 1991, primarily as a result of increased net income and lower inventory levels, offset somewhat by a reduction in accrued restructuring costs. Higher sales resulting from strong demand for new products and price reductions and other sales incentive programs, coupled with a decrease in operating expenses, contributed to the increase in net income. Inventory levels decreased as a result of higher sales levels and improved inventory management.

Improvement in cash flow from operations in 1994 will depend principally on the Company's ability to improve profit levels and reduce inventory levels.

Excluding short-term investments, net cash used for investments declined in 1993 compared with 1992 and 1991 levels. Net cash used for the purchase of property, plant, and equipment totaled $213 million in 1993, and was primarily made up of increases in land and buildings, manufacturing machinery and equipment, and leasehold improvements. The Company anticipates that capital expenditures in 1994 will be slightly below 1993 expenditures.

The Company leases the majority of its facilities and certain of its equipment under noncancelable operating leases. In 1993, rent expense under all operating leases was approximately $170 million. The Company's future lease commitments are discussed in the Notes to Consolidated Financial Statements.

On November 11, 1992, modifications were made to the terms of the Cupertino Gateway Partners partnership agreement. As a result of these modifications, the Company now consolidates its wholly owned subsidiary's 50.001% investment in the partnership. The Company previously accounted for this investment under the equity method. The Company recorded additional property, plant, and equipment of $139 million, relinquished related assets of $81 million, and assumed liabilities of $58 million as a result of this revised partnership agreement. This transaction has been excluded from the Company's Consolidated Statement of Cash Flows for 1993, because the change in accounting treatment did not involve a source or use of cash.

Net cash generated by financing activities increased in 1993 compared with 1992 and 1991, mainly because of a significant increase in short-term borrowings, which were used for working capital needs. Net cash generated by financing activities was partially offset by the repurchase of approximately 5 million shares of the Company's common stock in the open market under stock repurchase programs.

The Company's aggregate commercial paper borrowings at the end of 1993 were approximately $823 million, compared with $184 million and $149 million at the end of 1992 and 1991, respectively, which borrowings were incurred principally to finance increases in inventory levels in each period. As of October 29, 1993, the Company's commercial paper borrowings totaled approximately $936 million; its other short-term borrowings totaled approximately $80 million; and its cash, cash equivalents, and short-term investments totaled approximately $964 million. The Company expects that during 1994, its liquidity position will improve from recent levels, as the measures the Company has identified to reduce inventory levels are implemented and take effect. Although the Company believes that these measures will result in improved inventory management and liquidity in 1994, there can be no assurance that these measures will be successful.

The Company expects that it will continue to incur short-term borrowings from time to time to finance U.S. working capital needs and capital expenditures, because a substantial portion of the Company's cash, cash equivalents, and short-term investments is held by foreign subsidiaries, generally in U.S. dollar–denominated holdings. Amounts held by foreign subsidiaries would be subject to U.S. income taxation upon repatriation to the United States; the Company's financial statements fully provide for any related tax liability on amounts that may be repatriated.

On May 5, 1993, the Company filed an omnibus shelf registration statement with the Securities and Exchange Commission for the registration of debt and other securities for an aggregate offering price of $500 million. The securities may be offered from time to time in amounts, at prices, and on terms to be determined in light of market conditions at the time of sale. The Company believes that the shelf registration provides financial flexibility to meet future funding requirements and to take advantage of attractive market conditions.

The Company believes that its balances of cash, cash equivalents, and short-term investments, together with funds generated from operations and short- and long-term borrowing capabilities, will be sufficient to meet its operating cash requirements in the foreseeable future.

Consolidated Statements of Income

(In thousands, except per share amounts)

Three fiscal years ended September 24, 1993	1993	1992	1991
Net sales	$ 7,976,954	$ 7,086,542	$ 6,308,849
Costs and expenses:			
Cost of sales	5,248,834	3,991,337	3,314,118
Research and development	664,564	602,135	583,046
Selling, general and administrative	1,632,362	1,687,262	1,740,293
Restructuring costs and other	320,856	—	224,043
	7,866,616	6,280,734	5,861,500
Operating income	110,338	805,808	447,349
Interest and other income, net	29,321	49,634	52,395
Income before income taxes	139,659	855,442	499,744
Provision for income taxes	53,070	325,069	189,903
Net income	$ 86,589	$ 530,373	$ 309,841
Earnings per common and common equivalent share	$ 0.73	$ 4.33	$ 2.58
Common and common equivalent shares used in the calculations of earnings per share	119,125	122,490	120,283

See accompanying notes.

Consolidated Balance Sheets

(Dollars in thousands)

September 24, 1993, and September 25, 1992	1993	1992
Assets:		
Current assets:		
Cash and cash equivalents	$ 676,413	$ 498,557
Short-term investments	215,890	936,943
Accounts receivable, net of allowance for doubtful accounts of $83,776 ($83,048 in 1992)	1,381,946	1,087,185
Inventories	1,506,638	580,097
Prepaid income taxes	268,085	199,139
Other current assets	289,383	256,473
Total current assets	4,338,355	3,558,394
Property, plant, and equipment:		
Land and buildings	404,688	255,808
Machinery and equipment	578,272	516,335
Office furniture and equipment	167,905	155,317
Leasehold improvements	261,792	208,180
	1,412,657	1,135,640
Accumulated depreciation and amortization	(753,111)	(673,419)
Net property, plant, and equipment	659,546	462,221
Other assets	173,511	203,078
	$ 5,171,412	$ 4,223,693
Liabilities and Shareholders' Equity:		
Current liabilities:		
Notes payable	$ 823,182	$ 184,461
Accounts payable	742,622	426,936
Accrued compensation and employee benefits	144,779	142,382
Income taxes payable	23,658	78,382
Accrued marketing and distribution	174,547	187,767
Accrued restructuring costs	307,932	105,038
Other current liabilities	298,482	300,554
Total current liabilities	2,515,202	1,425,520
Deferred income taxes	629,832	610,803
Commitments and contingencies	—	—
Shareholders' equity:		
Common stock, no par value; 320,000,000 shares authorized; 116,147,035 shares issued and outstanding in 1993 (118,478,825 shares in 1992)	203,613	282,310
Retained earnings	1,842,600	1,904,519
Accumulated translation adjustment	(19,835)	541
Total shareholders' equity	2,026,378	2,187,370
	$ 5,171,412	$ 4,223,693

See accompanying notes.

Consolidated Statements of Shareholders' Equity

(In thousands, except per share amounts)

	Common Stock		Retained Earnings	Accumulated Translation Adjustment	Notes Receivable from Shareholders	Total Shareholders' Equity
	Shares	Amount				
Balance at September 28, 1990	115,359	$ 136,555	$ 1,312,156	$ 4,142	$ (6,033)	$ 1,446,820
Common stock issued under stock option and purchase plans, including related tax benefits	7,377	253,523	—	—	(744)	252,779
Repurchase of common stock	(4,350)	(111,213)	(73,464)	—	—	(184,677)
Repayment of notes receivable from shareholders	—	—	—	—	4,941	4,941
Cash dividends of $0.48 per common share	—	—	(56,509)	—	—	(56,509)
Accumulated translation adjustment	—	—	—	(6,519)	—	(6,519)
Net income	—	—	309,841	—	—	309,841
Balance at September 27, 1991	118,386	278,865	1,492,024	(2,377)	(1,836)	1,766,676
Common stock issued under stock option and purchase plans, including related tax benefits	4,093	155,388	—	—	—	155,388
Repurchase of common stock	(4,000)	(151,943)	(60,682)	—	—	(212,625)
Repayment of notes receivable from shareholders	—	—	—	—	1,836	1,836
Cash dividends of $0.48 per common share	—	—	(57,196)	—	—	(57,196)
Accumulated translation adjustment	—	—	—	2,918	—	2,918
Net income	—	—	530,373	—	—	530,373
Balance at September 25, 1992	118,479	282,310	1,904,519	541		2,187,370
Common stock issued under stock option and purchase plans, including related tax benefits	2,693	101,842	—	—	—	101,842
Repurchase of common stock	(5,025)	(180,539)	(92,915)	—	—	(273,454)
Cash dividends of $0.48 per common share	—	—	(55,593)	—	—	(55,593)
Accumulated translation adjustment	—	—	—	(20,376)	—	(20,376)
Net income	—	—	86,589	—	—	86,589
Balance at September 24, 1993	116,147	$ 203,613	$ 1,842,600	$ (19,835)	$ —	$ 2,026,378

See accompanying notes.

Consolidated Statements of Cash Flows

(In thousands)

Three fiscal years ended September 24, 1993	1993	1992	1991
Cash and cash equivalents, beginning of the period	$ 498,557	$ 604,147	$ 374,682
Operations:			
Net income	86,589	530,373	309,841
Adjustments to reconcile net income to cash generated by (used for) operations:			
Depreciation and amortization	166,113	217,182	204,433
Net book value of property, plant, and equipment retirements	13,145	14,687	6,955
Changes in assets and liabilities:			
Accounts receivable	(294,761)	(180,026)	(145,291)
Inventories	(926,541)	91,558	(316,182)
Prepaid income taxes	(68,946)	23,841	(97,445)
Other current assets	(96,314)	(87,376)	(5,738)
Accounts payable	315,686	69,852	16,509
Income taxes payable	(54,724)	100,361	42,308
Accrued restructuring costs	202,894	(57,327)	162,365
Other current liabilities	(24,007)	96,524	3,570
Deferred income taxes	19,029	100,933	8,038
Cash generated by (used for) operations	(661,837)	920,582	189,363
Investments:			
Purchase of short-term investments	(1,431,998)	(2,121,341)	(610,696)
Proceeds from short-term investments	2,153,051	1,472,970	944,533
Purchase of property, plant, and equipment	(213,118)	(194,853)	(218,348)
Other	(15,169)	(69,410)	(57,165)
Cash generated by (used for) investment activities	492,766	(912,634)	58,324
Financing:			
Increase in short-term borrowings	638,721	35,895	25,936
Increases in common stock, net of related tax benefits and changes in notes receivable from shareholders	85,289	120,388	197,028
Repurchase of common stock	(273,454)	(212,625)	(184,677)
Cash dividends	(55,593)	(57,196)	(56,509)
Other	(48,036)	—	—
Cash generated by (used for) financing activities	346,927	(113,538)	(18,222)
Total cash generated (used)	177,856	(105,590)	229,465
Cash and cash equivalents, end of the period	$ 676,413	$ 498,557	$ 604,147
Supplemental cash flow disclosures:			
Cash paid during the year for:			
Interest	$ 11,748	$ 8,778	$ 9,755
Income taxes	$ 250,987	$ 98,330	$ 265,755
Schedule of noncash transactions:			
Tax benefit from stock options	$ 16,553	$ 36,836	$ 60,692

See accompanying notes.

Notes to Consolidated Financial Statements

Summary of Significant Accounting Policies

Basis of Presentation

The consolidated financial statements include the accounts of Apple Computer, Inc. and its wholly owned subsidiaries (the Company). Intercompany accounts and transactions have been eliminated. The Company's fiscal year-end is the last Friday in September.

Revenue Recognition

The Company recognizes revenue at the time products are shipped. Provision is made currently for estimated product returns and price protection that may occur under Company programs. Historically, actual amounts recorded for product returns and price protection have not varied significantly from estimated amounts.

Foreign Currency Translation

Gains and losses resulting from foreign currency translation are accumulated as a separate component of shareholders' equity until the foreign entity is sold or liquidated. Gains and losses resulting from foreign currency transactions are immaterial and are included in the statement of income.

Financial Instruments

The Company hedges certain portions of its exposure to foreign currency and interest rate fluctuations through a variety of strategies and instruments, including forward foreign exchange contracts, foreign currency options, and interest rate derivative instruments. Gains and losses associated with these financial instruments and the underlying exposures are generally recorded currently in income. Gains and losses are deferred and included as a component of the related transaction when the instrument hedges a firm commitment. Gains from purchased foreign currency options used to hedge certain probable future transactions are also deferred and included as a component of the related transaction, while any losses on sold options are recognized currently in income. The interest element of the foreign currency instruments is generally recognized over the life of the contract.

Cash, Cash Equivalents, and Short-Term Investments

All highly liquid investments with a maturity of 3 months or less at the date of purchase are considered to be cash equivalents; investments with maturities between 3 and 12 months are considered to be short-term investments. Short-term investments are carried at cost plus accrued interest, which approximates fair value. A substantial portion of the Company's cash, cash equivalents, and short-term investments is held by foreign subsidiaries and is generally in U.S. dollar–denominated holdings. Amounts held by foreign subsidiaries would be subject to U.S. income taxation upon repatriation to the United States; the Company's financial statements fully provide for any related tax liability on amounts that may be repatriated.

Income Taxes

U.S. income taxes have not been provided on a cumulative total of $194 million of undistributed earnings of certain of the Company's foreign subsidiaries. It is intended that these earnings will be indefinitely invested in operations outside the United States. Except for such indefinitely invested earnings, the Company provides federal and state income taxes currently on undistributed earnings of foreign subsidiaries. The Company has not elected early adoption of Financial Accounting Standard No. 109, Accounting for Income Taxes (FAS 109). FAS 109 becomes effective beginning with the Company's 1994 fiscal year and will not have a material effect on the Company's financial position or results of operations.

Earnings per Share

Earnings per share are computed using the weighted average number of common and dilutive common equivalent shares attributable to stock options outstanding during the period. Loss per share is computed using the weighted average number of common shares outstanding during the period.

Inventories

Inventories are stated at the lower of cost (first-in, first-out) or market.

Property, Plant, and Equipment

Property, plant, and equipment is stated at cost. Depreciation and amortization is computed by use of declining balance and straight-line methods over the estimated useful lives of the assets.

Reclassifications

Certain prior year amounts on the Consolidated Statements of Cash Flows and on the Industry Segment and Geographic Information and Income Taxes footnotes have been reclassified to conform to the current year presentation.

Inventories

Inventories consist of the following:

(In thousands)

	1993	1992
Purchased parts	$ 504,201	$ 150,147
Work in process	284,440	94,790
Finished goods	717,997	335,160
	$ 1,506,638	$ 580,097

Notes Payable

As of September 24, 1993, notes payable represented unsecured commercial paper borrowings of approximately $823 million at varying interest rates. The carrying amount of the notes payable approximates their fair value due to their short maturities. The weighted average interest rate was approximately 3.3%, and the average days to maturity was 33 days. As of September 25, 1992, notes payable represented unsecured commercial paper borrowings of approximately $184 million at varying interest rates. The weighted average interest rate was approximately 3.5%, and the average days to maturity was 30 days. Interest expense in each of the 3 years ended September 24, 1993, was immaterial.

Restructuring of Operations

In the third quarter of 1993, the Company initiated a plan to restructure its operations worldwide in order to address the competitive conditions in the personal computer industry, including the increased market demand for lower-priced products. In connection with this plan, the Company recorded a $321 million charge to operating expenses ($199 million, or $1.72 per share, after taxes). The restructuring costs included $162 million of estimated employee-related expenses and $159 million of estimated facilities, equipment, and other expenses associated with the consolidation of operations and the relocation and termination of certain operations and employees.

The Company's 1993 restructuring plan consists of a series of actions, the majority of which have been initiated. The remaining actions are expected to be initiated during 1994. Spending associated with certain actions is expected to extend beyond the initiation of those actions. For example, lease payments under noncancelable leases generally extend beyond the closing of facilities. A portion of the employee-related actions was implemented in the fourth quarter of 1993. Although plans are in place to carry out the remaining actions, some plans may be refined as the Company continues to identify the best means of achieving reductions in its cost structure. The Company believes that the restructuring actions are necessary in light of competitive pressures on its gross margins as a percentage of net sales and in light of generally weak economic conditions worldwide. While no assurances can be given that the restructuring actions will be successful or that similar actions will not be required in the future, the Company has already realized some cost-reduction benefits in the fourth quarter of 1993, and expects to realize further benefits in the future.

In 1991, the Company recorded a $197.5 million charge to operating expenses under a plan to restructure its operations worldwide. The Company believed that the restructuring actions were necessary in light of its continued expectation of lower gross margins as a percentage of net sales and in light of generally weak economic conditions worldwide. Also in 1991, the Company recorded a reserve in the amount of $26.5 million in connection with certain trademark litigation filed against it by Apple Corps Ltd. and Apple Corps S.A. in 1989, which amount was paid in settlement of such litigation in 1992.

Commitments and Contingencies

Lease Commitments

The Company leases various facilities and equipment under noncancelable lease arrangements. The major facilities leases are for terms of 5 to 10 years and generally provide renewal options for terms of up to 5 additional years. Rent expense under all operating leases was approximately $170 million, $160 million, and $163 million in 1993, 1992, and 1991, respectively.

Future minimum lease payments under these noncancelable operating leases as of September 24, 1993, are as follows:

	(In thousands)
1994	$ 114,566
1995	95,238
1996	60,161
1997	43,089
1998	22,564
Later years	185,101
Total minimum lease payments	$ 520,719

Leases for facilities that were subject to the Company's restructuring actions initiated in the third quarter of 1991 and in the third quarter of 1993 are included in the preceding table. Future lease payments associated with these facilities were provided for in the Company's restructuring reserves recorded in 1993 and 1991, and therefore do not represent future operating expenses. Minimum lease payments may decline in the future, as the leases for facilities subject to restructuring actions are terminated or otherwise completed.

In July 1991, a subsidiary of the Company formed a partnership, Cupertino Gateway Partners, with a local real estate developer for the purpose of constructing a campus-type office facility to be leased to the Company by the partnership. The Company executed six noncancelable leases with the partnership to lease the buildings for terms of approximately 17 years. Modifications were made to the terms of the Cupertino Gateway Partners partnership agreement on November 11, 1992, and as a result of these modifications, the Company now consolidates its wholly owned subsidiary's 50.001% investment in the partnership. Because of the Company's consolidation of its investment, future minimum lease payments to the partnership of approximately $209 million have been excluded from the preceding table.

Off-Balance-Sheet Risk and Concentrations of Credit

Financial Instruments

At September 24, 1993, the Company had approximately $273 million ($538 million at September 25, 1992) in forward foreign exchange contracts in various currencies. Forward foreign exchange contracts not accounted for as hedges are carried at fair value. Deferred gains or losses on forward foreign exchange contracts accounted for as hedges were immaterial at September 24, 1993. The Company also enters into foreign currency options, both purchased and sold, generally to protect against currency exchange risks associated with certain firmly committed and certain other probable, but not firmly committed, transactions. The face value of the Company's foreign currency options with off-balance-sheet risk

of loss totaled approximately $2,691 million at September 24, 1993 ($577 million at September 25, 1992). While the notional amount of the foreign currency options discussed above reflects the volume of activity in those financial instruments at a single point in time, the notional amount at September 24, 1993, does not represent the Company's exposure to credit or market loss. Foreign currency options not accounted for as hedges are carried at fair value, with any gains and losses reflected in operating results. Deferred gains on foreign currency options accounted for as hedges were immaterial at September 24, 1993.

In addition, the Company has entered into interest rate risk management agreements (interest rate derivatives) with certain financial institutions. At September 24, 1993, the Company had outstanding interest rate derivatives with a total notional amount of approximately $179 million. Interest rate derivatives are carried at fair value. The agreements have maturities ranging from 3 months to 3 years and generally require the Company to pay a floating interest rate based on the 3-month or 6-month London InterBank Offered Rates and to receive interest at a fixed rate. Though the notional amounts of the Company's interest rate derivatives are an indication of the volume of these transactions, the amounts potentially subject to credit risk are generally limited to the amounts, if any, by which the present value of the counterparties' expected obligations exceed the present value of the expected obligations of the Company.

The value of any of these outstanding foreign exchange forward contracts, foreign exchange currency options, and interest rate derivative instruments as currently recognized in the consolidated balance sheet at September 24, 1993, may change in the future based on changes in foreign exchange and interest rate market conditions.

The estimates of fair values are based on the appropriate pricing models using current market information. However, in certain instances, judgment is required in estimating the fair values. The amounts ultimately realized upon settlement of these financial instruments will depend on actual market conditions during the remaining life of the instruments.

Concentrations of Credit Risk

The Company distributes its products principally through third-party computer resellers and various education and consumer channels. Concentrations of credit risk with respect to trade receivables are limited because of flooring arrangements for selected customers with third-party financing companies and because the Company's customer base consists of large numbers of geographically diverse customers dispersed across many industries. The counterparties to the agreements relating to the Company's

investments and foreign currency and interest rate risk management financial instruments consist of a number of major international financial institutions. The Company does not believe that there is significant risk of nonperformance by these counterparties because the Company continually monitors its positions and the credit ratings of such counterparties, and limits the financial exposure and the amount of agreements and contracts it enters into with any one party. The Company generally does not require collateral from counterparties.

Income Taxes

The provision for income taxes consists of the following: (In thousands)

	1993	1992	1991
Federal:	$ 13,637	$ 108,512	$ 106,162
Current	(23,757)	100,355	22,131
Deferred	(10,120)	208,867	128,293
State:	3,144	26,935	26,866
Current	633	13,891	(9,591)
Deferred	3,777	40,826	17,275
Foreign:	39,512	65,144	40,614
Current	19,901	10,232	3,721
Deferred	59,413	75,376	44,335
Provision for income taxes	$ 53,070	$ 325,069	$ 189,903

The foreign provision for income taxes is based on foreign pretax earnings of approximately $416 million, $611 million, and $464 million in 1993, 1992, and 1991, respectively.

Deferred (prepaid) income taxes result from timing differences between years in the recognition of certain revenue and expense items for financial and tax reporting purposes. The sources of timing differences and the related tax effects are as follows:

                                                                                              (In thousands)

	1993	1992	1991
Income of foreign subsidiaries not taxable in current year	$ 53,150	$ 71,429	$ 103,912
Warranty, bad debt, and other expenses	(80,126)	35,494	(96,349)
Depreciation	(3,796)	(3,398)	(11,989)
Inventory valuation	(16,835)	(1,940)	(16,691)
State income taxes	2,607	(10,959)	4,585
Other individually immaterial items	41,777	33,852	32,793
Total deferred taxes	$ (3,223)	$ 124,478	$ 16,261

A reconciliation of the provision for income taxes, with the amount computed by applying the statutory federal income tax rate (34.75% in 1993, and 34.00% in both 1992 and 1991) to income before income taxes, is as follows:

| | | | (In thousands) |
	1993	1992	1991
Computed expected tax	$ 48,532	$ 290,850	$ 169,913
State taxes, net of federal benefit	2,465	26,945	11,401
Research and development tax credit	(8,000)	(7,000)	(13,000)
Indefinitely invested earnings of foreign subsidiaries	(21,083)	(31,280)	(13,940)
Other individually immaterial items	31,156	45,554	35,529
Provision for income taxes	$ 53,070	$ 325,069	$ 189,903
Effective tax rate	38%	38%	38%

The Company's federal income tax returns for 1981 through 1988 have been examined by the Internal Revenue Service (IRS). All contested issues for the years 1981 through 1983 have been resolved. During 1990, the IRS proposed tax deficiencies for the years 1984 through 1986, and the Company made prepayments thereon in 1991. During 1993, the IRS proposed tax deficiencies for the years 1987 and 1988, and the Company made prepayments thereon in May 1993. The Company is contesting these alleged deficiencies and is pursuing administrative and judicial remedies. Management believes that adequate provision has been made for any adjustments that may result from these examinations.

Preferred Stock

Five million shares of preferred stock have been authorized for issuance in one or more series. The Board of Directors is authorized to fix the number and designation of any such series and to determine the rights, preferences, privileges, and restrictions granted to or imposed on any such series.

Common Stock

Shareholder Rights Plan

In May 1989, the Company adopted a shareholder rights plan and distributed a dividend of one right to purchase one share of common stock (a Right) for each outstanding share of common stock of the Company. The Rights become exercisable in certain limited circumstances involving a potential business combination transaction of the Company and are initially exercisable at a price of $200 per share. Following certain other events after the Rights have become exercisable, each Right entitles its holder to purchase for $200 an amount of common stock of the Company, or, in certain circumstances, securities of the acquiror, having a then-current market value of two times the exercise price of the Right. The Rights are redeemable and may be amended at the Company's option before they become exercisable. Until a Right is exercised, the holder of a Right, as such, has no rights as a shareholder of the Company. The Rights expire on April 19, 1999.

Stock Option Plans

The Company has in effect a 1990 Stock Option Plan (the 1990 Plan) and a 1987 Executive Long Term Stock Option Plan (the 1987 Plan). The 1981 Stock Option Plan terminated in October 1990. Options granted before that date remain outstanding in accordance with their terms. Options may be granted under the 1990 Plan to employees, including officers and directors who are employees, at not less than the fair market value on the date of grant. These options generally become exercisable over varying periods, based on continued employment, and generally expire 10 years after the grant date. The 1990 Plan permits the granting of incentive stock options, nonstatutory stock options, and stock appreciation rights.

The 1987 Plan permits the granting of nonstatutory options to certain officers of the Company to purchase Apple common stock at prices not less than 75% of the fair market value on the date of grant. Options under the 1987 Plan are not exercisable for 18 months after the date of grant, and then become exercisable at varying rates over the subsequent 7 years, based on continued service to the Company.

On August 5, 1993, the Board of Directors adopted a resolution allowing employees below the level of vice president to exchange 1.5 options at their existing option price for 1.0 new options having an exercise price of $24.25 per share, the fair market value of the Company's common stock on September 14, 1993. Options received under this program are subject to 1 year of additional vesting such that the new vesting date for each vesting portion will be the later of September 15, 1994, or the original vesting date plus 1 year. Approximately 4.1 million options were exchanged under this program.

Summarized information regarding the Company's stock option plans as of September 24, 1993, which includes the grants made under the exchange program described in the preceding paragraph, is as follows:

(In thousands, except per share amounts)

	Number of Shares	Price per Share
Outstanding at September 25, 1992	14,462	$7.50–$68.00
Granted	5,728	
Exercised	(1,730)	$7.50–$57.75
Expired or canceled	(5,364)	
Outstanding at September 24, 1993	13,096	$7.50–$68.00
Exercisable	6,219	
Reserved for issuance	17,909	
Available for future grant	4,817	

Restricted Stock Plan

On April 1, 1993, the Company's Board of Directors approved a Restricted Stock Plan for officers of the Company (the RSP), which became effective July 1, 1993, subject to shareholder approval in January 1994. The RSP is designed to provide an incentive for officers to continue to own shares of the Company's common stock acquired upon exercise of options under any of the Company's Stock Option Plans, thus more closely aligning officers' financial interests with those of the shareholders. The RSP provides that officers who exercise stock options and continue to hold the exercised shares for at least 3 years will receive up to three Awards of shares of restricted stock. Each such Award is for one-third the number of shares held for the requisite retention period. Each restricted stock Award granted pursuant to the plan becomes fully vested 3 years after the grant date, provided that the officer maintains continuous employment with the Company and that other vesting requirements are met.

Employee Stock Purchase Plan

The Company has an employee stock purchase plan (the Purchase Plan) under which substantially all employees may purchase common stock through payroll deductions at a price equal to 85% of the lower of the fair market values as of the beginning or end of the offering period. Stock purchases under the Purchase Plan are limited to 10% of an employee's compensation. In January 1993, the Company's shareholders approved an amendment to the Purchase Plan proposed by the Board of Directors to increase the number of shares reserved for issuance by 2 million shares. As of September 24, 1993, approximately 2.1 million shares were reserved for future issuance under the Purchase Plan.

Stock Repurchase Programs

In November 1992, the Board of Directors authorized the purchase of up to 10 million shares of the Company's common stock in the open market. Approximately 3.4 million shares were repurchased under this authorization in 1993. In September 1990, the Board of Directors authorized the purchase of up to 10 million shares of the Company's common stock in the open market. During 1993, 1992, and 1991, the Company repurchased approximately 1.6 million, 4.0 million, and 4.4 million shares, respectively, in the open market under this repurchase program.

Savings Plan

The Company has an employee savings plan (the Savings Plan) that qualifies as a deferred salary arrangement under Section 401(k) of the Internal Revenue Code. Under the Savings Plan, participating U.S. employees may defer a portion of their pretax earnings, up to the Internal Revenue Service annual contribution limit ($8,994 for calendar year 1993). The Company matches 30% to 50% of each employee's contributions, depending on length of service, up to a maximum 6% of the employee's earnings. The Company's matching contributions to the Savings Plan were approximately $11.1 million in each of 1993 and 1992 and $10.6 million in 1991.

Litigation

Apple v. Microsoft Corporation and Hewlett-Packard Company

In March 1988, the Company filed suit in the U.S. District Court for the Northern District of California (the Court) against Microsoft Corporation (Microsoft) and Hewlett-Packard Company (HP), alleging that their Microsoft Windows 2.03 and HP NewWave computer programs infringe the Company's audiovisual copyrights protecting the Macintosh user interface. Microsoft and HP each filed separate answers setting forth affirmative defenses and counterclaims against the Company seeking declaratory relief and unspecified monetary damages. The Court entered final judgment for Microsoft and HP on August 24, 1993, dismissing the Company's action. The principal rulings leading to that action are presented below.

In 1989, the Court ruled that a 1985 license agreement relating to Windows Version 1.0 did not constitute a complete defense to the Company's claim because the visual displays of Windows 2.03 are fundamentally different from those of Windows Version 1.0, but the visual display elements of Windows Version 1.0 that are used in Windows 2.03 are licensed. The Court concluded that the visual displays in Windows 2.03 that are not licensed are those relating to the use of overlapping main application windows and the appearance and manipulation of icons.

On April 16, 1990, the Company filed a motion for partial summary judgment, asking the Court to hold that the Company's copyrights for the Lisa® and Macintosh computers are valid and to strike the defendants' defenses challenging the validity and scope of protection of those copyrights. Microsoft and HP each filed a motion for partial summary judgment, challenging the validity of the Company's copyrights and seeking to narrow the scope of protection. Each also continued to argue that additional visual displays relating to overlapping main application windows and the use and manipulation of icons should be deemed licensed.

On March 6, 1991, the Court issued a ruling acknowledging the originality of the Company's copyrighted works. By an order dated June 15, 1991, the Court granted the Company's request to supplement its complaint to add Windows 3.0 and NewWave 3.0 to the lawsuit, but denied its request to add a claim against Microsoft for breach of the 1985 license agreement, rescission, and unfair competition.

By stipulation the parties agreed to the voluntary dismissal of the following claims: Microsoft's counterclaims for tortious interference with contract, intentional interference with prospective business advantage, disparagement of property, slander of title, and unfair business practices; HP's counterclaims for intentional interference with prospective and existing business relations and unfair business practices; and the Company's claim for unfair competition.

By an order dated July 25, 1991, the Court (i) dismissed Microsoft's claim that the Company breached the 1985 license agreement; (ii) dismissed an HP counterclaim to the extent that it raised the issue of the originality of the Company's copyrights; (iii) stayed all litigation on HP's antitrust counterclaim; (iv) held that the originality of the Company's copyrights had already been established and that the Company was not obligated to prove the originality of each element or feature of its works; and (v) ordered all discovery of fact witnesses to be completed by January 31, 1992, and all discovery of expert witnesses to be completed by February 28, 1992.

By an order dated August 14, 1991, the Court granted defendants' motion for reconsideration on the issue of originality, holding that defendants may attempt to establish that individual elements in the Company's copyrighted works are not original. According to the Court's order, to meet their burden, defendants would be required to prove that the Company's expression of component features was directly copied from prior work.

On April 14, 1992, the Court issued a ruling on motions filed by the parties, which substantially narrowed the scope of the issues in the case and was not favorable to the Company. The Court held that most of the Windows and NewWave interface elements either were licensed by the Company to Microsoft or could not be protected under the copyright laws.

On August 7, 1992, the Court entered an order disposing of various motions that had been filed by the parties, including the Company's motion for reconsideration of the Court's April 14, 1992, order. In the August order, the Court (i) held that many of the similarities alleged by the Company were not entitled to copyright protection; (ii) ruled that, with respect to Windows, four of the similarities may be entitled to protection but only against a standard of virtually identical copying and, with respect to NewWave, a few additional similarities alleged by the Company were protectible; and (iii) declined to extend protection to the overall arrangement and organization of the Macintosh work.

By an order dated April 14, 1993, the Court held that certain issues of fact remained with respect to the question of whether there is substantial similarity between unlicensed, protected expression in the Apple works and either Windows 2.03 or Windows 3.0 or HP's NewWave products. The Court ruled that a standard of "virtual identity" would be applied to the works.

By an order dated May 18, 1993, the Court (i) denied Apple's Motion for Reconsideration of the Court's April 14, 1993, ruling directing the application of the "virtual identity" standard; (ii) denied Microsoft's motion for summary judgment on Apple's contributory infringement claim; (iii) denied Apple's motion seeking a ruling that HP did not have a sublicense under the 1985 agreement; (iv) granted defendants' motion striking all copyrighted works but the Lisa work; (v) denied HP's motion for summary judgment that it is not jointly and severally liable with Microsoft; and (vi) granted in part and denied in part defendants' motions for summary judgment seeking the dismissal of the remaining items of similarity between the Apple work and defendants' works. The Court ordered the case to proceed to trial on the principal issue of whether defendants' works "as a whole" are "virtually identical" to Apple's Lisa work.

Following the entry of this order, in the interest of justice and to facilitate a prompt review on appeal of all of the Court's rulings, the parties stipulated to the entry of a judgment in favor of defendants. Specifically, Apple agreed not to oppose defendants' motions for summary judgment based on the "virtually identical" standard between the Lisa work and defendants' works. In view of Apple's nonopposition, on August 24, 1993, the Court entered judgment for defendants. On September 20, 1993, Apple filed a Notice of Appeal.

On September 21, 1993, the Court denied defendants' motions for an award of full defense costs and attorneys' fees under 17 U.S.C. §505, but allowed defendants to renew their motions should the Supreme Court alter the standard for the award of attorneys' fees in copyright cases after review of a case presently pending before it. The Court also denied without prejudice Microsoft's motion for reconsideration of the Court's prior ruling dismissing its counterclaim for breach of contract.

The case is now pending before the U.S. Court of Appeal for the Ninth Circuit.

In re Apple Securities Litigation (1993)

In July 1993, six civil class action complaints relating to the drop in price of Apple stock were filed in U.S. District Court against the Company and certain of its officers and directors, alleging violations of federal securities laws for alleged material misrepresentations and omissions of fact concerning the Company's business. The six cases were subsequently consolidated into *Rovner et al. v. Sculley et al.* by virtue of Pretrial Order No. 1, entered by the Court on August 6, 1993. Pursuant to that order, the consolidated class action is known as *In re Apple Securities Litigation,* Civ. No. C-93-20521-RMW (EAI). These suits were filed on behalf of the named plaintiffs and all others who purchased

the Company's common stock between October 15, 1992, and July 15, 1993. Plaintiffs seek an award of damages according to proof, with interest.

Subsequently, in August 1993, *Harris v. Sculley et al.* was filed on behalf of the named plaintiff and all others who purchased the Company's common stock between April 15, 1993, and July 15, 1993. It names as defendants the Company and certain of its officers and directors and is based on the same allegations as the class actions described above. The Harris suit is consolidated and subject to Pretrial Order No. 1, discussed above.

1993 Derivative Litigation

In August and September 1993, two derivative class action complaints relating to the drop in price of Apple stock were filed against the Company, as nominal defendant, and certain of its officers and directors. The suits, *Genduso v. Sculley et al.,* Civ. No. C-93-20581-RMW (EAI) (N.D. Cal. filed August 6, 1993), and *Selinger v. Sculley et al.,* Civ. No. C-93-3395-VRW (EAI) (N.D. Cal. filed September 13, 1993), both allege violations of California state law. On September 28, 1993, all parties entered into a stipulation that consolidated the derivative actions and stayed them in their entirety until the conclusion of the 1993 class action litigation.

Lemelson v. Apple

On September 25, 1992, Jerome Lemelson filed a complaint against the Company, Eastman Kodak Company, and Unisys Corporation in the U.S. District Court, District of Nevada, which complaint was amended on April 8, 1993, alleging infringement of two patents relating to information storage and retrieval systems. Unisys is being dismissed without prejudice from the action due to a conflict of interest pertaining to Lemelson's counsel. Mr. Lemelson seeks injunctive relief, damages in an unspecified amount, and an award of attorneys' fees and costs.

Grant v. Apple

On February 11, 1993, Richard B. Grant filed a complaint against the Company in the U.S. District Court for the Central District of California alleging infringement of a natural-language patent. Mr. Grant seeks damages in an unspecified amount and an award of attorneys' fees and costs.

The Company believes the suits cited above to be without merit and intends to vigorously defend against these actions. The Company believes the resolution of all these matters will not have a material adverse effect on its financial condition and results of operations as reported in the accompanying financial statements.

Industry Segment and Geographic Information

The Company operates in one principal industry segment: the design, manufacture, and sale of personal computing products. The Company's products are sold primarily to the business, education, home, and government markets.

Geographic financial information is as follows:

(In thousands)

	1993	1992	1991
Net sales to unaffiliated customers:			
United States	$ 4,387,674	$ 3,885,042	$ 3,484,533
Europe	2,001,593	2,017,840	1,882,355
Pacific and Canada	1,587,687	1,183,660	941,961
Total net sales	$ 7,976,954	$ 7,086,542	$ 6,308,849
Transfers between geographic areas (eliminated in consolidation):			
United States	$ 420,323	$ 934,673	$ 774,059
Europe	262,554	246,745	147,713
Pacific and Canada	1,374,039	979,566	1,099,448
Total transfers	$ 2,056,916	$ 2,160,984	$ 2,021,220
Operating income:			
United States	$ (253,499)	$ 245,810	$ 9,036
Europe	79,440	301,865	222,893
Pacific and Canada	286,572	246,181	227,690
Eliminations	(2,175)	11,952	(12,235)
Interest and other income, net	29,321	49,634	52,360
Income before income taxes	$ 139,659	$ 855,442	$ 499,744
Identifiable assets:			
United States	$ 2,534,545	$ 1,536,705	$ 1,440,332
Europe	973,741	767,765	734,836
Pacific and Canada	799,189	456,472	461,555
Eliminations	(49,838)	(43,716)	(56,693)
Corporate assets	913,775	1,506,467	913,567
Total assets	$ 5,171,412	$ 4,223,693	$ 3,493,597

Net sales to unaffiliated customers is based on the location of the customers. Transfers between geographic areas are recorded at amounts generally above cost and in accordance with the rules and regulations of the respective governing tax authorities. Operating income consists of total net sales less operating expenses, and does not include either interest and other income, net, or income taxes. U.S. operating income is net of corporate expenses. Identifiable assets of geographic areas are those assets used in the Company's operations in each area. Corporate assets include cash and cash equivalents, joint-venture investments, and short-term investments.

Report of Ernst & Young, Independent Auditors

To the Shareholders and Board of Directors of Apple Computer, Inc.

We have audited the accompanying consolidated balance sheets of Apple Computer, Inc. as of September 24, 1993, and September 25, 1992, and the related consolidated statements of income, shareholders' equity, and cash flows for each of the three years in the period ended September 24, 1993. These financial statements are the responsibility of the Company's management. Our responsibility is to express an opinion on these financial statements based on our audits.

We conducted our audits in accordance with generally accepted auditing standards. Those standards require that we plan and perform the audit to obtain reasonable assurance about whether the financial statements are free of material misstatement. An audit includes examining, on a test basis, evidence supporting the amounts and disclosures in the financial statements. An audit also includes assessing the accounting principles used and significant estimates made by management, as well as evaluating the overall financial statement presentation. We believe that our audits provide a reasonable basis for our opinion.

In our opinion, the consolidated financial statements referred to above present fairly, in all material respects, the consolidated financial position of Apple Computer, Inc. at September 24, 1993, and September 25, 1992, and the consolidated results of its operations and its cash flows for each of the three years in the period ended September 24, 1993, in conformity with generally accepted accounting principles.

Ernst & Young
San Jose, California
October 11, 1993

Financial Statements (excluding footnotes) from the Annual Reports of Federal Express Corporation and Ben & Jerry's Homemade, Inc.

CONSOLIDATED BALANCE SHEET ASSETS

	December 26, 1992	December 28, 1991
Current assets:		
Cash and cash equivalents	$ 7,356,133	$ 6,704,006
Accounts receivable, less allowance for doubtful accounts: $350,000 in 1992 and 1991	8,849,326	6,939,975
Income taxes receivable	306,193	
Inventories	17,089,857	8,999,666
Deferred income taxes	1,730,000	984,000
Prepaid expenses	208,996	107,325
Total current assets	35,540,505	23,734,972
Property, plant and equipment	39,312,513	28,496,080
Less accumulated depreciation	12,575,088	9,196,551
	26,737,425	19,299,529
Investments	25,200,000	
Other assets	728,885	21,598
	$ 88,206,815	$ 43,056,099

LIABILITIES AND STOCKHOLDERS' EQUITY

	December 26, 1992	December 28, 1991
Current liabilities:		
Accounts payable and accrued expenses	$16,858,919	$11,951,308
Income taxes payable	628,098	233,853
Current portion of long-term debt and obligations under capital lease		514,905
Total current liabilities	17,487,017	12,700,066
Long-term debt and obligations under captial lease	2,640,982	2,786,659
Deferred income taxes	1,319,000	1,300,000
Commitments and contingencies		
Stockholders' equity:		
$1.20 noncumulative Class A preferred stock – $1.00 par value, redeemable at $12.00 per share; 900 shares authorized, issued and outstanding, aggregate preference on voluntary or involuntary liquidation – $9,000	900	900
Class A common stock – $.033 par value; authorized 10,000,000 shares; issued: 6,239,575 shares at December 26, 1992 and 5,033,917 shares at December 28, 1991	206,327	166,541
Class B common stock – $.033 par value; authorized 3,000,000 shares; issued: 962,008 shares at December 26, 1992 and 986,888 shares at December 28, 1991	31,746	32,565
Additional paid-in capital	47,941,134	14,261,484
Retained earnings	19,984,461	13,309,121
Unearned compensation	(38,014)	(134,588)
Treasury stock, at cost: 66,453 Class A and 1,092 Class B shares at December 26, 1992 and 66,419 Class A and 1,075 Class B shares at December 28, 1991	(1,366,738)	(1,366,649)
	66,759,816	26,269,374
Total stockholders' equity	$88,206,815	$43,056,099

See accompanying notes.

STOCKHOLDERS' EQUITY
THIS IS CALLED THE "BOOK VALUE" OF THE OWNERS' STAKE IN THE COMPANY. IT INCLUDES PROCEEDS THE COMPANY RECEIVED FROM THE INITIAL AND SUBSEQUENT SALES OF STOCK TO THE PUBLIC, PLUS ACCUMULATED PROFITS, CALLED **RETAINED EARNINGS**.
THIS BOOK VALUE IS NOT THE SAME AS THE VALUE OF STOCK ON THE PUBLIC STOCK MARKET WHICH IS CALLED THE "MARKET VALUE". THE STOCK MARKET DETERMINES IN ITS OWN WAYS WHETHER THE COMPANY IS WORTH MORE THAN THE BOOK VALUE OF WHAT IT OWNS MINUS WHAT IT OWES. FOR EXAMPLE, A COMPANY'S STOCK PRICE CHANGES REGULARLY WITHOUT REGARD TO THE VALUE OF THE ASSETS & LIABILITIES IT USES TO RUN ITS BUSINESS.

LIABILITIES – WHAT THE COMPANY OWES.
- **CURRENT LIABILITIES** – BILLS, PAYROLL DUE, TAXES & OTHER OBLIGATIONS THAT HAVE TO BE PAID WITHIN A YEAR.
- **LONG TERM DEBT & OBLIGATIONS UNDER CAPITAL LEASES** – LOANS OR AGREEMENTS TO PAY FOR USE OF EQUIPMENT A YEAR OR MORE FROM NOW.
- **OTHER LIABILITIES** – MISCELLANEOUS OTHER FINANCIAL COMMITMENTS.

CONSOLIDATED STATEMENT OF INCOME

	December 26, 1992	Years Ended December 28, 1991	December 29, 1990
Net sales	$ 131,968,814	$ 96,997,339	$ 77,024,037
Cost of sales	94,389,391	68,500,402	54,202,387
Gross profit	37,579,423	28,496,937	22,821,650
Selling, general and administrative expenses	26,242,761	21,264,214	17,639,357
Operating income	11,336,662	7,232,723	5,182,293
Other income (expenses):			
Interest income	394,817	147,058	296,329
Interest expense	(181,577)	(736,248)	(868,736)
Other	(235,765)	(139,627)	(136,578)
	(22,525)	(728,817)	(708,985)
Income before income taxes	11,314,137	6,503,906	4,473,308
Income taxes	4,638,797	2,764,523	1,864,063
Net income	$ 6,675,340	$ 3,739,383	$ 2,609,245
Net income per common share	$ 1.07	$ 0.67	$ 0.50
Weighted average number of common shares outstanding	6,253,825	5,572,368	5,224,667

See accompanying notes.

STATEMENT OF INCOME

~ NET SALES ~ THIS IS THE TOTAL SALES OF THE COMPANY MINUS THE VALUE OF PRODUCT DISCOUNTED OR RETURNED.

~ COST OF SALES ~ WHAT IT COST TO MAKE & STORE THE PRODUCTS UNTIL THEY ARE SOLD. INCLUDES THE PACKAGING, LABOR COSTS, & STORAGE MACHINERY, & THE COST TO RUN INGREDIENTS, TO RUN PRODUCTION.

~ GROSS PROFIT ~ NET SALES MINUS COST OF SALES.

~ SELLING & ADMINISTRATIVE EXPENSES ~ THESE ARE THE COSTS OF MARKETING & SELLING THE PRODUCT AFTER IT HAS BEEN MADE, PLUS ALL OF THE ADMINISTRATIVE COSTS TO RUN THE COMPANY.

~ OPERATING INCOME ~ GROSS PROFIT MINUS SELLING, GENERAL & ADMINISTRATIVE EXPENSES (BEFORE TAXES) FROM HOW MUCH A COMPANY EARNS. THIS MEASURES THE CORE BUSINESS IT IS IN.

~ INCOME BEFORE TAXES, INCOME TAXES & NET INCOME ~ INCOME TAXES ARE THE AMOUNT OF FEDERAL & STATE TAXES PAID OR DUE BASED ON THE COMPANY'S BOOK INCOME. SUBTRACTING THOSE TAXES FROM INCOME BEFORE TAXES RESULTS IN NET INCOME OR THE "BOTTOM LINE." CONTINUED → (REMEMBER, BEN & JERRY'S HAS TWO "BOTTOM LINES.")

CONSOLIDATED STATEMENT OF CASH FLOWS

(29)

Years Ended	12/26/92	12/28/91	12/29/90
Cash flows from operating activities:			
Net income	$ 6,675,340	$ 3,739,383	$ 2,609,245
Adjustments to reconcile net income to net cash provided by operating activities:			
Depreciation and amortization	3,455,720	2,980,826	2,320,666
Provision for doubtful accounts receivable		100,000	88,000
Deferred income taxes	(727,000)	(294,000)	91,000
Amortization of unearned compensation	96,574	77,162	
(Gain) Loss on disposition of assets	(14,232)	13,250	3,666
Stock awards	57,000	302,601	
Changes in assets and liabilities:			
Accounts receivable	(1,909,351)	(1,995,530)	(1,462,567)
Income tax receivable/payable	(540,046)	(98,441)	390,413
Inventories	(8,090,191)	1,083,476	(6,086,592)
Prepaid expenses	(101,671)	10,601	72,363
Other assets	93,656		
Accounts payable and accrued expenses	4,907,611	4,399,156	3,198,786
Net cash provided by operating activities	3,903,410	10,318,484	1,224,980
Cash flows from investing activities:			
Additions to property, plant and equipment	(10,447,007)	(4,034,124)	(2,597,635)
Proceeds from sale of property, plant and equipment	105,084	70,000	42,500
Increase in investments	(25,200,000)		
Changes in other assets	(836,657)		
Net cash used for investing activities	(36,378,580)	(3,964,124)	(2,555,135)
Cash flows from financing activities:			
Borrowings on short-term debt		8,900,000	
Repayments of short-term debt		(8,900,000)	
Repayments of long-term debt and capital leases	(534,231)	(439,002)	(348,731)
Net proceeds from issuance of common stock	33,661,528	95,325	81,763
Payment of bond redemption costs		(102,867)	
Net cash provided by (used for) financing activities	33,127,297	(446,544)	(266,968)
Increase (decrease) in cash and cash equivalents	652,127	5,907,816	(1,597,123)
Cash and cash equivalents at beginning of year	6,704,006	796,190	2,393,313
Cash and cash equivalents at end of year	$ 7,356,133	$6,704,006	$ 796,190

See accompanying notes.

CONSOLIDATED STATEMENT OF STOCKHOLDERS' EQUITY

	Preferred Stock	Common Stock Class A	Common Stock Class B
	Par Value	Par Value	Par Value
Balance at December 30, 1989	$ 900	$131,909	$38,383
Net income			
Common Stock forfeited under restricted stock plan (306 Class A shares and 150 Class B shares)			
Common Stock issued under stock purchase plan (12,462 shares)		411	
Conversion of Class B shares to Class A shares (78,048 shares)		2,576	(2,576)
Conversion of subordinated debentures to Class A shares (644 shares)		21	
Balance at December 29, 1990	900	134,917	35,807
Net income			
Common stock issued under restricted stock plan (53,450 Class A shares)			
Amortization of unearned compensation			
Conversion of Class B shares to Class A shares (98,230 shares)		3,242	(3,242)
Conversion of subordinated debentures to Class A shares (847,804 shares)		27,976	
Common stock forfeited under restricted stock plan (40 Class A shares and 20 Class B shares)			
Common stock issued under stock purchase plan (12,292 Class A shares)		406	
Common stock contributed (89,624 Class A shares)			
Balance at December 28, 1991	900	166,541	32,565
Net income			
Common stock issued through public offering (1,170,000 Class A shares)		38,610	
Common stock issued under stock purchase plan (8,778 Class A shares)		291	
Common stock issued under restricted stock plan (2,000 Class A shares)		66	
Common stock forfeited under restricted stock plan (34 Class A shares and 17 Class B shares)			
Conversion of Class B to Class A shares (24,880 shares)		819	(819)
Amortization of unearned compensation			
Balance at December 26, 1992	$ 900	$ 206,327	$ 31,746

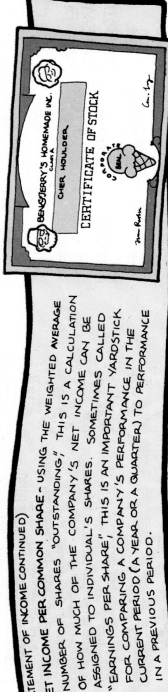

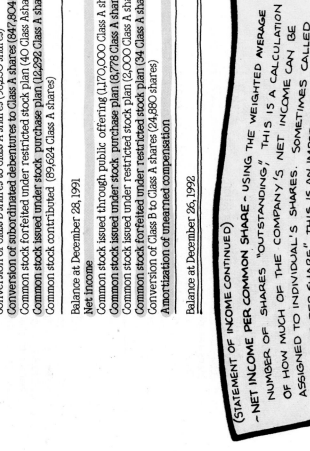

(STATEMENT OF INCOME CONTINUED)

- NET INCOME PER COMMON SHARE - USING THE WEIGHTED AVERAGE NUMBER OF SHARES "OUTSTANDING," THIS IS A CALCULATION OF HOW MUCH OF THE COMPANY'S NET INCOME CAN BE ASSIGNED TO INDIVIDUAL'S SHARES. SOMETIMES CALLED "EARNINGS PER SHARE," THIS IS AN IMPORTANT YARDSTICK FOR COMPARING A COMPANY'S PERFORMANCE IN THE CURRENT PERIOD (A YEAR OR A QUARTER) TO PERFORMANCE IN A PREVIOUS PERIOD.

31

Additional Paid-in Capital	Retained Earnings	Unearned Compensation	Treasury Stock Class A Cost	Treasury Stock Class B Cost
$6,302,851	$6,960,493	$ 0	($24,729)	($4,413)
	2,609,245		(534)	(264)
82,149				
4,978				
6,389,978	9,569,738	0	(25,263)	(4,677)
(53,450)	3,739,383	(211,750)	567,907	
		77,162		
5,925,527			(71)	(35)
94,919			(1,904,510)	
1,904,510				
14,261,484	13,309,121	(134,588)	(1,361,937)	(4,712)
33,467,490	6,675,340			
155,226				
56,934		96,574	(59)	(30)
$47,941,134	$19,984,461	$ (38,014)	$ (1,361,996)	$ (4,742)

See accompanying notes.

Consolidated Statements of Operations
FEDERAL EXPRESS CORPORATION AND SUBSIDIARIES

Years ended May 31 In thousands, except per share amounts	1993	1992	1991
REVENUES	$ **7,808,043**	$ 7,550,060	$ 7,688,296
OPERATING EXPENSES:			
Salaries and employee benefits (Notes 8 and 9)	**3,807,493**	3,637,080	3,438,391
Rentals and landing fees (Note 4)	**658,138**	672,341	650,001
Depreciation and amortization	**579,896**	577,157	562,207
Fuel	**495,384**	508,386	663,327
Maintenance and repairs	**404,639**	404,311	449,394
Restructuring charges (Note 13)	**(12,500)**	254,000	121,000
Other	**1,497,820**	1,473,818	1,551,850
	7,430,870	7,527,093	7,436,170
OPERATING INCOME	**377,173**	22,967	252,126
OTHER INCOME (EXPENSE):			
Interest, net (Note 1)	**(160,923)**	(164,315)	(181,880)
Gain on disposition of aircraft and related equipment	**4,633**	2,832	11,375
Other, net	**(17,307)**	(8,312)	(8,679)
Payroll tax loss (Note 13)	**—**	—	(32,000)
	(173,597)	(169,795)	(211,184)
INCOME (LOSS) BEFORE INCOME TAXES AND CUMULATIVE EFFECT OF CHANGE IN ACCOUNTING PRINCIPLE	**203,576**	(146,828)	40,942
PROVISION (CREDIT) FOR INCOME TAXES (Note 7)	**93,767**	(33,046)	35,044
INCOME (LOSS) BEFORE CUMULATIVE EFFECT OF CHANGE IN ACCOUNTING PRINCIPLE	**109,809**	(113,782)	5,898
CUMULATIVE EFFECT OF CHANGE IN ACCOUNTING FOR POSTRETIREMENT BENEFITS, NET OF TAX BENEFIT OF $34,287 (Note 9)	**(55,943)**	—	—
NET INCOME (LOSS)	$ **53,866**	$ (113,782)	$ 5,898
EARNINGS (LOSS) PER SHARE (Note 6):			
Before cumulative effect of change in accounting principle	$ **2.01**	$ (2.11)	$ .11
Cumulative effect of change in accounting for postretirement benefits (Note 9)	**(1.03)**	—	—
	$ **.98**	$ (2.11)	$ .11
AVERAGE SHARES OUTSTANDING (Note 6)	**54,719**	53,961	53,350

The accompanying Notes to Consolidated Financial Statements are an integral part of these statements.

Consolidated Balance Sheets

FEDERAL EXPRESS CORPORATION AND SUBSIDIARIES

May 31 In thousands	1993	1992
ASSETS		
CURRENT ASSETS:		
Cash and cash equivalents	$ 155,456	$ 78,177
Receivables, less allowance for doubtful accounts		
of $31,308 and $32,074	922,727	899,773
Spare parts, supplies and fuel	164,087	158,062
Prepaid expenses and other	63,573	69,994
Deferred income taxes (Note 7)	133,875	—
Total current assets	1,439,718	1,206,006
PROPERTY AND EQUIPMENT, AT COST (Notes 3, 4 and 11):		
Flight equipment	2,843,253	2,540,350
Package handling and ground support equipment	1,413,793	1,352,659
Computer and electronic equipment	947,913	851,686
Other	1,501,250	1,433,212
	6,706,209	6,177,907
Less accumulated depreciation and amortization	3,229,941	2,766,610
Net property and equipment	3,476,268	3,411,297
OTHER ASSETS:		
Goodwill (Note 1)	432,215	487,780
Equipment deposits and other assets (Note 11)	444,863	358,103
Total other assets	877,078	845,883
	$ 5,793,064	$ 5,463,186

The accompanying Notes to Consolidated Financial Statements are an integral part of these balance sheets.

	1993	1992
LIABILITIES AND STOCKHOLDERS' INVESTMENT		
CURRENT LIABILITIES:		
Current portion of long-term debt (Note 3)	$ **133,797**	$ 155,257
Accounts payable	**554,111**	430,130
Accrued expenses (Note 2)	**761,357**	799,468
Total current liabilities	**1,449,265**	1,384,855
LONG-TERM DEBT, LESS CURRENT PORTION (Note 3)	**1,882,279**	1,797,844
DEFERRED INCOME TAXES (Note 7)	**72,479**	123,715
OTHER LIABILITIES (Note 1)	**717,660**	577,050
COMMITMENTS AND CONTINGENCIES (Notes 11 and 12)		
COMMON STOCKHOLDERS' INVESTMENT (Note 6):		
Common stock, $.10 par value; 100,000 shares		
authorized, 54,743 and 54,100 shares issued	**5,474**	5,410
Additional paid-in capital	**699,385**	672,727
Retained earnings	**969,515**	906,555
	1,674,374	1,584,692
Less treasury stock and deferred compensation		
related to stock plans	**(2,993)**	(4,970)
Total common stockholders' investment	**1,671,381**	1,579,722
	$ **5,793,064**	$ 5,463,186

Consolidated Statements of Cash Flows

FEDERAL EXPRESS CORPORATION AND SUBSIDIARIES

Years ended May 31 In thousands	**1993**	1992	1991
OPERATING ACTIVITIES			
Net income (loss)	$ **53,866**	$ (113,782)	$ 5,898
Adjustments to reconcile income (loss) to net cash provided by operating activities:			
Depreciation and amortization	**579,896**	577,157	562,207
Provision for uncollectible accounts	**33,552**	31,670	59,721
Provision (credit) for deferred income taxes and other	**19,910**	(75,219)	36,935
(Gain) loss from disposals of property and equipment	**(5,648)**	1,810	(1,621)
Cumulative effect of accounting change	**55,943**	–	–
Changes in assets and liabilities, net of effects from purchases and dispositions of businesses:			
(Increase) decrease in receivables	**(41,535)**	(727)	20,431
(Increase) decrease in other current assets	**(5,813)**	61,749	(21,904)
Increase in accounts payable, accrued expenses and other liabilities	**13,651**	33,620	131,500
Other, net	**21,259**	4,543	(5,768)
Net cash provided by operating activities	**725,081**	520,821	787,399
INVESTING ACTIVITIES			
Purchases of property and equipment, including deposits on aircraft of $177,564 $212,291 and $92,587	**(1,023,723)**	(915,878)	(1,027,736)
Proceeds from disposition of property and equipment:			
Sale-leaseback transactions	**216,444**	400,433	275,347
Other	**5,984**	12,851	5,699
Purchase of businesses, net of cash acquired	**–**	–	(24,322)
Other, net	**1,992**	621	–
Net cash used in investing activities	**(799,303)**	(501,973)	(771,012)
FINANCING ACTIVITIES			
Proceeds from debt issuances	**878,499**	437,709	910,703
Principal payments on debt	**(737,334)**	(507,283)	(916,430)
Proceeds from stock issuances (includes treasury)	**24,512**	19,272	31,241
Purchases of treasury stock	**(472)**	(3,099)	(23,565)
Other, net	**(13,704)**	(4,962)	857
Net cash provided by (used in) financing activities	**151,501**	(58,363)	2,806
Net increase (decrease) in cash and cash equivalents	**77,279**	(39,515)	19,193
Cash and cash equivalents at beginning of period	**78,177**	117,692	98,499
Cash and cash equivalents at end of period	$ **155,456**	$ 78,177	$ 117,692
SUPPLEMENTAL DISCLOSURE OF CASH FLOW INFORMATION			
Cash paid for:			
Interest (net of capitalized interest)	$ **162,648**	$ 178,943	$ 190,054
Income taxes	**188,943**	89,729	36,500

Non-cash investing and financing activities:
In November 1992, approximately $73,000 of secured debt related to a portion of the purchase price of one MD-11 aircraft acquired by the Company was assumed by a third party in a sale-leaseback of the aircraft.

The accompanying Notes to Consolidated Financial Statements are an integral part of these statements.

Consolidated Statements of Changes in Common Stockholders' Investment

FEDERAL EXPRESS CORPORATION AND SUBSIDIARIES

In thousands, except common shares	Common Stock	Additional Paid-in Capital	Retained Earnings	Treasury Stock	Deferred Compen-sation
BALANCE AT MAY 31, 1990	$ 5,315	$ 639,676	$ 1,010,090	$ (21)	$ (5,873)
Purchase of treasury stock	–	–	–	(23,565)	–
Issuance of common and treasury stock under employee incentive plans (1,141,283 shares)	48	12,369	(4,483)	23,572	642
Amortization of deferred compensation	–	–	–	–	1,252
Foreign currency translation adjustment	–	–	3,700	–	–
Net income	–	–	5,898	–	–
BALANCE AT MAY 31, 1991	5,363	652,045	1,015,205	(14)	(3,979)
Purchase of treasury stock	–	–	–	(3,099)	–
Issuance of common and treasury stock under employee incentive plans (554,269 shares)	47	20,682	(287)	3,081	(2,792)
Amortization of deferred compensation	–	–	–	–	1,833
Foreign currency translation adjustment	–	–	5,419	–	–
Net loss	–	–	(113,782)	–	–
BALANCE AT MAY 31, 1992	5,410	672,727	906,555	(32)	(4,938)
Purchase of treasury stock	–	–	–	(472)	–
Issuance of common and treasury stock under employee incentive plans (655,938 shares)	64	26,658	(85)	468	(393)
Amortization of deferred compensation	–	–	–	–	2,374
Foreign currency translation adjustment	–	–	9,179	–	–
Net income	–	–	53,866	–	–
BALANCE AT MAY 31, 1993	**$ 5,474**	**$ 699,385**	**$ 969,515**	**$ (36)**	**$ (2,957)**

The accompanying Notes to Consolidated Financial Statements are an integral part of these statements.

PHOTO CREDITS

Page 770   Courtesy of Boeing Commercial Airplane Group
Page 783   Courtesy of Boeing Commercial Airplane Group

Chapter 21

Page 801   Courtesy of Kent Moore Cabinets
Page 803   ©Photri, Inc.
Page 804   Courtesy of Kent Moore Cabinets
Page 804   Photo courtesy of Hewlett-Packard Company
Page 807   Courtesy of Kent Moore Cabinets
Page 817   Courtesy of Kent Moore Cabinets
Page 824   Courtesy of Perkin-Elmer Corporation

Chapter 22

Page 845   Courtesy of Al Paul Lefton Company, Inc., on behalf of Rohm and Haas
Page 846   ©Nicholas Communications, Inc.
Page 849   Copyright photo courtesy of Dow Corning Corporation
Page 852   Copyright photo courtesy of Dow Corning Corporation

Chapter 23

Page 879   Courtesy of the Renton Coil Spring Company
Page 879   Courtesy of the Renton Coil Spring Company
Page 883   ©Nicholas Communications, Inc.
Page 889   Courtesy of the Renton Coil Spring Company
Page 893   Courtesy of Ford Motor Company
Page 894   Courtesy of the Renton Coil Spring Company

Chapter 24

Page 917   Courtesy of the Renton Coil Spring Company
Page 921   Courtesy of the Renton Coil Spring Company
Page 927   Courtesy of The Redhook Ale Brewery

Chapter 25

Page 955   ©Nicholas Communications, Inc.
Page 956   ©Nicholas Communications, Inc.
Page 962   ©Nicholas Communications, Inc.
Page 963   ©Nicholas Communications, Inc.

Comprehensive List of Accounts Used in Exercises and Problems

Current Assets

101	Cash
102	Petty cash
103	Cash equivalents
104	Short-term investments
105	Short-term investments, fair value adjustment
106	Accounts receivable
107	Allowance for doubtful accounts
108	Legal fees receivable
109	Interest receivable
110	Rent receivable
111	Notes receivable
115	Subscriptions receivable, common stock
116	Subscriptions receivable, preferred stock
119	Merchandise inventory
120	_____ inventory
121	_____ inventory
124	Office supplies
125	Store supplies
126	_____ supplies
128	Prepaid insurance
129	Prepaid interest
131	Prepaid rent
132	Raw materials inventory
133	Goods in process inventory, _____
134	Goods in process inventory, _____
135	Finished goods inventory

Long-Term Investments

141	Investment in _____ stock
142	Investment in _____ bonds
143	Long-term investments, fair value adjustment
144	Investment in _____
145	Bond sinking fund

Plant Assets

151	Automobiles
152	Accumulated depreciation, automobiles
153	Trucks
154	Accumulated depreciation, trucks
155	Boats
156	Accumulated depreciation, boats
157	Professional library
158	Accumulated depreciation, professional library
159	Law library
160	Accumulated depreciation, law library
161	Furniture
162	Accumulated depreciation, furniture
163	Office equipment
164	Accumulated depreciation, office equipment
165	Store equipment
166	Accumulated depreciation, store equipment
167	_____ equipment
168	Accumulated depreciation, _____ equipment
169	Machinery
170	Accumulated depreciation, machinery
173	Building _____
174	Accumulated depreciation, building _____
175	Building _____
176	Accumulated depreciation, building _____
179	Land improvements _____
180	Accumulated depreciation, land improvements _____
181	Land improvements _____
182	Accumulated depreciation, land improvements _____
183	Land

Natural Resources

185   Mineral deposit
186   Accumulated depletion, mineral deposit

Intangible Assets

191   Patents
192   Leasehold
193   Franchise
194   Copyrights
195   Leasehold improvements
196   Organization costs

Current Liabilities

201   Accounts payable
202   Insurance payable
203   Interest payable
204   Legal fees payable
207   Office salaries payable
208   Rent payable
209   Salaries payable
210   Wages payable
211   Accrued payroll payable
214   Estimated warranty liability
215   Income taxes payable
216   Common dividend payable
217   Preferred dividend payable
218   State unemployment taxes payable
219   Employees' federal income taxes payable
221   Employees' medical insurance payable
222   Employees' retirement program payable
223   Employees' union dues payable
224   Federal unemployment taxes payable
225   FICA taxes payable
226   Estimated vacation pay liability

Unearned Revenues
230   Unearned consulting fees
231   Unearned legal fees
232   Unearned property management fees
233   Unearned _____ fees
234   Unearned _____
235   Unearned janitorial revenue
236   Unearned _____ revenue
238   Unearned rent _____

Notes Payable

240   Short-term notes payable
241   Discount on short-term notes payable
245   Notes payable
251   Long-term notes payable
252   Discount on notes payable

Long-Term Liabilities

253   Long-term lease liability
255   Bonds payable
256   Discount on bonds payable

257   Premium on bonds payable
258   Deferred income tax liability

Owners' Equity

301   _____, capital
302   _____, withdrawals
303   _____, capital
304   _____, withdrawals
305   _____, capital
306   _____, withdrawals

Corporate Contributed Capital
307   Common stock, $_____ par value
308   Common stock, no par
309   Common stock subscribed
310   Common stock dividend distributable
311   Contributed capital in excess of par value, common stock
312   Contributed capital in excess of stated value, no-par common stock
313   Contributed capital from the retirement of common stock
314   Contributed capital, treasury stock transactions
315   Preferred stock
316   Contributed capital in excess of par value, preferred stock
317   Preferred stock subscribed

Retained Earnings
318   Retained earnings
319   Cash dividends declared
320   Stock dividends declared

Other Owners' Equity
321   Treasury stock, common
322   Unrealized holding gain (loss)

Revenues

401   _____ fees earned
402   _____ fees earned
403   _____ services revenue
404   _____ services revenue
405   Commissions earned
406   Rent earned
407   Dividends earned
408   Earnings from investment in _____
409   Interest earned
410   Sinking fund earnings
413   Sales
414   Sales returns and allowances
415   Sales discounts

Cost of Goods Sold Items

502   Cost of goods sold
505   Purchases
506   Purchases returns and allowances
507   Purchases discounts
508   Transportation-in

Manufacturing Accounts
520   Raw materials purchases
521   Freight-in on raw materials

530   Factory payroll
531   Direct labor
540   Factory overhead
541   Indirect materials
542   Indirect labor
543   Factory insurance expired
544   Factory supervision
545   Factory supplies used
546   Factory utilities
547   Miscellaneous production costs
548   Property taxes on factory building
549   Property taxes on factory equipment
550   Rent on factory building
551   Repairs, factory equipment
552   Small tools written off
560   Depreciation of factory equipment
561   Depreciation of factory building

Standard Cost Variance Accounts

580   Direct material quantity variance
581   Direct material price variance
582   Direct labor quantity variance
583   Direct labor price variance
584   Factory overhead volume variance
585   Factory overhead controllable variance

Expenses

Depletion, Amortization, and Depreciation Expenses

601   Amortization expense, _____
602   Amortization expense, _____
603   Depletion expense, _____
604   Depreciation expense, boats
605   Depreciation expense, automobiles
606   Depreciation expense, building _____
607   Depreciation expense, building _____
608   Depreciation expense, land improvements _____
609   Depreciation expense, land improvements _____
610   Depreciation expense, law library
611   Depreciation expense, trucks
612   Depreciation expense, _____ equipment
613   Depreciation expense, _____ equipment
614   Depreciation expense, _____
615   Depreciation expense, _____

Employee Related Expenses

620   Office salaries expense
621   Sales salaries expense
622   Salaries expense
623   _____ wages expense
624   Employees' benefits expense
625   Payroll taxes expense

Financial Expenses

630   Cash over and short
631   Discounts lost
632   Factoring fee expense
633   Interest expense

Insurance Expenses

635   Insurance expense, delivery equipment
636   Insurance expense, office equipment
637   Insurance expense, _____

Rental Expenses

640   Rent expense
641   Rent expense, office space
642   Rent expense, selling space
643   Press rental expense
644   Truck rental expense
645   _____ rental expense

Supplies Expense

650   Office supplies expense
651   Store supplies expense
652   _____ supplies expense
653   _____ supplies expense

Miscellaneous Expenses

655   Advertising expense
656   Bad debts expense
657   Blueprinting expense
658   Boat expense
659   Collection expense
661   Concessions expense
662   Credit card expense
663   Delivery expense
664   Dumping expense
667   Equipment expense
668   Food and drinks expense
669   Gas, oil, and repairs expense
671   Gas and oil expense
672   General and administrative expense
673   Janitorial expense
674   Legal fees expense
676   Mileage expense
677   Miscellaneous expenses
678   Mower and tools expense
679   Operating expense
681   Permits expense
682   Postage expense
683   Property taxes expense
684   Repairs expense, _____
685   Repairs expense, _____
687   Selling expense
688   Telephone expense
689   Travel and entertainment expense
690   Utilities expense
691   Warranty expense
695   Income taxes expense

Gains and Losses

701   Gain on retirement of bonds
702   Gain on sale of machinery
703   Gain on sale of short-term investments
704   Gain on sale of trucks

705   Gain on _____
706   Foreign exchange gain or loss
801   Loss on disposal of machinery
802   Loss on exchange of equipment
803   Loss on exchange of _____
804   Loss on sale of notes
805   Loss on retirement of bonds
806   Loss on sale of investments

807   Loss on sale of machinery
808   Loss on sale of _____
809   Loss on _____

Clearing Accounts

901   Income summary
902   Manufacturing summary